RESEARCH METHODS for COGNITIVE NEUROSCIENCE

Sara Miller McCune founded SAGE Publishing in 1965 to support the dissemination of usable knowledge and educate a global community. SAGE publishes more than 1000 journals and over 800 new books each year, spanning a wide range of subject areas. Our growing selection of library products includes archives, data, case studies and video. SAGE remains majority owned by our founder and after her lifetime will become owned by a charitable trust that secures the company's continued independence.

Los Angeles | London | New Delhi | Singapore | Washington DC | Melbourne

RESEARCH METHODS for COGNITIVE NEUROSCIENCE

AARON J. NEWMAN

Los Angeles | London | New Delhi
Singapore | Washington DC | Melbourne

Los Angeles | London | New Delhi
Singapore | Washington DC | Melbourne

SAGE Publications Ltd
1 Oliver's Yard
55 City Road
London EC1Y 1SP

SAGE Publications Inc.
2455 Teller Road
Thousand Oaks, California 91320

SAGE Publications India Pvt Ltd
B 1/I 1 Mohan Cooperative Industrial Area
Mathura Road
New Delhi 110 044

SAGE Publications Asia-Pacific Pte Ltd
3 Church Street
#10-04 Samsung Hub
Singapore 049483

Editor: Rob Patterson
Assistant editor: Katie Rabot
Production editor: Imogen Roome
Copyeditor: Christine Bitten
Proofreader: Neil Dowden
Marketing manager: Lucia Sweet
Cover design: Wendy Scott
Typeset by: C&M Digitals (P) Ltd, Chennai, India

© Aaron J. Newman 2019

First published 2019

Apart from any fair dealing for the purposes of research or private study, or criticism or review, as permitted under the Copyright, Designs and Patents Act, 1988, this publication may be reproduced, stored or transmitted in any form, or by any means, only with the prior permission in writing of the publishers, or in the case of reprographic reproduction, in accordance with the terms of licences issued by the Copyright Licensing Agency. Enquiries concerning reproduction outside those terms should be sent to the publishers.

Library of Congress Control Number: 2018955215

British Library Cataloguing in Publication data

A catalogue record for this book is available from the British Library

ISBN 978-1-4462-9649-3
ISBN 978-1-4462-9650-9 (pbk)

To my parents, Cynthia Anne Newman and Robert John Thompson

Contents

Preface xi
Acknowledgements xv
About the Author xvii
How to Use This Book xix

1 **The Organization of the Brain and How We Study It** 1

   Introduction 2
   From Cells to Networks 4
   Studying the Organization of the Brain 16

2 **Research Methods and Experimental Design** 35

   Introduction 36
   Basic Experimental Designs 37
   Experimental Set-up and Control 47
   Between- and Within-Subjects Designs 48
   Statistical Power and Replicability 49
   Interpretation and Inference 52
   Ethical Considerations 54

3 **Electroencephalography (EEG) and Event-Related Potentials (ERP) 1** 61

   Introduction 62
   What Are We Measuring? 63
   How Do We Measure It? 80

4 **Electroencephalography (EEG) and Event-Related Potentials (ERP) 2** 97

   Experimental Design 98
   Data Analysis 104

5 **Magnetoencephalography (MEG)** 133

   Introduction 134
   What Are We Measuring? 135
   How Do We Measure It? 138
   Experimental Design 167
   Data Analysis 169

6 Magnetic Resonance Imaging (MRI) — 177

- Introduction — 178
- What Are We Measuring? — 180
- How Do We Measure It? — 186
- Safety — 207

7 Functional MRI (fMRI) 1 — 215

- Introduction — 216
- What Are We Measuring? — 217
- How Do We Measure It? — 230
- Image Preprocessing — 237

8 Functional MRI (fMRI) 2 — 255

- Introduction — 256
- Experimental Design — 257
- Statistical Analysis — 280
- Functional and Effective Connectivity — 289

9 Structural MRI — 307

- Introduction — 308
- Linking Micro- and Meso-Scales of Cortical Organization — 310
- Morphometry — 315
- Computational Neuroanatomy — 318

10 Connectomics: Diffusion Tensor Imaging (DTI) and Tractography — 337

- Introduction — 338
- What Are We Measuring? — 339
- How Do We Measure It? — 343
- Data Analysis — 347
- Applications and Limitations — 360

11 Positron Emission Tomography (PET) — 371

- Introduction — 372
- What Are We Measuring? — 373
- How Do We Measure It? — 375
- Experimental Design — 390
- Data Analysis — 394
- Multimodal PET — 395

12 Near-Infrared Optical Imaging (fNIRI) — 403

- Introduction — 404
- What Are We Measuring? — 406
- How Do We Measure It? — 413

	Data Analysis	426
	Multimodal Imaging	436
13	**Transcranial Magnetic Stimulation (TMS)**	**443**
	Introduction	444
	How Do We Do It?	446
	What Are the Effects on the Brain?	465
	Considerations in Experimental Design	467
	TMS Combined with Neuroimaging	469
	Safety	477
14	**Transcranial Electrical Stimulation (tES: tDCS, tACS, tRNS)**	**483**
	Introduction	484
	How Do We Do It?	486
	What Are the Effects on the Brain?	499
	Considerations in Experimental Design	511
	Safety	514

Glossary	521
References	561
Index	583

Preface

Cognitive neuroscience is an exciting, multidisciplinary field aimed at understanding some of the most fundamental questions about what it means to be human: how our thoughts, feelings, motivations, and actions arise and, specifically, how they relate to the structure and activity patterns of the brain. The field of cognitive neuroscience has its roots in numerous fields of scientific endeavour throughout the twentieth century and before, but really came into its own in the late 1980s and early 1990s with the advent of non-invasive forms of brain imaging and neurostimulation. It so happens that the first non-invasive PET neuroimaging studies of cognition came out while I was in high school, and the first demonstrations of functional MRI were published soon after I started my undergraduate education. The potential of these tools fully captured my imagination and offered me a unique opportunity to study the relationship between mind and brain. I eagerly pursued the opportunities that I was fortunate to have, including doing my undergraduate honours thesis with Dr Mike McIntyre at the University of Winnipeg and National Research Council of Canada on an fMRI project only three years after the technique was developed. I was then lucky to pursue graduate education at the University of Oregon with Dr Helen Neville, a highly regarded ERP researcher who had just started working with fMRI and opened innumerable doors for me to learn from top people in the field, through collaborations at the National Institutes of Health and the McDonnell summer institute in cognitive neuroscience. My formal training culminated with a postdoctoral fellowship at the University of Rochester, where I was mentored by Daphne Bavelier, Elissa Newport, and Ted Supalla where, not only did I gain further experience with fMRI, but strong critical thinking and analytical skills that are at least as valuable as technical skills in any neuroimaging or other experimental technique.

As much as the power and promise of the methods of cognitive neuroscience excited me for what they could tell us about the relationship between brain and mind, I was equally fascinated by their technical aspects, and the broad cross-disciplinary collaboration and knowledge required to make them work. This included physics, physiology, biochemistry, computer science, mathematics, and statistics, as well as cognitive science. I also recognized that as useful as the techniques are, they all have limitations, and – while it takes significant work to master any one technique – in approaching questions from the perspective of a cognitive neuroscientist, it was important to understand what each technique had to offer, and have a variety of technical tools in one's toolbox, rather than being 'an fMRI person' or 'an ERP person'. Moreover, simply being an informed and critical consumer of the cognitive neuroscience literature requires a reasonably deep knowledge of the strengths and limitations of each technique, in order to be able to critically evaluate the information in a study and determine for oneself whether the conclusions are valid, as well as to relate those findings to research using other techniques.

I have had the privilege of being able to pass on my knowledge and passion for the techniques of cognitive neuroscience to hundreds of students and colleagues over my career, through my lab, workshops, and, most systematically, an undergraduate (and sometimes graduate) class for psychology and neuroscience students entitled 'Research Methods in Cognitive Neuroscience'. While I initially taught the class around my strengths, it quickly became apparent both that students had an appetite to learn about the full range of cognitive neuroscience techniques, and that I had a duty to give more even and balanced coverage to them all. In doing so, however, a significant barrier was that there was no textbook that provided uniform and consistent coverage of all the techniques, and many available materials assumed relatively high levels of background in areas such as physics, mathematics, and/or physiology and chemistry that could not be guaranteed among the people who wanted to learn about and use these techniques. While there are excellent texts on some specific techniques (most notably Steven Luck's *An Introduction to the Event-Related Potential Technique* [MIT Press, 2014], and Huettel, Song, and McCarthy's *Functional Magnetic Resonance Imaging*), these were too long and detailed for a course surveying a wide range of techniques, and were not matched by equivalent texts on the other techniques. I toyed with the idea of writing an introductory textbook to the techniques of cognitive neuroscience, but was, to be honest, somewhat intimidated by the prospect. Then one day, Michael Carmichael from Sage met with me on a routine sales visit and, hearing me complain about the fact that no publisher had a book suitable for my class, encouraged me to write the book, and provided extensive support through the process of drafting an outline and proposal for the book, including soliciting anonymous feedback from colleagues that helped further refine and shape the book you now hold in your hands. While the book took significantly longer – and *is* significantly longer – than initially planned (by approximately three years and 100,000 words; I now understand why editors are frequently described as 'long-suffering'), it is with no small amount of satisfaction and pride that I present it to you now.

In writing this book, I had in mind a range of readers, from undergraduates to faculty members, who are interested in the techniques of cognitive neuroscience and want to know more about them. Naturally, as a broad overview, this book cannot hope to make one an expert in any particular technique, nor go into the level of detail that a book devoted to one technique could do. As well, I have written this book for people coming from a wide range of backgrounds who may find the techniques of cognitive neuroscience useful, including psychology, linguistics, economics, business, information systems, computer science, etc. As such, I have tried to assume very little in the way of specific scientific background. This means that some readers may find the text at times basic or redundant with their previous training, and at other times lacking sufficient depth or precision. I have intentionally tried to limit the number of mathematical formulae or detailed descriptions of biochemical pathways, preferring instead to focus on allowing a conceptual understanding that – while glossing over details – hopefully is never factually incorrect. With that said, any inaccuracies are entirely my own and I eagerly invite any feedback from my readers that will make the second edition better.

While I have tried for relatively even coverage of techniques, this is not entirely realized in that some topics do receive more treatment. The first technique covered is EEG/ERP, and this receives two chapters, while most other techniques receive only one. While admittedly, this is in part due to my extensive experience with ERP, it is also because in the context of this technique, many concepts and fundamental topics are introduced that are essential for understanding the later chapters. It is also worth noting in this context that, from a pedagogical perspective, this book is very much intended to be read in the order it is printed, because later chapters assume, and build on, knowledge first presented in earlier chapters. I also elected to cover MRI across a total of five chapters – including two on fMRI and one on the basic physics of how MRI works – because MRI, and in particular fMRI, comprises the large majority of cognitive neuroscience studies published to date. Beyond simply meaning that this topic is likely of great interest to many readers, it means that the technique is rich in the variety of experimental designs and approaches to analysis that one may encounter, necessitating a fair amount of space to do them justice.

There are also numerous topics that are *not* covered in this book. In part, decisions to exclude topics were made to keep the length of the book reasonable, and to allow it to actually see the light of day in print! As well, I have chosen to focus on non-invasive techniques, even though there are a number of invasive techniques that fall squarely within the domain of cognitive neuroscience, such as intracranial EEG and optical imaging performed during neurosurgery. I have also chosen to provide very little coverage of lesion-deficit techniques, primarily because, from a pedagogical perspective, these are often covered in a separate course on neuropsychology in undergraduate curricula. Likewise, although I view computational modelling as a critically important area of cognitive neuroscience, it is neither an imaging nor a stimulation technique, and is commonly covered in separate courses. Another limitation is that, while I have used examples of published studies to demonstrate different techniques, this book focuses more on methods than applications. Relatedly, I have not covered topics such as real-time neuroimaging and brain–computer interfaces, and given relatively little coverage to others, such as multimodal imaging, primarily due to space and time constraints. The field of cognitive neuroscience is burgeoning, and this book is intended only to provide a first taste, and to form a groundwork for your understanding of the techniques – how they work and what their strengths and limitations are. I hope that it excites you and encourages you to use these techniques to make new discoveries, expand human knowledge, and make the world a better place.

August 2018
Halifax, NS

Acknowledgements

I have benefitted from the support and input of a large number of family, friends, colleagues, and students in the writing of this book. First and foremost, I would like to thank my wife, Diane, and children, Vikki and Rhianna, for their support, encouragement, understanding, and tolerance of late dinners during the many years it took to complete this project.

I would also like to acknowledge the feedback provided by students and colleagues, including the many students who were subjected to early drafts of various chapters in my class, and in particular Steph Attwater, Tim Bardouille, Jon Fawcett, Jon Garry, and Alex Rudiuk for their constructive feedback. Thanks are also due to the support and encouragement – and tolerance of the time this book took me away from the lab – of the members of my lab throughout this process, including Lyam Bailey, Lisa Beck, Yasmin Beydoun, Kathleen Cairns, Therese Chevalier, Colin Conrad, Katie Douglas, Ella Dubinsky, Graham Flick, Alena Galilee, Sreejith Gopalakrishnan, Cindy Hamon-Hill, Kelsey Holt, Emily Jarvis, Morgan Johnson, Zoe Lazar-Kurz, Clara Lownie, Heath Matheson, Emily McGuire, Sean McWhinney, Marie-Elssa Morency, Ali Muise, Kiera O'Neil, Emily Patrick, Brandie Stewart, Sam Stranc, Kaitlyn Tagarelli, Antoine Tremblay, and Francesco Usai.

A number of people at Sage have been instrumental in making this happen, and providing encouragement, support, and feedback along the way, including Katie Rabot, Amy Jerrold, Robert Patterson, Luke Block, Lucy Dang, and especially Michael Carmichael for encouraging me to start and supporting me through the proposal process.

I am also grateful to the innumerable software developers whose tools I have used in creating this book. These include Scrivener, in which the book was written and edited, and a number of packages used to create the figures, including Adobe Illustrator and Photoshop, Anaconda Python, BESA Simulator, EEGLAB, Matlab, MNE-Python, Maya, Python, and Surf Ice.

Finally, I would like to acknowledge my intellectual mentors whose influence infuses every page of this book, be it through education, inspiration, or modelling: Helen Neville, Michael Ullman, Daphne Bavelier, Elissa Newport, Mike McIntyre, W.G. Newman, Dick Aslin, Bruce Bolster, Richard Brown, Jim Clark, Dave Corina, Ray Klein, Mike Posner, Jackie Schachter, Evelyn Schaefer, and Bill Simpson – as well as those whose writing has inspired me, including Steve Pinker, Steve Luck, and Michael Gazzaniga. I would also like to thank all of the scientists whose work contributed to this one. I could not possibly have written this book without the hard work and lucid writing of the many people who are acknowledged in the references at the end of this book.

About the Author

Aaron Newman is a Professor in the Departments of Psychology & Neuroscience, Paediatrics, Psychiatry, and Surgery at Dalhousie University, as well as Director of the NeuroCognitive Imaging Lab. He completed his BA (Hons) at the University of Winnipeg, and his MSc and PhD in Cognitive Psychology at the University of Oregon, followed by a postdoctoral fellowship at the University of Rochester. His research has been supported by a Canada Research Chair and numerous grants from federal and provincial agencies, and private foundations, and has resulted in dozens of peer-reviewed scientific publications and over 100 peer-reviewed conference presentations. His research uses numerous cognitive neuroscience methods to address a wide range of topics including the cognitive neuroscience of language, neuroplasticity, sign language, deafness, hearing loss, second language acquisition, biological motion perception, aphasia, attention, paediatric pain, schizophrenia, and aging; as well as methodological papers relating to brain imaging techniques and analysis methods. In addition to his research, Dr Newman has a strong interest in encouraging the development and commercialization of science and technology for the benefit of society. To this end, he developed and directed the RADIANT neurotechnology innovation training programme, which led to the creation of numerous successful companies, and now directs the SURGE science sandbox, an organization providing students with training and support in innovation, commercialization, and entrepreneurship. Outside of work he enjoys cycling, running, swimming, playing a variety of musical instruments, and cooking. He lives in Halifax, Nova Scotia with his family.

How to Use This Book

Learning Objectives
Designed to structure your approach to the material each chapter addresses.

Chapter Introductions
Designed to give you a brief overview of what you will encounter in the chapter.

Chapter Summaries
Designed to summarize the key material in the chapter.

'Things You Should Know'
Designed to confirm that you have achieved each chapter's key goals.

Further Reading
Designed to point you in the right direction when you want to know more about a given topic.

1 The Organization of the Brain and How We Study It

LEARNING OBJECTIVES

After reading this chapter, you should be able to:

- Define the scope and objectives of the field of cognitive neuroscience.
- Identify the fundamental types of cells in the brain, and how they communicate with each other.
- Describe the basic organization of the brain, across micro-, meso-, and macro-anatomical scales.
- Explain the value of measuring behaviour in understanding both cognition and brain activity.
- List the various brain imaging and stimulation methodologies covered in this book, and categorize them based on the type of data they measure.

INTRODUCTION

Cognitive neuroscience is the field of study aimed at understanding how the brain produces thoughts, emotions, and behaviour. By and large, this field focuses on human beings specifically, and – given the general reluctance that most humans express to having their heads cut open – relies primarily on *non-invasive* methods for characterizing brain activity and structure. The field of cognitive neuroscience is quite new; although humans have a long-standing interest in the thoughts and behaviours of themselves and others, the idea that 'There could be a human neurobiology of normal cognitive processes' (Gazzaniga, 2018) was realized only three decades ago. Specifically, in 1988 a group of researchers from Washington University and the University of Oregon published the first studies of human cognition using **positron emission tomography (PET)** – a form of brain imaging that allowed researchers to localize changes in blood flow in the brain, using radioactively labelled oxygen (Petersen, Fox, Posner, Mintun, & Raichle, 1988; Posner, Petersen, Fox, & Raichle, 1988). Prior to this, the only ways to study brain activity in healthy, living humans employed **EEG**, which involves measuring brain electrical activity via electrodes attached to the outside of the head (or a related technique, **MEG**; however, this was restricted to a very small number of labs). Although as we will see in this book EEG is an extremely valuable tool, it does not provide accurate information as to *where* in the brain activity originates, and so left many unanswered questions. Other tools existed for studying brain–behaviour relationships, but these necessarily involved unhealthy brains, such as neuropsychological studies of people with developmental disorders or acquired brain damage, and direct electrical recordings from the surface of the brain made during neurosurgery.

A few scant years after the publication of the first PET studies, a number of other techniques were established for studying brain activity non-invasively, including **functional MRI (fMRI)** and **near-infrared optical imaging (fNIRI)**, as well as **transcranial magnetic stimulation (TMS)** for non-invasively and transiently perturbing brain function. These all contributed to the development of the new field of cognitive neuroscience, which was codified with the establishment of a dedicated, peer-reviewed scientific journal – the *Journal of Cognitive Neuroscience* – in 1989, and the first meeting of the Cognitive Neuroscience Society in San Francisco in 1993. These milestones were, however, the fruition of work going back decades earlier by trailblazers who were willing to ask the hard questions, and seek answers even within the extremely limiting constraints of existing technologies. Perhaps most importantly, these early investigators were willing to transcend the traditional disciplinary boundaries of cognitive psychology on the one hand, and neurophysiology and neuroanatomy on the other. As Michael Gazzaniga, founding editor of the *Journal of Cognitive Neuroscience*, wrote in the Editor's Note to its inaugural issue,

> Those cognitive scientists interested in a deeper understanding of how the human mind works now believe that it is maximally fruitful to propose models of cognitive processes that can be assessed in neurobiologic terms. Likewise, it is no longer useful for neuroscientists to propose brain mechanisms underlying psychological processes without actually coming to grips with the complexities of psychological processes involved in any particular mental capacity being examined. (Gazzaniga, 1989: 2)

This book focuses on these and other techniques that have revolutionized our understanding of the human brain, and the nature of human thoughts, feelings, and actions. These techniques have fascinated me for many years, dating back to when I was in high school and saw the pioneering PET research mentioned above reported in *Discover* magazine. In a fit of characteristic nerdiness, I remember bringing that issue of the magazine to school to show my friends, and my disappointment that they were not nearly as excited about it as I. Nevertheless, my interest persisted and I had the opportunity to first work with functional MRI during my undergraduate degree in 1995–96, thanks to the enthusiasm of my supervisor, Dr Michael McIntyre, and the National Research Council of Canada. Mike in turn connected me with Dr Helen Neville at the University of Oregon, who accepted me as a graduate student and provided me with amazing opportunities to learn EEG and fMRI, and connect with pioneering researchers from around the world. Among the many things I learned from Helen were that, as amazing as the tools of cognitive neuroscience are, they are only small windows into the workings of the brain, and are highly fallible. In consequence, it is vital to always question your data, inspect it closely (and repeatedly) for errors, and remember that results are only as good as the experimental design, and even then always very much subject to interpretation. Simply obtaining a result does not make it true.

FROM CELLS TO NETWORKS

Although our interest in cognitive neuroscience is in linking the brain with cognition and behaviour, as a first step it is critical to have an understanding of the organ we are studying and, in particular, of the levels of organization of the brain that we are able to study with the tools of cognitive neuroscience. This book will be most understandable if the reader has some prior background in both psychology and neuroscience; however, in this section we will review the bare essentials. This is intentionally a very simplified account and readers are encouraged to consult an introductory neuroscience textbook for a more detailed explanation.

Structural Units

The adult human brain weighs approximately 1.5 kg and is composed of roughly 86 billion **neurons** (nerve cells), and a roughly equal amount of non-neuronal cells (Herculano-Houzel, 2009; Purves et al., 2017). Neurons are the key players in the transmission of information throughout the brain and the body, forming synapses with other neurons so that electrical signals can be transmitted from one neuron to another. The non-neuronal cells are predominantly **glia**, which were traditionally viewed as 'helper' cells supporting neuronal functions (such as modulating activity), but which in recent years have come to be appreciated as important functional units in the brain as well (Magaki, Williams, & Vinters, 2017; Verkhratsky & Kirchhoff, 2007) and, as we will see, are also critical to generating the signal we measure with fMRI.

Neurons are, however, the main actors in cognitive function. There are many different types of neurons in the brain. One dominant type of neuron found in the **cerebral cortex** of humans (as well as most other mammals, birds, fish, and reptiles) is the **pyramidal cell**. Pyramidal cells are found primarily in brain structures supporting higher cognitive functions, including the cerebral cortex, amygdala, and hippocampus (Spruston, 2008), making them of particular relevance for cognitive neuroscience – although all types of neurons are no doubt important for brain function and cognition. Nevertheless, we will focus on pyramidal cells here to exemplify neuronal structure and function. As illustrated in Figure 1.1, pyramidal cells typically have a cell body or **soma**, from which extends a single **axon** that branches extensively, sometimes along its entire length and in other cases only at the end (the **tuft**). These branches are called **dendrites**, and these are where the majority of connections (both input and output) are made with other neurons. Dendrites also branch out from the soma, with the apical dendrites being those along the axon, and basal dendrites branching directly off the soma. Functionally distinct roles have been identified for different regions of pyramidal cells at an even finer-grained level, with several distinct subregions of both the apical and basal dendritic regions (Spruston, 2008).

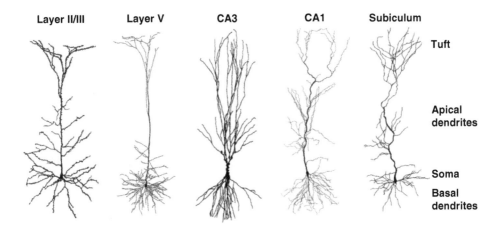

Figure 1.1 Pyramidal neurons from different parts of the brain, including layers of the cerebral cortex (leftmost two images; indicated by Roman numerals) and the hippocampus (rightmost three images). Labels on the right side indicate different regions of the cells. Reprinted from Spruston, 2008 with permission of Springer Nature

Neurons are densely connected with other neurons, over both short and long distances. It is these patterns of synaptic connections that allow the brain to carry out its complex representations and computations. Neurons communicate by way of both electrical and chemical transmission. At rest, neurons are electrically **polarized**, meaning that the **electrical potential** within the cell is negative relative to the space around the cell. Electrical potentials are covered in detail in Chapter 2, but for now we can simply say that there is potential for electrical charge to move between the outside and inside of the neurons (in the form of ions such as sodium, potassium, and calcium). A primary way for neurons to transmit information is to 'fire', or generate an **action potential**, in which case ion channels on the neuronal membrane open and allow the electrical charge inside the neuron to equilibrate with that outside the neuron – a phenomenon known as **depolarization**. This change in electrical potential starts at the soma and propagates down the axon, ultimately resulting in the neuron's firing being communicated to other neurons it is connected to. Importantly, axons are typically covered in a fatty coating called **myelin**, which serves as electrical insulation to both increase the speed of electrical transmission, and prevent the signal's strength from weakening along the length of the axon. The myelin sheath is actually provided by a specific type of glial cell, called oligodendrocytes. Figure 1.2 shows an example of an action potential travelling from a neuronal cell body, down its axon to the terminal where it communicates with another neuron.

The connections between neurons are called **synapses**, but it is important to understand that neurons are not directly physically connected to each other, but rather are separated by gaps, as shown in Figure 1.2. Thus when an electrical signal reaches the end of the axon, it does not directly propagate to the connected neurons.

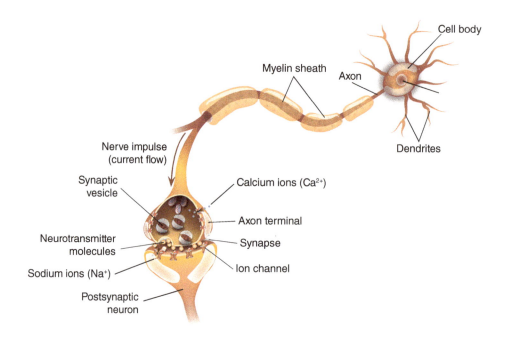

Figure 1.2   A schematic illustration of two neurons connected via a synapse

Instead, an arriving action potential triggers the release of chemical messengers called **neurotransmitters**. These chemicals are released by presynaptic ('sending') neurons to signal postsynaptic ('receiving') neurons by fitting into **receptors**: molecular structures on the neuronal membranes (outer walls of the cells) that fit the molecular shape of the neurotransmitter analogous to how a key fits a particular lock. The primary neurotransmitter used by neurons to excite other neurons (an excitatory neurotransmitter) is **glutamate**. There are three primary types of glutamate receptors: N-methyl-D-aspartate (NMDA), α-amino-3-hydroxy-5-methyl-4-isoxazolepropionic acid (AMPA), and kainate. Although all three receptor types are activated by glutamate, they differ in the types of cells and locations on cells that they occur, and their names reflect the fact that they can be selectively activated by specific chemicals other than glutamate – meaning that certain drugs can modulate the activity of one type of glutamate receptor with little or no effect on the other types. Using such drugs is a common way to investigate the role of particular neurotransmitters and receptors in brain function and cognition. Drugs that selectively target a particular type of receptor are called **agonists** for that receptor. In contrast, drugs that selectively block a receptor (meaning that the normal neurotransmitter will not activate that receptor) are called **antagonists**.

Not all neurotransmission is excitatory; many neurons actually *inhibit* other neurons, making them less likely to fire. The primary inhibitory neurotransmitter in the brain is **gamma-aminobutyric acid**, or **GABA**, for which there are two primary types of receptors (with much more logical names than the glutamate receptors): GABA$_A$ and GABA$_B$. In addition, there are other classes of chemicals, called neuromodulators and neurohormones, that affect neuronal activity. These act like neurotransmitters in the sense that they modulate neuronal function via receptors on the neurons. They differ from neurotransmitters in that rather than serving to communicate a transient action potential from one neuron to another at a very small scale across a synaptic junction, they are in many cases released into the intracellular space and act to modulate the function of larger numbers of neurons, making them more or less likely to fire in response to other inputs. Neuromodulators and neurohormones also act over longer time scales; while neurotransmitters act specifically at local synaptic junctions and are typically reabsorbed very quickly either by the neurons, or by surrounding glia (which then 'recycle' the neurotransmitters and send them back to the neurons), neuromodulators and hormones have longer lifetimes in the intracellular space prior to absorption or breakdown. **Neuromodulators** include serotonin, dopamine, norepinephrine, and acetylcholine, although some of these also act as short-acting neurotransmitters in some cell types and brain regions. Neurohormones function similarly to neuromodulators, and indeed the lines between the two are somewhat blurry, with different authors sometimes using one or the other to refer to the same chemical (Peres & Valena, 2011). However, **neurohormones** tend to refer to chemicals that are neuromodulatory, but produced in organs other than the brain and then travel through the body to the brain to modulate neural activity. In addition to the neuromodulators listed above, neurohormones include oxytocin, oestrogen, testosterone, vasopressin, insulin, and cortisol.

Networks of Neurons

Given the billions of individual neurons in the brain, it is not surprising that they form extremely complex, interconnected networks. The number of neurons connected to (that is, forming synapses with) another neuron varies widely by type and location of the cells, but estimates of around 10,000 connections per neuron are common. Within the cerebral cortex – the part of the brain that plays a primary role in most cognition (see next section) – there are many distinct regions that can be defined by the types and relative densities of cells present, the types of connections they have, and many other parameters. Even within a brain region, the cerebral cortex can be divided into distinct layers based on the locations and types of cells and connections. Typically six layers are defined within the cerebral cortex, although this may be further broken into sub-layers. This complex, layered organization of the cortex was first documented by Ramón y Cajal, who received the Nobel Prize in Physiology or Medicine for his work in 1906 (shared by Camillo Golgi, who invented the staining technique that made Cajal's work possible). Two of Cajal's drawings illustrating the laminal (layered) structure of the cerebral cortex are shown in Figure 1.3. Some layers are dominated by long-range inputs from other brain regions, while other layers contain horizontal cells – neurons with short-range connections that serve primarily inhibitory purposes.

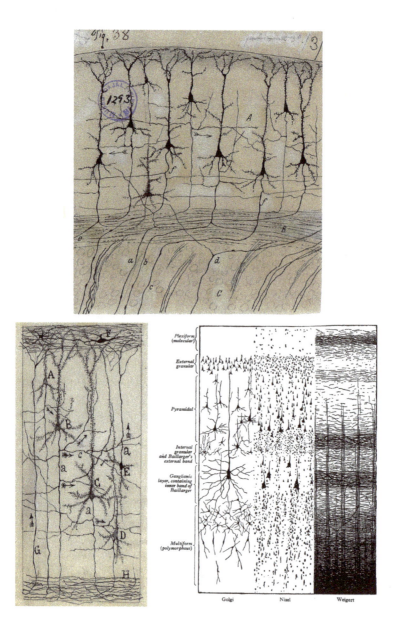

Figure 1.3 The laminar (layered) structure of the cerebral cortex, as illustrated by early anatomists. In all drawings, the outer surface of the cortex is at the top, and the bottom of the drawings is the white matter underlying the cortex. The top and bottom left drawings are by Spanish neuroanatomist Ramón y Cajal, using the Golgi staining method. The large cells are pyramidal neurons, arranged in a consistent manner with their axons running perpendicular to the cortical surface. Note how the bottom layers are dominated by long-range axonal connections to other brain areas, whereas the top layer contains more short-range, local connections to nearby cells. Middle layers contain medium-range connections. The drawing on the bottom right is by English anatomist Henry Gray, comparing three different types of stain (as indicated at the bottom of the drawing). These show how the cortical layers are differentiated based on the type and density of cell bodies, as well as the type and density of axonal connections. All images are in the public domain

Critical to brain function is the fact that synapses are not static, but dynamic connections. That is, synapses are not merely present or not, but the strength of a connection can vary widely. By 'strength' here we mean the extent to which the postsynaptic neuron's activity is affected by input from the presynaptic neuron. Not only can the strength of connections vary between synapses, but even for a given synapse, the strength can change over time. This is thought to be the most fundamental mechanism of learning, first hypothesized by Donald O. Hebb (Hebb, 1949) and made famous by the phrase, 'neurons that fire together, wire together' (commonly called the 'Hebb rule'). Hebb hypothesized that the strength of a synaptic connection was strengthened every time the firing of one neuron led soon thereafter to an action potential in a neuron it formed a synapse with. This was later demonstrated in living cells, in a process now known as **long-term potentiation (LTP)**. The weakening of synaptic connections is conversely known as **long-term depression (LTD)**.

In addition to these mechanisms, we now have evidence that neural connections can be modulated in many other ways. These include the fact that dendritic spines – the individual outgrowths on dendrites that form synapses – can grow and retract back on a scale of hours or even minutes, meaning that in addition to changing the strength of connections, synapses can literally appear and disappear with experience. Although such 'synaptic pruning' was long known as a key process in development – by which synaptic connections not strengthened by experience were eliminated – it is now recognized that this occurs on very short time scales and even in adult brains. As well, some brain regions, such as the hippocampus, are actually able to grow new neurons even in adulthood – in contrast to the older dogma that such neurogenesis occurred only in the early stages of brain development.

Levels of Organization

If we accept the basic estimates provided in the previous sections of 86 billion neurons in the brain, each with 10,000 connections to other neurons – and recognizing that such estimates are very approximate at best, and belie vast variability among brain regions, cell types, development and ageing within individuals, and perhaps even greater variability due to genetic and environmental variables between individuals – we could estimate roughly 86 trillion neuronal connections in an adult human brain. This is such an extremely complex structure for a human mind to even fathom trying to understand, made only exponentially more complex by the fact that the activity and even microstructure of the brain changes moment-to-moment on time scales as short as milliseconds. When we think about trying to characterize 'brain activity' with current state-of-the-art neuroimaging tools, we must first recognize how limited, fallible, and possibly even misleading this task is. Techniques such as EEG measure brain electrical activity with millisecond-level accuracy, but from at most a couple of hundred electrodes (and typically only dozens). In other words, we are attempting to sample 86 trillion dynamic connections with perhaps 64 sensors. Another technique, functional MRI, allows us to image changes in physiological activity in the living brain down to the level of 1 mm or less, yet even with this resolution each 1 mm^3 sample contains perhaps 100,000 neurons. Moreover, fMRI signal is a measurement of oxygen in small blood vessels, not a direct measure of any aspect of neuronal activity; how changes in oxygen relate, exactly, to the electro-chemical activity of neurons is poorly understood at best. Put simply, any of the methods discussed in our book – which are the best humanity has to offer at this time – are capable only of gross generalizations and best guesses concerning the true nature of brain activity. It is – to use a metaphor I heard from Dr Evelyn Schaefer, who attributed it to Dr Ulrich Neisser – as if we are attempting to determine what a massive factory does, based on knowing only what raw materials go in, what outputs emerge, and what we hear from a microphone held to the outside of the factory walls.

Fortunately for us the situation is not quite so dire, as the techniques we do have provide us with richer insights than a single microphone outside a factory – however limited they still may be. Moreover, although neurons comprise the cellular-level units of brain organization, it turns out that the brain is also organized at larger scales, including ones that the techniques introduced in this book are well-suited to measure. We can think of the brain as having at least three scales of organization: 'micro', 'meso', and 'macro'. The macro-scale is that of the lobes of the cerebral cortex (frontal, parietal, occipital, and temporal, see Figure 1.4), and other large, anatomically well-defined structures such as the hippocampus, cerebellum, pons, and so on. At this scale we can make gross generalizations of function, as are often

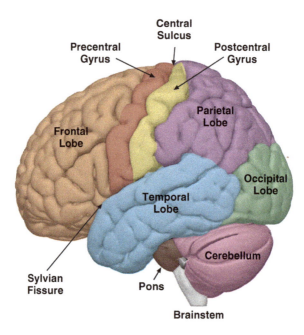

Figure 1.4 The lobes of the cerebral cortex, and major subcortical divisions of the brain. Also labelled are two major sulci that separate different lobes: the central sulcus separates the parietal and frontal lobes, while the Sylvian fissure separates the temporal lobe from the frontal and parietal lobes

seen in information aimed at the general public or children, such as 'the occipital lobe is for vision', 'the frontal lobe is for thought and action', or 'the hippocampus is involved in memory'. While all of these statements are true, they are too general to be of real use in cognitive neuroscience because they mask more fine-grained – and critically important – details. However, by and large cognitive neuroscience focuses on activity in the cerebral cortex, which is the most evolutionarily advanced part of the brain, and the one that plays the largest role in many aspects of cognition. However, this is not to discount the important roles of other parts of the brain, which also play necessary roles in many aspects of cognition.

At the other extreme is the micro-scale, where we have individual neurons (and sub-neuronal levels such as the study of neurotransmitters or subregions of neurons), cortical layers, and micro-structures such as columns. **Cortical columns** are clusters of neurons typically tens of microns in size, with distinct patterns of local connectivity running through the layers of the cerebral cortex, perpendicular to the outer surface of the brain. Columns have particular, repeating arrangements in a cortical area, which act as functional units. For example, in the **primary visual cortex** there are neurons that are tuned (that is, show the strongest response) to lines located in a particular part of the visual field, with a particular orientation. Similarly tuned neurons cluster in columns, such that within a region of cortex sensitive to a particular part of the visual field, there will be distinct columns tuned to lines of different orientations.

In between the macro- and micro-scales is the meso-scale of organization – the level of functionally and anatomically distinct 'brain areas'. This level of organization was first systematically documented by German neuroanatomist Korbinian Brodmann in his 1909 book *Localization in the Cerebral Cortex* (Brodmann, 1999 for English translation), based on his microscopic examination of slices of brain tissue stained to highlight cellular structures. Brodmann noted that the types of cells, how they were distributed across the layers of the cerebral cortex, and other micro-anatomical organizational factors differed across the brain, forming localized regions of consistent organization that were typically in the order of a few centimetres in size. Brodmann hypothesized that these systematic differences in **cytoarchitecture** must reflect differences in the functions that the different brain areas served. Brodmann's original map, along with an example of a cortical section showing the boundary between two cytoarchitectonically distinct areas, is shown in Figure 1.5.

Although these characterizations were based on anatomical work, generally performed post mortem (with the exception of the recent neuroimaging work), the notion of meso-scale organization was corroborated with work in the field of neuropsychology, which examines relationships between localization of acquired brain damage (for example, from stroke or injury) and functional deficits that can be measured through cognitive or other behavioural tests. This was first exemplified by Paul Broca, who in 1865 reported the case of a patient who had sustained brain damage and as a result, the only word he could utter was 'tan'. However, aside from this language deficit the person seemed otherwise cognitively intact, and was able to function relatively normally in his everyday life. After the patient died, Broca performed an autopsy and identified the inferior frontal gyrus in the left hemisphere as the localized site of brain damage, as shown in Figure 1.6. This led Broca to conclude

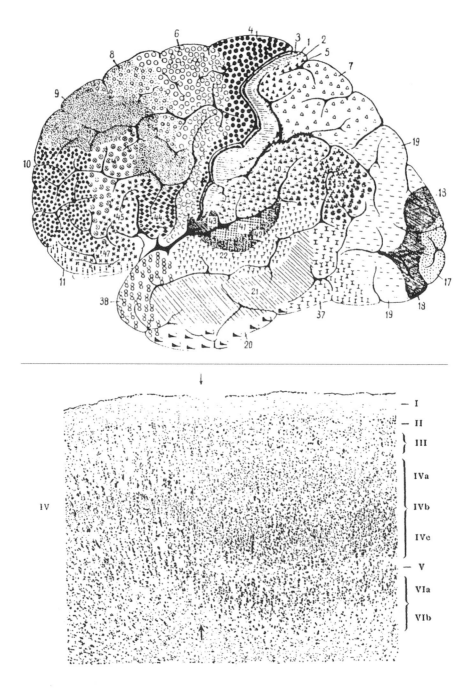

Figure 1.5 The original map of cytoarchitectonically defined cortical areas (left), published by Korbinian Brodmann in 1909. Areas are indicated by numbers and distinguished by filling with different symbols in the map. The bottom panel shows an example of a slice through the layers in the occipital cortex. The arrows indicate the boundary between areas 18 (left) and 17 (right); area 17 is the primary visual cortex, commonly referred to as V1. All images are in the public domain

that this brain region was the localized 'speech centre', and more generally that the brain was organized into functionally distinct areas (Broca, 1865).

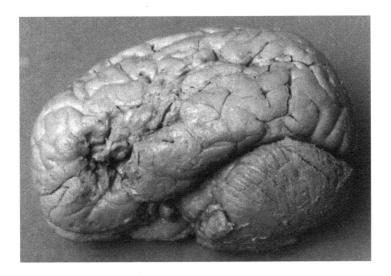

Figure 1.6 The brain of Paul Broca's patient 'Tan' (actually named M. Leborgne), extracted post mortem and showing the lesion to the left inferior frontal gyrus. Photograph by Bruno Delamain, reprinted from Dronkers, Plaisant, Iba-Zizen, and Cabanis, 2007 with permission of Oxford University Press

This notion of regional organization of the cerebral cortex was controversial into the early part of the twentieth century. In part, this was due to reactions against the nineteenth-century pseudoscience of phrenology – which also proposed localized meso-scale function, but conspicuously avoided systematic, scientific testing of hypotheses, and assumed that more 'developed' functions resulted in bumps on the skull due to the size of the brain regions responsible. In the twentieth century, more principled arguments and scientific evidence were brought to bear, most prominently through the work of Karl Lashley (1929) that involved lesioning the brains of animals such as rats. Lashley's findings suggested that large parts of the cerebral cortex could be damaged without affecting learning and memory, leading him to propose the principle of 'mass action' in which learning and memory functions were broadly distributed in the brain, rather than localized. Relatedly Lashley proposed 'equipotentiality', the idea that any part of the cortex could assume the functions of another if an area were damaged.

In spite of Lashley's ideas, further work along the lines Brodmann pioneered were carried out in the twentieth century by Vogt and Vogt (Vogt & Vogt, 1919), von Economo and Koskinas (Economo & Koskinas, 1925), and others. This work confirmed the existence of this meso-scale level of brain organization, based on cytoarchitecture and also **myeloarchitecture** (the microscopic structure of myelinated fibres; for example, the relative occurrence, distribution, and density of nerve fibres running horizontally, vertically, and/or diagonally within the cortex – as illustrated in the rightmost panel of Figure 1.3). Brodmann originally identified 43 cytoarchitectonically distinct areas within each cerebral hemisphere; subsequent work increased this number to between 150–200 areas, and recent neuroimaging work has similarly put the estimate at 180 (Glasser et al., 2016), as shown in Figure 1.7. This meso-scale level of organization is largely what we are able to examine with the non-invasive methods of cognitive neuroscience described in this book. Henceforth we will refer to meso-scale regions defined by cytoarchitecture, myeloarchitecture, or functional imaging simply as 'cortical areas'.

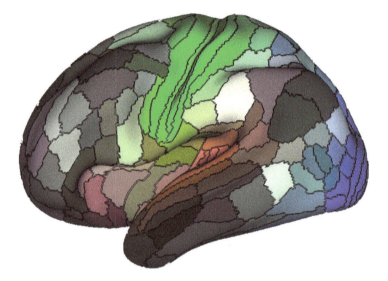

Figure 1.7 A contemporary cortical parcellation scheme produced by Glasser and colleagues (2016). Unlike most prior maps, which were based on post-mortem microscopic examination of stained tissue, this map is solely based on multiple measures derived from MRI scans in living humans, including both structural and functional information. This approach resulted in parcellation of each cerebral hemisphere into 180 distinct cortical areas. Reprinted from Glasser et al., 2016 with permission of Springer Nature

While the existence of such cortical areas is now widely accepted, their definition is still a subject of debate and active investigation. There are many possible ways to define a cortical area, including modern automated and computational versions of Brodmann's cytoarchitectonic approach, myeloarchitecture, the distribution of different neurotransmitter receptors, gene expression patterns, functional neuroimaging measures, and others. Different approaches will result in different borders between areas and even the number of areas. Recent work has attempted to merge multiple measures using advanced machine learning algorithms (Glasser et al., 2016). What we do know is that the meso-scale of organization does not map onto macro-scale gross anatomy in a systematic way. That is to say, although a given area will not be in the cerebral cortex of one individual and the hippocampus of another, within the cerebral cortex the exact location of an area may show considerable inter-individual variation. Thus the approach that was used in the early days of functional neuroimaging, of using the major **sulci** (folds) and **gyri** (bumps) on the cerebral cortex, has been shown to be invalid. Although major sulci, such as the **central sulcus** (separating the frontal and parietal lobes) and **Sylvian fissure** (separating the temporal from the frontal and parietal lobes) are universally present in healthy human brains, many smaller sulci vary considerably. We return to this important fact in later chapters, but for now it is an important detail to keep in mind.

The nice thing about the meso-scale anatomical and functional organization of the cortex is that it corresponds to the scales that we can visualize using non-invasive neuroimaging methods. However, this is not to say that there is not organization at a more fine-grained level within cortical areas, because indeed there is (for example, the micro-scale and cortical columns mentioned above). Indeed, with advanced high-resolution techniques such as fMRI, researchers have been able to image aspects of micro-level organization such as the closely interleaved areas of primary visual cortex that receive selective input from each eye – ocular dominance columns. As well, even without 'pushing the envelope' of **spatial resolution** in fMRI or other techniques, it is possible not just to image the activity of a particular cortical activity, but examine how this activity changes with experimental manipulations, or see regional variations within it. A recent trend in fMRI research is using 'multivariate' approaches to analysis that look not just at the level of activation in a region, but for systematic patterns of response across the region (for example, some pixels of the image may be consistently high in activation, while others are consistently mid-range, and yet others have consistently low levels of activation). In other words, we can ask more than simply whether a brain area, as a whole, is sensitive to experimental manipulations, but identify unique patterns of activation within that area. Work in this area has demonstrated that even for a given category of stimuli (for example, faces), individual exemplars of that category (individual faces) reliably evoke distinct patterns of activity.

Finally, a criticism that has often been levelled at functional neuroimaging is that it is simply 'neo-phrenology' – that labelling a particular cortical area as subserving a particular function does not provide particularly deep insights into how the brain functions. One concern is that in any given experiment, typically a number of brain areas are shown to be active using a technique like fMRI. Furthermore, across studies we often see the same brain area activated by very different tasks and stimuli, suggesting that many areas may serve more than one function. For example, the left inferior frontal gyrus is typically associated with the function of speech production, in line with Broca's discovery mentioned earlier (indeed, this area is often called 'Broca's area'). However, it is also associated with processing grammar in language, and in non-linguistic tasks such as learning to press buttons in a particular sequence. The challenge for cognitive neuroscientists is to determine whether this is because the area performs some sort of computations that are common to all of these tasks; because there are anatomically distinct subregions subserving different functions; because there are overlapping or interleaved – but distinct – sets of neurons subserving different functions; or because the same cells within the area support very distinct functions under different task conditions. This latter possibility is one of several reasons why work in cognitive neuroscience has shifted from the relatively simple 'neo-phrenological' approach to also looking at **connectivity** – how different brain areas work in concert with each other through their organization in larger networks of regions. The study of network-level connectivity is being pursued both through studies of the anatomical, structural connections between regions (the **connectome**), and through functional connectivity.

Thus broadly speaking, work in elucidating the organization of the human brain can be seen as involving a number of approaches, which can be pursued individually or multiply in any given study or research programme. The first approach is **segregation**, in which distinct areas are identified and associated with particular functions. Another approach is **connectivity**, in which the connections between segregated areas are identified. Each of these approaches can in turn employ either structural or functional methods. Finally, **functional integration** (Friston, 2011) aims to combine these approaches to yield a more complete account of brain function, involving how networks of regions work together to support cognition. The ultimate goal would be to understand the areas involved, how they are connected, and, finally, how information flows through the network over time.

STUDYING THE ORGANIZATION OF THE BRAIN

While this entire book is about methods for studying the organization of the brain, this section lays the groundwork by providing a broad overview of the different classes of methods used in this endeavour. Notably, I have chosen to start with behavioural methods because ultimately in cognitive neuroscience we wish to understand the relationships between brain activity, cognition, emotion, and overt behaviour. Long before we had high-tech brain imaging methods, humans were studying cognition by making systematic measurements of overt behaviour. This included approaches such as systematically manipulating the stimuli and/or task instructions given to research participants, and quantifying their responses using means such as response times, accuracy judgements, and ratings. While on their own these tell us little about the brain areas or networks involved in the performance of such tasks, they are nonetheless critical tools for understanding brain activity. Most cognitive phenomena are best characterized, defined, and measured using behavioural methods, and these data have led to the development of quite advanced theories of how the mind works. Such theories can then be tested and refined using brain imaging or stimulation methods. However, without a detailed understanding and description of the phenomena at the cognitive level, it would be very challenging to design – let alone interpret – meaningful studies of brain activity. For this reason, behavioural methods form the foundation of cognitive neuroscience, and are a critical consideration in the design of any neuroimaging or neurostimulation experiment. If behaviour is not measured during a study, the results may well be uninterpretable, or at least open to multiple interpretations. Among the many considerations are that assumptions about how people are performing a task (or how well they are performing it – or even *that* they are performing it) may be incorrect if performance data is not recorded, and as well performance may vary from person to person, or systematically between groups, in ways that are critical to interpretation of the imaging results. For example, people might naturally perform a task in one of two rather different ways (for example, different strategies), or one group of people (for example, older adults or children) may perform slower, and/or find the task more challenging, than the young adults that comprise the sampled population for many studies.

Behavioural Methods

Reaction Time Methods

Reaction time (RT; also called 'response time') studies – sometimes referred to as 'mental chronometry' – evolve measuring the amount of time it takes for someone to make some sort of overt response. Often this is a button press made by a finger, but it can also be any other type of muscle activity (for example, a foot tap, or a smile), the onset of speech, or really any other overt behaviour whose onset timing (or in some cases, offset) can be accurately measured. By far the most common type of RT study involves pressing a button, either on a computer keyboard or a specialized 'button box'. While individuals may vary in how quickly they can press a button, what is typically of interest in an experiment is how RT compares between different experimental conditions. For example, perhaps the simplest type of RT measure (which is often called 'simple reaction time') is having participants press a button whenever they detect a very brief flash of light, with the flashes presented at random intervals so as not to be overly predictable. If we ask people to perform this task as quickly as possible, then we can argue that the resulting RT, averaged over some number of trials, is a reasonably accurate measure of how long it takes for the person's retinal cells to detect the flash of light, communicate this to the visual cortex, and then for the information to travel from the sensory (visual) cortex to the motor cortex (which controls body movements), and for the motor cortex signal to be transmitted via peripheral nerves to the finger muscle to make a response (one might posit at least one additional process in the middle, whereby the visual information is evaluated and a decision to press the button is made). In other words, we have a measurement of the timing of brain activity based not on measuring the brain activity directly, but via the end result of the brain activity: a button press.

Of course, this simple RT measure has limitations as to what it can tell us about brain activity. For one, we cannot differentiate between the amount of time required for visual perception versus for initiating the motor response (or any intermediate steps), and as well we cannot separate the timing of brain activity from the time it takes for the signal to travel from the motor cortex to the finger. However, by adding more experimental conditions, we can gain much stronger insights. For example, if rather than simply detecting a flash of light, we present either a horizontal or vertical line on the screen (varying this randomly from trial to trial), and ask participants to press different buttons depending on the orientation of the line, then we can compare this to the simple reaction time condition (where all stimuli are the same, and no discrimination is required) by subtracting the average RT from the simple detection task from the average RT for the orientation judgement task. This is the subtraction method described earlier in this chapter: the difference in RT tells us how much time it took for the brain to make this judgement, independent of the other task-related factors like simply detecting the stimulus and preparing and executing a motor response.

RT differences can be exceedingly sensitive in some experimental paradigms. For example, in studies of attention the difference in RT between conditions may be as little as 10 ms (or even less), but over a large number of trials the variability in RT is so small that statistically reliable effects can be obtained. This sensitivity comes at a cost though: we are sensitive both to differences between conditions that are intended by the experimenter, and unintended ones as well. This is a critical consideration for any experimental design – thinking through all of the possible differences between experimental conditions, and trying to match them as closely as possible. For instance, in the example above we were comparing RTs in the horizontal/vertical line task with simple RTs to flashes of light. However, it is possible that making even simple decisions about the presence or absence of a line takes more (or less) time than making simple decisions about the presence/absence of a flash of light. Therefore, to isolate the time required for our judgement task, our control condition should involve a line detection, rather than flash detection. Another important consideration concerns psychological factors rather than just the physical properties of the stimuli. For example, if people find one type of stimulus or task more interesting than another, then the RTs may reflect both the intended differences between stimuli/tasks, and also the influence of attention.

Accuracy Measurements

The other staple measure of behavioural experiments in cognitive science is **accuracy**. This is, quite simply, whether the participant makes a correct response or not. 'Correct', of course, depends on the experimental context. In the simple RT paradigm described in the previous section, a correct response is one that follows a flash of light. Even in this simple paradigm 'accuracy' has some complexity to it, because it's possible that a participant could press the button even when there was no flash of light. This could happen for several reasons, including an 'itchy trigger finger' (that is, a response the person immediately realizes is wrong), a false detection (thinking they saw the stimulus when they did not), or a failure to follow the instructions (for example, someone who for whatever reason does not feel inclined to perform the task well, but instead presses the button randomly or continuously – as sometimes happens with students required to participate in experiments for class credit). Therefore it is important firstly to define a 'response window': minimum and maximum times after the stimulus in which to consider that a response was actually triggered by that stimulus. As well, in simple detection tasks it is often a good idea not to simply categorize responses as 'correct' and 'incorrect', but into four categories: hits (correct responses), misses (failing to respond when a response should have been made), false alarms (making a response when no response should have been made), and correct rejections (not responding when a response was not required). If the task involves different **response contingencies** – different responses to different stimuli, such as in the line orientation judgement task described in the previous section – it may be sufficient to classify each response as 'correct' or 'incorrect'; however, it may also still be worthwhile to determine the number of misses for each condition, or perform other analyses of errors. For example, if there are more than two response options, there might be systematic patterns in the types of errors people make.

In neuroimaging studies in particular, tasks that provide measures of accuracy can serve a different (or additional) purpose: ensuring that participants are actually paying attention and doing what the experimenter expects. In many neuroimaging studies experimenters include very easy tasks simply to ensure that the participant is paying attention to the stimuli. By keeping an eye on behavioural responses during the study, the experimenter can ensure that the participant is performing the task (and thus not asleep or otherwise inattentive), and hopefully performing it accurately as well. It is common in neuroimaging studies to report behavioural results that, on their own, provide little or no insight into how participants were performing the task. Rather, their primary purpose is to ensure that participants are paying attention to the stimuli, and performing the task in the way that the experimenters expect. In other cases, the interpretation of the neuroimaging data is bolstered by also demonstrating an expected pattern of differential accuracy across conditions.

Other Response Types

While accuracy and RT are the 'workhorse' measures in a large number of cognitive behavioural studies, any number of other types of measures are also available. For example, rather than binary 'yes/no' type responses, one may have a wider range of response options, such as ratings. A common form of **rating scale** is the **Likert scale**, which consists of a set number of response options (often five or seven) that run along a particular dimension. For example, one could ask people how much they like a variety of foods, and for each food the response options on a five-point Likert scale might be 'dislike strongly'; 'somewhat dislike'; 'neutral'; 'somewhat like'; and 'like strongly'. Likert scales are an example of a **discrete (or ordinal)** rating scale, that is, one with a fixed set of levels that the person must choose among. If greater sensitivity is desired, another option is an **analogue scale,** in which the possible responses are essentially continuous over a range. Again using the example of food preference ratings, rather than five discrete possible values, we could present the participant with a line with '0' at one end and '100' at the other, and ask them to simply point, or click with a mouse, at the spot along the scale that reflects their feeling about each food. Continuous scales are more sensitive, but in many cases Likert scales are sensitive enough for the purpose at hand (though scales with more possible levels – such as 11 or 12 – tend to be more sensitive and less skewed than with fewer options; Grant et al., 1999).

Another category of response type is **verbal responses**, such as naming a picture or repeating a list of memorized words. Many software packages can automatically compute response times based on when the onset of a vocal response is detected by a microphone, as well as saving the actual response to an audio file. While these are relatively easy to implement in behavioural studies, in neuroimaging research verbal responses can be trickier. For example, MRI scanners are extremely loud (on the order of 90 dB, which is at the upper limits of hearing safety – indeed, hearing protection is required inside an MRI scanner) and so it is often impossible to hear what participants are saying during a scan. However, noise-cancelling microphones have been used in this situation. In EEG, contractions of facial muscles – as occur during speech – can create artifacts in the data that make it more challenging to isolate the brain activity. A strategy that has been used to address this issue is delayed responses. For example, one could ask participants for verbal responses at the end of each MRI scan, although these are typically many minutes long and so this introduces a memory component as well, which may affect the results. In EEG, one could simply impose a short delay before asking for a vocal response, since typically the EEG activity of interest lasts for only a second or so after a stimulus.

A variety of other manual responses are possible as well. For example, Limb and Braun (2008) studied brain activity during musical improvisation by having experienced jazz pianists perform on a specially designed piano keyboard during fMRI scanning. Similarly, drawing has been studied using fMRI by having people draw using either a special electronic tablet, or simply paper and pencil, during fMRI scans (Gowen & Miall, 2007; Saggar et al., 2015). Other studies use motion capture, which provides three-dimensional tracking of a person's body (or parts thereof, such as the hands). This can be accomplished either via one or more cameras, or by sensors attached to various parts of the body. Motion capture can be valuable if the interest is not simply in the start or endpoint of a movement, but on variables occurring during the movement, such as the path or speed of a hand movement.

Ultimately, the choice of the behavioural measure(s) are determined by the needs of the study, but in neuroimaging the techniques themselves may impose certain limitations that require creative solutions to obtaining the desired measures. These issues, in particular the limitations imposed by different techniques, are discussed in greater detail in the chapters that follow.

Psychophysics

A special class of behavioural studies dealing with perception are those of **psychophysics**. This field was established in 1860 with the publication of Gustav Fechner's *Elemente die Psychophysik*, in which he defined psychophysics as 'an exact theory of the functionally dependent relations of … the physical and the psychological worlds' (Fechner, 1966: 7). In other words, Fechner sought to systematically relate psychological phenomena (perception) with physical ones (stimuli). Typical psychophysics experiments focus on individuals' abilities to detect simple stimuli or make discrimination judgements between them. For example, a person might be asked to sit in a dark room, stare at a blank screen, and press a button every time a flash of light is detected. By varying the brightness of the flash, one can determine the person's threshold for detection in terms of light intensity (Simpson, Braun, Bargen, & Newman, 2000; Simpson, Newman, & Aasland, 1997). In a discrimination experiment, one might have to determine which of two tones is louder, with the difference in loudness being systematically manipulated to find the threshold. Determining thresholds is usually done using a **staircase method**, in which the intensity (or difference in intensities, for discrimination experiments) is initially set below the expected threshold (making it undetectable), and then raised on subsequent trials until the participant can reliably detect it. Then, the staircase direction is reversed and the stimulus intensity is systematically lowered again until the participant can no longer detect it. This reversal process is repeated several times, and the threshold value is typically set to be the intensity level at which the person is able to accurately make the detection/discrimination 50% of the time.

Fechner and other psychophysicists sought to derive 'laws' or formulae relating perceptual judgements to stimulus intensity. For example, based on earlier work by E.H. Weber, Fechner defined 'Weber's Law' as a principle by which 'the magnitude of the stimulus increment must increase in precise proportion to the stimulus already present, in order to bring about an equal increase in sensation' (Fechner, 1966: 54). Fechner found that this principle generalized to different senses, such as detecting flashes of light or changes in weight – that it was not the absolute magnitude of the change (in brightness or weight) that determined people's ability to discriminate two stimuli, but the relative magnitude of the change. Thus the threshold for discriminating between two very small weights may be a matter of a few grams, whereas the threshold for discriminating between two much heavier weights would be much larger, on the order of tens or hundreds of grams.

While psychophysics is a relatively specialized domain of experimental psychology and cognitive science, it has wider relevance in areas such as neuroimaging. First of all, although general psychophysical principles or 'laws' generalize across individuals (indeed, most psychophysics studies focus on a large number of trials using only two to three individuals), individuals' thresholds can differ considerably. Thus in some cases it may be important to perform psychophysical threshold measurements prior to starting an experiment proper, to determine the appropriate stimulus levels for each individual so as to equate their performance and, as much as possible, subjective experience. As well, neuroimaging studies of psychophysical paradigms can be interesting and informative because we would expect that there is some relationship between perceptual experience and brain activity, which we might be able to measure. For example, some brain areas may respond in an intensity-dependent manner to stimuli – even when the stimuli are below the threshold for conscious perception – whereas other brain areas may respond only when a stimulus is consciously perceived. More mechanistically, psychophysical methods have been used to characterize the nature of brain responses and how they change with systematic manipulation of stimuli. For example, an early study employing visual psychophysics by Boynton and colleagues (Boynton, Engel Glover, & Heeger, 1996) was one of the first to carefully and systematically characterize how the fMRI response to individual stimuli varied as a function of stimulus parameters such as contrast and duration. This study provided valuable insight into the nature of the fMRI response that helped propel the field of fMRI forward.

Neuropsychology

From behavioural methods we now move to briefly cover the different classes of methods to study brain activity more directly. First among these, historically, is **neuropsychology** – or as it is now more commonly described in the research literature, **lesion-deficit** studies. Some of humankind's earliest insights into the brain as the seat of the mind and consciousness came from observations of people with brain damage, and the altered patterns of behaviour, thought, and consciousness that accompanied these. Throughout most of the twentieth century, lesion-deficit studies comprised the majority of sources of information we had about how cognitive processes related to different brain areas. This included studies of people with acquired brain injury (for example, through an accident, stroke, or other event), people who had undergone neurosurgery (for example, for the treatment of epilepsy, or tumour removal), or people who had a progressive or degenerative disease that specifically affected particular brain regions (for example, Alzheimer's or Parkinson's disease). In general, as implied by the name, lesion-deficit studies involve trying to determine how specific functional deficits are systematically related to damage (lesions) to particular brain regions. This line of inquiry provided significant insights into the functional organization of the human brain, and led to many influential theories of brain organization and cognitive function in domains such as language, memory, and movement. By and large, these results were confirmed with the advent of non-invasive brain imaging techniques such as PET and fMRI, leading many researchers in the early days to question why these expensive, high-tech imaging techniques were even necessary!

However, neuroimaging techniques have proven to have numerous advantages over lesion-deficit studies. One important limitation of much of the lesion-deficit literature in the twentieth century was the fact that the techniques available for characterizing lesion location were quite limited. While structural MR imaging was introduced in the 1980s, it took time to become widely available and used in hospitals; prior to that, the 'gold standard' technique for imaging the structure of the brain non-invasively was computed tomography (CT) scanning, which is essentially an X-ray of the head. CT scans have limited resolution and contrast (the ability to distinguish between different types of tissue), making identification and localization of lesions somewhat approximate. In particular, because scans were generally printed on film and evaluated 'by eye', most of the localization and generalization across individual patients was done qualitatively rather than in any systematic or quantifiable way. In other cases, no imaging was available and studies were limited to inferring lesion location from patterns of symptoms, such as simply knowing which cerebral hemisphere was affected (based on symptoms such as which side of the body showed motor deficits, or whether language – typically reliant on the left hemisphere – was affected). These limitations were unsatisfying at best, and in some cases it became apparent that very similar patterns of symptoms or deficits could result from damage to different parts of the brain. Another limitation of these studies was that, by definition, the subjects all had some sort of brain pathology. While this was exactly what made them scientifically interesting, it also meant that the symptoms observed could have resulted either from the obvious location of brain damage, or from other areas of damage that might not have been as obvious. As well, people may have partly recovered from the effects of the brain damage, possibly by recruiting different areas to serve a particular function, or some sort of 're-wiring' of the brain. Finally, most causes of brain damage do not affect brain areas randomly, which might be considered optimal from a scientific perspective. That is, if any brain area is equally likely to experience a lesion, then across the population we would have equal insight into the functions of all areas. However, diseases such as Alzheimer's have very characteristic patterns of brain damage, and even the damage caused by stroke is non-random. Rather, significant functional/cognitive deficits are most likely to occur with strokes involving larger blood vessels in the brain, and these are located in quite consistent locations across individuals. This means that we are able to derive more informative data from strokes about parts of the brain underlying these major arteries than about other, more distal areas.

With the advent and increasingly widespread availability of structural MRI and computerized methods of image analysis, lesion-deficit studies have entered a new era with increasing precision and reliability. The power of this approach, known as **voxel-based lesion-symptom mapping (VLSM)**, was first described by Bates and colleagues (2003) in a paper investigating aphasia – a broad category of disorders characterized by acquired language deficits following brain injury. Bates and colleagues took a group of people suffering from aphasia and had a neurologist trace the extent of each patient's brain lesion on their structural MR image. The brain images were then overlaid (using a method that compensated for differences in the size and shape of the brains), and for every point in the brain, patients were assigned to one group if they had a lesion there, and another group if they did not. The researchers then performed statistical tests between these two groups using a variety of language assessments as the **outcome measure**. As shown in Figure 1.8, the results showed that people who had deficits in speech production had the greatest lesion overlap in the left insula (the area tucked behind the frontal and temporal lobes), whereas people who had deficits in speech comprehension showed the most lesion overlap in the left posterior temporal lobe. Since then, the technique has been further refined and applied to a wide variety of different patient populations, allowing much more systematic insight into how brain damage affects cognition. While this does not mitigate other issues such as the potential other effects of pathology or compensation, it is a great improvement over the older and much more approximate techniques.

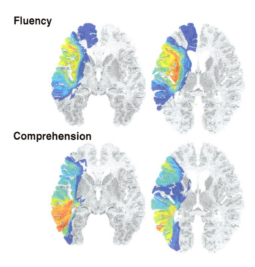

Figure 1.8 Example of voxel-based lesion-symptom mapping (VLSM) from Bates and colleagues (Bates et al., 2003). The top row shows correlations between lesion locations and deficits in speech production (fluency), in two slices through the brain, across a group of 101 people who had suffered a left hemisphere stroke and had some language deficits. The red areas are those that showed the most consistent relationship between lesion location and fluency deficits. The bottom row shows a similar correlation for the symptom of impaired auditory comprehension of speech, indicating that distinct lesion locations are associated with different functional deficits. Reprinted from Bates and colleagues, 2003 with permission of Springer Nature

Non-Neural Physiological Responses

Before turning to brain imaging proper, it is worth noting that there are a number of 'covert' methods that can be used to assess people's responses to stimuli without requiring that they make an overt, conscious response. One class of such measurements are generally called physiological (or psychophysiological) and include heart rate, respiration rate, skin conductance, skin temperature, and blood pressure. These parameters are under partial control of the autonomic nervous system, meaning that changes in these measures can indicate generalized arousal. These measures are somewhat nonspecific, in that such arousal can occur for several reasons, including stress, heightened attention or alertness, excitement, or as a result of certain drugs. However, in a controlled experimental context interpretation may be more constrained and these measures may provide an informative complement to other behavioural or neuroimaging measures.

Another measure that is frequently used in cognitive science studies is **eye tracking**. In essence, eye tracking is any technique that tracks the direction of a person's gaze over time. In cognitive science/neuroscience applications, this is typically done using specialized, high-speed cameras that shine infrared light on the eye and measure its reflectance. This method is able to isolate the pupil of the eye from the surrounding cornea, and use these features to track the movements of the pupils. Eye trackers can be stationary, typically placed on or near the computer monitor that the participant is viewing, or head-mounted, which works better for non-computer-based, 'real-world' situations as the participant is able to move their head in any direction without losing line-of-sight between the camera and their eyes. An example of a head-mounted eye tracker is shown in Figure 1.9.

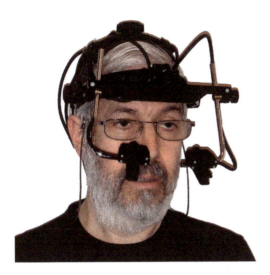

Figure 1.9 An example of a head-mounted eye tracker. The cameras are the black objects seen underneath each eye, which are aimed at, and remain in a fixed position relative to, each eye as the person moves their head. This allows for relatively natural movement. Other eye trackers are mounted on a computer or desk, and are effective only when the participant's head stays in a relatively consistent position, so that a direct line of sight between the eye-tracker camera and the eyes is maintained. Photo courtesy of Dr Raymond Klein, Dalhousie University. Used with permission

A first step in eye tracking is to perform a calibration in which the person is directed to focus their gaze on different locations in space in front of them (typically positions on a computer monitor). Once this is done, the eye tracker can identify where the person is looking with very high precision. A high-speed camera is required, taking an image at least 60 times per second, and often much faster (compared to standard video cameras that typically sample at 30 frames per second or less). This is necessary because most eye movements are not smooth, but are rather 'jumps' from one location to another (called saccades), which typically occur over very short time periods of about 200–250 ms. Eye tracking has found many uses in cognitive science, from investigating how reading occurs in real time to understanding how attention relates to the location of fixation. It has the advantage over most other overt forms of behaviour (such as button presses) in that eye movements often occur automatically or reflexively, and so can be used as a relatively non-invasive and covert means of assessing human performance. Another, somewhat more prosaic application of eye tracking is to ensure that people's gaze stays fixated on the point that the experimenter intends. For example, many studies of attention require participants to focus on a central fixation point on a screen, while attending 'covertly' to stimuli that occur elsewhere on the screen. Thus eye tracking can be used to ensure that fixation is actually maintained, and to alert the participant, and/or discard data, on trials when the desired fixation location is not maintained.

Another measure that can be obtained with eye-tracking equipment is **pupillometry**, the practice of measuring the diameter of the pupil. The pupil is the black centre of the eye, which is actually the opening that allows light to reach the retina. While its diameter adjusts automatically in response to changes in lighting, it is also influenced by a person's general arousal, similarly to skin conductance or other **physiological measures**.

Brain-Imaging Methods

We now turn to brain-imaging methods. While detailed discussion of these methods comprise the majority of this book, it is helpful at the outset to consider them collectively, so as to appreciate their relative merits and limitations. There are (at least) four important dimensions on which the different techniques vary. One is whether they measure brain structure or function. Structural techniques provide information about the anatomy of the brain. Since all brain activity relies on the structural 'matrix' of the brain, understanding brain structure is important. However, structure tends to be relatively stable over time, at least at the macro-anatomical scale (although as noted earlier, structure at the subcellular level has been documented to change over minutes and even seconds). Functional methods, on the other hand, capture some aspect of the moment-to-moment changes in some aspect of the physiological functioning of the brain and, in the context of cognitive neuroscience, typically about cognitive function as well.

Another dimension on which methods vary is the measured parameter. This is true both of structural and functional methods. For example, there are several types of structural imaging that can be performed using MRI scanners that are sensitive to very different aspects of brain anatomy, such as the density of cell bodies, or the presence of myelin (a fatty coating around neuronal axons, as discussed earlier and later in this chapter), or the orientation of connections between different brain areas. Functional imaging methods encompass an even wider range of physiological measures. Some, including EEG and MEG, are sensitive to the electrical activity of neurons. Since neurons communicate using electrical signals, this is considered a relatively 'direct' measure of brain activity (although the measurements are aggregates of the activity of large numbers of neurons, often from multiple, distinct areas). Other techniques are indirect, and require inferences between the measured variable and brain activity. For example, fMRI is sensitive to the concentration of oxygen in blood vessels in the brain. It turns out that oxygen levels tend to increase in relatively localized areas in response to increases in neuronal electrical activity, but nonetheless fMRI does not measure neuronal activity directly. Indeed, there is a very complicated relationship – involving a complex cascade of biochemical events – between increased neuronal activity and these localized changes in blood oxygenation.

The last two important dimensions are more continuous, as opposed to the categorical ones discussed so far. These are temporal and spatial resolution. **Temporal resolution** refers to the time scale that a technique is sensitive to changes over. Structural techniques obviously will generally have lower temporal resolution than functional techniques, since the parameters they measure change more slowly. Even among functional techniques, however, there is considerable variability in temporal resolution that is imposed both by what parameter is being measured, and how it is measured. For example, EEG has extremely high temporal resolution – EEG systems are capable of taking 10,000 measurements per second, and many important changes in neural activity can occur over the course of tens or even a few milliseconds. In contrast, although an fMRI image can be obtained in 100 ms or less, in common practice it takes 1–2 s to obtain a scan of the entire adult brain, meaning that the 'sampling rate' of fMRI is orders of magnitude slower than EEG. However, this is not as terrible as it might seem, because the blood oxygenation changes that fMRI measures occur over much slower time scales than electrical activity – typically several seconds.

Finally, spatial resolution refers to the level of spatial precision that a technique affords. While fMRI has lower temporal resolution than EEG, it has much higher spatial resolution. EEG is measured from electrodes placed on the outside of the head, typically using somewhere between 3 and 256 electrodes (64 being a common electrode count in cognitive neuroscience). Because of the relatively low number of sensors, and also the fact that electrical signals are distorted by the skull, localizing sources of electrical activity in the brain with EEG is challenging at best, and in optimal circumstances may be on the order of 1 cm (although often the resolution is much worse). In contrast, fMRI can localize activity with millimetre-level precision (or even sub-millimetre with advanced techniques), and the biggest spatial limitation of this technique is not the ability of the hardware, but the fact that the blood oxygenation changes that are measured change over a larger spatial area than the actual neural activity. Ultimately, there is no one best neuroimaging technique, nor is there a 'magical combination' of techniques that can unequivocally characterize all aspects of brain structure or function. Rather, cognitive neuroscientists must choose their tools based on a number of considerations, including the question at hand, their knowledge and experience, and available hardware (most of which is very expensive to purchase, and often to run as well). In some cases, researchers conduct **multimodal** neuroimaging studies by combining multiple techniques, such as EEG and fMRI. These may be done simultaneously; however, there are often practical constraints that make this challenging, and so in some cases the same experiment is performed on the same participants, once using one technique and once using another.

Structural Methods

The primary technique used to characterize human brain structure non-invasively is MRI. MRI scanners are, in very simple terms, sensitive to the concentration of water in the body relative to fat and other materials. The primary source of contrast (visual differences) in structural MRI is indeed between fat and water: the cerebral cortex – the outer layer of the brain, often referred to as 'grey matter' – contains primarily cell bodies that have a high proportion of water, while the underlying 'white matter' is mostly composed of connections between brain areas that are covered in a fatty coating known as **myelin**. The brain floats in **cerebrospinal fluid (CSF)**, which has an even higher concentration of water than grey matter. Thus a typical structural MR image will show clear visual distinctions (contrast) between grey matter, white matter, and CSF. Cognitive neuroscientists often use structural MRI as a primary measure to investigate factors such as the thickness of the cerebral cortex, or the integrity of white matter. These parameters can be affected by different disease states, as well as changing over the course of the lifespan. Advanced mathematical techniques have also been developed to characterize the shape of brain areas in quantifiable ways. It is also standard to acquire a structural MR image from every individual in a functional MRI study. This is because fMRI images are optimized to detect blood oxygenation changes, but this comes at the expense of good contrast between grey and white matter, and (generally) lower spatial resolution than structural MR images. Thus having a separate, optimized structural MRI scan aids in anatomical localization and especially in the necessary process of 'warping' each individual's uniquely sized and shaped brain to a standard template for averaging or comparison across individuals. Structural MRI scans are similarly useful for other imaging techniques, such as MEG and optical imaging, as well as in neurostimulation studies, for the anatomical precision they provide.

Another structural measure commonly used is diffusion-weighted imaging (DWI), which can be used to infer the orientation of nerve fibres within the white matter. The white matter contains a large number of different connections between brain areas, and DWI can be used to identify different tracts, and characterize parameters such as their integrity and thickness. DWI is an indirect measure, in that what it is actually sensitive to is the diffusion of water molecules. Because the myelin sheath around neuronal axons is high in fat, water does not cross the sheath, but instead preferentially diffuses parallel to the orientation of the axons.

Direct Functional Methods

The oldest non-invasive neuroimaging technique is electroencephalography, or EEG. This involves the application of electrodes to the outside of the head, which provide measurements of electrical activity coming from the brain. As already noted, EEG has exquisite temporal resolution; however, it also has a number of significant limitations. For one, the brain is not the only source of electrical signal picked up by EEG electrodes. A number of physiological artifacts, including contractions of face, neck, and shoulder muscles, eye blinks, and in some cases heartbeats all generate electrical signals that tend to be significantly larger than the brain signals. This can make it challenging to separate brain from non-brain signals. As well, numerous sources of electricity in the environment around the person can be picked up by the electrodes, creating additional artifacts. Another important limitation of EEG is that electricity conducts very well through the brain, and typically many brain areas generate electrical activity simultaneously. EEG electrodes measure the sum of all of this activity, which makes it difficult to separate signals that originated in different parts of the brain. This is made more difficult by the fact that the skull is a very poor conductor of electricity, which means that brain signals are both attenuated and blurred spatially, creating further challenges for localization. For these reasons, the primary strength of EEG is in its temporal resolution, as well as our amassed body of knowledge associating particular features of the EEG signal with specific cognitive processes. This allows researchers to characterize the timing and nature of some cognitive operations. This is typically done by time-locking the EEG signal to particular events of interest, such as the onset of stimuli, and then averaging together the time-locked data from numerous trials in an experiment. This helps isolate the brain activity that is reliably elicited by the stimuli, from noise that occurs randomly from trial to trial. When we analyse such time-locked EEG data it is usually called **event-related potentials (ERP)** or evoked potentials.

As a side note, it is worth mentioning that some cognitive neuroscientists question – or explicitly reject – the application of the term 'neuroimaging' to EEG, because of the limitations in localizing activity inside the brain. While this is an excellent topic to debate at the pub over a few beers, I unequivocally include EEG as a neuroimaging technique for several reasons. First of all, EEG data are typically represented and interpreted visually, either as time-varying waveforms from each electrode, or as maps of the head showing the strength of electrical potentials across the scalp. These are unarguably images. Moreover, the name 'electroencephalography' includes the root 'graph', the Greek word for writing – so EEG is a visual representation of electrical activity originating from the head. Finally, it is far more convenient and expedient to refer to 'brain imaging techniques' than to have to say something along the lines of 'brain imaging techniques and EEG' or 'neuroimaging techniques and that other measure of functional brain activity that some people refuse to call neuroimaging'.

A related technique is magnetoencephalography, or MEG. This is based on a fundamental physical principle, known as Ampère's circuital law or, more informally, the right-hand rule. This describes the fact that any time an **electrical current** flows through a conductor (such as the brain), a corresponding magnetic field is produced. Thus MEG uses extremely sensitive magnetic field detectors to measure the correlates of the electrical activity that EEG measures. Although they measure closely related signals, MEG has some advantages over EEG. Most notably, the skull does not affect magnetic fields as it does electrical current, and furthermore magnetic fields drop off sharply with increasing distance from their sources. For these reasons, localizing the sources of MEG activity within the brain tend to be more accurate with MEG than EEG, thus affording MEG better spatial resolution while at the same time preserving the excellent temporal resolution of EEG. Nonetheless, localizing the sources of MEG signals relies on certain assumptions and inferences, and so its spatial resolution is lower and less accurate than fMRI in most cases. MEG systems are also much more expensive to obtain and maintain than EEG systems, making MEG a far less commonly used technique. Both EEG and MEG can be considered 'direct' measures of neural activity.

Indirect Functional Methods

Indirect functional methods are those that infer brain activity through measurements of other physiological processes that are in some way influenced by neuronal activity. By far the most widespread of these (and indeed, of cognitive neuroscience techniques in general) is functional MRI (fMRI). As already noted, this technique uses an MRI scanner (involving strong magnetic fields and radio waves) to measure the concentration of oxygenated blood (or more precisely, the ratio of oxygenated to deoxygenated haemoglobin – the molecule that transports oxygen throughout the body) within the brain, with millimetre-level spatial resolution. Although its temporal resolution is somewhat limited – primarily by the relatively slow nature of the 'haemodynamic' response relative to electrical activity – fMRI is nonetheless able to characterize changes in activity over relatively short, and cognitively meaningful, periods of time in the order of a few seconds.

In addition to fMRI, however, there are several other non-invasive, indirect measures of brain action that are commonly used. One is **functional near-infrared optical imaging (fNIRI)**. This involves shining near-infrared light directly on the head using optical fibres, and measuring the transmitted light at nearby (2–3 cm) locations. Because the skull and other tissues of the head are relatively transparent to infrared light, the light is able to pass through to the brain and be reflected out again. Measurements of this transmitted light can be used to estimate the concentration of different chemicals in the brain. In fNIRI, the primary focus is on haemoglobin, and so fNIRI measures a signal closely related to that of fMRI. However, fNIRI has much poorer spatial resolution than fMRI because at safe intensities the light can only penetrate a few centimetres into the brain. As well, there are practical constraints on the number of 'optodes' used for transmitting and measuring light that limit spatial resolution over the surface of the scalp. However, fNIRI has some advantages over fMRI in that whereas fMRI requires very expensive hardware and imposes significant constraints due to the use of magnetic fields and radio waves (for example, many people with metal implanted in their bodies are ineligible for MRI), fNIRI is relatively inexpensive and has fewer constraints on who it can be used with. Indeed, one of the best use cases for fNIRI is with infants and very young children, who might not do well in an MRI scanner (which is very loud, and requires one to lie extremely still, and alone, in a small tube). Because it measures essentially the same physiological process as fMRI, fNIRI has similar temporal resolution. However, there is a second, less commonly used approach to fNIRI that has much higher temporal resolution – on the order of EEG or MEG. Often called event-related optical signal (EROS), this measurement of the 'fast' optical signal is relatively poorly understood but seems to be caused by changes in the size of neurons that occur when they fire. The cells swell up, decreasing the space between cells (extracellular space) and altering light transmission as a result.

Finally, there is **positron emission tomography (PET)**, which preceded fMRI by several years, and was thus the first non-invasive technique to provide accurate, high-resolution pictures of physiological processes occurring in the brain. However, PET measures the emission of radioactivity, and as such requires that a radioactive substance be introduced into the body, typically via injection or inhalation. While the levels of radioactivity used in PET scans are very safe, this limits the number of scans an individual can have in any given period of time, and also discourages many people from wanting to participate in studies, either due to a fear of radioactivity (or unnecessarily ingesting foreign substances more generally), or to not wanting injections. Functional PET imaging originally relied on radioactively labelled oxygen, and so the measurements were of oxygenated blood flow through the brain. However, fMRI quickly supplanted PET for several reasons, including the lack of a need to introduce a foreign substance into the body (fMRI relies on 'intrinsic contrast' – one that occurs naturally). As well, PET measurements of blood oxygenation have very poor temporal resolution, with each scan taking approximately 90 s and requiring time between each scan for the radioactive tracer to 'wash out' before the next scan. During each 90 s period only one experimental condition can occur, and so this makes experiments slow and tedious at best, and in some cases impossible if there is a need to examine randomly intermixed conditions, events that occur on very fast time scales, or other factors. In spite of these limitations, PET has found continued – if limited – use in cognitive neuroscience owing to the fact that many other chemicals besides oxygen can be radioactively labelled. These include various neurotransmitters, neuromodulators, and psychoactive drugs. While temporal resolution is still limited, PET is the only non-invasive technique that allows us to track the time course and spatial distribution of neuropharmacological agents in the brain, providing it with a unique niche in the cognitive neuroscientist's toolbox. As well, combined PET–MRI scanners have recently been developed that allow one to simultaneously obtain both types of data, making possible studies that combine structural imaging with fMRI measures of brain activation and neuropharmacological tracing using PET.

Manipulating Brain Activity

In addition to the bevy of neuroimaging techniques available, cognitive neuroscientists are also able to directly manipulate brain activity using **neurostimulation** techniques. These fall into two general types: magnetic and electrical stimulation. It is worth noting as well that many different drugs and other chemical compounds can be used to manipulate brain activity, and indeed often in much more targeted and specific ways than using non-invasive electrical or magnetic methods. However, these are considered invasive and fall outside the scope of this book.

Transcranial magnetic stimulation (TMS) relies on Ampère's circuital law (the right-hand rule) to induce very brief, but strong, electrical currents in the brain using a strong magnetic field. The stimulator is called a 'coil' because it contains many windings of copper wire through which a strong electrical current is passed. This creates a magnetic field which, when placed against a person's skull, induces an electrical current in the brain directly underneath. TMS has very high spatial precision, with the maximum stimulation occurring in an area of only a few cubic centimetres directly under the coil and dropping off quite sharply with distance. Depending on how it is applied, TMS can have inhibitory or facilitative effects on brain function, which last from seconds to up to an hour or more after stimulation. One common application of TMS is to use an inhibitory protocol to create 'transient brain lesions'; that is, to briefly disrupt the activity of a target brain area. From this, one can make inferences about the function of the area. While this could also be done using a neuroimaging technique to see if the area 'lights up' during a particular task, TMS has the advantage of demonstrating not only that the area is activated during the task, but that its activation is critically necessary for performance of that task. TMS can also be used to facilitate activity in a particular brain area, which can be of interest in training studies to improve cognitive performance, or in rehabilitation to improve recovery from a brain injury. As well, repeated TMS sessions over days and weeks have shown efficacy in treating some neurological and psychiatric conditions such as depression.

The other common type of non-invasive neurostimulation is transcranial electrical stimulation (tES). This involves passing a very weak current between two electrodes attached to the head, with the targeted brain area in between them. The currents in this case are far weaker than those used in TMS, and indeed tES is often referred to as 'neuromodulation' rather than stimulation, to reflect the comparatively moderate effects it has on brain activity. Like TMS, tES can have either inhibitory or facilitative effects on brain activity, depending on the parameters used for stimulation. However, the inhibitory effects would not be described as 'transient lesions' because they do not completely disrupt activity in an area. Rather, tES tends to alter activity in weaker, but still measurable ways. There are also a number of distinct types of delivering tES. The most common is direct current stimulation (tDCS), which involves simply passing a fixed level of current between the electrodes for a set period of time (typically 5–10 minutes). Another is alternating current stimulation (tACS), which involves modulating the current up and down sinusoidally. This is often used to entrain electrical brain activity, as it has been found (by combining tES with EEG) that certain brain rhythms can be induced or entrained using this technique. Finally, random noise stimulation (tRNS) involves alternating the strength of current randomly from moment to moment, rather than in a systematic sinusoidal fashion as in tACS. While less commonly used than the other techniques, tRNS seems to have similar effects to tDCS, but some evidence suggests the effects of tRNS are stronger and longer-lasting.

An important point to note about TMS and tES is that they are not actually measurements, but rather ways of influencing brain function. For this reason, experiments involving these techniques necessarily rely on one or more additional techniques to provide quantitative measurements of the effects of stimulation. Often these are behavioural measures such as RT, but as well studies may combine stimulation with some form of neuroimaging to more directly assess the effects of stimulation on brain activity.

SUMMARY

Cognitive neuroscience is a field of research focused on understanding relationships between mind and brain — how brain activity relates to cognitive functions such as memory, attention, reasoning, and language. The brain is organized, structurally and functionally, on multiple levels — which we can broadly classify as micro-, meso-, and macro-scale. Non-invasive cognitive neuroscience techniques operate primarily on the meso-scale of functionally and anatomically distinct regions approximately a few centimetres in surface area on the cerebral cortex. A variety of tools and techniques are available to cognitive neuroscience researchers, and can be classified on at least four dimensions, including whether they are reveal primarily structural or functional information; the physiological parameter they measure; their temporal resolution; and their spatial resolution. These include 'direct' measures of brain electrical activity (and its magnetic correlate), and 'indirect' measures such as of blood oxygenation. As well, there are neurostimulation and neuromodulatory techniques that allow researchers to manipulate brain activity in specific brain regions. The effects of neurostimulation can be excitatory/facilitative, or inhibitory/disruptive. In addition to using one or more neuroimaging and/or stimulation techniques, it is important in cognitive neuroscience studies to accurately measure and characterize behaviour during data acquisition. This is both to ensure that participants are performing the tasks intended, and in the manner intended. As well, behavioural measures can reveal important variability between tasks and/or individuals, which can significantly influence measures of brain activity and the effects of neurostimulation.

THINGS YOU SHOULD KNOW

- Cognitive neuroscience is the field of study that aims to understand the neural bases of cognition, emotion, and behaviour. It is a relatively young field that was enabled by the development of non-invasive neuroimaging techniques late in the twentieth century and continuing to this day.
- The primary cell types in the brain are neurons and glia. Neurons play the primary role in cognition, emotion, and action, while glia play largely supporting roles. However, glia are critical to normal brain function as well. Neurons communicate via electrochemical signalling. Chemical neurotransmitters and neuromodulators are the primary means of communication between neurons (and between neurons and glia). These chemical messengers modulate the electrical potential of neurons, and when a neuron 'fires' by generating an action potential, this is propagated along the neuron electrically, triggering the release of neurochemicals to signal other cells.

- The organization of the brain can broadly be described at three levels. The 'macro' scale is that of whole lobes, such as parietal and occipital. This is generally too broad for cognitive neuroscientific purposes. The 'meso' scale refers to brain regions that may be defined on the basis of differences in fine-grained cellular and connectivity architecture, and/or functional specialization. This is the primary scale of focus in cognitive neuroscience. The 'micro' scale is that of individual neurons, cortical columns, and other anatomical elements within a functionally or structurally defined brain region. In general, the non-invasive techniques of cognitive neuroscience lack the spatial resolution to study activity at the micro-anatomical scale.

- In empirical research, cognitive processes are generally operationally defined in terms of behavioural measures, such as the time it takes to make a response (response or reaction time – RT) and accuracy. Since the goal of cognitive neuroscience is to relate brain activity to cognition, it is critical to understand the cognitive processes under investigation, and to obtain behavioural measures to accompany the neuroimaging or neurostimulation data. Without behavioural measures, most cognitive neuroscientific data is challenging to interpret. It is far preferable to measure behaviour than to assume that particular cognitive operations are occurring in an experiment. Exceptions to this include studies of brain structure, and of brain activity during resting states.

- There are many types of non-invasive tools used in cognitive neuroscience today. These can be broadly categorized based on whether they measure structural parameters, provide direct measures of electromagnetic brain activity, provide indirect measures of brain activity such as blood oxygenation, or modulate brain activity by electrical or magnetic stimulation.

FURTHER READINGS

Chipman, S.E.F. (Ed.) (2017). *The Oxford Handbook of Cognitive Science*. Oxford: Oxford University Press.

Gazzaniga, M.S., Ivry, R.B., & Mangun, G.R. (2018). *Cognitive Neuroscience* (5th ed.). London: W.W. Norton & Company.

Passingham, R. (2016). *Cognitive Neuroscience: A Very Short Introduction*. Oxford: Oxford University Press.

Postle, B.R. (2015). *Essentials of Cognitive Neuroscience*. Hoboken, NJ: Wiley-Blackwell.

Purves, D., Augustine, G.J., Fitzpatrick, D., Hall, W.C., LaMantia, A-S., and White, L.E. (2017). *Neuroscience*. Oxford, UK: Oxford University Press.

Ward, J. (2017). *The Student's Guide to Cognitive Neuroscience* (3rd ed.). London: Psychology Press.

2 Research Methods and Experimental Design

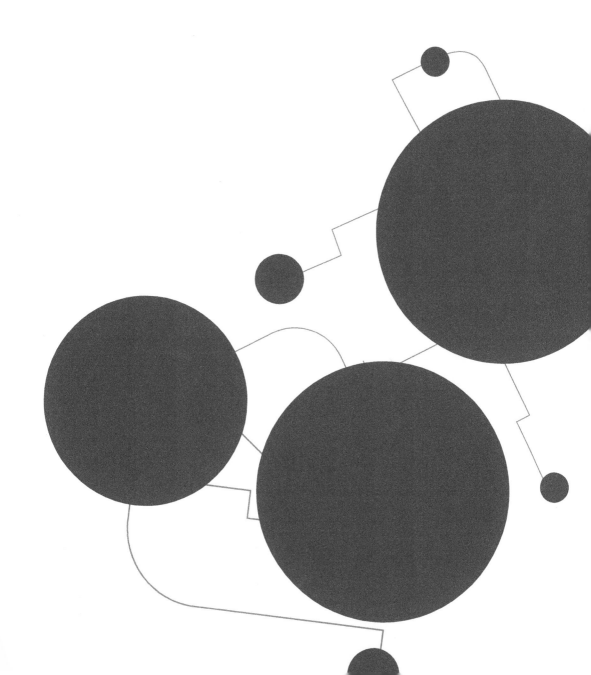

LEARNING OBJECTIVES

After reading this chapter, you should be able to:

- Explain what independent and dependent variables are, and what contrasts between levels of a variable are.
- Explain the logic and value of subtractive and additive factors designs.
- Describe how multiple variables can be systematically manipulated in factorial and parametric designs, and distinguish between the two.
- Explain why manipulating psychological conditions is preferred to comparing between different physical stimuli in neuroimaging experiments.
- Describe the difference between within- and between-subjects designs.
- Explain the concept of statistical power and its relationship to sample size.
- Explain the difference between forward and reverse inference in interpreting neuroimaging results.
- Identify key ethical issues raised by cognitive neuroscience.

INTRODUCTION

Before digging into the 'meat' of this book – detailed explanations of each cognitive neuroscience method – it is important to lay some groundwork in the fundamental methods of experimental design for cognitive neuroscience. If you have previously conducted research in experimental psychology, cognitive science, or a related field – or taken a general research methods class in this area – you may be able to give this chapter a quick overview as a refresher. If you do not have such a background, however, understanding the material in this chapter is the foundation on which all the other chapters rest.

We start by defining variables, and then covering the simplest experimental designs, in which we compare two levels of a single variable. We then expand this to include multiple variables as well as increased numbers of levels of a given variable, and continuous variables. We move on to discussing some basics of experimental setup and control. In addition to basic experimental design, we touch briefly on statistics. While teaching statistical analysis is beyond the scope of this book, there are some basic concepts and considerations that are necessary for understanding how neuroimaging data are analysed and interpreted. As in the rest of the book, I have focused here on conceptual understanding rather than formulae or other technical details – so those without prior training in statistics need not be afraid! Finally, we conclude with a discussion of research ethics, and in particular aspects of this topic that are unique to cognitive neuroscience. Our ability to peek inside the brain, both at structure and function, and to link this with thought raises a number of important ethical and privacy issues that everyone should consider as the techniques of cognitive neuroscience find an increasing role in larger society.

BASIC EXPERIMENTAL DESIGNS

Variables

Fundamentally experimentation in cognitive neuroscience involves the manipulation of one or more **variables** – specific, well-defined dimensions or properties that can have different values. For example, if we wish to compare brain responses to loud and quiet auditory tones, then 'loudness' (or to use a fancier term, 'amplitude of the tone') is the variable and the levels are 'quiet' and 'loud'. However, we would not simply want to define the levels qualitatively and subjectively as 'quiet' and 'loud'; rather, we would like to quantify the loudness variable in an objective way. This is because a fundamental tenet of empirical research is that it be carefully and systematically documented, and **replicable** – meaning that when we report on the study, we should describe our methods in sufficient detail that the reader could replicate the experiment and (hopefully) the results. The volume of auditory stimuli is typically quantified in deciBels (dB) and so we might define as levels of our variable 40 dB for 'quiet' and 70 dB for 'loud'.

An important thing to keep in mind is that there are, broadly speaking, two types of variables. **Continuous variables** are those whose values vary on a continuum. For example, the brightness of a visual stimulus is a continuous variable; images do not get brighter or darker in discrete steps, but rather in a continuous fashion. In contrast, **categorical variables** (also called **factors**) are variables that have discrete levels. For example, if we are doing an experiment with words, we could have one category of nouns, and one category of verbs. Words do not vary on a continuum of 'more noun-y' to 'more verb-y' – they are one or the other (admittedly, some words can act as both a noun or a verb in different contexts, but we will avoid linguistic minutiae for the sake of explanation here). In many cases though, for the purposes of an experimental design we might choose to treat a continuous variable as categorical, so that we can compare between set levels. This is what was done in the example in the first paragraph of this section: although the loudness of a sound is a continuous variable, we somewhat arbitrarily defined discrete categories of 'loud' and 'quiet' sounds. In this case we **operationally defined** our categories of loudness based on specific values on an otherwise continuous scale.

Another dimension on which we can define variables is with respect to their role in a given experiment. **Independent variables** are ones that are explicitly and intentionally manipulated by the experimenter. In the example above, we were interested in how human participants differ in their responses to the loud versus quiet stimuli, so loudness was an independent variable. Independent variables can be discrete or continuous; often continuous variables are operationalized as discrete levels for the purposes of an experiment (as in our example of quiet and loud stimuli), because it is conceptually and/or pragmatically simpler to do so. That is to say, on the conceptual side it can be easier to talk about 'loud versus quiet' than 'a range of loudness'; on the pragmatic side, it is easier to create and run a study with only two levels of loudness than trying to develop stimuli that capture the full range of human hearing. Naturally, however, the choice of continuous or categorical variable heavily depends on the actual research question. While stimuli are one way that experimenters can manipulate independent variables, there are other ways as well. For example, one could keep the stimuli present, but have participants perform two different tasks on the stimuli, and compare how task affects the outcome. It is also important to note that an independent variable can be defined as a property of a given individual, rather than a stimulus or task. For example, we could compare the performance (or brain activation) between a group of people with a particular disease (for example, Alzheimer's disease) and a group of neurologically healthy people (typically called a **control group**). In this case, which group an individual was would be an independent variable. While not 'manipulated' by the experimenter in the sense of causing some people to develop Alzheimer's disease, this would nonetheless be a variable that was designed and controlled by the experimenter in performing the recruiting for the study.

At a minimum, an experiment requires at least two levels of one independent variable, since experimentation depends on systematic manipulation of variables, combined with measurements of the resulting outcome of that manipulation. This leads us to the other classification: as well as at least one independent variable, an experiment requires at least one **dependent variable** – a response that we measure from the subject. Dependent variables are so-called because they are 'dependent' on the experimental manipulation (that is, the independent variable). As described in the previous chapter, in a cognitive neuroscience experiment this could be a button press (for example, press one button for quiet tones, and another for loud ones), from which we could derive RT and/or accuracy, or some measure of brain activation. For the most part, dependent variables in cognitive neuroscience experiments are continuous measures, whether they be RT, or brain activation as measured by some imaging method. One notable exception to this, however, is accuracy – in many studies, a response is either 'correct' or 'incorrect', and never something in between.

Subtractive and Additive Factors Designs

The experimental design described in the previous section – in which we compare the magnitude of a dependent variable between two levels of an independent variable (or, we could say, two conditions) – is the most basic and fundamental method in cognitive neuroscience and perhaps cognitive psychology more generally; the **subtraction method**. This approach was invented by the Dutch experimental psychologist F.C. Donders in the nineteenth century. The basic premise of the subtraction method is that if we hold all possible variables constant except for one which we manipulate (for example, loudness of the tone), then the difference in our dependent measure (be it response time or brain activation or whatever) represents the effect of the experimental manipulation.

An important thing to always keep in mind is that the subtraction method relies on the assumption of **pure insertion** – that inserting the additional cognitive process (or more generally, the experimental manipulation) does not alter any other aspects of how the person performs the task. For example, if one were interested in face perception, one might contrast brain activation when people are viewing faces with a control condition in which blurred or otherwise scrambled images of faces were presented – to control for activation associated with visual perception generally, rather than faces specifically. However, because faces are inherently more interesting to look at than fuzzy, scrambled blobs, people might pay more attention to the faces, creating a violation of pure insertion – because the control condition differs from the target condition in both visual features, and the amount of attention that the images attract.

The logic of the subtraction method is extended in **additive factors designs**, which involve several conditions in which variables of interest are systematically manipulated. For example, in one of the first non-invasive neuroimaging studies ever published, Steve Petersen, Mike Posner, and colleagues (Petersen et al., 1988) used additive factors to investigate brain areas involved in word reading. This used PET imaging (see Chapter 11) to measure activation levels in specific parts of the brain using radioactively labelled oxygen. While the interest was in brain areas involved in reading words, it turns out that word reading involves multiple cognitive processes, including (at least) visual perception, letter recognition, whole-word recognition, mapping letters to their associated sounds, and ultimately recognizing the meaning of the word (semantic processing). Thus simply contrasting words with a black screen in a subtractive design would reveal brain areas involved in word recognition, but it would be impossible to distinguish areas specifically involved in accessing word meanings from areas involved in visual perception more generally, or from areas specialized for letter recognition or letter-to-sound mapping.

Petersen and colleagues' study thus involved several conditions designed to incrementally engage different processes involved in reading, based on careful consideration of what these processes might be. The key subtraction contrasts between these conditions are shown in Figure 2.1. In the top row of the figure, areas active during passive word perception were isolated by subtracting signal recorded during a 'fixation' condition in which people viewed a blank screen. Different areas were activated for auditory presentation of the words (primarily in the superior temporal cortices) versus visual presentation (occipital cortices). However, when the passive perception condition was subtracted from a condition in which people had to repeat the words they heard or saw (second row of the figure), very similar areas of the motor cortex were activated. Since the sensory perception of words was present in both the passive and repeat aloud conditions, activation associated with this level of processing was subtracted out. The next higher order of contrast was aimed at identifying areas involved in semantic processing. For this, the researchers contrasted

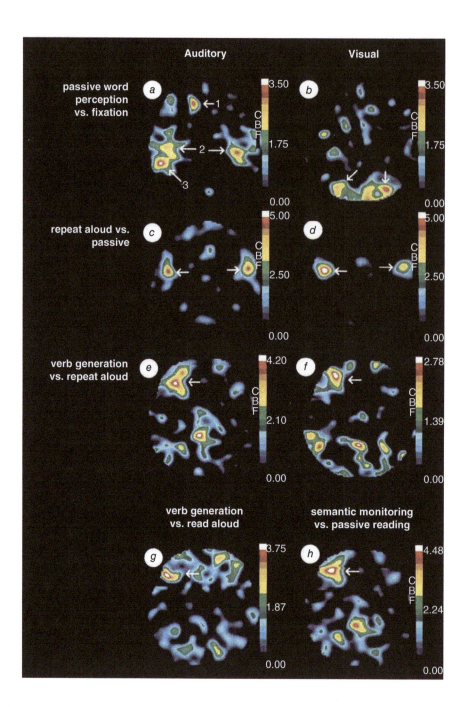

Figure 2.1 Results of a series of contrasts in an additive factors design. Panels (a) and (b) show the contrast of passively hearing (a) or seeing (b) words relative to baseline condition of simply seeing a fixation point. Although no anatomical underlay is shown, the auditory stimuli primarily activated superior temporal cortex bilaterally (primary auditory cortex), whereas visual stimuli primarily

Figure 2.1 (Continued)

activated primary visual cortex in the occipital lobe. The next level of contrast used passive perception as the control condition, subtracted from repeating the words aloud. Here, similar patterns of activation were seen for auditory (c) and visual (d) presentation formats. The third contrast used repeating aloud as the control condition for generating a verb based on the heard (e) or viewed (f) noun. Thus each level of the contrast is designed to isolate one additional cognitive operation. The bottom two panels are two different contrasts designed to tap into semantic (meaning-related) processing, by using two different tasks that both require processing the meaning of the word relative to control conditions designed to isolate the semantic from lower-level processes. Adapted from Petersen et al., 1988 with permission of Springer Nature

activation between simple repetition of each word, and generating a verb in response to a noun (for example, if *BREAD* was presented, the participant might say 'eat'). This highlighted activation in the left inferior frontal gyrus (historically referred to as Broca's area, based on Broca's original findings with his patient 'Tan', described in the previous chapter) – again, regardless of whether presentation was auditory or visual. As well, motor cortex was absent in this contrast, because speaking aloud was common to both tasks. The final row in the figure shows a contrast designed to test whether 'semantic processing' in a general sense activates a specific brain area, across different tasks and contrasts. Thus in the bottom row, we see the results of two different contrasts both designed to subtract simpler sensory and motor activations from semantic processing. The result was that indeed, a similar left frontal region was active in both semantic tasks.

Although from a contemporary psycholinguistic perspective, the details of the stimuli and tasks used in Petersen and colleagues' study could be (and have been, in later studies) improved upon, the logic of the additive factors method is sound and remains central to experimental design in cognitive neuroscience. In spite of this, the logic is not universally well-understood or implemented, and numerous manuscripts are rejected by journals specifically because this logic was not understood or followed carefully enough (or reviewers thought of possible confounds that the researchers had not anticipated or could not control). This often leads to ambiguity as to whether the experimental contrast really isolates brain areas associated with the process that the authors claim.

Factorial Designs

Factorial designs involve the systematic manipulation of two or more experimental factors. One can think of a simple subtractive design as manipulating a single factor (the difference between the two conditions) that has two levels (control and experimental). A factorial design is simply an expansion of this to manipulate multiple variables, typically in a systematic, **fully crossed design** – meaning that each possible combination of variables is tested. This is easily conceptualized visually, as shown in Table 2.1. The most obvious application of factorial designs is simply to test the effects of multiple variables in a single experiment. For example, if one were studying word processing, one could ask which brain areas showed differences between reading nouns and verbs, and also the effects of word frequency – whether less commonly occurring words require more brain activation associated with word retrieval than more frequent words. One could do two separate subtraction design experiments, one contrasting nouns and verbs, and the other contrasting low- with high-frequency words; however, it would be a more efficient use of resources to conduct a single experiment testing both these variables.

Table 2.1 A schematic of a simple factorial design. This would be called a 2 × 2 factorial, because each factor (variable) has two levels. By extension, if each variable had three levels, this would be a 3 × 3 factorial. In contrast, if we had three variables, each with two levels, it would be a 2 × 2 × 2 factorial design

		Factor A	
		Level 1	Level 2
Factor B	Level 1	A1B1	A2B1
	Level 2	A1B2	A2B2

The more powerful feature of factorial designs, however, is what they buy the experimenter in terms of generalizability. Certain unresolvable questions could arise when trying to interpret these two separate experiments. For example, in the noun/verb experiment, the researcher would need to choose what frequency of words to use – perhaps only high-frequency ones, or perhaps a mixture of frequencies (matching, of course, the frequencies of the words in the noun and verb conditions). Similarly, for the frequency experiment one would need to decide what types of words to use. Of course, one could use a mixture of words in each experiment, or make an arbitrary decision, but one would not know the extent to which the results of each experiment depended on the choice of words made. It could be, for example, that the difference in activation between high- and low-frequency words is greater for nouns than verbs. One easy way to test for this is a factorial design.

Factorial designs offer both greater experimental efficiency (in terms of being able to test multiple variables in a single experiment), and greater generalizability of the results. Imagine that we conducted a 2 × 2 factorial design experiment to investigate these same questions. The design of this is shown in Table 2.2. In this fully crossed design, high- and low-frequency nouns and verbs are all presented, leading to four experimental conditions. (Note that because all the stimuli are words, we do not really need a separate control condition, such as consonant strings – our interest is specifically in the contrast between words of differing type and frequency, not how these compare to non-word stimuli.) In analysing the results, we could look for a **main effect** of word type, which would be the difference in activation between nouns and verbs, averaged over (or, 'collapsed across') the two levels of frequency. Likewise, the main effect of word frequency would be obtained by contrasting high- with low-frequency words, collapsed across nouns and verbs. In both these cases, we would be confident that these activation maps generalized across word frequency (in the noun–verb contrast) and word type (in the frequency contrast). Moreover, we could test whether there were **interactions** between these two variables – this addresses the question posed above of whether nouns and verbs show different frequency effects. For example, to determine whether frequency differentially affects the two word types, one could examine the simple contrast between high- and low-frequency nouns and, separately, the contrast between high- and low-frequency verbs. One could also ask whether noun–verb differences exist, say, only for low-frequency words by contrasting low-frequency nouns with low-frequency verbs. In behavioural research, it is common to examine the formal test of the interaction effect in an analysis of variance (ANOVA), and then if the interaction is significant, follow this up with **post hoc tests** (the simple contrasts referred to above, for example, between high- and low-frequency nouns only). However, in neuroimaging it is more common to simply conduct and report the post hoc tests without reporting the interaction test. This is in part because, usually, the researcher has specific hypotheses concerning the interactions, so conducting these tests is justified regardless of whether the interaction term is significant; a significant interaction term is not usually informative on its own. Rather, a significant interaction just indicates some difference beyond the main effects that would need to be followed up by post hoc tests anyway.

Table 2.2 A schematic of a 2 × 2 factorial design contrasting verbs with nouns, and visual with auditory presentation

		Word Type	
		Noun	Verb
Word Frequency	High	Noun High Freq	Verb High Freq
	Low	Noun Low Freq	Verb Low Freq

Factorial designs clearly offer certain advantages over simple subtractive designs. However, as in all neuroimaging studies, it is important to not let the design get too complex. In behavioural research, it is not uncommon to have numerous factors and several levels of each. However, attempting to analyse and interpret such designs can get very complicated, especially in a neuroimaging context where there are the added dimensions of space (different locations in the brain, determined by the spatial resolution of the technique) and/or time. Thus it is often better to use simpler factorial designs and conduct multiple studies, rather than investing significant time designing and running 'the ultimate study' only to find when it's time to analyse the data you can't make any sense of the results.

Parametric Designs

Parametric designs are another approach that can give the experimenter a greater understanding of the relationship between an experimental manipulation and brain activation. Parametric designs involve investigating how activation changes as some experimental variable (parameter) is changed over a range of levels. For example, in studying visual perception, parametric manipulations could include varying the size, contrast, or brightness of a stimulus, while holding all other parameters constant. Subtraction designs are essentially the simplest sort of parametric design, with only two levels of a parameter. However, if one increases the number of levels of the parameter, additional insight is possible. For instance, if one wished to know which brain areas were sensitive to the luminance of a visual stimulus, one could simply conduct a subtraction-design experiment contrasting a brighter with a dimmer stimulus. While this would identify areas sensitive to this contrast, it would tell us relatively little about the response properties of these areas – how the areas respond to other levels of the stimuli. If we doubled the brightness of the 'bright' stimulus, would we see double the level of brain activation? By using a parametric design, we could manipulate brightness over a range of levels to determine whether there was a simple linear relationship between brightness and activation levels, or a more complex relationship (recall from the previous chapter that psychophysics research has revealed that human perception indeed actually operates on a logarithmic, rather than linear scale). One might also find that some brain areas have optimal rates or levels of stimulation, such that as the experimental parameter increases, brain response increases up to the optimal level of this parameter, and then begins to decrease (an inverted-U shaped function).

Another example of the use of parametric designs is in studies of learning, where either time or performance on the task to be learned are used as the parameter of interest. The simplest approach to conducting a learning study is to perform a scan prior to the learning experience, and a second scan afterwards. This would identify areas that change in activation from what we might call the 'naïve' state to the 'educated' state. Some brain areas might show reduced activation after learning (perhaps due to more efficient processing), whereas others might show increased activation (due to their performing a function they are now trained to handle). However, such a pre/post design would hide many potentially interesting mechanisms involved in learning; some brain areas might be involved only in the learning *process*, such that they are not activated prior to learning, nor once the task is mastered. For example, a brain region called the anterior cingulate gyrus (among others) is involved in detecting errors in performance, which is critical to learning – since awareness of errors is a signal that leads to improved performance. Thus prior to learning, we might not see anterior cingulate activation because participants didn't know that they were making errors on the task, and in the post-learning scan, participants' performance might be error-free and thus again anterior cingulate activation would not be observed, even though it was critical to the learning process. Thus pre/post scanning might not highlight these areas at all. However, if we performed brain imaging not only pre- and post-training, but also at regular intervals during the learning process (or even continuously, if the learning task could be performed in the scanner over a reasonable period of time), then we would be able to characterize not only what changed from the naïve to the educated state, but how changes evolved over time. Brain areas involved in learning might show interesting patterns such as linear increases or decreases over time. Ideally, one would record behavioural performance during all of the scans as well, so that one could examine correlations between brain activation and performance.

Even outside of learning tasks, behavioural data can be the key to an insightful parametric design, using either a within- or between-subjects design. In a within-subjects design, one could correlate brain activity with a behavioural parameter such as reaction time, subjective ratings of the emotional valence (intensity) of a variety of images, or some other parameter. Thus rather than coding the parametric 'level' of each stimulus beforehand and using the same set of levels for all participants, one could use a range of stimuli expected to elicit a range of responses, and use the behavioural data from each individual to analyse their data.

An example of this approach is an fMRI study by Bode and colleagues (2018) that looked at decision making. Typically, decisions are made faster when they are easier to make – for example, when deciding what a picture is showing, it is easier to make this decision if the picture is clear than if it's degraded in some way, such as if it is blurry. A simple parametric manipulation to identify brain areas associated with making decisions about noisy images could thus manipulate the quality of the stimuli (for example, low-medium-high); however, since response times (RTs) are correlated with how difficult it is to make a decision, the results would be a combination of brain areas involved in making the decision, and those involved in planning the response after the decision had been made. Therefore Bode and colleagues examined correlations between fMRI signal and both quality of the stimuli (amount of noise in the image), and, separately, RTs. Critically, in examining the correlation with RTs, the researchers held the noise level in the stimuli constant, so that this would not confound the results (so the variability in response time was the natural trial-to-trial variability in RT, rather than the noise-related variability). The results, shown in Figure 2.2, demonstrated that indeed several brain areas (such as the inferior parietal lobe and middle frontal gyri) were present in both correlations, suggesting that their correlation with stimulus quality was related to planning motor responses. However, other areas, such as the superior and inferior frontal gyri, did not show correlation with RT and thus could be more confidently associated with the decision-making process that occurs prior to planning the motor response.

Parametric approaches can also be useful in between-subjects designs. In this case, rather than correlating brain activity with some within-subjects parameter, like stimulus intensity or time, activity is correlated with a variable that varies across individuals. For example, in studies of second language learners, variables such as the age at which the second language was learned, or the fluency achieved in that language, could be used as parameters. Although it is also common to simply group people into groups (for example, early learners versus late learners), statistical analyses are more sensitive (often by a factor of 30–50%) when a parametric or

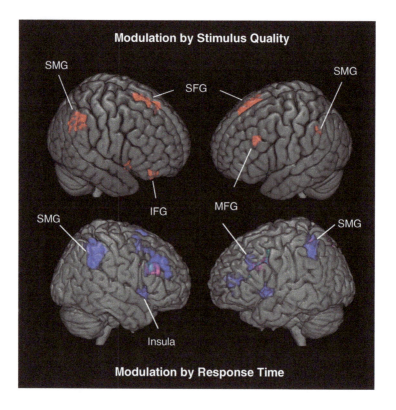

Figure 2.2 Example of a parametric fMRI study design in which correlations with both an experimentally controlled factor and behavioural results were conducted and compared. The top panel shows brain areas whose BOLD response was modulated by stimulus quality (the amount of noise added to images of objects, which was low, medium, or high). Response times (RT) are on average slower when the images are noisier. The bottom panel shows areas whose BOLD response was modulated by RT, within each level of stimulus quality. In other words, the variation in RT was due to random trial-to-trial variance, unrelated to the level of noise in the stimuli. Several brain areas showed similar modulation in both cases, indicating that the stimulus quality-related modulation could be attributed to time involved in preparing a response, rather than identifying the images in the presence of noise. However, some areas were modulated by stimulus quality but not RT, suggesting that they may be more directly involved in object recognition in the presence of noise. Adapted from Bode et al., 2018 with permission of Elsevier

correlational approach is used to analyse the data than when data that vary over a continuum are 'lumped' into two categories, often based on a fairly arbitrary cut-off.

Another application of parametric designs is to determine which brain areas are *not* sensitive to a particular experimental manipulation. In a classic study, Price and colleagues (1992) presented participants with auditory speech played at different rates. The superior temporal gyrus (auditory cortex) showed a steady increase in activation level with increasing speech rate. However, Wernicke's area (an area at the junction of the temporal and parietal lobes long associated with speech comprehension) showed consistent activation across all speech conditions relative to a baseline condition, with no modulation by speech rate. This pattern of results led the authors to conclude that while the auditory cortex is sensitive to low-level parameters of auditory stimuli, such as speech rate, Wernicke's area responded in a rate-independent fashion. This supported the **hypothesis** that Wernicke's area is involved in higher-level comprehension processes but not lower-level sensory decoding, since comprehension was comparable across the different rates of speech presentation.

EXPERIMENTAL SET-UP AND CONTROL

In any study in experimental psychology or cognitive science, careful control over the conditions of the experiment – such as the stimuli used, the instructions given to the participant, and so on – are vital for the data to be interpretable. Likewise, experimental manipulations – such as the factors defining different experimental conditions – need to be systematic and carefully measured and controlled. This is one of the most fundamental tenets of empirical science in general, and certainly in the domain of studying human minds and behaviour, since humans are inherently sensitive to these factors. In cognitive neuroscience, if anything even tighter control is often required. One important reason for this is that the brain is exquisitely sensitive to many things, including physical properties of stimuli, that may not affect the behavioural outcomes of an experiment. For example, imagine an experiment in which participants hear the names of different objects (for example, *fish*; *rock*) and have to determine for each word whether the object is living or not (commonly called an 'animacy judgement'). It may be the case that the spoken words were not all recorded at the same time, and perhaps on average the words for animate objects are louder in the experiment than those for inanimate objects. As long as all the words were audible, this would probably not affect people's ability to discriminate between animate and inanimate words, and so this systematic difference between stimulus categories – while not optimal – might not be a significant cause for concern in a behavioural study (although even there, one could speculate that RTs might be faster for louder stimuli). However, in a brain-imaging study this systematic difference in loudness could have much larger effects, because areas of the auditory cortex respond more strongly to more intense sounds. Thus the brain activity recorded in this experiment would likely be different between the animate and inanimate stimulus conditions – however, it would be challenging to know which brain areas showed differences due to the intended experimental manipulation (animacy) and the unintentional physical difference between the stimuli (loudness). Although one could propose that any differences in the auditory cortex were attributable to the differences in loudness, whereas differences in other brain areas were due to the experimental manipulation, this would be at best shaky ground. This is because loudness might affect brain activity in other areas, and conversely it is theoretically possible that animacy affected auditory cortex activity. Moreover, with some techniques such as EEG, we cannot easily or reliably ascertain the exact brain areas generating the recorded activity, so we would not even be able to apply this rationale.

The importance of this consideration was enshrined as the **Hillyard Principle** by author and researcher Steve Luck, in honour of his PhD supervisor Steve Hillyard (who also trained my PhD supervisor, Helen Neville, and numerous other groundbreaking ERP researchers). The principle is, 'Always compare brain activity elicited by the same physical stimuli, varying only the psychological conditions' (Luck, 2014). This principle is an ideal that cognitive neuroscientists should endeavour to follow whenever they can, controlling stimuli as tightly as possible and, if feasible, **counter-balancing** stimuli across conditions (so that the same stimulus is used in every condition). Of course, this is not always possible – in many cases inherent, fundamental differences between stimuli are exactly what defines the experimental conditions and/or phenomena of interest. However, even in those cases experimenters should think deeply and carefully about this issue, and figure out how to minimize the possible influence of physical differences between stimuli across experimental conditions. As well, if such differences exist and cannot be controlled for, analyses should be performed to determine whether there were effects of these systematic differences. In some cases, additional control conditions or even experiments might be required to determine the effects of such physical differences.

BETWEEN- AND WITHIN-SUBJECTS DESIGNS

As we have learned, any experiment requires some contrast between levels of one or more variables. In neuroimaging experiments, at a bare minimum we would need to compare brain activity between two conditions. Often one of these is considered the 'experimental' condition – or the condition of interest – and the other is the 'control' condition which serves as a reference or baseline for the comparison. For example, in Petersen and colleagues' (1988) PET experiment discussed above under 'Subtractive and Additive Factors Designs', one contrast was between false fonts and consonant strings – so false fonts served as the control condition and consonant strings as the experimental condition for that contrast. This (and indeed, all the contrasts in Petersen et al.'s study) would be considered a **within-subjects** comparison, because each individual participant experienced both conditions. Alternatively, some experiments include **between-subjects** comparisons, in which different participants experience different conditions. With virtually all neuroimaging techniques – certainly those that measure functional activation, as opposed to structural imaging methods – within-subjects contrasts are necessary because these techniques produce measurements that are in 'arbitrary units'. That is to say, the absolute value of an individual measurement is meaningless in its own right; it is only meaningful in comparison to a measurement made under some other experimental condition (or baseline condition). Furthermore, with any neuroimaging technique, individuals vary (often widely) in both their baseline measures of activity, and in the size of the effects of an experimental manipulation. Thus within-subjects contrasts give us the most (and sometimes only) accurate measures of the effects of an experimental manipulation.

Within-subjects designs are thus generally the most powerful and convincing designs. This is true even in non-neuroimaging experiments, simply because each individual acts as their own control. In contrast, between-subjects designs are subject to concerns that the two groups of individuals being compared might vary along many important dimensions. While it is common practice to try to match groups on factors such as age, sex, and education level, there are so many possible influences on behaviour and brain activation that this still leaves open many possibilities for systematic, and uncharacterized, differences between the groups. Thus while the researcher would like to conclude that any difference observed between groups is due to the experimental manipulation, there are inevitably many other possible explanations for the difference.

With this said, however, it is important to recognize that there are many situations in which between-subjects designs are unavoidable. For example, difference between individuals may be precisely the subject of an investigation. This is true in the case of studies of people who have a particular disease or condition – very often studies of such populations compare them to a control group of healthy people. Obviously, unless it were possible to obtain measurements both before and after the onset of the disease, a within-subjects design would be impossible. Another case in which between-subjects designs may be required is if an experimental manipulation is expected to have lasting consequences that could impact the results of further experimentation. For example, if one wanted to compare the effects of a drug with those of a placebo, one might need to use a between-groups design if, once people had taken the drug, it would be obvious to them whether they received drug or placebo (such as with many psychoactive drugs). Likewise, if one were comparing two different methods of teaching a skill, one would require a between-subjects design because people could not un-learn the skill after learning it one way. A final case is where neurostimulation is used. The effects of neurostimulation often last for 30–60 minutes or more – and the durations vary between individuals. Thus, if one wanted to compare the effects of different stimulation parameters, without requiring participants to spend many hours in the lab, or come back to the lab on many different days, one might opt for a between-subjects design.

Finally, there is no reason not to have both between- and within-subjects manipulations. For example, if we are comparing between groups (a between-subjects design), we might also have several experimental conditions, and contrasts between them, that each person in each group experiences. These are called **mixed designs**.

STATISTICAL POWER AND REPLICABILITY

It is strongly recommended that anyone venturing into cognitive neuroscience take several statistics classes, and this is a topic that is outside of what can reasonably be covered in the present book. However, there are some fundamental topics that any consumer of the cognitive neuroscience literature should be familiar with. First of all, any measurement we make is subject to **variance** – that is, whether we are measuring response times or brain activation or anything else, each measurement is likely to be somewhat different (and sometimes very different) from the other measurements, even from the same individual under the same experimental conditions. There are numerous causes of variance, including the fact that our measurement instruments are sensitive to variables beyond our control, and the fact that biological systems (such as those controlling everything from button presses to brain activity) are influenced by a vastly greater number of variables than we can ever hope to control or even measure in a given experiment. Thus in virtually every experiment, we are not interested in any single measurement, but in the average across multiple measurements of each type, for each experimental condition, etc. In computing statistics to determine whether our measurements differ between experimental conditions, we would calculate the average (also called the mean) for each condition, and also the variance around each of these average values. In some cases it may be that the mean values in two conditions differ, but when we consider the variability in our measurements, we lack the confidence to declare that the two mean values are truly, reliably different. For us to declare a difference to be 'statistically significant', we need to have confidence not only that the means differ, but that they are sufficiently different, given the variance, that it is likely that if we repeated the experiment, we would obtain a similar difference.

The notion of statistical significance can be misleading, however. A significance value is typically reported as p – the probability that the result obtained in the experiment could happen by chance, if a large number of replications of the experiment were conducted. In many areas of psychology and cognitive neuroscience, the threshold for statistical significance is set at $p<.05$, meaning that the likelihood of obtaining the result by chance is less than 5 in 100. What is misleading about this value is that for a given experiment, the p value is calculated based only on the data collected in that particular experiment. Thus the p value is entirely dependent on the random sample of people who participated in the experiment, and likely many other random factors as well (such as the time of day when the experimenter was running the study, the time of year, where the experiment was conducted, etc.; in a neuroimaging experiment, the quality of data from an individual might be influenced by how well the EEG electrodes were attached, how still the person lay in the MRI scanner, and related factors). Thus if the experiment were replicated, the mean and variance measures obtained would doubtless be different from the first study, and it is quite possible that they would not achieve statistical significance the second time around.

The depth and significance of this issue has recently received great attention in experimental psychology and other fields, and has been dubbed the **replicability crisis** – the fact that numerous statistically significant findings published in academic journals have not been subsequently replicated. One important factor driving this is that statistically significant results are typically more interesting than non-significant ones, and so they are much more likely to be published in journals – especially because one factor that many scientific journals use to determine whether or not to publish a paper is the anticipated 'impact' of the finding (Ioannidis, 2005). This is called **publication bias** and likely means that there are vast numbers of experiments that have never been published – and may even contradict published and widely accepted results – because the results were not statistically significant. This is not to say that all non-statistically significant results should be published, as there are many other reasons why a significant effect might not be obtained, such as methodological flaws. However, it is an important consideration and one that has been identified as problematic in neuroimaging studies as well as in behavioural sciences.

One important factor in determining statistical significance is the number of samples (measurements) obtained in an experiment. In general, variance decreases as the sample size increases, typically in an exponential fashion – meaning that, as an approximation, we get a precipitous drop in variance going from one to ten samples, but in going from ten to 100 samples we don't get a ten-fold drop in variance, but only approximately an equivalent decrease to that obtained in going from one to ten. In other words, more data is better, but we get diminishing returns with increasing numbers of samples. The concept of **statistical power** is a formalized way of estimating the sensitivity of an experiment to the sample size or, put another way, power calculations can be used to estimate how much data would be needed to obtain a statistically significant effect of a given size. However, power calculations are – like p values – entirely dependent on the data that have been collected, and so are in essence mere guesses than may help guide researchers, but provide no real guarantees. The existence of publication bias further means that power calculations based on published results may be overly optimistic with respect to the size of the effect and the number of participants needed in future studies (Anderson, Kelley, & Maxwell, 2017).

While it is not possible in this short account to fully discuss these issues, let alone provide solutions (and indeed, these are 'moving targets' that are under intense, ongoing discussion in the scientific community), there are a couple of key points to take away. First of all, in designing a study one needs to be aware of the issues around statistical power, and consider the available evidence from the prior literature in determining both the number of trials to include in each experimental condition, and the number of individual participants to include. Perhaps the greatest issue in the neuroimaging literature around statistical power is that all neuroimaging methodologies require specialized, expensive equipment, and many neuroimaging techniques involve very high per-participant costs (for example, MRI scanning often costs approximately US$500 per hour, with an hour being the typical time required for each participant in the scanner). As well these are often shared facilities with many researchers competing for access. Thus there may be practical constraints that make it challenging to recruit large numbers of participants. As well – and primarily for the reasons described here – historically many neuroimaging studies have used relatively small numbers of participants, leading to a perception in the field that these low numbers are acceptable. However, this is rapidly changing and there is now a much greater awareness and sensitivity within the neuroimaging community to issues of power and sample size (Button et al.,

2013a, 2013b; Cremers, Wager, & Yarkoni, 2017; Luck & Gaspelin, 2016; Mumford, 2012; Mumford & Nichols, 2008).

INTERPRETATION AND INFERENCE

The results of any experiment are open to interpretation, and (as anyone who has had a manuscript peer-reviewed knows) it is usually the case that different interpretations are possible, if one makes different assumptions. This is true of any data in cognitive neuroscience, and is perhaps exacerbated relative to behavioural measures due to the fact that all of the measures we have of brain activity and structure are indirect and inferential in one or more ways. For example, fMRI measures blood oxygenation and not electrical activity, and although EEG does measure electrical activity, this is averaged at the scalp electrodes from many different regions of the brain. Interpretation is certainly facilitated by good experimental design, sufficient statistical power, the use of appropriate analysis methods, and a solid understanding of the literature. Nonetheless, it is critical to always remember that we are making inferences, and that we need to question our assumptions.

One very common approach to data interpretation in cognitive neuroscience is **reverse inference**. This term, first introduced to the neuroimaging literature by Poldrack (2006), refers to the practice of inferring that a particular cognitive process was engaged, based on the observation of activation in a particular brain area. This is in contrast to 'forward inference', in which the design of the experiment isolates a specific cognitive process, and the pattern of brain activation observed in the experiment is taken to reflect that cognitive process. For example, if we contrast brain activation, using fMRI, between two conditions – one in which people see moving dots, and another in which the dots are stationary – we would interpret the areas that are more active during visual motion as being those that support the cognitive process of perceiving visual motion.

Reverse inference typically occurs when experiments are less constrained, or when a brain area is identified as activated that was not necessarily predicted **a priori**. For example, imagine that we performed an fMRI experiment of spatial working memory, in which people had to remember the locations, and order, of a series of stimuli shown on a screen. In one condition the stimuli were all white squares, and in the other condition each square was a different colour. Imagine that in the contrast between the conditions, our fMRI data showed stronger activation in two brain areas for the coloured squares relative to the white ones: in a region of the occipital lobe, and in the left inferior frontal gyrus. Based on prior literature, the occipital activation could be predicted, as there is a region of the visual cortex that specifically responds more strongly to coloured than non-coloured stimuli. However, the frontal activation would be more surprising, because this region is not typically associated with colour perception. However, this region – often labelled 'Broca's area' – is often activated in tasks involving speech production (even 'covert speech' in which people say words 'in their head' rather than aloud). Thus – by reverse inference – we might conclude that, because in the 'colour' condition the squares were all different colours, participants adopted a strategy of covertly saying the names of the colours as memory aid. In other words, we are relying on the results of past neuroimaging studies to obtain a post-hoc interpretation of our data.

It is important to stress that there is nothing inherently wrong with reverse inference. Indeed, in the absence of strong predictions about the outcomes of the data – as in exploratory or very novel study designs – or in the presence of unexpected regions of activation, reverse inference is sensible and represents a type of **abductive reasoning** in which the most likely cause is inferred, based on an observed result and an informed understanding of the possible causes of the result (Poldrack, 2011). However, often reverse inference is found in the 'Discussion' section of journal articles reporting on neuroimaging experiments, and often the basis for the inference is a very selective review of the past literature. It is thus very easy for an author to be biased by the set of papers they happen to have read, or other prior beliefs. Poldrack (2006, 2011) has noted that there are far superior ways of performing reverse inference than simply relying on one's own knowledge or intuition. This is through the use of large, online databases of past neuroimaging results. One in particular is the Neurosynth database (http://neurosynth.org; Yarkoni, Poldrack, Nichols, Van Essen, & Wager, 2011). To create this database, researchers developed a way of extracting both the activation patterns from published neuroimaging studies, and an automated text analysis to identify key terms in the paper to characterize the activation patterns (for example, 'memory', 'language'). Using this database, one can perform a more principled reverse inference, by getting actual data on which types of tasks or cognitive operations are commonly found to activate a brain region. This is not a perfect method, in particular because some brain areas show very high 'base rates' of activation across many studies, tasks, and cognitive operations, as shown in Figure 2.3. Thus interpretation of activation

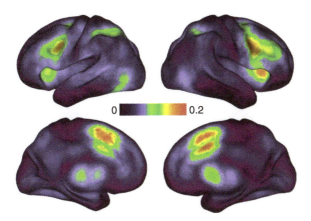

Figure 2.3 Base rates of activation across nearly 3,500 published fMRI studies. The colour scale indicates the proportion of studies reporting activation in a given region. Reprinted from Yarkoni et al., 2001 with permission of Springer Nature

via reverse inference within these regions in particular should be made cautiously, if at all. Conversely, other brain regions activate under much more specific conditions, allowing more reliable inference. In general, the important thing to remember here is that while we might colloquially think of particular brain areas subserving specific functions in a very neo-phrenological way, we must be aware of our biases and the limitations of our knowledge. We must both carefully distinguish the conclusions we derive from forward versus reverse inference, and be especially sceptical of both our own, and others', interpretations based on reverse inference – especially if it is of the 'casual' form.

ETHICAL CONSIDERATIONS

Cognitive neuroscience research holds great promise for humanity: we hope that by better understanding relationships between mind and brain, we may gain greater insight into what it means to be human, and the principles and factors that lead to different patterns of thought and behaviour, and also the ability to better diagnose and treat brain-based conditions. At the same time, this research raises many ethical considerations. Some are relatively generic considerations in any research involving human beings. For example, the Canadian *Tri-Council Policy Statement: Ethical Conduct for Research Involving Humans* (Canadian Institutes of Health Research et al., 2014) defines three core principles for the ethical conduct of research: respect for persons, concern for welfare, and justice (the obligation to treat people fairly). In virtually every country and research institution, researchers are bound by a code of ethics such as this, and must submit proposed research for review by an independent body (such as an institutional review board or research ethics board) prior to initiating the research, to ensure adherence to ethical principles. While some researchers may consider this a nuisance, such oversight was developed in response to numerous documented cases of unethical research occurring in academic and other institutions. While some of these clearly reflected a lack of respect for the rights of research participants, in other cases the violations reflected factors that the researchers had not considered, and/or perspectives on the cost–benefit ratio of the research that were skewed by researchers' own interests or unconscious biases. Ethics review boards thus serve a vital role in protecting research participants – and ultimately researchers and institutions – both from malfeasance, and unintended or even unappreciated potential consequences of the research.

Core to ethical research involving humans is that participants should provide free and **informed consent** to participate in the research. This means that, prior to conducting the research, the researchers should inform potential participants as to what will happen in the study, and any possible risks or undesirable consequences (as well as any potential benefits). Potential participants must also be given the opportunity to ask any questions they have, and demonstrate a clear understanding of any risks (in other words, a researcher should engage in the informed consent process with the potential participant, rather than simply instructing them to read and sign a consent form). They must also be informed that their participation in the experiment is voluntary, and that they can discontinue their participation at any time without penalty (or of any limits on voluntariness or discontinuation – for example, if the study involves administering a drug, it may not be possible to stop the effects of the drug immediately, but the participant may request that the experimenter stop making measurements). While some types of deception may be justifiable in certain cases – such as when certain knowledge might bias people's behaviours or the research outcomes – these must always be clearly indicated to (and approved by) the review board, and participants should be informed of the deception as soon as reasonably possible (such as immediately at the end of the experiment).

In cognitive neuroscience, additional, specific ethical considerations arise that are not necessarily present in other areas of research with human subjects. This has led to the establishment of **neuroethics** as a field of scholarly study, with its own society and journal. While all of the techniques covered in this book are considered safe when performed in accordance with established best practices and safety guidelines, some do carry greater risk than one might experience in one's day-to-day life. For example, PET scanning involves introducing radioactive substances into the body, and transcranial magnetic stimulation involves strong electrical stimulation that can cause unpleasant muscle contractions and, in people with certain risk factors, generalized seizures. Moreover, participating in neuroimaging research may have indirect, but significant, consequences. For example, MRI studies produce high-resolution images of the brain's structure and physiology. It is possible – and indeed, occurs with some non-trivial frequency – that a previously undiagnosed disease could be identified in the course of an MRI study involving an otherwise healthy individual (Illes & Borgelt, 2009; Morris et al., 2009). While most people might be happy to have an early diagnosis of a serious condition, there may be other, less desirable consequences. For one, if the condition is serious but untreatable, people may experience despair and reduced quality of life that would otherwise have been delayed until the condition became symptomatic. As well, diagnosis of a 'pre-existing condition' can preclude people from obtaining life insurance, or significantly increase costs associated with health and life insurance (Anonymous, 2005; Illes, Desmond, Huang, Raffin, & Atlas, 2002).

Neuroethics

Another dimension of ethical consideration in cognitive neuroscience research is largely more future-oriented, but non-trivial even in the present day. That is, as we gain greater insight into how the brain functions, and the ability to interpret brain imaging scans with greater precision, we approach an era in which we can literally 'read' people's minds. This presents significant considerations around privacy and people's rights to keep their thoughts to themselves – an emerging area known as **neuroprivacy** (Hallinan, Friedewald, Shutz, & de Hert, 2014; Ienca, 2015; The Committee on Science and Law, 2005). Already we have seen published 'neuromarketing' studies investigating whether brain responses can be used to predict consumer behaviour. In one high-profile study (McClure, Li, Tomlin, Cypert,

Montague, L. & Montague, P., 2004), researchers compared brain activation patterns when people tasted the soft drinks Coke® and Pepsi®, either with or without brand labels, and found that the labels significantly impacted brain activation patterns. This, and subsequent research, have raised concerns that marketers could use brain imaging to influence consumer behaviour and cause people to make decisions that they otherwise would not make, that have detrimental long-term consequences.

In addition to neuroprivacy, another significant consideration is the potential to use brain-imaging and neuro-stimulation techniques to alter human thoughts and behaviour. While this may have obviously beneficial implications, such as the treatment of psychiatric conditions and neurological diseases, it could also find more sinister uses. For example, such techniques could be used to cause people to comply, against their will, with institutional or governmental desires. More seemingly benignly, some neurostimulation studies have suggested that these techniques can actually boost cognitive performance, in domains such as learning and memory. This raises concerns around a neural 'arms race' or driving greater inequality, as some people choose – or are simply able to afford to choose – to be enhanced, while others do not or cannot make that choice (Hyman, 2011). These and other topics have engendered significant and lively ongoing discussion and debate, and provide an important societal context that anyone working in the field of cognitive neuroscience should be familiar with.

SUMMARY

This chapter focused on fundamental concepts in experimental design that cut across all neuroimaging techniques and disciplines within cognitive neuroscience. Any experiment requires the systematic, controlled manipulation of independent variables by the experimenter, and the measurement of dependent variables. Dependent variables in neuroimaging studies are typically whatever measure of brain activation the technique provides, while in behavioural studies these are typically RT, accuracy, or whatever behaviour the researcher is measuring. The simplest experimental designs use the subtraction method to identify the difference between two conditions (two levels of an independent variable); the additive factors method expands this to include more levels of a variable, and/or additional variables, that are contrasted to isolate different cognitive processes. Designing experiments is a 'human intelligence task', meaning that it is crucial for the experimenter to think deeply through the experiment, and have good operational definitions of the cognitive processes under investigation. The experimenter must think of how best to isolate a particular process, and critically about what factors might confound the results or lead to alternative interpretations, because there is very often no gold standard or quantitative way to determine whether an experimental design makes sense or not, other than through the application of logic and critical thinking.

In all experiments it is important to limit the number of variables manipulated, but this is all the more true in neuroimaging studies due to the rich, complex data provided by these techniques. As well, some brain areas and cognitive processes are very sensitive to factors that might not be as critical in designing behavioural experiments, such as the physical properties of the stimuli. The ideal experimental design follows the Hillyard Principle, in manipulating only the psychological/task conditions of the experiment, while keeping the physical stimuli constant. While this is not always possible, it is always critical to consider how unintended or seemingly incidental differences between conditions could influence the outcomes of an experiment. It is also generally best to design within-subjects experiments, so that participants act as their own control and the influence of individual differences on the effects of the experimental manipulation are minimized. This is, however, subject to practical limitations and so sometimes between-subjects designs are necessary.

In any experimental design it is also crucial to think about the kinds of effects that are predicted, their magnitude, and the amount of variance in the measurements that will be obtained. Any cognitive neuroscience experiment will be analysed using statistics, and making strong claims about the results of a study – and expecting that these results would generalize or replicate in other studies – is dependent on having sufficient statistical power.

Finally, we covered ethical issues in cognitive neuroscience, including research ethics and domain-specific considerations of neuroethics. The ability to measure and even manipulate brain activity creates a number of considerations that are not encountered in other areas of behavioural or human science. These include both incidental findings of previously undiagnosed disease, and the implications of being able to gain some insight into – or even manipulate – an individual's private thoughts and feelings by way of their brain activity.

THINGS YOU SHOULD KNOW

- Independent variables are those manipulated by the experimenter, while dependent variables are the outcomes that are measured in an experiment. Experiments focus on how contrasts (differences) between levels of one or more independent variables affect the dependent variable.

- Subtractive and additive factors designs can isolate a particular cognitive operation by examining a contrast in which all factors are held constant, differing only in the presence or absence of the cognitive operation investigated. Doing this properly depends on careful, logical reasoning on the part of the experimenter.

- Factorial designs involve contrasts between two or more levels, of each of two or more independent variables. Such designs are critical if the experimenter predicts that the variables interact; that is, that the effects of manipulating one variable depend on the other variable. Parametric designs involve measuring the dependent variable over a range of levels of one or more independent variables. Generally speaking, factorial designs involve the manipulation of categorical variables, whereas parametric designs involve the manipulation of continuous variables.

- Differences in physical stimuli (for example, brightness, loudness) can have a significant impact on measures of brain activity (including activity related to perception and attention) that may be independent of the predicted impact of an experimental manipulation on cognition. For this reason, it is always preferable to compare brain activity in response to the same physical stimuli, manipulating only the psychological condition (such as task, or the participant's expectations). This has been termed the Hillyard Principle.

- In between-subjects designs, participants are split into different groups and receive different treatments or experimental manipulations, and the dependent measures are compared between groups. In within-subjects designs, every participant experiences every condition, or level of the independent variable(s). Mixed designs combine within- and between-subjects manipulations.

- Statistical power refers to the likelihood of detecting an experimental effect, if it is in fact present. Statistical power is influenced by the amount of noise, or variance, in the data, as well as the sample size. Results from studies with low power are less likely to replicate in future experiments. Underpowered studies can be of particular concern in neuroimaging research due to the high cost per participant of running the studies.

- In interpreting neuroimaging studies, forward inference is the practice of associating a pattern of brain activity with a particular cognitive operation or process based on the design of the study and a priori hypotheses. Reverse inference, by contrast, occurs when a researcher observes activity in a particular brain region – often not predicted a priori – and infers the presence of a particular cognitive process based on past literature concerning the function of this brain area. While reverse inference represents a sound practice of scientific reasoning in the presence of uncertainty, it can be undermined by bias on the part of the researcher. Reverse inference based on large databases that systematically review the published literature is preferable to selective reviews of the literature.

- The rise of neuroimaging and neurostimulation techniques has led to the development of neuroethics as a field of scholarly study. This impacts on consideration of ethical issues in the design of experiments using these techniques, as well as the future implications of these technologies as their accuracy and reliability increase. Key issues include neuroprivacy, cognitive enhancement, and the possibility of diagnosing previously undetected illness.

FURTHER READINGS

Farah, M.J. (Ed.) (2010). *Neuroethics: An Introduction with Readings*. Cambridge, MA: MIT Press.

Harrington, M. (2010). *The Design of Experiments in Neuroscience* (2nd ed.). London: Sage Publications.

Illes, J. (2017). *Neuroethics: Anticipating the Future*. Oxford: Oxford University Press.

Klein, G., & Dabney, A. (2013). *The Cartoon Introduction to Statistics*. New York: Hill & Wang.

McBride, D.M., & Cutting, J.C. (2018). *Cognitive Psychology: Theory, Process, and Methodology* (2nd ed.). London: Sage Publishing.

3 Electroencephalography (EEG) and Event-Related Potentials (ERP) 1

LEARNING OBJECTIVES

After reading this chapter, you should be able to:

- Explain what EEG measures, and what the acronym stands for.
- Explain the neural origins of the EEG signal.
- Explain the difference between EEG and ERPs.
- Discriminate between time- and frequency-domain views of EEG data.
- Define an ERP component in terms of four parameters.
- Describe the basic hardware components required to record EEG.
- Explain the concept of differential amplifiers, and specify the minimum number of electrodes required to record EEG.
- Describe best practices for running an EEG study.

INTRODUCTION

Electroencephalography, or EEG, is the oldest non-invasive neuroimaging technique. It is also one of the simplest technically, involving electrodes placed on the scalp and connected to an amplifier. The electrodes record electrical activity generated by large groups of neurons acting in synchrony. EEG was first recorded by Hans Berger, a German psychiatrist and neurologist who was interested in studying the relationship between brain and mind. Berger published the first report of EEG in 1929; however, at first his results were not believed by the scientific community. In 1934, however, Adrian and Matthews published evidence that confirmed Berger's initial report, and made the findings more credible by providing an explanatory account of how the relatively slow fluctuations in electrical activity related to the better-understood and much faster-occurring action potentials. Adrian and Matthews noted that, 'Recording [the slow waves we now call EEG] would seem to offer the most direct method of investigating cortical activity, but for the difficulty that they are certainly summated effects compounded out of the potential changes in many neurones' (p. 440) and concluded that these waves corresponded 'to a summation of the brief responses of individual neurones' (p. 471). Soon after, the first **event-related potentials (ERPs** – sometimes also called **evoked potentials** or **EPs**) were recorded by Pauline and Hallowell Davis (Davis, Davis, Loomis, Harvey, & Hobart, 1939; Davis, 1939). The distinction between EEG and ERP is an important one in the field, and quite simply EEG refers to continuous recordings of ongoing electrical brain activity, whereas ERPs are EEG signals time-locked to particular events, such as the presentation of a specific stimulus or a motor response. As we will see, both EEG and ERPs are used in cognitive neuroscience; however, ERPs are the more commonly used technique because they allow us to associate brain activity with specific, experimentally controlled events.

As this is the first chapter describing a neuroimaging technique, a number of key concepts are introduced that are common to many, if not all, techniques of cognitive neuroscience and so we will spend some time explaining these concepts. Rest assured, the time invested understanding concepts of data acquisition and signal processing will serve you well in chapters to come.

WHAT ARE WE MEASURING?

Physiological Basis of the EEG Signal

EEG is recorded from electrodes (typically numbering 3–256) placed on the scalp, which are connected to an amplifier that boosts the size of the signals before saving them digitally on a computer, as shown in Figure 3.1. EEG can also be recorded directly from the cortical surface via electrodes placed during neurosurgery, but in this chapter we focus on non-invasive recordings. The EEG electrodes measure electrical activity generated by the brain; however, we cannot measure the activity of individual neurons. This is because the brain contains millions of neurons, located relatively far away from the EEG recording electrodes. Rather, the EEG signal represents the summed activity of many neurons. Indeed, the physics of EEG impose a number of constraints on interpretation of the signals that may be viewed as both a blessing and a curse. They are a blessing in the sense that they serve to filter and simplify the incredibly complex activity of the brain. However, the 'curse' is that this limits our ability to understand brain activity using this technique, and to interpret the results. Indeed, much of what we know about EEG comes from a 'black box' approach of recording activity under different experimental conditions, observing what EEG signals are produced, and developing interpretations of what these EEG signals mean through inference based on what changes or stays the same across experimental manipulations.

One important constraint on EEG is that the number of sources of information that we have (the number of electrodes) is far lower than the number of neurons in the brain, or even the number of functionally distinct brain areas that exist. However, simply increasing the number of electrodes is not useful above a certain point, because of other factors. Firstly, electrical signals conduct very well through the brain, so an EEG signal recorded from a particular electrode represents not only activity of the brain directly under that electrode, but activity from many other areas of the brain as well. Thus activity measured at any given electrode is the sum of the activity of many brain regions. Secondly, the skull is a relatively poor conductor of electricity. One effect of this low conductivity is that electrical signals are blurred, spatially, by the skull. Thus EEG electrodes placed close together on the scalp record virtually the same information from the brain. Together these two factors impose a limit on the spatial resolution of scalp-recorded EEG,

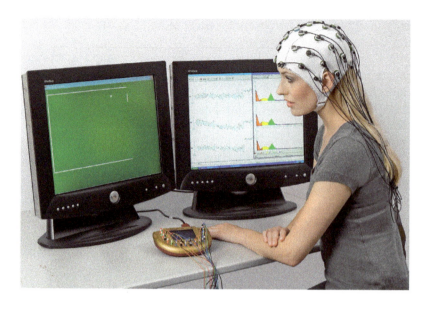

Figure 3.1 An example of an EEG system. The participant is wearing an elastic cap with electrodes, which feed into the amplifier (the gold object in the centre of the table) which then connects to a computer to record the data. In an experiment, the participant typically views stimuli on a computer monitor (left) while EEG is displayed for the experimenter on another monitor (right). Image provided courtesy of Brain Products GmbH

meaning that more electrodes is not necessarily better – a topic that is discussed further below.

Another constraint on EEG is that individual neurons acting alone produce relatively weak signals. For a signal to be detected by EEG it must be quite strong, because it must be conducted from its source to the recording electrodes, through the poorly conducting skull. What is picked up by EEG scalp electrodes, then – as observed by Adrian and Mathews in considering even the earliest EEG recordings – is the summed activity of many neurons acting in synchrony, with similar anatomical location and alignment.

This brings us to an important concept for understanding the generation and propagation of EEG signals – the electrical **dipole**. 'Dipole' refers to something that has two ends, or poles, that are opposite in some way. The magnetic poles of the Earth are a familiar example. When talking about electricity, a dipole is something that has a positive charge at one end and a corresponding negative charge at the other. A battery is a common example of this. Brain areas that generate an EEG signal detectable at the scalp also have a dipolar configuration. In practice, this generally occurs when a fairly large group (a 'field') of neurons within a particular anatomical location are aligned with each other, as shown schematically in Figure 3.2. This group of neurons will form an **equivalent current dipole (ECD)** when, overall, one side of the field (the side with the cell bodies in the example shown) has a positive charge, and the other end (with the axons in the example) has a negative charge. In the human brain, the cortex contains large numbers of pyramidal neurons whose shape and anatomical organization lend themselves to creating ECDs that are measurable at the scalp. Groups of neurons that are physically aligned with each other and synchronously activated, thus able to generate EEG signals measurable at a distance, are referred to as **open fields**. Other possible configurations of neurons, whose activity would collectively cancel out and thus not generate a detectable EEG signal at the scalp, are referred to as **closed fields**. Examples of these are also shown in Figure 3.2.

It is also important to consider what sort of activity these neurons exhibit and how this relates to the corresponding EEG signal. The form of neural activity that is probably most familiar are action potentials: the firing of an individual neuron when the electrical potential of its membrane exceeds its firing threshold, which causes a current to travel down the neuron's axon to the terminal, where the action potential triggers the release of neurotransmitters which in turn affect the potential of other neurons. The duration of action potentials is very brief, however, so synchronization across neurons is relatively unlikely. As well, signals propagate down the axon via saltatory conduction (whereby the signal 'jumps' from one section of the axon to the next, because axons are insulated with myelin alternating with nodes of Ranvier where ion channels open and close as a signal passes through them). This means that if two adjacent axons are conducting action potentials that occur at slightly different points in time, the same spatial location on the two neurons may be depolarizing in one axon and re-polarizing at the other, in which case their potentials would cancel each other out when measured from a distance by EEG.

Another component of neural activity, and one that changes more slowly, is postsynaptic potentials. These are the electrical potentials of the membranes of the cell bodies of neurons, which are influenced by incoming signals from other neurons. Postsynaptic potentials essentially represent the sum of all of the incoming excitatory and inhibitory signals to a neuron, over some period of time ranging from tens to hundreds of milliseconds. Because the inputs are summed over time, there is more opportunity for the postsynaptic potentials of multiple neurons to be synchronized (in other words, have similar changes in potential at the same time), and thus summate to produce a signal that is detectable at the scalp. In neurons, if the cell body is depolarized by incoming excitatory postsynaptic potentials (EPSPs), then the body becomes relatively positively charged relative to the axon of the neuron (which has not been affected by the incoming EPSPs) – thus forming an electrical dipole between the cell body and axon, as depicted in Figure 3.2.

Thus at any given point in time, the EEG signal measured at a particular location on the scalp will be the sum of all of the ECDs active in the brain whose fields are oriented towards that electrode. Because of the volume conduction of EEG signals through the brain, the activity of a given ECD will in principle actually be detectable at any location on the scalp, either as a negative or positive voltage. However, the signal will be stronger at locations that are directly aligned with the poles of the ECD, and also at electrodes that are closer to the source of the signal. Note, however, that these two factors can work against each other, making inference about the location of the ECD difficult: a dipole oriented tangentially to the scalp (as shown in Figure 3.3C), and close to the skull may generate strong electrical potentials both at electrodes that are close to it (which are physically close, but not aligned with the axis of the dipole), and at electrodes farther away (which are physically distant, but

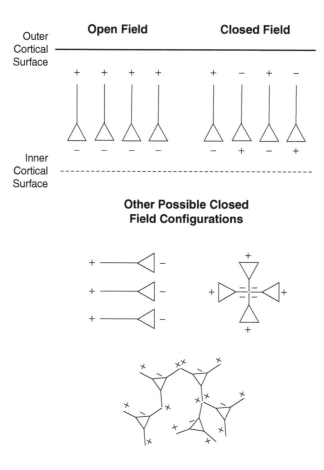

Figure 3.2 Schematic examples of open and closed field configurations of neurons. To generate a measurable EEG signal at the scalp, neurons must be oriented parallel to each other, and have similar electrical polarization across their long axis

aligned with the axis of the dipole). This is one of the many problems inherent in determining where a given EEG signal comes from in the brain, which will be discussed later in this chapter.

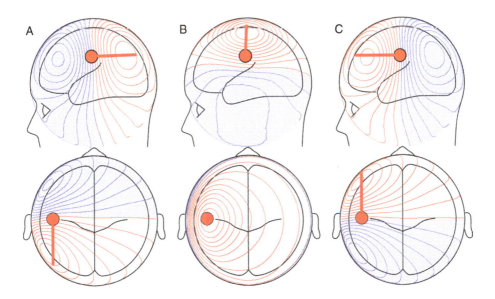

Figure 3.3 An example of a single electrical dipole (shown as a red dot, with the line extending from it indicating the direction of the positive pole) located approximately in the motor cortex, and how its electrical fields would project across the scalp depending on the dipole's orientation. In A, the positive pole is pointed towards the back of the head. The red contour lines with white background show areas of the scalp where a positive EEG potential would be recorded, with the peak potential at the centre of the smallest (middle) circle; progressively weaker positive potentials would be recorded at each contour line moving away from the centre circle. The blue shaded areas indicate where a negative potential would be recorded, with the maximum negative potential again in the centre of the smallest circle. B and C show how a dipole with the same electrical potential ('activation') strength, in the same location in the brain, would generate very different scalp topography patterns depending on its orientation. Because dipoles are largely generated by pyramidal neurons oriented tangentially to the scalp, the three different cases shown here could arise simply by the dipole's being located on either the left side, right side, or top of a gyrus on the cortex

ERP Components

EEG recordings thus represent the summed activity of all the ECDs active in the brain at that point in time that have open field configurations, as well as noise. Noise can come from various sources, including the person being recorded from (for example, muscle activity) and the environment (for example, electromagnetic fields generated by nearby electrical equipment). How do we differentiate these and characterize the brain activity of interest?

The basic logic of using **event-related potentials (ERPs)** as a measure of brain activity is that over a number of trials in an experiment involving the same types of stimuli and task demands, brain activity related to this type of stimulus and task should be consistent, whereas the noise should not – noise should be random with respect to our experimental manipulations. Thus if we average together the brain activity across multiple trials, time-locked to some experimentally controlled event of interest (such as the onset of the stimuli), then the influence of the noise on the resulting average should be reduced, while the true, consistent signal should be enhanced. Such averaged, segments of EEG data, time-locked to events, are what we refer to as ERPs. In the ideal case, the **signal-to-noise ratio (SNR)** will increase as the square root of the number of experimental trials included in the average. This assumes that the signal and noise are independent, the signal is truly consistent across the trials, and the noise is random with a mean of zero and consistent variance. In reality, any of these assumptions may not actually be true. For example, the brain activity may vary from trial to trial based on individual characteristics of the stimuli, the subject's attention level, or other factors. Likewise, some aspects of noise may be correlated with stimulus presentation, for example if a subject blinks every time a visual stimulus is presented (something ERP experimenters in fact go to lengths to prevent). Nevertheless, it is generally true that more trials lead to better SNR.

The number of trials (events) required per condition to obtain a reliable ERP effect can vary depending on several factors. These include the size of the ERP effect of interest, and how much noise there is in the data (which can be influenced by the design of the experiment, the EEG system used, the EEG recording environment, and the individual subject). While generally, 'more is better', the fact that SNR increases with the square root of the number of trials means that there are diminishing returns from more trials. The number of experimental conditions and how long each experimental trial takes are also limiting factors. Thus in studies of the auditory brainstem response, which is very small but is elicited by very brief 'click' sounds, it is not uncommon to use 10,000 trials per subject. Each 'click' is very brief and they can be presented in very rapid succession, so 10,000 trials only take a few minutes to conduct. However, in studies of sentence processing, experimenters use far fewer trials because of the amount of time required for people to read each sentence and make a response for the experimental task; a sentence processing study involving 200 sentences may take over an hour for data collection. Because of these complexities, there is no hard-and-fast rule for choosing the number of trials; typically this decision is made based on review of the prior literature and/or the researcher's previous experience working in a particular domain.

Once data are collected from multiple subjects and averaged together across trials and participants, a **grand average** waveform is obtained at each electrode. More details on all of the steps required to get to this point in data analysis are provided later in this chapter; for now we want to focus on the end result. An example of grand averaged waveforms from an experiment are shown in Figure 3.4. The waveform at each electrode basically consists of a series of positive and negative peaks. The effects of interest in the experiment are called **components**, and are commonly – though not necessarily – associated with particular peaks. A common definition for an ERP component is a feature of the averaged waveform that has a consistent (a) polarity (positive or negative), (b) timing, (c) scalp distribution (where on the scalp it is largest), and (d) eliciting conditions. For example, the onset of a visual stimulus (the eliciting condition) typically evokes a series of components referred to as the P1-N1-P2 complex; a convention in ERP research is to label early components according to their polarity (positive or negative) and their sequence (so, P1 is the first positive peak, P2 the second positive peak, etc.). The P1-N1-P2 complex has been labelled in the bottom panel of Figure 3.4. It is important to remember from our description of ECDs that positive and negative polarity both represent brain activation – when first introduced to ERPs some people think that negative peaks represent activity decreases, or neural inhibition. However, when a particular ECD is active it generates both positive and negative electrical potential; what is measured at a given electrode simply depends on the orientation of the ECD. Inhibition would be reflected in a smaller amplitude peak (or no discernible peak at all).

The labelling of components can be confusing for a newcomer to the field of ERPs. First of all, an alternative convention for labelling components – and one that is used most of the time for later components – is to label peaks according to their polarity and latency. Thus the P1 is sometimes called the P100, because it tends to peak around 100 ms. The timing and scalp distribution of components is also often complex. For instance, there are actually three distinct visual N1 components, in that the first negativity in the waveform peaks at different latencies over different parts of the scalp, and these can be differently affected by experimental manipulations. Furthermore, certain types of visual stimuli elicit specific components that are not seen for visual stimuli more generally. For example, faces elicit a distinct component, labelled the N170 (because it peaks at 170 ms post-stimulus onset) over the posterior temporal lobe – typically largest at electrodes on the mastoid process, the bony area behind the ear. Other visual stimuli also elicit N170-type components, but these differ in their scalp distribution and sensitivity to eliciting conditions. For example, the N170 elicited by faces is larger for inverted than upright faces, and is larger over the right than the left hemisphere. In contrast, an N170 is also elicited by printed words, but in this case it is larger over the left than right hemisphere, and is larger for real words than non-words (strings of consonants) or false fonts (letter-like symbols). Component labels are also often used to refer to different components in very different domains. For example, the onsets of auditory stimuli also elicit a series of components labelled the P1-N1-P2 complex. However, the scalp distribution of these components is different for visual and auditory stimuli: the visual P1-N1-P2 complex is largest over the occipital cortex, whereas the auditory P1-N1-P2 complex is largest over midline frontal electrodes. These differences in scalp distribution are due to the fact that the components are

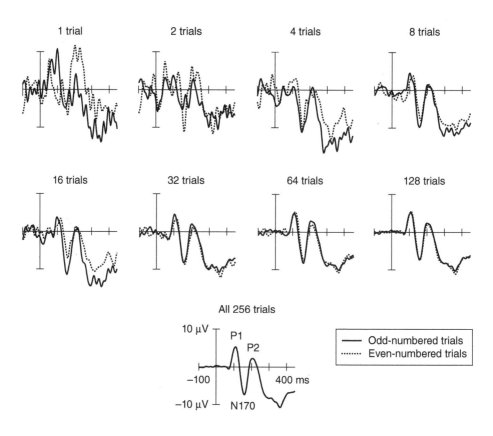

Figure 3.4 Effects of averaging trials on ERP waveforms from a single participant. All trials are from the same experimental condition: viewing upright faces. The top two rows show averages of different numbers of trials (or, in the case of the top right, un-averaged single trials). The solid lines represent averages of one set of trials (selected from odd-numbered trials), the dotted lines represent averages of different trials (even-numbered). The top row demonstrates that not only are averages composed of low numbers of trials noisier than those composed of larger numbers, but also the averages are less consistent (that is, less overlap between odd- and even-numbered trials). The bottom panel shows the average of 256 trials for this particular experimental condition presented to the participant, with the first three prominent components – P1, N170, and P2 – labelled (a total of 300 trials were actually presented, but some were removed due to artifacts caused by eye blinks). The data shown are from an electrode placed over the right mastoid, referenced to the average of 128 electrodes covering the scalp

generated in distinct brain regions (visual versus auditory sensory cortices). The timing of the auditory and visual P1-N1-P2 complexes also differ; however, the timing of these early sensory ERP components are sensitive to experimental factors such as the brightness or loudness of the stimuli.

The P1-N1-P2 complex and the N170 are examples of a set of **exogenous components**, so-called because they are elicited by external, sensory factors. Although the amplitude (size) and timing of these components can be influenced by stimulus and/or manipulations, exogenous components are generally 'obligatory' in the sense that they are elicited by stimuli regardless of whether the participant is paying attention to them (or, often, even when people are unconscious). Other components depend more heavily on the task and the subject's mental experience of the events, and are referred to as **endogenous components**. An example of an endogenous component is the P3, which is elicited specifically by relatively infrequent, task-relevant stimuli. For example, if the stimuli in an experiment consist of a series of pictures of cats and dogs, and the cats occur 80% of the time but subjects are instructed to respond only when they see a dog, then dog stimuli will elicit a P3 effect (which is a positivity, generally maximum just behind the top of the head peaking around 300 ms after stimulus onset). However, if the dogs and cats occur with equal frequency, or the subject does not have to make a special response to the rarer stimuli, then the P3 will be smaller or undetectable in the ERP waveforms. Another example of an endogenous component is the N400. This component is elicited by (among other things) words whose meaning does not fit into the context of the words preceding it in a sentence. For example, in the sentence 'He drove to the beach in a banana', the word 'banana' will evoke a negativity peaking around 400 ms over the top of the head relative to a semantically appropriate word like 'car'. However, there is nothing special about the word 'banana' that evokes the N400 component; the same word would not evoke this N400 effect in a sentence like 'The monkey went to the beach and ate a banana'. It is important to remember however that the exogenous/endogenous distinction is somewhat fuzzy – for example the N1, which we called an exogenous component, can vary in its amplitude depending on whether or not the person is attending to the stimulus or not – an endogenous factor.

As a side note, you may have noticed that whereas previous components were referred to by a letter indicating their polarity along with the sequential number of their peak (for example, P1, N1, P2, N2, P3), the N170 and N400 are named based on the timing of its peak. This is a relatively common convention in the ERP literature: early peaks are labelled sequentially, while later ones are labelled according to their timing, but this convention is not 100% consistent. Often the timing information in the label can be confusing as well; for instance, the P600 component (elicited by syntactic violations in sentences) had a peak latency of approximately 600 ms when first discovered and named thus (Osterhout & Holcomb, 1992); however, in subsequent work it was discovered to have variable latency (e.g., Newman, Ullman, Pancheva, Waligura, & Neville, 2007). Most investigators still refer to it as the P600 though, reflecting the power of habit and convention. As well, many components are labelled according to their eliciting conditions and/or other features of the waveforms, such as 'error-related negativity' (ERN), or 'left anterior negativity' (LAN). The naming conventions for ERP components typically arise 'organically' in the field as a component is discovered and perhaps initially referred to differently by different investigators. Indeed, in some cases components that were independently discovered in different experimental contexts – and given different labels – are later recognized as being the same component due to commonalities in polarity, timing, and scalp distribution, along with the characterization of a common underlying cognitive process in the two experimental contexts (e.g., MacLeod, Stewart, Newman, & Arnell, 2017). Timing is probably a more consistent convention in the literature overall, even though it is recognized that the timing is approximate and experimental factors may influence peak timing.

In spite of the consistency with which particular peaks occur in time under certain experimental conditions, and our conventions for naming those peaks, in many cases these waveform peaks do not represent the time at which any particular brain area or ECD reaches its peak activity. This is because the scalp-recorded waveforms are the sum of all EEG-measurable activity at a given point in time. As Figure 3.5 shows, a peak electrical potential in the scalp-recorded ERP waveform may actually occur at a time in between the times at which the activity of two underlying generators (ECDs) peaks. We refer to the peaks of these underlying generators as latent components, which we cannot directly observe but which combine to yield scalp-recorded components. As well, the absolute amplitude of the ERP is difficult to interpret because it is influenced by preceding and subsequent peaks, and the timing and amplitude of many components (especially early ones more strongly associated with sensory-perceptual processes) are quite sensitive to low-level stimulus factors such as intensity (for example, brightness or loudness), contrast, and size. Thus the optimal way to use ERPs as a research technique is to compare the waveforms between two or more different conditions, ideally with all participants seeing all of the stimuli/conditions (a within-subjects design). As much as possible, differences in the stimuli between conditions should be minimized, except for the factors under experimental manipulation. Thus, for example, in the N400 sentence processing experiments like the one described above, it is common practice to generate two versions of each sentence that differ only in whether the 'target' word is semantically appropriate or not. The semantically appropriate and anomalous words themselves should be matched on as many properties as possible, such as their length, how frequently they occur in the language, their part of speech (for example, both nouns), and possibly other factors such as their imageability. Likewise, in the P3 experiment described earlier, the pictures of the dog and the cat should be similar in size, overall luminance, etc.

The advantage of comparing ERPs elicited under such closely matched conditions is that such comparisons isolate effects of the experimental manipulation from extraneous factors. Waveform peaks cannot be guaranteed to reflect peaks in underlying neural activity – or even activity of single brain areas/processes as opposed to overlapping activity from multiple brain regions. As well, '0 µV' is arbitrary and defined by a short baseline period immediately preceding the stimulus, so the actual voltage value at any given point in an ERP epoch has no independent meaning. Thus waveforms from individual ERP conditions are, in many cases, not very informative. The **subtraction method** provides a solution to this problem, by focusing on differences between waveforms elicited in two closely matched experimental conditions that differ only in the feature that is of experimental interest. This isolates the brain activity associated with these experimental differences. (The subtraction method is

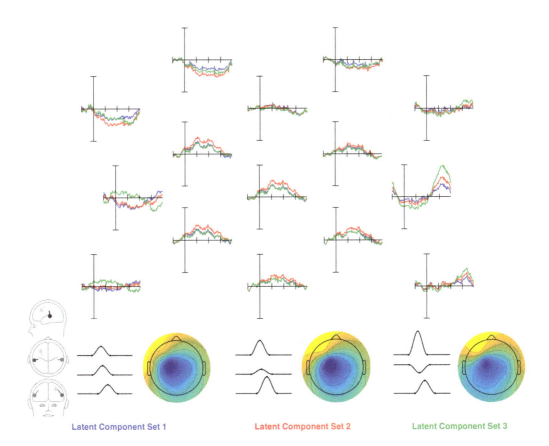

Figure 3.5 Simulated data showing how different patterns of activation of three dipoles (latency components) can create nearly indistinguishable patterns of ERPs at the scalp. Three dipole sources were modelled, located approximately in the superior temporal lobes of each hemisphere, and the left frontal lobe (the diagram at bottom left shows dipole locations and orientations). Across the bottom of the figure are the three different time courses of activity of these three sources, along with the projections of the summed activity of these latent components at the scalp. Although there are subtle differences in the scalp topography, these patterns would likely be statistically indistinguishable from each other. The top part of the figure shows the ERP waveforms at 15 electrode locations covering the scalp. In these projections, some random noise has been added to the data, similar to what would be found in real data (the noise is about 10% of the amplitude of the latent components). As with the scalp maps, the waveforms are quite similar across the three different combinations of latent component activity. Notably, the largest apparent differences between the different latent component sets are not where the dipole project their maximum potentials (that is, not near the vertex of the head, where the scalp maps show the darkest), but at electrodes that are quite peripheral. Another important point to note is that although there are three distinct dipoles contributing to the scalp-recorded ERP activity, it would be difficult, if not impossible, to determine this based on the scalp-recorded activity, because of the way the dipoles' activity sum at the scalp

also a standard approach to designing and analysing fMRI experiments, as we will see later in this book.) It is thus common to plot **difference waveforms**, which are created by subtracting the waveforms from one condition from those of another. Difference waveforms allow the experimenter to see clearly the times at which the conditions differ, without being distracted or potentially biased by the appearance of the peaks in the individual conditions' waveforms (which, as noted above, may not correspond to peaks in latent components anyway).

An example of the subtraction method is shown in Figure 3.6. Activity is compared between biological and scrambled motion. Biological motion comprised short

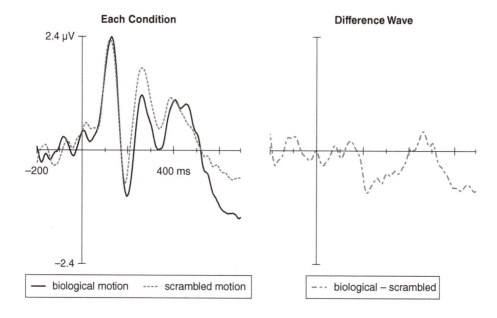

Figure 3.6 The left panel shows the ERPs elicited by two different experimental conditions, as described in the text. A sequence of early components can be seen, including the P1 at 100 ms, the N1 just before 200 ms, the P2 at approximately 250 ms, and the N2 at approximately 250 ms. The right panel shows the difference wave created by the subtraction biological - scrambled motion. Note that the peaks (greatest differences) in the difference wave do not necessarily correspond directly to 'component' peaks or troughs in the waveforms of the individual conditions. For example, biological motion's first peak negativity in the difference wave is at approximately 200 ms, which corresponds to the 'slope' between the N1 and P2 in the individual-condition waveforms, rather than to either the peak time of the N1 or the P2. Furthermore, this difference is maintained from approximately 200-600 ms, which overlaps with the N1, P2, and N2 components. This underscores the point that the component peaks visible in the individual-condition ERP waveforms may not reflect the brain activity that is modulated by a particular experimental manipulation. Waveforms are derived from an experiment originally published in White, Fawcett, & Newman, 2014

videos of people performing actions such as walking or chopping wood; these were shown as white dots placed on the joints of the body, against a black background. Thus there was no outline of a body, rather the impression of a human form was derived from the patterns of motion. The other (control) condition was scrambled motion, obtained by scrambling the locations of the dots in the biological motion videos to preserve the low-level features of the stimuli (number of dots, speed and distance of movement), but eliminate the coherent percept of a body. The figure shows that the timing of the between-condition differences did not correspond to the timing of the obvious component peaks in the individual-condition waveforms. This is not always the case – sometimes peak differences do correspond in time with individual-condition waveform peaks; for example, the P3 and N400, although visible as peaks in the difference waveforms, are also visible as prominent features in the waveforms of the deviant conditions that elicit them.

At a minimum, difference waveforms can be used as a form of **mental chronometry**, to determine the earliest point at which the subject's brain makes a distinction between the two experimental conditions. However, typically much more can be inferred from differences by referring to the published ERP literature on similar experimental designs. For example, the P3 is thought to reflect 'context updating' whereby new information is integrated with recent events held in working memory, and the P3 reflects novel information relevant to the individual. This process seems to be supra-modal, or generic, in that similar P3s can be obtained for visual, auditory, somatosensory, or other stimuli. Thus observing a P3 in an experiment not only tells us when the brain registered the experimental manipulation, but also that the context-updating process was involved, which in turn tells us that the information was relevant to the individual (since irrelevant information does not elicit a P3). Indeed, when the N400 component was discovered in response to semantic expectation violations in sentences (Kutas & Hillyard, 1980), the researchers were surprised because they had predicted a P3 response. Observing a distinct component for semantic anomalies led the researchers to conclude that this component – the N400 – reflected a language-specific process related to integrating the meanings of words. In other words, the N400 showed that semantic information in sentences was processed differently from the more generic context-updating process reflected by the P3. Another example of how difference waves can be informative again relates to the P3. Farwell and Donchin (1991) created a computerized device that allowed people to spell words using only their brainwaves. The 'P3 speller' works by showing all the letters of the alphabet in a grid on a screen, and asking the user to focus their attention on the letter they want to 'write'. Then, in random order rows and columns of the grid flash. All of these flashes elicit visual evoked potentials; however, the flashes that highlight the letter the person is attending to elicit a P3 due to their task relevance (the attention the user is paying to that letter). Thus by comparing differences between ERPs elicited by highlighting different rows and columns, the chosen letter can be identified after a sufficient number of flashes.

Another way of using difference waves is to compare waveforms from a single condition, from corresponding electrodes over either hemisphere. For example, the **lateralized readiness potential (LRP)** is a component that rises as people prepare to make a motor response, such as pressing a button. The LRP is larger over the motor cortex of the hemisphere contralateral (opposite) to the hand that will move, and so the LRP is obtained as the difference between the waveforms from electrodes C3 and C4, which are over the left and right motor cortex, respectively.

The use of difference waveforms may allow experimenters to get closer to the activity of underlying ECDs that relate to the experimental effect and associated neurocognitive process of interest, to the extent that these may be masked by overlapping activity of ECDs that are not specifically modulated by the experimental manipulation. However, it is still important to remember that just like the peaks in the waveforms of individual conditions, these difference waves may reflect the activity of multiple ECDs/brain areas and that the activity of all contributing areas may not be simultaneous but rather partially overlap in time. This is a fundamental limitation of the ERP technique, and perhaps the most important thing to keep in mind when interpreting ERP results. Numerous efforts have been made to attempt to separate the contributions of different generators to these ERP effects, some of which we will discuss later. However, all of these approaches are based on assumptions and inferences, and so do not perfectly solve the 'black box' problem inherent in EEG/ERP.

Oscillatory Signals

Our description of ERPs so far has focused on what is referred to as the **time domain**, meaning that brain activity is examined as a function of time. Another way of visualizing and analysing the data is in the **frequency domain. Frequency** refers to how many times something happens in a given time interval. Typically we talk about frequency of waveforms in terms of the unit Hertz (Hz), which is defined as the number of cycles (peaks or troughs in the sine wave) per 1 second of time. The frequency of a simple waveform such as a sine wave is easy to determine simply by looking at it. For example, Figure 3.7 shows examples of sine waves of different frequencies; the frequency can be determined visually by simply counting the number of peaks (or troughs) that occur in the space of 1 second. Human EEG is characterized by a number of **frequency bands** (ranges) that are associated with different conscious states as well as different aspects of cognitive processing. Table 3.1 describes these different bands and associated processes. It is important to understand that although one particular frequency may be most dominant or obvious to the naked eye in a segment of EEG data, any data actually comprises a mixture of different frequencies.

Mathematically, it is possible to both compose a complex waveform from a series of sine waves – as shown in Figure 3.7 – and conversely to decompose such a complex waveform into its component frequencies. A **Fourier series** is a combination of waveforms of different frequencies. Figure 3.7 shows an idealized Fourier series consisting of a set of component sine waves at frequencies within each of the bands defined for human EEG shown in Table 3.1, along with 60 Hz noise that is typically

Table 3.1 EEG frequency bands, defined based on their association with different cognitive functions and states of consciousness. Note that alpha and mu bands cover the same frequency range; activity in this frequency band is labelled 'alpha' more generally, and particularly when it is generated over occipital cortex, whereas mu is the label applied to this frequency range specifically when the activity is recorded over motor cortex during movements or imagined movements

Band Name	Frequency Range (Hz)
Delta	< 3
Theta	4–7
Alpha [occipital cortex]	8–14
Beta	15–30
Gamma	> 30
Mu [motor cortex]	8–12

present due to electromagnetic interference (60 Hz noise is discussed in more detail later in this chapter). Real EEG data never looks this simple owing to the fact that there is a much broader range of frequencies in real data, and the power (amplitude) of these frequencies is rarely constant for any length of time.

A consequence of the fact that we can break a complex waveform down into a Fourier series is that we can take any waveform in the **time domain** (which is the 'normal' way that we look at EEG data, as electrical potential varying over time – shown in the top panels of Figure 3.7) and perform a mathematical operation (known as a **Fourier transform**) that allows us to view it in the **frequency domain** (shown in the bottom panel of Figure 3.7). A frequency-domain representation collapses over time, so that rather than time on the x axis, frequency is plotted; amplitude (referred to as **power** in the frequency domain) is plotted on the y axis. Thus in the bottom of Figure 3.7 we see clear peaks in the frequency domain corresponding to the frequencies of each of the component waveforms in the top panels, with the power (height) of each peak corresponding to the amplitude of the sine waves in the top panels. (Note that the decrease in amplitude with increasing frequency in this plot follows the pattern observed in real EEG, in which power is approximately proportional to 1/frequency.)

The relevance of all this to EEG research is that an alternative to analysing ERP components in the time domain is to examine the effects of experimental manipulations in the frequency domain. Frequency-domain analysis typically focuses on changes in **power (amplitude)** in particular frequency bands that occur time-locked to experimental events of interest. So in fact the distinction between time- and frequency-domain analyses is an oversimplification; typically analyses that consider frequency are **time-frequency analyses**. Thus they are the equivalent of ERPs, but in the frequency domain. Two types of event-related changes in the frequency domain are possible, typically referred to as **event-related synchronization (ERS)**

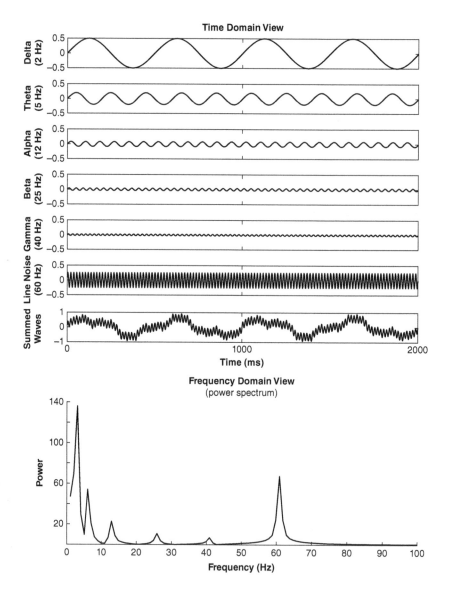

Figure 3.7 An example of Fourier series composition/decomposition. The top panel shows a set of sine waves of different frequencies, in the time domain (that is, time is on the x axis of the plot). In this example, the sine wave frequencies were chosen to correspond to the different major frequency bands listed in Table 3.1, along with a 60 Hz which corresponds to the electromagnetic noise typically present in EEG data. The first six plots show individual sine waves; the seventh plot shows the sum of the individual frequency components above it. The bottom panel shows this summed waveform in the frequency domain, after applying a Fourier transform to the summed waveform. The x axis now represents frequency, and clear peaks are present at the frequencies at each of the components of the summed waveform

and **event-related desynchronization** (**ERD**). ERS occurs when power in a frequency band increases following an event of interest, while ERD is the opposite – a decrease in power after event onset. Perhaps the easiest example of ERS and ERD to obtain is related to the alpha rhythm, in the 8–14 Hz frequency band. An example of this is shown in Figure 3.8. Very clear alpha oscillations are typically evoked over occipital electrodes when a person closes her or his eyes – an example of ERS where alpha power increases time-locked to the event of eye closure. ERD occurs when the subject opens his or her eyes again, at which point the alpha typically disappears from the EEG. An important thing to note here is that although the terms 'synchronization' and 'desynchronization' are commonly used to describe changes in power, these terms reflect an unproven hypothesis – namely that power changes are solely attributable to changes in synchrony between neurons within a brain area. In fact, power changes could arise for other reasons, including simply reduced postsynaptic potentials as a result of decreased input to that brain region.

Figure 3.8 A simple example of event-related synchronization (ERS) and desynchronization (ERD). Continuous EEG recorded from an electrode over the occipital lobe is shown. The dashed vertical lines represent events triggering synchronization/desynchronization. Increases in alpha power can be seen as the increased amplitude and clear 10 Hz oscillation in the periods marked as 'ERS'. Note however that some alpha power is evident even in the 'ERD' periods

In addition to looking for ERS or ERD – frequency band changes associated with experimentally controlled events – frequency domain analysis can be applied over longer periods of EEG data. One example of this is in 'resting state' experiments where EEG data is recorded for some period of time (for example, 1–10 minutes) while the participant is at rest, either with his or her eyes closed or open and staring at a fixation point. The power in different frequency bands is then analysed, averaged over a number of seconds (for example, 30-second segments may be used, with each segment overlapping 50% with the one preceding it, and 50% with the one after it). The same analysis can also be applied to task-related EEG data, if the subject is performing a consistent task over an extended period of time (for example, reading words presented at a steady rate). Such analyses can reveal 'state-level' patterns of brain activity that is related to general aspects of task performance such as sustained attention (or 'default mode' brain activity that occurs when no specific task or stimuli are given, in the case of resting state data), rather than transient, event-related activity.

Another application of frequency domain analysis is to what are called 'steady state' stimuli. These are stimuli that alternate on and off at a rate comparable to frequencies in the EEG that are particularly sensitive to the stimuli. For example, steady state visual evoked potentials (SSVEPs) are elicited by flashing a visual stimulus on and off at a rate within the alpha band (8–14 Hz). This type of stimulation 'drives' the alpha rhythm at the rate of the stimulation. An example application of this is to present similar stimuli (for example, white circles) on each side of a computer screen while the subject is instructed to maintain fixation on a cross in the centre of the screen. If the circle on the right flashes at 8 Hz, and the circle on the left at 12 Hz, we will see two peaks in the frequency plot of the data – at 8 and 12 Hz. If we further direct the subject's attention to one or the other side of the screen at different points in the experiment, we will find that power in the 8 Hz band increases when attention is directed to the right side of the screen, while power in the 12 Hz band will increase when attention is directed to the left side of the screen. Similar steady-state effects can be obtained in the auditory and tactile modalities as well.

HOW DO WE MEASURE IT?

Data Acquisition

EEG is measured by electrodes placed on the scalp. The electrodes are simply small sensors made of some conductive material, connected to wires that in turn plug into an EEG **amplifier**. Common materials for electrodes include tin, silver/silver chloride, and gold, though other materials such as graphite have been experimented with. In clinical settings, EEG electrodes are commonly placed on the head individually, attached with a sticky paste. In research settings, it is more common to use a cap in which the electrodes are fixed in specific locations. Caps have the advantages of relatively quick set-up, and faster clean-up; applying electrodes individually takes more time and the paste is harder to wash out, but the positioning of electrodes can be more precisely done in relation to an individual's head size and shape, and the paste allows for recordings that can last for extended periods of time, even during sleep. Other variants include caps into which individual electrodes can be plugged, nets in which elastic connects the electrodes, leaving the hair accessible between elastics and electrodes, and headbands that contain relatively few electrodes. Some examples of EEG caps and nets are shown in Figure 3.9. The electrodes do not normally touch the scalp directly, but rather sit a few millimetres from the scalp and a conductive gel is injected through a small hole in the electrode to make the connection with the scalp (in some systems, sponges soaked in electrolyte solution substitute for the gel). This system reduces noise because the physical movement of the electrodes against the scalp can create noise; the gel serves as a flexible connection that is resistant to this effect. Some EEG systems use dry electrodes which make direct physical contact with the scalp and do not require a conductive medium like gel. While this reduces set-up and clean-up time, dry electrodes are inherently much more sensitive to noise – gel and paste form a highly conductive path for the electrical signal to travel from the scalp to the electrode, and are flexible enough that the effects of electrode movement are reduced. The quality of data collected with dry electrodes is generally poorer than with 'wet' electrode systems, leading most researchers to avoid dry electrode systems unless there is a specific benefit that outweighs the reduction in data quality.

Figure 3.9 Examples of different EEG caps and systems. Across the top row, the left image shows a conventional 32-channel system with disc-type passive electrodes. The middle cap features 64 active electrodes, each of which has a small circuit board on the electrode itself, which includes a pre-amplifier to boost the signal (and thus reduce environmental noise) and a coloured LED to facilitate impedance checking. Both of these first two systems use electrolyte gel to make the contact between electrode and scalp. The right cap is a 256 channel system in which electrodes are embedded in sponges which are soaked in a liquid electrolyte solution rather than gel, and the electrodes are connected by transparent elastics forming a net, rather than using a cap made of stretchable material as in the left two caps. The bottom row shows additional EEG hardware. The left image shows a cap with active electrodes, an interface box (centre), and the amplifier (top right) and battery (bottom right). The right image shows a net (left) with the associated amplifier (right) and a computer that would control data acquisition and perform analysis. Top left and centre, and bottom left images provided courtesy of Brain Products GmbH; top and bottom right images provided courtesy of Electrical Geodesics, Inc.

Electrode positions vary from system to system, but most follow a standard known as the **International 10–10 System**, as shown in Figure 3.10. This system is based on the use of standard landmarks on the head, measuring the distances between them and then placing electrodes at evenly spaced distances from each other along the lines defined by the landmarks. The landmarks commonly used are the **nasion** (the indent at the bridge of the nose), the **inion** (the depression at the base of the skull, centred left-to-right), which define the distances along the anterior–posterior dimension, and between **peri-auricular points** located in the area of each ear – just above the tragus in the zygomatic notch. The **vertex** of the head is defined as the point 50% of the distance between these two pairs of points. This electrode position is labelled **Cz** (for 'central zero'), and the labelling of other electrode positions follows a standard system of letters and numbers based on 10% increments of the anterior–posterior and left–right measurements (American Clinical Neurophysiology Society, 2006). This system is still often referred to as the 'International 10–20 System', harkening back to a time when fewer electrodes were used and a combination of 10% and 20% increments were used; there is also a 10–5 system involving 5% increments and thus allowing higher-density (more electrodes) recordings, although this is not widely used or clinically accepted. It is important to note in research settings where the electrodes are fixed to a cap or net, the actual distances between electrodes may not be exactly 10% once the cap is on an individual's head, because head shapes differ. Thus in common practice the electrode positions are approximations. However, in clinical settings electrodes are attached individually to the scalp using a glue-like paste (called colloidon), and are placed at precise 10% increments.

The electrodes connect to an amplifier, which boosts the very small signals recorded from the scalp prior to their being recorded. Amplification serves to make the EEG signals easier to measure and quantify. Amplifiers also perform analogue-to-digital conversion – the continuous (analogue) EEG detected by the electrodes is converted to a digital signal that represents the voltage at discrete points in time. It is typical to digitize EEG data at **sampling rates** of between 100–1000 Hz (Hz, or Hertz, is a unit indicating the number of samples recorded per second). The amplified, digitized signals are then output to a computer for visualization and recording. Many amplifiers have additional inputs for other sensors (for example, to measure other physiological signals such as heart rate and respiration), as well as a 'trigger port' which is an input from a computer or other device that allows markers to be recorded in the EEG data file that are precisely time-locked to external events of interest, such as stimuli presented by a computer to the participant.

One of the most important concepts to understand about EEG recording is the fact that we are always measuring a *difference* in electrical potential between two locations. Indeed, electricity itself is a dynamic force, and any measurement of electrical potential is by definition a differential measurement. Electrical potential is an important concept to understand. It may be most intuitive to think of electricity as something that flows through a conductor, such as a wire. This flow of electricity is known as **current**, and involves the movement of charged particles (electrons) through a conductor. However, electrical **potential** is a more common measurement

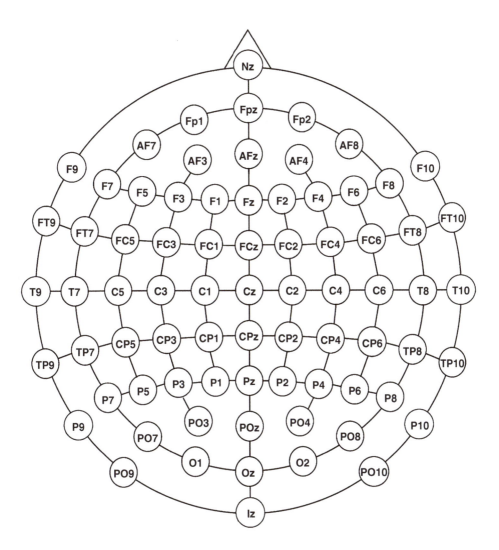

Figure 3.10 The electrode positions and names in the International 10-10 System. Letters generally refer to the lobe of the brain over which the electrodes are (approximately) positioned; 'z' stands for 'zero' and represents the midline of the scalp, running from the nasion (Nz) to the inion (Iz). Electrodes on the left side of the midline are assigned odd numbers and those on the right side have even numbers. Note that TP9 and TP10 typically fall over the mastoids – the bony, hairless area behind the ears that is often used as a reference in EEG recordings. They may thus alternatively be labelled 'LM' and 'RM', respectively

than current. Electrical potential is not current flow; rather, it is literally the potential for current to flow. Sources of electricity always have potential, even when current is not flowing. Thus the wall outlet in a typical North American home has a potential of 120 V, regardless of whether any device is actually attached to the outlet and drawing current. Similarly, batteries store electrical potential. For example the 'AA' type of battery used in many handheld devices has an electrical potential of 1.5 V, meaning that the difference in charge between the positive and negative terminals is 1.5 V – again regardless of whether anything is connected to the battery. This potential sets a limit on the amount of current that could flow between the terminals if a conductor connected them; however, the actual current flow depends on the properties of the conductor, such as resistance.

An analogy that may be helpful in understanding the concept of electrical potential is that of water. Imagine that we have a bowl of water sitting on a table. This bowl of water has a certain potential, which is the amount of water that *could* fall to the ground if the bowl was tipped. If we were actually to tip the bowl, the rate at which the water moves (for example, litres per second) would be equivalent to electrical current. However, the potential is simply the difference between the amount of water in the bowl, and the amount of water on the floor (which we could measure in litres). In electricity, potential is typically measured in units of Volts (V) relative to **ground**, where ground is literally the electrical potential of the Earth itself; the Earth is considered to have zero electrical charge so serves as a good reference point. Returning to EEG, this principle of electrical measurement means that the electrical activity measured at any electrode placed on the scalp (typically quantified in microvolts – µV – or millionths of a Volt) is actually the potential difference between that electrode and the ground. In EEG systems, the earth is not used as the ground – to do so would create a safety hazard (stray electrical current could pass through the person connected to the electrodes, leading to electrocution), and reduce the overall sensitivity of the system to the very small potentials measurable at the scalp. Instead, a ground circuit (or 'floating ground') is created within the EEG amplifier to serve as 'zero voltage'. Measuring the difference between an electrode on the scalp and the amplifier's circuit ground, however, will reflect not only the brain activity around the electrode on the scalp, but *all* of the electrical charge in the subject's body, including accumulated static electricity. To cancel out this effect, the ground circuit is connected to an electrode placed somewhere on the subject's body. The location of this **ground electrode** is arbitrary, and for convenience it is typically somewhere on the head, included in the montage of electrodes in the cap that is used.

While this arrangement isolates brain activity at the **active electrode** (the one on the scalp at which we want to measure brain activity) from static electrical charge in the body, it is not sufficient for clean (that is, low-noise) EEG recordings. The circuitry of the amplifier will inevitably contain some amount of electrical noise itself, due to electrical noise in the environment and within the amplifier itself. Thus the measurement of electrical potential between the active electrode and the amplifier's ground circuit will reflect both electrical activity at the scalp and the noise present in the ground. To deal with this problem, EEG recording uses **differential amplifiers**. In such systems, a minimum of three electrodes are required for EEG recording, the active and ground electrodes, and a **reference electrode** (in practice, a larger number of active electrodes are used). The electrical potential is measured at the active electrode relative to ground (A–G), and the potential at the reference electrode is likewise measured relative to the ground (R–G). Then what is actually recorded is the difference between the active and reference electrodes (A–G) – (R–G), and any noise specific to the ground circuit is cancelled out in this subtraction. This configuration, in principle, restricts what is recorded from the active electrode to the electrical potential present at that location, eliminating noise from the rest of the body, the ground circuit, and the environment. In practice, some noise will still be present in the recordings due to imperfections in the amplifier circuitry, the quality of the connections between the electrodes in the scalp, and the fact that different locations on the body (and even the head) may vary slightly in the noise that they contain.

There are some important implications of the use of differential amplifiers for the recording and interpretation of EEG data. Firstly, the quality of the connection between each electrode and the scalp is critical. This is typically measured as **impedance** (conceptually similar to resistance). The impedance threshold for good-quality recordings varies between EEG systems depending on their engineering, but the guidelines of the system used should be adhered to, and efforts should be made to ensure not only low, but comparable, impedance at all electrodes. Impedance is typically lowered by rubbing the electrolyte gel or solution into the scalp, which works both by getting the gel deeper into the skin and also gently abrading the dead outer layer of skin cells. A clean scalp is a good starting point for low-impedance recordings, so having participants wash their hair prior to coming for a study is good practice.

In terms of the interpretation of EEG recordings, the important thing to remember is that the potential recorded at each (active) electrode is actually the difference between that site and the reference site. One effect of this is that active electrodes near to the reference electrode will show very little signal unless there happens to be a strong source within the brain, in between these electrodes and close to them. A consequence of the fact that EEG recordings are differences between two sites is that the actual potential recorded at a particular scalp location will vary depending on what location is used as a reference (but will not, typically, vary with the location of the ground). Historically, it was common to use a reference location away from the head (for example, the collarbone) because it was thought that this would be 'neutral' with respect to brain activity. However, this is inconvenient and based on a false assumption, because the body is highly conductive and so brain activity is measurable at any location on the body. As well, noise cancellation may actually be worse for a reference farther from the head, because the sources of the noise may vary in strength more than for a reference location on the head. Thus in most modern systems it is common to use a location on the head, such as the mastoid bones (the bony area behind the ear, just below the hairline), on the tip of the nose, or the top of the head.

The choice of reference electrode location will determine how the recorded data look (specifically, the amplitude and polarity of the potential at each electrode). Fortunately, as discussed below under 'Preprocessing', it is very easy to re-reference the data to another electrode location later. This means that, in practice, the choice of reference electrode location during data acquisition should be made more on the basis of convenience than for any other reason. Indeed, in many EEG systems the reference and ground electrode locations used during recording are fixed and cannot be changed.

Signal and Noise

Like all research techniques, collecting good-quality EEG data relies not just on the equipment, but the expertise and care of the experimenter. EEG data quality is arguably even more dependent on the care taken by the experimenter than some other imaging techniques. This is because EEG is particularly sensitive to various sources of noise, and so the experimental procedures must account for this susceptibility. Noise in EEG comes from a number of sources. To start with, we should clarify that in EEG, **noise** is defined as any variance in the recorded EEG data that is not of interest to the experimenter. This is a very broad definition, and includes electromagnetic noise in the recording environment, physiological noise from the experimental participant (that is, signals generated by sources other than the brain), and even signals from the brain that are not of interest in the experiment. A term that is often used in EEG research to describe transient noise in the data is **artifact**. This term can refer to both physiological and non-physiological noise.

These different sources of noise are controlled in different ways, and understanding how to control them depends on understanding where they come from. We will start with electromagnetic noise. A fundamental rule of physics, **Ampère's circuital law,** describes the fact that any electrical current will induce a magnetic field, and correspondingly any magnetic field will induce an electrical current in a nearby electrical conductor. Colloquially, this relationship is often referred to as the **right-hand rule**, because if you hold your right hand with the thumb extended and fingers curled, the relationship between electrical current and magnetic field is shown: for a current flowing in the direction of the thumb, the corresponding magnetic field will flow in the direction of the curled fingers (though in reality the magnetic field entirely circles the conductor). This is illustrated in Figure 3.11. In an EEG recording environment, we have wires connecting the electrodes on the scalp to the EEG amplifier, with current (the signal from the electrodes) flowing through the wires. As conductors, these wires are able to have current induced in them by nearby magnetic fields – and note that, unlike electricity which requires a conductive medium, magnetic fields travel easily over distance through the air. Critically, in the environment we typically have other sources of electromagnetic signals as well. These include lights, computers, monitors, and anything else connected to an electrical outlet, as well as (potentially) other sources such as cell phones, two-way radios (often used by facilities personnel in universities and hospitals), and other devices that generate a wireless signal. All of these devices generate magnetic fields, and can therefore induce current in the EEG wires.

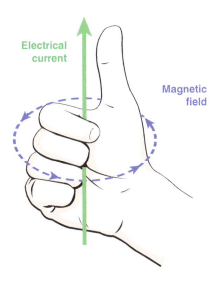

Figure 3.11 The right-hand rule, a mnemonic for Ampère's circuital law, illustrating the relationship between an electrical current and its associated magnetic field. Given a current flowing in the direction that the thumb of one's right hand is pointed (green arrow), the induced magnetic field will flow in the direction of one's curled fingers (blue dashed line)

Much of this induced noise is associated with devices connected to electrical mains systems (for example, anything connected to an electrical outlet; overhead lights), and the electricity supplied in these systems is an alternating current (AC) that fluctuates at a rate of either 50 or 60 Hz (different countries have different standards; for example, North America uses 60 Hz while Europe uses 50 Hz). Thus the noise induced in the EEG conductors fluctuates at this frequency, as shown in Figure 3.12. Care should always be taken in the EEG recording environment to control and mitigate the effects of line noise. This can be done through simple means such as ensuring that any electrical wires are as far away from the recording subject as possible, and in some cases shielding the effects of noise from the subject. Many wires (for example, computer monitor cables) are shielded by having a grounded, conductive sheath placed over the wires. On a larger scale, many EEG labs record data inside a shielded booth, or **Faraday cage**. This is a room enclosed in a conductive material, such as copper, with the conductive material connected to an **electrical ground**. Anything inside a Faraday cage is largely isolated from electromagnetic sources outside the cage. However, in practice the efficacy of Faraday cages in EEG research is less than complete, because typically there are electrical devices such as video monitors and/or speakers inside the recording booth. Any wires running from the outside to the inside of the Faraday cage will act as antennae to carry outside electromagnetic noise into the booth, unless they run through filtered connections between the outside and inside of the booth. It is also possible to place devices such as monitors outside the booth (booths can have shielded windows) or to build Faraday cages to surround individual pieces of equipment within the booth. Ultimately, however, the cost and effort involved in properly shielding the EEG subject from outside electromagnetic noise may not be worth the benefits. Because electrical mains noise is highly regular, and occurs at a higher frequency than is usually of interest in EEG data (which, for most studies, is typically below 30–40 Hz), it is generally possible to remove most of the effects of mains noise from the data by filtering (see the next section for more details). This said, it is still valuable to reduce noise in EEG recordings as much as possible for a number of reasons. Sources of noise other than electrical mains may be less regular in their frequency or strength over time, making filtering much less effective – and electrical wires running to the recording booth can act as antennae to conduct outside signals such as from two-way radios and large electrical equipment that do not generate purely 50 or 60 Hz noise. Finally, it is important for the experimenter to monitor the quality of the EEG data as it is being recorded, in order to control for any problems that may occur. The more noise that is present in the EEG signal, the harder it will be for the experimenter to assess whether problems are occurring that could be corrected.

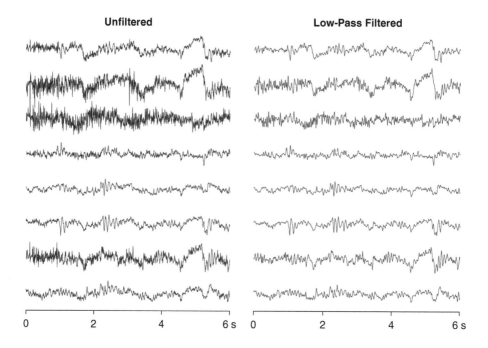

Figure 3.12 A six-second segment of raw EEG, shown without (left) and with (right) high-frequency noise removed by applying a 30 Hz low-pass filter. The high-frequency noise included 60 Hz electrical line noise as well as noise from other, unidentified sources

Other sources of electromagnetic noise may have very different frequencies, and possibly varying ones. For example, most audio headphones use electricity to drive their speakers, and the frequency and intensity of the electricity used varies with the sound being produced. Headphones placed on an EEG subject's head and creating sounds will induce highly variable, and very large, artifacts that are difficult to remove and may wash out the EEG data. For this reason, careful control over the recording environment, and the equipment used in the experiment, is critical to obtain good-quality data. For auditory presentation, speakers placed some distance away from the subject are preferable to headphones; if headphones are required, there are models available that keep the electromagnetic sources relatively distant from the head, and use air tubes to carry the sound from its source to the ears.

The other important source of noise in EEG recordings is physiological. As noted above, EEG signals from the brain can themselves be noise depending on the experimental context. Other important sources of physiological noise include eye movements, eye blinks, muscle movements (especially facial muscles), chronic muscle tension, and heartbeat (EKG). The eyes generate electrical artifacts because each eyeball is effectively an ECD, with polarity reversing between the retina and the front of the eye. When the eyes move, the orientation of this dipole changes, and this will be reflected in EEG recording electrodes on the scalp due to electrical conduction. A characteristic feature of eye-movement artifacts is that any eye movement results in a negative shift in potential on one side of the eye, and a corresponding positive shift on the other side of the eye, maximal along the axis of the eye movement. These can be easily identified by examining the data from electrodes near the eyes; many labs place electrodes close to the outside of each eye to monitor for horizontal eye movements, though these can also be detected in nearby scalp electrodes (for example, F3/4 and F7/8). Eye blinks also generate EEG artifacts. The skin is a good conductor of electricity, and when the eyelids touch they form a new path for current to flow. Blinks result in large, peaked artifacts that reverse in polarity above and below the eyes. This is why it is useful to have electrodes placed above and below at least one of the eyes – this arrangement will facilitate blink identification because the polarity inversion will be evident when comparing the electrodes above and below the eye.

Besides the eyes, muscles (especially facial and neck muscles) can generate large EEG artifacts. These artifacts are generated by the nerves that innervate the muscles; this 'noise' in the EEG signal is of interest in other research fields, where it is known as the electromyogram (EMG). The frequency range of EMG can span 0.5–350 Hz, but in the EEG signal it is typically recognizable as relatively high (> 30 Hz) frequency. Common causes of EMG artifact include muscle tension (which is often easily fixed by asking the participant to relax her/his muscles), jaw clenching, or speaking. This does make it difficult to record clean EEG data under experimental conditions that require speaking or other body movements. EMG artifacts can be removed to some extent by filtering; however, because the signal is more complex and variable over time than line noise, and can include frequency bands of interest for EEG, eliminating the sources of EMG noise during the recording is preferable to a 'hope we can filter it later' approach.

Head movements can often induce another artifact as well: a physical artifact created by the movement of the wires running from the electrodes to the amplifier. These artifacts are created through induction because the wires (conductors) are moving through space (containing varying magnetic fields). Some EEG systems use shielded wires for which this artifact is much less of a concern, but it is generally a good idea to ask participants to remain as still as possible during the experiment. In studies requiring movement, wireless EEG systems can be used. Artifacts can also be generated by the physical movement of the electrodes relative to the scalp. This is not typically a significant concern for most systems, as the electrode gel or solution acts as a flexible connection and minimizes the effects of small movements; this is more of a concern with dry electrode systems, however. As well, if a participant scratches her head and moves the electrodes an artifact may be produced.

Artifacts can also be generated by changes in skin conductance. These are commonly known as **skin potentials** and are generated by increased electrical conductance across the surface of the skin due to sweat (which, as an electrolyte-rich liquid, is a very good conductor). Skin potentials manifest in the EEG as very low-frequency drift: the tracing for the electrode will not go horizontally across the screen but instead trend – often dramatically – upward or downward. Decreasing electrode impedance will help to reduce skin potentials, but the best approach is prevention by ensuring adequate climate control within the EEG recording environment.

A final physiological artifact worth mention is from the heartbeat. The heart generates a characteristic, complex electrical waveform with every beat, which is commonly referred to as the EKG. This can sometimes be picked up in some EEG electrodes, although it is relatively uncommon. Because the heartbeat is relatively low frequency (roughly 0.5–2 Hz under resting conditions) and unlikely to be synchronized with experimental stimuli, this artifact is not typically a major concern for EEG data quality.

As mentioned above, even EEG itself may be considered noise, if it is brain activity unrelated to the experiment. For example, alpha waves are characteristic EEG waves generated in the occipital cortex. These are often generated when a person closes his or her eyes, but can also be generated when people are tired or bored. Thus in a long, boring experiment, the experimenter may see alpha waves generated. These are not of experimental interest, and alpha waves are often quite large relative to other EEG signals. Thus even though the alpha waves are being generated by the brain, they are considered 'noise' because they are not of experimental interest. EEG effects of no interest such as this can be some of the most problematic for an experimenter because they occur in the same source (the brain) and at similar frequencies to the experimental effects of interest, and so cannot typically be filtered out or removed by most techniques. It is thus important for the experimenter to consider why these artifacts occur and try to optimize the experimental design; for example, by giving participants frequent breaks, making the task as interesting as possible, keeping the task as short as possible, not running experiments at times when people are likely to be tired, and so on.

Practical Considerations

In describing the different artifacts above, we touched on some strategies to help improve data quality. Here we will summarize and expand upon these. There are three general times when data quality can be controlled: before the participant arrives (through proper set-up of the recording environment and experimental design), when preparing the participant (by proper application of the electrodes), and during the recording (by providing feedback to the participant).

Proper set-up of the recording environment should include creating a space for the experimental participant to sit that is comfortable, acoustically quiet, and free of distractions. An acoustically and radio frequency-shielded booth is ideal, although a small, quiet room is adequate and used in many labs. A comfortable chair should be provided, to help minimize discomfort and associated muscle tension. However, for most experiments it is desirable for the participant to stay awake, so the chair should not be too comfortable! It is also a good idea that the chair not have a high back, so that the participant's head will not touch the chair back – this can produce artifacts in the data through the mechanical movement of the electrodes and wires. The environment should be climate-controlled to ensure that the subject is comfortable; in particular too hot an environment is problematic because sweating can induce skin potentials. As much as possible, it is also a good idea to control the presence of electrical line noise near where the participant will sit. This primarily involves minimizing the number of conductors (especially electrical and computer wires) near to the participant. Because the strength of magnetic fields decreases with the square of the distance, moving wires that are near to the participant's chair to a location even a foot farther away can often substantially decrease the amount of line noise in the recordings. It is common to have the computers being used for the experiment outside of the recording booth/room, with only the minimum necessary equipment (for example, video monitor, speakers, response device) inside the recording space. It is also useful that all electrical equipment near the participant be grounded; for example, laptop computers with ungrounded electrical plugs generate substantially more line noise in the data than desktop computers with grounded connections. Some troubleshooting and experimentation is typical in setting up an EEG lab to identify the optimal configuration.

Experimental design is also a consideration that can affect EEG data quality. Because blinks create artifacts, it is a good idea not to design stimuli that are likely to induce blinks, such as sudden, bright visual stimuli or loud auditory stimuli. Because eye movements create artifacts, it is a good idea to ensure that visual stimuli can be easily viewed without eye movements. For example, in studies that use written sentences as stimuli, the sentences are typically presented one word at a time, in the centre of the screen. Experiments may also be designed in ways that allow participants specific times to blink in between critical trials. For example, if the participant has to initiate each trial with a button press, s/he can blink between trials. In other cases frequent breaks can be given to allow blinking. Because physical movements create artifacts, it is a good idea to minimize movement requirements. Studies that require button press or verbal responses typically have a delay between stimulus onset and the prompt to respond, to ensure that the physical movement occurs after the post-stimulus period during which the EEG is of interest (often 1 second, though this varies with the EEG effects under investigation). Finally, while fatigue affects performance under any circumstance, in EEG it is of particular concern because numerous artifacts may occur (for example, alpha waves, increased blinking, body shifting, stretching, yawning). Thus it is a good idea to design experiments that last an hour or less, and provide breaks during the experiment. Some labs have found that playing background music can also help participants feel more alert, so long as the music does not interfere with the experiment itself.

Proper set-up of the EEG participant also contributes significantly to data quality. It is always a good idea to have all equipment and forms prepared before the participant arrives, and to proceed with the study in a calm, organized manner – if the experimenter acts stressed, this may lead to less comfort and more tension in the participant. Care should be taken with preparation of the exposed skin where electrodes will be placed, and to the placement of the electrode cap and any free electrodes. Connections between the electrodes and the head should be as physically secure as possible (for example, in a snug-fitting cap). Electrode impedances should be measured, and lowered to levels appropriate for the system as discussed in the previous section. This is typically done by rubbing the scalp at each electrode location to work the gel in better and loosen dead skin cells. Exposed skin can be prepared with rubbing alcohol or an exfoliating cleanser prior to electrode application to lower impedance. Because the reference and ground electrodes affect the data at all other (active) electrodes, particular care should be taken to ensure that these have low impedance. Because participant and comfort are important, it is always good to attend to a participant's needs. Many EEG labs offer snacks (such as candy) and drinks (including caffeinated ones) to participants to aid in their alertness.

During recording, it is vitally important to monitor the EEG signals from all electrodes. This allows the experimenter to take action during the study to improve data quality, as needed. Many different actions might be required, depending on the situation; thus it is important for experimenters to know how to recognize and differentiate different types of artifacts. Most commonly, a participant may show muscle tension or blink particularly frequently. In these cases, verbal feedback to the participant is usually very effective. As well, impedance may go up at some electrodes over time, resulting in increased line noise and drift in those channels. This can be corrected by taking steps to lower impedance at those electrodes. If a participant gets bored or sleepy during the experiment, an increase in alpha band activity is often seen. When this is observed, it is a good idea to pause the experiment, give the participant a break, and possibly offer a stimulating snack and/or beverage. For all of these reasons, it is a good idea to programme breaks into the experiment, perhaps every 10–15 minutes. This both gives participants regular intervals to reduce fatigue, and provides the opportunity to check impedances or give feedback to the participant.

SUMMARY

EEG is the oldest non-invasive neuroimaging technique, first developed in the 1930s. It measures the summed electrical activity of many brain regions, due to the fact that electricity is conducted well through the head. Thus EEG data provides poor information as to the location in the brain of activity. However, EEG has exquisite temporal resolution, making it an excellent choice for studies interested in the timing of neurocognitive activity. The primary source of electrical activity measured by EEG is postsynaptic potentials, and not action potentials. Although electricity is volume-conducted through the head, not all electrical activity manifests as measurable EEG signals. This is because activity can only be recorded at the scalp when large numbers of neurons are oriented parallel to each other, and have synchronized postsynaptic potentials.

Much research focuses on ERPs, which are EEG signals time-locked to particular events of interest (such as the onset of stimuli), and typically averaged over many trials. Averaging is important because EEG has an inherently low signal-to-noise ratio (SNR), but SNR improves non-linearly with the number of trials averaged together. ERP components are features (peaks or troughs) of a waveform that have characteristic polarity, timing, scalp topography, and eliciting conditions. Certain components have been associated with particular cognitive operations through many repeated experiments, and so the presence and/or size of these components is often the focus of studies investigating a particular cognitive process.

EEG is normally recorded by placing electrodes on the scalp (usually with a conductive electrolyte gel or solution to improve the quality of the contact), and connecting these electrodes to a differential amplifier. The amplifier serves to both boost the signal, and cancel out environmental noise. Noise is cancelled by the fact that the electrical potential measured at each 'active' electrode on the head is actually the difference in electrical potential between that electrode and a reference electrode placed elsewhere on the body, and in fact the potential at each of these electrodes is measured relative to a third, ground electrode. Differential amplifiers rely on common-mode rejection, which eliminates any signal that is identical at both electrodes. Since electromagnetic noise from the environment should be largely similar at different parts of the head, this is effective in removing much environmental noise, such as from electrical lights and other equipment. However, other types of noise are still present in most EEG data, including that generated by muscles, blinks, skin conduction, head movements, and heartbeats. Recording clean EEG data requires careful attention to detail; perhaps more than most other cognitive neuroscience techniques.

THINGS YOU SHOULD KNOW

- EEG stands for electroencephalography, and it measures electrical activity generated in the brain via electrodes placed on the scalp.

- EEG is generated primarily by postsynaptic potentials, which are modulations of neural cell membranes by incoming signals from other cells. To be recorded at the scalp, large numbers (thousands or even millions) of neurons must be arranged parallel to each other in an 'open field' configuration, and have postsynaptic potentials that oscillate synchronously with each other.
- Event-related potentials, or ERPs, are EEG signals time-locked to particular events of interest (such as the onset of stimuli), and averaged across many trials to improve the signal-to-noise ratio (SNR).
- While EEG is often viewed in the time domain – plotting electrical potential as a function of time – it can also be fruitfully examined in the frequency domain. This involves applying a Fourier transform, collapsing over a period of time (ranging from milliseconds to many minutes) to identify the amplitude of the signal (power) in different frequency bands. Frequency bands are defined by the number of cycles (peaks and troughs) per second, in units of Hertz (Hz). Human EEG is categorized into at least five frequency bands: delta, theta, alpha (or mu), beta, and gamma.
- In the time domain, ERP components are characteristic features of a waveform that have consistent polarity, timing, scalp distribution, and eliciting conditions across individuals and experiments. Components are typically associated with particular cognitive processes, and so they are often the focus of study in ERP experiments. Because of volume conduction, a component defined in this way may be generated by multiple brain areas operating over the same time period, or even different brain areas active at slightly different, but overlapping, times.
- Recording EEG requires electrodes placed on the scalp, connected to an amplifier that boosts the signal and removes some environmental noise. Data from the amplifier are typically streamed to a computer for digital storage and analysis.
- EEG relies on differential amplifiers, which subtract electrical noise that is common to pairs of electrodes. Specifically, recording EEG requires a minimum of three electrodes: active, reference, and ground. Data are observed at each active electrode, and reflect the subtraction [A–G] – [R–G].
- Recording clear EEG data requires careful attention to detail in the preparation of the participant, how the electrodes are connected, and instructions and feedback provided to the participant before and during the experiment. In applying electrodes, a key factor is reducing the impedance between electrode and scalp as much as possible. This is done through cleaning the skin under each electrode, rubbing to move hair and remove dead skin cells, and to ensure good contact between the electrolyte gel/solution and the scalp (or direct electrode–scalp connection in the case of dry electrodes). For the cleanest data, it is also good practice to encourage the participant to keep their muscles relaxed, and minimize blinking and body movement during the study.

FURTHER READINGS

Cohen, M.X. (2017). Where does EEG Come From and What Does It Mean? *Trends in Neurosciences*, *40*(4), 208–218.

Luck, S.J. (2014). *An Introduction to the Event-Related Potential Technique* (2nd ed.). Cambridge, MA: MIT Press.

Luck, S.J., & Kappenman, E.S. (Eds.) (2011). *The Oxford Handbook of Event-Related Potential Components*. Oxford: Oxford University Press.

Picton, T.W., Bentin, S., Berg, P., Donchin, E., Hillyard, S.A., Johnson, R. Jr., Miller, G.A., Ritter, W., Ruchkin, D.S., Rugg, M.D., and Taylor, M.J. (2000). Guidelines for using human event-related potentials to study cognition: Recording standards and publication criteria. *Psychophysiology*, *37*(2), 127–152.

4 Electroencephalography (EEG) and Event-Related Potentials (ERP) 2

LEARNING OBJECTIVES

After reading this chapter, you should be able to:

- Explain why it is best to control psychological/task conditions in an ERP experiment, while holding physical stimuli constant.
- Describe the important considerations in stimulus timing for ERP experiments.
- Describe common sources of noise in EEG recordings, and how to minimize them.
- List the common steps involved in preprocessing EEG/ERP data.
- Describe the different types of filtering commonly applied to EEG data, and how to determine appropriate cut-offs.
- Recognize different types of artifacts in EEG recordings, and explain how best to deal with them in preprocessing.
- Identify the common dependent measures used in, and common approaches to, statistical analysis of ERP data.
- Explain the differences between event-related synchronization and desynchronization.
- Explain the difference between forward solution and inverse problem, and the challenges posed by source localization of EEG/ERP data.

EXPERIMENTAL DESIGN

Stimulus Features

One of the most important considerations in ERP research is matching the stimuli between conditions. Although stimulus control should be considered important in any experimental design, including for behavioural studies, the effects of stimulus differences in EEG data may be magnified. This is because some ERP components – particularly early components most strongly related to sensory processing – are exquisitely sensitive to low-level stimulus features such as size, brightness, and contrast. Thus if there is a systematic difference in any of these properties between the stimuli used in different experimental conditions, it will be impossible to know if an observed ERP difference between conditions is due to the experimental manipulation or a stimulus confound (this of course assumes that the experiment is not aimed at investigating the effects of varying some low-level stimulus property).

There are a number of different ways to address this issue. Perhaps the most ideal approach is to apply the 'Hillyard Principle', mentioned in Chapter 2: 'To avoid sensory confounds, you must compare ERPs elicited by exactly the same physical stimuli, varying only the psychological conditions' (Luck, 2014: 134).

Hillyard is known for his pioneering ERP research on attention (Hillyard & Anllo-Vento, 1998; Hillyard, Hink, Schwent, & Picton, 1973; Mangun, 2013). In a classic application of this principle, an experiment would compare ERPs evoked by, for example, a white square presented on the left side of a computer screen for 100 ms between conditions in which the subject was either cued to pay attention to that side of the screen, or cued to attend to the right side of the screen. Thus the stimulus was exactly the same in the two conditions, and all that varied was where the subject's attention was directed. Often in such experiments attention is directed to one side of space by requiring subjects to respond to stimuli presented there – however, this would create a 'psychological' confound if some stimuli (on the attended side) were to be responded to, whereas other stimuli (on the unattended side) were not. The solution to this is to have two types of stimuli: 'target' stimuli that the subject is instructed to respond to when seen on the attended side (in this example, perhaps red squares), and 'standard' stimuli that the subject is instructed not to respond to (the white squares). To compare the effects of identical stimuli on the attended and unattended sides, only the ERPs in response to the white squares (standards) would be analysed. It would be important to balance all experimental factors, so both target and standard stimuli should be equally likely to appear on either side of the screen, with equal numbers of stimuli presented on each side. Because the targets are used to provide subjects with a task, but ERPs to these stimuli are not of experimental interest, they could be less frequent that standard stimuli (perhaps only 10–20% of the total stimuli). This would ensure that most of the trials were used for ERP analysis.

Obviously, the Hillyard Principle cannot always be applied in an experiment. For example, if we wish to compare ERPs evoked by upright and upside-down (inverted) images of faces, the stimuli are necessarily different. However, in this case it would be advisable to ensure that each face image is presented in each condition (that is, each face presented both upright and inverted), and that nothing besides the orientation of each image was varied. This would restrict stimulus differences to the one of experimental interest. In such a case, it would also be advisable to keep the 'psychological conditions' matched – if participants were instructed to make a button-press response to one type of stimulus (say, inverted faces) but not to the other, then the to-be-responded-to stimuli might be expected to elicit greater attention/arousal as well as ERPs associated with preparing a motor response – so it would be better to have participants press one button for upright faces, and a different button for the inverted ones.

Timing

Because of the high temporal resolution of EEG, stimulus timing is a significant consideration. This manifests in a number of different ways. First of all, it is important to ensure that there is a high degree of synchrony between when the stimulus computer initiates the presentation of a stimulus, when that stimulus actually is presented to the participant, and when the EEG system receives the marker code (or trigger) from the stimulus computer indicating the onset of that stimulus. The first of these, synchrony between when the computer initiates the stimulus and when the stimulus hardware actually presents the stimulus, may seem trivial, but it is not. A number of factors come into play here, primarily related to the mechanics by which stimulation devices like video monitors and speakers produce stimuli. Video monitors do not have instantaneous responses; rather, they re-draw every pixel on the screen at a regular interval known as the **refresh rate**, which is typically the same as the electrical line frequency (50 or 60 Hz depending on the country). A 60 Hz refresh rate means that the shortest duration a visual stimulus can appear on a screen is 16.67 ms (1000 ms/60 Hz), and it also means that if the request to draw/update an image comes from the computer at a time other than exactly at the start of a refresh cycle, there will be a delay between the time the computer 'thinks' that the stimulus appeared, and when it actually did – of up to 16.67 ms. If the stimulus computer blindly sends a trigger code to the EEG computer at the same time that it sends the message to draw a visual stimulus on the monitor, without considering the monitor's refresh rate, the code could misrepresent the actual onset of the visual stimulus to the subject by the duration of the refresh cycle. Given that some timing differences in EEG are in the order of 20 ms (for example, the peak of the N170 component between upright and inverted faces), this degree of timing uncertainty could distort or even eliminate our ability to detect an experimental effect.

There are two primary ways to address this issue for visual stimuli. One is to use a monitor with a higher refresh rate. For example, current monitors targeted towards the video gaming market have refresh rates of above 120 Hz, bringing the refresh cycle down to 8 ms or below. Regardless of the hardware, it is advisable to use specialized software that synchronizes stimulus presentation with the refresh rate of the monitor. In this case, the software will ensure that the code to initiate stimulus display is synchronized with the start of a drawing cycle on the monitor, and the code sent to the EEG computer can be timed with this as well. Numerous commercial stimulus presentation packages, as well as open-source libraries for programming languages such as Python, have this capability. Regardless of the approach used, it is critical that the experimenter test the timing of the visual stimuli relative to the EEG trigger codes. This can be accomplished using a photodiode (which detects light flashes) that sends a trigger directly to the EEG amplifier; the timing of the codes sent by the photodiode can be compared with the timing of codes sent by the stimulus program and the mean and standard deviation of the asynchronies computed.

Auditory stimuli present similar issues, although the sources of timing delays can be more variable depending on the hardware – speakers and headphones do not have refresh rates but may nevertheless have characteristic delays. These delays can be measured in a similar fashion to that described above for visual stimuli – a hardware device can be built or purchased that sends a trigger code to the EEG system whenever a sound exceeding a particular threshold is detected by a microphone. Given the constraints of a particular hardware set-up, the timing inaccuracy of auditory stimuli should be at a minimum for simple stimuli such as simple sine wave tones. However, complex auditory stimuli such as speech may induce additional variability. Careful editing of such stimuli is essential to ensure that there is no silent gap at the beginning of each sound file. Another consideration is that, for example for speech stimuli, different words may be identifiable at different times after their onset, depending on the particular phonemes and their uniqueness. Such factors can be difficult to control and may lead to variance in the timing of the ERP components across trials.

Another timing-related consideration is the duration of the stimuli, and the **inter-stimulus intervals (ISIs)**. Sensory systems typically produce characteristic ERP responses not only to the onset of a stimulus, but to its offset as well. These offset-related ERPs are typically lower amplitude than the onset effects, but are not negligible. Thus one might wish to ensure that the duration of the stimuli is sufficiently long to separate the onset- from offset-related components. Another approach would be to use variable-duration stimuli so that the offset-related components would be expected to cancel out when trials are averaged together. The inter-stimulus interval, or more specifically the **stimulus onset asynchrony (SOA)**, between stimuli is also an important consideration. If stimuli are presented too closely together in time, the ERP components elicited by each stimulus may overlap and thus be difficult to separate (mathematically deconvolve) from each other. Thus expectations concerning the amount of time after stimulus onset that ERP effects will be detectable should be factored into timing considerations. Beyond overlap of ERP components, another consideration is refractoriness – the fact that after an initial stimulus, the amplitude of ERPs evoked by subsequent, similar stimuli will be somewhat attenuated. The extent of refractoriness varies depending on the type and intensity of stimuli (being maximal for simple, highly repetitive stimuli), but at its extreme one could fail to see any distinctive response to individual stimuli if they are presented too closely together in time. On the other hand, full recovery from refractoriness typically takes several seconds, which could result in a long, boring experiment for participants. Thus it may not be reasonable to design stimulus timing around full recovery from refractoriness, but nevertheless this is a consideration that should not be overlooked.

Stimulus Presentation and Response Collection Hardware

As we have discussed, electromagnetic noise can be a serious concern in EEG data. Noise is generated, among other things, by equipment typically used for stimulus presentation, including computer monitors and headphones. It is thus ideal to keep all stimulation equipment as far away from the subject as possible, since electromagnetic noise drops off with the square of the distance from the source. Most acoustic headphones are problematic for EEG because they use electricity to generate the sounds they produce, which will induce significant artifacts in the EEG since the headphones are right near the recording electrodes. Generally, using 'free field' sound presentation (speakers placed farther from the subject) is preferred if it is feasible for the experiment. However, in some cases the experimenter may wish to separately control the stimulation presented to each ear, which is only possible with headphones. In this case, there are special headphones available for audiological research that place the sound- (and noise-) generating hardware farther from the subject's head, and deliver the sound to the ears via tubes that fit into foam earplugs.

Hardware used for collecting behavioural responses, such as a keyboard or button box, also runs the risk of transmitting electromagnetic noise to the subject. This is largely dependent on the hardware design and so testing is essential to ensure that this doesn't happen. More generally, the experimenter should pay careful attention to how wires are run in the EEG recording room, keeping them as far away from the subject as possible. Sometimes simple actions like moving a power cord can drastically reduce noise in the EEG recordings.

Participant Movement

Head movement can be a serious concern in EEG recording. Movement of the electrodes relative to the scalp can induce artifacts in the data, as can movement of the wires connected to the electrodes. Thus the ideal experimental design does not require the participant to move, and involves instructing the participant to stay as still as possible. Small movements such as those required to make a button press response are not a concern, but larger movements may be. Different EEG systems vary in their sensitivity to these effects, and wireless systems have been developed that are specifically designed for experiments requiring the participant to move. Nevertheless, careful thought and extensive pilot testing are required if one wishes to record clean EEG from moving people.

One type of movement that is particularly difficult to deal with is speaking. Because speech involves the activity of so many muscles in and around the face, it will induce very significant motor artifacts in the EEG data. One approach to this in studies interested in speech production is to only analyse EEG data collected immediately prior to speech production. This can be effective in revealing brain activity associated with preparing a spoken response, but it is obviously rather limiting if the experimenter is interested in the brain activity that goes on during speech. Another approach is to attempt to remove the speech-related artifacts from the data, using principles similar to those described above for removing ocular artifacts. Just as EOG electrodes are used to record ocular artifacts, EMG electrodes can be placed on the face and neck to capture speech production-related artifacts. Specialized signal-processing techniques (discussed later in this chapter) can then be used to attempt to isolate the artifacts from EEG data, and remove them. It is important to emphasize, however, that these post-hoc data clean-up methods may be imperfect at best, and require significant investment of time to develop and validate. Thus it is always preferable to avoid artifacts wherever possible than to attempt to remove them after the fact.

Designing for Simplicity

Compared to research using exclusively behavioural measures, EEG and other cognitive neuroscience methods require significantly more time spent on data acquisition, processing, and analysis. Thus there is a common temptation to try to squeeze several experimental manipulations into one study, in an effort to get the most 'bang for the buck' in terms of the amount of data collected per subject. However, in the end this can often work against the experimenter. One thing to consider in designing an experiment is the complexity of the model that will be required for data analysis. Analysis of variance (ANOVA) and related variants of the general linear model are a very common way to approach data analysis. Because EEG data have both spatial and temporal dimensions, the complexity of the ANOVA model applied to EEG/ERP data is often more complex than for a comparable behavioural study. The effect of an experimental manipulation will likely differ at different electrode locations, since ERP components have a spatial distribution over the scalp. For this reason, it is common to include one or more factors in the ANOVA related to electrode position. This may be as simple as electrode identify, or a two-dimensional approach such as coding the location of each electrode along the left–right and anterior–posterior dimensions. It is common to simplify the levels of these dimensions by grouping electrodes into regions of interest (ROIs); for example, creating levels such as left–midline–right and perhaps three to five levels along the anterior–posterior dimension. Nevertheless, such an approach will mean that in addition to the experimental factors of interest in the ANOVA, there will be additional factors related to electrode position.

Thus in the simplest possible experimental design – looking for a difference between two experimental conditions – the ANOVA model might have three factors: the experimental factor along with left–right and anterior–posterior factors. In this case a significant experimental effect that modulated an ERP component with a particular scalp distribution would involve a three-way interaction between these factors, since the difference between experimental conditions would be larger at some combination of the left–right and anterior–posterior dimensions than at other combinations. If we expand on our hypothetical design, imagine that we wanted to examine the effects of various features of a word on N400 amplitude. We could select word frequency (how often the word appears in normal usage – coded as high/low), imageability (how easy it is to visualize the concept associated with the word – also coded as high/low), and length (number of letters – coded as long/short). In this case, our ANOVA model would contain five factors and a significant five-way interaction might be obtained if all three dimensions of the words affect N400 amplitude. The presence of such an interaction would necessitate a very large number of post-hoc tests in order to interpret – so many, in fact, that the interaction might be very hard to interpret at all! This is especially true because increasing the number of post-hoc tests also increases the probability of Type I error (finding false positives), and so multiple comparison correction should be applied to the post hoc tests, which may result in an overly conservative analysis. This is not to say that such designs should always be avoided, but merely to suggest that (as with any experimental design) the experimenter think through the planned approach to data analysis, and what pattern(s) of results will be required to support the experimental hypotheses, prior to executing the study. A series of simpler studies might ultimately be easier to interpret than running one complex study whose results are not interpretable.

Another dimension of complexity in ERP data analysis is time. Different components and experimental effects might occur at different points in time, and sometimes a manipulation may have effects over more than one temporal epoch. For example, sentences containing syntactic violations such as *Yesterday I wanted the eat to banana* typically elicit an enhanced negative potential from 300–500 ms (labelled the LAN) followed by an enhanced positive potential (called the P600) from approximately 600–800 ms. Thus separate analyses will be performed on mean amplitudes over the two different time windows where these effects are predicted.

Another suggestion is to design ERP experiments around specific components. This has several benefits. For one, if the experimental hypothesis centres around a single component, then only one time window may need to be analysed. Conversely, if one does not have a prediction a priori as to when the experimental effects will occur, one may have to conduct analyses over a number of time windows, which again would necessitate multiple comparison correction. Another significant benefit of designing a study around a particular component is that one can draw on the body of prior research concerning that component. This makes it much easier to interpret the results of the study in terms of the neurocognitive processes associated with that component.

DATA ANALYSIS

Preprocessing

Signal processing refers to any operations performed to modify the data prior to visualization or statistical analysis. The goal of signal processing is to optimize, as much as possible, our sensitivity to the experiment-related brain activity and our ability to detect an effect of an experimental manipulation, if it is present. It is important to understand that modifying the data in the ways we will describe is not 'cooking' the data or otherwise trying to make effects appear that are not truly present. On the contrary, our goal is to remove noise and thus increase the SNR of our data as much as possible. As we have already discussed, there are many sources of noise that can contaminate EEG data. While it is critical to minimize the presence of noise in the data as much as possible at the time of recording, it is impossible to record data using EEG (or for that matter, any other neuroimaging technique) that contain only brain activity – noise is inevitable. However, noise is ultimately variability in the experimental measurements, and our ability to detect statistically significant experimental effects, should they exist, is reduced when variability increases. Thus signal processing comprises a variety of techniques that help to reduce noise and increase our sensitivity to experimental effects.

Filtering

Filtering is a set of techniques that reduce certain frequencies in the data, with the primary goal of making it easier to detect signals in the range of frequencies not filtered. As mentioned earlier, **frequency** refers to how many times something happens in a given time interval. We learned earlier that the term 'frequency' is used to refer to how many times per second the EEG was sampled at each electrode. When describing the data itself, we commonly use frequency to describe the number of cycles (peaks and troughs) that occur in a unit of time. Recall that it is mathematically possible to break any waveform down into a set of different sine waves of differing frequencies, using a Fourier transform; this set of simpler waveforms is called a Fourier series. Mathematically, there are many implementations of filters, such as finite impulse response (FIR), infinite impulse response (IIR), Butterworth, Bessel, and others. Each have advantages and disadvantages in different applications, but the details of these are beyond the scope of this book. What is important to understand, however, is that filters can be described in general terms by how they affect the data. A **low-pass filter** attenuates high frequencies (allowing low frequencies to 'pass through' the filter), while a **high-pass filter** attenuates low frequencies. These filters are typically described by their cut-off frequency; for example a 0.1 Hz high-pass filter attenuates frequencies below 0.1 Hz. A **band-pass filter** is a combination of low- and high-pass filters (passing through a frequency band between the high-pass and low-pass frequency cut-offs). It is common to apply band-pass filtering to EEG data to reduce low-frequency noise (such as drift from skin potentials) and high-frequency noise (such as EMG artifact). A **notch filter** does the opposite of a band-pass filter, reducing frequencies in a particular band between its high- and low-frequency cut-offs. The most common application of a notch filter in EEG is to reduce line noise, by applying a notch filter at the frequency of the electrical mains (50 or 60 Hz, depending on the country).

The **filter responses** of each of these types of filters is shown in Figure 4.1. Filter response plots show the effects of applying a filter, in the frequency domain. One important thing to note in these plots is that the filters do not reduce all frequencies below the cut-off to zero. Rather, there is a **transition band** (shaded in grey in Figure 4.1) over which the power is gradually attenuated before dropping to its maximally reduced value. This transition band is often called the **roll-off** of the filter, and is a necessary feature. If the transition band is too narrow (that is, the roll-off is too steep), the filter can introduce artifacts in the data, which manifest as 'ripples' in the time domain. In other words, filtering with too narrow a transition band will reduce some frequencies in the data, but introduce artifacts at other frequencies. The width and shape of the filter roll-off is dependent on the type of filter applied, and the cut-off; in general, narrower bands are required at lower frequencies, as seen in the band-pass panel of Figure 4.1. It is thus necessary to understand the nature of the filters one is applying when working with EEG data. In general, mature EEG data analysis software packages provide filters that have been well tested, but it is important to read and understand the documentation to ensure this step is done correctly.

Figure 4.2 shows time- and frequency-domain representations of some example EEG data, before and after different types of filtering. The left panels show the power spectra (another term for frequency-domain plots) of the data and the right

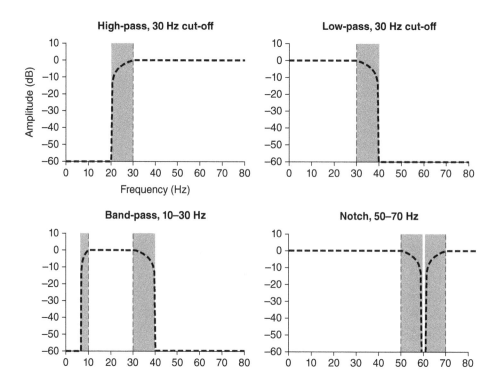

Figure 4.1 Responses, in the frequency domain, of different categories of filters. The grey shaded areas represent the transition band (or roll-off), over which the signal is partially attenuated

panels show a 15 s segment of the EEG data (in the time domain) from six channels. Starting with the top panels, in the raw data power spectrum we see a pattern that is quite typical of EEG data: the power drops off exponentially with increasing frequency (the 1/f effect mentioned in the previous chapter); there is a peak just below 10 Hz (corresponding to the person's alpha frequency); and there is a very large spike at 60 Hz (corresponding to electrical line noise). In the time domain, the segment of data shown demonstrates all of these features: the low-frequency power is manifest as slow drift in all channels, but especially in F3 and C3 in the earlier portion of the segment; alpha is notable especially around 5–6 s in channels C4 and P4 (and also in these and other channels at other times); 60 Hz noise is present as high-frequency fluctuations throughout the segment; and finally there is a large burst of high-amplitude, high-frequency noise between 12–14 s (which probably was caused by head movement and/or muscle contraction).

Moving down in Figure 4.2, we can see first the effects of applying a 30 Hz low-pass filter. The cut-off frequency is indicated by a dashed line in the power spectrum, and we can see that the power (amplitude) of the EEG drops off dramatically above this frequency. In the time domain, we can see that this filter markedly reduces the high-frequency noise, including both the 60 Hz noise throughout and the high-amplitude

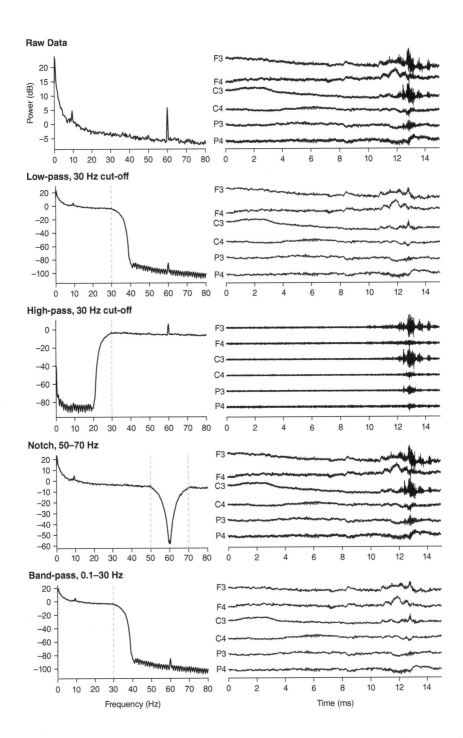

Figure 4.2 The same EEG data is shown in its raw form (which was collected with a 150 Hz low-pass filter and no high-pass filtering) and after various filters are applied. Left panels show the frequency-domain representations (power spectra) of the entire dataset (approximately 45 min of data), while the right panels show a 15 s segment of the data in the time domain. Note that the y-axis scale for the power spectra is adjusted in each case to capture the actual range of power in the data

noise from 12–14 s. However, we can see that this 12–14 s noise burst also included a lower-frequency component which was not removed by the filter. A couple of other things are notable about the power spectrum for the filtered data. First of all, the roll-off of the filter can be clearly seen with a transition band of approximately 10 Hz. Secondly, the 60 Hz peak is still visible; however, it is of no concern because of the overall attenuation of frequencies below 40 Hz. Conversely, we can see that the frequencies above 30 Hz are well preserved, including the alpha peak. The alpha peak looks much smaller than in the raw data, but this is because the scale of the y axis of the frequency plot has been dramatically increased to account for the effects of filtering the higher frequencies. Finally, there are 'ripples' at frequencies > 40 Hz. These are a side effect of the filter (in particular the with of the transition band), but are of no consequence because all of the frequencies are well attenuated by the filter.

The next filter that was applied is a high-pass filter with the same 30 Hz cut-off that we applied for the low-pass filter. A 30 Hz high-pass filter is not something that would normally be applied to EEG data, but for illustrative purposes here it provides a nice contrast to the 30 Hz low-pass filter. In the frequency domain, we see essentially a mirror image of the panel above: the width of the transition band is similar, and although the 1/f decline in power at lower frequencies is still visible, even the lowest frequencies are well attenuated. The result in the time domain is very flat EEG at each channel, because the low-frequency drift has been completely removed, as has the alpha that was visible in the raw and low-pass filtered data. However, the higher-frequency noise, including 60 Hz, is still very much present in the data. Below this we see the effects of applying a 50–70 Hz notch filter, which is a way of reducing electrical line noise while otherwise preserving high frequencies. The plots show that this behaves as expected, with maximal attenuation of 60 Hz and roll-off on either side between 50–60 and 60–70 Hz. The time-domain representation looks very much like the raw data, since the notch filter is selective for 60 Hz noise and thus does not have much effect on the other high-frequency noise in the data.

Finally, the bottom panel of Figure 4.2 shows the effects of a 0.1–30 Hz band-pass filter. This is a very typical setting for ERP studies. Because the low-frequency cut-off is 0.1 Hz, it is basically impossible to see the effects of the filter at the low end of the band in the power spectrum. However, even though the power spectra for the 30 Hz low-pass and this band-pass filter look very similar, the effects of the low-frequency cut-off are quite apparent in the time domain: the band-pass filtered data shows reduced low-frequency drift, for example for electrode F3.

It is common to band-pass filter data to be used in ERP analysis using high-pass cut-offs of 0.01–0.3 Hz, and low-pass cut-offs of 30–40 Hz. As noted above, it is important to be aware of the roll-offs of the filters one is using, and also to examine the data before and after filtering to determine whether any untoward effects occurred during filtering. Figure 4.3 shows data from a study by Tanner, Morgan-Short, and Luck (2015) which investigated filter artifacts on ERP data from a real sentence processing experiment. As the high-pass filter cut-off starts to encroach on the range of frequencies of interest in the EEG data, experimental effects of interest are attenuated, while at the same time complex interactions of inappropriate filter settings with the data create artifactual differences between the two experimental conditions.

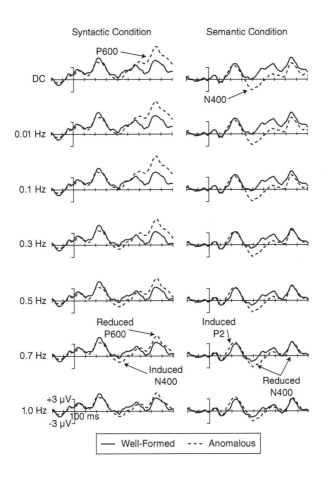

Figure 4.3 Artifacts that can be induced in ERPs by high-pass filters. Data are from a sentence processing experiment in which two types of anomalies were presented: violations of grammatical rules (Syntactic Condition) and of meaning expectancy (Semantic Condition). Well-formed control sentences were also included for each sentence type. The top row shows the data with no high-pass filtering applied (the term used for this in the EEG literature is DC for 'directly coupled'). The syntactic condition shows a component typical of this type of violation – an enhanced positivity for anomalous relative to control sentences, labelled the P600. Likewise, the semantic condition shows a typical effect for this type of violation – an enhanced negativity peaking around 400 ms called the N400. Little, if any, effect of filtering is seen on either of these effects with high-pass cut-offs of 0.01 or 0.1 Hz. However, starting at 0.3 Hz both components begin to show attenuation by filtering. Furthermore, induced differences between the conditions that are not present in the unfiltered data begin to emerge. Beginning with the 0.3 Hz cut-off and increasing from there, we see an induced N400 in the syntactic condition and an induced P2 in the semantic condition. The authors of this study showed that high-pass cut-offs of 0.01–0.1 Hz were optimal in terms of maximizing the statistical sensitivity to the actual effects while minimizing the risk of spuriously identifying filter artifacts as statistically significant experimental effects. Data reprinted from Tanner et al. (2015) with permission of John Wiley and Sons

Generally these sorts of filters are applied offline, meaning they are applied in software to the data after they are recorded. During recording, a wider range of frequencies is typically collected; however, some filtering is needed during acquisition. The reason to record the data with less filtering is to preserve as much information in the raw data as possible; information that is filtered out prior to recording can never be re-created; after recording, any offline filtering can be undone by going back to the raw data. Strictly speaking, high-pass filtering is not required, although it is common to use a 0.01 Hz high-pass filter to reduce the effects of low-frequency drift in the data (such as skin potentials caused by perspiration). Although this drift can be filtered out later, it can make monitoring of the EEG during recording more difficult. A low-pass filter, however, is *always* required when recording EEG. The reason for this is to eliminate the induction of a particular type of artifact, called aliasing, that is caused by the sampling rate. Recall that sampling rate is the rate at which the continuous data are sampled and recorded; typically rates between 100–1000 Hz are used. The sampling rate sets the upper limit of frequencies that can be recorded in the data – if we record at 100 Hz, clearly there is no way that we could detect a 200 Hz signal. However, without filtering out frequencies higher than our sampling rate, information at higher frequencies will still be recorded – but inaccurately due to the lower sampling rate. This inaccuracy takes the form of power at an artificially low frequency in the data. The reason for this is shown in Figure 4.4. Because we are not sampling quickly enough, we only capture parts of the signal, and the spacing of our sampled points is such that we 'catch' the signal at different points in its cycle at each sampling time. When we connect the dots of these time points, the result is a distorted version of the original signal.

To eliminate aliasing, we must apply a low-pass filter at a frequency below the sampling rate. The highest frequency we can accurately record for a given sampling rate is known as the Nyquist frequency, and is defined as half of the sampling rate. In actual practice the low-pass cut-off used should be at most one third of the sampling rate, or even lower. This is illustrated in Figure 4.4. The figure shows two examples of a 10 Hz signal, and what happens when the sampling rate is two and three times the frequency of the signal. In both cases, the sampled data (the dashed black lines) is sufficient to determine the presence of a 10 Hz signal. That is, if we count the peaks in this 1 s sample of data, we will find 10 peaks. However, compared to the true signal (the grey line), the amplitude of the sampled 10 Hz signal is not consistently as high, because our sparsely sampled points do not always capture the peak. This has two consequences. First of all, the power of the measured 10 Hz signal will be lower than the true signal. In an experiment where the power at 10 Hz was of interest, this would obviously be a problem, and even in an ERP experiment if there was a component of interest that was about 50 ms wide (which is the width of one peak of a 10 Hz signal), we would underestimate its true amplitude. The second consequence is that aliasing introduces low frequencies into the data that are not present in the true signal. In the top panel of Figure 4.4 this would be approximately a 1 Hz signal, because the peaks are underestimated in the first half of the 1 s time window, and the troughs are underestimated in the second half. In the bottom panel the aliased signal would be approximately 0.5 Hz. While the 1/3 rule generally

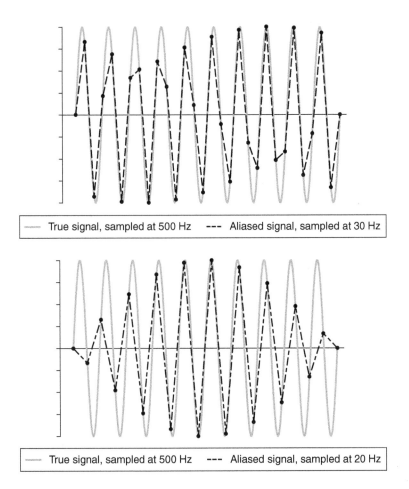

Figure 4.4 Examples of aliasing. The true signal is a 10 Hz sine wave. When sampled at a sufficiently high rate (in this case, 500 Hz), this signal is well represented, as shown by the solid grey lines. However, when the sampling rate is too low aliasing occurs. The effects of aliasing are shown for sampling rates of 30 (top) and 20 Hz (bottom)

works well, another approach to setting the low-pass filter is to base it on the highest frequency that one hopes to have in the recorded data, which may be well under 1/2 or even 1/3 of the sampling rate.

Artifact Detection, Removal, and Correction

Filtering can be effective in removing certain types of artifacts from EEG data – in particular, artifacts that are fairly consistent over time (or at least fluctuate systematically for part of the recording period) and occur in frequency ranges outside that of the brain activity we are interested in measuring (which, for a large majority of

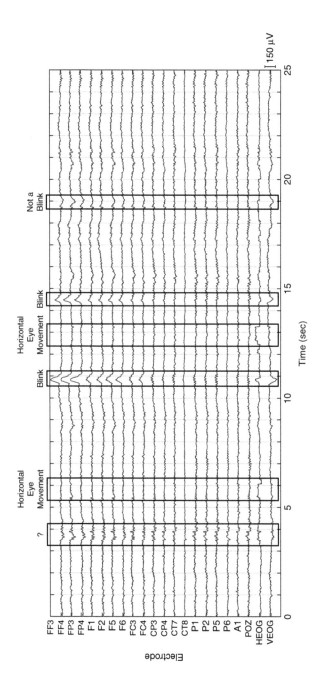

Figure 4.5 Examples of common artifacts found in EEG data. A 25 s segment of continuous EEG is shown for a number of channels (electrodes), with different types of artifacts marked and labelled. HEOG is the horizontal eye channel (a bipolar recording representing the difference in potential between the outer canthi of the left and right eyes), and VEOG is the vertical eye channel, recorded from an electrode placed under one eye and referenced to the average of the left and right mastoids (as all other electrodes were). The nature of the first segment of artifact (marked with a '?') is unclear – the fact that the waveforms are relatively high amplitude and quite consistent across many channels suggests that this is an artifact, but as is sometimes the case with EEG, visual inspection alone does not tell us what its origin is. The other artifacts are more readily identifiable by certain hallmarks. For instance, horizontal eye movements typically manifest as square wave-like deflections in the HEOG channel. Blinks show opposite-polarity deflections in above and below the eyes, so comparison of the VEOG channel with those above the eyes (the channels starting with 'F') helps identify these. Note that the last segment marked is labelled 'not a blink' because, although the shape of the EEG waves in this segment is roughly similar to that in the marked blinks, the polarity is the same in VEOG and the 'F' channels

cognitive neuroscience ERP studies, is in the range of approximately 1–25 Hz). However, not all artifacts in EEG data meet these criteria. Some of the most disruptive artifacts come from eye blinks and eye movements, which we collectively refer to as **ocular artifacts**. Examples of blinks and horizontal eye movements are shown in Figure 4.5 and could also be seen in Figure 4.2. Ocular artifacts are of relatively high amplitude compared to EEG, and can significantly obscure EEG data. It is important to note that these artifacts are not just detectable around the eyes – they propagate across the scalp to electrodes that are quite far away from the eyes. Other artifacts that may occur include those induced by sudden movements (such as sneezing), or by touching the electrodes. Because ocular artifacts tend to be the most prominent, we focus here on those.

There are several ways to deal with ocular artifacts. The first is to try to minimize their presence in the data through the design of the experiment and the procedures used during data collection. While blinking and eye movements normally occur unconsciously, they can to a large extent be controlled consciously, so simply informing participants that they should try to minimize their blinking and eye movements can be effective. The experimenter should always monitor the EEG during recording, and can provide feedback to participants who show excessive ocular activity in a further attempt to reduce it. As well, where possible the design of the experiment should allow for designated blink periods in between trials. This is often done by making studies self-paced, or inserting mandatory break periods at regular intervals in the experiment. This approach can be combined with cues that remind subjects not to blink during critical parts of the trials, such as a box which appears immediately prior to the onset of critical stimuli. An advanced and technically demanding approach is to use an eye tracker to monitor for ocular artifacts during the experiment. An automated algorithm running in real time on the eye-tracking data can identify blinks and eye movements and send signals to the EEG data recording computer to ignore the trials with ocular artifact, and also to inform the stimulus presentation computer to 'recycle' the trial and present it later. In this way, the experiment can be run with no ocular artifacts or loss of data. Another important recommendation concerning EEG recording is that a number of electrodes be placed around the eyes. These are commonly referred to as **electrooculogram (EOG)** electrodes because their primary purpose is to detect ocular artifacts and not brain activity. A typical arrangement involves electrodes placed above and below at least one eye and electrodes placed on the temples lateral to each eye (commonly called the outer canthi of each eye) to detect the horizontal component of eye movements.

In spite of the experimenter's best efforts, the data will inevitably contain some ocular artifacts. Historically, the way to deal with these during data processing was to remove these trials. They can either be identified manually, by the researcher scrolling through the EEG from each trial and identifying trials for removal that have obvious artifacts. This process can be automated by using algorithms designed to detect blinks, such as rejecting any trial where the change in amplitude over a short time period exceeds some criterion such as 75 or 100 µV (since typically no EEG effects of interest are nearly this large). This approach tends to be very reliable, although because the algorithms may not detect all artifacts, it is advisable for the experimenter to review the data manually after automated artifact rejection.

The downside of the trial rejection method for dealing with artifacts is that it reduces the number of trials that contribute to the average. Since signal-to-noise ratio improves with the square root of the number of trials, reducing the number of trials will tend to lower our signal-to-noise ratio, making detection of an experimental effect less likely. As well, people may vary in how much they blink or move their eyes, so this approach may result in different participants contributing differentially to the across-subject average, which is not an ideal situation. Some experimental designs may also inherently induce ocular responses, at least in some people – such as particularly bright visual stimuli or loud auditory stimuli. Thus an alternative approach to artifact rejection is **artifact correction**. In this approach, artifacts are identified and classified, and then removed in some way from the data while preserving the non-artifactual components of the data. One approach to this is using regression (Gratton, Coles, & Donchin, 1983). Ocular artifacts are identified in the EOG electrodes using an automated algorithm, and any signal that correlates with the artifacts is removed from each other electrode. While generally well accepted, this approach can in some cases overestimate or underestimate the size of the artifact and so is imperfect.

An alternative approach is using a signal processing technique known as **independent components analysis** (ICA; Makeig, Bell, & Jung, 1996). The ICA algorithm attempts to identify a number of different 'components' in the data that are statistically independent of each other. A given component can be more or less strongly present at a given electrode, or on a particular trial, and components that contain artifact can be removed from the data without affecting the other components. Since ocular artifacts come from independent sources from brain activity (that is, the eyes rather than the brain) and can be reasonably expected to have different time courses and magnitudes than brain activity, ICA readily identifies these and can be highly effective in removing them. ICA can also be effective in isolating and removing other artifacts, including muscle noise, alpha artifact, and noise that may arise from individual electrodes having a poor connection (Delorme, Sejnowski, & Makeig, 2007). However, caution should be exercised by the experimenter as an incomplete understanding of what the algorithm is doing, or what the components represent, could result in removing actual task-related brain activity. A related technique, **principal components analysis (PCA)**, can also be effective at removing ocular artifacts but has been shown to be less effective overall in removing other types of artifacts (Jung et al., 1998).

Re-Referencing

As noted earlier, the choice of reference electrode during recording is often determined by convenience, or by the EEG system manufacturer, and may not be ideal for interpretation of the results of a given experiment. Different reference locations may be standard in different research areas, and/or more or less suitable for detecting a particular effect depending on its scalp distribution. It is easy enough in most analysis software to re-reference the data. This is done simply by subtracting the data recorded at the new reference channel, time point by time point, from the data of every other channel. Because we are subtracting a constant value from every electrode, the overall scalp distribution – in terms of the differences in amplitude between electrodes across the scalp – will not change. However, the actual potential value at each electrode site can change considerably, so depending on the reference chosen a particular component could have large, small, or zero potential, and be positive or negative. An example of this is provided below, but first we will discuss the merits of different reference location choices.

Arguably the most 'neutral' approach is to use the average reference, by computing the average potential at all electrodes at each time point, and subtracting this from each individual electrode. The net potential of the head, considering all neural sources, is theoretically zero since every generator of an EEG effect can be considered a dipole with equally strong negative and positive poles. In practice, however, what is recorded is not the ideal. First of all, the strength of electrical potentials will attenuate somewhat with distance from the source, and especially due to intervening tissues – mainly the skull, whose thickness and thus impedance varies across the head. More importantly, we are unable to place electrodes at equally spaced locations all around the head, because if nothing else the neck gets in the way, and in reality most EEG electrode montages have most or all of their electrodes located over the top half of the head (although some systems feature many electrodes lower down in part to facilitate more accurate computation of an average reference). If all of the electrodes are over the top of the head, and a particular EEG effect is broadly distributed over the top of the head (as many are), then the average potential across the recording electrodes may in fact include the effect of interest. Thus subtracting this average from all electrodes may actually attenuate the experimental effect – the exact opposite of what we would want. For this reason, it is common to use a single location (such as the tip of the nose or the nasion), or a pair of comparable locations on either side of the head. It is advisable not to use a single location on one side of the head, because if there is an overall difference in the laterality of the EEG potential (and many EEG/ERP effects are lateralized), a lateralized reference may induce a bias in the re-referenced data.

Although mathematically, re-referencing is very simple, its effects on ERPs can be complex and are often the topic of intense discussion among experts. An example can demonstrate why this is. Figure 4.6 shows sample data from a group of twelve people who participated in a face processing experiment. On each trial, participants saw either an upright face, or an inverted one (rotated 180°). The data in Figure 4.6 are the grand average across all upright face trials and all participants, referenced in four different ways: to the average of all electrodes, the nasion, averaged mastoids, or the **vertex** (electrode Cz). These are all common reference sites to use in EEG studies, although the vertex is more commonly used during recording, with re-referencing occurring afterwards, since many ERP effects are large at the vertex. The nasion is probably the most common reference site for face processing studies, although the average reference is also common (the data in this example were obtained using a 128-channel recording system with quite comprehensive coverage of the scalp, including more ventral areas, so an average reference was a reasonable choice). The average of the two mastoids (electrodes TP9 and TP10) are also common reference in many ERP studies, although less so in studies of face processing because one of the main effects of interest tends to be largest at or near these electrodes. This effect is known as the N170 (so-named due to its polarity and timing), and is typically associated with a positive peak at the vertex.

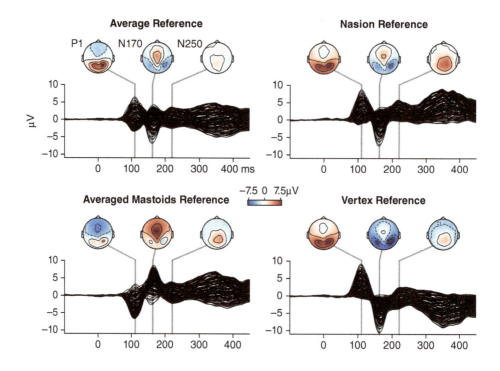

Figure 4.6 Scalp topography of the ERP effects elicited by upright faces, from the grand average of 12 participants obtained using a 128-channel EEG system. Each of the four panels shows the data referenced to a different location. In each panel, the top figure shows the scalp topography at three time points when the ERP components are largest, corresponding to the P1, N70, and N250 components typically reported for face stimuli in the literature. The bottom of each panel shows a 'butterfly' plot in which tracings of each electrode are overlaid. Data are replotted from Matheson and Newman (2008)

Figure 4.6 shows the data as 'butterfly' plots, showing the waveforms at all 128 electrodes overlaid on one axis to emphasize where the potentials deviate the most from baseline. As well, scalp topography maps are shown for three time points, selected as those where peak potentials occurred. These correspond to components typically obtained in face processing studies: the P1, N170, and N250. Examination of this figure shows that regardless of the reference, the largest potentials can be observed to occur at the same time points, and with generally the same scalp distributions. However, the amplitude of the components differs quite a bit. For example, with the averaged mastoids reference, the N170 is only negative right around the peak of this effect (the two dark areas in the corresponding scalp map), with a maximum negative voltage seen in the butterfly plot of approximately −2.5 μV. In contrast, using a vertex reference the negativity extends over much more of the scalp, and the maximum values are over −10 μV. Similar variability can be seen for the other components and references as well. Thus we can see that the choice of reference in this case seems to have little impact on our ability to detect where the experimental effects are largest across the scalp, although the magnitude of the potentials will certainly vary with reference location.

The situation gets more complicated, though, when we compared ERPs between different conditions. Recall that looking at ERPs to a single experimental condition is rarely very useful; what we should focus on are the differences between carefully controlled experimental conditions. In the case of our example, the stimuli in the two conditions differed only in their orientation. The typical finding is that the N170 to inverted faces is slightly delayed, and higher amplitude, than for upright faces, especially over the right hemisphere; as well the P1 and N250 are larger for inverted faces. Figure 4.7 shows the difference

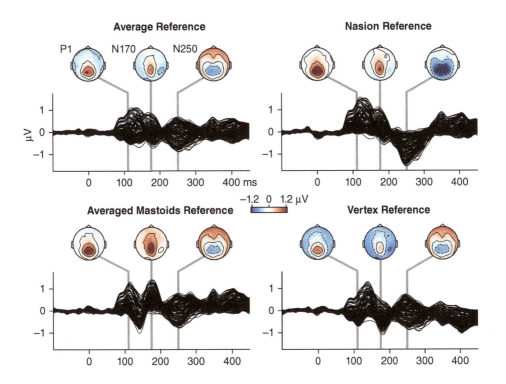

Figure 4.7 Data from the same experiment as in Figure 4.6, but showing the difference waves computed as inverted–upright faces

waveforms computed as inverted–upright, again with four different reference locations. Looking first at the N170, we see that indeed the scalp distributions show a greater negativity over ventral temporal-occipital scalp regions for inverted than upright faces, and that this effect is most pronounced over the right hemisphere – regardless of choice of reference. Critically, however, the magnitude of this experimental difference is very dependent on the choice of reference. This is shown even more clearly in Figure 4.8: at the right mastoid electrode – the typical peak of the inverted–upright N170 difference – the amplitude of this experimental difference varies by roughly a factor of ten, from –0.1 (for the averaged mastoids reference) to more than 1 µV (for the vertex reference)! Similarly, the right panel of Figure 4.8 shows the difference waves at the vertex electrode, where the difference is zero for the vertex-referenced data (which is expected), and largest for the averaged mastoids-referenced data. Thus our ability to detect an experimental effect – at least at a given electrode – could differ depending on our choice of reference.

Epoching

Epoching, also known as segmentation, is the process of 'chopping' the EEG data into short segments around experimental events of interest – in other words, moving from (continuous) EEG data to ERP data. Typically, during data collection the computer presenting the stimuli sends 'codes' or markers to the EEG recording computer, indicating precisely the time and type of each event of interest. Epoching involves finding those codes and extracting the EEG for a short period before, and a somewhat longer period after, each code of interest. The data immediately prior to the event code is used as the baseline for the post-code potentials, so after segmentation the average potential of this time period is subtracted from each post-stimulus time point within the epoch. This serves to account for drift and other random factors and ensures that 'zero' potential for the data of experimental interest is consistent across electrodes and trials. The time periods used for epoching depend on the experimental design, and the ERP effects of interest. Commonly the baseline period ranges from 50–500 ms, and the post-stimulus period may range from 250–1000 ms or more depending on the expected timing of the experimental effects. An important consequence of this procedure is ensuring (in the experimental design) that the experimental conditions immediately prior to the events of interest are neutral (or as neutral as possible) and, most importantly, comparable across conditions. If the stimulation or expected cognitive processing can be expected to be different between conditions immediately prior to the time-locking event of interest, then the brain activity measured with EEG may differ between conditions prior to the event of interest. In this case, it would be impossible to know whether any observed differences between conditions after the event were in fact due to the event itself, or preceding differences.

Epoching may involve more complex criteria than simply finding particular event codes of interest. For example, one might wish to only select events to which the participant made a correct response, in which case an event code subsequent to the

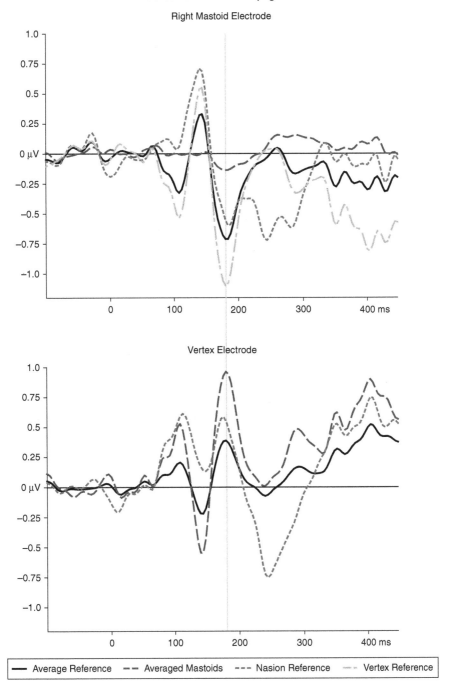

Figure 4.8 Difference waveforms from the same data shown in Figure 4.7, plotted for two specific electrodes. These correspond to two common reference locations, and are also where the largest experimental effects are typically reported in face-processing ERP experiments. Note that in the bottom panel, the waveform for the vertex-referenced data is a flat line overlapping the x-axis, because the data at the reference location are necessarily zero

target event would also have to be examined. Similarly, one might wish to separately categorize the ERPs to stimuli depending on what type of event preceded them. Thus the process of epoching is not simply segmenting EEG data into short segments, but also of 'binning' these segments into categories of experimental interest.

Subsequent to epoching, trials within each experimental category are typically averaged together for each participant. Averaging allows us to examine the ERP response for each category of stimulus and to visualize differences between conditions. The averages for each participant are then averaged together, across subjects, to create a **grand average**. While this is normally the point at which data are plotted for interpretation and display in manuscripts or other presentations, it is important for the experimenter to examine the averages of each participant's data prior to including it in the grand average. This allows for quality control, ensuring that nothing looks amiss in an individual's data that might signal a problem in the preprocessing steps; indeed it is good practice to visualize the data after each processing step to catch problems when they occur and ensure that the ultimate grand average is not contaminated by artifacts.

Extracting Measures for Statistical Analysis

A number of approaches are commonly used for statistical analysis of ERP data, and many others are currently being explored as alternative possibilities. Much of ERP research focuses on specific components – peaks or troughs in the data that have reliable polarity, timing, scalp distribution, and experimental eliciting conditions – and how these components vary as a function of some experimental manipulation. Thus statistical analysis depends on extracting some measurement of the size (amplitude) and/or timing (latency) of that component, for each subject in each condition. The various measures that are commonly used are illustrated in Figure 4.9. **Peak amplitude** is the electrical potential at the peak of a specific component. Typically the researcher has a prediction, based on previous research, as to when a particular component will peak. Since the timing of the peak of a particular component varies over some range across individuals (and indeed, across trials within an individual), the most intuitive way to identify a peak is to use an algorithm that picks the maximum positive or negative amplitude, at each electrode and for each participant, within the time window when the component is predicted to appear. For example, an N1 component might be defined as the most negative amplitude between 100 and 200 ms. A variant of this is **peak-to-peak amplitude**, which measures the difference between the amplitude of adjacent positive and negative peaks (such as the difference between P1 and N1 amplitude).

This approach is problematic, however, for several reasons. For one it is highly sensitive to noise. The largest (or smallest) value within any distribution of data is not representative of the average of some larger sample of the data. As well, peak amplitude will be strongly affected by the filtering (particularly low-pass filtering, because peaks are a high-frequency aspect of the data) and the algorithm may fail to properly identify the true component peak if an earlier or later component with larger amplitude occurs at the beginning or end of the time window. Thus an

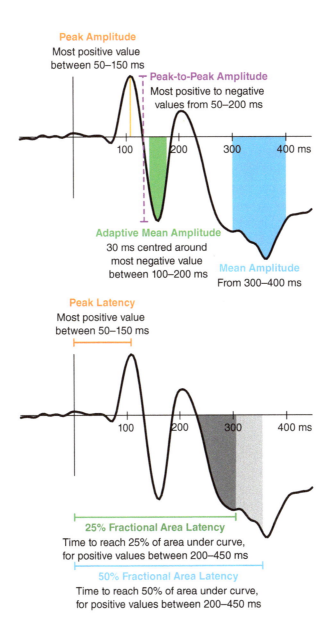

Figure 4.9 Common dependent measures that can be extracted from ERP waveforms for statistical analysis. Amplitude measures are shown in the top panel, while latency measures are shown in the bottom panel

alternative is to compute the **mean amplitude** within some time window. If the experimenter is interested in the size of a component with a fairly narrow peak, one approach is to identify the **adaptive mean amplitude** (or mean peak amplitude), by first finding the maximum value within the desired time window (the peak), and then computing the average of a few time points on either side of that value (for example, the average of five or seven time points centred on the peak amplitude). For other components, a clear peak may not be obvious (for example, the N400 commonly studied in language processing studies has more of a plateau shape). In these cases, the mean amplitude over a larger time window (for example, 100–200 ms) is commonly used.

One of the strengths of the EEG/ERP technique is its high temporal resolution. While simply analysing the amplitude of specific components that occur over particular, but relatively constrained time windows exploits this high temporal resolution, another approach is to use the actual timing of an effect as the dependent variable in an analysis. This is generally referred to as **latency**, and it can be measured in several different ways. Conceptually, one may be interested in when the *onset* of a particular ERP component or effect occurs, or in when it *peaks*. Identifying the timing of a component peak – its **peak latency** – is subject to the same concerns as measuring peak amplitude discussed in the previous paragraph, in terms of being sure to define an appropriate time window, ensuring that the 'peak' identified is not the tail of a different component occurring at the beginning or end of the time window, and the sensitivity to high-frequency noise. An alternative to quantifying the peak latency is using the **fractional area latency**. This involves defining a time range over which the area under the curve is computed (typically the time range over which the component of interest occurs), then identifying the time point at which a particular fraction of this total area is obtained. Thus one could define 50% of the total area as representing the mid-point of the component, as an alternative to trying to identify the peak amplitude. Fractional area latency can also be used to define the onset of a particular ERP component. Onsets can be tricky to define, because the ERP waveform is continuous over time and contains noise as well as preceding components. Thus operationally defining the onset as, for example, the point in time at which the area under the curve reaches 10% or 25% eliminates the need to identify the exact onset time, and is more robust to noise in the data.

A somewhat contentious issue in the ERP literature concerns how to choose the time windows for peak or mean amplitude measurements. From the perspective of objective, hypothesis-driven, reproducible research, it is best to choose the time window prior to running the experiment. This would normally be guided by a review of the prior literature of the ERP component(s) of interest, to identify the time window when the component normally occurs. However, this can be problematic because the timing of ERP components is sensitive to stimulus characteristics, the task involved, and even the overall experimental context (such as room lighting or background noise). As well, there may be sufficient variability in the published literature that one either has to pick a wide time window, or pick one of several windows. If the timing that is predicted a priori does not actually match the timing of the component that is observed once the data are collected and averaged, then the component (or more specifically, the difference in the waveforms between experimental conditions) may only partially overlap the time window chosen for analysis. As a result, the statistical analysis may not reveal a significant effect. An alternative approach often seen in ERP studies is that an approximate time window is chosen a priori, but adjusted once the data are collected, based on visual inspection of the data. While this has the advantage of titrating the analysis to the effects present in the data, it is scientifically questionable practice because it amounts to 'cherry picking' results once the data are collected, rather than testing an a priori hypothesis. In exploratory studies this may be acceptable, but this is different from hypothesis-driven research, and may result in findings that are not replicable. An ideal solution to this is to run a small pilot study using the intended paradigm, using this to characterize the timing of the experimental effects and generate hypotheses for a replication of the study using a larger number of participants. Alternatively, there are approaches that investigate multiple time windows, or include time as a factor in the analysis.

Mass Univariate Analysis

All of the advice provided here on experimental design should be taken as guidelines rather than hard-and-fast rules. Science is by its nature dynamic and it is important to use the right tools to answer a research question (assuming they are used correctly), rather than simply following rules. Indeed, many important scientific discoveries come from 'thinking differently'.

An approach that contradicts the advice provided in the text concerning simplicity and focusing on a single component, but does try to address issues discussed in the previous section around choosing the appropriate time window for analysis, is what has been termed **mass univariate analysis** (Groppe, Urbach, & Kutas, 2011). In this approach, differences between conditions are computed by way of t-tests at every time point and every electrode. Thus if one had a dataset with 64 electrodes and a 1000 ms post-stimulus epoch to analyse, one might compute 64,000 t-tests. In practice, EEG data is typically recorded at sampling rates of 250–500 Hz (that is, every 2–4 ms) and the data is not expected to change very much over a few milliseconds, so for mass univariate analysis the data are typically down-sampled to a lower rate such as 100 or even 50 Hz. As well, the developers of this approach suggest that the time range for analysis be restricted to the window in which the experimenter expects experimental effects to occur, which may not be before 100 ms post-stimulus presentation for example. Nevertheless, even with 50 Hz sampling this would result in 45 x 64 = 2,880 t-tests. This would clearly necessitate some form of multiple comparison correction, since at a typical significant threshold of $p < .05$ we would expect 5% of the 2,880 t-tests (144 of them) to be significant by chance. A number of approaches to multiple comparison correction can be used, which are described in the citation provided above.

The advantage of the mass univariate approach is that it is unbiased by the experimenter's expectations. In a typical analysis using a measure such as mean amplitude, the experimenter is expected to make a prediction concerning the timing and scalp distribution of the experimental effect before collecting the data. If this prediction is partially wrong, the time window and/or set of electrodes chosen for data analysis may only partially overlap with the actual experimental effect, which may make identifying an actual effect as statistically significant less likely. The mass univariate approach is 'data driven' and so can accurately capture the timing and scalp distribution of the effect in the data rather than trying to make it fit into a particular 'mould'.

There are benefits and costs to this approach. The developers suggest that it may be useful in exploratory data analysis, either when a researcher doesn't know where or when to expect experimental effects, or when the researcher has a prediction but is open to the possibility of other, unpredicted differences occurring and wishes to capture those. The developers nevertheless suggest that if a researcher has a strong a priori hypothesis concerning the component affected by the experimental manipulation (in terms of both timing and scalp distribution), then a component-driven analysis approach using mean amplitude or another measure may be more sensitive. In addition to greater sensitivity to a predicted effect, a component-centric data analysis approach may have greater validity because the results confirm an a priori hypothesis. Exploratory analyses normally generate hypotheses for future experiments.

Frequency Domain Analysis

As with the time domain, analysis in the frequency domain can be performed in several ways. One approach to frequency domain analysis is to filter the data to remove information at frequencies above and below the frequency band of interest (a type of bandpass filtering, described in the section on signal processing below). The filtered data thus represent the activity only in the frequency range of interest. Another approach involves applying a **Fourier transform** from the time to the frequency domain. Then, data can be plotted as a function of frequency (averaged over the time window of interest, which can be the entire epoch or smaller segments of the epoch) and one can look for peaks at particular frequencies (or differences between conditions at particular frequencies). A third approach is to use what are called **wavelets** – essentially short segments of a sine wave of a particular frequency – in a mathematical operation known as convolution which essentially 'slides' the wavelet across a segment of EEG data to find the point at which it fits best. This best fit should represent the point when the peaks in the EEG data best line up with the peak in the wavelet.

Another factor to consider in a frequency-domain analysis is time. In the simplest case, one can compute power within a frequency band, or across a range of frequencies, over an entire EEG recording, or over epochs time-locked to events of interest. Often these epochs may be longer than those used in time-domain ERP analyses, because accurately measuring power at low frequencies requires segments of data long enough to actually capture those frequencies. Another approach is a **time-frequency analysis**, which examines power at different frequencies as a function of time. This is commonly employed on epochs of data time-locked to events of interest. Rather than looking at average frequency over the entire epoch, however, a wavelet or other approach is used to compute power as a function of time. The result is that the researcher can identify whether power in a particular frequency band increases or decreases at a consistent time relative to an experimental event of interest. For example, Figure 4.10 shows data from a sentence-processing experiment conducted by Davidson and Indefrey (2007). This employed a typical paradigm in which participants read sentences that could end coherently, or with a semantic or syntactic violation. Such experiments typically employ time-domain analyses, with the N400 component being elicited by semantic violations and the P600 elicited by syntactic ones. However, Davidson and Indefrey used a wavelet analysis over epochs spanning 2 s before and after each target word to create the time-frequency plots shown in Figure 4.10. Each panel of this figure shows time on the x axis and frequency on the y axis. Focusing on the rightmost panels, which show the difference between each violation type and control (well-formed) sentences, we can see that the two violation types have distinct frequency-domain effects. Semantic violations elicited increased

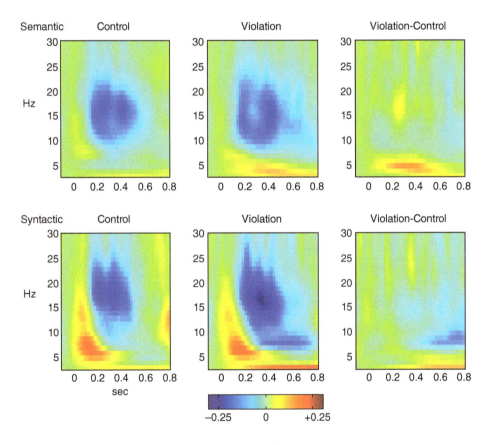

Figure 4.10   Time-frequency plots from a study of semantic and syntactic violations in sentence processing. In each panel, time is on the x-axis and frequency on the y-axis; increased power is shown in white and decreased power in black. Reprinted from Davidson and Indefrey, 2007 with permission of Elsevier

power in the theta band from approximately 200–500 ms, whereas syntactic violations elicited decreased power in the alpha and beta bands from approximately 400–800 ms. The authors further noted that the changes in power were inversely related to the amplitude of the components in the time domain (for example, trials with larger N400s had lower theta-band power), and the scalp distributions of the frequency-domain effects were distinct from those of the time-domain components. This illustrates that both time- and frequency-domain analyses can provide interesting – and complementary – information.

Another application of time-frequency analysis can overcome a key limitation of ERP analyses, which are almost always performed on grand-averaged waveforms.

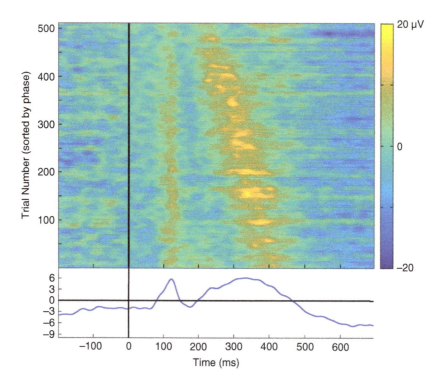

Figure 4.11 A set of ERPs elicited on 500 trials of a visual processing experiment, from a single subject, at electrode T6. The trials have been sorted by their phase in the theta (3-6 Hz) band. Each line of the top panel represents a single trial; the bottom panel shows the average ERP waveform of all 500 trials. Two components are notable in the average waveform: an early positive peak at 100 ms and a later, more sustained positive component from approximately 200-450 ms. However, the phase-sorted individual trials reveal that while the early positive component has very consistent timing across trials, the later component's onset varies across a range of approximately 100 ms. Thus the average ERP waveform suggests a much wider-duration component than was actually present on any individual trial

This averaging process, while useful because it increases our ability to identify what is common across many trials versus the non-systematic noise in the data, can mask trial-to-trial, variation in the EEG signal that is nevertheless consistently related to the experimental manipulation. Frequency-domain analysis is more flexible in its approach to single-trial analysis, because an increase in frequency may consistently occur over trials, even when the **phase** (timing of the peaks) of the oscillations is not consistent across trials. Thus whereas ERP analysis depends on peaks occurring at relatively consistent times across trials – so that in the averaging across trials this peak becomes clearer – frequency-domain analyses applied to individual trials may find that power in a particular frequency band increases even when a clear effect in the averaged time-domain ERP is not present. Figure 4.11 shows a plot in which individual trials are sorted according to their phase (when the peak of a particular frequency band occurs). This plot shows that the component that appears as a positivity from 200–450 ms in the average ERP waveform actually has a duration of only 100–150 ms on any given trial, but that its onset varies over a range of roughly 100 ms, leading to temporal smearing in the average. In a case such as this, further analysis could be performed to determine whether this phase shift correlated with any properties of the stimuli or the participant's performance (for example, reaction times).

Source Localization

Understanding how brain activity relates to cognition necessitates an appreciation of the brain's activity over time and space. As we have emphasized in this chapter, EEG is particularly good at revealing the time course of brain activity. However, it is less well-suited at identifying the locations in the brain in which the signals are being generated. This is because the so-called **inverse solution** of finding the set of sources that generate a particular pattern of scalp electrical activity is mathematically ill-posed – there are in principle an infinite number of possible configurations of electrical potential-generating sources inside the head that could all result in the same pattern of scalp potentials. For this reason, it is often called the **inverse problem** rather than 'solution'. In practice, not all possible solutions are neurophysiologically valid – for example, we know that EEG is not generated in the ventricles of the brain (which are filled with cerebrospinal fluid) or in the white matter (which consists primarily of axons but not cell bodies where postsynaptic potentials occur). Nevertheless, even with anatomical and neurophysiological constraints any scalp potential map still has many possible generators, which can vary in their location, dipole orientation, strength, and number.

In spite of the ill-posed nature of the source localization problem, many efforts have been made to develop source localization algorithms for EEG/ERP data. While there are many different families of these, they all essentially attempt to compare different possible **forward solutions** – estimates of expected scalp electrical potential maps given a particular set of generators in the brain. Forward solutions are in principle relatively simple to compute, because if one specifies the location, orientation, number, and strength of the dipoles there is a unique solution for how these project outward in space. However, computing an accurate forward solution to model a particular individual's EEG data is more complicated. This is because many factors affect the measured scalp topography. These include the thickness of the skull (which varies across the skull as well as across individuals), the exact shape and sulcal folding patterns of the brain, the size and shape of the brain and of the skull, and the noise in the data. The simplest (and least accurate) forward solutions assume the head, including the brain, is shaped like a perfect sphere, with uniform skull thickness. From there, different approaches get increasingly complex, with the ultimate approach being to obtain a structural MRI of the participant's head as well as accurate 3D measurements of the location of each electrode on that person's head during the EEG recording. Even with this level of accuracy, however, source localization algorithms tend to be highly sensitive to noise in the data, and it can be challenging to validate or compare source localization algorithms because there is no 'ground truth' reference to compare the solutions to.

Although EEG/ERP source localization has serious limitations, it can also be a useful tool. In particular, source localization can theoretically overcome the significant limitation of ERPs discussed earlier, namely that of overlapping latent components. Recall that the scalp topography at any given point of time is the sum of all EEG-measurable activity going on in the brain at that point in time. Source localization offers a means of disentangling these overlapping time courses of activity, because each source will have its own time course of activity. Thus it offers the opportunity to characterize latent components rather than simply relying on their overlapping projections to the scalp. Caution is nevertheless advisable since an inaccurate source solution could potentially generate an erroneous set of latent components.

Caveats notwithstanding, it is not uncommon to perform source localization on EEG/ERP data. The validity of these solutions is often assessed with reference to prior knowledge; for instance, ERPs evoked by visual stimuli should evoke activity with sources located primarily in the occipital lobes, at least for early components such as the P1-N1-P2 complex. Indeed, the best way to use EEG source localization is for confirmatory, rather than exploratory, purposes – in other words to test a hypothesis about the time course of activity in a specific brain region, rather than 'fishing' to determine which regions might be involved. Source localization is also used with MEG data, and for several reasons the solutions can be more accurate for MEG. Thus this topic is discussed at greater length in the next chapter.

SUMMARY

Designing experiments using ERPs or EEG requires a solid understanding of how the technique works, its limitations, and its strengths. Like most neuroimaging measures, ERP responses are very sensitive to features of stimuli, including physical properties such as size, brightness, loudness, and timing. Ideally, an experiment should compare ERP responses to the same physical stimuli under different psychological/task conditions so as to eliminate the possibility that any observed differences between conditions are due to the stimuli. While in practice this is often not possible, as many questions depend on differences between stimuli, nevertheless experimenters should always consider possible unintended stimulus effects and take steps to minimize these.

EEG recordings are subject to many sources of noise, including electromagnetic interference from the environment, head movements, and physiological artifacts such as eye movements, blinks, skin potentials, and muscle potentials. Many of these artifacts register as electrical potentials that are much larger than the EEG itself, creating serious problems for data analysis. While signal-processing techniques can help reduce or remove some artifacts, it is by far preferable to minimize the presence of these artifacts during recording. This is achieved both through careful monitoring of the EEG data during recording, and thoughtful experimental design to minimize the occurrence of artifacts (for example, minimizing the need for head or body movement; giving participants opportunities to blink between trials).

Preprocessing involves a number of steps performed on EEG data prior to statistical analysis, to improve the quality of the data and maximize the likelihood of finding experimental effects, if they are present in the data. These include high- and low-pass filtering to remove low- and high-frequency artifacts, respectively; removal of trials with excessive artifacts; correction for common artifacts like blinking, using approaches such as regression or ICA; re-referencing the data to a different electrode(s) than that used during recording; and segmenting the continuous EEG into epochs time-locked to events of interest to create ERPs. Properly applying each of these steps requires a solid understanding of their effects. Once data have been preprocessed, statistical analysis can be performed. For ERPs, this usually involves computing peak or mean amplitude within a particular time window (ideally defined a priori, based on hypotheses), and/or the latency of the onset or peak of a particular component. Because many EEG systems have large numbers of electrodes, it is common to select specific electrodes for data analysis, or to group electrodes into regions of interest (ROIs). As well, data can be analysed in the frequency domain, in which case power in specific frequency bands and temporal windows is used as the dependent measure (a time-frequency analysis). When large numbers of statistical tests are performed, some form of multiple comparison correction should be applied to minimize the likelihood of obtaining spurious results. Another step sometimes performed in data analysis is source localization, which attempts to solve the inverse problem – identifying the locations in the brain from which measured EEG activity arose. However, the inverse problem is mathematically ill-posed (has an infinite number of possible solutions), making the results of such efforts often unreliable.

THINGS YOU SHOULD KNOW

- Because brain activity is sensitive both to the physical properties of stimuli and the cognitive processes activated by stimuli and tasks, physical differences in stimuli between experimental conditions can confound the interpretation of EEG data. For this reason, it is preferable to hold stimuli constant between experimental conditions, manipulating only the psychological conditions.

When this is not possible, researchers should be mindful of this possible confound and attempt to control for differences between stimuli.

- EEG has exquisite temporal resolution, but this also means that ERP experiments are very sensitive to the timing of stimuli and cognitive operations. Relatively small delays or variability in stimulus timing (on the order of 10–20 ms) can drastically change the timing of ERP components, or make these effects difficult to identify if their timing does not overlap sufficiently in the grand average. In EEG experiments it is important to use stimulus presentation software specifically designed to have very precise timing, and also to confirm the reliability of timing prior to running the experiment.

- Sources of noise in EEG data include environmental electromagnetic interference, head and body movement, and physiological artifacts including blinks, muscle contractions, and skin potentials caused by sweating. It is important to minimize these during EEG recording through the design of the experiment, and attentive monitoring of the EEG during the experiment, and providing constructive feedback to participants if they produce excessive artifact.

- Preprocessing EEG data involves a series of steps to improve the signal-to-noise ratio (SNR) and sensitivity to experimental effects. These steps include filtering, artifact identification and removal, artifact correction, re-referencing, and segmenting the data into epochs time-locked to events of experimental interest.

- High-pass filters attenuate low-frequency artifacts, while low-pass filters attenuate high-frequency artifacts. Bandpass filters combine high- and low-pass filters, while notch filters remove a specific band of frequencies while leaving higher and lower ones untouched. Filters necessarily have roll-offs around their specified cut-offs, meaning that not all frequencies beyond the cut-off are entirely removed from the data. As well, filters can actually induce unintended artifacts into the data. For these reasons, it is important to use the minimum amount of filtering necessary to remove artifacts in the data.

- Because EEG/ERP data is so rich in information, often comprising hundreds of time points over dozens of electrodes, various data-reduction techniques are typically performed to obtain dependent measures for statistical analysis. Common dependent measures in ERP (time-domain) analysis include peak amplitude, mean amplitude, peak latency, and onset latency. In ERD/ERS (frequency-domain) analysis, the most common dependent measure is power within a specified frequency band. All of these measures are typically obtained within pre-specified time windows of interest. As well, researchers often select individual electrodes, or combine electrodes into regions of interest (ROIs), rather than analysing every electrode individually.

- Event-related synchronization (ERS) refers to increases in EEG power within a specific frequency band, time-locked to an experimental event of interest. Event-related desynchronization (ERD) refers to time-locked decreases in power. However, the terms (de)synchronization should not be interpreted literally, because many factors other than increased or decreased synchronization of neural activity can influence EEG power.

- The forward solution refers to predicting a pattern of scalp electrical potentials, given knowledge of the number, location, orientation, and activation strength of the generators of these potentials in the brain. Forward solutions are relatively simple to calculate. The inverse problem refers to predicting the number, location, orientation, and activation strength of the neural generators on the basis of scalp-recorded EEG/ERP data. The inverse problem is mathematically ill-posed, meaning that there are an infinite number of possible solutions to this problem for any observable pattern of scalp potentials. Performing source localization with EEG data involves attempting to solve the inverse problem, using the forward solution. There are many approaches to this, but because there is no 'gold standard' to compare the results to (that is, a known correct solution for real human EEG data), and because EEG data tend to be very noisy, EEG source localization can be unreliable.

FURTHER READINGS

Luck, S.J. (2014). *An Introduction to the Event-Related Potential Technique* (2nd ed.). Cambridge, MA: MIT Press.

Picton, T.W., Bentin, S., Berg, P., Donchin, E., Hillyard, S.A., Johnson, R. Jr., Miller, G.A., Ritter, W., Ruchkin, D.S., Rugg, M.D., and Taylor, M.J. (2000) Guidelines for using human event-related potentials to study cognition: Recording standards and publication criteria. *Psychophysiology*, 37(2), 127–152.

5 Magnetoencephalography (MEG)

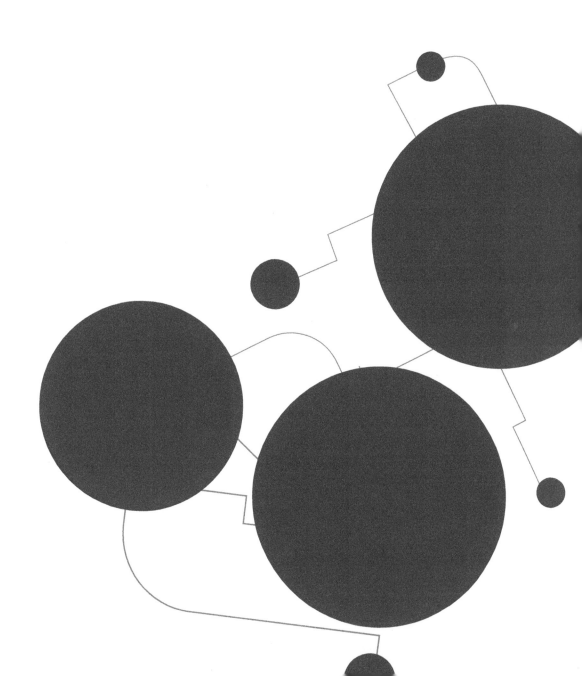

LEARNING OBJECTIVES

After reading this chapter, you should be able to:

- Explain how magnetic fields are generated by electrical activity in the brain.
- Describe the relationship between EEG and MEG, and explain why a particular EEG effect might look different when measured with MEG, or not be visible at all.
- Name the different types of MEG sensors and describe how each works, including the orientations of dipoles that each is sensitive to.
- Describe common sources of noise in MEG recordings, and how these are mitigated.
- Explain the standard preprocessing and analysis steps applied to MEG data.
- Explain why source localization is generally more reliable for MEG than for EEG.
- Name three general classes of source localization algorithm, and explain the strengths and weaknesses of each.
- Describe considerations in experimental design that are specific to the MEG technique.
- Describe the strengths and limitations of MEG relative to EEG.

INTRODUCTION

Magnetoencephalography (MEG) is a technique closely related to EEG, first developed by David Cohen in 1968. However, rather than recording brain electrical potentials with electrodes placed on the scalp, magnetic fields are measured using devices called **magnetometers** and **gradiometers** that are arranged in a helmet. The magnetic fields measured by MEG are generated by electrical activity in the brain, just like the signals recorded by EEG. Indeed, much of this chapter builds on the technical foundation developed in the preceding chapters. In the chapters on EEG we described Ampère's circuital law (the right-hand rule), by which electrical current flow induces a magnetic field, and vice-versa. This same principle allows us to measure the brain's electrical activity using magnetic field sensors. In spite of the fact that MEG is in principle sensitive to the same forms of brain activity as EEG, in practice it is different in many respects. Firstly, peak MEG activity locations on the scalp will differ from the locations of EEG/ERP peaks due to the right-hand-rule relationship between electrical current and magnetic fields. Secondly, magnetic fields drop off rapidly with distance, whereas EEG signals are volume-conducted through the head – so MEG is more sensitive to activity on the cortical surface than deeper activity; this also adds an additional useful constraint in source localization. Finally, MEG is much more technically demanding and expensive. MEG is more sensitive to environmental electromagnetic noise than EEG, so it requires very expensive shielding. As well, the magnetometers must be cooled close to absolute zero to function, and so must be kept bathed in liquid helium. As a result, the costs of MEG are closer to those of MRI than of EEG, meaning that MEG scanners are typically multi-user facilities. MEG scanners are less ubiquitous than MRI scanners, however – while MRI has many revenue-generating clinical applications, MEG has relatively few. Given the high cost and technical complexity, one might wonder why anyone would ever choose MEG over EEG. The greatest advantage of MEG over EEG is that the physics of the magnetic signal are such that source localization is generally more reliable than with EEG, allowing MEG a combination of high temporal and spatial resolution – although caveats about the accuracy of source localization remain. Those caveats notwithstanding, it is more common to see MEG data reported in terms of time-varying activity in different brain locations, than in terms of sensor-level signals as is the norm with EEG/ERP.

WHAT ARE WE MEASURING?

The physiological basis of the MEG signal is essentially the same as for the EEG signal. Open fields of pyramidal neurons whose postsynaptic potentials fluctuate in synchrony with each other are the primary source of MEG activity. A critical difference between MEG and EEG signals, however, is that the magnetic fields induced by electrical current flow in the brain wrap around the conductors (neurons). This is illustrated in Figure 5.1, where we see that for an intracellular electrical current flowing along a neuron from dendrites to axons creates a magnetic field around the neuron. The location of the open field along the cerebral cortex becomes critical here, because pyramidal neurons are largely oriented perpendicular to the surface of the cortex. Thus as can be seen in Figure 5.1, only magnetic fields generated by neurons whose axons are aligned tangentially to the scalp will radiate outside of the head. This means that MEG is primarily sensitive to activity of neurons along the banks of sulci on the cortex, because neurons on the gyri and in the depths of the sulci will be oriented such that their magnetic fields do not radiate outside of the head where the MEG sensors are.

The physical relationship between electrical and magnetic fields creates some important differences between MEG and EEG. Firstly, since EEG signals are orthogonal to MEG signals, EEG will in principle be most sensitive to neurons on the gyri – since those are oriented with their dipoles projecting directly outward from the head (see Figure 5.1). Secondly, electrical potentials conduct through the volume of the head quite well, so neurons along the banks of the sulci will generate potentials that may not be detectable (at least weak) at electrodes directly above the active region, but these potentials will be detectable by EEG at locations on the scalp farther away. In contrast, magnetic fields are not readily conducted through the brain, but rather drop off rapidly – approximately exponentially – with distance. As a result they are

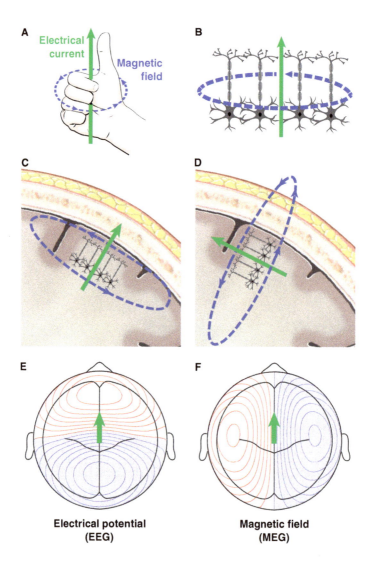

Figure 5.1 A magnetic field is induced by any electrical current, following Ampère's circuital law – also known as the right-hand rule. This is illustrated in A, showing that if one makes a 'thumbs-up' gesture the thumb points in the direction of current flow (blue arrow), and the magnetic field is induced flowing in the direction indicated by the curled fingers (black dashed line). B shows this for an open field configuration of pyramidal neurons: a dipole is created by current flow from cell bodies to axons, which induces a magnetic field around the neurons. In C and D, we see examples of currents and associated magnetic fields induced by open fields of neurons located in two different positions within the cerebral cortex. Note that these illustrations are highly schematic and the neurons are not drawn to scale! In C, the active open field is located along a part of the cortex parallel to the skull. So while the electrical potential would be detected by an EEG

Figure 5.1 (Continued)
electrode positioned above this field, the magnetic field around it stays entirely inside the head, and would not be detected by an MEG sensor. In contrast, D shows a similar open field of active neurons located on the banks of a sulcus. Here, the electrical dipole is oriented parallel to the scalp and so an EEG electrode located above this field would not detect the activity - rather, we would see zero electrical potential at this location (although the activity would be detected at electrodes farther away). However, the magnetic field induced by this current flow would exit and then re-enter the head above the open field, and would thus be detectable by an MEG sensor placed there. The bottom two panels further illustrate the relationship between EEG and MEG. In E and F, a single electrical dipole is shown, located along the midline of the head with current flowing towards the front of the head (this is not a realistic situation as there is no cortex along the midline, but this serves to illustrate the basic principle). E shows the scalp distribution of electrical potential, while F shows the distribution of the associated magnetic field, with showing the field exiting the head, and blue showing the field re-entering the head

less detectable at locations more remote from their source. As well, because the skull is a poor conductor of electricity, EEG signals get blurred by the skull, and thus in many cases there will be quite a bit of overlap between the scalp potentials generated by neurons on the gyri and along the banks of the sulci. In contrast, magnetic fields are almost entirely unaffected by the skull, so they are not blurred the way EEG signals are, leading to activity that appears more focal with MEG than EEG.

The relationship between depth and strength of the MEG signal is shown in Figure 5.2. In practice, it is not clear how much signal is actually missed simply because it is generated deep in a sulcus. On one hand it has been estimated, based on in vitro measurements and computational modelling, that a minimum of 50,000 neurons acting synchronously are required to generate a measurable MEG signal (Hansen, Kringelbach, & Salmelin, 2010). While this may sound like a fairly large number of neurons, this many neurons can be found in a patch of cortex approximately 1 mm in diameter. So certainly, focal areas of activity that are in principle strong enough to be detected by MEG might be missed if they are located too deep in a sulcus. On the other hand, the area of cortex activated in a functional imaging experiment is typically well over 1 mm in diameter, so activation may extend enough to include neurons both on the banks of sulci and on the adjacent gyrus or sulcus. This is not always the case though: activation may be more focal. For example, in mapping the motor or somatosensory representations, the peaks of activation of adjacent fingers tend to be relatively small and close together, on the order of millimetres. In spite of this close proximity, MEG has been shown to be able to resolve these small spatial differences. Likewise, early visual cortex areas have a fine-grained **retinotopic** organization whereby areas representing different parts of the visual field may be separated by one or only a few millimetres, and this too has been detected using MEG (Hagler et al., 2009; Perry, Adiamian, Thai, Holliday, Hillebrand, & Barnes, 2011).

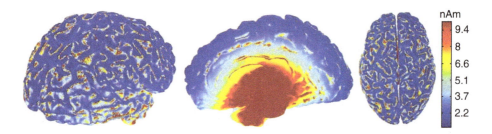

Figure 5.2 Empirical data from a single individual, demonstrating how MEG sensitivity decreases with the depth of the source. This is shown as the strength of a source that would be required to generate a detectable MEG signal. Reproduced from Hillebrand and Barnes, 2002 with permission of Elsevier

HOW DO WE MEASURE IT?

Data Acquisition

Detecting Magnetic Fields

MEG recordings are done using devices that measure magnetic fields, or more specifically **magnetic flux**, which is change in magnetic fields. Although this may seem like a subtle distinction, it is actually very important: MEG specifically measures changes in magnetic fields, rather than static fields. MEG sensors need to be extremely sensitive because the magnetic fields generated by the brain are very small – on the order of 10^{-15} Tesla (T; Tesla is a standard measure of magnetic field strength). By comparison, the Earth's magnetic field (which causes the needle on a compass to point north) is $25^{-65} \times 10^{-6}$ T and a common fridge magnet is approximately 10^{-3} T in strength. The minute strength of the brain's magnetic fields thus require very sensitive instruments to measure. The only device sensitive enough to measure the brain's evoked magnetic fields is the **superconducting quantum interference device (SQUID)**. One basic requirement of the sensitivity required for MEG is that the sensors must be cooled to a temperature near absolute zero. At these temperatures, materials become superconducting – that is, they have almost zero resistance to current flow. This is the only way to allow the tiny magnetic fields from the brain to induce a current in the sensor. In MEG systems, typical superconducting materials include niobium, lead, or mercury, which have critical temperatures at which they switch to the superconducting state of below 10 K (–263°C). Keeping the sensors this cool requires bathing them in liquid helium, which is only liquid below 4.2 K. The need for liquid helium to maintain the superconductivity of SQUIDs is a significant, ongoing cost of maintaining a MEG system. Liquid helium is a scarce resource worldwide, and therefore costs continue to steadily increase. While some MEG systems are equipped with helium recovery systems, in other systems the helium boils off at a steady rate and must be refilled every few weeks. A contemporary MEG scanner is shown in Figure 5.3.

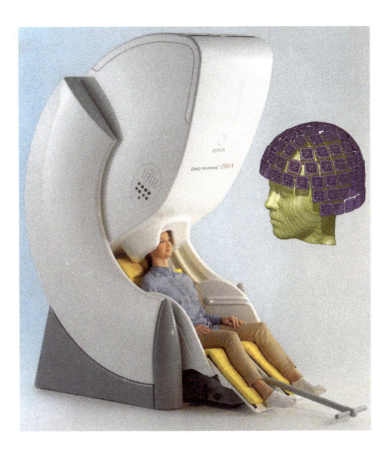

Figure 5.3 An example of an MEG scanner. The person's head is inside the helmet of the scanner, which contains the MEG sensors. The inset shows the arrangement of the sensors inside the helmet, relative to the head. The scanner has an integrated seat which can be raised or lowered (using the handle seen extending from between the person's feet) to ensure a snug fit of the helmet to the head. Much of the space above the head is devoted to a dewar, containing the liquid helium necessary to keep the MEG sensors cooled to near-absolute zero. This enables the superconducting properties of the sensors that is necessary for MEG to function. Images courtesy of Elekta

Even beyond keeping the materials cool enough to allow superconductivity, the required level of sensitivity for MEG requires further complex engineering. A schematic diagram of SQUID is shown in Figure 5.4 – it consists of a thin 'washer' approximately 1 mm square, broken by a thin gap which is bridged by an electrical insulator. This is known as a **Josephson junction** (named after Brian Josephson, who received the Nobel Prize in 1973 for his work developing this) and allows for the measurement of changes in electrical current flowing through the SQUID. SQUIDs operate by passing a constant 'bias' current through the SQUID; by the right-hand rule the strength of this current is altered if there is any change in the magnetic field around it, and this is how the brain's magnetic fields are measured – as the amount of change from the default bias current. The Josephson junction is critical to this process because it has a special property: it passes current unaltered when the current is low, but at higher current levels it creates a high-frequency alternating current. The SQUIDs do not sense the magnetic fields of the brain directly though, because their small surface area – while essential to their sensitivity levels – provides poor coupling to the magnetic fields. Thus the SQUIDs are connected to **flux transformers** that are also made of superconducting material and run from the SQUIDs themselves to locations closer to the subject's head in the MEG helmet. The shape of the flux transformers determines their sensitivity. This fact allows different types of flux transformers that are sensitive to different aspects of the brain's magnetic field.

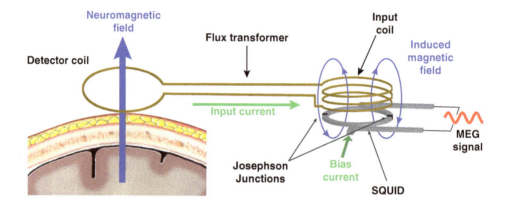

Figure 5.4 Simplified diagram of a MEG sensor. The left side shows the detector coil which would be inside the helmet, close to the participant's skull. When a neuromagnetic field is produced by the brain, with the proper orientation relative to the sensor, the field induces a current in the detector coil. This current is transmitted via a conductor to the input coil. Collectively, the detector coil, input coil, and conductors connecting them comprise the flux transformer. Because there is current flowing through the coil, a magnetic field is induced around the input coil. The SQUID (grey ring) is located next to the coil, so that when a magnetic field is induced in the coil, it in turn induces a current in the SQUID. This induced current generates an electrical potential difference across the SQUID, on either side of the Josephson junctions. This potential difference is directly proportional to the magnetic flux at the detector coil, and is recorded as the MEG signal

There are three different types of flux transformers used in MEG scanners. The simplest type of flux transformer is a **magnetometer**, shown in the left panel of Figure 5.5. A magnetometer consists of a single coil or loop of wire arranged such that the flat surface of the loop is parallel to the surface of the MEG helmet (and by extension, the subject's head), with leads to and from the SQUID. Any magnetic field impinging on the loop will induce a current in it via the right-hand rule. A problem with the simple design of the magnetometer is that it records all magnetic fields, including both those of neural origin and environmental background noise. Thus in modern MEG systems a flux transformer configuration known as an **axial gradiometer** is typically used instead. As shown in the middle panel of Figure 5.5, axial gradiometers have a second loop that is wound in the opposite direction from the first, located farther away (~5 cm) from the head. Axial gradiometers are one of a more general class of sensors (gradiometers) that are sensitive to gradients in magnetic fields – magnetic fields that vary along a spatial dimension. More specifically, gradiometers are sensitive to the difference in magnetic field strength

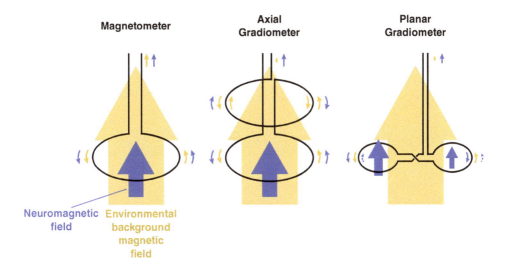

Figure 5.5 Schematic diagram of the configurations of magnetometers and gradiometers. The magnetic fields are shown as large arrows, and the current induced by these fields in the measurement coils is represented by the smaller arrows. Magnetometers consist of a single loop of wire, and suffer from the problem of being sensitive to both signal from the brain and noise from external sources. Axial gradiometers address this problem by having a second loop of wire in the coil, farther from the head and wound in the opposite direction to the loop close to the head. Because of its distance from the head (a few centimetres), this second loop is insensitive to magnetic fields emanating from the scalp but is still affected by other magnetic fields in the environment. Because of the right-hand rule, this opposite-direction winding serves to cancel out any signal that is induced in both loops by the same source. Both magnetometers and axial gradiometers are sensitive to the component of magnetic fields perpendicular to the scalp. Planar gradiometers also employ two loops with opposite windings to cancel out environmental noise. However, the loops are in a figure-8 pattern which makes them sensitive to magnetic fields that vary over short distances across the head (the parallel component of the fields)

between the two loops of coil. Axial gradiometers are sensitive to magnetic field gradients along lines moving out from the surface of the scalp; because of the right-hand rule, any magnetic field present (and equivalent) at both loops will cancel out, so only fields that drop off with distance from the scalp are measured. This is because the magnetic field induces currents following in opposite directions in the two loops, due to their opposite windings. Since environmental magnetic noise tends to be uniform around the head, the axial gradiometer configuration should cancel out such environmental noise, while preserving neural signals because they drop off over much smaller distances, and so are not detected at the coil rather away from the head.

A second gradiometer configuration, the **planar gradiometer**, has the two coils in the same plane, equal distance to the scalp, in essentially a figure-8 configuration. This is shown in the right panel of Figure 5.5. Like axial gradiometers, the reverse winding in the two loops of the planar gradiometer serves to cancel out the effects of any magnetic field that impinges on both loops. However, the fact that both loops are close to the scalp makes planar gradiometers more sensitive to different neuromagnetic field patterns than axial gradiometers. Specifically, since gradiometers are sensitive to the difference in magnetic field between the two loops of the gradiometer, planar gradiometers are sensitive to neuromagnetic fields that change over the distance between the two loops, along the surface of the scalp.

The spatial sensitivities of these different gradiometers are known as their **lead fields**, which describe the orientation of the current that would yield the maximum output of the sensor at that location in space. To understand the lead fields of axial versus planar gradiometers, first recall that MEG is primarily sensitive to dipole sources that are oriented parallel to the surface of the head. The magnetic field of such a source can be imagined as circles centred on that dipole and radiating out of the head, as shown in Figure 5.1. Visualized from outside the head, this magnetic field can be drawn as arcs emanating on one side of the dipole and re-entering the head on the other side of the dipole. This is shown in the top left panel of Figure 5.6. This magnetic field, measured at any point along the scalp, can in turn be described as having two 'components' – one measured orthogonal to the scalp (the **perpendicular**, or radial, **component**) and one running tangentially to the scalp (the **parallel component**). The perpendicular component is maximal right where the magnetic field 'emerges' from the scalp, while the parallel component is maximal at the apex of the arc of the magnetic field, just where it changes in its path from travelling away from the scalp, to where it starts travelling back towards the scalp.

Axial gradiometers (and magnetometers) are most sensitive to the perpendicular component of the magnetic field. The perpendicular component has equivalent values on either side of the dipole at a given distance from the dipole, but with opposite signs (since on one side of the dipole, the magnetic field is flowing out of the head, whereas on the opposite side it is re-entering the head). In contrast, planar gradiometers are most sensitive to the parallel component of the magnetic field. A given dipole will have a particular, fixed orientation and so its parallel component outside the head will have a single maximal direction. One important distinction between

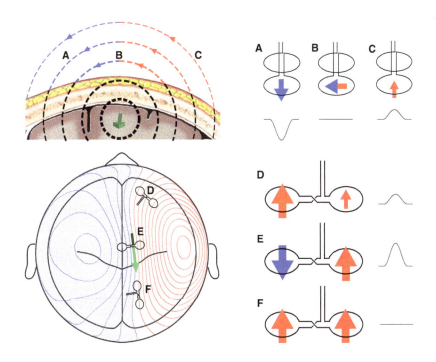

Figure 5.6 Examples of sensitivity profiles of axial (A–C) and planar (D–F) gradiometers to different magnetic field patterns and strengths. The top left panel shows a coronal cross-section of the head, with an electrical dipole source represented as the green arrow, pointing towards the viewer. The dashed lines represent the magnetic field induced by this dipole, with the thickness of the lines schematically representing the fact that field strength decreases with difference. Where the field manifests outside the head, field lines flowing out of the head are shown in red and those entering the head are shown in blue. The letters A, B, and C represent locations of axial gradiometers, corresponding to the diagrams in the top right panel. In the right panel, A shows a gradiometer positioned over a relatively strong field (close to the dipole) entering the head, and below this is the MEG signal that would be recorded if the dipole increased and then decreased in activity over a brief period of time. B shows that an axial gradiometer positioned directly over the dipole would not detect any activity, because at this position the magnetic field has no perpendicular component but rather is parallel to the head. C shows an axial gradiometer positioned over the outward-flowing part of the magnetic field, but because it is further from the source the measured signal is weaker. The bottom left panel shows the magnetic field map as viewed from the top of the head, again with red lines representing fields exiting the head, and blue lines representing fields entering the head. D shows a planar gradiometer positioned over the outward-flowing part of the field, but the magnetic field is stronger under one loop than the other. On the bottom right the magnitude of the magnetic fields are represented by the size of the arrows and the resulting signal detected by the planar gradiometer is shown on the far right. In E the gradiometer is centred over the dipole, such that one loop is over the field exiting the head and the other over the field entering the head. Because of the large difference in the magnetic field between the two loops, the resulting signal is very strong. F shows a gradiometer positioned such that both loops are along the same magnetic field line, and so the field is identical in orientation and strength at the two loops. As a result, the measured signal – representing the difference between the two loops – is zero

axial and planar gradiometers is that while axial gradiometers are equally sensitive to dipoles regardless of their orientation (assuming the dipoles are tangential to the scalp), planar gradiometers are maximally sensitive to dipoles of a particular orientation. Indeed, dipoles oriented 90° to the optimal orientation of a planar gradiometer are essentially invisible to it. For this reason, planar gradiometers are always arranged in pairs at each sensor location in MEG systems, oriented 90° relative to each other.

Both types of gradiometer are sensitive to magnetic fields in the brain, but provide complementary information. Some MEG systems have been manufactured with exclusively one or the other type of sensor. However, the maximum sensitivity to brain activity and dipolar orientation is achieved by combining both types of sensors. The most common commercially available MEG systems currently on the market use a combination of two planar and one axial gradiometer at each of 102 locations in the MEG helmet, providing comprehensive coverage of the head with a total of 306 sensors. Examples of evoked MEG data from each type of sensor are shown in Figure 5.7.

'Wearable' MEG

An exciting recent development in MEG technology is the first report of a 'wearable' MEG system (Boto et al., 2018). This system uses an entirely different technology than the standard MEG systems described above. Rather than using SQUIDs, this system relies on **optically pumped magnetometers (OPMs)**. These sensors rely on shining a laser with a specific wavelength (795 nm) through glass vials filled with ^{87}Rb (a weakly radioactive isotope of the element rubidium). A property of ^{87}Rb ions is that they polarize – or align themselves – with a laser beam of this wavelength. Most usefully, the orientation of the ^{87}Rb ions in the laser beam changes when an external magnetic field is applied. This weakens the amount of light transmitted by the laser through the glass cell. Therefore, by measuring the amount of laser light transmitted, we get a measurement of the strength of the magnetic field around this sensor. The primary advantage of these sensors over SQUIDs is that they operate at room temperature (actually, the ^{87}Rb has to be heated to 150°C), and so the system does not require the sensors to be embedded in a large dewar of liquid helium. As a result, each sensor is relatively small and light, and can be attached to the head using a plastic holder. In Boto and colleagues' report, a face-and-head mask was 3D printed for each individual participant based on a 3D MRI scan of their head, allowing a custom fit with enough support to hold each sensor, as shown in Figure 5.8. Because the sensors are held in a fixed position relative to the head, and do not require the bulky helium dewar, the system allows for relatively free movement of the individual, which opens up many possibilities not possible with existing MEG technology. As well, custom-fitting the sensors to the head ensures they are all at a close, and relatively fixed, distance (rather than, for example, the sensors being at variable distances in a helmet, and farther away from the head for people with smaller heads), and that the sensors move with the head, eliminating the need for motion correction.

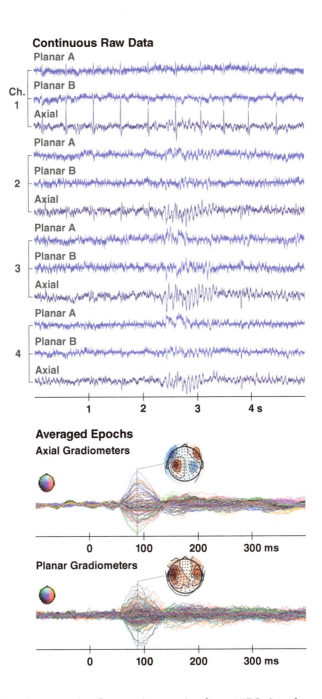

Figure 5.7 Top: An example of several seconds of raw MEG data from four sensors of an Elekta Neuromag MEG system. The data are taken from a recording from an adult presented with a variety of auditory and visual stimuli, and are shown for four sensors located over the occipital lobe (visual cortex). On this system, each sensor has three gradiometers in the same location: one axial and

Figure 5.7 (Continued)

two planar (the latter oriented 90° relative to each other). Note in the continuous data the electrocardiogram artifact (large spikes) in the first axial gradiometer channel, as well as the burst of alpha rhythm in the second, third, and fourth sensors – particularly in the axial gradiometers. Bottom: Butterfly and scalp topography plots of epochs time-locked to the onset of auditory stimuli presented to the left ear, averaged across 72 trials. The colours of the lines in the butterfly plot indicate the position of their corresponding sensors on the head, as shown by the legend on the left. The auditory evoked response is clearly visible, peaking at 88 ms post-stimulus onset. The scalp topography plots show the distribution of the magnetic fields over the head for each sensor type. For axial gradiometers, red shows fields exiting the head and blue, fields entering the head. Note that the planar gradiometer data is shown on a monochromatic scale (no negative values) and represents the magnitude of change (gradient) in magnetic field between the two loops of each gradiometer. Although the raw data includes separate recordings for each of the pair of planar gradiometers at each sensor location, these are combined in the scalp map because they reflect gradients along two perpendicular axes parallel to the scalp surface. In other words, one of the pair measures changes approximately front to back, and the other approximately left to right. Note also that the most intense changes in the planar gradiometer scalp map are positioned in between the largest blue and red spots of the axial gradiometer map, reflecting their relative sensitivities to the parallel versus perpendicular components of the magnetic fields. Data are from the 'sample_audvis_raw' example dataset recorded at the MGH/HMS/MIT Athinoula A. Martinos Center Biomedical Imaging and available in the MNE-Python software package (Gramfort, 2013)

This system still has limitations however. Neuromagnetic signals are very tiny relative to external sources such as the Earth's magnetic field, regardless of the sensor type used. Thus these sensors are still used in a shielded room as traditional MEG is (see below). Even in this shielded room, weak external magnetic fields are present, and movement of the OPMs through this field create large artifacts. Thus each sensor is equipped with electromagnetic coils that measure and cancel out changes in the external magnetic fields. As well, this system is still in the prototype stage and currently offers limited coverage of the head. It does provide an exciting glimpse into the future of MEG technology, however.

Head Position

An important consideration in MEG scanning is that the head of the person being scanned is positioned inside the scanner in what is often referred to as a 'helmet'. Unlike an EEG cap, this helmet is not snug-fitting, but rather a hard plastic portion of the MEG scanner that is made big enough to accommodate most head sizes. This means that the head is in fact free to move inside the helmet; however, head movement during a MEG scan is not desirable. Because the sensors are located in fixed

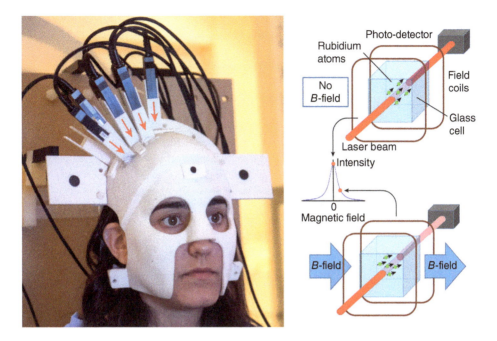

Figure 5.8 A wearable MEG system using optically pumped magnetometers (OPMs). In the left-hand photo, the sensors (marked with red arrows) can be seen over the right sensorimotor cortex of an individual. These are held in position by a 3D printed mask custom-fitted to the individual's head and face. The left panel shows a schematic diagram of how OPMs function: in the absence of an external magnetic (B) field, ^{87}Rb ions in the OPM align with a laser beam shining through them. When an external magnetic field impinges on the sensor, however, the ions are moved out of alignment with the laser. This results in a decreased strength of the laser beam at the photo-detector, which provides a measurement of the external magnetic field strength. Reprinted from Boto et al., 2018 with permission of Springer Nature

positions inside the helmet, if the head moves then the position of the sensors relative to the brain changes, which is problematic since we assume a fixed relationship between the sensor and head locations. MEG systems typically address this issue through the use of **head position indicators** (**HPIs**) attached to the participant's head. These are simply small metal coils, typically coated in plastic, attached to wires that connect to the MEG system. A common configuration is to place one on each temple and one on the nasion (bridge of the noise), though greater numbers of coils can provide greater accuracy and redundancy (for example, one on either side of the forehead and one behind each ear). After being attached to the head (often with tape), the locations of these coils on the head are digitized using a device connected to the MEG system that records positions in three dimensions. This device typically has a stylus, the tip of which is touched to each HPI coil (though other approaches such as camera-based systems can also be used). The stylus is also used at this time to digitize the shape of the head, typically by tracing around the head to provide comprehensive coverage. This 3D digitization is used later in analysis for accurate representation of the head shape and the positions of the MEG sensors relative to the head shape. If a structural MRI scan of the participant's head and brain is also available, the 3D digitized tracing of the head is also valuable for co-registering the MEG data with the individual's brain anatomy. Each HPI generates a unique signal that is detected by the MEG scanner. Head position can either be recorded once at the beginning of the scan, occasionally throughout, or continuously. Continuous scanning of the HPI coils is ideal so that compensation can be made for any changes in head position post-scan. In spite of this measure, it is ideal that the participant be instructed to move her/his head as little as possible – and that head movement is monitored and feedback provided if excessive motion is detected. The motion correction algorithms are only really effective over a limited range of movements, so movements of more than a few millimetres can render the MEG measurements inaccurate – errors which can be propagated and magnified in subsequent steps such as source localization.

Combined MEG-EEG

EEG can be recorded simultaneously with MEG. MEG systems often come with EEG amplifier hardware built into the MEG scanner, so that an electrode cap can be plugged into the MEG scanner and the EEG data saved in the same file as the MEG data. Third-party, MEG-compatible EEG systems are also available from various vendors. MEG and EEG have different sensitivity patterns, both because signals from the same generator are related to each other via the right-hand rule, and because of the fact that MEG is preferentially sensitive to sources on the banks of cortical sulci while EEG is more sensitive to deeper and volume-conducted sources. This is illustrated in Figure 5.9. Because MEG and EEG provide complementary information, simultaneous recording of both can have two advantages. Firstly, the EEG data can act as an additional source of information for, and constraint on, source localization. Secondly, if a study is focused on using MEG to develop a richer understanding of a commonly recorded ERP component, it can be useful to have the actual ERP data from each individual in the MEG study. At a minimum, this can confirm that the ERP component of interest is being elicited in the MEG study, since the same component as measured with MEG will necessarily have a different spatial distribution across each type of MEG sensor; timing can even vary somewhat between MEG and EEG (likely due to how different latent components separate in the two measures). Further, one could perform analyses such as correlating the amplitude of the ERP component in each individual with source-localized MEG activity in different brain regions. This could be useful if multiple regions are active; not all of these regions might contribute to both the MEG and ERP components, so a correlation analysis could help clarify the MEG–EEG relationship. The downside to simultaneous MEG–EEG recording is that EEG set-up extends the overall duration of the procedure, often significantly, and the data analysis becomes more complex as well.

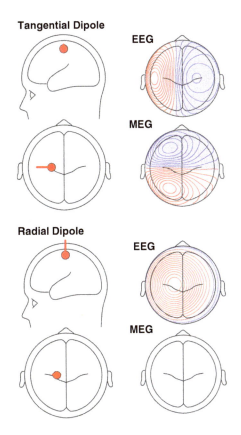

Figure 5.9 Comparison of electrical potential and magnetic field scalp topography maps resulting from particular dipole orientations. The top panel shows a dipole source tangential to the cortical surface. The two drawings on the left show the position of the dipole (red circle) and its orientation (red line). On the right are the scalp distributions generated by that dipole, as they would manifest in EEG and MEG recordings, respectively. For EEG, red represents positive electrical potential while blue represents negative. For MEG, red represents magnetic fields exiting the head and blue fields entering the head. The bottom panel shows a radial dipole source. The location of this dipole in the head is identical to that in the top panel, but the orientation is changed. Note that this radial source is invisible to MEG since the magnetic fields remain entirely inside the head

Signal and Noise

Shielding

As noted earlier, the size of the magnetic fields generated by the brain is tiny relative to the magnetic fields generated by most electronic devices as well as metal objects moving through space. Elevators or passing vehicles even tens of metres away from the scanner can induce significant artifacts (for example, one MEG system was placed too close to a subway tunnel and could only be used in the middle of the night when the subway was not running). Much smaller metal items closer to the scanner can also create artifactual magnetic fields – for example, office chairs used at the operator's console. Although low-pass filtering is always used with MEG to prevent aliasing (as in EEG), and high-pass filtering is usually performed as well, these are not sufficient to remove all artifacts. In particular, many sources of noise are so large, compared to MEG, that they can 'swamp' the MEG sensors because they greatly exceed the range of values that the sensors can record. In this case the recordings look like flat lines and no useful data can be extracted.

Because of MEG's extreme sensitivity, recordings can only be successfully performed in shielded environments. There are essentially two strategies for shielding, passive and active. **Passive shielding** involves surrounding the scanner room with several layers of metal, including copper, aluminium, and **mu-metal**, a special blend of metals specifically designed to deflect magnetic fields (primarily nickel and iron, along with copper and chromium or molybdenum). The shielding is designed to be highly **magnetically permeable**, meaning that it does not actually block magnetic fields, but rather provides a path for magnetic fields to flow around the shielding rather than through it. Mu-metal is particularly effective for lower frequencies, while aluminium is more effective for higher frequencies. Each of these materials has a limited capacity for deflecting magnetic fields before it becomes saturated. Therefore, to provide sufficient shielding for a MEG scanner multiple layers of shielding are required, using a mix of metals. To be fully effective such shields are very thick and heavy (10–15 tons), and must be placed on a heavy concrete pad or other specially reinforced flooring. A concrete pad is advantageous because it can also attenuate vibrations transmitted through the building that could generate MEG artifacts. The weight of the room and desirability of vibrational isolation places limitations on where the shielded room can be located since the floors of typical buildings are not engineered to handle such weight.

Active shielding takes a very different approach – the impinging magnetic fields are measured by coils of wire placed in various configurations around the room, and then subtracted from the MEG recordings. This approach does not replace mu-metal shielding, but on its own can provide significant noise reduction. Thus for sites that cannot accommodate a fully sufficient mu-metal shield (for example, because the floor could not support the considerable weight of such a shield), a thinner mu-metal shield is complemented by active shielding. Regardless of the approach taken to shielding, the complexities of engineering and cost of materials mean that the cost of the shielded room can represent a significant proportion (for example, half) of the overall cost of an MEG system.

Properly designed and installed room shielding is effective in attenuating the external magnetic fields entering the MEG scanner room. However, such shielding is never perfect. Some further attenuation can be obtained via coils placed inside the MEG scanner itself, but sufficiently far away from the subject's head so as not to record brain activity. In addition to these measures, it is important to control sources of magnetic noise within the recording room itself. Any electronic equipment used in the room will generate magnetic fields that can render the MEG recordings unusable. For this reason, the best approach is to keep all such equipment outside the room when possible. This places considerable limitations on devices used for stimulus presentation and behavioural monitoring. Typically a projector is placed outside the room, aimed through a hole in the shielding wall towards a (non-electronic) screen in front of the participant. The hole in the wall does not allow magnetic interference to enter because it is designed around a **waveguide**, a metal tube whose diameter-to-length ratio is designed to prevent electromagnetic fields from passing through it. Waveguides are also used to run any cables in and out of the shielded room; however, any metal wires running through the waveguide can act as antennae to carry in electromagnetic interference. To prevent this, many response devices (such as button boxes) are available that rely on fibre optic technology rather than electricity. Acoustic stimulation can be another challenge. Speakers inside the room can be a source of electromagnetic noise, and typical headphones are unusable because they use electricity and/or magnets to drive the speakers, which are located next to the head. As with EEG, specialized headphones that use air conduction through small tubes can be used to keep the electromagnetic generators of the sound far from the participant. Speakers can be used if properly designed and shielded, and kept as far away from the MEG scanner itself as possible. It is also important to realize that many sources of electromagnetic interference, such as cellular phones and computers, should not be brought into the MEG scanner room even when a scan is not taking place. The fields generated by these can negatively affect the MEG scanner and it may take considerable time for these effects to dissipate, and/or recalibration of the MEG sensors may be required.

Physiological Noise

Another significant source of noise is the participant being scanned. Eye movements, blinks, and muscle artifacts are detected by MEG as they are by EEG, and similar approaches to controlling them can be used, including providing the participant with instructions as to when not to blink, and recording EOG. Muscle activity can be recorded using EMG electrodes if much muscle activity is expected during parts of the scan where the neuroimaging data are of interest, though it is not routinely recorded otherwise. Cardiac artifact is another significant source of noise in MEG (see Figure 5.7), and so EKG (electrocardiogram) recordings should ideally be obtained as well for artifact removal. Any metal on the participant can be a source of magnetic noise, for two reasons. One is that metal objects may have become magnetized over time, and thus generate magnetic fields of their own. The other reason is that any metal moving in the magnetic field will generate artifacts. Thus as the participant moves (including breathing), any metal on their body or clothing creates artifacts. Thus participants should remove all jewellery and other metal prior to entering the MEG recording room, as well as any clothing that has metal on it such as buttons, snaps, or zippers. Under-wire brassieres are also a source of noise (since the metal wire moves with every breath) and so female participants should be advised to wear a different type of undergarment when coming for their MEG scan.

Some participant-related artifacts are unavoidable. Dental work that contains metal, including braces, wires, posts, bridges, and some types of fillings, can be a problem and some people with these items are simply not eligible for MEG scans. Implanted metal plates or pins, especially in the head, can also be a problem, and implanted electronic devices such as pacemakers, cochlear implants, deep brain stimulators, and insulin pumps should not even go close to the MEG scanner. Another potential source of noise, which may be surprising to some people, are personal beauty products. Many types of make-up, hair products, and tattoos have metal particles in them that can affect magnetic recordings. Participants should be advised not to use any make-up or leave-in hair products prior to coming for a MEG scan, and should be asked about tattoos.

Prior to starting the MEG experiment, the participant should be placed in the MEG and the data quality examined. This can help determine whether questionable factors such as dental work are an issue for that individual. If artifacts are detected, steps should be taken to attenuate these if possible. For example, a demagnetizer (de-Gausser) can be used to attempt to 'scramble' residual magnetization in implanted metal items. This may or may not be effective, and improper use may increase, rather than reduce magnetization. As well, the demagnetizer can exert magnetic force on implanted ferromagnetic objects so it should not be used if there is a danger of the implanted metal moving, and it should never be used near implanted electronic devices.

Signal Processing

Many of the steps of data preprocessing and analysis are similar for MEG data as for EEG data. It is common to filter the data to a narrower range than was used during online recording, to segment the data into epochs around event codes of interest, and to perform artifact rejection or correction to remove ocular and other artifacts. However, there are other steps that are specific to MEG data. Often additional data, such as continuous head-motion tracking and data from noise sensors built into the MEG scanner, are not automatically used for artifact correction during data recording; rather these corrections are applied in an offline step after the scan is completed. These are usually done in software specific to the MEG vendor and so it is best practice to perform these corrections prior to other preprocessing steps.

It is possible to analyse MEG sensor-level data in the same ways that EEG/ERP data are analysed; for example, by computing peak or mean amplitudes within specific time windows of interest and performing statistical comparisons between conditions. However, for MEG systems with more than one type of sensor, this analysis would have to be performed twice: once for the magnetometers/axial gradiometers, and once for the planar gradiometers (note that although planar gradiometer data are recorded from orthogonally oriented pairs of sensors, these are typically combined for analysis into a single 'root mean square' measure which always has a positive sign, and represents the overall magnetic field strength across the planar gradiometers at a given location). This results in multiple measures of the same effect, which will have different scalp distributions and may vary in magnitude between sensor types. This could result in challenges for interpretation since it could be difficult to tell simply from the sensor-level data whether effects with similar timing were the same effect (from the same brain generators) reflected differently by the different patterns of sensitivities of each type of MEG sensor, or distinct effects. While there are multivariate analysis approaches that could integrate data from multiple sensor types into one analysis, this is not common practice. An additional consideration when averaging data across individuals is that while EEG electrodes are applied in a set of standardized locations that are defined relative to the size of each person's head – and so should approximately lie over the same brain regions across individuals – with MEG the sensors are in fixed locations, and the head is free to move inside the scanner. Thus the position of a given MEG sensor relative to a particular brain region may vary much more between individuals than the position of an EEG electrode. Since MEG data are more amenable to source localization than EEG data (especially for systems with both axial and planar gradiometers) – and source localization potentially provides richer information about the neurocognitive processes of interest – it is increasingly common for MEG researchers to perform source localization and focus solely on those results for data analysis and reporting. There are a number of different approaches to source localization, however, which may not give consistent results. Thus it is essential for MEG researchers to understand the fundamentals of how the different source localization algorithms work, and their strengths and limitations. This is what we discuss in the next section.

Source Localization

The basic concepts of source localization were introduced in the preceding chapter on EEG. In this chapter we will go into detail on some of the more common methods for performing source localization. It is important to emphasize a certain level of caution when interpreting source localization results, both as a researcher and as a consumer of the research literature. In spite of the fact that the physics of magnetic field propagation and MEG sensors mean that source localization solutions are better-constrained for MEG than EEG, all of the methods available are estimations or possible solutions, based on certain assumptions about the data. The mere fact that multiple solutions are available – and under active development – should be an indication that there is no one 'right' solution, and that any solution may not be correct. This means that the localization information provided by MEG should not be considered as reliable or accurate as that provided by fMRI or PET. While those techniques have their own limitations, the means by which activity is localized are universally accepted and do not rely on untested assumptions.

While the developers of MEG source localization algorithms spend considerable time and effort to test and validate these approaches, the tests themselves are subject to limitations. Firstly, there is no way to know what the 'ground truth' is. It is common to evaluate source localization algorithms using data collected from simple paradigms such as finger-tapping or presenting a simple visual stimulus such as a black-and-white checkerboard, or auditory pure tones. Since the locations of primary motor and sensory cortices are well known, it is comparatively easy to validate the accuracy of these approaches. Indeed, since within primary motor and sensory cortices there are reliable topographic organizations – such as the retinotopic organization of visual cortex whereby there is a mapping between locations in the visual field and locations on the occipital cortex – one can do more than simply confirm localization to the generally correct brain region, testing whether the algorithm accurately represents the known organizational patterns of a given region. However, the fact that a particular algorithm is accurate and reliable for such straightforward motor and sensory paradigms does not necessarily entail that it is accurate for other patterns of brain activity. For example, if multiple generators in different parts of the brain are simultaneously active, there is no guarantee that an algorithm will produce correct results simply because it performs well in a simple, single-generator experiment.

Another approach to testing source localization algorithms is to use simulated data, in which the sources are precisely known because they are set by the experimenter. Commonly noise is also added to these datasets (ideally noise recorded from a MEG scanner, for example from someone sitting in the MEG scanner but not performing any task). This is a more powerful way of testing accuracy, in the sense that the ground truth is known, but the accuracy of an algorithm with one set of simulated data may not generalize to other sets of data – for instance, simulated data with sources in different locations, different properties of the noise, or individual differences in head shape. With simulations, however, it is possible to systematically move the simulated source throughout the brain to assess the accuracy of the algorithm at every possible location. While any approach has limitations, the simulation approach is the most widely used method for testing and comparing source localization algorithms.

Another possible validation approach, for paradigms where more complex patterns of activation are expected, is to compare source localization results with data from other techniques, such as fMRI, neuropsychological, and intra-operative mapping studies. While these can certainly be used to guide expectations regarding MEG source localizations, there is no guarantee that MEG will be sensitive to all or even the same set of active regions as these other techniques. Each technique has a unique 'sensitivity profile' to the types and locations of activity. For example, fMRI might detect activity in a closed field configuration of neurons that MEG is blind to. Recall as well that the physics of magnetic field propagation, as well as individual differences in brain anatomy, entail that MEG is not equally sensitive to activation in every part of the brain – MEG is primarily sensitive to activity along the banks of cortical sulci. However, this does not mean that MEG is entirely insensitive to deeper sources – merely that it is less sensitive, and that the variability in sensitivity between individuals will increase with distance from the sensors. Noise levels are also variable across participants and noise can contribute significantly to the (in)accuracy of source localization.

None of this is to suggest that source localization is inappropriate or non-scientific. It is merely to encourage an appropriate level of critical evaluation when viewing and interpreting source localization results. Source localization algorithms can be thought of as ways to model the data, based on certain assumptions. As with any model, these are possibly wrong, but are nevertheless a representation of the data given to them. It is always useful to both understand the assumptions made by the source localization algorithm, and to evaluate the results of any one study in light of the larger literature to determine whether there is converging evidence to support the results. In what follows we will discuss a number of different source localization approaches that are widely used. This is not an exhaustive review, and a failure to mention any particular approach does not imply anything about its validity. The goal here is to provide the reader with a conceptual understanding of classes of approaches that they are most likely to encounter in the lab and in the literature, and how these approaches differ from each other.

General Issues in Source Localization

There are a number of factors to consider that may affect the accuracy of any source localization approach. One has to do with the shape of the head and brain. The simplest approaches to source localization treat the head as a set of concentric spheres – representing the surface of the brain, the skull, and the scalp (and possibly other tissues such as the dura mater covering the brain). Assuming a spherical shape makes the mathematical computations simpler; however, it is clear by simply looking at anyone's head that this is an incorrect assumption that may result in inaccuracies. An alternative is to use a realistically shaped head model. A common approach to realistic head modelling is to use a standard reference model obtained from averaging the anatomical MRI scans of a large number of people ('standard' reference brains for this purpose are readily available and widely used in this field, as discussed in more detail in the chapters on MRI). Besides more accurately representing the shape of the head, having an anatomical MRI also allows one to place further constraints on the source localization algorithm: if we assume that the recorded MEG activity was generated only in the grey matter of the cerebral cortex, then there are many fewer possible locations for dipoles to be located and the inverse solution thus becomes somewhat less ill-posed – although there are still in principle many possible forward solutions that could generate a particular pattern of sensor-level data. An important consideration is that simulation studies using a single, standard head-shaped model cannot take into account how the increased variability stemming from individual differences in brain size and shape may affect the results. However, the most accurate models use an anatomical MRI scan of the actual person from whom the MEG data being used for source localization were obtained. This obviously depends on having access to an MRI scanner as well as MEG, and the necessary funds to perform both types of scans, which can substantially increase the cost and logistical complexity of the study.

The benefits of using a realistically shaped head model vary with the source localization algorithm used. A study (Tarkiainen, Liljeström, Seppä, & Salmelin , 2003) using simulated MEG data with real MEG noise compared source localization accuracy for spherical and realistically shaped models, with and without information on the conductivity of the different tissues (since conductivity, particularly of the skull, will affect the recorded data). The authors found that the amount of noise and the depth of the source had a greater impact on source localization accuracy than the choice of head model, and that while the most realistic models yielded the most accurate localizations, the gains in accuracy were typically on the order of only a few millimetres. This level of variability is unlikely to meaningfully impact the interpretation of the results, since this is at the limits of the spatial resolution of MEG or EEG anyway. However, a limitation of this study was that it used only a single point source in each simulation, localized using a very simple approach (dipole modelling, which is described below). It is therefore uncertain whether the results generalize to more realistic cases with multiple active sources; one study that addressed this question concluded that the benefits of more realistic head models become more pronounced when multiple sources are active (Lalancette, Quraan, & Cheyne, 2011). As well, some approaches to source localization, such as the distributed source models discussed below, depend critically on having a realistic head model.

Beyond shape, another consideration is what tissues in the head to model. The primary goal in modelling the tissues in the head (other than the cortical surface) is to determine how the propagation of electrical currents or magnetic fields is affected by the tissues. Tissues with low conductivity (most notably the skull, but also the scalp) attenuate and smear electrical signals particularly; magnetic fields are also somewhat affected by the skull. It turns out that what affects signal propagation is specifically the boundaries between different tissue types. For this reason, head models used in source localization are called **boundary element models (BEMs)**, and these model the surfaces of tissues as thin layers, rather than explicitly modelling the thickness of each layer. This can be seen in Figure 5.10, which shows an example of a realistic, three-layer BEM. Note that the skull is not represented as a single layer, but rather that the inner and outer layers of the skull (the boundaries) are separately modelled. A three-layer BEM like this would typically be used for EEG source localization, whereas a single-layer model (the inner skull) would be sufficient in MEG source localization, because the magnetic fields are not differentially affected in any significant way by the different tissue types.

Noise in the data can also have a significant impact on the accuracy of source localization – perhaps more than the choice of head model or source localization algorithm. Thus it is advisable to perform any steps that can be done to improve the SNR of the data, prior to source localization. This includes standard preprocessing procedures such as filtering, and artifact removal or correction. Tarkiainen and colleagues (2003) found that increasing the level of low-pass filtering from 100 to 40 Hz (thus removing more high-frequency noise) resulted in increased localization accuracy when using dipole fitting, and that this effect was more pronounced as the depth of the sources from the cortical surface increased. Another way to improve SNR is to average across trials, since SNR increases with the square root of the number of trials in the average. This can improve localization accuracy for some methods, such as dipole fitting (the first method discussed below), but it may be counter-productive for other methods, such as beamformers (discussed later) – the accuracy of beamformer calculations increases with the amount of data provided, and so including all of the individual trials rather than the average can actually increase accuracy (though see Brookes et al., 2010 for a method that uses trial averaging to improve the accuracy of beamformers to distinguish activity at nearby locations). This underscores the

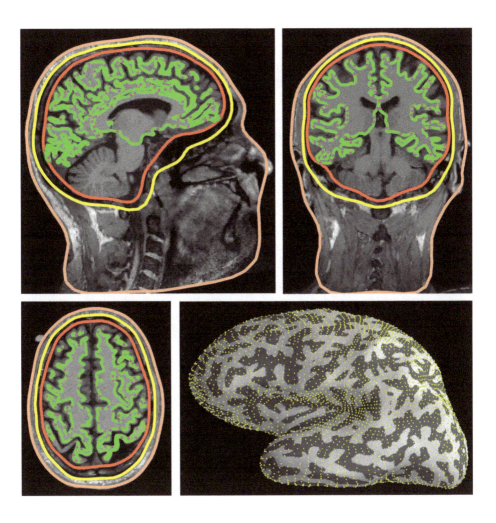

Figure 5.10 Example of a three-layer boundary element model of the head, combined with a cortical surface model, for use in source localization. The layers are defined from a T1-weighted anatomical MRI scan. The two top panels and bottom left panel show the three layers of the head that are modelled: the skin (pink), outer skull (yellow), and inner skull (red). Note that for the purposes of mathematical modelling, each layer is represented as a continuous, closed surface – so even though the skull does not actually surround the brain completely, it is modelled even beneath the brain, inside the head; likewise the 'skin' layer connects along the bottom of the field of view of the MRI scan, even though this is actually inside the neck of the person. The green layer represents the outer surface of the white matter (which is also the inner surface of the cerebral cortex). Note that this is not one of the layers of the head model but rather the surface on which dipoles would be modelled; the three layers of the head model are used to estimate how signals are altered as they pass across those boundaries between different tissues. The bottom right panel shows an inflated view of the cortex of the left hemisphere. The purple dots in the head model panels, and the yellow dots in the inflated surface view, represent the dipoles modelled on the cortical surface

importance of understanding how a particular source localization algorithm works prior to attempting to use it. Regardless of whether trials are averaged or not, it is clearly advisable to include as many trials as possible for each experimental condition in a study design, and ideally equal numbers of trials in each condition.

Some researchers go further and perform source localization on data averaged across all participants in a study, rather than averaging the data after performing source localization on each individual. This practice introduces several concerns, however. Firstly, since each individual's head will have been in at least a slightly different location in the MEG scanner, simply averaging data from each sensor across subjects will introduce accuracy errors because the position and distance of a given point in the brain from each sensor will vary across individuals. Some correction for head position would need to be performed using data from the head position indicators. As well, each individual's head and brain are a different size and shape, so ideally at a minimum some scaling for head size (based on the head shape digitization performed at the beginning of the scan) should be performed. Better yet, **spatial normalization** – an approach that involves not only scaling but actually adjusting the shape of each individual's brain to match the reference brain – would be performed. However, any of these adjustments to the data can introduce error and thus reduce the accuracy of the source localization for that individual. These normalization steps would of course still need to be performed after source localization in order to average data across subjects, but at least if the source localization is performed first, its accuracy will not suffer from the normalization procedure. Thus in the end, it is not obvious that the gains in SNR from averaging across individuals would offset the errors introduced by the steps necessary to allow such averaging.

Dipole Modelling

Perhaps the simplest and most long-standing approach to source localization is based on the assumption, discussed in the chapter on EEG, that electrical brain activity can be modelled by dipoles. Technically, a dipole is a point source, meaning it is infinitely small, exists at a particular location in the brain, and has negative and positive poles of equal electrical strength with some orientation. Several examples of simple dipole models were shown in the EEG chapters. In practice, of course, we know that one of these assumptions is not true: the sources of electrical activity in the brain that we can measure with MEG or EEG are not infinitely small, but rather are collections of many hundreds or thousands of neurons (mostly pyramidal cells) whose electrical potentials vary in polarity between their soma (cell bodies) and axons. However, a point dipole located in the centre of such a collection of neurons is a fairly reasonable simplification.

In essence, dipole modelling is an iterative process that involves placing a dipole at a particular location inside the head and assigning to it a particular orientation and strength, then computing the forward solution to determine its expected scalp topography (or more precisely, sensor-level data). This scalp topography is then compared to the actual data and the difference between the predicted and actual data are computed. This gives a measure of the goodness-of-fit. Then, one of the parameters of the dipole (location, orientation, or strength; technically each dipole has six parameters because location is specified along three dimensions, and orientation along two) is changed slightly (usually by a pre-specified amount, but in a randomly chosen direction), the forward solution is again computed, and the difference between this topographic map and the real data are computed again. If the goodness-of-fit generated by this set of dipole parameters is better than the previous iteration (that is, a smaller difference between the model and the data), then a further change of the same parameter, in the same direction, is made and the goodness-of-fit again calculated. If the goodness-of-fit is worse, the preceding model is returned to, and a different change in parameters is made (for example, a change of the same parameter in the opposite direction, or change of a different parameter). This process is repeated until the best fit is determined – the model that generates the smallest difference from the actual data. This process is called **least squares estimation** because the metric used is actually the square of the difference between the model and the data (which is done because this elegantly eliminates negative values, resulting in measures of the absolute size of the difference regardless of which quantity is larger), and the goal is to find the minimal (least) squared difference.

While this model-fitting process is relatively straightforward, in practice it is much more complicated and subject to uncertainty. First of all, there is a very large set of possible dipole locations, orientations, and strengths, and because the inverse problem is ill-posed, many of these possible combinations could produce equally good fits to a particular dataset. Typically the researcher makes an assumption as to where the dipole is located and how it is oriented based on prior literature or other information. However, without an exhaustive search it is possible for the algorithm to get 'caught' in a **local minimum** – a set of parameters that does not generate the absolute best goodness-of-fit, but simply the best fit given a particular set of starting parameters and a particular set of (randomly selected) changes to those starting parameters. One way to avoid local minima is to run the algorithm repeatedly – since different random selections of parameters should not all end up at the same local minimum. Different sets of starting parameters can also be tested to determine whether they converge on a common solution. However, recall that by definition the inverse problem is mathematically ill-posed because there are a potentially infinite number of possible dipole solutions that could generate the same pattern of sensor-level data. Thus some guesses about dipole location – and constraints on how far the dipole can move from that starting location – are necessary in order to find a unique and reasonable best-fitting solution. At the same time, the need to pre-specify dipole locations means that dipole fitting is operator-dependent, and thus the results can differ depending on who is using the algorithm and what assumptions s/he makes. One advantage of having MEG data obtained from multiple sensor types (both axial gradiometers and orthogonal pairs of planar gradiometers, and possibly EEG as well) is that the known lead fields of these different types of sensors can impose additional constraints that help 'triangulate' the dipole location(s) and reduce the number of possible solutions.

Another problem with dipole fitting is that for many experimental conditions and brain states it is likely – if not guaranteed – that more than one area of the brain is involved in generating the measured pattern of activity. A single dipole model is at best usually only valid for specific types of simple conditions, such as a small stimulus presented in a particular part of the visual field or movement of a single finger. Thus ideally the experimenter should have an idea of how many dipoles to use and roughly where each is located, which is in most cases unknown. Changing the number of dipoles can significantly alter the results of dipole fitting; for example, the best-fitting single-dipole solution for activity generated by a pair of brain areas is a dipole located midway between the two true sources. Thus assumptions made in this regard can significantly influence the results and lead to erroneous interpretations. One could still implement a 'multi-start' approach that involves fitting many different models comprising different numbers of dipoles and starting locations. However, again because of the ill-posed nature of the inverse problem, as the number of parameters increase there is increasing likelihood that two or more very different models will have comparable goodness-of-fit values. A priori predictions can be used to guide the number and starting locations of dipoles, but this again raises the issue of operator dependence. If the assumptions made are incorrect, the dipole solution will likely be as well.

Distributed Source Models

Distributed source models take a very different approach from dipole modelling, although at their heart they are actually based on the same principle: computing a forward solution based on dipoles and comparing this to the data. The critical difference from dipole modelling is that distributed source models simultaneously fit a dipole at every location on the cortical surface, rather than making assumptions about the number of dipoles and where they should be. Finding the optimal source solution then depends on determining what the optimal strength (signal amplitude) of each dipole is to best match the observed data. This approach accounts for the fact, known from other imaging methods such as fMRI, that brain activation is rarely as focal as a single dipole model would suggest, and in fact is often distributed over relatively large (up to several square centimetres) areas of cortex.

Although technically a distributed source model could be computed for a 3D matrix encompassing the whole space inside the head, virtually all available approaches constrain the model to locations that are neurobiologically plausible, such as the cerebral cortex. The first step in computing a distributed source model is thus to create a model of the surface of the brain (either from a standard brain or the individual's anatomical MRI) and **tessellate** it – a process of representing the surface as a set of roughly equally sized triangles (with the variability in their size being driven by the need to fit as best as possible to the shape of the brain surface). This is shown in Figure 5.11. A dipole is then placed at each of the vertices (corners) of these triangles. The spatial resolution of the model is determined by the number of triangles and vertices; typically there are in the order of 10,000 vertices, resulting in a resolution of 5–10 mm, which is reasonable given the effective spatial resolution of MEG and time required for computation. An important consequence of this large number of dipoles is that distributed surface models are inherently underdetermined – that is, there are more parameters to estimate than there are independent sources of data (the MEG sensors; at best there may be ~300 sensors). The mathematical consequence of this is that, like the inverse problem in general, the distributed source solution is ill-posed and has an infinite number of possible solutions. In order to make the solution tractable, constraints need to be applied – known mathematically as **regularization**. One constraint that is already implied by using a cortical surface model is that the range of possible solutions is limited to the surface of the brain, but this constraint is insufficient. Additional constraints are needed, and different distributed source models differ primarily in their approaches to regularization.

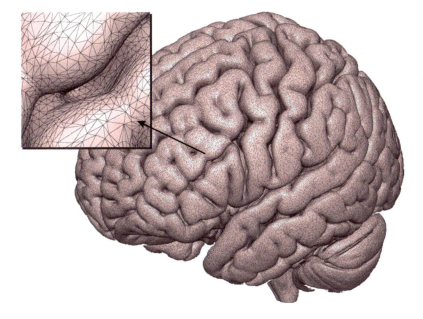

Figure 5.11 A tessellated cortical surface. The smooth, continuous cortical surface is represented as a set of discrete triangles, defined by a set of points on the cortex (vertices). The size of each triangle can vary according to the shape of the brain. The inset at top left shows a zoomed view of the region indicated by the arrow. Image produced using the Surf Ice software package (www.nitrc.org/projects/surfice)

One distributed source modelling approach is known as **minimum norm estimation (MNE)**. The primary regularization used by this approach is to assume that the correct solution is the one that minimizes the overall difference between the data and the model, while keeping the average amplitudes of the entire set of dipoles to a minimum. Because signal strength drops non-linearly with depth from the surface of the brain, a consequence of MNE is that it is biased towards solutions where most of the activity is on the outer surface of the brain. Modern implementations of MNE thus employ an additional regularization, a parameter which 'penalizes' shallow sources in favour of deeper ones (Lin, Witzel, Ahlfors, Stufflebeam, Belliveau, & Hämäläinen, 2006). Correct tuning of this parameter produces relatively even sensitivity to sources of varying depths, at least within the cortex; this regularization cannot fully compensate for the fact that MEG is inherently less sensitive to deeper sources. Another regularization that can be applied is **noise normalization**. This approach recognizes that noise levels may not be the same at every dipole across the surface of the brain, and converts the data to z statistics by dividing the estimated strength by the variance of that estimate, at each dipole individually. Two commonly used versions of noise normalization are **dynamic statistical parametric mapping** (dSPM; Dale et al., 2000) and **standardized low-resolution brain electromagnetic tomography** (sLORETA; Pascual-Marqui, 2002). Figure 5.12 shows an example of a dSPM solution.

Distributed source models have advantages over dipole modelling because they do not suffer from operator dependence in specifying the number and starting locations of the dipoles, and seem to better fit our understanding that brain activity in many experimental paradigms is not highly focal but rather distributed. However, all of these techniques are inherently low resolution, and likely overestimate the spatial extent of activation in many cases.

Beamformers

Beamformers are a class of signal-processing technique originally developed for radar, but which have been found to have applications in a wide variety of domains. A **beamformer** is a spatial filter – effectively a set of weights (multipliers) applied to the data from each MEG sensor – such that the signal from every location in the brain volume other than the region of interest is suppressed (Baillet, 2011; Barnes, Hillebrand, Fawcett, & Singh, 2004; Brookes et al., 2008, 2010; Hillebrand & Barnes, 2005). This is based on models of how a signal propagates from each location in the brain to each sensor. As with distributed source models, beamformers can fit dipoles only along the pre-specified, tessellated cortical surface, or they can operate on a three-dimensional grid whereby the space inside the head is sampled with a consistent spatial resolution by first dividing it into **voxels** (cube-shaped 'volume pixels') of a consistent size, typically 1–4 mm on each side of the cube. Then, for each voxel (or a subset of voxels deemed to be of interest), the appropriate weighting matrix is computed to filter out the signal from all other locations, leaving the time series data associated with that particular location. Each source location in a beamformer analysis is often called a **virtual electrode**. Just as with dipole or distributed source models, beamformers assume a dipole at each location in the head where source modelling takes place. But whereas distributed source models attempt to find the optimal balance of dipole strengths across the entire set of dipoles simultaneously to model the sensor-recorded data, beamformers instead use the forward solutions from voxels of non-interest to build the spatial filters – essentially characterizing the data from the voxel of interest as what cannot be attributed to the dipoles at other locations. Nevertheless, each voxel in the beamformer result is still a dipole with a

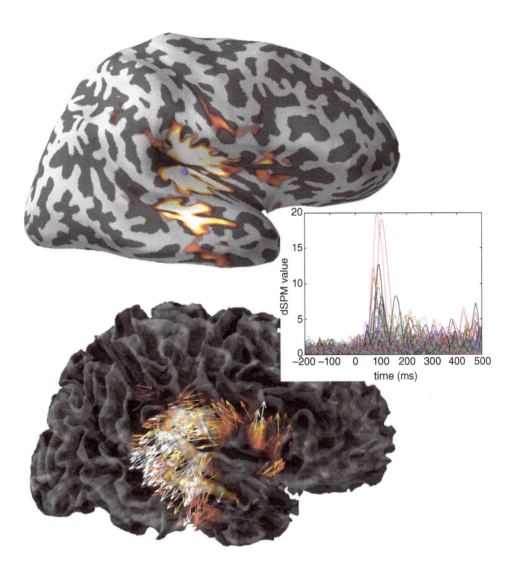

Figure 5.12 Example of a distributed source model, using dSPM noise normalization. The top panel shows the inflated cortical surface of the right hemisphere, with areas showing activation levels above a statistical threshold shown with a colour scale indicating intensity of activation ranging from red (weaker) to yellow (stronger). Consistent with the fact that the data are from an auditory stimulation experiment, the activation is focused in the superior temporal lobe. Time courses from the 100 strongest dipoles on the cortical surface are shown in the middle bottom panel. The bottom panel shows the same source localization solution, but uses arrows positioned at each of the distributed sources to represent the orientation of the dipoles; the colour still represents activation intensity. For this figure the cortical surface is not inflated, as this would distort the dipole orientations. Data are from the 'sample_audvis_raw' example dataset recorded at the MGH/HMS/MIT Athinoula A. Martinos Center Biomedical Imaging and available in the MNE-Python software package (Gramfort, 2013)

particular strength and spatial orientation. An example beamformer result is shown in Figure 5.13.

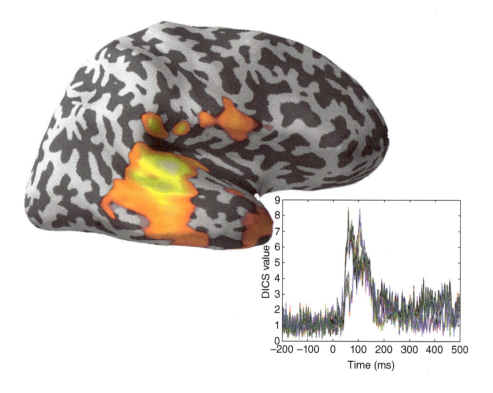

Figure 5.13 Results of a beamformer applied to the same auditory stimulation dataset as the distributed source solution shown in Figure 5.12. This used a type of beamformer known as dynamic imaging of coherent sources (DICS) (Gross, Kujala, Hamalainen, Timmermann, Schnitzler, & Salmelin, 2001). Time courses for the 30 strongest dipoles are plotted in the bottom right panel. Data are from the 'sample_audvis_raw' example dataset recorded at the MGH/HMS/MIT Athinoula A. Martinos Center Biomedical Imaging and available in the MNE-Python software package (Gramfort, 2013)

Because they can sample the entire space inside the head systematically, beamformers can be performed using a spherical head model – in contrast to distributed source models which require a model of the surface of the cortex. However, the accuracy of beamformers increases if the head model is more representative of the head of the actual person whose data is being source-localized, so constraining the source localization to the cortical surface using the individual's own anatomical MRI is likely to increase accuracy. On the other hand, a more detailed but inaccurate head model, or poor registration between the MEG sensor locations and the head model, can result in lower accuracy (Hillebrand & Barnes, 2003).

As with distributed source models, the SNR of beamformers get worse with increasing distance from the sensors (towards the centre of the head), and the approach for compensating that is regularization. A side effect of this regularization is a loss of effective spatial resolution as depth increases; however, this is also an inherent limitation of the MEG technique itself.

The use of spatial filters allows source imaging at a very fine resolution with beamforming; however, this has a potentially negative consequence. Because the spatial filter suppresses activity that is detected at locations other than the target voxel, if there is a high correlation between the activity at the target voxel and some other location in the brain, then the spatial filter will remove that activity from its estimate of the activity at the target voxel. In other words, if the activity of two sources are highly correlated over time, then beamforming will be poor at detecting them, or may not detect them at all. However, beamformers are robust to partial correlations, and so this limitation is only true in cases where the data are quite highly correlated (although there is no hard-and-fast rule, correlations over 0.5 would typically be considered 'high'; however, this also depends on the strength and SNR of the source). Even for highly correlated sources, correction algorithms have been developed. It is also the case that even when two brain areas show correlation, the strength of this correlation is typically not consistent over time. As a consequence, the use of longer-duration segments of MEG data when computing beamformers will decrease the likelihood of this type of error. This issue of correlated sources becomes important particularly for research studies interested in 'functional connectivity' – how different brain areas modulate each other. Functional connectivity is typically defined as the correlation between time courses from different brain regions. However, such correlations are commonly weaker than 0.5, so beamformers can still be used for this purpose; as well there are techniques to measure functional connectivity other than linear correlation that can be used. Functional connectivity is discussed in greater detail in the chapter on functional MRI.

It is important to understand that the fact that highly correlated sources may cancel each other out does not mean that beamformers cannot detect activity that is spread out over an area larger than the size of a single voxel. Indeed, Figure 5.13 shows a very smooth, extensive activation, which is typical for beamforming and consistent with the effective spatial resolution of MEG. The distributed source localization results occur because the weighting matrices for adjacent voxels are highly similar (since they are spatial filters for almost the same location), and so there is comparatively little suppression of signals by the beamformer for nearby voxels. The problem of correlated signals described above is with regard to source locations some distance from each other (several centimetres). However, the weighting matrices do by definition differ from voxel to voxel, and so the source signal strength at the voxel exhibiting the highest level of activity within a region will tend to reduce the beamformer-reconstructed activity of the voxels around it. Thus whereas distributed source models may tend to overestimate the spatial extent of activation, beamformers may tend to underestimate it. However, this general observation is highly dependent on the particular source localization algorithm and the parameters used with that algorithm; a comparison of Figures 5.12 and 5.13 suggests that in this case the beamformer resulted in a more spatially distributed solution. A related consequence of the way spatial filtering works is that if there are two activation peaks that are highly correlated and relatively close to each other, the beamformer will erroneously place a single peak of activation in between the two actual sources. However, in practice this may often not be a significant concern unless the activations are very strong and focal. Indeed, another consequence of spatial filtering to be aware of is that beamformer-reconstructed sources with higher levels of activation will be more focal than sources with weaker activity, because the high activation will induce greater spatial filtering of nearby voxels. This again runs contrary to distributed source modelling, where stronger activations may end up being smeared over a larger area.

An important consideration for spatial filtering is that the brain volume must be sampled at a sufficiently high spatial resolution, because if the brain is undersampled, the peak location of activity might be missed (especially if it is relatively focal), and thus filtered out by the beamformer rather than detected. On the other hand, a paradoxical feature of beamforming is that better SNR and a larger number of MEG sensors can actually make signal detection more difficult. This is because both of these factors increase the effective spatial resolution of the beamformer, which in turn increases the likelihood of suppression of nearby signals; in noisier data and/or with fewer sensors, the spatial filter can only act over larger brain regions.

Comparison of Source-Localization Algorithms

Because of the nature of spatial filters, beamformers and distributed source models can be viewed as complementary approaches to source localization, and asking 'which is better?' may be an overly simplistic question (or, alternatively, have an overly complex answer). Distributed source models are generally thought to overestimate the spatial smoothness, and thus spatial extent, of brain activation. Their inherently low spatial resolution makes them unsuited to do high spatial resolution imaging, especially where differential activation of nearby cortical regions is expected – for example, retinotopic mapping in the occipital lobe or tonotopic mapping in the auditory cortex. In contrast, retinotopic mapping has been successfully performed using beamforming (Brookes et al., 2010). On the other hand, distributed source models are unaffected by correlated activity in different brain areas, while beamformers may less reliably detect activity that has multiple peaks over a restricted area, or that is correlated between brain areas that are some distance from each other. As an example of the latter case, a transient, simple auditory stimulus presented to both ears will evoke sensory-related activity in the superior temporal lobes (**primary auditory cortex**) bilaterally. This activity will thus be highly correlated between the two, spatially discrete cortical regions and thus a beamformer would fail to detect either area of activation; though a solution to this is to compute the beamformers for each hemisphere separately (Herdman, Wollbrink, Chau, Ishii, Ross, & Pantey, 2003). One strength of beamformers is that while they are negatively affected by correlated (that is, time-locked) activity between brain areas, they are able to detect consistent activity across trials that is not time-locked to stimulus presentation. This can occur in frequency domain analyses where either there are no time-locking events (such as in data collected during the resting state), or there are consistent changes in power within a particular frequency band after a particular stimulus event, but these changes are not phase-locked – in other words, the peaks and troughs within the frequency band do not consistently line up across trials. Other approaches, which depend on first averaging data across trials to improve SNR, are unable to detect these changes because the averaging process would largely cancel out any changes that are not time-locked to the stimulus events.

Ultimately, the choice of source-localization algorithm, as well as the interpretation of the results should thus be informed by a good understanding both of the strengths and limitations of the technique, and the experimenter's prior expectations concerning the spatial distribution and extent of activation. It is also important to understand that all approaches to source localization are attempts to create a solution to a mathematically ill-posed solution – that is, one that has a virtually infinite number of possible solutions. The mathematical computations and parameters used in any source-localization approach represent one possible solution to the ill-posed problem, based on certain assumptions and extensive testing as to what seems to work best. As a result, different source-localization approaches will almost inevitably lead to at least somewhat different results given the same dataset. This can be seen in comparing Figures 5.12 and 5.13 – although in those two figures the results are broadly consistent with each other, and with prior expectations for cortical responses to auditory stimuli. Determining which the 'right' solution is not straightforward, either. With real data, the ground truth is never known, because each individual, and each dataset, has its own characteristics. Even if one had data from a method with relatively unambiguous localization information, such as fMRI or PET (though see caveats in those chapters concerning localization accuracy), those techniques do not measure the same thing (magnetic fields) as MEG and so could not be relied upon as ground truth. Thus it is important to always keep in mind that source-localization results are models, not literal representations of data, and to take source-localization results with at least a grain of salt (if not more).

EXPERIMENTAL DESIGN

Due to the great similarity in what EEG and MEG measure, and their temporal resolutions, virtually all that was discussed in the previous chapter concerning experimental design for EEG is equally applicable here for MEG. Perhaps the only factor worth mentioning specifically here is that source localization approaches in particular benefit from having larger amounts of data. This includes not only the number of trials, but the number of time points available in each segment or trial epoch. Increasing the number of time points can be achieved both by a high sampling rate (1000 Hz is common for MEG), and longer segment lengths (extending perhaps 1–2 s both before and after the onset of each stimulus). Longer pre-stimulus baseline epochs may be more important for MEG than EEG, for two reasons.

One is that for certain source-localization methods such as beamformers, accurate detection and localization of the signal is related to contrasts between the pre- and post-stimulus epochs, and noise estimates are based on the amount of data available for each of those periods. If fewer data points are present in the pre-stimulus period, estimation of the baseline may be noisier (have higher variance) than for the post-stimulus period, which may be problematic. The same reasoning applies if one wishes to perform a frequency-domain analysis, because calculation of pre- and post-stimulus power in different frequency bands should be done on the same quantities of data, and indeed lower frequencies can only be accurately estimated from longer segments of data. The need for longer baseline periods than in EEG may also inform decisions about SOA (the timing between successive stimuli), to ensure that there is minimal overlap between stimuli in different epochs, or that there is sufficient random variability that subsequent stimuli are not closely time-locked to each other.

Another consideration arises if source localization is of critical importance to the study. As noted earlier in this chapter, MEG does not have uniform sensitivity to sources throughout the brain. It is maximally sensitive to activity occurring in the cerebral cortex close to the surface of the scalp, and less sensitive to deeper structures such as the hippocampus and brainstem. This does not mean that MEG is blind to sources in these locations, but the reduced sensitivity can result in lower spatial accuracy in localizing sources, and/or less ability to detect signals at all. Here again, including as many trials per condition as possible will aid in the ability to detect and accurately localize signals. At the extreme, Parkkonen and colleagues (Parkkonen, Fujiki, & Makela, 2009) demonstrated that it is possible to measure auditory brainstem responses (ABRs) using MEG. ABRs are a sequence of peaks typically recorded using EEG, generated within the first 10 ms after a brief auditory stimulus such as a click is presented. While easily recorded by EEG due to volume conduction of the electrical signals, they were considered a challenge for MEG because they are generated in auditory nuclei deep in the brainstem. Nevertheless, Parkkonen et al. were able to record these signals with MEG – using approximately 16,000 repetitions of the stimulus per subject – and provided evidence from dipole modelling that these signals were in fact generated in the brainstem. While this number of trials is obviously infeasible for many experimental designs (here, each stimulus was a brief 'click' and the experiment took about 30 min), it does illustrate that experimental design can overcome some factors commonly perceived to be inherent limitations of the MEG technique.

In a less extreme example, Riggs and colleagues (Riggs, Moses, Bardouillle, Herdman, Ross, & Ryan, 2009) conducted a recognition memory experiment in which participants viewed 200 images of indoor and outdoor scenes and were later tested for their memory of these images among a set of distractor images. Brain activation in the hippocampus was of interest because this structure is involved both in encoding such images into memory and in later retrieving them, and activation differs between familiar and novel images. Because the hippocampus is buried deep in the medial temporal lobe, it sits far from any MEG sensors and is considered a challenging target for source localization. Riggs and colleagues compared three different approaches to beamformer analysis and were able to recover hippocampal activity, including the predicted differences between familiar and novel images. The analysis approach that worked best operated in the frequency domain, measuring the degree to which the peaks in a particular frequency band (in this case, theta: 4–6 Hz) lined up across trials – a technique called inter-trial coherence (ITC). The authors speculated that this worked better than an approach based on amplitude of the beamformer-derived signal, because amplitude-based measures are penalized more with increasing depth than coherence measures. This experiment demonstrates both the feasibility of using MEG to study activity even in deep sources, and the importance of comparing and understanding different source-localization approaches.

DATA ANALYSIS

In general, MEG data is broadly similar to EEG and approaches to analysis are likewise very similar. The raw data are a set of time series from multiple sensors, which are then preprocessed to improve SNR and then either analysed as sensor data or as source-localized time series. Regardless of whether they are sensor or source data, analysis can occur in the time domain or in the frequency domain. In the time domain, component-based analyses can be conducted in which peak or mean amplitudes within certain time windows (ideally specified a priori) are analysed, or correlations between time series can be conducted to examine functional connectivity. In the frequency domain, both power (amplitude) and coherence (correlation of peaks across trials, and/or between sensors or brain areas) in different frequency bands can be analysed. In general the same statistical approaches can be used for MEG as EEG data, such as *t*-tests, ANOVAs, and other variants of the general linear model. Regardless of the approach used, however, one important consideration is with regard to multiple comparisons. While we touched on it in the previous chapter, here we will discuss this issue in more depth.

The Multiple Comparison Problem

In the previous chapter we described an approach to ERP data analysis called mass univariate analysis, in which between-condition *t*-tests are performed at every electrode and time point. We noted that while this approach is unbiased by predictions about where or when an experimental effect might occur, this comes at the cost of an increased risk of false positives – finding results that meet the threshold for statistical significance simply by chance. This occurs because a conventional p value used in statistical null hypothesis testing sets the probability of such false positive events, and a conventional threshold such as .05 is fine when performing a single test – since 95 times out of 100 a significant result would not be found by chance – but when performing hundreds of tests, it means by definition that 5% of them will appear significant when in fact they are not.

A similar problem exists for most MEG data, regardless of whether source localization is performed or if the sensor-level data is analysed. A typical modern MEG scanner has upwards of 100 sensors, and signals may be more focal at the MEG sensors than at EEG electrodes, because there is less smoothing by the intervening tissues. Thus where in EEG research often multiple electrodes are analysed together in a single region of interest (ROI), this is not as reasonable an approach with MEG. So if one were using a modern MEG system with 100 sensors, each of which had three gradiometers (one axial and two planar), then the analysis would involve 300 comparisons if each sensor was treated independently – multiplied by the number of time points that were being analysed (as noted earlier, data from the pairs of planar gradiometers are often combined prior to data analysis, but this still leaves 200 contrasts to contend with). The problem becomes vastly greater if a distributed-source or beamformer approach is used, as these generate time series at thousands of voxels in the brain.

It is possible to simplify the analysis by reducing the number of statistical comparisons considered, for instance by analysing data averaged over a time window of interest, rather than all time points, and/or at specific sensors or locations in the brain where the effects are expected to be maximal. However, these are not always appropriate for the research question, and even when they are there are likely to still be multiple comparisons, albeit fewer than if all time points and locations were analysed.

There are a number of different approaches to dealing with the multiple comparison problem. The one most commonly taught in introductory statistics classes is the Bonferroni correction, which involves dividing the desired p threshold by the number of tests performed. Thus if one were to perform ten tests with a desired overall p of .05, then one would need to apply a threshold of $p = .05/10 = .005$ to each individual test. This approach is problematic for neuroimaging data, however, since the number of tests is typically in the tens or even hundreds of thousands, and so the resulting p threshold becomes so low as to be difficult to obtain. The Bonferroni approach is thus considered overly conservative for neuroimaging data. In fact there is a good, principled reason not to use Bonferroni correction as this approach assumes that each statistical test is independent of every other test. However, in neuroimaging data we expect that brain activity measured at each voxel in the brain (or at each sensor) is in fact correlated with the data from adjacent and nearby brain regions (or sensors), as well as some more distant areas that are functionally connected to a given brain area – so the individual tests are not truly independent.

One commonly used alternative to Bonferroni correction, both in neuroimaging and other areas (such as genetic microarrays), is the **false discovery rate (FDR)**, introduced by Benjamini and Hochberg (1995) and first applied to neuroimaging by Genovese and colleagues (2002). In brief the approach works by controlling the proportion of discoveries (p values that exceed the desired univariate or single-test threshold, such as .05) that are false positives, based on a ranking of the p values (with the smallest – most significant – p value ranked the highest). Thus the approach is adaptive depending on characteristics of the data, in particular the total number of discoveries but also the total number of tests and the desired level of significance. A number of variants of the FDR approach are available, and have been compared in some papers (Groppe et al., 2011).

A third type of approach uses **nonparametric statistics**. An advantage of nonparametric approaches is that they do not make any assumptions about the variance or other aspects of the data – they are data-driven approaches and merely assume that the data collected are representative of the more general population to which one would want to generalize. They are however more computationally intensive than more familiar (parametric) statistical methods such as ANOVAs and t-tests, and can be less powerful. The two main nonparametric approaches are bootstrapping and randomization methods (Nichols & Holmes, 2001). In both cases, estimates of the activity levels are made many times with different randomized subsets of the data. In **bootstrapping**, the data are randomly sampled with replacement, meaning that the same data point (subject or trial, depending on the level of the analysis) could be represented multiple times whereas other data points could not be present at all in a particular sample. In **randomization** all of the data are used, but on each iteration of the estimation, each data point (typically a trial in a single-subject analysis, or the average across trials for a given condition and subject in a group-level analysis) is randomly assigned to one condition or the other, rather than being assigned to its true condition. In this way, one can estimate how much more likely the difference between the conditions in the true experiment is from any random set of assignments of data to conditions (since if there is no true difference, then the two samples really are random samples from a single population).

In both bootstrapping and randomization approaches, 1000 or more randomized samples are created and a between-condition difference statistic (for the purposes of explanation, we will use t but in principle any statistic can be used) is computed for each sample, at each voxel or sensor. Once this is done, the maximum t value for each sample (that is, across all voxels or sensors in that sample) is found; collectively the values of all of these maximum t values form the **permutation distribution** of this statistic. Assuming a desired p value of .05, the t value is obtained by comparing the conditions using their actual labelling to the permutation distribution; if the actual t value is within (or above) the range of the top 5% of t values in the permutation distribution, we consider this a significant result. Put another way, the threshold for significance is the t value at the 95th percentile of the permutation distribution. This process controls for multiple comparisons because the threshold for significance is defined by the maximum statistic values that are likely to be found by chance, across a very large sample of randomized relabellings of the data – each of which contained the same number of statistical tests as the dataset with the correct labellings. Therefore any t value in the dataset with the actual labelling that exceeds the threshold is considered significant in the face of multiple comparisons. While nonparametric statistics are considered to be more robust for neuroimaging data – including MEG and fMRI – than parametric approaches, an important consideration is that they tend to be less sensitive than parametric methods (Eklund, Nichols, & Knutsson, 2016; Hillebrand & Barnes, 2005), and in some cases considerably less sensitive. In practice, this means that although a researcher can have confidence in effects that are found to be significant using a properly applied nonparametric approach, other effects might be missed, resulting in 'false negatives'.

SUMMARY

Electrical current flow – the movement of charged particles – create a magnetic field according to Ampère's circuital law (also known as the right-hand rule). Because of this, electrical brain activity gives rise to very small magnetic fields that can be measured at the scalp using MEG. Because these magnetic fields – produced by hundreds or thousands of synchronously active neurons arranged in open field configurations – are so small, MEG must be conducted in a magnetically shielded room, and use very sensitive detectors super-cooled in liquid helium. These superconducting quantum interference devices (SQUIDs) can be connected to different types of sensors, which differ in the orientation of magnetic field that they are sensitive to. Magnetometers and axial gradiometers are maximally sensitive to the radial components of magnetic fields as they enter or exit the head. Conversely, planar gradiometers are maximally sensitive to tangential components of magnetic fields, which run parallel to the surface of the scalp. Two planar gradiometers with orthogonal orientations are required to capture the full possible range of tangential magnetic field orientations at a given location. The term 'gradiometer' refers to sensors with one pick-up coil close to the scalp, and another with opposite winding further away from the scalp. Because both the near and far windings will pick up environmental noise, but only the near winding will pick up brain activity, gradiometers help to reduce the amount of environmental noise in MEG recordings. However, shielding the room and elimination of other sources of noise are still necessary, including ensuring that the person being scanned has no metal on their clothing or in their body, and using stimulation and response equipment that does not generate magnetic fields within the shielded MEG recording room.

Because the head fits loosely inside the MEG helmet, the relationship between sensor locations and specific locations on the scalp is less fixed than with EEG. For this reason, it is common to track the head position using head-position indicators, and correct for any movement of the head relative to the MEG sensors during preprocessing. There are limits on the efficacy of this, however, so the head should always remain as still as possible during scanning. This can be a problem for children especially, whose smaller heads pose additional problems because of the greater distance between the brain and the sensors. Another common step in preprocessing that is unique to MEG is correction for environmental noise by subtracting recordings of the noise made by sensors in or around the shielded room, and/or on the scanner itself. Other preprocessing steps are similar to EEG, including filtering and correction or removal of artifacts created by eye blinks, eye movements, and heartbeat.

Although MEG data can be analysed at the sensor level, like MEG, it is more common to perform source localization and interpret the time series data from specific brain locations that show modulation with the experimental manipulation.

This is both because with MEG there are often data from multiple sensors at each scalp location (meaning sensor-level analysis would need to be performed multiple times), and because the physics of magnetic field propagation create more constraints on source localization than with EEG. While electrical potentials volume-conduct through the head, meaning that EEG signals can be strong even far away from their sources, magnetic fields drop off sharply with the square root of distance. As a result, there is somewhat less ambiguity in source localization for MEG than EEG. Three common classes of source localization algorithm are dipole fitting, distributed source models, and beamforming. Dipole fitting can have highly variable results because it is heavily dependent on choices made by the researcher concerning the number, location, orientation, and strength of the dipoles. Distributed source models offer a better solution in many cases because they assume dipoles at every location on the surface of the cerebral cortex, and find the optimal combination of dipole strengths to explain the measured data. This reduces the operator-dependence of the results relative to dipole fitting. However, in some cases – such as with early sensory components that have one or two sources that can be relatively easily predicted (for example, primary auditory cortex) – dipole fitting is a more appropriate and robust approach to use. Beamforming uses the data from all sensors to create a spatial filter that isolates activity originating from a given location in the brain from activity at all other locations. This can be applied to pre-specified regions, or systematically across the whole brain surface (like distributed source models) or whole brain volume (like fMRI). Beamforming can be unreliable when the activity in multiple brain locations is highly correlated, although in most cases this is not an issue. Source localization is highly sensitive to noise and thus requires a high signal-to-noise ratio (SNR). This may necessitate many more trials than would be required for sensor-level analysis or in an equivalent EEG study where source localization was not the goal. As well, longer pre-stimulus baseline periods may be required to obtain low noise in the baseline period, which is necessary to detect significant post-stimulus activation. As well, the sharp drop-off of magnetic field strength with distance means that activity in deep brain regions may be difficult to detect, or require large numbers of trials.

Relative to EEG, MEG has comparable temporal resolution but better spatial resolution due to the physics of magnetic field propagation. As well, set-up time is shorter for MEG than EEG as there is no need to manually lower impedance at every sensor location. However, MEG is significantly more expensive than EEG and so in cases where source localization is not required, EEG may be a better choice.

THINGS YOU SHOULD KNOW

- Whenever an electrical current flows through a conductor, a magnetic field is induced with a spatial relationship described by the right-hand rule. This is how magnetic fields, measured by MEG, are produced by brain activity.

- The basis of the MEG signal is similar to EEG. Like EEG, hundreds or thousands of neurons must experience synchronized changes in polarization, and be

arranged in an open-field configuration, in order to generate a measurable magnetic field at the scalp. Because of the right-hand rule, the distribution of magnetic flux across the scalp will be very different from the distribution of electrical potentials. Differences in scalp topographies between EEG and MEG are further enhanced by the fact that, while electrical signals volume-conduct through the head, MEG signals drop off sharply with distance. Depending on the location and orientation of a neural generator, it might produce measurable EEG and MEG signals, or only one or the other.

- The primary types of MEG sensor are magnetometers, axial gradiometers, and planar gradiometers. Magnetometers and axial gradiometers are primarily sensitive to radial components of magnetic fields, while planar gradiometers are primarily sensitive to tangential components of magnetic fields. Typically, two planar gradiometers with orthogonal orientations are used in each sensor location in order to capture the entire range of possible tangential magnetic field orientations. These sensors all rely on superconducting quantum interference devices (SQUIDs), which must be cooled in liquid helium and well-shielded from external noise.

- MEG is very sensitive to electromagnetic noise from the environment, as well as physiological noise and movement artifacts from the body of the person being scanned. Environmental noise is attenuated through passive or active shielding of the room containing the MEG scanner, as well as by the use of gradiometers (rather than magnetometers), whose design includes reverse-winding loops distal from the head which help cancel out environmental noise that is equivalent at both loops of the gradiometer. Movement artifacts are reduced by ensuring that the person being scanned does not have any metal on their body or clothing (because metal moving through space induces magnetic fields, even simply with breathing). Physiological artifacts, including heartbeat and eye blinks and movements, are removed offline during data preprocessing.

- A number of preprocessing and analysis steps for MEG data are similar to EEG data, including filtering, artifact removal and/or correction, and segmentation into epochs of interest. However, prior to these steps, MEG-specific preprocessing may include correction for head motion (based on recordings made from head position indicators during the scan) and removal of environmental artifacts measured by external sensors during the scan. Unlike EEG data, MEG data are not recorded relative to a reference sensor and so re-referencing is not necessary. Another consideration is that with MEG, there may be more than one data recording at each sensor location; for instance, there may be recordings from an axial gradiometer and two orthogonal planar gradiometers. These may be analysed in parallel, or combined in some way such as in source localization.

- Source localization of MEG data can be somewhat more constrained than for EEG data. This is because the magnetic fields drop off sharply with distance, creating less ambiguity of the depth and location of a generator than with EEG. As well, if multiple sensor types are used (for example, both axial and planar gradiometers), the different sensitivity patterns of these sensor types can be used to further constrain the source localization.

- Three common classes of source-localization algorithms are dipole fitting, distributed source models, and beamforming. Dipole fitting requires pre-specification of the number of sources (dipoles), as well as guesses as to the location, orientation, and strength of each. As a result, the results of dipole fitting may be highly operator-dependent and not replicable. Distributed source algorithms address this issue by fitting dipoles at each of many locations across the cortex, meaning that the user does not need to pre-specify the details of each dipole. Distributed source models tend to produce very blurry, low-resolution solutions. Beamforming can operate either across the brain volume or surface, or on a pre-specified set of locations. Beamforming applies a spatial filter, derived from all sensor data, to isolate the activity originating from a specific location in the brain. The nature of this spatial filtering means that beamforming is less reliable when two or more sources are highly correlated (that is, have similar time courses of activity).

- The considerations for MEG experiment design are similar to EEG, although the fact that the person's head must remain in the MEG helmet, and that the stimulation and response collection equipment must not generate electromagnetic fields, impose some additional constraints on what is possible. Experimenters may also consider including longer pre-stimulus baseline periods in MEG than EEG designs, to reduce the amount of noise in the baseline estimations. Finally, the fact that MEG signal strength drops with distance means that studies investigating activity originating in deep (non-cortical) structures, like the brainstem or hippocampi, may need to average data over far more trials than would be required with EEG to get a reliable signal.

- MEG's greatest strength relative to EEG is that source localization is generally considered more constrained, and thus more reliable. As such, it can be considered to have somewhat higher spatial resolution than EEG. MEG has similar temporal resolution to EEG, and like EEG can be considered a direct measure of neural activity. Disadvantages of MEG relative to EEG are the high costs of the equipment and shielding, as well as the ongoing costs of liquid helium. As well, the SNR of MEG can be low, especially for deep sources or source localization of cognitive (as opposed to sensory) brain activity.

FURTHER READINGS

Hansen, P.C., Kringelbach, M., & Salmelin, R. (Eds.) (2010). *MEG: An Introduction to Methods*. Oxford: Oxford University Press.

Papanicolaou, A.C. (2009). *Clinical Magnetoencephalography and Magnetic Source Imaging*. Cambridge: Cambridge University Press.

Supek, S., and Aine, C.J. (2014). *Magnetoencephalography: From Signals to Dynamic Cortical Networks*. Heidelberg: Springer.

6 Magnetic Resonance Imaging (MRI)

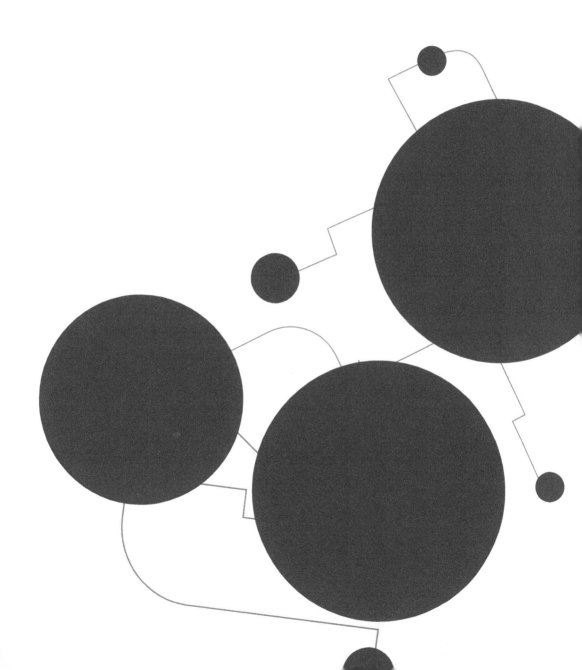

LEARNING OBJECTIVES

After reading this chapter, you should be able to:

- Explain the role that hydrogen ions play in MRI, and describe their physical properties that are relevant to obtaining MR images.
- Define the concepts of the net magnetization vector, precession, and resonance, and how these are influenced by an external magnetic field.
- Explain the process of excitation and how the net magnetization vector is influenced by a radio frequency pulse.
- Define and contrast the processes of T1 recovery and T2 decay.
- Explain how T1 and T2 contrast are obtained in an MRI scan.
- Explain the difference between T2 and T2* decay.
- Identify whether a structural MR image was obtained with T1 or T2 contrast.
- Explain the function of magnetic field gradients in obtaining a 3D MR image, and distinguish the roles of slice selection, frequency encoding, and phase encoding.
- Define the concepts of spatial frequency, 2D Fourier decomposition, and *k* space, and explain their relevance to MR image reconstruction.
- Explain what an MRI pulse sequence is.
- Identify common safety risks of MRI, and explain precautions that should be taken prior to bringing a person within the field of an MRI scanner.

INTRODUCTION

Magnetic resonance imaging (MRI) is a medical imaging technique that has revolutionized both clinical medicine and cognitive neuroscience. Within cognitive neuroscience, MRI scans can be used in many different ways to examine brain structure and function. Functional MRI (fMRI) is far and away the most commonly used functional neuroimaging technique; in any given year there are more than double the number of published papers in Medline referencing this technique than any other technique. The first papers demonstrating functional MRI were published in 1992 (Bandettini, Wong, Hinks, Tikofsky, & Hyde, 1992; Kwong et al., 1992; Ogawa et al., 1992), and since that time use of the technique has exploded. While fMRI has some important limitations, as we will see, it offers highly accurate localization of brain activity without the ambiguities inherent in EEG or MEG source localization. As well, because MRI scanners are able to acquire high-resolution structural scans of the brain in the same session as the functional data, the fMRI data can easily be displayed as coloured activation maps on these images, resulting in compelling images that have highly intuitive interpretations – or at least apparently intuitive interpretations – compared to the 'squiggly lines' of EEG for example. Also contributing to the prevalence of fMRI is the fact that although MRI machines are very expensive, their use in clinical medicine is so widespread that they are fairly ubiquitous and accessible. This means that researchers interested in using fMRI do not have to necessarily raise the funds to purchase the scanners (although the mere presence of an MRI scanner does not mean it is suitably configured for a particular research purpose). In contrast, MEG scanners have roughly comparable price tags but have relatively few clinical indications, and so are a rarity in hospitals, even today. The accessibility and appeal of fMRI led to the development of a large community of users and some relatively established and commonly accepted approaches to data analysis, along with software packages implementing these. In addition to fMRI, a number of other uses of MRI have found widespread application in cognitive neuroscience, in particular diffusion tensor imaging (DTI, which can be used to make inferences about the white matter tracts connecting different brain regions), and morphometry, which attempts to relate features of brain structure to characteristics such as the effects of particular experience (including long-term changes in conditions such as deafness, as well as changes over shorter periods such as in training studies) or disease states (for example, Alzheimer's disease). Because MRI is such a widespread and multi-faceted technique, this book devotes five chapters to the topic, covering the various functional and structural applications of the technique in cognitive neuroscience. But first, it is important to understand the fundamentals of how MRI works in general. This knowledge will help you understand how the different applications of MRI in cognitive neuroscience work, as well as what their limitations are and why these limitations exist.

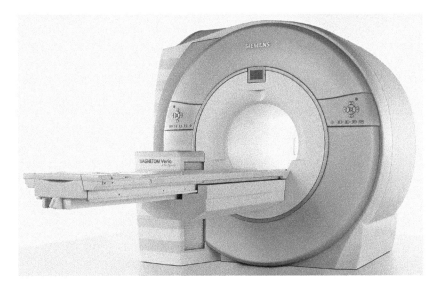

Figure 6.1 A typical MRI scanner. Image copyright Siemens AG, Munich/Berlin; used with permission

WHAT ARE WE MEASURING?

In different applications of MRI, we actually measure different things, such as blood oxygenation (fMRI), the relative amounts of fat compared to water in tissue (structural MRI), the movement of water molecules (diffusion MRI), or the amounts of different chemical compounds (MRI spectroscopy). However, in all of these cases, and indeed in virtually all applications of MRI to human beings, MRI is ultimately measuring energy released from hydrogen (H) atoms. Hydrogen is ubiquitous in the body: our bodies are composed almost entirely of water, and hydrogen is a component of water (H_2O) as well as other important physiological compounds such as glucose and fats. The mechanisms by which MRI scanners are able to produce so many different measures of brain structure and function, all through the hydrogen atom, are fascinating and significantly more complex than the much more direct relationship between electrical activity in the brain and the measurements made by EEG or MEG. Understanding how MRI works will require some appreciation of physics as well as physiology, but the basic concepts can be understood conceptually without requiring a background in mathematics or physics (Hanson, 2008).

Hydrogen Atoms and Magnetic Fields

Hydrogen is the simplest atom in the universe. You may recall that there are three fundamental types of subatomic particles: protons, which have a positive electrical charge; electrons, which have a negative electrical charge; and neutrons, which have no charge. Hydrogen atoms are composed solely of a single proton, whereas other types of atoms include greater numbers of protons, as well as electrons and neutrons. For this reason, in many cases (including the present chapter), the terms 'proton' and 'hydrogen atom' can be used interchangeably. Protons spin constantly around an axis, much as the Earth spins around its axis (this is a general property of atoms that have more protons than neutrons). Continuing our analogy with the Earth, the spin of a proton gives it a **magnetic moment**, meaning that it acts as a magnetic dipole – with poles we can refer to as 'north' and 'south' – and will experience force in a magnetic field. A proton also has a characteristic **angular momentum**, a fundamental characteristic proportional to its inertia and speed. Any atom that has a magnetic moment and angular momentum is considered an **MR-active nucleus**, and could be detected using MRI. However, in practice MRI hardware must be tuned to a particular nucleus, and virtually all MRIs for human use are tuned to hydrogen. A schematic diagram of a spinning proton is shown in Figure 6.2.

Because they have magnetic properties, protons are influenced by external magnetic fields. A useful analogy is a compass, which contains a needle made of a magnetic material. The needle points to north because it aligns itself with the Earth's magnetic field. However, if you bring a stronger magnet near the compass (such as a fridge magnet), the needle will align itself with the position of that

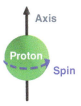

Figure 6.2 A schematic representation of a proton (hydrogen ion), showing its axis and the direction of rotation or spin. This spin creates the magnetic moment (field) of the proton

magnet due to the stronger field. Protons operate essentially like compass needles. Inside the body, the orientation of protons is generally random, as they are influenced by the Earth's magnetic field, but also local, microscopic magnetic fields of other protons, atoms, and molecules in the body. Recall that magnetic field strength drops off exponentially with distance, so even very small magnetic fields can have significant influence over short distances at the atomic level. In the presence of a relatively strong external magnetic field, however, the orientations of the protons will be pulled into alignment with that magnetic field. An essential component of any MRI scanner is a very strong magnet, whose field runs along the length of the bed that the person lies on in the scanner. This strong magnetic field of the MRI scanner is often called B_0. The strength of B_0 is a fixed property of the scanner, and MRIs are typically described by their magnetic field strength, which is measured in Tesla (T). Typical scanners used in cognitive research are 1.5, 3, or 7 T, although lower-field scanners are used in some clinical work, and scanners up to 9 T have been produced for use in human research. By comparison, the Earth's magnetic field is in the order of tens of microTesla (10^{-6} T), and a typical fridge magnet is in the order of tens of milliTesla (10^{-3} T). The field of an MRI system is so strong that the scanner must be kept in a magnetically shielded room, and no ferrous or otherwise magnetic materials can be taken into the room, or they would be drawn into the centre of the MRI at high speed (see also the section on MRI safety at the end of this chapter).

Inside the body, the influence even of the strong magnetic field from an MRI scanner exerts only a relatively weak (though measurable) influence on the orientation of the protons. Thus the orientations of the many protons in the body inside an MRI scanner will still be largely random, but with a slight net overall tendency to be more aligned with the field of the scanner than any other direction. In fact, less than ten out of every million protons is actually aligned with B_0 in a typical human MRI scanner, but this is nevertheless sufficient to create a measurable effect due to the large number of protons in the body (on the order of 10^{27}). The degree of alignment of the protons with B_0 is a function of the strength of the magnetic field, and so stronger MRI systems induce greater alignment of the protons, which ultimately (for reasons discussed below) leads to better signal quality. While the orientation of any individual proton is insignificant in MR imaging, we can compute the net magnitude and orientation of all the protons in a particular sample (such as the entire head, or a smaller portion of it): this is called the **net magnetization vector** (**NMV**). As you are reading this chapter, the NMV of your head is likely to be approximately zero, because your protons have completely random orientations. However, when someone lies in an MRI scanner, the NMV of their body will be aligned with B_0 and thus have a magnitude greater than zero. This is shown in Figure 6.3. This is the essential first step in MR imaging – aligning the NMV of the body with B_0. Subsequent steps involve perturbing this NMV and then measuring the result.

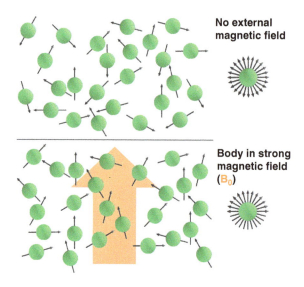

Figure 6.3 The orientation of axes of individual protons is largely random when not in a magnetic field (top). However, when in a strong magnetic field, such as an MRI scanner (bottom), there is a weak tendency of the protons to align with the axis of that external magnetic field (B_0; large orange arrow). The summed orientation of all the protons in a sample can be described by the net magnetization vector (NMV). In the top panel, since all possible orientations of proton are possible (top right), the NMV is essentially zero. However, in a strong magnetic field, the majority of protons will have orientations roughly aligned with the magnetic field, and so the NMV will be non-zero, and oriented parallel to B_0

Precession and Resonance

In the presence of a static magnetic field – B_0 – protons will tend to align their axes with this field. Previously we learned that protons spin around this axis. However, protons also experience a second type of movement, which is a rotating 'wobble' around the central axis. This is called **precession**, and can be visualized as the axis of the proton (the line between its two poles) being tilted slightly away from, and rotating around, the axis of B_0, as shown in Figure 6.4. Moreover, the protons precess at a precise rate, determined by the strength of the magnetic field, according to the **Larmor equation**:

$$\omega = B_0 \times \lambda$$

In this simple multiplication formula, ω is the precessional speed (also known as the **Larmor frequency**, and typically expressed in megahertz – MHz – where 1 MHz = 1000 Hz), B_0 is the strength of the magnetic field, and λ is the **gyro-magnetic ratio**. The gyro-magnetic ratio is a fixed property of any MR-active nucleus relating its magnetic moment to its angular momentum; for hydrogen the value of λ is 42.57 MHz/T. Therefore in the presence of a 1 T MRI scanner, the hydrogen atoms precess at 42.57 MHz; in a 3 T MRI scanner, they precess at $3 \times 42.57 = 127.71$ MHz. Providing you with these numbers may seem very specific, given the conceptual approach of this textbook, and indeed in the day-to-day use of an MRI scanner there's typically no need to know these values. However, the precessional speed of hydrogen atoms is critical to understanding how MRI actually works; this brings us to the topic of resonance.

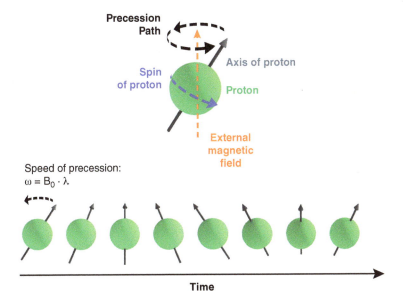

Figure 6.4 In the presence of a strong magnetic field, protons both align with that field, and precess around it. Precession (black dashed arrows) is different from the spin of the proton (dashed blue arrow), and occurs only in the presence of an external magnetic field. The bottom panel shows a proton at different points in its precessional path over time

Resonance is a general phenomenon whereby energy can be transferred from one material to another if both are oscillating at (or tuned to) to the same frequency. Musicians may be intuitively aware of this – for example, if a guitar is sitting on a stand and a key is played on a piano nearby, the corresponding string of the guitar that is tuned to that note will vibrate. In this case, the piano caused oscillating sound waves which had sufficient energy to travel through the air to the guitar, and make its string vibrate. However, only a string tuned to vibrate at the same pitch (frequency) is able to absorb this energy – this is resonance. Another example is pushing someone on a swing: if the pushes are timed synchronously with the movement of the swing, they add energy and help the person swing higher; if, however, the pushes go against the direction of the swing, they slow the swinger. This is essentially the same manner in which MRI scanners work. Protons precess at their resonant (Larmor) frequency, and any energy applied to them at that resonant frequency will be absorbed by the protons, whereas energy at other frequencies has no effect on the protons. In the case of MRI, the Larmor frequency is in the **radio frequency** (RF) range, and so radio waves are used. During MR image acquisition, an RF transmission coil transmits RF energy at the Larmor frequency of hydrogen into the head of the person being scanned, and as a result this energy is absorbed by the protons.

An important feature of radio waves is that, physically, they can be considered magnetic fields that change direction in time. As noted earlier, we induce precession by applying a second magnetic field perpendicular to B_0; we can now say more specifically that in an MRI scanner, it is the radio waves that are transmitted in a plane perpendicular to B_0. Thus there is now 'competition' between B_0 and the RF magnetic field to determine the orientation of the protons.

Thus the result of applying RF energy is that the NMV 'tips' from being aligned with B_0 (also called the **longitudinal plane**) towards being aligned with the **transverse plane** that the RF energy is being transmitted in. This is called **excitation** and is illustrated in Figure 6.5. It is common on MRI scanners to quantify the amount of RF energy used in terms of the **flip angle** of the RF pulse, and so using the amount of energy required to put the NMV in the transverse plane is referred to as a 90° flip angle.

A 90° flip angle is quite common as it generates the maximum possible MRI signal, because the receiver coil that measures the MRI signal is also aligned with the transverse plane. This is illustrated in Figure 6.6. The receiver coil is effectively a loop of conductive wire, and so as the precessing NMV passes through the receiver coil, it induces an electrical current via the right-hand rule, which forms the basis of the MRI signal. The strength of the signal thus depends on the length of the NMV as it projects onto the transverse plane. This is important to understand: the length (size) of the NMV is proportional to the degree to which protons align with B_0; however the length of the NMV projected onto the transverse plane is proportional both to the strength of B_0 and the flip angle. This is shown in Figure 6.5 – although the absolute length of the NMV shown in the figure is the same for the 45° and 90° flip angles, the projection of the NMV into the transverse plane – and thus the strength of the recorded signal – is greater for the 90° flip angle.

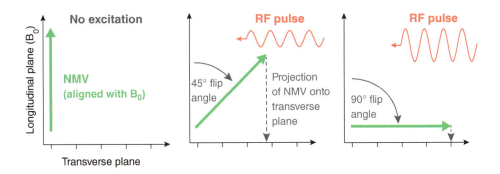

Figure 6.5 Excitation. The left panel shows the NMV of a sample of protons (such as the head) aligned with a strong magnetic field (B_o), which we call the longitudinal plane. Excitation involves applying RF energy at the resonant (Larmor) frequency of the protons in the B_o, and in a plane orthogonal to B_o (the transverse plane). Because RF energy is a time-varying magnetic field, it draws the NMV towards the transverse plane, as shown in the right two panels. This 'flip' of the NMV is proportional to the intensity of RF energy applied, and so RF energy can be quantified in terms of flip angle. Because the MRI signal is recorded in the transverse plane, the magnitude of the MRI signal is proportional to the projection of the NMV into the transverse plane, as shown by the dashed grey arrows. A 90° flip angle creates the maximum recorded MRI signal

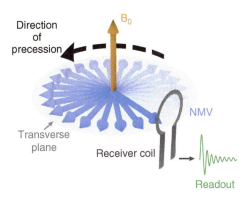

Figure 6.6 Schematic diagram of an MR receiver coil (grey) and its positioning relative to the transverse (B_o, orange) and longitudinal planes of the net magnetization vector. When the NMV is flipped by 90°, precession occurs in the transverse plane, as shown by the blue arrows. Since the receiver coil is oriented in the transverse plane, the magnitude of the recorded signal is proportional to the size of the NMV in the transverse plane

Excitation – the input of RF energy to the body via resonance – actually has two primary effects that are important for MR imaging. In addition to tipping the NMV into the transverse plane, RF energy also causes **phase synchronization** (or **coherence**) of the protons with the RF signal input. Recall that phase refers to the relative positions of the peaks and troughs of an oscillation over time; two waveforms may have the same frequency but have different phase values, as shown in Figure 6.7. In the absence of external RF energy, all of the protons in the head are precessing at the same (Larmor) frequency, but their phases will be random. When an RF pulse is applied, the phases of all of the protons will align with the phase of the input RF pulse, thus becoming coherent. After the RF pulse is turned off, the phases will gradually desynchronize and become random (incoherent) again. The effect of phase synchronization is to create a very strong NMV in the transverse plane. This is because, in addition to being proportional to the strength of B_0, the NMV is affected by the degree of coherence of the phases of all the precessing protons. If the protons are highly incoherent, then the NMV projected into the transverse plane is short, because at any given time some protons' poles are passing over the receiver coil. This results in a weak signal because the signal from some protons is effectively cancelled out by those crossing the receiver coil immediately before or after. In contrast, when coherence is high, all (or really, a majority, as there is always a degree of randomness or noise) of the protons' poles cross the receiver coil at the same time, generating a strong signal, as shown in Figure 6.7.

HOW DO WE MEASURE IT?

These two phenomena, tipping the NMV and phase synchronization, together allow us to obtain MR images. As shown in Figure 6.6, the piece of hardware that collects the imaging data – the MR receiver coil – is positioned such that it only detects the precession of protons when the NMV is in the transverse plane. Thus in the equilibrium (incoherent) state, no measurable signal is detected by this coil since the NMV is aligned with the longitudinal plane. However, when the NMV is flipped into the transverse plane, the coherent precession of the protons is now detectable by the receiver coil. The signal is induced in the coil due to the right-hand rule: the magnetic field created by the precessing protons induces an oscillating electrical current in the coil. This signal would be minimal if the phases of the protons' precession were incoherent, but when they are coherent they summate to induce a large signal in the coil, oscillating at their rate of precession (the Larmor frequency). Thus the 'raw' MRI signal is actually simply an oscillating waveform. How this gets converted into a two- or three-dimensional image is a topic we will cover in the next section, but first we need to explore the nature of this signal a bit more.

At this point we need to introduce the variable of time into our understanding of how MRI signals are obtained. Above we have referred to the RF transmitter being turned on and off, and indeed MR imaging is dependent on rapid and precise alterations of RF energy being transmitted and not. More generally, we can think of the

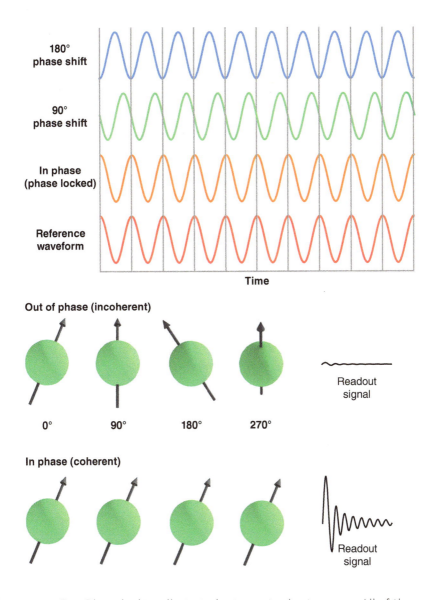

Figure 6.7 *Top*: Phase locking illustrated using a simple sine wave. All of the waves have the same frequency (in this case, 10 Hz, although protons precess much faster in reality). The value of the sine wave at any point in time represents the position of the axis of a proton in its precessional path. Relative to the reference waveform shown at the bottom in red, the orange wave is phase-locked, or 'in sync'; the green waveform is phase shifted by 90°; and the blue waveform by 180°. *Bottom*: schematic of four protons precessing either out of phase or in phase. The waveforms to the right of the proton images show the relative magnitude of the recorded signal: coherent precession results in a much larger signal

process of obtaining an MR image as a **pulse sequence** – a sequence of pulses of RF energy (and as we will learn soon, other events as well) over time. Indeed, the term 'pulse sequence' is used to refer to the type of program run on an MRI scanner that determines what type of images are obtained, and their quality. This can be visualized as the sequence of events occurring over the course of a scan, as seen in Figure 6.8.

A first important thing to note about the pulse sequence in Figure 6.8 – which is true of all MRI pulse sequences – is that the RF transmission is not constant during the scan. Rather, it is on for brief, regular periods. In between these, the signal is read out from the receiver coil. This alternation of excitation and readout is necessary, among other reasons, because reading from the transmission coil when an RF pulse was being applied would simply result in measuring that RF pulse. This alternation is also necessary because the relative timing between RF energy transmission and receiver sampling is critical to determining the type and quality of image obtained.

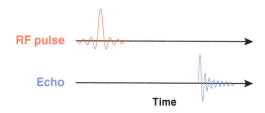

Figure 6.8 A simple MRI pulse sequence diagram, showing the relative timing of an RF pulse and the signal readout from the receiver coil. The readout is called an 'echo' because it is a reflection of the RF pulse

Recall that applying RF energy causes two events: the NMV flips into the transverse plane (assuming a typical 90° flip angle) and the phases of precession of the protons become coherent. As soon as the RF pulse is turned off, the protons begin to revert to their pre-RF-excited state – the NMV begins to tip back towards the longitudinal plane (the axis of B_0) and the phases of the individual protons lose coherence. Collectively, these two phenomena are called **relaxation**, but each phenomenon also has its own name. The return of the NMV to the longitudinal plane is referred to as **T1 recovery**, while the dephasing is known as **T2 decay**. It is important to understand that while these two processes begin at the same time (when the RF pulse is turned off), they are distinct phenomena, and are independent of each other (see Figure 6.9). T1 recovery and T2 decay are influenced by different factors, and they have different time courses – T1 recovery times are typically significantly longer than T2 decay times.

T1 recovery occurs as protons give up their energy to the surrounding environment (the **molecular lattice**). The time course of T1 recovery is an exponentially increasing function, as shown in Figure 6.10, and occurs more quickly in fat than water (as discussed below, we focus on fat and water here because they are the

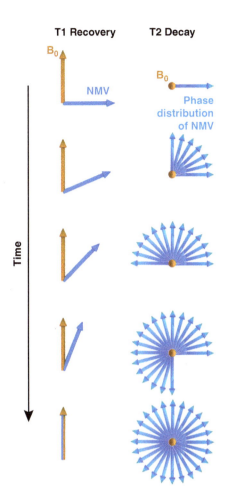

Figure 6.9 The two relaxation phenomena in MR imaging. T1 recovery (left) is the return of the NMV to alignment with B_o after excitation by an RF pulse. In this view, the longitudinal plane is vertical (orange arrow, B_o) and the transverse plane is horizontal. T2 decay is the gradual dephasing of protons after the RF pulse is turned off. This is visualized here looking down onto the transverse plane, with B_o pointing directly out of the page towards the viewer. Note that T1 recovery and T2 decay actually have different time courses, and are illustrated on the same timeline here only for convenience

two main components of brain tissues that influence MR contrast). The rate of T1 recovery for a particular type of tissue can be described by its **T1 relaxation time**, which is defined as the time it takes for 63% of the longitudinal relaxation to recover. Figure 6.10 shows that the T1 relaxation time is shorter in fat than in water. T2 decay also has an exponential time course, but a decreasing one since it describes the loss of coherence over time. This is shown in Figure 6.10, where it can be seen that, as with T1 relaxation, T2 decay occurs more quickly in fat than water. Again, the rate of T2 decay can be quantified by a number, the **T2 relaxation time**, which represents the time it takes for a 63% reduction of the NMV in the transverse plane or, put another way, for transverse magnetization to reach 37% of its maximum value.

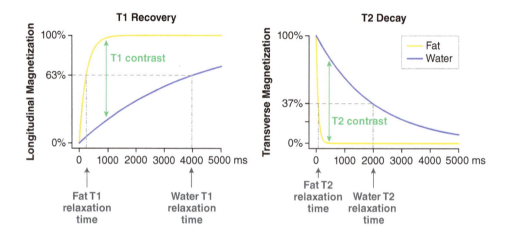

Figure 6.10 T1 recovery and T2 decay curves as a function of time at 1.5 T, shown for the two different tissue types that are of primary importance in creating contrast in structural imaging of the brain: fat and water. Note that T2 decay has a faster time course than T1 recovery

As noted above, T1 recovery and T2 decay are influenced by different factors, although both occur more quickly in fat than in water. T1 recovery time depends on how easily the surrounding lattice can absorb energy from the protons. Fat molecules are densely packed and are inherently good absorbers of energy, so they allow for rapid transfer of energy from protons. In contrast, water molecules are less densely packed and have higher inherent energy, making it harder for them to accept energy from excited protons. Thus energy transfer is less efficient and consequently slower.

T2 decay, in contrast, occurs due to interactions with the magnetic fields of molecules surrounding the protons. When the RF energy is turned off, there may seem to be no principled reason why dephasing should occur – since protons precess at a fixed rate (their Larmor frequency), once they are precessing coherently they should continue to do so in the absence of a change in the magnetic field. In reality, however, the spins of protons near to each other interact because of their magnetic moments. These interactions cause some protons to precess at slightly faster rates and others at slower rates, leading to T2 decay. These interactions occur more rapidly in the densely packed fat molecules than in the more spread-out water molecules so, like T1 relaxation, T2 decay occurs more quickly in fat.

Another phenomenon that can be measured is known as **T2* decay**. This is also dephasing, but occurs much more rapidly even than T2 decay, in fact over only tens of milliseconds. T2* decay is caused by small, local inhomogeneities in the magnetic field, which can be caused by magnetic properties of some molecules (for instance, haemoglobin in blood) as well as by the fact that magnetic field inhomogeneities are caused near the boundaries of different tissue types – for example, between fat and water, or at the boundaries of the brain and the cerebrospinal fluid that envelops it, but even between blood vessels and brain tissue. Although these differences in magnetic field strength are very small compared to the B_0 field of the MRI scanner, they nevertheless exert measurable influence on the microscopic environment around the protons. T2* decay is particularly important in fMRI, as we will discuss in the next chapter.

Contrast in MR Images

The fact that different tissue types, like fat and water, have different T1 and T2 recovery times is the basis for **contrast** in an MR image – that is, differences in intensity (brightness) between different tissue types. Figure 6.11 shows examples of two different MRI scans of a human head, with different **contrast weightings**. In both cases, we see the contrast as differences in intensity of the image between grey matter, white matter, and cerebrospinal fluid (CSF). These tissue types are the primary source of contrast in anatomical MR images due to their differences in fat/water content: grey matter is composed primarily of cell bodies, which have a low fat content and a relatively high water content; white matter is composed primarily of axons, which have high fat content due to the myelin sheath that insulates the axons; and CSF has a higher water content even than grey matter since it lacks cellular structures. Optimizing the contrast between grey matter, white matter, and CSF results in the best renderings of anatomical structure, and this is done by adjusting scan parameters so as to maximize the difference in T1 and/or T2 contrast between these tissue types. You may have noticed the green arrows in Figure 6.10 highlighting contrast: these arrows are at the times when the T1 and T2 recovery curves are maximally different – thus providing the best signal contrast between the images. Understanding how these times are used requires further elaboration of MRI pulse sequences.

Although Figure 6.8 showed a simple pulse sequence involving only a single RF pulse and readout (echo), in reality during an MRI scan a large number of RF pulses are used, spaced at regular intervals. The time between each RF pulse during the scan is called the **repetition time (TR)**. In a T1-weighted image (one designed to maximize T1 contrast), the first 90° RF pulse flips the NMV into the transverse plane, and when the pulse is turned off T1 recovery begins; however, the TR is set such that the second RF pulse occurs before full T1 recovery has occurred. Thus at the time of the second RF pulse, the NMV has recovered only partially – and critically, differently for different tissue types. Because T1 recovery is faster in fat than water, the NMV in fatty tissues (like white matter) will have recovered more than

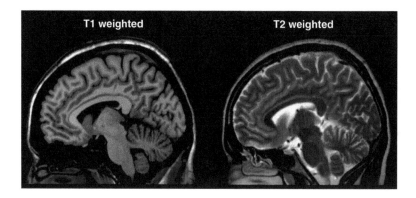

Figure 6.11 Examples of T1- and T2-weighted MR images, both shown for a midline slice through the head in the sagittal plane. Images generated using FSLview software from the 'Colin' single-subject template brain (Aubert-Broche, Evans, & Collins, 2006; Holmes, Hoge, Collins, Woods, Toga, & Evans, 1998). Copyright © 1993–2009 Louis Collins, McConnell Brain Imaging Centre, Montreal Neurological Institute, McGill University. Used with permission

tissues with higher water content. Thus when the second (and each subsequent) 90° RF pulse occurs, the NMV is flipped past the transverse plane because the effect of the second pulse is additive with the residual transverse magnetization in the tissues. This is shown in Figure 6.12. As can be seen in this figure, the result is that the **transverse component** of the NMV is longer for fat than for water. The transverse component is the projection of the NMV into the transverse plane – essentially obtained by drawing a vertical line from the end of the NMV for each tissue type to the transverse plane. The transverse plane is important because this is where the receiver coil is positioned, so the projection onto the transverse plane determines the size of the signal that will be measured. Tissues with higher fat content therefore appear brighter in T1-weighted MR images, because they have a longer transverse component. Thus to maximize fat–water contrast (or in the brain, grey matter–white matter–CSF contrast) the TR in T1-weighted images is set at the time where the T1 recovery curves for fat and water are maximally different. This ensures that the projection of their respective NMVs into the transverse plane will be maximally different. The result is that in T1-weighted images fat is bright and water is dark. A typical T1-weighted image of the brain looks rather intuitively like a black-and-white photograph, since white matter will be white, grey matter will be grey, and CSF will be essentially invisible (black). A typical T1-weighted image is shown in the left panel of Figure 6.11.

In other cases, a T2-weighted image is desired, such as the one in the right panel of Figure 6.11. Recall that T2 decay refers to the decrease in phase coherence (dephasing) in the transverse plane. Thus to obtain a T2-weighted image we need to pick parameters that maximize the contrast in T2 decay between fat and water – a time when significant dephasing has occurred for fat, but relatively little for water.

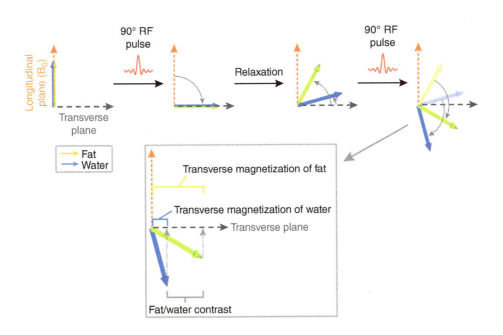

Figure 6.12 How contrast is generated in MR images over repeated excitation cycles. Moving from left to right, a first 90° flip angle RF pulse causes the NMV for both fat (yellow) and water (light blue) to be flipped into the transverse plane. The next panel shows a point in time (at which partial recovery has occurred. The NMV for fat has recovered more than for water, since the T1 recovery time for fat is shorter. The rightmost panel shows the NMVs immediately after the second 90° RF pulse, which occurred at the time of the middle panel, when recovery was different for fat and water. As a result, both NMVs are flipped past 90° (since the second pulse is additive with the residual effects of the first). However, their previous partial recovery leads to the projection of the NMV into the transverse plane (grey arrows, bottom panel) for fat being longer than for water. Thus a greater MR signal will be recorded for fat than for water, resulting in brighter spots on the MR image. This is because the receiver coil is positioned in the transverse plane, so the projection of the NMV into the transverse plane determines the MR signal strength

T2 contrast is primarily dependent on a different scan parameter than T1 contrast: the **echo time (TE)**. This is the time between the RF pulse and readout of the signal from the receiver coil (since what is read out is essentially an 'echo' of the RF signal sent in to the tissue). By reading out the image at a time when fat has significantly dephased, but water has not, we obtain an image of the brain in which white matter (fat) is dark (because it is highly dephased and contributes little signal), while grey matter and CSF are brighter. Referring back to Figure 6.10, we can see that the TE that maximizes this contrast is relatively short compared to the TR that is optimal for a T1 weighted image. The influence of T1 contrast in a T2-weighted image is minimized by using a TR that is longer than what would be used in T1-weighted imaging – a time at which full or almost-full recovery has occurred for both fat and water.

Spatial Encoding of MR Images with Gradients

Thus far we have discussed how contrast is obtained in MRI images, and noted that MRI pulse sequences are designed to maximize the contrast between different tissue types. However, we have made no mention of how to obtain a 2D **slice**, or a 3D image, of a structure such as the brain. Indeed, in contrast to EEG or MEG – in which the number and density of the sensors is directly related to the spatial resolution of the resulting data – high-resolution MR imaging can be performed with a single RF coil (although multi-channel coils do exist, and can provide improvements in image quality as well as how long it takes to obtain an image; these are beyond the scope of this book however). Understanding how 2D and 3D MR images are formed builds on our understanding of the Larmor equation. Recall first that excitation is dependent on the match between the frequency of the RF pulse and the resonant (Larmor) frequency of the protons. Secondly, recall that the Larmor equation tells us that protons' resonant frequency is determined by the strength of the magnetic field that they are in. A consequence of this is that if different protons (in different locations) are experiencing different magnetic field strengths, then an RF pulse tuned to excite the protons at one magnetic field strength will not excite those experiencing a different field strength. This is the principle used for spatial encoding of MR images.

At first the notion of different magnetic field strengths might seem surprising, since the entire head of the subject during an MRI scan of the brain is inside the bore of the scanner, which has a fixed field strength such as 1.5, 3, or 7 T. However, MRI scanners have additional hardware inside them that allow for the creation of magnetic field **gradients** – changes in the strength of the magnetic field over one dimension of space. Along such a gradient, the strength of the magnetic field at the very centre of the scanner is equal to the labelled field strength of the scanner, but along one dimension (for example, bottom to top, or left to right) the field strength increases gradually going in one direction from the centre, while in the opposite direction field strength decreases gradually. This is depicted in Figure 6.13. In the figure the magnetic field strength is lower at the bottom of the head, and higher at the top, and as a consequence the Larmor frequencies that will excite tissue at the top of the head will not excite the bottom. Indeed, MRI scanners are typically capable of sub-millimetre resolution, meaning that the slope of the gradients used creates distinguishable Larmor frequencies across distances of less than a millimetre. Thus there is a direct relationship between the slope (steepness) of the magnetic field gradient used, and the resolution that is possible in an MR image.

A 3D image of an anatomical structure such as the brain is typically acquired as a series of 2D **slices**. Each slice has a particular thickness (for example, 1 mm for an anatomical image), and is composed of a 2D grid of individual elements (for example, a 256 x 256 array of squares, 1 mm on a side). An MRI slice can essentially be thought of as being like a digital photograph, which is composed of a grid of pixels; however, the MR slice – although typically viewed as a 2D image – has a particular thickness as well. Thus the elements comprising MR images are called **voxels** (volume pixels), which are the 3D equivalent to pixels.

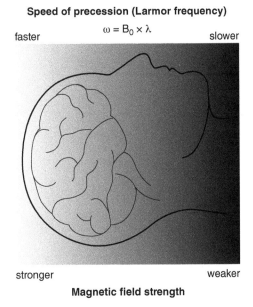

Figure 6.13 A magnetic field gradient, represented schematically within the bore of an MRI scanner. At the centre of the bore the magnetic field is the field strength of the MRI system (for example, 3 T). Moving away from the centre in one direction (rightward in this image), field strength decreases along the gradient while in the opposite direction field strength increases. The effect of this is to change the resonant (Larmor) frequency of protons along this spatial dimension

Acquiring 2D or 3D MR images involves the use of gradients along three orthogonal spatial dimensions. These are typically labelled x, y, and z, with z running parallel to B_0 (along the bore of the scanner), y running vertically, and x running horizontally. This is illustrated in Figure 6.14. In the simplest type of MR image acquisition, these gradients are applied to one spatial dimension at a time over the course of the pulse sequence. There are, however, many different variations on this theme which affect the properties of the image; some of these are discussed in later chapters. For now we will go through the most straightforward sequence used to acquire a single 2D slice. For the sake of explanation, we will use an example in which the person being scanned is lying on their back in the MRI (which is the typical position), and we are acquiring a set of slices in the axial plane. As shown in Figure 6.14, three different image planes are typically defined in anatomical imaging: **axial** is as if you were looking at the brain of a person lying down, viewed from the feet; **sagittal** is looking at the person from the side; and **coronal** is as if you were facing the person. Since a participant lies on their back in the MRI scanner during brain imaging, we can also define a 3D, x–y–z coordinate system relative to the brain that parallels that described above for the scanner. Thus we define x as the right–left dimension of the axial slice, y as the anterior–posterior dimension, and z as the dorsal–ventral (up–down) dimension along which the slice will be specified.

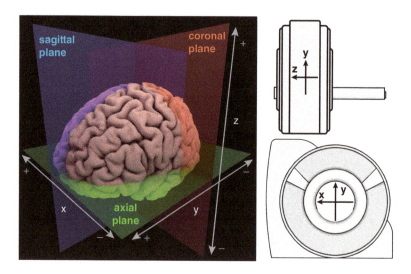

Figure 6.14 The three primary spatial axes, and planes of view defined in medical imaging, relative to both the MR scanner bore (right) and the brain as it is typically positioned in the bore (left)

The first step of the pulse sequence is **slice selection**; one slice is acquired at a time. Slice selection involves inducing a gradient – the **slice selection gradient** – along the axis that will be divided into slices. In our example, since we want axial slices, this means inducing a gradient along the z dimension – the long axis along the bore of the scanner. This is shown in Figure 6.15. The slice selection gradient is turned on immediately before RF excitation, and stays on during the excitation phase, as shown in Figure 6.16. The frequency of the RF pulse is tuned to the Larmor frequency of the particular position along the z axis of the slice we wish to image. The thickness of the slice is determined by the slope of the gradient (with steeper slopes producing thinner slices), and the **bandwidth** of the RF pulse – the range of frequencies in the pulse. The RF pulse is thus a narrow range of frequencies with a peak at the desired frequency for the target slice, and some roll-off on either side of it. The steepness of this roll-off determines the bandwidth. In Figure 6.16 note that the slice selection gradient is actually briefly reversed immediately after the RF pulse. The effect of this is to undo the effects of the slice selection pulse: the slice selection gradient briefly changed the rate of precession of protons along the z dimension, and a side effect of this is that when the gradient is turned off, the phase of the protons at different locations along the gradient direction will be different – since the ones that sped up 'got ahead' of the ones that slowed down. The brief reversal of the slice selection gradient 'rewinds' the phases of the protons along the gradient so that they are all in phase again. If this was not done, some residual gradient in the precessional frequencies of protons along the slice selection dimension might remain when the next RF pulse was sent, which could lead to interactions that interfered with selective excitation of slices acquired after. As well, for reasons we will learn below, it would interfere with accurate reconstruction of the signal *within* the slice. The result of the slice selection step is that protons within the target slice are excited, with their NMV flipped into the transverse plane, while protons at all other locations in the brain are not excited. Thus at readout, we can be confident that our signal is originating only from that slice. However, we still need to be able to resolve the signal from distinct 2D locations within that slice. This is where the additional gradients come in.

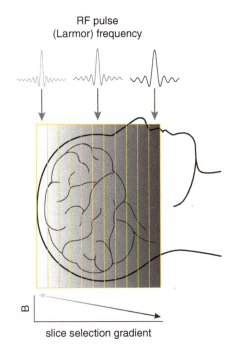

Figure 6.15 A magnetic field gradient along a spatial dimension changes the Larmor frequency of protons along the gradient. In MR imaging, a single slice is selected for imaging at a given point in time by applying a gradient along the slice dimension (here, the z axis) and then transmitting an RF pulse at the Larmor frequency of the targeted slice, as determined by its position along the gradient

Two-Dimensional Image Reconstruction

Understanding how a 2D MR image (slice) is created depends on understanding how we can encode 2D information in a single 1D waveform (which is all the receiver coil of the MRI records). The answer lies in a method that should now be familiar from previous chapters: Fourier analysis. Up until now we have considered Fourier transforms only in one dimension: time. Recall that the Fourier transform allows

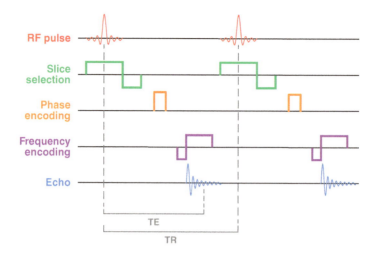

Figure 6.16 Pulse sequence diagram showing slice selection, frequency encoding, and phase encoding steps

us to convert a time-varying waveform into a frequency-domain representation, because any complex waveform can be decomposed into a weighted combination of simpler sine waves – where by 'weighted' we mean that the amplitude of some of the constituent sine waves are greater than for others. This was illustrated in Figure 3.7. However, to reconstruct a 2D image we need to take our understanding of Fourier analysis a step further, into the second dimension.

Just as a 1D signal can be decomposed into component sine waves, so can 2D patterns such as images (whose two dimensions we call x and y) be decomposed into a combination of 2D sine waves. Examples of 2D sine waves – commonly called **sine wave gratings** – are shown in Figure 6.17. Although at first glance these may look like alternating black and white bars, closer inspection reveals that they change continuously from black through grey to white. The white corresponds to the peaks of a sine wave, and the black to the troughs. One can imagine that sine wave gratings are like rippling sand dunes on a desert, or – less poetically – as if we were viewing a sine wave from above, rather than the typical 'side view' as shown in the top panel of Figure 6.7. In the 1D (temporal) domain we refer to the frequency of a sine wave in terms of cycles per unit time (typically cycles per second, or Hz); in the 2D (spatial) domain we refer to the **spatial frequency** of a grating in terms of cycles per unit space (for example, per millimetre). Thus we can say that the gratings in the bottom row of Figure 6.17 have higher spatial frequency than those in the top row. As well, note that the gratings in the right column of the figure are tilted at an angle. These were created by a combination of sine waves running along the x and y axes. In the top right panel, the lines in the image run at a 45° angle because the frequencies along the x and y axes are equal. In the bottom right panel, the frequency along the x axis is higher than along the y axis, resulting in a tilt of less than 45°.

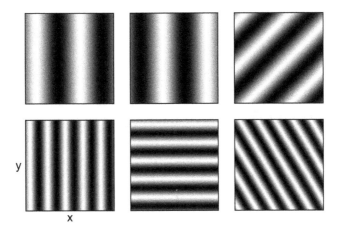

Figure 6.17 Examples of 2D sine wave gratings

So, just as any 1D waveform can be decomposed through a Fourier transform to a weighted combination of sine waves, any 2D image can be decomposed into a weighted set of sine wave gratings. Conducting a 2D Fourier transform essentially involves determining the individual weights of a very large set of gratings, since they can vary in their spatial frequencies along two dimensions, x and y. For a 1D Fourier transform, the result is a frequency spectrum (as we saw in the EEG chapters), with frequency along the x axis and power (the weighting of that frequency) on the y axis. The result of a 2D Fourier transform requires us to plot power for each possible combination of spatial frequency along the x and y axes of the original image, therefore we plot spatial frequency along the two axes of a 2D frequency spectrum, and power is represented as the brightness at each pixel in the image. In MR imaging, the frequency spectrum of a 2D image is called **k space**; an example of this is shown in Figure 6.18. The top row shows a drawing of Joseph Fourier (after whom the transform is named), along with the 2D Fourier transform (k space) of the drawing. By convention, k space is plotted with zero in the centre of the graph, and so the power at the lowest frequencies along each spatial dimension of the image are represented by the brightness of the centre of k space; higher spatial frequencies are plotted in the periphery of k space. Thus each point in k space actually represents information about every spatial location in the MR image – but only some of the information. This is illustrated in the bottom two rows of Figure 6.18: if we reconstruct the image using only the centre of k space, we get a blurry version of the image, since it only contains the low spatial frequencies of the image. This is in effect a low-pass filter of the image. Conversely, if we reconstruct the image from only the periphery of k space, excluding the centre, the result is a high-pass filtered version of the image, showing only the edges or high spatial frequencies. Put another way, the centre of k space is responsible for the image contrast, while the outside of k space is responsible for the sharpness of the image.

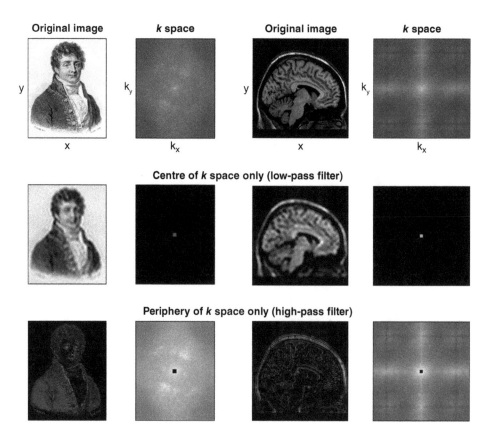

Figure 6.18 K space is the frequency-domain representation of a 2D image. In the top row, the left two columns show a line drawing (of Joseph Fourier, after whom the transform is named) and its k space representation, while the right two columns show an MR image of a brain and its k space representation. The middle row shows the same images reconstructed from only the centre of their respective k spaces, while the bottom row shows the images reconstructed from only the periphery of k space. By convention, k space is drawn with the origin (0, 0) in the centre of the plot, so the centre of k space contains information about low spatial frequencies, while the periphery contains high-frequency information. Original image of Joseph Fourier from 'Portraits et Histoire des Hommes Utiles, Collection de Cinquante Portraits,' Societe Montyon et Franklin, 1839–1840, obtained from commons.wikimedia.org/wiki/File:Joseph_Fourier.jpg

Another way of thinking of k space is in terms of what sine wave grating each location in k space represents. This is illustrated in Figure 6.19. The dimensions of k space are called k_x and k_y – since k_y reflects frequencies along the y axis of the original image, moving vertically from the centre of the image corresponds to horizontal gratings of increasing frequency; moving away from the centre along k_x corresponds to vertical gratings of increasing frequency. Most of k space, however, corresponds to gratings that run at some angle, representing a combination of different spatial frequencies along k_x and k_y. Also note that k space is symmetrical around zero – in other words, there are negative spatial frequencies along both axes. These actually correspond to the same spatial frequency, but with the opposite phase. For example, the figure shows two gratings with x frequencies of –2 and 2, respectively, with the phase difference reflected in whether the bar on the left side of the grating is dark or light.

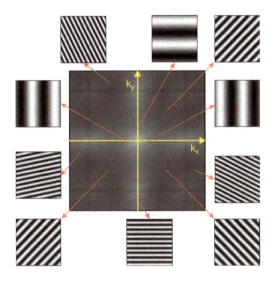

Figure 6.19 Different positions in k space represented as 2D sine wave gratings. The origin (0,0) of k space is in the centre, so we can see that a grating with vertical bars corresponds to a location along the k_x axis where k_y = 0, whereas a horizontal grating corresponds to a point along the k_y axis where k_x = 0. Most locations in k space represent combinations of non-zero frequencies along both axes, resulting in angled gratings. Negative spatial frequencies reflect gratings with the same spatial frequency as a positive value, but opposite sign; this is evident in comparing the relative positions of the black and white stripes in the two gratings with vertical bars.

As stated above, the 2D Fourier transform of an image is just a combination of a (typically very large) set of sine wave gratings of varying combinations of spatial frequencies along the two dimensions. Any 2D image – be it a drawing, photo, or MRI scan of a brain – can be decomposed into a weighted set of sine wave gratings, and conversely the set of these weightings – the k space representation of the image – can be used to reconstruct an image. With this in mind, we are now ready to understand how we can go from the 1D waveform recorded by the MRI scanner to a 2D image of a slice of some tissue such as the head. In MR imaging, we use magnetic field gradients to determine the weighting of each of a large set of sine wave gratings for the slice being imaged, and from this create a k space representation of the slice. Then, the image is reconstructed by subjecting the k space representation to an inverse 2D Fourier transform.

Moving through *k* Space

Deriving this 2D Fourier transform of a slice of tissue in MR imaging essentially involves creating this large set of individual sine wave gratings, and determining how well each matches the slice of tissue being imaged. We create these gratings and determine their weighting by using gradients along the *x* and *y* dimensions of the slice. Since magnetic field gradients change the precessional speed of the protons in the tissue, the result is that at any given point in time, the phase of the precessing protons will vary along the gradient (since faster-precessing protons' phases will get ahead of those of slower-precessing protons), in a continuous fashion. Since protons precess very fast, over the length of the gradient there will be a number of points, evenly spaced along the gradient, where the protons have the same phase. As a result, if we plot the phase of the protons along the gradient (so, along one dimension of our MRI slice) we will get a sine wave whose spatial frequency corresponds to the distance over space between protons that have the same phase at that particular point in time. This phenomenon is known as **phase roll** and is illustrated in Figure 6.20.

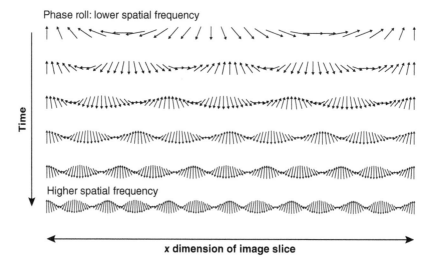

Figure 6.20 The result of applying a magnetic field gradient along a single spatial dimension is to change the speed of precession of the protons along the gradient. This results in a 'phase roll', whereby at any given point in time the phases of the protons along the gradient will vary in a continuous fashion, according to a sine wave. Arrows have been plotted to emphasize the sinusoidal shape created by the phase roll. The spatial frequency of the phase roll will continue to increase with time as long as the gradient stays on, because the faster-precessing protons will gradually move farther ahead of the slower ones

Keeping our explanation to a single gradient applied along a single spatial dimension for the moment, recall that the MRI records only the net signal averaged across all locations along the gradient. Thus when a phase roll is applied, the resulting MRI signal should actually be zero because there are (roughly) the same number of locations with each possible phase, so the opposing phases will cancel each other out. However, this is only true if the sample was homogeneous (for example, a container of water). However, if the spatial frequency of the phase roll happens to match the spatial frequency of contrast variation across the image, then the MRI signal would be larger than if the tissue were homogeneous across the image. For example, if there is white matter at the locations along the spatial gradient of the phase roll where the arrows are pointing up, but grey matter or CSF at the locations in between, we would get a relatively strong signal in a T1-weighted image because the strong signal from the fat in the white matter would not be completely cancelled out by the signal from the intervening locations, since they were composed of a type of tissue that generated less signal. In other words, when the spatial frequency of the phase roll across the gradient matches with the spatial frequency of the contrast (structure) of the tissue being imaged, a relatively strong signal will be generated, and so a greater weighting for that particular sine wave grating will contribute to the ultimate image formation.

Figure 6.21 shows the extension of this same idea to two dimensions. Gradients have been applied along both the x and y dimensions and so we get phase rolls along both these dimensions, which interact to yield a complex 2D pattern. It is relatively easy to imagine how this 2D map of phase angles corresponds to a sine wave grating: the stripes of the grating would run diagonally from the bottom left to top right of the image. Figure 6.22 shows a parallel to Figure 6.19, but with 2D phase rolls rather than sine wave gratings drawn.

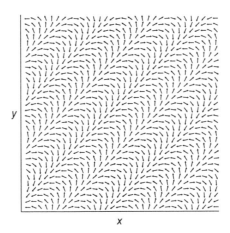

Figure 6.21 Phase roll in two dimensions. Gradients have been applied along both the x and y axes; the interaction of these results in a diagonal pattern of phase roll. This would correspond to a sine wave grating with its 'stripes' running diagonally from the top left to bottom right

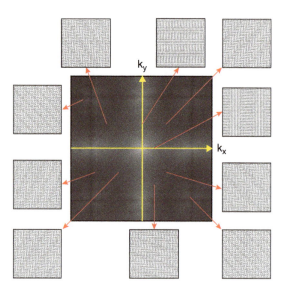

Figure 6.22 Relationship between 2D phase roll plots and k space, analogous to Figure 6.20

Another important point to consider is that the spatial frequency of the phase roll will increase continuously over time as long as the gradient is turned on. This is because the different speeds of precession, over time, will increase the differences in phase between protons at different locations. This can easily be visualized by imagining three people running on a circular track, at different speeds: a few seconds after the start of the race, the runners will be close together. However, as time goes on, assuming each person runs at a fixed rate, the faster runner will get increasingly ahead of the slower runners. Thus we can derive information about different spatial frequencies depending on the exact time at which the signal is sampled. In practice, the signal is read out over a specific range of time to obtain a specific range of spatial frequencies. This is called 'moving through k space' or, alternatively, 'filling' k space. How the gradients are applied along the x and y dimensions of the MRI slice over time is determined by the pulse sequence, which in turn determines the manner in which k space is filled during image acquisition.

We will now walk through a conventional 2D acquisition sequence. If we look at the pulse sequence diagram in Figure 6.16, we see that the x and y gradients are applied at different times, and have different names. The y gradient is called the **phase encoding gradient**, and the x gradient is called the **frequency encoding gradient.** This terminology can be a bit confusing – there are good reasons for these labels, but it is important to remember that ultimately, they are both used to encode the *spatial frequencies* present in the tissue. The purpose of these gradients is to place the MRI signal in a particular location in k space, and then read out the signal over a period of time as the spatial frequency of the phase roll changes due to the differing precessional frequencies along the gradient.

The way that the gradients are applied determines a number of properties of the image, including how long it takes to acquire and what sorts of artifacts may be present in the image. The most straightforward type of acquisition is the one shown in Figure 6.16, where the y (phase encoding) gradient is applied first, followed by the x (frequency encoding) gradient. Acquiring such an image requires a number of phase encoding steps for each 2D slice, in which the entire pulse sequence is repeated with a different strength of the phase encoding gradient. Because a steeper gradient induces a greater spatial frequency in the phase roll along the axis of the gradient, this process means that each phase encoding step (that is, one cycle through the pulse sequence) fills a different row of k space, or a different line along the k_y axis. This is shown in Figure 6.23.

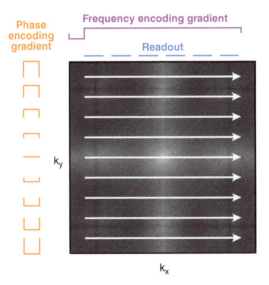

Figure 6.23 Movement through k space induced by magnetic field gradients. The strength of the phase encoding gradient (applied in this case along the y axis of the scanner) determines the position of the signal readout along the k_y axis, with steeper gradients (represented as taller orange bars) leading to positions farther from the middle of k space. After the phase encoding gradient has been applied and turned off, the frequency encoding gradient (purple) is turned on, along the x dimension of the scanner. This gradient is first applied in one direction along x, which 'winds' the 2D phase roll of the image to a location at the left side of k space. Then, the direction of the gradient is reversed and readout of the signal begins. Because the frequency encoding gradient stays on during readout, the phase roll will gradually unwind (decrease in spatial frequency) to zero, and then increase again. Readout occurs at discrete times during the application of the frequency encoding gradient; each sampling time represents one voxel along the k_x dimension. Once one row of k space has been filled in this manner, the phase encoding gradient is applied again with a different gradient strength, to fill the next row of k space

Normally the process of filling k space proceeds from the top to the bottom, one row at a time. Thus the steepest phase encoding gradient is applied first; the steepest gradient will create the greatest phase roll and thus correspond to the highest spatial frequency, which corresponds to the top line in k space. Each subsequent phase encoding step will use a shallower gradient, approaching the centre of k_y. A zero phase encoding gradient will fill the centre line, and after this the slope of the gradient begins to increase again, but in the opposite direction (so, if the gradient initially ran from the back to the front of the head, now the gradient will slope from front to back) to fill the bottom half of k space. The number of phase encoding steps determines the number of voxels along the y axis in the MRI image. Note in Figure 6.16 that the phase encoding gradient is applied, and then turned off, prior to the readout of the MRI signal. This is why it is called a 'phase encoding' gradient – because once the gradient is turned off, prior to readout, the precessional frequencies along this axis return to the Larmor frequency, but a phase roll along this axis has been induced.

Following the phase encoding gradient, the frequency encoding gradient is applied and then readout begins. Although the basic principle behind the frequency encoding gradient is the same as for phase encoding – to induce a phase roll – the fact that it is kept on during readout means that its effects on the ultimate MR signal are a bit different. The first thing to notice about the timing of the frequency encoding gradient shown in Figure 6.16 is that prior to readout, it is switched on in one direction (for example, so that the right side of the head experiences a stronger magnetic field than the left), then at the time that readout begins, it is switched to the opposite direction (so that now the left side of the head experiences the stronger magnetic field). This trick has the effect of 'winding' the phase roll along the frequency encoding gradient in one direction, so that at the start of readout, the phase roll across the frequency encoding direction has its maximal spatial frequency. This places us at the left edge of k space. Then, as readout commences, the reversal of the gradient along the frequency encoding direction has the effect of gradually slowing down the protons that were precessing fastest prior to readout, and speeding up the ones that were precessing slowest. The effect of this is that the spatial frequency of the phase roll along the x axis gradually decreases over time, reaching zero and then increasing again as the effect of the reversed frequency encoding gradient takes effect – ultimately resulting in a high spatial frequency caused by higher precession at the opposite end of the x axis from that induced by the first frequency encoding gradient. As you may have noted in the figures, negative and positive values of spatial frequency are effectively opposite phases of the gratings: the locations of the black and white bars in the sine wave gratings are reversed.

In this way, the signal read out by the MRI over time corresponds to movement through k space along the k_x axis, from left (when the effects of the initial frequency encoding gradient induce a maximal spatial frequency phase roll), through the centre (when the reversed gradient cancels out the initial phase roll), to the right edge of k space (where spatial frequency is again maximal, due to the effects of the reversed gradient). Although the process of moving along k_x is continuous (in contrast to the discrete steps of filling the lines of k space in different phase encoding steps), the

MRI signal is sampled only at discrete intervals. The number of intervals corresponds to the resolution of the resulting MR image along the x axis, which is often called the number of frequency encoding steps. It is most common to acquire square images, so the number of phase and frequency encoding steps will be equal.

As a final point, you will notice that any k space plot of an MR image is always brightest in its centre. This is essentially an artifact of how the images are created: when one or both spatial encoding gradients are zero (or close to zero), this means that the spatial frequency across that axis is zero, and so all of the protons along that dimension are precessing in phase. Thus regardless of the tissue composition, we will record a relatively large MR signal because of the phase locking across the protons all the way along the axis.

Armed with this basic understanding of the steps involved in generating a MR image, we are now ready to explore specific applications of MRI in cognitive neuroscience. In each of the following chapters on MRI we will refer to concepts such as contrast and k space to explain how individual imaging techniques differ from each other, why they work the way they do, and importantly, how the physical basis of image acquisition imposes limits on the technique and can induce artifacts in the images.

SAFETY

In routine use, MRI is an extremely safe technique. It has been in use for several decades, and there is no evidence of harm from either short- or long-term exposure to the strong magnetic fields or radio waves used. There are, nevertheless, three important safety considerations when working around MRI. These include the dangers inherent in a strong magnetic field; possible heating due to the use of RF energy; and effects that can be induced by the rapid switching on and off of magnetic field gradients.

First and foremost, an MRI scanner has a very strong magnetic field (for example, 1.5, 3, or 7 T) that is always on – even when the machine is not scanning, and even when the machine is switched 'off' for the night. This magnetic field is not present when an MRI scanner is being transported from the manufacturer to the site where it will be installed, but it is created when the machine is first installed. Bringing an MRI 'up to field' (that is, to full strength) is a slow and somewhat delicate process that requires trained engineers – so not something that one would want to do on a regular basis – and once the process is completed, the machine can remain at field for years. Because of the strength of the magnetic field, and the size of the space over which the field has to be full strength (that is, the entire bore of the scanner, large enough to accommodate a large human body), the field is both strong and can extend for many metres around the scanner. Even ten or more metres away from the scanner, its magnetic field is strong enough to pull ferromagnetic objects out of a human hand and into the bore of the scanner at high velocity. There are numerous video demonstrations of this available online, which the reader is strongly encouraged to seek out. Indeed, several deaths have been caused by accidents in which someone brought such an object (such as an oxygen tank) into the scanner room when someone was in the scanner. For this reason, MRIs are always housed in specially shielded rooms (which also keep radio waves from the rest of the environment from contaminating the images), and anyone entering the MRI room should be screened by a trained MR technician. Even loose change or other small metal objects in a pocket can become dangerous projectiles. Any equipment that needs to be used inside the MRI room needs to be certified as MR-safe; specialized medical and research equipment is made specifically with MRI safety in mind.

The strong magnetic field also presents some danger for people with metal inside their bodies. However, the static field is usually not a significant concern, as most medical devices designed for implantation are made of non-ferrous materials because MRI is such a widely used diagnostic tool. However, this is not universally true, and so databases containing MRI safety information provided by medical device manufacturers are available and should be consulted if there is any question. In many cases as well, implanted devices such as pins or plates are firmly attached to bone and over time, fuse with the body making them unlikely to move. A larger concern with implanted metal, however, is the effects of gradient fields. Magnetic field gradients are turned on and off rapidly and repeatedly during any MRI scan. These rapid changes can have several effects. Firstly, they can create small but repeated movements of metal objects. This can be of significant concern for things like aneurysm clips (used to patch blood vessels in the brain), wires from implanted electrical devices, and stray pieces of foreign metal which may enter the body, such as small pieces of metal from metal grinding or welding, or shrapnel. As well, because of the right-hand rule, rapidly changing magnetic fields can induce currents in loops of conductor in the body, such as wires (also, when being scanned one should never hold their hands together as this creates a conductive loop through the arms, which can result in unpleasant nerve stimulation). Another potential risk is tattoos, as some inks contain small metal flakes as part of the colouring (even if the ink does not appear magnetic). While many people with tattoos have been scanned without incident, it is possible that uncomfortable or even painful heating could occur, depending on the size of the tattoo, the infused, and if the tattoo is on the part of the body being scanned. Likewise, any jewellery and body piercings should be removed. Collectively, burns caused by conductive loops and tattoos comprise the majority of injuries reported in MRI scanning.

The risks of metal objects – implanted or not – are easily mitigated through careful screening. Any MRI centre will have a routine screening questionnaire that everyone who is to be scanned will complete, and that is then reviewed by a trained MRI technician. If this reveals any concerns, the technician will inquire further, and possibly consult a device safety database or follow up with a physician. In some cases people may not be eligible for an MRI scan; in some extreme cases, if the MRI is medically essential then surgery may be performed to remove the incompatible device.

Another risk of MRI is heating. The RF energy used during a scan is, by definition, deposited into the body, and over time during a scan this can actually raise the temperature of the tissue. However, the amount of heating can be quite accurately calculated based on the weight of the person, and the software running MRI scanners is required by law to have controls in place that prevent any significant heating from occurring. For this reason, a person's weight is always entered into the scanner console prior to starting the scan, and it is important to use an accurate number. Because of these built-in controls, heating is generally not a significant concern for an MRI participant. However, these constraints may actually limit some of the scan parameters, and especially for some participants. Notably, children's smaller mass makes them more susceptible and thus some types of scan that can safely be run on adults may not be possible to do with small children.

A final consideration is of a very different nature: in some cases, especially when an ostensibly healthy person has an MRI scan for research purposes (as opposed to clinical diagnostic reasons), the scan may reveal a previously unknown medical condition. These are called **incidental findings** and can range from entirely benign to life-threatening; the incidence of clinically significant findings has been estimated to be between 2 and 4%, although this increases with age (Morris et al., 2009). This issue has attracted significant concern from bioethicists (Anonymous, 2005; Illes et al., 2002; Illes & Borgelt, 2009; Morris et al., 2009) and is an important consideration during the informed consent process for any MRI research study. There are two primary concerns here. First of all, the potential participant should be informed that they may learn of a serious medical condition of which they were previously unaware, and what the potential consequences of this are. While this might be positive in the sense of diagnosis and treatment, it could also negatively affect people's eligibility for insurance, their employment, or other factors. Secondly, it is also possible that the person will have a medical condition that is not detected during the MRI scan. This could occur for several reasons: when someone has an MRI for diagnostic purposes, the set of scans performed are chosen by the referring physician with particular concerns in mind. For example, different scans might be done if a brain tumour was suspected, as opposed to multiple sclerosis, or Parkinson's disease. In the case of a research scan, the choice of scans is driven by the research question, and limited by the time available and the cost of running the MRI. Therefore the appropriate scans to detect a particular condition may not be performed. Moreover, even if there is some diagnostic information present in the scans, the condition may not be detected because the researchers are not trained to perform diagnosis, and therefore do not know what to look for. Some things may be obvious to anyone with experience looking at healthy brain scans, but other things may not. This consideration means that the potential MRI participant should not think that by participating in a research study they are getting a 'free MRI' or that any diagnosis will be performed. As well, the informed consent process should include wording that makes it clear that the participant understands this and will not hold the researchers accountable if a later diagnosis is made.

SUMMARY

Virtually all human MR imaging – including all of the techniques discussed in this book – relies on the magnetic properties of hydrogen atoms, which are ubiquitous in the human body. The fact that different types of tissue differ in their hydrogen concentrations, and how the hydrogen atoms are bound into molecules, is the

basis for obtaining contrast between different tissue types in an MR image – which allows us to distinguish, for example, grey matter, white matter, and cerebrospinal fluid in a structural MRI of the brain. Hydrogen atoms – or protons – have a single positive charge and spin around a central axis. This spin creates a magnetic moment, meaning that protons act as magnetic dipoles with a north and south pole along the axis of their spin. Protons also experience a second type of movement, precession, which is a circular 'wobble' around the axis – similar to a spinning top it starts to tip towards the ground. Normally inside the body, protons' axes have random alignments as they are influenced by the Earth's magnetic field, as well as magnetic interactions between atoms and molecules within the body. However, when placed in a strong magnetic field, the protons in the body have a weak tendency to align with that magnetic field. This does not mean that all protons align perfectly with the external magnetic field, but that the net magnetization vector (NMV) – representing the net orientations of all protons in the body – tends to align with the field. An MRI scanner has a strong magnetic field that is always on, so when lying in an MRI scanner an individual's NMV aligns with the magnetic field of the scanner (which is termed B_0).

Simply aligning the NMV of the body with the scanner's B_0 is not sufficient to create an MR image. A critical next step is excitation, wherein the alignment of the NMV is perturbed. This is done through the mechanism of resonance, whereby radio frequency (RF) energy is transmitted to the body at a specific frequency. This is known as the Larmor frequency, and corresponds to the speed of precession of the protons. The precessional speed – and thus Larmor frequency – are determined by the strength of the magnetic field. RF energy applied at the Larmor frequency is absorbed by the protons. Because RF energy is actually a type of magnetic field that changes direction over time, applying RF energy is equivalent to applying a second magnetic field, and the RF energy is transmitted in a plane perpendicular to B_0. The result is that the RF energy pulse causes the NMV to tip away from alignment with B_0 (which we call the longitudinal plane), into the orthogonal (transverse) plane. The RF pulse also causes the precessional phases of the protons to align, creating a stronger coherent, oscillating pattern (phase locking). Because the receiver coil – which measures the MR signal – is aligned with the transverse plane, the degree to which the RF pulse tips the NMV, as well as the degree of phase locking, determine the strength of the MR signal. Another critical determinant of MR signal strength is the type of tissue. Relaxation occurs more quickly in tissues that can dissipate energy more rapidly, notably fat. Relaxation is slower in water (and cerebrospinal fluid), and intermediate in grey and white matter (though white matter contains more fat, and has shorter relaxation times). Relaxation actually involves two distinct processes: T1 recovery is the speed of return of the NMV to alignment with B_0, while T2 decay is the dephasing that occurs once the RF pulse is turned off, and phase locking is reduced due to interactions between the magnetic fields of protons and their surrounding environments. The timing of certain MRI scan parameters should be chosen based on the T1 or T2 relaxation curves depending on the type of contrast desired in the image, to maximize contrast between fat and water, or more specifically between the tissue types of interest (for example, grey and white matter). Because MR scanning involves many repeated cycles of excitation and relaxation, T1 contrast is dependent on the time between RF pulses, termed TR, as this determines the amount of relaxation time before the next excitation pulse. In contrast, T2 contrast depends on the time between each excitation and signal readout (termed TE), because this determines how much dephasing will have occurred prior to readout.

Critical to 2D and 3D MR imaging is the concept of magnetic field gradients. Gradients are systematic linear variations in magnetic field strength along one spatial dimension. Because the Larmor frequency is dependent on magnetic field strength, creating a magnetic field gradient along one spatial dimension means that an RF pulse of a particular frequency will selectively excite protons only in a specific position along that gradient. Slice selection involves applying a gradient along one dimension (the slice plane) during the RF pulse, which causes only protons within that slice to be excited. Then, a gradient is applied along a second, orthogonal dimension (phase encoding), which creates a 'phase roll' whereby the precessional phase of protons varies systematically along this dimension. This effectively creates a 2D sine wave grating along the phase encoding direction. Finally, the phase encoding gradient is turned off and a gradient along the third orthogonal dimension (frequency encoding) is applied during signal readout. This creates a phase roll along the frequency encoding direction, whose frequency increases the longer the gradient is left on. In this way, over time the readout signal includes information about a range of spatial frequencies in the image. The MR signal that is read out is a one-dimensional sequence of numbers, which contain rich information of many frequencies and phases. The slice selection-phase encoding-frequency encoding steps are typically repeated many times to obtain information about different spatial frequencies within each slice. This results in an image in *k* space, which is the 2D Fourier transform of 'real' space. Locations in *k* space correspond to particular combinations of spatial frequency and orientation in real space, and the inverse Fourier transform can be applied to a *k* space image to create a 'real' space image.

While MRI is a very safe technique for most people – as there are no known long-term effects of the magnetic fields or RF waves used – the strong magnetic field creates a number of safety risks that need to always be kept in mind. Firstly, any material that will be attracted to a magnetic field (ferromagnetic metals) should be kept far away from an MR scanner. The magnetic field of an MRI scanner is so strong that virtually any metal object carried into the MRI room is likely to be ripped from a person's hand or pocket with life-threatening force and speed. Scanners are typically located in shielded rooms that demarcate a safe distance, and so in general ferromagnetic materials should be kept outside of the MRI room. As well, people with metal in their bodies may be ineligible for MRI scans. Although most surgically implanted metal is non-ferromagnetic, these materials may still move slightly or heat up during MRI scans – especially loops of metal such as implanted wires. Non-surgical metal objects in the body, such as metal slivers from metal working, or shrapnel from injuries, can pose similar dangers. Therefore it is critical that anyone entering the MRI room – for a scan or even as an observer or experimenter – be safety-screened by a trained professional. MRI researchers should also consider the ethical and practical implications both of the fact that research MRI scans may reveal previously unknown pathologies, and also that non-diagnostic scans may not reveal pathologies that do exist.

THINGS YOU SHOULD KNOW

- Hydrogen ions, or protons, are ubiquitous in the human body and are the primary basis for the MRI signal. Critical to generating the MR signal are the fact that protons spin around an axis, creating a magnetic moment with 'north' and 'south' poles.

- The net orientation of the axes of all protons in the body (or the part of the body being scanned, such as the head) is referred to as the net magnetization vector (NMV). Normally proton orientations are random, resulting in an NMV of zero. However, because protons have a weak tendency to align with an external magnetic field, in an MRI scanner the NMV aligns with the strong field (B_0) of the scanner.

- Protons are able to absorb radio frequency (RF) energy whose frequency matches the speed of their precession, a phenomenon known as resonance. Because RF energy is a type of magnetic field, applying RF energy in a plane perpendicular to B_0 results in both tipping the NMV towards the RF pulse (out of the longitudinal plane, into the transverse plane), and bringing the precessional phases of the protons into alignment – a process collectively called excitation. Because the readout coil from which the MRI signal is measured is in the transverse plane, excitation also creates the signal that is ultimately measured.

- Once the RF pulse is turned off, relaxation occurs, which has two dimensions: T1 recovery and T2 decay. T1 recovery is the return of the NMV to alignment with the longitudinal plane, while T2 decay is the loss of phase synchrony (dephasing) among the precessing protons. The speed of both types of relaxation differ between tissue types, being much faster for fat than water. These two aspects of relaxation are the basis of two primary types of contrast between tissues in structural MR images. T1 contrast is obtained by choosing a TR (time between RF pulses) that optimizes the difference in T1 recovery between different tissue types. T2 contrast is obtained by choosing a TE (time between RF pulse and readout) that maximizes differences between the tissues in T2 decay.

- T2* decay is a special, more rapid type of T2 dephasing that is caused by very localized magnetic field inhomogeneities. This is the basis of conventional fMRI contrast, because deoxygenated haemoglobin (the oxygen transporter molecule in blood) causes small magnetic field disruptions.

- Magnetic field gradients are systematic variation (slopes) in magnetic field strength along a particular spatial dimension. These are the basis of creating 2D and 3D MR images, because in varying magnetic field strength, we also vary the Larmor frequency of protons along that dimension. This is used in slice selection to excite only one slice of the image. As well, the phase and frequency encoding steps in image acquisition involve creating 2D 'phase rolls' across the slice by manipulating the precessional phase and frequency of protons.

- Although the MR signal that is measured by the readout coil is a single time series, the use of frequency and phase encoding gradients allow this signal to be decomposed into a *k* space image, in which different locations correspond to different spatial frequencies and orientations of 2D sine wave gratings. The strength of the signal at each location in *k* space reflects the degree to which that 2D sine wave grating is represented in the image being scanned. By applying an inverse 2D Fourier transform, a *k* space image can be converted into a 'real' space image.

- An MRI pulse sequence describes the sequence and timing of the RF pulse; slice, phase, and frequency encoding gradients; and readout of the MR signal. The parameters of the pulse sequence largely determine the type, contrast, and quality of an MR image.

- MRI scanners have a strong magnetic field that is always on, even when the scanner is 'turned off'. This magnetic field is so strong that any ferromagnetic materials brought into the MRI room will be drawn into the centre of the scanner with great force and speed, creating significant safety hazards. For this reason, no ferromagnetic materials should be brought into the MRI room, and specialized, MR-safe equipment should be used (for example, for stimulation and response collection). As well, any individual entering the MR room – whether for a scan or as an observer or helper – should be safety-screened by a trained professional. Some people should never enter the MRI room, and other people may be safe to enter, but should not be scanned due to risks of implanted metal moving or heating up.

FURTHER READINGS

Hanson, L.G. (2015). *Introduction to Magnetic Resonance Imaging Techniques*. Available at: http://eprints.drcmr.dk/37/2/MRI_English_letter.pdf.

Westbrook, C. (2015). *MRI at a Glance* (3rd ed.). Chichester: Wiley-Blackwell.

7 Functional MRI (fMRI) 1

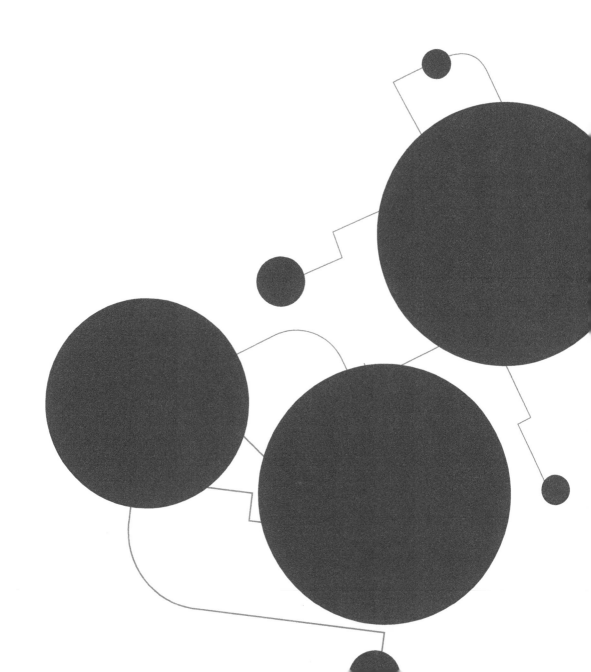

LEARNING OBJECTIVES

After reading this chapter, you should be able to:

- Define and explain BOLD contrast.
- Explain the value of calibrated BOLD, and how it is performed.
- Define the haemodynamic response function (HRF), including its typical timing characteristics.
- Explain how BOLD signal is related to neural activity.
- Contrast EPI with conventional MRI pulse sequences, and explain the costs and benefits of EPI.
- Describe the preprocessing steps commonly applied to fMRI data, and the motivation for each.
- Explain how motion correction is performed on fMRI data, what the limitations of this process are, and why these limits arise.
- Explain spatial normalization of MR images, and describe three approaches to this process.

INTRODUCTION

Functional MRI (fMRI) is the most widely used technique in cognitive neuroscience. Its introduction in 1992 revolutionized (or, some might argue, defined) the field of cognitive neuroscience. Although PET (see Chapter 10) already was able to localize brain activation in vivo, PET scans were very expensive and required introducing radioactive material into the person being scanned; as well PET scanners were relatively uncommon and had poor temporal resolution. In contrast, MRI scanners were already quite common, and the fMRI technique – while not possessing the millisecond-level resolution of EEG or MEG – offered good temporal resolution, allowing a much wider range of experimental designs than PET. Functional MRI remains one of the most powerful and flexible tools for cognitive neuroscience, although like any technique it has limitations. Generally speaking, fMRI is sensitive to the concentration of oxygen in the blood, which is correlated with neuronal activity. However, an important limitation of the technique to consider is that fMRI is always an indirect measure of brain activity.

As discussed in the previous chapter, MRI uses a combination of magnetic fields and radio waves to create images. Functional MRI capitalizes on two properties of the haemoglobin molecules that transport oxygen from the lungs throughout the body to the tissues that need it: they contain iron, and they change their molecular configuration depending on whether oxygen is bound to them or not. These properties led to a series of experiments in the 1980s and 1990s that culminated in the publication in 1992 of seminal papers from three independent research groups, demonstrating that MRI could be used to map functional activation in the brain (Bandettini et al., 1992; Kwong et al., 1992; Ogawa et al., 1992). Since that time these techniques have been refined and extended, and an immense amount of innovation has occurred in the areas of MRI hardware and software, data analysis techniques, and experimental design. Functional MRI has now unquestionably revolutionized our understanding of the brain.

WHAT ARE WE MEASURING?

The BOLD Effect

Functional MRI relies on the fact that the **haemoglobin** molecules that transport oxygen in the blood to different tissues contain iron, and more specifically that the haemoglobin molecules actually change their shape depending on whether or not oxygen is bound to them. Furthermore, the magnetic properties of haemoglobin are different depending on whether it has oxygen bound to it (oxyhaemoglobin, or oxy-Hb) or not (deoxyhaemoglobin; deoxy-Hb). Specifically, deoxy-Hb is **paramagnetic**, whereas oxy-Hb is not. Paramagnetic molecules have unpaired electrons, creating a magnetic moment (spin) that can align with external magnetic fields. This means that deoxy-Hb – but not oxy-Hb – is affected by the strong magnetic field of an MRI scanner. Most importantly, because they have magnetic properties, deoxy-Hb molecules alter the strength of the magnetic field surrounding themselves, including nearby water molecules (which are the primary source of protons, and thus MRI signal, in the body). As a result, the presence of deoxy-Hb increases the rate of loss of transverse magnetization, and specifically **T2* decay**. As introduced in the previous chapter, T2* decay is very rapid dephasing (faster than T2) that occurs specifically due to interactions of protons with very localized magnetic field inhomogeneities associated with surrounding molecules – in this case deoxy-Hb. The properties of haemoglobin in MR imaging were first reported by Thulborn and colleagues (1982), who showed that T2* decay was proportional to the ratio of oxy-Hb to deoxy-Hb. In other words, higher concentrations of (paramagnetic) deoxy-Hb caused more rapid T2* decay. In the same study, the authors showed that this effect was magnified by increasing the strength of the magnetic field. While Thulborn and colleagues' work was done in vitro (that is, in test tubes), subsequent work showed that the effects were obtained in vivo as well: in 1990 Ogawa and colleagues demonstrated differences in MR image contrast of live rat brains depending on the concentration of oxygen in their blood.

In a series of experiments using a very strong magnetic field (7 T), Ogawa and colleagues (Ogawa, Lee, Nayak, & Glynn, 1990b) demonstrated that it was possible to visualize blood vessels as small as 50 μm in diameter, using a pulse sequence sensitive to T2* (called a gradient echo sequence). In one experiment, rats either breathed normal room air (which has an oxygen concentration of about 20%), or they breathed 100% oxygen, which led to extremely high levels of oxygen saturation of the blood and thus very little deoxy-Hb. Comparing the images, many dark lines were observed in the 20% oxygen condition compared to the 100% condition. These were the veins in the brain, and the effect was attributed to the faster dephasing, and consequent signal drop, caused by the higher concentration of deoxy-Hb in the 20% oxygen condition. Ogawa and colleagues labelled this change **blood oxygenation level dependent (BOLD)** contrast. Importantly, they noted that this effect extended beyond the haemoglobin molecules themselves, and indeed beyond the walls of the blood vessels into the surrounding tissues, which they described as a form of amplification of the signal produced by the oxy-Hb:deoxy-Hb ratio. This is an important point to note for two reasons. Firstly, it means that BOLD changes can be imaged even using voxel sizes that are significantly larger than the capillaries that the oxy-Hb:deoxy-Hb ratio is changing in. At the same time, this does place an ultimate limit on the precision of spatial localization using BOLD fMRI. It is important to keep in mind, however, that since the changes in BOLD contrast occur in blood vessels, and not in neurons, there are additional constrains on fMRI's spatial precision.

Two years after the first demonstrations of the BOLD contrast, the first human fMRI studies were published, essentially simultaneously, by three independent labs. In one study, Ogawa and colleagues (1992) presented visual stimulation (flashing lights) to participants for 100–150 s, alternating with periods of darkness. Kwong and colleagues (1992) used a similar paradigm, alternating 60 s of visual stimulation with darkness. Both experiments reported reliable increases in MR signal in the occipital lobe (where visual input is known to be processed) during visual stimulation compared with darkness. Kwong and colleagues' study also showed similar changes in BOLD signal in **primary motor cortex** in a different experiment, in which participants alternately closed and opened their hands compared to not moving their hands. A similar motor task was used in a study published by Bandettini and colleagues (1992) in the same year. While Ogawa's study used a specialized, high-field MRI scanner (4 T), the other two studies used 1.5 T scanners of the type commonly found in hospitals at the time. Although all of these scanners used highly modified hardware and software, the fact that fMRI was possible on standard hospital-grade 1.5 T scanners meant that research would not have to rely on expensive, research-dedicated hardware but could be performed on machines that were already present in many hospitals. Today clinical scanners (which are now mostly 3 T) are largely capable of fMRI either 'off the shelf' or with standard upgrade packages sold by the manufacturers. In many cases fMRI research is conducted on clinical scanners during off-hours or dedicated research time, while on the other hand the popularity of fMRI has led to the establishment of research-dedicated MRI centres at many sites.

Physiological Basis of the BOLD Effect

The ground-breaking studies demonstrating the feasibility of fMRI using BOLD contrast opened the door to an explosion in cognitive neuroscience research. At the same time, they posed perplexing questions concerning what, exactly, was being measured with BOLD fMRI. In all of the studies of brain activation using fMRI, the T2*-weighted images showed increases in signal at times when a brain area was expected to be more activated – for example, in the occipital lobe during visual stimulation. While it makes intuitive sense that fMRI signal should increase when brain activity increases, upon closer examination we would actually predict the opposite effect. Neural activation is, by definition, an increase in neural activity. Since physiological processes generally require oxygen, increased activity should increase oxygen demands in active areas – leading to a relative increase in deoxy-Hb relative to oxy-Hb, if more oxygen is being extracted from the haemoglobin. Deoxyhaemoglobin causes more rapid T2* dephasing, which means that when deoxy-Hb levels are higher, BOLD signal should be *weaker*. Recall that this was what Ogawa and colleagues (Ogawa, Lee, Kay, & Tank, 1990a) showed: higher levels of deoxy-Hb created black lines in the MR image where the veins were, indicating lower signal levels at higher deoxy-Hb concentrations. Thus if increased neural activity leads to increased oxygen consumption and thus higher levels of deoxy-Hb, then during activation BOLD signal should actually decrease – contrary to what is observed in fMRI studies.

This paradox led to several hypotheses concerning the relationship between changes in neuronal activity levels and blood oxygen levels. To understand these, it is important to first have a basic understanding of cellular metabolism – how energy is produced and used in the body. The primary source of energy for cellular processes, including neuronal activity, is **adenosine triphosphate (ATP)**, a molecule derived from glucose (a simple sugar). Glucose can be converted to ATP through two possible pathways – aerobic and anaerobic. **Aerobic metabolism** requires oxygen, which is used in a complex chain of biochemical events including the tricarboxylic acid (TCA) cycle, the electron transport chain, and oxidative phosphorylation. Aerobic metabolism produces 38 molecules of ATP from each molecule of glucose, consuming six molecules of oxygen in the process and producing carbon dioxide (CO_2) as a by-product. The alternative method of converting glucose to ATP is **anaerobic metabolism**, which does not require oxygen. This process is far less efficient than aerobic metabolism, yielding only two ATP molecules from every glucose molecule, rather than 38. Thus aerobic metabolism is by far the most common form in the body; anaerobic metabolism typically occurs only when there is not enough oxygen available to support aerobic metabolism. One familiar experience of this is during highly demanding exercise, such as running hard, or climbing a long flight of stairs. At some point during this exertion one begins to feel a 'burn' in the muscles; this sensation is produced by the lactic acid that is a by-product of anaerobic metabolism, and indicates that the level of effort has exceeded what can be sustained through aerobic metabolism.

In the brain, the primary demand for ATP comes from the ion pumps on the outer membranes of neurons. A neuron at rest has a negative electrical potential relative to the extracellular environment, due to higher concentrations of sodium and calcium outside than inside the cell; in contrast, potassium concentration is higher inside the cell. When action potentials reach a cell, neurotransmitters typically trigger ion channels to open, creating localized changes in membrane potentials. As well, when a neuron fires (an action potential), channels in the cell wall open and allow a flood of sodium and calcium ions into the cell, and of potassium ions out of the cell, causing a rapid change in the electrical potential across the cell membrane. In order for the cell to recover from the action potential, re-establishing its resting potential to allow for a future action potential, sodium and calcium must be pumped out of the cell, and potassium pumped in. The activity of these pumps requires ATP; collectively the activity of these pumps is estimated to account for approximately 75% of the energy consumption in the primate brain, as shown in Figure 7.1. The next most significant energy costs come from propagating action potentials – 10% – and recycling neurotransmitters – 12% (Attwell & Iadecola, 2002).

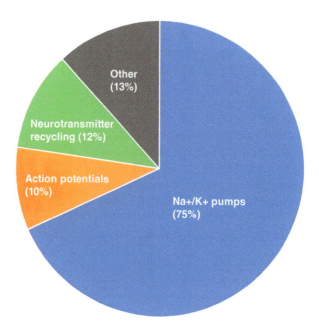

Figure 7.1 Major sources of energy demands in the brain, as a proportion of total energy consumption

It is important to realize that the brain is always active; even when no specific stimulation or cognitive activity is occurring, neurons maintain baseline levels of activity. As such, the 'activations' typically studied with brain imaging are increases over and above these levels, not a change from entirely quiescent neurons to ones that are firing. Indeed, the increases in firing rates associated with specific activation (such as visual stimulation) are relatively small and transient compared to the baseline levels of activity. It is thus reasonable to assume that baseline levels of brain activity are supported through aerobic metabolism, since this is more efficient than anaerobic metabolism and is the primary metabolic pathway in the body generally. This has been confirmed by PET imaging, which is capable of measuring rates of glucose and oxygen metabolism in the brain. The question relevant to understanding the BOLD signal is whether transient increases in neuronal activity levels, such as those induced in cognitive neuroscience studies, are supported by increased aerobic metabolism, or whether the brain treats these like 'sprints' and resorts to anaerobic metabolism to support increases in firing rate above baseline.

The original studies investigating this question actually precede the development of human fMRI. Fox and colleagues (Fox, Raichle, Mintun, & Dence, 1988) used PET to measure the cerebral metabolic rates of both oxygen ($CMRO_2$) and glucose (CMR_{glu}), as well as the rate of cerebral blood flow (CBF). These scans were performed during both a resting condition (lying quietly with eyes closed) and a visual stimulation condition. During visual stimulation, CBF and CMR_{glu} both increased by approximately 50% above resting levels in the visual cortex; however, $CMRO_2$ only increased by 5%. The researchers calculated that the large majority of the increase in glucose metabolism – over 90% – was not associated with increases in oxygen consumption, strongly implicating anaerobic metabolism. This speculation was strengthened by other studies that had shown increases in lactate levels during transient brain activation in other animals; then in 1991, Prichard and colleagues demonstrated lactate increases in the human brain during visual stimulation (Prichard et al., 1991). Further support for anaerobic metabolism came from an influential paper by Pellerin and Magistretti (1994). This paper demonstrated a critical role for **astrocytes** (another very common, non-neuronal cell type in the brain) in recycling the excitatory neurotransmitter glutamate: removing it from the synaptic cleft after it is used for neural signalling, converting it to inactive glutamine, and then transporting it back into the synaptic terminals of neurons. This process consumes ATP through anaerobic glycolysis, and astrocytes are commonly found in close proximity to blood vessels, allowing them to easily obtain the necessary glucose from the blood. Thus Pellerin and Magistretti's work suggested that increased anaerobic metabolism during brain activation might not be due to neurons having energy needs in excess of what aerobic metabolism could provide, but rather because of increase glutamate recycling in astrocytes – which has been termed the **astrocyte-neuron lactate shuttle hypothesis**.

In contrast to these early studies, more recent research has provided strong converging evidence that neural activation is supported primarily by aerobic metabolism, with a relatively minor contribution from anaerobic metabolism. A few years after the first published BOLD fMRI studies, Malonek and Grinvald (1996) investigated this mechanism using invasive optical imaging in an animal model. This type of imaging allows researchers to separately measure concentrations of oxy-Hb and deoxy-Hb, as well as total blood volume. Malonek and Grinvald found that deoxy-Hb actually did increase immediately after visual stimulation, consistent with an increase in *aerobic* metabolism. However, within 1–2 s there was a more substantial increase in oxy-Hb levels, accompanied by increases in blood flow and volume which counteracted the increased deoxy-Hb. Malonek and Grinvald concluded that the reason the BOLD fMRI effect manifests as an increase in signal, even though oxygen consumption does increase, is that activity-dependent increases in blood flow rapidly overcompensate for the small increases in oxygen consumption. They characterized this phenomenon as 'watering the entire garden for the sake of one thirsty flower' (p. 554), and suggested that this mechanism existed to ensure an adequate supply of oxygen for active neurons. Subsequent research has increased our understanding of this mechanism, although it is not yet fully understood and several theories exist (Buxton, Griffeth, Simon, Moradi, & Shmuel, 2014; Hoge, Atkinson, Gill Crelier, Marrett, & Pike, 1999; Lin, Fox, Hardies, Duong, & Gao, 2010). It has been demonstrated that increased flow is caused by **vasodilation** – an increase in the diameter of the blood vessels – both in the capillaries (the smallest blood vessels, where oxygen is actually exchanged with surrounding tissue) and the arterioles that feed into the capillaries, as well as the veins that drain the capillary beds. At least two distinct mechanisms can trigger local vasodilation in the brain. One is increased levels of CO_2 – this is a general physiological mechanism that seems to have evolved to ensure adequate blood supply. The other is directly related to neural activity, by way of astrocytes.

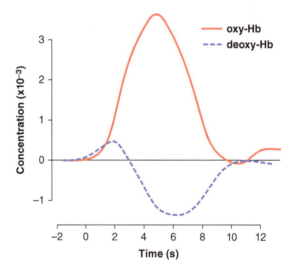

Figure 7.2 Optical imaging data from Malonek and Grinvald (1996), showing the concentrations of oxy- and deoxy-haemoglobin (Hb) in the visual cortex during the onset of brief (4 s) visual stimulation (indicated as 0 on the time axis). Deoxy-Hb shows a rapid initial increase (slightly prior to the increase in oxy-Hb), suggestive of an initial increase in local oxygen consumption. However, this is then swamped by a much larger influx of oxygenated blood. Adapted and redrawn from Malonek and Grinvald, 1996

A further important contribution to our understanding of the physiological basis of the BOLD effect came from Takano and colleagues (2006), who demonstrated a pathway by which neural activity could trigger vasodilation via astrocytes. In a series of experiments, Takano and colleagues demonstrated that neural activity leads to calcium ion increases in the 'end feet' of astrocytes, which wrap around arteries. Increased neural activity lead to increased calcium ion concentrations in the astrocytic end feet, which in turn trigger increased levels of the enzyme COX-1. This enzyme converts the fatty acid arachidonic acid into prostaglandins and thromboxanes – hormones which cause vasodilation. Takano and colleagues further confirmed Pellerin and Magistretti's findings that the increase in astrocyte activity was triggered by synaptic release of glutamate. Thus, increased neural activity results in greater release of glutamate in the synaptic cleft, which is then taken up and recycled by astrocytes. Calcium levels in astrocytes increase with elevated glutamate levels, which in turn trigger the release of hormones that cause violation of the blood vessels that the astrocytes are in contact with. In this way, neural activity can trigger vasodilation; Takano and colleagues showed that this process takes approximately 1 s for neural activation to trigger vasodilation. Critically, nothing about this pathway relies on oxygen levels – neural activity can trigger vasodilation and subsequent

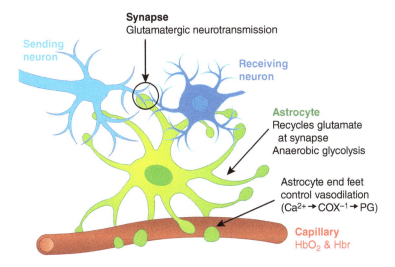

Figure 7.3 Schematic diagram of the astrocyte-neuron lactate shuttle (ANLS) model. Action potentials arriving at a brain area lead to the release of the excitatory neurotransmitter glutamate, which binds to receptors on the receiving neuron, evoking excitatory postsynaptic potentials. The glutamate is then released from the receptors back into the synaptic cleft, where it is taken up by astrocytes for recycling. This recycling process inside the astrocytes uses anaerobic glycolysis to obtain the necessary energy. As well, glutamate increases levels of calcium (Ca^{2+}) inside astrocytes. These increased calcium levels lead to increases in the enzyme COX-1, which in turn activates the hormone prostaglandin. This chemical pathway occurs in the end feet of the astrocytes that wrap around capillaries, and the prostaglandin triggers vasodilation (increased diameter) of the capillaries, leading to increased blood volume and flow

local increases in blood flow, volume, and oxygen concentrations irrespective of any actual changes in local oxygen concentration. An important consequence of this is that, because arteries are highly saturated with oxygen whereas veins are not (since oxygen has been extracted from the blood as it passes from the arteries, through the capillaries to the veins), the changes in oxygen concentration in the blood that are associated with vasodilation are proportionately larger in the veins than in the arteries or capillaries. This places a limitation on the spatial precision of BOLD fMRI, because peak levels of BOLD signal change are likely to be detected 'downstream' of the location of actual neural signal change.

This limitation is an important one, and has been called 'the great brain versus vein debate' (Menon, 2012). In the early days of fMRI, there was significant concern about whether fMRI signals truly localized neural activity, or whether the peak BOLD signal changes were all downstream of active regions, in the draining veins. Indeed, the draining veins have been shown to make greater contributions to BOLD signal than capillaries at lower magnetic field strengths like 1.5 T. Thus at 1.5 T, and even at the fairly common 3 T field strength, draining veins can make a significant contribution to BOLD signal and so some degree of mislocalization occurs. This is mitigated by the fact that the draining veins are quite close to the capillary beds, and studies using these field strengths typically employ voxels on the order of 3 × 3 × 3 mm in size. Voxels of this size would typically include both the capillary beds and draining veins, so the level of imprecision ultimately has little or no impact because the scans lack the spatial resolution for the distinction between vein and brain to be significant. However, some research questions depend on very high-resolution imaging, at 1 mm or lower. The demand for this level of resolution has driven the adoption of higher field strength scanners, and now there are many 7 T scanners in research centres around the world. This is because as field strength increases, the relative amount of signal from the capillary beds increases. Thus while 3 T scanners may be technically capable of obtaining 1 mm resolution fMRI images, the signal in these would be dominated by draining veins, whereas at 7 T the capillary beds make a more significant contribution.

Returning to the question we started this section with, the paradox of increased BOLD signal – reflecting increased oxy-Hb:deoxy-Hb ratios – in response to increased neural activity and aerobic metabolism is explained through the dilation of blood vessels leading to greater perfusion of the active tissue (and draining veins) with oxygen. Other studies have looked at the relationship between CBF and $CMRO_2$ in greater detail. Understanding this is critical to interpreting BOLD signals in terms of neural activation – if vasodilation leads to increased blood flow that is disproportionately higher than the increases in $CMRO_2$, then changes in BOLD signal observed in fMRI experiments would be likewise disproportionately greater than actual changes in neural activity. The data suggest that in fact there is a relatively consistent relationship between CBF and $CMRO_2$, with ratios of approximately 2–4 (in other words, changes in CBF are in the range of 2–4 times greater than changes in $CMRO_2$). However, although flow and oxygen metabolism are correlated, this ratio does vary based on a number of factors. For example, some studies have suggested that different experimental manipulations can have differential effects on CBF and $CMRO_2$ – changes in stimulus factors have a greater impact on CBF, whereas 'intrinsic' cognitive changes (such as changes in attention) affect $CMRO_2$ to a greater degree.

Another important consideration is the baseline state. Because BOLD fMRI is not a quantitative measurement – meaning that the signal levels recorded in fMRI studies are in arbitrary units and cannot be interpreted as reflecting a specific level of oxy-Hb:deoxy-Hb ratio or any other quantity – fMRI activation levels are always measured relative to a **baseline condition**. This baseline is commonly a condition in which the person being scanned stares at a simple cross or other visual stimulus. Several factors of the baseline state impact the magnitude of activation-related BOLD changes, primarily due to how these factors impact baseline oxygen concentrations. One such factor is the proportion of oxygen being taken from the blood in the baseline state – the **oxygen extraction fraction**. In conditions where this is relatively low, baseline oxy-Hb levels are relatively high and so there is less 'dynamic range' for the oxygen concentration to increase during activation. In other words, the amount of possible increase in BOLD signal during activation is smaller. Similarly, high CBF is associated with greater oxygen levels, so high baseline CBF can also reduce the dynamic range. Conversely, situations such as low baseline CBF or high oxygen extraction can increase the dynamic range of BOLD responses. As well, low haematocrit (the concentration of oxy-Hb-containing red blood cells) can reduce the dynamic range of the BOLD signal. These different baseline situations can arise in particular in comparisons between populations. Factors such as age, exercise, smoking, drugs, and disease can all impact oxygen extraction fraction and CBF, meaning that any apparent differences in fMRI signals between two groups may not actually be due to differences in neural activation, if the groups differ in these other factors. Even within a group, individual differences may influence outcomes. For example, numerous studies have demonstrated that caffeine, which causes **vasoconstriction**, leads to stronger task-related fMRI signals due to the increased dynamic range afforded by lower CBF in the baseline state. Thus people who have recently consumed caffeine may be 'better activators' than others.

Basic research into the relationships between CBF, $CMRO_2$, and neural activation, as well as concerns about how to control for individual- and population-level differences in non-neural factors affecting the BOLD response, have led to the development of **calibrated BOLD fMRI** (Mark, Mazerolle, & Chen, 2015). This refers to a group of methods in which both physiological and neural activation factors are systematically manipulated. Using a biophysical (mathematical) model, calibrated BOLD makes it possible to calculate $CMRO_2$ with a high degree of accuracy. This technique was introduced by Hoge and colleagues (1999), who developed a way of measuring both CBF and BOLD signal in a single fMRI scan (by alternately collecting flow-sensitive and T2*-weighted images, such that both are obtained every few seconds), while at the same time manipulating the proportion of CO_2 in the air participants breathed, and the contrast of a visual stimulus. The technique pioneered by Hoge and colleagues works by inducing **hypercapnia** – elevated blood CO_2 levels – which in turn triggers vasodilation and increased blood flow as the body attempts to compensate and flush the CO_2 away, while providing increased O_2.

Hypercapnia is induced by having participants use a breathing apparatus during the MRI scan, which allows precise control of the relative levels of O_2 and CO_2 in the air that is inhaled. By measuring the changes in CBF and BOLD signal that occur over a different levels of CO_2, and systematically co-varying the contrast of the visual stimulus (higher contrast triggers higher neural activation), experimenters can extrapolate these values to determine a maximum possible BOLD signal (which would be obtained in the theoretical case of 100% oxy-Hb and no deoxy-Hb). This value is in turn used to calculate $CMRO_2$. More recently, related methods have been developed that rely on manipulation of O_2, rather than CO_2, levels. This **hyperoxic** method is more comfortable for the participant, because hypercapnia induces feelings of not being able to breathe properly, which can lead to panic in some people.

The importance of calibrated BOLD fMRI is being increasingly recognized in studies comparing different populations. As noted above, age, disease, and pharmacologic agents can all affect the BOLD signal through non-neural factors such as baseline CBF and metabolism. In addition to 'global' effects of such factors on the brain generally, more local effects can be observed in people with brain abnormalities such as stroke, Alzheimer's disease, and cerebrovascular disease. In these cases the magnitude of BOLD signal change from baseline to active conditions can vary substantially between different parts of the brain, which could in turn lead to erroneous conclusions from fMRI data. It is thus important in fMRI studies involving such between-group comparisons (or even within-group comparisons over time, for example when studying recovery from stroke) to assess regional variation in **cerebrovascular reserve** (**CVR**; also known as cerebrovascular reactivity), which is a measure of the amount of change in BOLD signal that different brain areas undergo as a function of CO_2 levels.

As a final note, the astute reader might note that the brain contains both excitatory and inhibitory neurons. Thus increased 'activity' seen with fMRI could in principle be attributable to increased firing rates of inhibitory neurons, rather than increased activation of excitatory neurons. The evidence does not suggest that this is the case, however. In general, inhibitory neurons comprise a smaller proportion of cells in the brain than excitatory. Moreover, the physiological processes involved in inhibitory synaptic activity differ from those of excitatory activity, in that they are much less reliant on ATP-consuming ion pumps – and thus less likely to drive the BOLD effect. This is, however, a relatively under-studied area and questions still remain concerning the relative contributions of excitatory and inhibitory neural activity on BOLD signal.

Properties of the BOLD Response

We have now established that the BOLD signal increases during neural activation, due to increases in oxygenated blood volume caused by dilation of blood vessels in response to changes in metabolic activity that are driven by synaptic activity. This cascade of events takes time to happen, and as a result the time course of the BOLD response to neural activation is quite different from the timing of the actual neural responses. Thus while the initial responses to a stimulus can be seen in EEG or MEG data after 50 ms or less (as early as a few seconds for auditory brainstem responses), fMRI responses evolve over many seconds. The shape of the BOLD fMRI response over time is called the **haemodynamic response function (HRF)**. Although the exact shape of the HRF varies between individuals and even between brain areas within individuals, it has a general characteristic shape and time course as shown in Figure 7.4. The HRF takes 1–2 seconds after an eliciting event to begin to rise, peaks after 6–8 seconds, and returns to baseline after approximately 12 seconds. Often, the return to baseline is followed by an 'undershoot' which lasts until roughly 15–18 seconds post-stimulus onset. This time course of the HRF is what would be seen to a brief, transit stimulus (such as in the visual cortex, in response to a brief visual image).

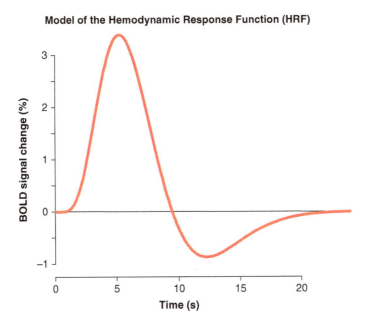

Figure 7.4 An example haemodynamic response function (HRF), representing a model of the time course of BOLD signal from the brain in response to a transient stimulus. Note the slow timing of this response compared to EEG or MEG

A first question to ask is how sure we are that BOLD fMRI changes actually reflect neural activity and, if so, what aspect of neural activity they reflect. The first part of this question – whether fMRI reflects neural activity – was well supported in the affirmative even in the first human fMRI studies, where signal changes were localized to those brain regions predicted a priori to show differences; for example, the occipital cortex for visual stimuli and the motor cortex for hand movements. However, this still leaves open the question of what aspect of neural activity the BOLD signal reflects. In a series of seminal experiments, Logothetis and colleagues (Logothetis, Pauls, Augath, Trinath, & Oeltermann, 2001) made direct recordings from electrodes implanted in the visual cortex of monkeys while simultaneously recording BOLD fMRI activity. The electrical recordings included both multi-unit activity (MUA) measurements (the spiking activity representing action potentials of neurons) and local field potentials, which reflect the slower changes in postsynaptic potentials (LFPs). The LFPs are thus sensitive to the same type of activity that is measured with EEG and MEG – although of course the latter techniques measure activity at the scalp and thus represent the summed activity of many brain regions, whereas LFPs represent changes localized to the area right around the electrode implanted in the cortex. Logothetis and colleagues' data showed that although both multi-unit and LFP recordings correlated with BOLD fMRI responses, the relationship was much tighter between BOLD and LFPs. The conclusion from this is that fMRI activity primarily reflects the relatively slow changes in postsynaptic potentials that result from the input delivered to a brain area, rather than the spiking output of that brain area. In this sense, fMRI can be taken to measure signals similar to what EEG or MEG measure (although with important caveats as discussed below).

The timing of the HRF is clearly very sluggish compared to the actual neural responses that induce it. This is attributable to the fact that, as discussed earlier, the BOLD response is an indirect reflection of neural activity, filtered through several physiological steps including neurotransmitter release and recycling, chemical messengers, and eventual vasodilation. As well, BOLD signal is biased towards the veins that drain the capillary bed serving the active neurons, so some of the signal delay may be due to the time it takes the influx of oxygenated blood to actually reach these veins. Furthermore, there is no reason to expect that the timing between the neural response and vasodilation is constant in different areas of the brain, or even within the same area, across different events or levels of neural activity. This has been demonstrated empirically in numerous studies. The timing and shape of the HRF itself is highly variable between individuals, and even between brain areas within individuals. Aguirre and colleagues (Aguirre, Zarahn, & D'esposito, 1998) examined HRF variability in the motor cortex in a simple button pressing task, and found that the peak of the HRF had a range of approximately 3–6 s between individuals. Other studies have reported ranges of 4–6 s (Buckner, Koutstaal, Schacter, Dale, Rotte, & Rosen, 1998) and 6–11 s (Birn, Saad, & Bandettini, 2001), using different tasks and examining different brain areas. Beyond the timing of the peak of the response, the shape has been shown to vary in other ways, including the time between stimulus onset and the initial rise of the HRF, and in whether or not there is an undershoot prior to a return to baseline. Beyond this natural range of variation in healthy individuals, as Handwerker and colleagues (Handwerker, Gonzalez-Castillo, D'Esposito, & Bandettini, 2012) put it, 'Virtually every examined disease state, age difference, or ingested substance causes changes in HRF shape' (p. 1019). This includes very commonly ingested substances like caffeine and Ibuprofen. The impact of this variability is nontrivial: data analysis of 'event-related' fMRI experiments (see below) relies on correcting BOLD signal with a model of the HRF, and models that are off by 2 s can reduce the estimated magnitude of the response by nearly 40% (Handwerker et al., 2012). One possible solution would be to run an initial scan for each participant in an fMRI study to estimate their individual HRF shape; however, this can vary from voxel to voxel and region to region within individuals, and many researchers are reluctant to spend valuable scan time on such 'reference' scans rather than scans that will yield publishable data. Other approaches to this problem include analysis methods that allow flexibility in fitting the shape of the HRF, but these can increase the complexity of the analysis and make interpretation more difficult.

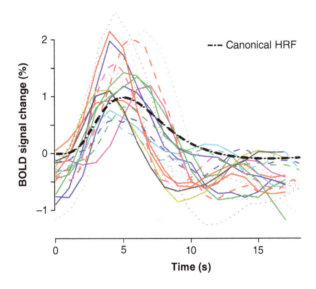

Figure 7.5 Individual variability in the shape and timing of the HRF. The black dashed line shows the canonical (mathematical model) HRF; each other line represents the HRF recorded from an individual. The data were obtained from primary motor cortex (M1) in a simple task where participants pressed a button as quickly as possible in response to a visual stimulus. Adapted from Handwerker, Ollinger, & D'Esposito, 2004 with permission of Elsevier

Although variability in HRF shape can reduce the sensitivity of the data analysis applied, nevertheless there is enough consistency and robustness across individuals that an average response can typically be measured in a properly powered experiment. The concerns raised here are most significant in two situations. One is in comparing different populations, who may show systematic differences in HRF shape and/or timing. In this case, researchers run the risk of vascular differences being mistaken for neural ones, and so approaches such as estimating the HRF in individuals – or even using calibrated fMRI as discussed above – may be warranted. The other situation where the timing of the HRF is a particularly important consideration is in so-called 'functional connectivity' analyses, which examine relationships in activity between different brain areas. These are discussed in greater detail below; for now we will simply say that one should proceed with extreme caution in making inferences about the timing of neural activation based on the timing of the HRF. While with EEG or MEG the relative timing of different events can be taken to literally reflect the sequence of neural activation, with fMRI this inference is tenuous at best, and often likely wrong. In other words, the relative timing of the BOLD response (for example, the onset or peak of the HRF) between brain areas should not be taken to represent the relative timing of the underlying neural activation in these brain areas.

Another consideration in contrasting EEG/MEG data with fMRI is that since the signals rely on such different mechanisms, there is no reason to expect that these techniques will all be sensitive to the same brain activation. EEG and MEG are most sensitive to open field configurations of neurons, with postsynaptic potentials that change coherently across the open fields. Thus there are numerous possible configurations of neurons, and patterns of activity, that will not give rise to a measurable EEG or MEG signal but could be detected by fMRI. Conversely, changes in the coherence of postsynaptic potentials could affect EEG or MEG signals without affecting fMRI signals, if the overall level of neural activity remained the same but was simply less correlated between neurons.

HOW DO WE MEASURE IT?

Pulse Sequences for fMRI

As noted above, BOLD fMRI relies on T2*-weighted images. Because T2* decay occurs much more quickly than either T1 relaxation or T2 decay, this necessitates very fast pulse sequences. The ability to acquire MR images very quickly is also critical to functional imaging because, as we saw in the previous section, the timing of the BOLD response is such that we need to be able to obtain a series of images relatively quickly (ideally every 1–2 s) in order to accurately characterize the shape of the response. Conventional (structural) MRI pulse sequences require in the order of 3–10 minutes to acquire a single image of the whole brain; clearly such timing would make fMRI impossible. Fortunately, pulse sequences have been developed that allow very rapid T2* weighted imaging. These allow TRs (repetition time – the time between each consecutive acquisition of a particular slice in the image, or effectively the time it takes to acquire all of the slices once) on the time scale necessary for fMRI. The most common pulse sequence used in BOLD fMRI is call **echo planar imaging (EPI)**. Another frequently used pulse sequence is spiral imaging. The two sequences differ in how they traverse k space; however, both have in common their sensitivity to T2* contrast, and relatedly their ability to scan through k space very quickly in comparison to conventional pulse sequences.

The idea of EPI was originally developed in the 1970s by Sir Peter Mansfield (Mansfield, 2001; Stehling, Turner, & Mansfield, 1991), who went on to receive the Nobel Prize in Physiology or Medicine for this and related work on MRI. The key innovation in this technique is filling all of k space after a single RF excitation.

In contrast, recall that traditional pulse sequences fill k space in a stepwise fashion, conducting one phase encoding step per excitation. Given that each slice in a typical fMRI image may contain 64 × 64 or even 128 × 128 voxels, EPI represents an increase of 64 or 128x in the speed of acquisition over a traditional phase encoding scheme. Since a typical T1- or T2-weighted image can take several minutes to acquire, this speed increase was necessary to make time-resolved MRI possible. To scan this fast, the MRI's gradients need to be stronger than for most other types of sequences (gradient strength is a feature of the MRI hardware itself), and be able to switch direction very rapidly. In fact, Mansfield's development of EPI was entirely theoretical until the late 1980s and early 1990s, when advances in engineering finally yielded MRI hardware capable of performing these scans – which in turn coincided with the timing of the first published human fMRI studies.

Rapid and frequent gradient switching is key to EPI scanning. In an EPI pulse sequence, excitation and slice selection are followed by activation of the frequency and phase encoding gradients (G_x and G_y) to move to one corner of k space. After the time required to fill the first line of k space, the G_x gradient is reversed, and at the same time the G_y gradient is adjusted to fill the next phase line of k space. This contrasts with the typical approach described in the previous chapter, in which each phase encoding step requires a separate RF excitation and slice selection process. Instead, in EPI all the lines along the phase encoding direction of k space (k_y) are filled after a single excitation/slice selection pulse. In this way the frequency encoding of the second line of k space occurs in the opposite direction from the first line. This process continues, zig-zagging back and forth through k space until it is filled. This process is shown in Figure 7.6.

The process just described obtains an entire MR image slice in one excitation step. On modern scanners, the time required to traverse all of k space to acquire a single slice through the brain can be as short as 20 ms. In a typical fMRI scan, a set of slices (usually 3–4 mm thick, or less) is obtained that cover the entire brain, top to bottom, on each TR. Thus one TR comprises a series of single slice acquisitions that are assembled to form a 3D brain volume, a process which takes typically from 1–3 seconds depending on the scanner hardware, software, and the thickness of the slices. Thinner slices necessitate more slices for a given amount of brain coverage, and so increased resolution requires increased time. Modern scanners are capable of whole-brain acquisitions in less than one second, although TRs in the order of 2 s are still very common. In general, one should aim for full-brain coverage at the desired spatial resolution, and then set the TR as short as is possible given the constraints the scanner hardware imposes based on the spatial resolution and number of slices. Although shorter TRs lead to larger data files (since there are more individual time points, and each time point comprises a 3D image with upwards of 100,000 voxels), which are more demanding on storage and processing, the advantages gained include more accurate resolution of the time course of the haemodynamic response, and greater statistical sensitivity to experimental effects. The latter benefit accrues from the fact that in analysing the time course of an fMRI image, each time point contributes information, and from a statistical standpoint, degrees of freedom, leading to greater statistical power.

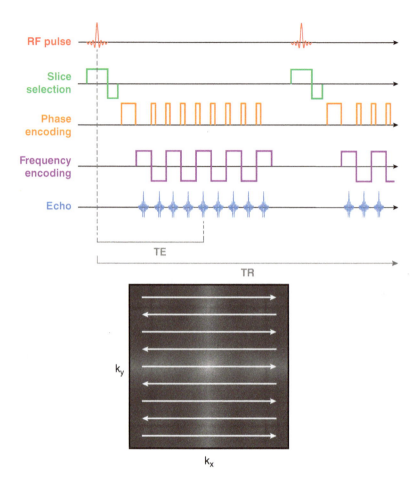

Figure 7.6 EPI pulse sequence trajectory through k space. Unlike the more conventional pulse sequence shown in the previous chapter, in EPI all rows of k space are filled after a single excitation (RF pulse and slice selection gradient). Thus the phase encoding gradient is applied multiple times, with different strengths, and the frequency encoding gradient rapidly switches directions at the end of each row of k space. In this way a single slice can be captured in as little as 100 ms, and enough slices to cover the whole brain can typically be obtained in under 2 s

The rapid switching of strong magnetic field gradients is not only demanding on MRI hardware, but it creates images that are very sensitive to distortion. Firstly, proper reconstruction of the images requires that the data from every second line of k space be properly realigned since the frequency encoding direction changes by 180° with every phase encoding step. Inaccuracies in this step can lead to 'ghosting' in the images whereby a faint image of the brain appears overlaid on the image, but shifted halfway along the phase encoding direction. Since phase encoding in EPI images is typically the anterior–posterior dimension, this means that a 'ghost' of the front of the brain would appear overlaid with the middle of the brain. This can be avoided with proper implementation of the pulse sequence and reconstruction algorithm however. A more common and problematic artifact arises due to inhomogeneities in the magnetic field within the area being scanned. While the magnetic field of MRI scanners is made to be extremely homogeneous during installation, and regular quality assurance procedures and maintenance will maintain this homogeneity, this is disrupted by the presence of a head in the MRI scanner. The many different tissue types in the head (predominantly air, bone, fat, muscle, and water, and also dental work) all have distinct magnetic properties, and in particular the boundaries between different materials are problematic because the magnetic field properties change dramatically at these points. Thus while the application of a magnetic field gradient (such as G_x and G_y) to a homogeneous medium such as water would produce a truly linear slope in the magnetic field strength, local inhomogeneities in the brain create a more uneven gradient, which in turn leads to distortions in the reconstructed image. In particular, signal loss occurs because the actual Larmor frequency at a location of high inhomogeneity is relatively far from what would be predicted from the application of the gradient. In EPI images, the most dramatic examples of these artifacts – called **magnetic susceptibility** artifacts – occur in the parts of the brain nearest to air pockets inside the head: the inferior frontal lobe (orbitofrontal cortex), which is directly above the sinuses, and the inferior temporal lobes above the ear canals. These artifacts are shown in Figure 7.7.

Another artifact that occurs as the result of the demands of EPI scanning is geometric distortion of the images. EPI images often look smeared, particularly at the front of the head, and the front of the head may also appear to have a 'bite' taken out of it, as shown in Figure 7.7. These are due to the fact that in an EPI acquisition there is only one TE for the entire set of phase and frequency encoding steps. Thus the TE is optimal only for the centre of k space, and increasingly sub-optimal for the more distal portions of k space. This is in contrast to conventional pulse sequences, in which the TE occurs at the same time after every phase encoding step. Thus in EPI, more time elapses between some phase encoding steps and the readout time than others, leading to greater signal decay prior to readout. Moreover, these effects are amplified by any magnetic field inhomogeneities in the head. In effect, rather than the trajectory through k space being a precise set of horizontal lines along the frequency dimension alternating with vertical 'blips' in the phase direction – as shown in Figure 7.6 – the trajectory through k space will be a distorted version of this, with the horizontal lines being somewhat angled or even wiggly, and some phase blips occurring before a frequency encoding line reaches the far edge of k space.

These artifacts can be reduced through a number of methods. A number of acquisition strategies can be used, including **shimming** – corrections for local inhomogeneities using additional hardware coils – and applying additional gradients (for example, in the slice selection direction) for correction. In some cases, slight adjustments to the position and angle of the slices can reduce susceptibility artifact, and distortions are also reduced when slice thickness is thinner. Another way to reduce spatial distortions is to use **parallel imaging**. This requires special head coils (the RF receiver around the head is in during scanning) that have multiple receiver coils placed around the head (typically 8–32 coils or 'channels'). Because each coil samples the head from a different position, the nature of the spatial distortions in each differ and when the images from all channels are averaged, the distortions are reduced.

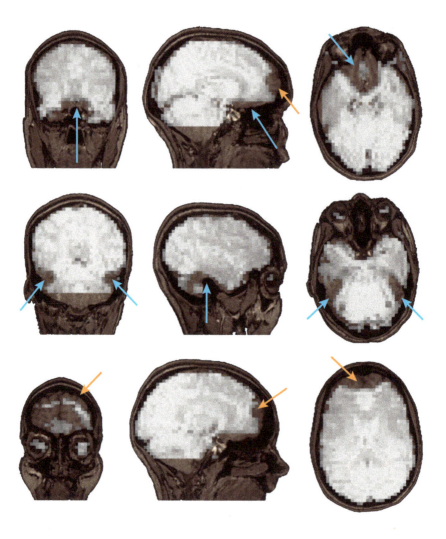

Figure 7.7 EPI susceptibility artifacts and geometric distortion. An EPI image (greyscale) is overlaid on a high-resolution T1-weighted structural scan from the same individual; images were acquired on a 3T scanner. This highlights the areas of the brain that are characterized by signal dropout in the EPI images. Blue arrows point to magnetic susceptibility artifacts in the orbitofrontal (top-row) and inferior temporal (middle-row) regions. Orange arrows point to geometric distortion in the frontal pole

Multi-channel coils have several other advantages, including improvements in SNR and reduced acquisition time. Faster imaging is possible because each individual coil actually samples k space more sparsely than when a single-channel coil is used, requiring less time; since multiple coils are sampling k space in parallel, however, the sampling of k space in the reconstructed image is as good or better than with a single-channel coil. Another approach is to acquire a **magnetic field map**. This is done using a separate MRI sequence (and so requires some extra scan time) that will characterize how the field is distorted by the presence of the individual's head. This map is then used in post-processing to 'unwarp' the EPI images. This unwarping will produce EPI images that more accurately reflect the true shape of the brain. However, since the warping conflated signals from different spatial locations, it is mathematically impossible to separate these after the fact, which means that the brain's shape will appear more accurate (and thus easier to co-register with the structural image; see below), but inaccuracies in the spatial localization of BOLD signal will be present in the areas that originally had artifact.

An alternative pulse sequence for BOLD fMRI is called **spiral imaging**. This is similar to EPI in that it is a scheme for traversing all of k space in a single excitation step; however, the path through k space is a spiral rather than a zigzag, as shown in Figure 7.8. This trajectory is obtained by oscillating both the G_x and G_y gradients synchronously. Spiral imaging is less demanding on the gradient hardware, because changes in gradient strength occur gradually, rather than abruptly and dramatically. It is also more efficient than EPI, because in EPI the phase encoding 'blips' take time but do not directly contribute to the data readout, and so the scan time can be reduced which will contribute to reduced geometric distortions in the image. Although magnetic field inhomogeneities still cause both susceptibility artifacts and geometric distortions in spiral images, the shape of these spatial distortions is different due to the different path through k space. One way of partially compensating for this is to perform 'spiral in-out' imaging. While in a typical spiral scan, the k space trajectory is from the centre of k space outward, in a spiral in-out scan two sequential acquisitions are made (with separate excitation pulses): one starting from the centre of k space, and one starting at the edge of k space and spiralling inward. Since the geometric distortions are magnified as the time between excitation and readout, combining the 'in' and 'out' spiral trajectories helps to cancel out much of this distortion. In practice, EPI pulse sequences are more widely available on commercial MRI scanners than are spiral sequences, and so spiral imaging is less widely used.

Typically an fMRI experiment for an individual participant involves a number of scans, and typically takes between 45–90 min depending on the complexity of the experiment. Because participants have to lie still and try to move as little as possible during the experiment, it is ideal to keep experiments on the shorter side because as time wears on, participants may become bored, tired, and uncomfortable and data quality may suffer. A common structure for an experiment would be to start with a 'scout' scan, which typically takes less than 1 min to acquire and provides information concerning where the person's head is positioned in the scanner, and allows the operator to position the slices for the other scans according to the specific anatomy of the individual. This is then followed by several fMRI 'runs', defined as

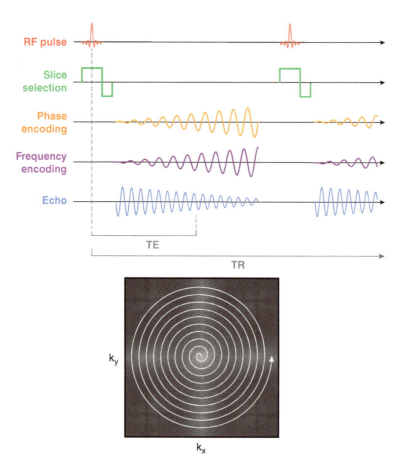

Figure 7.8 Spiral pulse sequence trajectory through *k* space. As with EPI, spiral imaging fills all of *k* space for a single slice in one excitation. However, rather than rapidly switching the phase encoding gradient on and off, and reversing the frequency encoding gradient, the strength of both gradients is continuously modulated in a sinusoidal fashion. This creates the spiral trajectory shown in the bottom panel. Spiral pulse sequences are less taxing on the gradient hardware, and are associated with different distortion artifacts than EPI, but are less widely available on different scanner platforms

periods of continuous scanning when the experiment is conducted. Typically runs last approximately 5 min, although in principle they could be much shorter or much longer (20 min or more). However, experience suggests that 4–6 min is a reasonable amount of time to expect a person in the scanner to hold still and stay focused on the task; in between runs the participant can rest, scratch an itch, etc. Shorter runs are a less effective use of scanner time, both because of the increased amount of 'down time' between scans cutting into the proportion of time that data is being collected, and also the fact that fMRI statistical power is in part dependent on the number of samples taken during a scan – so, for example, it would be harder to detect activation in five 1 min scans than in a single 5 min scan.

An anatomical (typically T1-weighted) scan is also routinely obtained in fMRI studies because the functional images are optimized for BOLD contrast, rather than anatomical (grey matter/white matter/CSF) contrast. Anatomical scans facilitate both localization of activations on the individual's brain, and co-registration of activations across the individuals in the study (this is discussed in more detail later in the chapter). Finally, other pulse sequences may be run depending on the research question and data-processing stream. These could include magnetic field mapping sequences used to correct for image distortions, as discussed above, or other structural scans such as for volumetric, morphometric, or diffusion tensor imaging (these techniques are discussed in the following two chapters). The relative timing of these different scans is at the discretion of the researcher (with the exception of the scout scan, which is necessarily obtained first); however, since people tend to become increasingly fatigued as the scan wears on, there is value in running the fMRI scans first and other scans after – or interspersing functional and other scans to give people breaks between the functional scans (which may be desirable in some experimental designs).

IMAGE PREPROCESSING

As with all neuroimaging techniques, fMRI data requires **preprocessing** prior to statistical analysis. The goals of preprocessing are to reduce noise and therefore improve data quality, and ultimately our ability to detect experimental effects in the data.

Filtering

As we have seen, a typical first preprocessing step for neuroimaging data is filtering, to remove effects of non-interest. However, the frequency range of interest for fMRI is very different from EEG or MEG, since we are measuring a different thing (the HRF) and sampling at a much lower rate: TR values in fMRI tend to be in the 1–2 s range, which equates to a sampling rate of 1–0.5 Hz. By the Nyquist theorem, we are therefore limited to measuring quite low frequency fluctuations (below 0.33 Hz for a TR of 1 s, or below 0.167 Hz for a TR of 2 s). Since the HRF typically has a time to peak of about 6 s and returns to baseline after 12–20 s, this means that the highest frequencies we would expect associated with BOLD signal would be < 0.1 Hz. On the other hand, BOLD fMRI signal is contaminated by other, higher-frequency physiological artifacts, in particular from respiration and pulse. Because these have relatively high frequencies relative to the fMRI sampling rate, they are aliased into the recorded fMRI signal as low-frequency components, and so high-pass filtering is typically applied to fMRI data to remove these artifacts. The exact frequency cutoff depends on the experimental design (specifically the highest expected frequencies associated with the experimental manipulation, convolved with the HRF), but are generally in the range of 0.1–0.2 Hz.

Motion Correction

A second, virtually essential preprocessing step is **motion correction**. As we learned in the previous chapter, spatial encoding in MRI scanning is determined by the spatial gradients. Because these are part of the MRI hardware, and are centred on the centre of the bore of the MRI scanner, it is important that the head being scanned is located in the centre of the bore. In practice, an initial 'scout' image is acquired prior to any other scanning, and this is used to position the slices for all structural and functional MRI scans relative to the actual position (and size and shape) of the person's head. However, this all assumes a fixed head position. If the head moves at all, serious problems occur – for several reasons. Firstly, because fMRI scanning occurs over time and multiple samples are acquired (a typical 5 min scan with a 2 s TR yields 300 images of the brain), if the head moves then the part of the brain that was in a given voxel will not be located in that voxel after movement occurs. If nothing else, this will cause abrupt changes in signal if the two locations in the brain have different signal levels. However, this concern is greatly amplified because scanning relies on the application of multiple magnetic field gradients at different times. So if the head moves between slice selection and readout, then the part of the brain that was excited by the RF pulse will not be in the same position relative to the other gradients during frequency and/or phase encoding. Also, subsequent RF pulses may result in above- or below-expected amounts of excitation in certain parts of the brain, because an area that was excited by one pulse may be excited by the next pulse as it moves into the plane of a different slice (relative to the original slice plane). As well, if the movement results in a different tissue type (or no tissue at all) being in a voxel, then very dramatic changes in the signal intensity at that voxel will occur. This is most pronounced at the edges of the brain, because the brain itself yields a relatively large signal relative to the CSF – so a voxel may contain (bright) brain at one point in time and (dark) CSF at the next sampling time, after the movement. This results in large 'spikes' in the fMRI time series that are significantly larger than the small (typically a few per cent) changes associated with normal BOLD signal. These artifacts are illustrated in Figure 7.9. As well, the overall shape of the brain image may change with head movement due to the susceptibility and spatial distortion artifacts inherent in echo planar and spiral imaging pulse sequences. These large motion spikes can end up being mis-identified as activation during analysis, especially if they happen to correlate with experimental factors such as the appearance of stimuli or button presses.

All mainstream fMRI analysis software packages include a motion correction algorithm that attempts to identify and correct for head motion. This is done using a relatively simple image processing approach whereby one time point (typically either at the start or midpoint of the run) is chosen as a reference and each other ('target') time point is compared to this by subtracting the two images. The algorithm then iteratively moves the target brain image slightly in different directions (shifts – commonly called translations – and rotations) and re-computes the difference between the two images to find the transformation that yields the smallest possible difference. Although effective up to a point, motion correction approaches

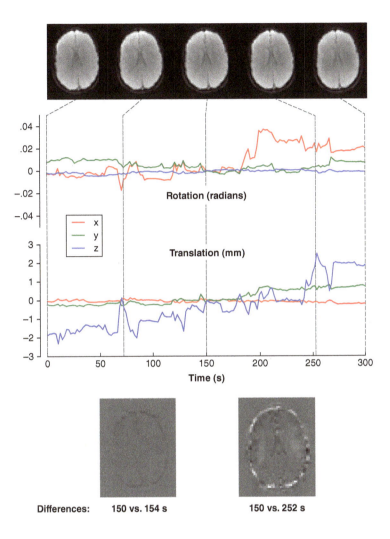

Figure 7.9 Motion detection and correction for fMRI. The top row shows a single slice from an EPI time series, at five different time points (dashed grey lines) across a 5 min scan. Although all of the images look roughly the same to the naked eye, a motion detection algorithm found some rotation over time, as well as (for fMRI) a significant amount of translational movement in the z plane. Rotations around each principal axis are shown in the second row, and translations in each plane in the third row. Note in particular the 'spikes' of motion on the order of 1.5-2 mm at the second and fourth time points highlighted. The bottom row, left panel shows the difference between the middle time point (150 s) and a time point 4 s (two acquisitions) later, while the bottom right panel shows the difference between the middle time point and 252 s, corresponding to the second large translation in z. The difference between these two time points highlights the extreme values (bright and dark spots) created by head motion. As well, the fact that the structural anatomy is more visible in the latter image (for example, skull outline, ventricles in the middle of the brain, outline of each hemisphere) reinforces the fact that motion artifacts are most pronounced at the edges of different tissue types

are fundamentally limited by the physics of MRI. Too large a movement results in uncorrectable artifacts because it is impossible to accurately account for the effects of movement of heterogeneous tissue through a complex set of magnetic field gradients as well as the supra- or super-additivity effects of the RF pulses. Thus the general rule of thumb is that only movements of about half of the size of the voxel can be adequately corrected for. In a typical scan with 3–4 mm voxels, this means that head movements of 1.5–2 mm may result in unusable data. Scans with smaller voxels sizes will have smaller tolerances and thus be more sensitive to motion artifacts. These are very small movements – indeed, so small that many people might not realize they are making them. Thus it is always important both to emphasize to participants how important it is to stay still during scanning, and to take preventative measures such as packing the space between the head and the head coil with foam. Other types of head restraints (such as masks or bite bars) may be used, but these generally make people uncomfortable and so may ultimately not result in better data quality. Another option (primarily used with children and some clinical populations) is to train people to hold still outside of the scanner. This can be done in a mock MRI scanner with a built-in camera system that tracks head movement and provides feedback when movement exceeds a threshold – for example, by temporarily pausing a movie that the person is watching. A recent advancement is to implement this game on a tablet so that children can train at home, lying on a bed with the tablet held in a special frame above their head and using the tablet's built-in camera to track movement.

Spatial Smoothing

Spatial smoothing is the application of a spatial filter, but can be thought of as 'blurring' the fMRI image prior to analysis. Although this might seem to go contrary to the goal of achieving high spatial resolution brain imaging, there are several good reasons that spatial smoothing is almost always recommended. Firstly, it helps to reduce noise in the image. At the level of brain organization we are typically interested in with fMRI, activation is expected to be spread out over relatively extended areas of brain tissue encompassing more than a single voxel, or even a few voxels. Thus when imaging at a typical resolution of 2–4 mm voxels, it is reasonable to predict that highly focal 'effects' (only a few voxels in size) are attributable to noise rather than brain activation. Spatial smoothing reduces such 'pointillistic' noise. This can be observed in Figure 7.10. Typically smoothing is done using a Gaussian **kernel** – the 2D or 3D equivalent of a Gaussian (normal) distribution – as shown in Figure 7.11. The size of the smoothing kernel is typically described by its width at half of its maximum height (**full-width at half-maximum; FWHM**). A rule of thumb is to use a smoothing kernel whose FWHM is 1.5–2 times the voxel dimensions of the input image. Thus for $3 \times 3 \times 3$ mm voxels, a kernel of 4.5–6 mm would be appropriate.

Another advantage of spatial smoothing is that, according to the **matched filter theorem,** if we filter an image with a kernel that matches the expected size of the features in the image we are looking for (in our case, 'blobs' of brain activation), we should enhance those relevant details while reducing the influence of noise from

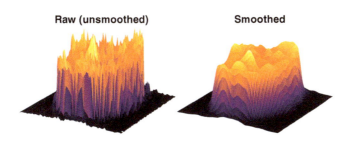

Figure 7.10 A comparison of data in a 2D slice before (left) and after (right) spatial smoothing. Both images are representations of a single slice from a BOLD EPI image, but with the intensity at each voxel represented both by height and colour to highlight the changes in smoothness. Note how the voxel-to-voxel variability is greatly reduced in the smoothed image. Overall, amplitudes are smaller after smoothing, however the major peaks are retained, but are more distinctive due to the reduction in noise. Figures generated with code adapted from Dr Matthew Brett, University of Birmingham, with permission

Figure 7.11 An example of a 2D Gaussian smoothing kernel that could be applied to a slice of an fMRI image. Effectively, the centre of this kernel would be placed at each voxel in a 2D slice, and the resulting, smoothed, value at that location in the image would be the sum of the original intensity value at that voxel, plus a proportion of the values at surrounding voxels as determined by the height of the kernel at each surrounding voxel. For example, if the kernel overlapped a certain voxel where the height of the kernel was half of its maximum, then half of the intensity of that voxel would be added to the intensity of the centre voxel being smoothed. Figure generated with code adapted from Dr Matthew Brett, University of Birmingham, with permission

smaller and (to a lesser extent) larger spatial features in the image. This is apparent both for the area of activation in Figure 7.12, and even for the grey-white-CSF contrast in the underlying greyscale in the figure: the major anatomical features are clearer in the 6 mm smoothed image than either the 4 or 9 mm, suggesting that in this case 6 mm is the closest match to the spatial frequency of these anatomical features.

Another reason to perform spatial filtering is that many fMRI analysis approaches base the identification of spatially extended clusters of activation on algorithms that assume that the noise in fMRI images has a Gaussian distribution; while this has been shown to be approximately true anyway, applying a Gaussian filter brings the data more into line with this expectation, making the statistics more reliable. Finally, spatial smoothing can help account for small inaccuracies in alignment of brains between individuals, as discussed in the next section.

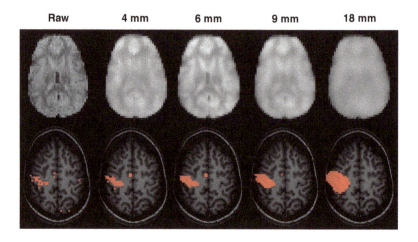

Figure 7.12 Spatial smoothing. Top row shows a slice of an EPI image with no smoothing ('raw'), and increasingly large Gaussian kernels. Note that the 6 mm kernel best highlights the structural anatomy of the image (grey-white-CSF contrast). This suggests that 6 mm is a better match to the actual spatial frequencies in the image than either smaller or larger kernels. The bottom row shows statistical maps from the same person, showing (in red) the contrast in BOLD signal when they tapped their fingers together with their right hand relative to no movements – again with different smoothing kernels. As expected, this activation is focused in primary motor cortex in the hemisphere opposite to the hand involved. Although the un-smoothed data shows activation that most closely matches the shape of the cortical grey matter, the smoothed images show this activation over larger areas, which can help to facilitate overlap in group averages. As well, note the numerous small red spots in the un-smoothed image, and how most of them disappear with smoothing (suggesting they were random noise) while the spot on the medial (midline) surface of the left hemisphere increases slightly in size and remains present in the 4 and 6 mm (and to some extent 9 mm) smoothed images. This suggests that, rather than being random noise, this small area is likely a true activation. The fact that this small area of activation disappears at larger smoothing kernels, while the larger area of activation remains and increases in size, is consistent with the matched filter theorem

Spatial Normalization

One of the first problems that fMRI researchers had to address in averaging data across individuals was that everybody's head (and brain) is a different size and shape, as illustrated in Figure 7.13. However, data analysis is almost invariably done for each voxel separately, so we need to have a way of ensuring that across individuals, the same voxel in the MRI volume corresponds to the same part of the brain. This process is called **spatial normalization**. The initial way of doing this was borrowed from neurosurgery; French surgeons Talairach and Tournoux (1988) had produced an atlas of the brain, labelling different areas and providing spatial coordinates in a 3D Cartesian frame. This atlas was based on a single brain (that of a deceased elderly woman, which had been preserved in formaldehyde), and a method was provided to adjust the size of any other brain to this reference. This method involved marking two small, but readily identified structures in the midline of the brain: the anterior and posterior commissures. These are small white matter bundles that connect the two cerebral hemispheres, and are quite easily seen on a T1-weighted structural MRI. The line through these two commissures defines the horizontal plane of this coordinate system, and the longitudinal fissure dividing the two hemispheres defines the vertical plane; the third dimension is defined as orthogonal to these other two planes. The brain is then divided into 12 sections and each is scaled to match the size of the reference brain. Coordinates are measured in millimetres, with the centre of the system (0, 0, 0) defined as the anterior commissure.

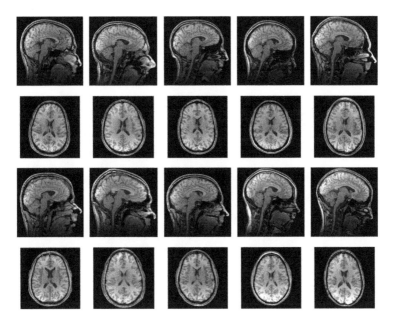

Figure 7.13 T1-weighted images from ten individuals who participated in an fMRI study, showing approximately the same locations in the brain. Note the wide differences in brain size and shape that are evident at the level of gross anatomy

The research community quickly identified problems with this system. One issue was that the reference brain was likely a choice of convenience for Talairach and Tournoux, but was not representative of the typical healthy young adult brain in vivo – which comprises the bulk of the population used in fMRI studies. Secondly, the scaling approach was very approximate and could obviously not match the size and shape of any two brains at the level of spatial resolution typical of fMRI (millimetres), and could not account for variations in size and shape below the level of the 12 'chunks' of brain used in the Talairach and Tournoux system. As well, the Talairach and Tournoux process relied on having a skilled user manually identify and mark the necessary anatomical landmarks in each brain; an automated approach was desirable. Addressing these problems required two different things: a better reference brain and better alignment algorithms.

Although ultimately our goal is to have the BOLD fMRI data spatially normalized to the template, in most cases the template is provided as a T1-weighted structural image, because these have high spatial resolution and excellent grey-white-CSF contrast. Typically, then, spatial normalization occurs in three steps: first, a structural image from the individual participant is aligned to their (motion-corrected) functional data; second, the participant's structural image is normalized to the (structural) template brain; and, finally, those two mappings (participant's structural to participant's functional, and participant's structural to template) are mathematically combined to create the mapping from the participant's functional data to the standard

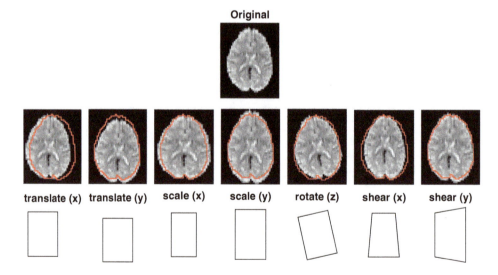

Figure 7.14 Linear affine spatial registration, as used in normalizing individual brains to a common space. The top row shows the original image. The middle row shows examples of the different types of affine transformations that can be applied; the red outline shows the original brain shape, while the greyscale image shows the transformed image. The bottom row shows the same transformations applied to a simple rectangle

space template. Mapping the participant's functional to their structural image is achieved using a process virtually identical to that used for motion correction (finding the optimal set of translations and rotations to minimize the difference between the images), except in this case adjustments are made to the algorithm because the structural and functional images have different weightings, so we cannot expect that the image contrast will compare between the two images. As well, compensation for spatial distortion of the fMRI images can be made (for example, applying magnetic field map correction). In the second step, the structural image from the participant is adjusted to match the size and shape of the template brain. This uses the same iterative fitting approach; however, because the two brains will have different shapes and sizes, more parameters are adjusted in the mapping process. Thus in addition to translation along and rotation around each axis, scaling (stretching or shrinking) can be applied along each of the three dimensions, and also 'shears' along each dimension that allow for greater geometric distortion (for example, making the brain narrower in the front but wider in the back). This approach is called **affine linear registration**; Figure 7.14 illustrates the different types of transformations that can be applied, and Figure 7.15 illustrates the steps in affine registration from an individual's EPI to a template structural image.

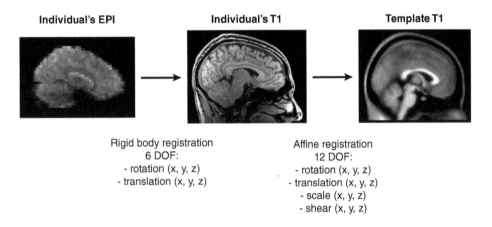

Figure 7.15 The process of linear spatial normalization. In one step, the individual's high-resolution, T1-weighted structural image is registered to the template T1 image (such as the MNI152 standard brain). This step uses affine linear registration to adjust the size and shape of the individual's brain to match the template as closely as possible. In a second step, the individual's EPI image is registered to their own T1 weighted image. Typically a single time point, or average across time, is used to calculate the transformation since the EPI images will have already been motion corrected. This step uses only rigid body registration, because there is no reason to think that the actual size or shape of the person's brain would change between the two scans. Finally, the two sets of registration parameters – one mapping from the individual's T1 to the template, and the other mapping from the EPI images to the individual's T1 – are mathematically combined. This combined transformation is then used to normalize the individual's EPI images to the template

Although affine registration is far more accurate than the Talairach and Tournoux approach, it is still only an approximation based primarily on matching the overall size and shape of the brain. The more fine-grained details, such as individual gyri and sulci, will in general be matched reasonably well, but inaccuracies of several millimetres or more can be reasonably expected. Given that areas of activation are expected to be spatially extended, and also because the same functional area may not lie in exactly the same anatomical location relative to the gross anatomy across individuals (that is, an activated area may be on the gyrus of one subject and in the adjacent sulcus of another), and further because of spatial smoothing, this level of accuracy was historically well-accepted in the fMRI community and a large proportion of published papers used such linear registration. However, in the quest for even higher accuracy – which may be advantageous in identifying very focal activation, differentiating activations between nearby regions (as in mapping relationships between stimulation of specific locations on the retina and their corresponding activations in the visual cortex), or in some structural imaging techniques as discussed in the next chapter – alternative approaches have been developed that yield higher spatial accuracy. One is **non-linear registration**, which uses 2D basis functions (sine wave gratings). In this approach, affine registration is first used to get a best linear fit, and then additional warping is done to apply non-linear ('curvy' or 'wavy') adjustments to the shape of the brain. This is illustrated in Figure 7.16. The template and individual participant's brains are each characterized by a set of

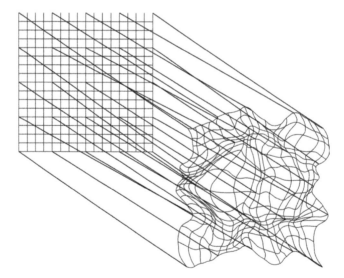

Figure 7.16 Non-linear normalization using basis function warping. After matching the 2D basis functions (Fourier transforms) of the individual's T1 to the template, the size and shape of individual voxels from the original image (left) are adjusted in localized, non-linear ways (right) to obtain the best match to the template. Reprinted from Ashburner and Friston (2007) with permission

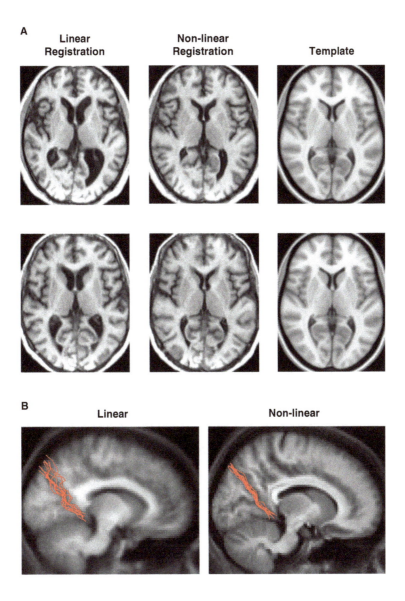

Figure 7.17 Comparison of the results of linear versus non-linear registration of T1 structural images to a standard template. Panel A shows axial slices from two individuals (top and bottom rows, respectively), after linear (left column) and non-linear (middle column) registration. The template (which is identical for both cases) is shown in the right column. In B, the parieto-occipital sulcus was traced on the brains of ten individuals (red), after linear (left) and non-linear (right) registration. The results are superimposed on the template brain to which they were registered. In both A and B non-linear registration shows clear improvements in the similarity of the registered brains to the template, although some variability always remains. Images in panel A reproduced from https://fsl.fmrib.ox.ac.uk/fsl/fslwiki/FNIRT (retrieved 10 February 2018) with permission of J. Andersson and M. Jenkinson; images in panel B reprinted from Andersson, Jenkinson, and Smith (2007) with permission of the authors

weightings on 2D sine and cosine basis functions (essentially, a 2D Fourier decomposition is performed), and then the algorithm determines the optimal making to 'warp' the individual's basis functions to match those of the template image. This can yield improvements in the accuracy of registration that are significant enough to be visible to the naked eye, as shown in Figure 7.17.

An rather different alternative approach to spatial normalization is **spherical surface-based normalization** first pioneered by Fischl, Sereno, Tootell, and Dale (1999). The rationale for this approach was the recognition that the primary interest in most fMRI studies is not the whole brain volume, but the cortical surface. Moreover, this surface is continuous but heavily folded. Because of this folding, some regions of the cortex that are close to each other in 3D space – such as either side of a sulcus – are actually quite distant from each other along the cortical surface. However, an approach that adjusts brain size and shape in 3D space may conflate data from these distant areas in the same voxels. The approach developed by Fischl and colleagues involves extracting the cortical surface from a high-resolution structural MR image (for example, a T1 weighted image), cutting the brain along the midline to separate the two hemispheres, and then 'sealing' the cut so each hemisphere is represented as a continuous (but still folded) surface. Then, each hemisphere is computationally inflated into a sphere, using a transformation that minimizes the amount of spatial distortion (stretching or squishing) required. This is illustrated in Figure 7.18. An important feature of this transformation is that it is entirely reversible, so that although the shape changes, it is still possible to map each location on the sphere back to its original position in the folded brain. The template brain is likewise inflated to a spherical shape, and then the individual brain is aligned to the template. By inflating both brains to spherical shapes, there is no problem in matching the size or shape of the brain. Rather, the algorithm focuses on aligning the folding patterns (gyri and sulci) between individuals. Because this approach focuses explicitly on aligning cortical features, it is less prone to blurring anatomically defined areas across individuals, compared to other methods. Although the brain is represented as a smooth sphere, the locations of the gyri and sulci are still identifiable because the inflation process computes 'convexity' values that reflect the curvature of the original brain at each point on the smoothed surface; gyri have negative convexity values and sulci have positive ones. By examining the convexity values and their variance, the algorithm is able to match the positions of the folds across subjects, with an emphasis on best-matching the major sulci (for example, central sulcus and Sylvian fissure) that both dominate cortical shape and are least variable between individuals. Increasingly, fMRI researchers are recognizing the value of analysing and viewing activation maps on inflated surfaces rather than 2D slices or folded surfaces. Although inflation for analysis and/or visualization purposes is possible after using affine or non-linear warping algorithms, this surface-based alignment approach provides a more integrated and principled approach to the problem. That said, all of these registration methods are widely used and accepted in the field, although it is important to keep in mind that the same data may yield slightly different results depending on which algorithm is used.

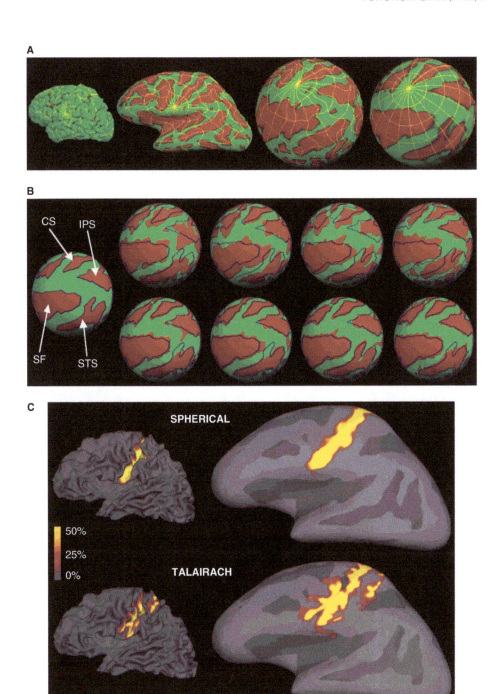

Figure 7.18 The spherical surface-based normalization method developed by Fischl and colleagues. (A) shows the steps of inflation of the cortical surface, from the original brain (left) to an inflated brain-like shape, to a sphere. The

Figure 7.18 (Continued)

right-most panel shows the average of 40 individuals in this spherical space. The final step would be to align the gyri and sulci of the individual's spherical brain to that of the template. (B) shows the hemispheres of four people before (top row) and after (bottom row) normalization to the template brain (left; arrows and labels indicate major sulci that drive the matching process). (C) shows the anatomical localization of the central sulcus across 11 individuals, comparing spherical normalization with the original method of Talairach and Tournoux (1988). While the spherical normalization produced a coherent, smooth, and connected average sulcus - consistent with the true anatomy of any individual - the Talairach process resulted in less overlap (red as opposed to yellow), and even areas that are disconnected from each other - inconsistent with true anatomy. Note that Talairach normalization is less accurate than linear affine or non-linear warping algorithms as well. Republished with permission of John Wiley & Sons Inc., from Bruce Fischl et al. (1999)

We now return to the issue of an ideal reference brain. Recall that the Talairach and Tournoux reference was based on the brain of a single, deceased woman in her 80s. The brain had been fixed in formaldehyde and sat out of the body for some period of time, both of which likely led to spatial distortions relative to a healthy living brain, suspended in CSF and perfused with blood. To develop a better reference brain, the Montreal Neurological Institute (MNI; later as part of the International Consortium for Brain Mapping – ICBM) developed a template based on structural MRI scans of hundreds of healthy young adults. A spatial average of all of these scans was obtained (using linear registration to minimize the differences between the brains as a group) and this was in turn referenced to the original Talairach and Tournoux brain, to allow with comparability with that coordinate system, which was already the standard in the field. This standardized atlas has gone through several iterations to improve its quality; as of this writing the most widely used version (and the one distributed with all major fMRI analysis software packages) is the MNI152, based on 152 brains but referenced to an original average of 305 other brains using more advanced algorithms. However, it is very important to understand that the MNI and Talairach coordinate systems are not the same. They are quite similar; however, in matching the overall size and shape of the average healthy brain to the Talairach and Tournoux template, the centre of the coordinate system shifted from being in the centre of the anterior commissure, to several millimetres away. Likewise, the exact positions of many other areas changed slightly as well. It is important to keep this in mind when interpreting the spatial coordinates that are typically used to identify the foci of activations in fMRI papers: if one paper used Talairach coordinates and another used MNI coordinates, some adjustment is required to compare them. This is well documented and several sources are available on the internet to convert between the two. It is also important to read the 'Methods' sections of all papers because some authors erroneously use the term 'Talairach coordinates' to refer to 3D Cartesian coordinates in general, even when the MNI system was actually used.

SUMMARY

Functional MRI relies on blood oxygenation level dependent (BOLD) contrast, which arises due to the magnetic susceptibility of deoxyhaemoglobin (deoxy-Hb). Deoxy-Hb causes rapid T2* dephasing, resulting in a lower signal in a T2*-weighted MR image. Although increased neural activity may trigger increased oxygen consumption, which would be predicted to yield an increase in deoxy-Hb and a consequent drop in BOLD signal, this drop – when seen at all – occurs only in the first 1–2 s after neural activity onset. Subsequent to this, the increases in neural activity trigger local vasodilation, which increases the volume of blood and the proportion of oxygenated haemoglobin (oxy-Hb) in the region, resulting in increased BOLD signal. The changes in vasodilation are thought to be caused by a complex cascade of chemical transmitters, mediated by astrocytes. BOLD signal is in arbitrary units, and the magnitude of the signal – and the extent to which it changes in response to experimental conditions – is highly variable both within and between individuals with respect to amplitude and timing. The time course of the BOLD signal in response to a stimulus or other event is called the haemodynamic response function (HRF). Although the HRF tends to start rising approximately 2 s after stimulus onset, peak after 6–8 s, and return to baseline by 10–15 s, this varies considerably by brain region and individual. The BOLD response is also influenced by drugs (including caffeine and nicotine) and disease states, making comparisons between groups sometimes challenging. For these reasons, techniques such as calibrated BOLD have been developed to quantitatively relate BOLD signal amplitude changes to oxygen consumption. As well, some studies run 'localizer' scans to characterize the shape and timing of the BOLD response in brain areas of interest, which are then used to analyse the data from the experimental conditions of interest.

While conventional MRI scans take minutes to collect a single brain volume, fMRI is only possible due to pulse sequences that allow much faster data acquisition, on the order of a few seconds. The primary pulse sequence used in fMRI is echo planar imaging (EPI). This technique involves applying all phase encoding steps in a single TR (after a single RF pulse), with a rapid frequency encoding step after each phase encoding step, allowing complete sampling of k space with a single excitation. While this allows very rapid scanning, there are some costs to EPI imaging, notably magnetic susceptibility artifacts and geometric distortion. As well, voxel sizes for BOLD imaging tend to be several times larger than for structural MR imaging, in order to obtain reasonable SNR. An alternative pulse sequence for fMRI is spiral imaging. In this technique, k space is traversed in a spiral pattern by sinusoidally varying the phase and frequency encoding gradients in synchrony, again with all of k space being sampled after a single excitation (RF pulse). Spiral imaging is less demanding on the gradient hardware of MRI systems, because the phase and frequency gradients change continuously, rather than switching the direction of their slopes very rapidly as in EPI.

However, spiral imaging has its own unique artifacts. Because EPI sequences are more widely implemented on different MRI scanners, and because modern hardware is capable of keeping up with the gradient switching demands of EPI, EPI is much more common than spiral imaging.

As with EEG and MEG data, fMRI data requires a number of preprocessing steps prior to statistical analysis to increase SNR and sensitivity to experimental effects. One step is temporal filtering to remove low-frequency artifacts. Another is motion correction, to compensate for small head movements during the scan. A limitation of motion correction is that, because MRI uses magnetic field gradients over space to obtain images, head movements of more than about 2 mm cannot be properly corrected for. This is because head movement will result in dramatic changes in the precessional phase and frequency of protons at a given location in the scanner. Another common step in preprocessing is spatial filtering, or smoothing. This is done to remove noise that occurs randomly at individual voxels, while enhancing the ability to detect activation of comparable size to the smoothing kernel, according to the matched filter theorem. Another critical step in fMRI processing is spatial normalization. Because every person's brain is unique in its size, shape, and sulcal/gyral anatomy, it is not possible to simply average together fMRI data across individuals without compensating for these spatial differences. Spatial normalization is the process of adjusting the size and shape of each individual's brain to match some standard reference template brain. There are several techniques for this. The most venerable is the method originally proposed by Talairach and Tournoux for neurosurgery, which involves manually identifying landmarks to divide the brain into sections, then scaling each section to best match the size of a reference brain. However, this is a very approximate technique and has been supplanted by automated algorithms. Among these are linear affine registration, which involves applying translations (shifts) and rotations around each spatial axis (x, y, and z), a global scaling factor, and then adjustments to the size of the brain along each spatial dimension individually, as well as shears to change the shape of the brain. While linear affine registration does an adequate job, the accuracy of spatial normalization can be improved by following the linear affine step with non-linear warping. While linear affine registration adjusts the size and shape of the brain on a 'global' scale, nonlinear warping allows for more fine-grained local adjustments, yielding a better fit for smaller features such as the ventricles and individual gyri and sulci. A very different approach to spatial normalization is spherical surface-based normalization, in which the cortical surface of each cerebral hemisphere is extracted, inflated to a sphere, and then warped to a spherical template on the basis of sulcal and gyral anatomical landmarks. A final point concerning spatial normalization is that the process requires a standard template brain to serve as the reference that individuals' brains are matched to. These templates also define the coordinate space that is used to report the location of activations in fMRI analyses. The most widely used template was developed at the Montreal Neurological Institute (MNI) and is based on the average of hundreds of healthy young brains. However, in comparing activation locations between studies it is important to note which template and coordinate system was used.

THINGS YOU SHOULD KNOW

- Blood oxygenation level dependent (BOLD) contrast is the basis of virtually all fMRI studies, and derives from the fact that deoxy-Hb causes distortions in the local magnetic field that are not caused by oxy-Hb, and which cause rapid signal decay in T2*-weighted MR images. Because changes in neural activity are associated with changes in blood oxygenation, BOLD provides an indirect measure of neural activity.

- Calibrated BOLD involves systematically manipulating blood O_2 and CO_2 levels and measuring the resultant changes in BOLD signal. This allows more precise calculation of oxygen consumption as well as the ability to quantify BOLD signal in meaningful units, whereas typical un-calibrated BOLD is in arbitrary units. Calibrated BOLD is especially useful when comparing fMRI activations between different groups who may vary in their haemodynamics for reasons such as medication or disease state.

- The haemodynamic response function (HRF) describes the time course of the BOLD signal in response to a transient event such as a stimulus or response execution. The typical human HRF has an onset approximately 2 s after the event onset, peaks after 6–8 s, and returns to baseline after 10–15 s. However, the shape and timing of the HRF varies considerably between brain regions within an individual, as well as between individuals. While a standard shape can often be assumed for all individuals in an fMRI study, more robust results may be obtained by using localizer scans to characterize the HRF prior to the experimental conditions of interest.

- BOLD is an indirect measure of neural activity. Changes in neural activity (postsynaptic potentials and, to some extent, neural firing rates) cause a complex cascade of neurochemical changes, mediated by astrocytes, that result in increased vasodilation of capillaries around the area of increased activity. Increased capillary size results in a net increase in the concentration of oxy-Hb relative to deoxy-Hb, leading to an increased BOLD signal.

- The pulse sequence most commonly used for fMRI is echo planar imaging (EPI). In EPI, all of k space is traversed after a single excitation, by rapidly switching the phase encoding gradient on and off, while also rapidly switching the direction of the frequency encoding gradient and performing readout with each switch. While this allows for very fast imaging relative to conventional MRI, EPI is associated with characteristic artifacts, including signal dropout due to magnetic susceptibility, and geometric distortions.

- Preprocessing fMRI data typically involves steps of temporal filtering, motion correction, spatial filtering (smoothing), and spatial normalization.

- Motion correction compensates for the effects of small head movements during a scan. However, it is limited by the fact that spatial encoding in MRI relies on systematic differences in the precessional phase and frequency of protons over space. As a result, movements of more than approximately 2 mm may render fMRI data unusable.

- Spatial normalization involves adjusting the size and shape of an individual's brain to match a standard template. This is necessary to average activation across participants in a study, due to the large range of individual differences in brain size and shape. Common approaches include linear affine registration, non-linear registration, and spherical surface-based normalization.

FURTHER READINGS

Huettel, S.A., Song, A.W., and McCarthy, G. (2014). *Functional Magnetic Resonance Imaging* (3rd ed.). Oxford: Sinauer Associates.

8 Functional MRI (fMRI) 2

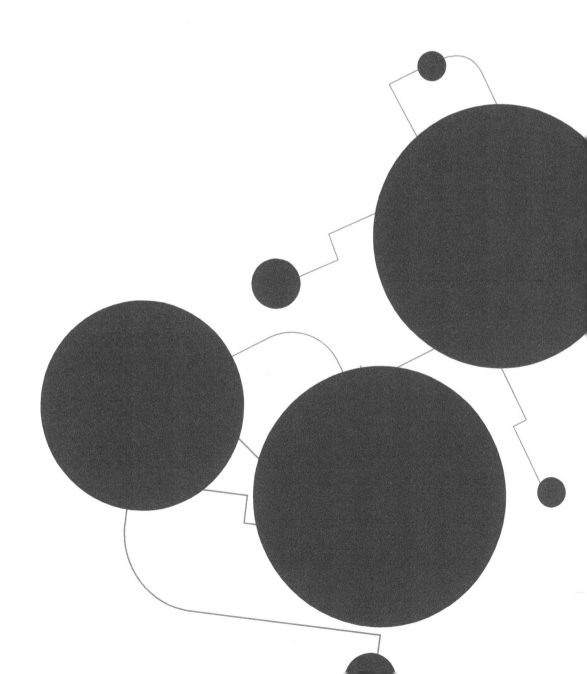

LEARNING OBJECTIVES

After reading this chapter, you should be able to:

- Compare and contrast blocked and event-related fMRI designs.
- Explain how the BOLD HRF influences decisions regarding the timing between trials in fMRI designs, and how temporal jittering can improve SNR in event-related fMRI designs.
- Explain why a baseline condition can be critical to the interpretation of experimental contrasts in fMRI studies.
- Describe the logic and utility of conjunction and disjunction analyses.
- Explain the logic and advantages of fMRI-adaptation designs.
- Describe common approaches to statistical analysis of fMRI experiments, and compare mass univariate and multivariate approaches to analysis.
- Explain the importance of multiple comparison correction in fMRI analysis, and compare different approaches that can be used.
- Define and contrast functional and effective connectivity analyses.

INTRODUCTION

In the previous chapter we introduced and characterized the BOLD signal that is the basis of fMRI. Understanding the neural origins of this signal, as well as its timing (the HRF), are important precursors to understanding the relatively unique considerations in designing and interpreting fMRI experiments. In the previous chapter we also covered the basic preprocessing steps needed to prepare the data for statistical analysis. In the present chapter, we focus on the design and analysis of fMRI experiments. The first part of the chapter covers different approaches to experimental design, including advantages and disadvantages of the various common approaches. This builds on the basic types of experimental design introduced in Chapter 2, but also introduces a number of approaches that have arisen specifically due to the nature of fMRI data and the HRF. As well, statistical analysis of fMRI data is discussed in the context of different experimental designs. While much of the chapter is focused on designing and analysing experiments with the aim of determining which brain areas are sensitive to an experimental manipulation, the final part of the chapter focuses on methods for examining relationships between activity between different areas. These approaches, known broadly as functional and effective connectivity take us beyond 'neo-phrenology' to considering the brain as a large-scale, integrated network.

EXPERIMENTAL DESIGN

In designing fMRI experiments, an appreciation of the origin and nature of the BOLD signal is essential, because it places constraints on what can be done. Perhaps most obviously, the timing of the BOLD response places limits on how quickly we can present stimuli and still be able to recover the HRFs to individual items. However, other factors place constraints on the sorts of questions that can be fruitfully asked (or at least, answered) with fMRI. For example, due to both the sluggishness of the BOLD response, and uncertainties in the precise relationship between the timing of neural responses and BOLD signal changes, fMRI is not well suited to asking questions about the time course of neural activity – at least not with the precision allowed by other techniques such as EEG or MEG, which can resolve events that differ in the order of tens or hundreds of milliseconds. As we have seen, it is questionable whether the timing of the BOLD HRF accurately reflects relative timing of activation in different brain areas. It is still possible to recover information over longer time courses with fMRI, however. For example, in working memory tasks one can distinguish activity during different phases of a trial such as initial stimulus presentation (encoding), the maintenance period during which people retain the encoded information, and a response period where memory is tested. These typically take place over many seconds, and so are comfortably within the temporal resolution of the HRF. In the sections that follow we will see different examples of fMRI designs that both accommodate these limitations, and try to move beyond them in clever ways.

Blocked Designs

For the first several years of fMRI experimentation, studies exclusively employed **blocked designs**, in which experimental conditions were presented in 'blocks' that lasted typically between 20–100 s. The simplest blocked designs are called **boxcar designs**, owing to their characteristic time course in which the blocks involving the stimulus/task of interest (often call the target or experimental condition) alternates with a control condition, as shown in Figure 8.1. For example, in Ogawa and colleagues' initial demonstration of the feasibility of human fMRI, participants viewed a flashing red and green checkerboard (the experimental condition, designed to activate visual cortex) alternating with periods of darkness (the control condition). This alternation is essential because fMRI is not a truly quantitative method – the intensity values in the fMRI time course are in arbitrary, meaningless units. Thus the only way to tell if a brain area is activated is to compare BOLD signal in a condition when activation is expected, with a condition in which it is not. This **subtraction method** was discussed in Chapter 2, and was introduced to neuroimaging by Michael Posner in the 1980s during his involvement in the first PET neuroimaging studies of cognition, with colleagues at Washington University in St. Louis (Petersen et al., 1988; Posner et al., 1988; Posner & Raichle, 1994). The logic is that all brain areas will have some baseline level of neural activity and BOLD signal; only areas that are involved in the particular task under investigation will show increases in BOLD signal during that task, and so the subtraction of [task − baseline] will identify those areas.

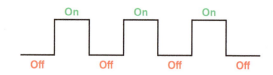

Figure 8.1 Simple block design with one experimental ('on') and one control ('off') condition, alternating

Researchers initially employed blocked designs both because each fMRI image took several seconds to acquire (and so stimulation had to continue over at least this period), and because of concerns that the fMRI signal was relatively insensitive – so activity needed to accumulate over some extended period of time in order to be distinguished from the baseline. Indeed, even before studies were conducted aimed specifically at characterizing the time course of the HRF, simple visual inspection of the time course of the BOLD signal showed that it rose over the course of several seconds before plateauing. This suggested that the fMRI response to a single or short series of events would not rise as much as that for a longer block, and so would be harder to detect statistically. Furthermore, the initial approaches to fMRI data analysis involved conducting t-tests between the signal averaged over the 'on' time points and the signal averaged over the 'off' time points, and so it made sense to design the stimuli such that the 'on' and 'off' periods each had numerous time points to average together. This also allowed the earliest fMRI researchers to capitalize on statistical analysis methods pioneered for PET scanning (Friston, Frith, Liddle, & Frackowiak, 1991) which, as we will learn later, is inherently limited to blocked designs. Subsequent work with event-related fMRI designs (discussed in detail in the next section) has proven that it is possible to obtain reliable signals from short periods of stimulation and even single events, but at the same time confirmed that blocked designs are more sensitive due to the greater signal change that occurs over longer periods of stimulation or task performance.

The advantage of blocked designs comes from the fact that while the HRF to a single event has a characteristic shape (as seen in the previous chapter), the HRFs evoked by multiple events that occur close together in time will overlap and add together in a fashion that is roughly linear. In other words, if one predicts the strength of the BOLD signal to multiple events by simply drawing the HRF for each single event and then adding these together at the time points where they overlap, this prediction is very consistent with the actual fMRI signal obtained. This is discussed in greater detail (and with some caveats) in the next section. Because the signals summate over time in this way, a blocked design will yield larger signal changes than an event-related design, in which single stimulus events are separated by larger baseline periods and/or stimuli of other experimental conditions.

While the simplest blocked designs are the boxcar type described above, more complex designs involving more than two conditions are possible, and commonly used. For example, in Newman and colleagues (Newman, Supalla, Hauser, Newport, & Bavelier, 2010a, 2010b) we investigated brain activation associated with three different aspects of American Sign Language (ASL) sentences. One condition involved sentences that conveyed grammatical information through word order (as in English, ASL places subjects before the verb and objects after, as in the sentence *John kissed Mary*), a second condition involved sentences that conveyed information through grammatical markers (in ASL, these are movements of the hands through space; some spoken languages, such as German, use suffixes called case markers for this purpose), and a third condition added 'narrative' devices including emotional facial expressions and body shifts not seen in the other conditions. This design followed additive factors logic, in that word order was present in all three conditions, and the grammatical devices in the second condition were also present in the third (narrative) condition. In the fMRI study, experimental blocks each consisted of videos of an ASL signer producing a series of three sentences of the same type, with each block lasting 21 s. These blocks were presented in random order (so that participants could not predict what type of sentence was coming in the next block), alternating with baseline blocks (these lasted only 15 s, since this was long enough for the HRF to return to baseline after the preceding stimulus block). Also intermixed with the three experimental conditions were 21 s blocks of three control conditions. Each of these types of control blocks involved the same ASL sentences used in one of the experimental conditions, but the sentences were played backward, and three sentences were digitally overlaid. Thus these control blocks contained exactly the same visual stimuli as the experimental blocks (thus controlling for low-level visual features including face and body perception, and perception of specific types of human movements), but were not understandable as language. It is worth noting that the control stimuli were not 'perfect' in the sense that while experimental stimuli involved a single signer, the control stimuli contained six arms, three heads, etc. (which only partially overlapped due to the signer's movements). However, in pilot testing we found that native ASL signers could understand single, backward ASL sentences quite easily – so backward sentences did not isolate language comprehension from lower-level features of the stimuli. Our logic in using overlaid backward sentences was that although they were not perfectly matched to the experimental stimuli, since they contained *more* of the features we were trying to control for, this only helped our efforts to isolate linguistic processing. Schematic diagrams of the block design are shown in Figure 8.2. While this example is somewhat complex, it illustrates some of the 'real world' considerations that go into fMRI experimental design, and the fact that efforts must sometimes be made to accommodate the fact that perfect subtractive logic is not always possible to effect.

A critical consideration when using the additive factors or subtraction method is the assumption of **pure insertion**. This is the assumption that the difference between the two conditions being compared is exclusively the difference intended by the experimenter – that the variable that is 'added' can be inserted into the stream of cognitive processing without any interaction with other processes. For example, using

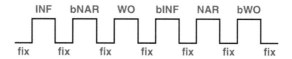

Figure 8.2 Complex block design with three experimental conditions (INF, WO, NAR), three control conditions (bWO, bINF, bNAR), each alternating with a fixation baseline condition (fix). Experimental and control blocks were 21 s long, while fixation blocks were 15 s long

the Petersen and colleagues (1988) experiment discussed in Chapter 2, directly comparing real words with false font strings to identify brain areas associated with accessing the meaning of words violates pure insertion because several other processes are involved, such as letter recognition and phoneme identification. Another example would be a typical face-processing experiment, in which BOLD signal is contrasted between images of faces and non-face control stimuli. One type of control stimulus is images of faces that have been scrambled in some way, so that the overall size, brightness, and contrast of the images are preserved but there is no recognizable face or face-like features. While this represents good control of low-level stimulus properties, there is a potential violation of pure insertion in that faces are inherently more interesting to look at than blurry blobs. Thus the faces and control stimuli vary both in their 'face-ness' and in the level of attention that is directed to the stimuli. There are numerous possible ways of dealing with potential violations of pure insertion. For example, one could employ a task that requires participants to play attention to all stimuli (for example, pressing one button if the stimulus is a face, and another if it is not), or change the control stimuli so that faces are compared with, say, pictures of real objects that are matched in size, brightness, and contrast. Often there is no 'perfect' solution to violations of pure insertion, but thoughtful experimental design can at least ameliorate this concern. For example, one could both use a task that requires equal attention to all stimulus types, and employ multiple control stimulus types – so in our face-processing example, one might include scrambled faces, real objects, and pictures of landscapes as control items, and take as face-processing specific brain areas only those that are consistently activated in multiple contrasts between faces and other types of pictures (for example, Kanwisher, McDermott, & Chun, 1997).

Event-Related Designs

While blocked designs were essentially the only type of fMRI experimental design for the first several years of research in the field, scientists quickly recognized their limitations. One is that the stimuli and task used in a block all necessarily need to be of the same type – that is, part of the same experimental condition. While this may be fine for some research questions, often in cognitive neuroscience unpredictability or the element of surprise is necessary. This is most obvious in experiments such as the 'oddball' designs described earlier in the context of ERP studies (where a P3 and/

or MMN component is elicited), where the experimental effect is elicited precisely because a single stimulus is distinctive from those preceding it – and typically the task instructions require the participant to respond to the oddball stimuli in a way different from other stimuli. There is no way to elicit this effect in a block lasting for tens of seconds, because once the first oddball stimulus has been presented, one needs to present more 'standard' stimuli before another oddball stimulus can be presented. More generally, a wealth of evidence demonstrates that presenting similar stimuli repeatedly results in speeded, more accurate responses and attenuated brain activation compared to less predictable stimuli.

Another type of experimental design that is not amenable to blocked designs are those in which each trial comprises multiple, distinct stages that need to occur in relatively rapid succession. Studies of short-term memory are a prime example of this: in a typical paradigm, some stimuli (such as a series of letters) are presented (the encoding phase), then a retention interval follows during which people are required to hold the items in memory, followed finally by a test phase in which memory is checked; for example, by presenting a letter and asking if it was part of the originally presented set on that trial. While one could conduct a series of such trials in a blocked fMRI design, there would be no way to differentiate brain activation associated with encoding from retention, or testing, because all would have occurred during the block. Another topic in the field of memory concerns what kind of brain activity predicts later memory. For instance, one might want to present a list of words to a person and then later test their memory for those words. Of interest would be whether there was different activation during the initial encoding of words that were later correctly remembered, compared to those that were forgotten. This is obviously only possible if one can isolate the fMRI responses to individual words in the list, which is not possible in a block design. More generally, block designs do not allow researchers to analyse trials separately depending on the participant's response.

Recognizing these limitations, in the late 1990s researchers began exploring the possibility of so-called 'event-related' fMRI (er-fMRI, sometimes called 'single-trial' designs), with the goal of recovering the HRFs to individual stimuli. For example, Boynton and colleagues (1996) presented simple moving visual chequerboard stimuli (which excite visual cortex strongly) with durations from 3–24 s, with 12 s periods of a plain grey screen in between each stimulus. Their results showed some of the first published examples of what are now recognized as typical event-related (not blocked) HRFs, with the duration of peak activation increasing steadily as the duration of the stimulus increased. McCarthy and colleagues (McCarthy, Luby, Gore, & Goldman-Rakic, 1997) implemented a typical P3 ERP oddball paradigm in an fMRI study, using letter strings as stimuli. Letter strings were presented with a **stimulus onset asynchrony** (**SOA**; the time from the onset of one stimulus to the onset of the next) of 1.5 s, with one letter string (*OOOOO* – standards) occurring approximately 95% of the time and another (*XXXXX* – oddballs) occurring randomly in 5% of the trials. This rate of stimulus presentation was quite fast relative to the HRF (which takes approximately 6–8 s to peak), so there was a large amount of overlap between the BOLD responses to each stimulus – so much overlap, in fact, that it was not possible to visualize the HRFs for each individual stimulus. However, in areas sensitive to the experimental manipulation, a distinct and statistically significant rise in the signal occurred following oddball stimuli, which peaked approximately 4 s after the onset of the oddballs. Signals time-locked to standard stimuli did not show any such rise – they were essentially flat because there was a more or less constant response to the standard stimuli due to their overlap in time. The significant activations in response to oddballs occurred in regions predicted to be involved in this task on the basis of previous electrical recordings in monkeys (dorsolateral prefrontal cortex and the inferior parietal lobe), adding credibility to the findings. Another early example of an er-fMRI study investigated the memory encoding question mentioned above. Wagner and colleagues (1998) compared brain responses to the initial presentation of stimuli in a short-term memory experiment that were later remembered, with ones that were not remembered. The researchers found greater activation in a number of brain regions for later-remembered items. Since it cannot be predicted beforehand which trials an individual will later remember, this study was only possible using an event-related design that could characterize the responses to individual trials, rather than only blocks of trials.

These and numerous other experiments demonstrated that blocked designs were not necessary in order to obtain a statistically reliable fMRI signal. These studies also led to further studies investigating how the HRFs to different trials summate when they overlap in time. If experimenters want to measure the response to each individual stimulus in an experiment without any overlap (as opposed to just examining differential activation, as McCarthy and colleagues did), the experiment would take a long time and be very boring for participants, because each individual stimulus would have to be separated by 12 or more seconds of a low-level baseline condition in order to allow the HRF to return to baseline between each trial. Some early studies indicated that overlapping HRFs combine in an approximately linear fashion (Dale & Buckner, 1997). In other words, if one first presents a series of stimuli spaced 12 s or more apart in time (termed a 'slow event-related design'), and then presents stimuli spaced more closely together (so that their HRFs overlap – a 'fast event-related design'), the time course of the fMRI data from the fast design will be almost identical to the time course that would be predicted by taking the average HRF from the slow design and placing it at each point in time where an event occurred in the fast design, then adding the HRF signal values where they overlap. The additivity of overlapping HRFs is shown in Figure 8.3.

Later studies demonstrated that this linearity is not guaranteed, and is dependent on the type of stimulus and the brain region investigated (Heckman, Bouvier, Carr, Harley, Cardinal, & Engel, 2007; Horner & Andrews, 2009; Huettel, Obembe, Song, & Woldorff, 2004). In general, the evidence has suggested that the HRFs in rapid event-related designs are under-additive if all of the stimuli that are presented in rapid succession are similar to each other – that is, the actual response to multiple closely spaced stimuli is somewhat weaker than would be predicted from a slow event-related design. More linearity and less under-additivity is observed when the stimuli are more variable. For example, if the same stimulus (such as a black and white chequerboard) is presented repeatedly, under-additivity is observed in the fast event-related design. However, if the stimuli are of a particular category but vary

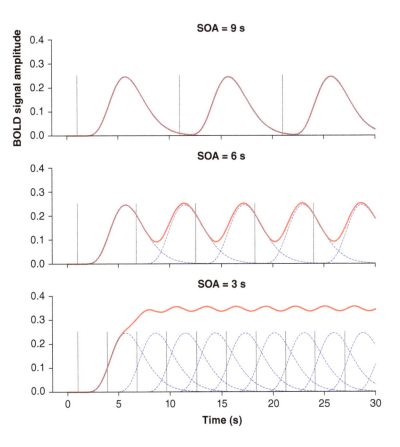

Figure 8.3 Convolution of stimulus time series with the predicted HRF, for different SOAs. The vertical grey lines represent the onset of each stimulus, the dashed blue lines represent the predicted HRF to each individual event resulting from the convolution of the HRF model with each grey line. For simplicity, the model of the HRF used here was a simple gamma function with no undershoot. The red lines represent the sum of the HRFs to all events. For the 9 s SOA, there is no overlap of the individual HRFs and so the blue and red lines are perfectly overlaid. However, as SOA becomes shorter, the overlapping HRFs sum together

along some dimension (for example, 2D sine wave gratings that vary in the orientation their lines), then greater linearity of the response is seen between the slow and fast event-related designs. Moreover, the differences between fast and slow event-related designs also tend to be larger in areas that are particularly sensitive to the stimuli used. For example, Horner and Andrews (2009) showed greater differences between fast and slow er-fMRI designs to pictures of faces than to pictures of places in a region of the fusiform gyrus that typically shows strongest responses to faces. The multiple studies on this topic have converged on the explanation that the under-additivity in fast event-related designs can be explained by **neural adaptation**:

the phenomenon that neurons tend to show reduced firing rates upon repeated presentation of stimuli that they are sensitive to. Slow event-related designs allow more time for recovery between individual stimulus presentations, and thus show less adaptation. Adaptation also explains why varying stimulus properties reduces the attenuating effect of fast designs: within a brain region that is sensitive to a particular type of stimulus – for example, the oriented lines in sine wave gratings – different populations of neurons are tuned to different parameters of that stimulus – such as the orientation of the lines. Thus although the same general brain area will respond to gratings of any orientation, different neurons will respond preferentially to different orientations, and so if a series of gratings of different orientations are presented in a fast event-related design, less adaptation of the BOLD response will occur than if a single orientation was presented repeatedly because different neurons within that area are stimulated by each orientation.

Of course, in most cases the reason a researcher would choose an event-related design in the first place is to be able to present stimuli from different conditions in random order – so concerns over the effects of repeated presentation of the same stimulus, or multiple stimuli of one experimentally defined category, might seem to be of little consequence. However, an appreciation of the potential for linear summation versus under-additivity is important in designing an experiment, for several reasons. Firstly, even in a block design, a stronger signal will be obtained when the stimuli within the block are more varied (within the parameters of what defines the experimental condition for that block) than if they are less variable. Secondly, since overlapping HRFs do summate, presenting a short series of trials of a single experimental condition in rapid succession within a fast event-related design (mini-blocks) can be expected to yield a stronger BOLD response than either a slow event-related design or constant alternation of different conditions (compare the amplitude of the response between the 6, 3, and 1.5 s SOAs in Figure 8.4) – and a stronger BOLD response will tend to yield a more robust effect when the data are analysed. Thus consideration of the potential for adaptation should factor into choosing stimuli and arranging them in the experimental sequence.

Finally, understanding how overlapping HRFs summate is essential for understanding how the data from er-fMRI experiments are analysed, which in turn informs good design of an experiment to ensure that it's actually possible to analyse the data. For example, the 1.5 and 3 s SOA conditions in Figure 8.4 demonstrate that it is easily possible to design an er-fMRI experiment that yields no recoverable signal. For this explanation we will start with the simplest case: analysis of a block design involving only a single experimental condition alternating with a control condition. Analysis of such a design can involve simply correlating the fMRI time series at each voxel with function such as a square wave or a sine wave. However, a more accurate model is to **convolve** the stimulus time series (which would look like a series of spikes when each stimulus was on, as in Figure 8.4) with a model of the HRF. Convolution is a mathematical operation that can be understood as taking the HRF model and sliding it over the stimulus time series, multiplying the HRF model by the stimulus time series. This is how the red, predicted HRF line was generated from the grey spikes representing the stimuli in Figure 8.4. Equivalently, one

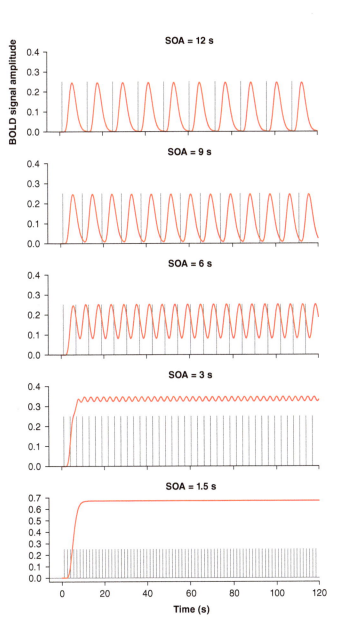

Figure 8.4 Linear additivity of HRFs to individual events, as a function of SOA. The onset of each event (stimulus) is shown as a grey vertical line, and the predicted HRF to that stimulus as a red line. The SOA = 12 condition (top) reflects a 'slow' er-fMRI design in which the HRF has time to return to baseline before the next event. As SOA becomes progressively shorter, the HRFs to individual events start to overlap. The result is that the BOLD signal does not return to baseline after each event, and at the shortest SOAs (3 and 1.5 s), the resulting BOLD response is essentially a flat line after an initial ramp-up at the start of the run. As well, increasing overlap results in a higher overall BOLD signal; indeed, the 1.5 s SOA had to be plotted with a different amplitude scale. Although the amplitude of the BOLD signal is larger with shorter SOAs, this does not mean that the signal will be more detectable. This is because without a return to baseline after each event, it is difficult to distinguish the flat response in the 1.5 or 3 s SOA conditions from what would be expected in brain areas not responsive to the stimulus (which would also be a flat line, though perhaps without the ramp-up at the start; because the units of fMRI BOLD signal are arbitrary and vary across the brain, active areas would not be distinguished from a non-active areas simply by having larger BOLD signal values). Note that this linear summation only holds if the individual stimuli are distinct from one another, but from the same experimental condition (for example, pictures of different faces)

can imagine placing a copy of the HRF model on a timeline, starting at each time point where a stimulus was presented, and adding the HRFs together at time points when they overlap. Analysis of an er-fMRI study involves this same process: the stimulus time series is convolved with a model HRF, and then the time series from each voxel in the fMRI scan is correlated with this predicted HRF time series. From Figure 8.4 it is clear that the more-or-less linear overlap of HRFs to closely spaced events means that if the SOA between events is a constant value, then short SOAs are problematic as the resulting time series lacks sufficient stimulus-related variation over time to distinguish task-related from unrelated voxels – because both are predicted to yield relatively flat responses. This is in fact desirable in blocked designs, because the point there is to capitalize on this summation of individual HRFs. Indeed, as shown in Figure 8.5, shorter SOAs yield stronger predicted BOLD responses. However, this only works in blocked designs because the intervening 'off' blocks serve to create the necessary systematic variation in predicted BOLD response.

Two critical insights allowed er-fMRI to flourish even with short SOAs. The first, as we have already seen from the study by McCarthy and colleagues (1997), is that if the stimuli comprise at least two distinct categories that are expected to yield different-strength responses (for example, standard versus oddball), then systematic variation in the BOLD signal is predicted. The other insight was that even if there is only a single category of stimulus, it is possible to create systematic variation in the predicted BOLD response by 'jittering' the SOA. That is, rather than using a constant time interval between stimuli, we vary it – for example in a range between 2–12 s. Longer SOAs allow more time for the HRF to start to return to baseline, at least partially – thus moving the summed HRF away from a flat line. Having longer baseline intervals of up to 12 s (sometimes called 'null events') allows for more or less complete return to baseline, which helps create the strongest fluctuation in BOLD response. Examples of the effect of jittering are shown in Figure 8.6. From these we can see that, relative to a fixed SOA, with jittered SOAs we can both increase the amount of systematic variation in the predicted BOLD response, and gain a much stronger signal (at least at some points in the time series, where more events occur closely together); moreover, jittered SOAs also allow us to increase the number of events presented in a given amount of time, which further helps boost the BOLD signal.

Given the random spacing of events, one can imagine a wide range of possible jittered time series, even given a fixed number of stimuli and scan duration. Different temporal sequences will vary in how optimal they are for detecting the signal associated with the experimental manipulation. A measure of the optimality of different designs (including blocked and event-related) has been developed called **efficiency**, which is a function of the variance in the predicted fMRI time series (Friston, Zarahn, Josephs, Henson, & Dale, 1999). Greater variance in the predicted time series yields greater efficiency, consistent with the observation that a randomly jittered design is better than a design with closely and evenly spaced trials. This measure of efficiency also provides a way of comparing different experimental designs to find one that provides a good balance of unpredictability, a relative lack of 'dead time' for the participant, and maximal sensitivity to experimental effects. Various software tools are available to facilitate the design of event-related fMRI experiments based on efficiency and other measures.

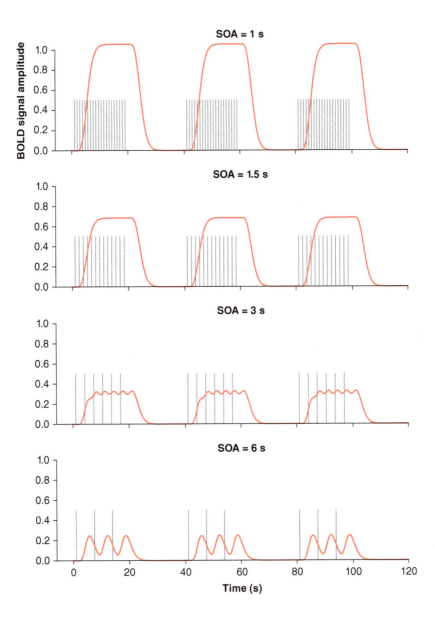

Figure 8.5 Predicted BOLD response (red lines) for block design fMRI runs, with different SOA within the blocks. Onset of each event is marked with a vertical grey line. The HRF was modelled using a simple gamma function with no undershoot, time-locked to the onset of each event. More closely spaced events cause greater summation of the individual HRFs, and thus stronger predicted BOLD signal. Note, however, that very short SOAs may not be possible with some experimental designs, due to the time required for each stimulus to be sufficiently processed by the participant, and a response (if any) to be made

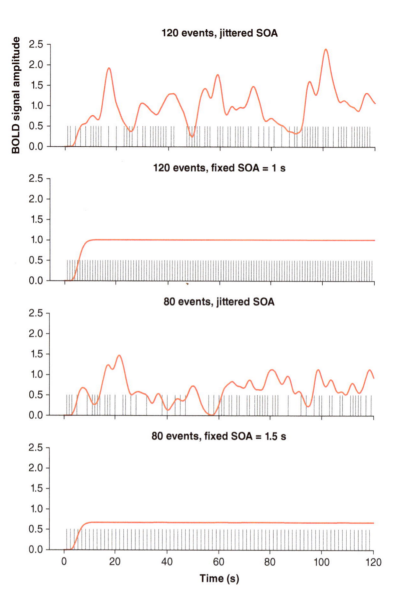

Figure 8.6 Effects of jittering SOA on predicted BOLD response in an er-fMRI design. Grey vertical lines represent stimulus onsets, and the red lines are the predicted BOLD response based on convolving the grey lines with a model of the HRF. Jittering the SOA creates systematic variance in the predicted BOLD response that is unlikely to occur by chance in brain areas not sensitive to the experimental manipulation. Conversely, fixed SOAs yield an effectively flat predicted BOLD response that would be indistinguishable from the time course of brain areas that were not sensitive to the experimental manipulation. The top panel further demonstrates that far more stimuli can be included when a jittered SOA is used without loss of the ability to detect the systematic BOLD response, which in turn creates stronger fluctuations in signal that are more likely to be detected and yield statistically significant results

An additional consideration in this regard is for multi-phase experimental designs, such as the type of short-term memory study described above. Recall that in such a design, each trial comprises distinct encoding, retention, and response phases. Firstly, note that each trial is much longer in this type of design than in a simpler study in which individual stimuli are presented in relatively rapid succession, possibly with a response made to each as quickly as possible after stimulus onset. Thus each trial is necessarily long in duration, and will thus have a relatively long SOA. Moreover, if the three phases of the trial occur at fixed times relative to one another (say, 2 s for encoding, 10 s for retention, and 2 s for response), then we again face the problem of predicted HRFs that overlap in time and create an essentially flat predicted fMRI time series. While we might be able to distinguish activation during the trial, overall, with baseline activation, we would not be able to resolve the differential activation in each phase of the experiment. To overcome this, we need to jitter the onset of each phase of the trial relative to the other phases. Although within a trial, the study design might apply greater constraints than in a simple, short-trial study (for example, we probably wouldn't want a 10 s encoding phase followed by only 2 s for retention), jittering even within a range that makes sense given the cognitive structure of the design will improve the design's efficiency. Another option is to eliminate one phase of the trial on a subset of trials. For example, one can reduce the contingency between the retention and responses phases by only requiring a response on 50% of trials (Henson, 2006). Since participants cannot know during the encoding or retention phases whether or not they will be prompted for a response, they should still perform the tasks similarly, and typically it is activation during the retention phase that is of greatest interest in such studies.

Baseline Conditions

In the preceding sections we have discussed subtractive and additive factors designs and the importance of carefully designing the control condition and stimuli to ensure that the subtraction between experimental and control conditions isolates the cognitive process(es) of interest. The logic of additive factors originates in behavioural reaction time studies, where it is assumed that given a certain amount of time required to perform a particular cognitive operation or operations, when we add an additional cognitive operation, the increase in reaction time is attributable to the time required for that additional operation. However, when applied to BOLD fMRI, the picture becomes more complex. This is because unlike reaction times, which are measured in units of time where zero has a clear definition, BOLD signal is measured in arbitrary units that are meaningless except in a relative sense – that is, how much of an increase we see between the control and experimental conditions. Because the brain is always perfused with oxygenated blood, there is always some baseline level of BOLD signal everywhere in the brain, even when a person is not performing any task that a particular brain area is involved in. Furthermore, many brain areas actually show a *reduction* in BOLD signal during task performance relative to a more 'neutral' **baseline condition** such as lying still with eyes closed, or staring at a blank screen or a fixation cross – without any specific task instructions.

Thus henceforth it will be important to remember the distinction between control conditions – during which stimuli and/or tasks are presented to control for factors of non-interest that are present in the experimental condition – and baseline conditions (during which no stimulus or task is used, or a simple, unchanging stimulus such as a fixation cross is present).

Decreases in brain activation measures were noted even in the earliest fMRI and PET functional neuroimaging studies, and are sometimes referred to as 'deactivations' or 'negative BOLD' – although it is important to keep in mind that they reflect reduced BOLD signal, but not necessarily neural inhibition – and again that BOLD is measured in arbitrary units, so 'negative BOLD' is meaningful only relative to BOLD signal measured in some other condition. These task-related BOLD decreases were first addressed directly by Binder and colleagues (Binder, Frost, Hammeke, Bellgowan, Rao, & Cox, 1999), who postulated that during **resting states** in neuroimaging experiments (that is, during times when no explicit stimulation was provided), people engage in conceptual processing – which Binder and colleagues suggested might include awareness of one's body position and internal signals, future planning, encoding ongoing experience into episodic memory, and tracking the passage of time. More subjectively, and perhaps a bit tongue-in-cheek, one could describe this as 'what people do when they're bored' since lying still in an MRI scanner staring at a blank, unchanging screen is perhaps one of the least interesting things one can do! Binder and colleagues provided support for the notion of such general conceptual processing during the unconstrained resting state by showing that a very similar set of brain areas showed greater activation in multiple subtractive contrasts: a passive resting condition relative to making judgements about auditory tones; when performing semantic judgements (about the meanings of words) relative to the same tone task; and when performing semantic judgements relative to performing phonetic judgements (that is, about speech sounds).

A large amount of subsequent fMRI work has been conducted around the resting state, which we come back to in a separate section below under 'Functional Connectivity'. For now, the important point to consider is that during task performance, some brain areas show decreased BOLD signal relative to a neutral baseline condition. The implication of this for subtractive designs is that even when greater signal is observed in a particular brain area for an experimental than a control condition, *both* conditions might actually show reductions in BOLD signal relative to a more neutral baseline condition. In other words, a pure subtraction between two conditions could reflect either a true increase in activation for the experimental relative to the control condition, or a smaller decrease in BOLD signal for the experimental relative to the control condition – or even no difference between the experimental condition and a neutral baseline condition, but decreased BOLD for the control condition. The many possibilities are illustrated in Figure 8.7.

There are several implications of the fact that fMRI subtractions are not baseline-independent. Firstly, any simple subtractive design should be interpreted with caution. While any significant difference between experimental and control conditions can be interpreted as sensitivity of that brain region to the experimental contrast, the more specific interpretation of the neurocognitive

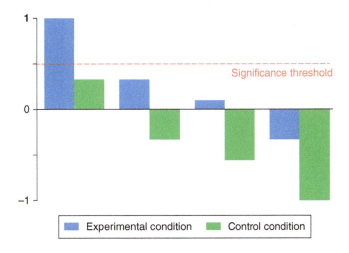

Figure 8.7 Different patterns of BOLD response in subtraction designs can result in the same apparent result in the subtraction image, even though their interpretations could be very different. This figure shows four different possible levels of BOLD activation across two conditions, 'experimental' and 'control', all relative to BOLD signal measuring in a baseline condition (for example, starting at a fixation cross). This baseline BOLD level is set to zero and indicated by the black line. The dashed red line shows the hypothetical size of signal change from baseline (represented as 0 on the y axis) required for activation in a given condition to be considered statistically significant, or 'activated', relative to a neutral baseline condition such as viewing a blank screen. Thus only in the first (leftmost) situation would we consider there to be significant activation in the experimental condition. However, in all four examples the magnitude of the difference in BOLD signal between the experimental and control conditions is the same. Thus without including a baseline condition, it would be impossible to know, simply from the experimental–control subtraction, whether the observed differences at any given voxel reflected truly 'interesting' activation (that is, significantly activated in the experimental condition relative to both baseline and the control condition) or a difference of no interest (or, at least, requiring a different interpretation)

function of that region will likely differ depending on whether the area shows greater or lesser BOLD signal in (at least) the experimental condition relative to baseline. A common approach to including the baseline in fMRI data analysis is to **mask** the difference in BOLD signal between the experimental and control condition, with the experimental–baseline contrast. In other words, report only the activations that are both significant for experimental–control, and experimental–baseline contrasts. This is illustrated in Figure 8.8, using data from a study in which a group of people viewed movies of people making communicative hand gestures, and control movies containing similar biological motion, but that were not interpretable as communicative gesture (Newman, Supalla, Fernandez, Newport, & Bavelier, 2015). As well, the study included a baseline condition which involved viewing a still frame of the gesturer. The figure shows that the simple gesture–control contrast yielded apparent 'activation' in numerous brain areas (red), however when this contrast was masked with the areas that were also significant in the gesture–baseline contrast (blue), a far more restricted set of brain areas resulted (purple). The interpretation of the results might have been very different if the baseline condition had not been included.

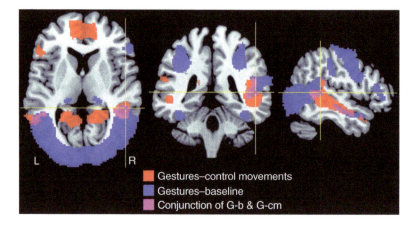

Figure 8.8 The importance of including a baseline condition and using it to mask contrasts between experimental and control conditions. In this example the interest is in brain areas that show stronger BOLD signal to communicative gestures than non-communicative hand and arm movements. Areas shown in red are from the contrast between viewing videos of communicative gestures, and non-communicative biological motion. Areas shown in blue are the contrast between the communicative gestures and a baseline condition (passive viewing of a still image of the gesture model). Areas shown in purple are those that were significant in both contrasts. The crosshairs indicate the location of brain area STSp (superior temporal sulcus, posterior), commonly implicated in biological motion processing, in the three views of the brain. Note the numerous areas shown in red that would have been erroneously considered 'active' if only the experimental-control contrast had been included, without using the baseline condition for masking. Data are redrawn from a study published by Newman and colleagues (2015)

It should also be kept in mind that in many cases, the functional role of a particular brain area may be well understood enough, based on the previous literature, that the inclusion of a baseline condition in further studies is not always necessary. For example, area V5 of the visual system (in lateral occipital cortex) is well documented to be sensitive to visual motion – both relative to static visual displays and neutral baselines. Thus, in designing or interpreting a study contrasting moving with stationary visual stimuli, one could be quite confident in ascribing V5 activity to motion-related processing, even in the absence of a baseline condition.

While one may rely on the previous literature in some cases, in other situations it may be valuable – and perhaps even essential – to include a baseline condition as well as experimental and control conditions in an fMRI design. Fortunately, the duration of the baseline periods need not be equivalent to that of the experimental or control stimulation. Our understanding of the temporal dynamics of the HRF tell us that it takes about 12–15 s for BOLD signal to return to baseline levels following stimulation, and so a baseline interval in the range of 12–20 s should normally be sufficient, even if the stimulation blocks are longer. Furthermore, the general consensus is that relatively few baseline periods are necessary within an fMRI run to adequately estimate the baseline BOLD signal level. Thus in many studies, baseline periods are included only at the beginning and end of a block design run (with the intervening blocks alternating between experimental and control conditions); in other studies, a few baseline periods may be interspersed with stimulation blocks, but perhaps only half to one-third as many baseline blocks as experimental/control blocks are used.

In event-related fMRI designs, baseline estimation can be achieved by having occasional, extended inter-stimulus intervals ranging in duration from 8–15 s (in many er-fMRI designs, these are no longer than 8–10 s). These are sometimes called 'null events' to indicate that they take approximately the same time as 'real' events; however, this terminology may be confusing because they are not really events at all, but the absence of events (and in data analysis, one does not treat the null events as an experimental condition – rather, they implicitly form the baseline against which event-related activation is compared). Such extended baseline periods are not strictly required in an er-fMRI design, any more than they are in a block design; one could present events in rapid succession (though still with jittered ISIs), and simply contrast activation between two or more conditions. However, because of the importance of having sufficient variance in the predicted BOLD signal over time in er-fMRI designs (as described in the previous section), it is generally advisable to include such baseline periods in any er-fMRI design.

Conjunctions and Disjunctions

A different approach to experimental design – and one that is somewhat unique to neuroimaging research and not typically used in behavioural studies – is **conjunction analysis** (originally called **cognitive conjunctions**). First introduced by Price and Friston (1997), this approach is more flexible than a factorial design in that it does not require multiple, fully crossed variables. The logic behind conjunction designs is quite intuitive: if two (or more) experimental conditions share a common cognitive factor or factors, then the brain areas supporting these shared cognitive operations should be significantly activated in each of those experimental conditions relative to each condition's baseline. The different conditions might not be expected to yield exactly the same activation maps; conjunction analysis shows only the areas that are significantly active in all experimental conditions of interest, and not any areas that are uniquely activated in one condition. In mathematics and formal logic, this is called an 'intersection' operation. An example of a conjunction map is shown in Figure 8.9.

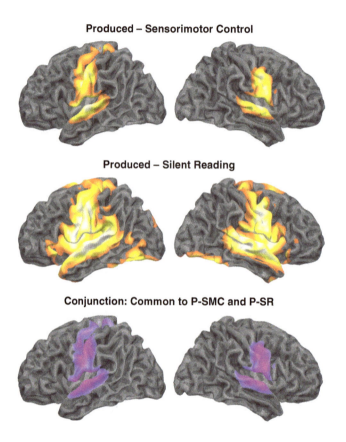

Figure 8.9 Example of an fMRI conjunction analysis. The top two panels show two different contrasts from an experiment in which people viewed a single English word on each trial. Each word was associated with instructions to either say the word aloud (Produced condition), read the word silently (Silent Reading), or read the word silently while saying 'yes' aloud (Sensorimotor Control). The goal of the study was to identify areas associated with the 'production effect', which is a behavioural phenomenon in which words read aloud are later remembered better than words read silently. Because subtracting the silent reading from the produced condition would not control for the motor-related brain activity involved in speaking, nor perceptual activation associated with hearing one's voice, the sensorimotor control condition was included. However, the silent reading condition was also included because this is the standard way that the

Figure 8.9 (Continued)

production effect is normally elicited in behavioural studies (though behavioural data from this experiment demonstrated a similar memory advantage for the produced condition relative to sensorimotor control). The conjunction analysis in the bottom panel represents brain areas that were significantly activated in both the produced-sensorimotor control, and produced-silent reading contrasts. Areas that were common to both contrasts can be most confidently associated with the behavioural production effect, because they reflect both (a) a well-controlled contrast (produced-sensorimotor control) and (b) a second contrast that is not as well-controlled, but generates the same target behavioural effect. Data are from a study by Newman and colleagues (Newman et al., 2018)

Cognitive conjunctions allow much more flexibility in experimental design than factorial designs. For example, imagine that rather than investigating word type and frequency, as in the example given for factorial designs above, we wanted to identify brain areas specialized for word processing, irrespective of whether words are read or heard, as well as brain areas specific to only reading (but not hearing) words, and to only auditory word processing (but not reading). This would not be possible in a factorial design – we could not simply substitute 'visual/auditory' as a factor in place of, say, frequency in the above factorial design. This is because directly contrasting visual and auditory stimuli can be expected to yield a wide range of differences since they stimulate different sensory systems, and may engage partially non-overlapping cognitive processes as well. A factorial design requires conditions that are well matched on variables of no interest, as in a subtraction design. However, with a conjunction design, we could address these issues. For example, visual words could be contrasted with consonant strings as a control condition, and auditory words could be contrasted with auditory control stimuli (various transformations, such as playing sounds backward and applying specific types of filtering, are good at preserving most of the low-level acoustic features of speech while rendering it unintelligible). Then, we could examine the conjunction of brain regions that were significantly activated both in the visual words–visual control contrast, and the auditory words–auditory control contrast. This would isolate the brain areas common to word perception across sensory modalities.

One could also examine the **disjunction** maps for each condition, which would show areas significantly activated in only one or the other condition. Care should be taken in interpreting disjunction maps, however. Intuitively, one might think that an area that's shown as active in condition A but not condition B is more active in A than B. While in a sense this is true, it is not the same as the area being *significantly* more active in condition A than B. This would have to be assessed through a statistical contrast between A and B (such as a *t*-test). In many cases, the size of the difference (and/or the variance in the size of the difference) between two conditions is small enough that although activation crosses the threshold for statistical significance in one condition but not the other, the direct statistical comparison does not yield a significant difference.

Conjunctions can naturally be extended beyond the case of two experimental conditions of interest – one could look for the overlap of three, four, or even more conditions, although as mentioned above, one should aim for simplicity in fMRI experimental designs and not go overboard with the number of conditions included. Another important point to consider is the difference between conjunctions and conducting a single analysis collapsing across the experimental conditions. In the latter case, in performing the analysis one would simply treat the two experimental contrasts (A–control and B–control) as equivalent (that is, as if they were all A–control). This has both advantages and disadvantages, and the choice depends on the research question. This latter analysis approach would potentially be more sensitive, because we would have two data points per subject, rather than one, which would increase statistical sensitivity to true effects (recall the advantage in SNR gained by increasing the number of trials in an experiment). On the other hand, the areas seen as significant in this combined analysis might not actually reflect true overlap between the conditions – an area that was strongly activated only in condition A might still appear as active in the combined map, simply because it was consistently and strongly activated in condition A, along with weaker activation in condition B (that was not significant in condition B alone). In contrast, a conjunction analysis first tests whether each condition is significant on its own, and then shows the overlap between those conditions. A conjunction analysis is thus generally the better approach because we can be certain that the areas identified in the conjunction are truly significantly activated in each of the input conditions alone. Conjunction/disjunction analyses can also be performed between groups of participants. In this case, activation maps for the two groups would be taken from the same experimental contrast (rather than two different experimental conditions) and the brain areas significantly activated in both groups would be shown by the conjunction between them.

fMRI Adaptation (fMRI-a)

Factorial and parametric designs are likely to be familiar to many readers due to the fact that they are common in many areas of research, including psychology. **fMRI adaptation (fMRI-a)** designs, however, were developed to address an issue that is rather specific to this neuroimaging technique: each voxel in an fMRI scan encompasses many tens or hundreds of thousands of neurons. Within a brain area specialized for a particular function, individual neurons (or localized groups of functionally related neurons, such as cortical columns) are generally tuned to different parameters of the stimuli. For example, in many areas of visual cortex, including primary visual cortex, cortical columns are tuned to the orientation of simple lines. Thus some neurons are tuned to vertical lines, some to horizontal, and some to other angles of orientation. This organization can be readily identified using invasive techniques such as recording from individual neurons, but the spatial scale of this organization is not obtainable using conventional fMRI techniques – a typical fMRI scan using $3 \times 3 \times 3$ mm voxels would be expected to contain many columns with different orientation tunings. Because of this, we would expect that, on average, lines of any orientation would be likely to yield equal activation in a voxel containing neurons tuned to line orientation. In practice, by chance some voxels might have more columns tuned to horizontal lines, and others more voxels tuned to vertical lines, etc. – but nonetheless the spatial resolution of fMRI is too coarse to identify individual cortical columns or other fine-grained levels of neural organization.

fMRI-a was designed to overcome this limitation, and essentially tap into a level of spatial resolution that fMRI does not inherently have. The principle of this is based on a virtually universal property of neurons – **adaptation** – which is that their firing rates decrease if the same stimulus is presented repeatedly. In fact, this occurs even if the stimuli vary, as long as they have in common whatever property the neuron is tuned to; thus presenting a series of horizontal lines of different colours would lead to adaptation of neurons tuned to horizontal orientation, but not neurons tuned to colour. In the fMRI context, this means that if a brain area has multiple neural populations tuned to different values of a stimulus property (like line orientation), then activation should steadily decrease with repetition of stimuli that share a particular value of that property (such as horizontal lines). Once this adaptation has occurred, if a stimulus is presented of the same general category that the region is tuned to, but with a different value of the tuning parameter (such as vertical lines), then the region should show an increase in activation levels – release from adaptation – and then re-adapt as the same stimulus is repeated.

This technique was pioneered by Grill-Spector and colleagues, in a paper published in 1999 (Grill-Spector, Kushnir, Edelman, Avidan, Itzchak, & Malach, 1999). The researchers were interested in a part of visual cortex known as the lateral occipital complex (LOC), located in the anterior-lateral region of the occipital lobe, close to the boundary with the temporal lobe. LOC had been implicated in object recognition in numerous studies, showing greater activation to objects than non-object visual stimuli such as textures or visual noise in a number of subtraction-design fMRI studies. As well, parametric studies had shown that LOC responses were constant across four-fold changes in the size of the stimulus, as well as the location of the stimulus in the visual field. This was interpreted as suggesting that LOC was not performing lower-level perceptual functions (which would be predicted to be sensitive to size and stimulus location, as seen in areas such as primary visual cortex) but rather the higher-order cognitive function of object recognition. However, Grill-Spector and colleagues noted that different neural populations in the LOC might in fact be sensitive to lower-level properties such as size; however, because of the coarse level of resolution of fMRI the activation of these different populations within each voxel would lead to similar levels of fMRI activation regardless of stimulus size. In other words, two entirely separate populations of neurons within each voxel might respond to small and large stimuli, but when activation was averaged over the voxel (which is all fMRI can provide), activation would be identical for different-sized stimuli.

To distinguish between these possibilities, and with the intent of more strongly establishing the object-specificity of LOC, Grill-Spector and colleagues conducted a series of fMRI-a experiments based on modifications of a block design. In one of these experiments, shown in Figure 8.10, blocks each consisted of a series of images of objects, including a variety of animals and cars. These alternated with two types of control blocks: visual textures (noise) and scrambled images. Critically, different experimental blocks were designed to produce different amounts of adaptation. One block (labelled '1' in the figure) involved the repetition of the same image 32 times throughout the block, while the others involved differing numbers of different images ('2' involved the alternation of two images, 16 times each, etc.). Thus condition '1' was expected to produce the greatest adaptation, and '32' the least (as it consisted of 32 unique images). The top right panel of Figure 8.10 shows the time course of fMRI data from area LOC. While all object blocks elicited greater activation than control stimuli, the effect of adaptation is clear when comparing the different experimental blocks: the '1' condition shows relatively weak activation that adapted to a level comparable to the noise condition about halfway through the block, '32' shows strong activation that was maintained throughout the block, and the intermediate conditions show differing levels of adaptation.

Having demonstrated adaptation in an fMRI experiment using the property of object identity, Grill-Spector and colleagues went on to conduct several other experiments to determine which stimulus properties LOC might adapt or not adapt to. Over these experiments they demonstrated that LOC voxels were more sensitive to changes in illumination and viewing angle, and less sensitive to changes in the size or position of the stimulus. The fMRI-a technique also revealed two functionally distinct subdivisions in LOC that were defined by their different adaptation properties across the different experimental manipulations. Thus fMRI-a can be an effective technique for characterizing the functional specificity of brain areas in a way that is potentially more sensitive than other types of experimental design.

Condition-Rich and Time-Continuous Designs

Some fMRI research takes a rather different approach to experimental design and data analysis from the traditional approach of implying many trials of stimuli falling into relatively few categories (experimental conditions). **Condition-rich** designs employ relatively large numbers of experimental conditions, often treating individual stimuli as conditions, rather than grouping these into categories (for example, for face stimuli, each individual is treated as a separate condition, rather than averaging across all faces) (Kriegeskorte, Mur, & Bandettini, 2008). Such designs evolved within the context of multivariate approaches to data analysis (discussed in the next section), where the aim is to characterize unique response patterns across voxels within brain areas, as well as between areas. To the extent that a brain region responds similarly to different exemplars of a particular category (such as faces), the distributed pattern of activation within a voxel should show consistency across exemplars, but this can only be determined if each exemplar is treated individually. Condition-rich designs also allow for exploratory analyses in which, rather than focusing analysis on a single hypothesis-driven research question (for example, does the fusiform face area distinguish between faces and other types of visual objects?), one can categorize

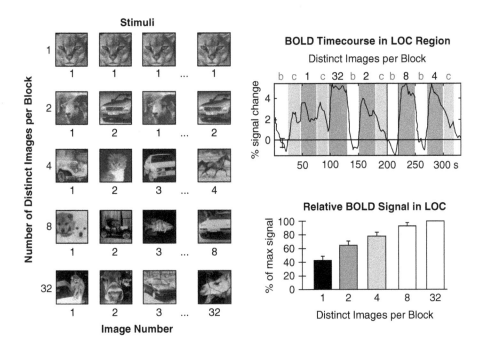

Figure 8.10 Design and data from an fMRI-a experiment, published by Grill-Spector and colleagues (1999). Of interest was BOLD fMRI activation levels during blocks in which 32 images were presented, with an SOA of 1 s. The left side of the figure shows examples of stimulus sequences in different experimental blocks: '1' presented an identical stimulus 32 times, '32' presented 32 unique images, and the other conditions involved intermediate levels of repetition. The right top panel shows the fMRI BOLD time course from the lateral occipital cortex (LOC) region, which is commonly implicated in visual object recognition. Blocks shown in dark grey involved presentation of photos; the number above the block indicates the number of distinct images in the block. As well, the experiment included blocks of visual control images (textures and scrambled images), which are shown as light grey blocks and labelled 'c', and baseline blocks consisting of a blank screen, labelled 'b'. For the image blocks, note the differences in both peak activation levels, and how activation declines over the course of the block, as a function of the number of distinct images. The right bottom panel shows the relative mean amplitude of BOLD signal in LOC as a function of the number of distinct images in the block, relative to the activation level in the 32 distinct images condition. Adapted with permission from Elsevier from Grill-Spector et al. (1999)

stimuli along multiple dimensions (for example, face/non-face, animate/inanimate, by colour, by size, by shape) and identify brain regions or activity patterns that vary systematically with these dimensions.

Time-continuous designs take the concept of condition-rich designs even further, by using stimuli that vary continuously over time (such as having people watch a movie for the entire scan), and treating each individual time point in the fMRI time series as a separate condition (Hasson, Furman, Clark, Dudai, & Davachi, 2008; Haxby, Gobbini, Furey, Ishai, Schouten, & Pietrini, 2011). These time points can be labelled according to what stimulus categories are present at each point in the movie (for example, faces, cars, outdoor scenes), or alternatively the analysis can focus on the degree to which similar patterns of brain activation occur across individual viewers at specific time points.

While condition-rich and time-continuous designs may seem grossly unconstrained from the perspective of traditional experimental design in cognitive science or neuroscience, they are generally meant to address different questions. For example, rather than testing a hypothesis that certain stimulus categories are treated differently by the brain, these designs allow for 'late commitment' (Kriegeskorte et al., 2008) wherein one presents the brain with rich, naturalistic information and allows a data-driven identification of the relevant dimensions that the brain activation represents.

STATISTICAL ANALYSIS

Univariate Analysis

Statistical analysis of fMRI data is not unlike that of other types of neuroimaging or behavioural data. The most common way to analyse a functional time series (individual run) is to use multiple linear regression, as described earlier in the chapter: a time series is created for each experimental condition of interest that indicates when each stimulus event (or block) occurred, and this is convolved with a model of the HRF. This model time series is then regressed against (correlated with) the time series at each voxel in the brain individually – that is, a 'mass univariate' analysis approach. Since typically an experiment comprises multiple runs per subject, and multiple subjects, multiple levels of analysis are required. The output of the multiple regression on an individual run yields a coefficient (sometimes called a parameter estimate, or beta weight) at each voxel, for each condition in the run; these essentially indicate the strength of 'activation' at each voxel for that condition. More precisely, they reflect how similar the BOLD time series is in each voxel to the modelled HRF. These coefficients, along with the variance around the estimates of the coefficients are used as the input to a second-level analysis, across runs within each participant. This second-level analysis thus yields a statistical map of coefficients averaged across runs for that subject. The results of the second-level analysis then serve as the input to the third-level analysis, which tells us what the pattern of activation is across subjects. These higher levels of analysis typically involve common statistical approaches such as t-test, ANOVAs, or linear mixed effects. Although this is a very common way of performing an analysis, different experimental designs require different approaches, making this topic far more complex than can be adequately addressed in this brief section. There are, however, numerous authoritative books on the topic and the manuals provided with most fMRI analysis software packages provide extensive information, with examples, on this topic.

Multiple Comparison Correction

The aspect of fMRI statistics that is perhaps most important to understand is the issue of multiple comparisons. This was raised earlier in our discussions of ERP and MEG analysis, but it is perhaps most significant in fMRI. This is because analysis is performed separately on each voxel in the MR image, and these images typically contain hundreds of thousands of voxels (for example, a set of 30 slices covering the brain, each 64 × 64 voxels, comprises 122,880 voxels). Statistical analysis typically yields p-values, and in many disciplines $p < .05$ is generally considered statistically significant. However, this criterion sets the likelihood of obtaining a 'significant' result by chance (a 'false positive') at 5/100. Thus even in an fMRI image containing only random noise, we could expect 5% of the voxels to appear 'significant'; in our example above, this would mean 6,144 false positives. For this reason, we need some better way of controlling the false positive rate.

The typical approach to controlling the false positive rate taught in introductory statistics classes is the Bonferroni correction. In this method, the desired p value (for example, .05) is divided by the number of tests performed, and the resulting value is used as the threshold for determining whether each individual test is significant. For example, if we perform ten tests then the Bonferroni-corrected p threshold for significance of each test is $.05/10 = .005$. Thus a Bonferroni correction for our example fMRI study would set the p threshold at approximately .0000004 (.05/122,880). However, this very strict p threshold might make it difficult to find any significant activation, and so we might end up missing true activations (that is, in controlling our false positive rate, we would unacceptably inflate our false negative rate). In practice, the number of voxels tested can be reduced significantly by restricting the analysis to the brain itself, ignoring the surrounding tissue and air space around the head, but this still generally results in tens, if not hundreds, of thousands of statistical tests being performed. Another issue with Bonferroni correction is that it assumes that the outcome of each test is independent of every other one, but this is not the case in fMRI – we actually expect the signal from adjacent voxels to be correlated, for several reasons. Firstly, activated brain areas are in most cases likely to be larger than single voxels, so adjacent voxels' results are likely to be correlated, rather than independent. As well, the physiology of the BOLD response – specifically, the fact that we are measuring changes in blood oxygenation in vessels around active tissue – further increases the likelihood that adjacent activated voxels will show correlated results. Finally, we further increase the correlation of the data from adjacent voxels by the spatial smoothing that is typically applied in fMRI data preprocessing.

To address this issue, various approaches to **multiple comparison correction** have been developed for, or adapted to, fMRI. One of the first was based on a branch of mathematics, **Gaussian random field theory** (GRFT), which prior to fMRI was considered a purely theoretical area with no practical applications. However, mathematician Keith Worsley, working with colleagues at the Montreal

Neurological Institute and elsewhere in the early days of fMRI, realized that this could be fruitfully applied to address the multiple comparison problem (Worsley, 2001; Worsley, Evans, Marrett, & Neelin, 1992). GRFT deals with Gaussian (normal) distributions in three dimensions, and as discussed in the previous chapter under 'Smoothing', this is a good approximation of how signal and noise are distributed in fMRI images. What GRFT provides is a way of estimating how likely it is that a cluster of contiguous voxels should all have values above a particular threshold level. Thus rather than testing for significance in a massively univariate sense (at each voxel), the GRFT approach applies a threshold, uncorrected for multiple comparisons, to each voxel, but then – critically – determines a p value for each cluster of supra-threshold voxels, where a 'cluster' is defined as all voxels above the individual voxel p threshold that are adjacent to each other. This cluster-level probability reflects an estimate of the likelihood that a cluster of that many supra-threshold voxels could occur by chance. This approach also strikes a balance such that it is sensitive both to small but strongly activated clusters and larger but overall less strongly activated clusters. Another common approach involves using the **false discovery rate (FDR)** (Genovese, Lazar, & Nichols, 2002). This approach, which is widely used in genetics where large numbers of candidate genes must be screened, tries to minimize the rate of false positives adaptively, based on the distribution of p-values in the dataset under consideration. Another well-regarded approach is non-parametric, permutation-based testing, which was discussed in Chapter 5 in the context of MEG (Nichols & Holmes, 2001).

Recent work in this area has drawn attention to the fact that the multiple comparison correction approaches historically used in published fMRI studies may have been overly lenient, contributing to published results that do not replicate (Button et al., 2013b; Eklund et al., 2016; Poldrack et al., 2017). These issues have their roots in several factors, some of which are not unique to fMRI or even neuroimaging (such as pressure to publish, and a bias in the literature towards publishing positive but not null findings), and some of which are more specific to fMRI (such as the high cost of acquiring the data, leading to relatively small sample sizes in individual studies). Lenient procedures for multiple comparison correction have also been identified as a significant source of problems in this regard. The positive outcome of this increased scrutiny is that fMRI analysis software packages are changing default parameters to use more stringent thresholds, and peer reviewers are becoming more sensitive to issues of power and statistical sensitivity. Nevertheless, as a critical consumer of the fMRI literature it is important to have an appreciation of the importance of multiple comparison correction, and the complex issues involved.

Region of Interest Analysis

In our discussion of mass univariate analysis and multiple comparison correction, we assumed that the analyses were applied to every voxel in the fMRI image (or at least every voxel in the image that was located in the brain). This 'whole-brain' approach to analysis is perhaps the most common way of approaching fMRI analysis, and is arguably the most objective. However, in many cases a researcher may have specific questions and/or hypotheses regarding specific brain areas – defined either anatomically or functionally. For example, in studying visual object processing the inferior temporal cortex is often of interest, whereas in studying language processing, researchers often focus on peri-Sylvian areas (that is, around the Sylvian fissure, including the inferior frontal gyrus, superior temporal gyrus, and inferior parietal lobe). Whole-brain analysis can certainly be used in these situations since, if activation in the expected areas is indeed modulated by the experimental design, the analysis should identify them. However, there may be theoretically well-motivated reasons to restrict the statistical analysis to one or more **regions of interest** (ROIs). One obvious advantage of doing so is that the multiple comparison problem is much-reduced relative to a whole-brain analysis, since an ROI necessarily has far fewer voxels than the whole-brain image. By reducing the number of tests that need to be corrected for, one can gain sensitivity to relatively small experimental effects. Another advantage is that by specifying the ROI a priori (before running the analysis), one avoids issues of circularity that might arise with more vague pre-specification of hypotheses (for example, simply stating 'the inferior parietal lobe'), followed by **post hoc** 'confirmation' in which any pattern of activation obtained in a whole-brain analysis that overlaps with the broad area predicted is taken as confirmation of the hypothesis. As well, one might be interested in fine-grained patterns of activity within an ROI (see the next section on multivariate analyses) that is defined on the basis of specific parameters.

There are generally two ways of specifying an ROI: based on anatomy, or function. **Anatomically defined ROIs** may be based on gross sulcal/gyral landmarks (for example, the inferior frontal gyrus, or the intraparietal sulcus), or on probabilistic atlases based on cytoarchitecture or other micro-anatomical features. Using anatomical landmarks, one can choose to manually trace the ROI on each individual's structural MRI scan (without spatial normalization); this is an extremely tedious and labour-intensive process, however. An alternative is to spatially normalize all participants' brains and then either manually trace the region once, or use an existing MRI-based atlas that has the area already defined. The latter is generally a preferable approach from the point of view of replicability, since other researchers would have access to the same atlas and be able to use consistent anatomical definitions. Anatomically defined ROIs – especially if using a standard atlas – have the advantage of being replicable; however, they are limited by the fact that studies have suggested that there is not a consistent relationship between gross anatomical landmarks and either the underlying cytoarchitecture or functional localization. For this reason, many researchers prefer **functionally defined ROIs**. As the name suggests, these are defined based on fMRI mapping. For example, if one wishes to investigate activation patterns in the fusiform face area, one can functionally define this region on the basis of an fMRI scan contrasting faces with control stimuli. In general, it is advisable to base functional ROI definition on data from a separate scan from the data that the ROI will then be used to analyse. Continuing our face example, one might run a single blocked fMRI run alternating between faces and control stimuli as the functional localizer, and then separate scans with the stimuli and tasks of experimental interest. Otherwise one runs the risk of circularity in analysing a dataset once to define the ROI, and then re-analysing the same data for a second purpose.

Multivariate Analysis

An alternative class of analyses to mass univariate approaches are described as **multivariate** approaches. Fundamental to multivariate analyses is that they simultaneously consider the signal at multiple voxels, rather than performing independent, parallel analyses at each voxel. This approach was first described by Haxby and colleagues (Haxby et al., 2001) in a study examining cortical activation in response to images of different object categories. Their analysis focused on voxels in the inferior temporal lobe, an area commonly involved in visual object recognition. Within this region, there are specific areas that show stronger BOLD signal for certain object categories than others, such as the 'fusiform face area' that responds more strongly to faces than other objects. However, rather than focusing on areas defined by the category to which they respond most strongly, Haxby and colleagues asked whether the distributed pattern of BOLD signal strength across *all* voxels in the object-sensitive inferior temporal cortex (hereafter called the ROI, or region of interest) could predict which category of object was being viewed. To do this, they collected fMRI data across multiple runs in a blocked design, with 24 s blocks of stimuli from a given category alternating with 12 s rest blocks. They then performed a typical, first-level mass univariate multiple regression analysis on each run's data to determine the strength of the BOLD response of each voxel to each stimulus category.

In a typical univariate approach, the next steps would have been to conduct a group-level mass univariate analysis to determine which voxels showed significant differences between object categories. However, what Haxby and colleagues did instead was to create a vector (a long string of numbers) for each stimulus type containing the BOLD activation values for every voxel in the ROI – regardless of whether the voxel was 'significantly activated' or not. They created separate vectors in this way for the data from the even and odd-numbered runs from each individual, so that they had two sets of data from each person for each condition. Finally, they calculated the strength of correlation between the odd- and even-numbered runs both within and between stimulus categories. Specifically, they wanted to determine whether the vectors representing the distributed pattern of activity in the even-numbered runs for a given stimulus type were more strongly correlated with the distributed activity patterns for the same stimulus type in the odd-numbered runs, than with distributed activity patterns for other stimulus categories. This is indeed what they found: the distributed pattern of activity in one set of runs was able to predict, with 96% accuracy, which category of stimulus was being viewed in the other set of runs.

While in principle this correlation still could have been primarily driven by very strong responses in the voxels that were most selective for a particular object category (for example, those that respond more strongly to faces than any other category), this was found not to be the case. Haxby and colleagues performed several follow-up analyses, including computing the correlations after removing the voxels that showed the strongest category-specific responses, and obtained similar results. While these findings do not undermine the fact that certain brain regions may show selectively stronger responses to one stimulus category than others, they do suggest that the most 'selective' brain regions are not the only ones involved in processing information of a specific type. Instead, it seems like the distributed pattern of activation over a larger brain area contains information that is specific to the type of stimulus (or task) involved. For this reason, in multivariate analyses the data are not typically spatially smoothed, since this would decrease the unique informational value of each voxel.

The approach used by Haxby and colleagues is a type of linear decoding approach, which falls into a more general class of multi-voxel pattern analysis (MVPA). Vast numbers of studies have been performed using MVPA subsequent to Haxby and colleagues' pioneering paper, and these approaches are now very much in the mainstream of fMRI research (and are also being applied to source-localized MEG data). Many current approaches involve using machine learning algorithms to identify and characterize the features of distributed activation patterns that best distinguish between different conditions and, in many cases, have yielded impressive results. For example, Formisano and colleagues (Formisano, De Martino, Bonte, & Goebel, 2008), based on activation in auditory cortical regions of the superior temporal cortex, were able to reliably determine what phonemes were being spoken and the identity of the speaker using multivariate analyses. Similarly, vision studies have shown that it is possible to reliably reconstruct complex natural images being viewed by people based on their fMRI activation patterns (Kay, Naselaris, Prenger, & Gallant, 2008). Recent work has also demonstrated consistency between distributed patterns of neural activation and how neurally inspired computational models of visual recognition (deep neural networks) represent visual information (Cichy, Pantazis, & Oliva, 2014).

One widely used approach to MVPA is called **representational similarity analysis (RSA**; Kriegeskorte et al., 2008). This extends the logic of Haxby and colleagues' original study by using condition-rich or time-continuous designs combined with explicit models of how information in the stimuli or tasks might be represented by the brain. These models can be conceptual (for example, categories such as faces, houses, tools, etc., or semantic properties such as animate/inanimate) or computational (ranging from simple models such as high- or low-pass filtering of images, to complex models that apply more sophisticated and theoretically motivated computations).

In RSA, the first step is to obtain activation maps for each individual stimulus (or time point, in a time-continuous design), using traditional mass-univariate approaches – though again the resulting statistical maps are not thresholded, but rather we obtain a value for each voxel representing its difference in BOLD signal for the stimulus relative to baseline. These activation maps are commonly then grouped into ROIs determined by the focus of the study (for example, specific inferior temporal lobe regions for a study of visual object processing). Although whole-brain data could also be used, it is common for researchers to focus on ROIs, and sometimes an interest is in comparing activation patterns between brain regions, which depends on defining those regions and treating the data from each separately. Once the activation patterns for each stimulus and ROI are obtained, correlations between the maps for each pair of conditions (stimuli) are computed within each ROI. This yields a 'dissimilarity matrix' – a measure of the 'distance' (or dissimilarity) between activation patterns for each pair of stimuli; this value represents as a single number the extent to which activation patterns for any pair of stimuli are similar or dissimilar (although the technique is called representational similarity analysis, the developers chose *dis*similarity as their preferred measure because it has certain computational advantages). This is illustrated in Figure 8.11. This step is important for several reasons. For one, it reduces a complex, distributed pattern of activation to a single number, and moreover the numbers represent not the activation pattern for an individual stimulus, but the relationships between activity patterns for different stimuli. Another benefit of this approach is that it is agnostic with respect to the actual distributed pattern of activation within the brain area, which means that across individual participants in a study, we do not need to worry about issues of anatomical overlap. That is to say, two people might have very different patterns of activation within their fusiform face area to the same face stimulus, but in RSA this doesn't matter – because comparisons between the fine-grained activity patterns are done entirely within each individual. What ultimately matters at the group level is the extent to which each pair of stimuli elicits similar or dissimilar activation patterns across subjects. For example, to the extent that the fusiform face area is specialized for processing face information, across individuals this region should consistently yield higher similarity measures for pairs of faces, than for pairs involving a face and some non-face stimulus.

Having obtained the stimulus dissimilarity matrices for each subject, the next step in RSA is to compute similar dissimilarity matrices for each model of how the stimulus is represented. For example, in Kriegeskorte and colleagues' (2008) original description of RSA, they ran each stimulus image through a number of computational models of how the visual information might be represented in the brain. These ranged from simple high- and low-pass filtering, to more complex models of how primary visual cortex (V1) neurons encode information (based on Gabor patches, which are essentially 2D sine waves of a particular orientation, representing a specific part of the visual field). Thus for each model, we obtain a matrix showing how similarly (or dissimilarly) the model treats each pair of images. Effectively, what we are doing is positing that if a model is reflective of how a brain region actually represents the stimulus information, then the pattern of dissimilarities between stimuli generated by the model should match the pattern of dissimilarities in activation of that brain area. Thus the next step in RSA is to compare how similar each pair of dissimilarity matrices is – in other words, we compute the dissimilarity matrix of dissimilarity matrices. These can be quantified statistically, and also visualized in different ways. For example, Figure 8.12 shows both the matrix of dissimilarities between models and ROIs, and a visualization of these that groups more similar representations (be they models or brain areas) together.

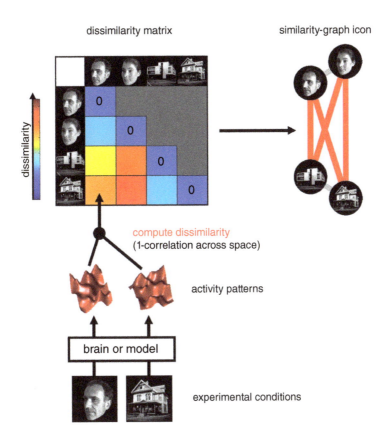

Figure 8.11 An example of a dissimilarity matrix used in representational similarity analysis (RSA). In this simple example, four stimuli were used, which fell into two categories: faces and houses (left, bottom). Distributed activity patterns within an ROI were obtained for each individual stimulus (left, middle). Then, correlations between the distributed activation patterns for each pair of stimuli were computed, to create the dissimilarity matrix (top left). Note that dissimilarity is computed as one minus the correlation value, yielding positive-valued numbers ranging from zero (identical) to 2 (perfectly negatively correlated). The top right panel shows an alternative visualization in which dissimilarity values are simplified as either 'similar' (grey lines) or 'dissimilar' (red lines). Image adapted from Kriegeskorte and colleagues (2008) under the Creative Commons Attribution License (CC BY)

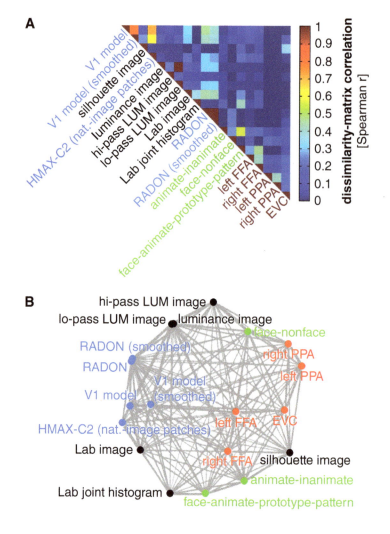

Figure 8.12 End result of the RSA performed by Kriegeskorte and colleagues (2008) and described in the text. The top panel (A) shows the matrix of dissimilarities between distributed activation patterns in several brain ROIs (names in red) in response to 96 unique images, and multiple models of representations of those images. Names in black are simple computational models; names in blue are complex computational models; names in green are conceptual models. The bottom panel (B) shows the result of applying a transformation (multidimensional scaling) to these results, which groups ROIs and models according to their similarity; points that are closer in this visualization can be considered to represent the image information in more similar ways. Reproduced from Kriegeskorte and colleagues (2008) under the Creative Commons Attribution License (CC BY)

FUNCTIONAL AND EFFECTIVE CONNECTIVITY

Functional Connectivity

Within a few years of the introduction of fMRI, a novel approach to data analysis was developed that is widely termed **functional connectivity** or **fcMRI** (Biswal, Yetkin, Haughton, & Hyde, 1995). Functional connectivity analysis involves computing correlations (or covariance) in BOLD signal between different brain areas. This can be contrasted with the approach of correlating BOLD signal with an independently specified reference time series determined by the timing of some external event such as stimulus presentation or motor responses. It is important to note that in this context the word 'connectivity' does not mean *structural* connectivity – direct axonal (white matter) connections between brain areas (but see Chapter 10). A correlation in BOLD signal implies some synchronization of activity or other interaction between the correlated areas, but – critically – this could be modulated either by direct structural connectivity, indirect connectivity through one or more intervening brain regions, or the influence of another brain region sending signals to the two functionally connected brain areas – or even a chance correlation between two brain areas whose activity is not truly correlated. These caveats notwithstanding, this technique provides a potentially very powerful way of understanding brain activity using fMRI (and other techniques; functional connectivity analyses can be performed using MEG, EEG, and optical imaging data as well). While standard task-related fMRI analysis approaches can identify a set of brain regions activated during a particular task, fcMRI can provide insight into how these areas interact as coherent networks, rather than a set of isolated areas. In this way, functional connectivity is one way to move the discipline of fMRI beyond 'neo-phrenology' towards understanding the brain as a network – or a set of networks.

Functional connectivity analyses can be performed both on task-based fMRI data, and on 'resting state' scans in which the person being scanned is instructed simply to lie still – either with eyes closed or open, and possibly with a mark on a display to fixate on – without any other task to perform, typically for between 5 and 15 minutes. In a task-based functional connectivity analysis, one can naturally expect that all brain areas relevant to the experimental manipulation will show correlated BOLD signal, since by definition 'activated' areas are those whose BOLD signal correlates with the experimental manipulation (for example, boxcar time series or more complex block or event-related designs); thus all active areas can be expected to be correlated with each other. However, in a functional connectivity analysis one can specifically examine the time series only during the task-related blocks or events. In this case, all areas will be 'on' relative to the baseline or control condition periods of the scan. However, by focusing exclusively on activity during only the 'on'/task-related time periods, functional connectivity analyses can determine whether some of the brain areas show stronger correlations in activity during those 'on' blocks.

As noted, functional connectivity analyses can be performed on **resting state fMRI (rs-fcMRI**, or simply **rs-fMRI)** data. From the perspective of an experimental psychologist or cognitive scientist, this may seem odd: the resting state is very unconstrained – people are typically told merely to rest quietly, either with their eyes closed or open – and so we do not have any objective insight into what sort of cognitive activity is going on during such states. Indeed, it is entirely reasonable to think that different people would be engaged in rather different mental activities. However, hundreds, if not thousands, of rs-fMRI studies have been conducted to date and the patterns of functional connectivity that emerge from them are quite consistent, suggesting either that there is more commonality among what people do in these states than might be thought, or that what is reflected in rs-fcMRI data is not so much reflective of specific, moment-to-moment neurocognitive activity so much as of the inherent patterns of connectivity or correlated activity between brain regions, even when particular networks are not actively engaged in a particular task. A typical rs-fcMRI map is shown in Figure 8.13

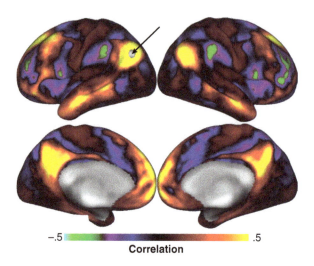

Figure 8.13 Example of a resting state functional connectivity (rs-fcMRI) map. During all scans participants kept their eyes open and fixated on a cross on a screen. The arrow points to the seed voxel, located in the left inferior parietal cortex. Areas in yellow showed the strongest positive correlation with the BOLD time course in the seed region, while areas in green showed the strongest negative correlations; areas in black showed weak or no correlation. Data were collected across four 15 min resting state runs per subject, at 7T with 1.6 mm spatial resolution. Reprinted from Vu and colleagues (2017) with permission of Elsevier

Indeed, one of the major applications of rs-fcMRI is in comparing between different groups or populations of people: because people perform no task, there is no possibility that observed differences between groups are due to differences in task performance. In contrast, this is a real concern in task-related fMRI comparisons between groups. For example, one might wish to compare BOLD signal in a group of people with Alzheimer's disease (who have memory impairments) to that of a group of age-matched, healthy controls in a memory task. Likely, there would be differences in BOLD signal between the groups. However, one would be challenged to know whether the observed differences between groups were related to the causes of the memory deficits in the Alzheimer's group, or instead were an effect of the fact that the Alzheimer's group performed the task less well (so, for example, they may have had to work harder, spending more mental computation time on each trial; alternatively they may simply have not fully processed information on some or all trials). Although a rs-fcMRI scan would not solve the cause-and-effect question, it allows us to look for differences in brain activity that we at least know cannot be attributed to differences in task performance. In this way, a primary use of rs-fcMRI is as an **endophenotype** or biomarker of a particular disease or other state. This could be used diagnostically, for instance to identify a particular disease (possibly before overt behavioural symptoms manifest), as well as to monitor the efficacy of a particular treatment (on the assumption that functional connectivity patterns would become more normal if the treatment was effective). It is important to note, however, that in comparing functional connectivity patterns between groups we are at something of an inferential disadvantage: typically in experimental cognitive neuroscience, we aim to observe consequences (brain activity) based on causes (experimental manipulations), and we use control conditions to increase our confidence that the experimental manipulation caused the observed changes in brain activity. On the other hand, with rs-fcMRI the researcher typically does not explicitly manipulate anything, but makes the inference that any observed difference in fcMRI between groups (or over time) are causally related to the defining characteristics of the groups. Because groups may vary along many different dimensions, besides the one of primary research interest (for example, a patient group may be on more medications, get less exercise, have less social interaction, etc. than a control group), the ability to draw causal links is often weaker. This is, of course, not exclusively a problem with rs-fcMRI but a more general challenge to any study that does not involve experimental manipulations and control, including the structural MRI techniques discussed in the next two chapters.

There are two common approaches to analysing functional connectivity patterns. The first, as described above, involves computing correlations in BOLD signal between different brain areas. This can itself be performed in two general ways. One is **seed-based correlation**, in which one chooses a particular voxel or small area of the cortex as a 'seed' and correlates the BOLD time courses from all other voxels in the brain with this seed time course. The choice of seed region will naturally have significant effects on the patterns of functional connectivity that result. One common approach is to choose a voxel within a known (or hypothesized) network, since all regions that are part of that network should correlated with this region's activity. Figure 8.13 shows an example of a seed-based correlation, with the seed located in the left inferior parietal cortex – a common choice when investigating what is often called the 'default mode network' (Fox, Vincent, Van Essen, & Raichle, 2005).

An alternative approach, **network-based correlation**, is to use a large number of seed regions, and compute correlations among each pair of seeds. It is well-established that there is a high degree of smoothness or inherent correlation among nearby voxels in fMRI signal, so it is unnecessary to use every voxel in the brain in such an analysis. Typically, these approaches use between 90 and 300 seed regions or **nodes**; the choice of the exact regions and their number can have a significant impact on the results; however there is still much research and little agreement on the best choices for these parameters. One approach is to pick regions based on anatomical labels (for example, each gyrus on the cortex); however, other researchers argue that since any particular gross anatomical label may have functionally distinct subregions, it is better to divide the brain into a larger number of areas that are all of approximately the same size. Computing the pair-wise correlations among all of the seeds yields a large matrix of correlation values; these can then be thresholded to isolate the strongest correlations, and these network maps can further be analysed using approaches such as **graph theory** – a line of mathematics developed for analysing complex network relationships. Graph theory-based analysis can identify features such as **hub** regions that show functional connectivity with disproportionately large numbers of other areas, and **modularity** whereby groups of brain areas that show high correlations with each other are largely separated from other such densely interconnected networks. The brain has been characterized using the graph theory approach as having **small-world properties**, meaning that it consists of a number of densely interconnected modules (sub-networks) which are connected globally through a set of short paths (that is, any given node is linked to any other one through a relatively low number of intervening nodes). An example of a graph theory analysis is shown in Figure 8.14.

The second predominant approach to functional connectivity analysis is using **independent components analysis (ICA)**. This is a signal processing method designed to separate complex signals into a set of components that are maximally statistically independent of each other (this technique was also discussed in the context of EEG artifact removal). In its implementation in fMRI, ICA identifies maximally distinctive spatio-temporal patterns within an fMRI dataset, such as an rs-fMRI scan (Damoiseaux et al., 2006). Each pattern, or component, has a characteristic time course that is present in all voxels within that component – although the strength (amplitude) of the time course can vary across voxels. Also, although a consistent pattern of BOLD signal over time is present at each voxel in that component, it explains only a part of the variation in the time course for each voxel. In other words, the time course of an individual voxel will not necessarily look like the time course of the component that the voxel is a part of. This is important to understand because it means that a given voxel may participate in more than one spatial component, since its time course can be decomposed into multiple contributing patterns of variation.

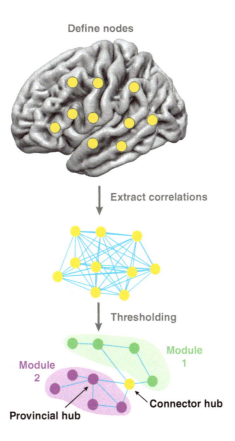

Figure 8.14 An example of a graph theory analysis applied to fcMRI data. A set of brain regions of interest (nodes, shown in yellow) are first defined by the researcher. Then, the BOLD fMRI time series from each node is extracted, and correlations between these time series are computed for every pair of nodes (indicated by the thickness of the blue lines). These correlations are then thresholded to retain only the strongest correlations, which define the paths (connections between nodes, shown as blue lines) in the network. Principles from graph theory are then applied to define features such as modules (a subset of nodes that show relatively high connectivity with each other) and hubs (individual nodes that connect to a relatively large number of other nodes, either within a module – provincial hubs – or between modules – connector hubs)

An advantage of ICA is that it does not rely on any prior assumptions or guesses on the part of the researcher as to what to choose as a seed region, or how many and which regions to use, as is required in a network-based correlation analysis. ICA instead uses all the voxels in the data and typically yields a large number of components in an entirely 'data-driven' approach. On the other hand, in addition to functionally connected neural networks, many ICA components will capture systematic noise in the data such as cardiac and respiration artifacts, head movement, and non-physiological sources such as scanner drift. Although this can be a good thing – in the sense that signal and noise are separated based on their having distinctive spatial patterns – it also means that it is up to the researcher to decide which components are 'signal' and which are 'noise'. There are several principled ways of making these decisions: for instance, physiological noise is very regular over time and has distinctive temporal frequencies; head movement is characterized by occasional, transient changes predominantly at the edges of the brain. However, there is still a degree of subjectivity in deciding which ICA components actually reflect brain activity of interest. One approach to doing this is, rather than deciding at the level of individual rs-fMRI runs or subjects which components are interesting, to combine ICA maps from many scans across many subjects together, and use clustering algorithms to identify components that occur consistently across individuals with similar spatial patterns (Damoiseaux et al., 2006). An alternative approach is to combine all of the scans from a group of people and use this as the input to ICA, thus identifying one set of components across the entire set of subjects. This can be followed by a step where these group-level components are regressed against each individual subject's scan to determine the degree to which that component is present in each individual (known as 'dual regression' ICA; Mackay, Filippini, & Smith, 2009).

Although functional connectivity approaches are very popular, they have some inherent limitations. Firstly, as noted earlier, functional connectivity does not equate to structural connectivity, and correlations between BOLD activity in multiple brain areas could have several different interpretations (Menon & Dougherty, 2009). Secondly, it is important to note that changes in functional connectivity (that is, correlation values between two voxels or regions) do not necessarily reflect actual changes in the relative strength of interaction between the areas, nor can the direction of causation of any changes be inferred. For example, it can be shown mathematically that even in a simple network with three nodes, a change in the strength of correlation between one pair of nodes can cause a change in the correlation between other, indirectly connected nodes. A further mathematical limitation is that changes in the amount of noise in the data can alter the estimated correlations (functional connectivity) between regions, even if the true correlation values themselves do not change. Thus if we are comparing rs-fcMRI between two groups, and one group's data are noisier (for example, due to more head movement), then between-group differences might be identified but misinterpreted as real differences in brain activity. Limitations such as these do not undermine the use of functional connectivity approaches; however, they do impose important limitations on the conclusions that can be drawn from such analyses – a limitation which is not always evident in the discussion sections of functional connectivity papers.

Effective Connectivity

Given the limitations of functional connectivity approaches, researchers have developed a second class of analysis tools to measure **effective connectivity**, in which the direction of influence between functionally connected brain regions can be

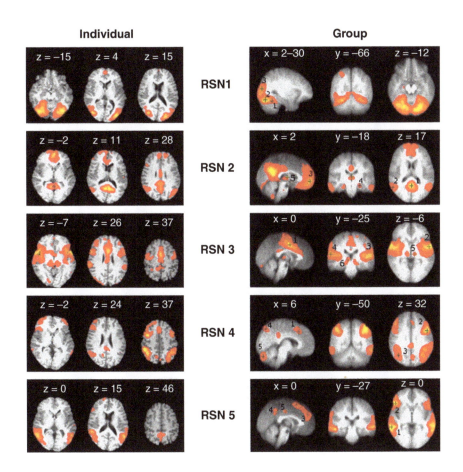

Figure 8.15 An example of five resting state networks (RSN) identified using ICA. The left panels show the networks identified in a single individual, while the right panels show the networks that were consistently identified across a set of ten individuals. Each network shows consistent spatiotemporal patterns of activity during the resting state. Reprinted from De Luca, Beckmann, De Stefano, Matthews, & Smith (2006) with permission of Elsevier

estimated – or more generally, effective connectivity attempts to provide explanations or inferences of causality for functional connectivity. These methods go beyond simple correlations and are generally applied to task-based studies, rather than rs-fMRI data, because they typically rely on experimentally induced changes in activity as the basis for making inferences about the causal direction of those changes.

Granger Causality

The first method we will discuss can actually be applied to both task-based and rs-fMRI data. This method is called **Granger causality analysis (GCA)**, which is part of a larger class of models known as multivariate autoregressive models. GCA can be understood as an extension of basic correlation analysis. In computing a correlation between two time series, we normally look at how similar the two time series are over time. Effectively, this means we are comparing the values of the two time series at each point in time. In GCA, we extend this to look at the relationship between the data at a particular point in time in one brain area, and the data at a slightly later (or earlier) point in time in another area (the technical term for this is autoregressive modelling). In this way we can determine whether the data in one brain region 'predict' the data at a slightly later time in another brain area. If so, we can say that one area 'Granger causes' activity in another area. This is illustrated in Figure 8.17. Ideally, this could be interpreted as the neural activity in the 'Granger causing' area being propagated to, and causing (or at least influencing), the neural activity in the second area. However, GCA results should be interpreted with extreme caution. Recall that the shape and timing of the HRF varies considerably between brain regions, even within individuals. GCA makes the strong, but untestable, assumption that this variance is directly related to differences in the underlying neural activity that drives the haemodynamic response. However, the temporal relationship between neural activity and BOLD response can be influenced by many factors, and is not well understood. Thus it is impossible to test whether the directionality suggested by GCA is valid or not. GCA is also based on several other assumptions that are known to be violated in fMRI data, which raise further questions about its suitability and about whether it should truly be considered a form of effective, as opposed to functional, connectivity analysis (Friston, 2011).

Psychophysiological Interactions

Another approach to effective connectivity is called **psychophysiological interactions (PPI)**. Essentially, this involves determining whether the correlation in BOLD activity between two regions (or more generally, between one region and the rest of the brain) changes with an experimental manipulation. As noted above, changes in correlations within networks are themselves insufficient to infer causal relationships. What makes this inference possible in PPI is that the effect of the experimental manipulation is explicitly taken into account, by first multiplying the experimental time course (that is, the stimulus and/or response time series) by the BOLD time course from the seed or 'reference' voxel, as illustrated in Figure 8.17, and then correlating the result with other voxels in the brain. In this way, the reference time series contains information about how the experimental manipulation modulated activity in the seed region, whereas in functional connectivity analysis (or GCA), experimental manipulation is not taken into account. This is why functional connectivity analyses can be performed on resting state data – but it also makes clear that PPI analysis is only possible on data in which there was an experimental manipulation, and not on rs-fMRI data.

As an example, imagine a task during which people navigate a maze in a computer game (O'Reilly, Woolrich, Behrens, Smith, & Johansen-Berg, 2012). Two areas known to be involved in spatial navigation are the prefrontal cortex and the

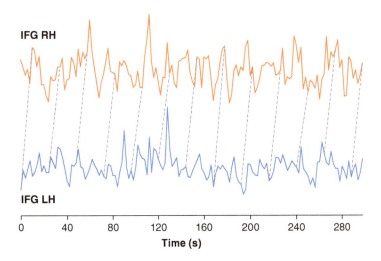

Figure 8.16 An example of Granger causality analysis. The two time series represent BOLD signal from two different brain areas, the inferior frontal gyrus (IFG) in the left (LH; blue) and right (RH; orange) hemispheres, extracted from an individual who was reading the story over the course of the entire five-minute fMRI run. Granger causality analysis was performed on lags ranging from 1 to 8 time points, and the strongest correlation between the two time series occurred at lag 6 (that is, 12 s; $p = .022$). We can therefore say that the signal in the left IFG 'Granger causes' changes in activity in the right IFG. This is illustrated by the dashed grey lines, which show the correspondence between points in the left IFG time series and those lagged 6 time points later in the right IFG

hippocampus. Both might be activated in this task relative to a control condition in which participants view a 'fly-through' of the maze without controlling their movement. A PPI analysis could help us differentiate between two possible interpretations: one, that the two areas were simply both engaged in spatial navigation in some way; and the other, that the two areas acted in concert during navigation, in a way that was different than when simply watching the fly-through. Under the second condition, the greater interaction between the areas would result in stronger correlations in BOLD signal during the experimental than the control condition. In other words, rather than simply looking at correlations of the overall BOLD time series (that is, across the entire scan, including experimental and control blocks or trials), or just during the experimental condition, we would compare the strength of correlation between brain regions during the experimental condition with the strength of correlations during the control condition. Although in this example we have described only two brain areas, as noted earlier in PPI analysis one can specify one 'seed' region of interest (ROI), and examine PPIs with every other voxel in the brain, or with a limited set of other voxels or ROIs that are of theoretical interest.

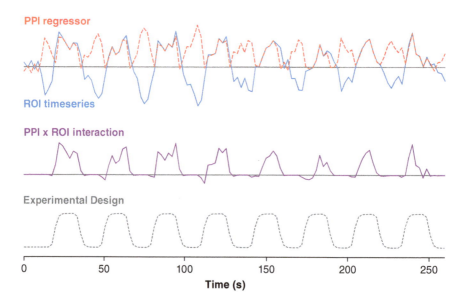

Figure 8.17 Regressor time series used in psychophysiological interaction (PPI) analysis. The grey time series at the bottom shows the boxcar experimental design convolved with the predicted HRF, alternating between two conditions every 15.4 s. The blue line is the averaged BOLD time series from a region of interest (for example, hippocampus in the example in the text). The PPI regressor is created by multiplying the boxcar time series with the ROI time series. The result is that the PPI regressor is correlated with the ROI time series during the 'on' blocks, but anti-correlated with the ROI time series during the 'off' blocks. Of interest in the PPI analysis is the interaction between these two time series, which is shown in the purple line. The anti-correlation between the PPI regressor and the original ROI time series results in a model that tests for correlations with the activity of the ROI only during the 'on' blocks; the correlation during the 'off' blocks is set to zero. In a PPI analysis, areas found to be 'effectively connected' to the ROI are those whose activity correlates with the PPI x ROI interaction – in other words, the areas that show a stronger correlation with the ROI during the 'on' blocks than the 'off' blocks

The advantage of PPI over the more basic fcMRI analyses described above is that because the experimental modulation is taken into account, we can have confidence that changes in functional connectivity are related to the experimental manipulation. Furthermore, PPIs represent task-specific changes in the relationship between two brain regions over and above any changes in signal that they show as a direct effect of the task manipulation. PPI does have several limitations, however. Firstly, it is not a terribly powerful method, and so may not yield any significant (or replicable) results. Since er-fMRI designs have inherently lower power than blocked designs, PPI is more likely to fail to find any significant relationships in event-related designs. A further, more conceptual limitation of PPI analysis is that it cannot tell us the directionality of any observed changes in the strength of relationship between two areas. Continuing with the above example, if we did find stronger correlations between prefrontal and hippocampal regions during navigation than passive viewing, we would not be able to say whether prefrontal cortex influenced hippocampal activation, or vice-versa – only that they showed functional connectivity that was task-related. Thus although PPI can be considered an 'effective connectivity' technique to the extent that it gives us greater faith than simple functional connectivity analysis can as to the nature of the change in correlation between areas – that is, that the change is both indeed a change in 'connectivity' rather than activation levels of one or more brain regions, and that it is related to a specific experimental manipulation – PPI still falls short of being able to tell us the direction of flow of information through a neural network.

Dynamic Causal Modelling

A more advanced approach has been developed in an attempt to overcome the limitations of GCA and PPI, to allow us to make inferences about the directionality of functional connectivity relationships in task-related fMRI. This approach, **dynamic causal modelling (DCM)**, attempts to estimate the strength and direction of changes in BOLD signal over time (Friston, 2011; Friston, Harrison, & Penny, 2003). It does so by using an explicit model of the relationship between how neural activity is modulated by external input (the experimental manipulation), combined with a second model of how that neural activity relates to the observable BOLD signal. Note that this is more sophisticated than a typical fMRI analysis, which attempts to directly model the relationship between the experimental manipulation and the BOLD response, without a mediating model of the neuronal activity. Another important feature is that as a modelling technique, DCM does not simply test one hypothesis against a null hypothesis, as is done in typical fMRI and fcMRI analysis (that is: Is there activation or not? Is there a correlation between two brain areas or not?). Rather, DCM tests the relative evidence that the data provides in favour of each of a set of possible alternative models describing connectivity between brain regions. A third distinguishing feature is that, whereas a functional connectivity model provides only a single connectivity value between a pair of regions (the correlation), in a DCM connectivity values are specified separately in each direction between each pair of regions. This is critical because it allows us to test the directionality of the connectivity ('activation flow') – the connectivity value in one direction can be larger than in the opposite direction. The parameters of a DCM (the values that are estimated and can vary between the different models being compared) include both these connectivity values (correlations) between each pair of regions and – critically – explicit values estimating how much the connectivity values change as the result of an experimental manipulation. Within DCM, one can test multiple hypotheses as to whether any particular pair of regions are functionally connected, as well as the directionality of how that connectivity changes with a manipulation (effective connectivity).

As an example, refer to the simple model in Figure 8.18. In this example, we are interested in the connectivity between three brain regions, and how this changes with an experimental manipulation. Carrying on from the spatial navigation example used above in the discussion of PPI, we could imagine that Context 1 is the fly-through condition and Context 2 is the subject-controlled navigation condition. Since we are dealing here with a DCM model involving three brain regions, we could expand our ROIs from the previous example to include the hippocampus, prefrontal cortex, and inferior parietal cortex. The figure shows a possible difference between these two contexts, specifically an increased connectivity strength from the prefrontal to hippocampal node. Note that we can model the directionality of this connection because we have separate connection strengths for each direction between pairs of reciprocally connected nodes. Although this simple example includes only three nodes, DCM can scale to larger networks. However, in doing so many more models must be compared, which increases computational demands. For example, a network with only six nodes has 32,768 different possible connectivity models! At present, the computational complexity of DCM limits the number of nodes in these models to around eight; however, with advances in both the algorithms underlying DCM and the computational power available, this limit can be expected to steadily increase. This would allow for DCM to be used for **network discovery**, in the same way

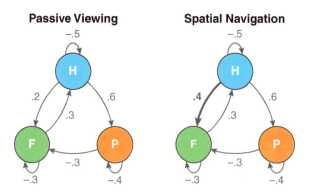

Figure 8.18 An example of a simple three-node neural network model that could be used in dynamic causal modelling (DCM). This is based on a hypothetical example in the text, comparing effective connectivity between two experimental contexts: passively viewing a fly-through of a virtual 3D maze, and actually navigating through it. The three brain areas (nodes) of interest are the hippocampus (H), a region of the frontal lobe (F), and a region of the parietal lobe (P). Arrows indicate effective connections between nodes; note that not all nodes are predicted to be connected in both directions in this model. In this hypothetical example, spatial navigation increases the effective connectivity from the hippocampus to the frontal cortex, as shown by the thicker arrow and increased connectivity value. Adapted from a diagram by Karl Friston (2011)

that graph theory (discussed earlier) allows one to test all possible pairwise connections between a large set of nodes. Critically, however, DCM offers the advantage of information concerning the directionality of influence, which graph theoretical approaches do not. Ultimately, DCM will have to deal with the same questions raised earlier in the context of graph theory: what is the most appropriate way to choose the number and location of the nodes? However, at this point because DCM is relatively limited in the number of nodes it can practically handle, it is more commonly used in cases where the researcher has explicit, a priori predictions about the key regions involved in a particular network – for example based on task-related fMRI analyses or even on functional connectivity analyses.

While DCM can be considered the most rich and complex approach to attempting to understand how brain networks are connected, it does have some limitations. DCM originally required an experimental manipulation, or data from two different groups, to provide the systematic context leading to the observed changes in connectivity. However, recent advances allow the network discovery approach to be applied to rs-fMRI data as well, making this less of a concern. As well, DCM is limited in the complexity of the networks it can be applied to, although this could change with future developments. A more fundamental and significant concern is that DCM's advantage over other functional connectivity measures relies on its mathematical models relating experimental manipulations to neuronal activity on the one hand, and neuronal activity to BOLD responses on the other. This necessarily requires an explicit model of the HRF. As discussed earlier in this chapter, there is no single correct model of the HRF across all brain regions within an individual, let alone across individuals. Thus the accuracy of DCM is inherently limited by how the HRF is modelled. DCM does have some advantage over simple convolution of the HRF with the stimulus time series, because it integrates the intermediate step of relating experimental manipulations to BOLD responses via an explicit model of predicted neural activity. Nevertheless, the results can only be as accurate as this model, and it can be demonstrated that inaccuracies in the model can affect the results.

For example, Handwerker and colleagues (2012) applied DCM to simulated fMRI data (used so that the 'truth' was known). They compared DCM estimates in a simple case involving two nodes that were modulated by an er-fMRI manipulation in exactly the same way. This meant that the two nodes had no effective connectivity – although their responses were correlated with each other, this was because the experimental manipulation affected both areas; the experiment did not induce any change in the strength of the correlation between brain regions. However, to test the ability of DCM to deal with variable HRFs, Handwerker and colleagues compared DCMs when the same HRF model was used for both nodes, with a case in which one of the nodes (Node 2) was convolved with an HRF whose timing was lagged by 1 s relative to the first node. This means that the timing of the (modelled) brain activation did not change – only the relationship between the brain activation and the BOLD response. DCM nevertheless indicated in this latter case that Node 1 predicted Node 2's activity; in other words, DCM erroneously suggested effective connectivity that did not exist in the underlying neural responses, but rather was due to differences in the coupling between neural activity and BOLD response in the two brain areas.

Further research is needed to better understand how robust DCM is across a range of plausible differences in HRFs.

SUMMARY

The design of fMRI experiments must necessarily take into account the unique nature of the BOLD HRF, in particular its sluggish timing relative to direct measures of neural activity like EEG or MEG. Blocked designs involve presenting multiple trials of the same experimental condition in a row (a block), alternating with blocks of other experimental conditions. This allows the BOLD response to summate over the duration of the block, resulting in a relatively strong signal. In contrast, event-related fMRI designs must account for the fact that stimuli occurring closely together in time will produce overlapping BOLD responses. If these BOLD responses occur at fixed intervals, it can be difficult or even impossible to distinguish the responses from different trials. However, by jittering (varying) the inter-stimulus intervals, BOLD signal can be recovered without having to wait for the BOLD signal to return to baseline after each trial.

Another consideration in fMRI designs is that the BOLD signal is arbitrary and only meaningful with reference to the magnitude of the BOLD signal in some comparison condition. As a result, the interpretation of a direct contrast between two different experimental conditions may be complicated by the fact that one, or both, conditions might show reduced BOLD signal relative to a neutral baseline condition such as viewing a fixation cross. For this reason, it is often a good idea to include such a low-level baseline condition as well as conditions control for stimulus or task features in subtractive designs.

Conjunction analyses can be used to draw stronger conclusions from fMRI analyses, by identifying brain regions that are significantly activated across multiple experimental contrasts. If these contrasts are each thought to involve a specific cognitive process, then by showing conjunction one can have greater confidence that the brain activation pattern is related to the cognitive process. Disjunction analyses can likewise be used to identify brain areas involved in one contrast, but not in another. Finally, fMRI-adaptation designs can be used to characterize distinct populations of neurons within a given brain region or voxel. Adaptation refers to a decrease in BOLD signal with repeated presentation of the same stimulus or stimulus category. If the brain region responds with increased response when some feature of the stimulus is altered, this can indicate that unique neurons within the region respond to the differentiating features of the 'de-adapting' stimuli.

Statistical analysis of fMRI data typically involves several levels of analysis. The first-level analysis usually involves using multiple regression on the time series of each fMRI run to identify voxels whose BOLD signal systematically varies (correlates) with some aspect of the experimental design. If there are multiple runs for each participant, these are combined within individuals in a second-level analysis. Finally, data are combined across participants (and/or between groups of individuals) and statistically analysed, often using familiar statistical techniques like t-tests, ANOVAs, and linear mixed effects. A mass univariate approach is usually applied, in which the same statistical test is applied at every voxel in the image. This creates a significant multiple comparison problem, because conducting so many separate statistical tests is likely to yield many false positive results (Type I error). For this reason, it is critical to employ some form of multiple comparison correction that is appropriately validated for fMRI data. Alternatives to the mass univariate approach include a variety of multi-voxel pattern analysis (MVPA) approaches that examine distributed patterns of BOLD signal strength across all voxels in a region of interest, or the whole brain, as a function of stimulus features or experimental conditions. MVPA can provide unique insights that complement traditional mass univariate analyses.

In addition to examining activation patterns in specific brain regions, fMRI data can be used to examine interactions between different brain areas. Functional connectivity methods examine correlations in BOLD signal between different brain areas, but cannot provide insight into the direction of influence – which area's activity leads to changes in the activity of another area. Effective connectivity techniques allow researchers to estimate the directionality of influence between different brain areas, but are limited by the assumptions that they rely on in making these estimations.

THINGS YOU SHOULD KNOW

- Blocked fMRI designs involve presenting experimental conditions in blocks of trials of the same type, each of approximately 30 s duration, and alternating with blocks of other experimental conditions. Event-related (er-fMRI) designs involve randomly interleaving trials of different experimental conditions. Blocked designs typically provide the best SNR and experimental design efficiency, but limit the types of experiments that can be performed (for example, if an element of surprise or unexpectedness is required). Event-related designs are more flexible with respect to the types of experimental designs they allow, but can have lower SNR and efficiency than blocked designs.

- The fact that the BOLD HRF takes 10–15 s to rise, peak, and return to baseline imposes limits in how closely trials can be placed together in er-fMRI designs. Randomly jittering the inter-stimulus intervals between trials can help improve the efficiency of an er-fMRI design relative to allowing sufficient time for the HRF to return to baseline after each trial.

- Statistical analysis of fMRI data typically employs a 'mass univariate' approach, in which the same statistical test is applied to every voxel in the image. Individual time series are usually analysed using multiple linear regression, by convolving the time series of each experimental condition with a model of the HRF, and comparing this to the time series at each voxel. At the group level, common statistical methods such as t-tests, ANOVAs, and linear mixed effects are typically used.

- Multivariate analysis techniques are a class of alternatives to mass univariate analysis of fMRI data. While there are a number of different types of multivariate analysis, in general they consider and compare the distributed patterns of activation across voxels, either within regions of interest or across the whole brain. This approach recognizes the fact that fMRI data may contain systematic relationships between BOLD signal and experimental contrasts besides simply which individual voxels show changes above a given statistical threshold.

- A significant consideration in mass univariate analysis is the risk of Type I error (false positives) due to the large number of statistical tests performed. For this reason, some form of multiple comparison correction should be applied. There are many approaches to this, some of which are less rigorous than others. It is important to be mindful of the advantages and disadvantages of different multiple comparison approaches, as well as different thresholds for significance for a given method, as these can significantly influence the results. In particular, being too liberal at this stage may yield results that are not replicable.

- It is often critical in fMRI experiments to include a baseline condition – such as having participants stare at a fixation cross – to establish the BOLD signal level when no stimulation or task is occurring. This is because the BOLD fMRI signal is measured in arbitrary units, and so the BOLD signal 'activation' levels have no objective, independent interpretation. When contrasting directly between two experimental conditions, such as 'target' and 'control' conditions, significant differences may not always represent stronger 'activation' in the target relative to the control condition, because one or both conditions might show reduced BOLD signal relative to baseline. Interpretation of the results of a contrast might be very different if one or both conditions show reduced BOLD signal relative to baseline, compared to showing increased signal relative to baseline.

- Conjunction analyses involve identifying brain regions that show significant activation across different experimental contrasts. This can allow researchers to make stronger inferences about the nature of cognitive operations performed by brain areas. Disjunction analyses, in contrast, highlight brain areas that are activated in one experimental contrast but not in the other.

- fMRI-adaptation designs capitalize on the fact that neuronal firing rates – and BOLD activity – show decreases over time when the same stimulus, or class of stimulus, is presented repeatedly. Such designs can provide sensitivity to different populations of neurons that may co-exist within a given voxel or cortical region. If different populations of neurons, tuned to different stimulus features, exist in an area, then BOLD signal in that area should show a 'rebound' from adaptation when one population is adapted, then another is stimulated.

- Functional connectivity refers to the analysis of correlations in activity between different brain regions. Functional connectivity analyses cannot inform us as to the direction of influence of the regions involved, however. In contrast, effective connectivity analyses provide estimates of the direction and strength of influence of one brain area on another. However, an important limitation of both types of analysis is that they cannot determine whether two functionally or effectively connected areas have direct anatomical connections, or whether their activity is mediated through one or more intervening anatomical regions.

FURTHER READINGS

Penny, W.D., Friston, K.J., Ashburner, J.T., Kiebel, S.J., and Nichols, T.E. (Eds.) (2006). *Statistical Parametric Mapping: The Analysis of Functional Brain Images*. New York: Academic Press.

Poldrack, R.A., and Mumford, J.A.. (2011). *Handbook of Functional MRI Data Analysis*. Cambridge: Cambridge University Press.

9 Structural MRI

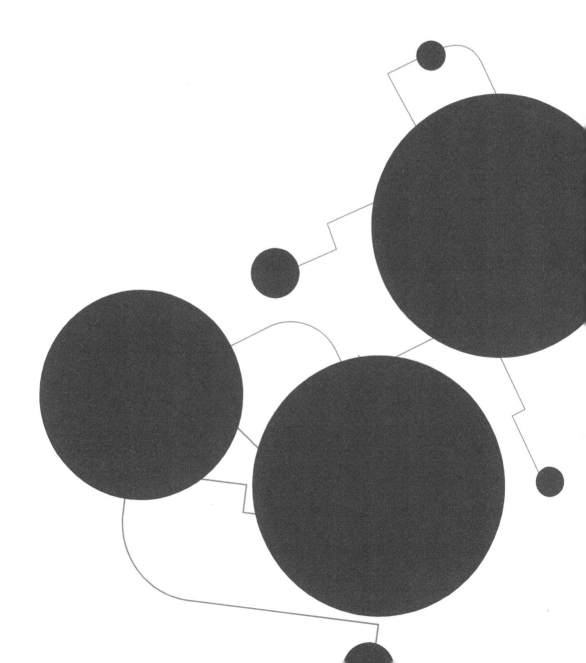

LEARNING OBJECTIVES

After reading this chapter, you should be able to:

- Define and contrast cytoarchitecture and myeloarchitecture.
- Explain what probabilistic cytoarchitectural maps are, and how they can be used in MR imaging.
- Define morphology, and contrast manual and computational morphological approaches in structural brain imaging.
- Describe how MR imaging can be used to create maps similar to those obtained through cytoarchitecture.
- Explain the basic steps involved in a typical computational neuroanatomical analysis.
- Contrast the dependent measures used in voxel-based, deformation-based, and tensor-based morphometry.
- Describe two approaches to estimating cortical thickness.

INTRODUCTION

Structural neuroimaging has a unique position within cognitive neuroscience. Clearly, an understanding of neuroanatomy is relevant – since the brain is the centre of cognition – but at the same time, most cognitive neuroscience methods (other than lesion-deficit studies) focus on dynamic measures of brain activity – those that change over short periods of time. Because experience – perception, cognition, and action – is transient, it naturally makes sense that in order to understand human experience we need measures that have sufficient temporal resolution to capture the associated changes. Neuroanatomy is relatively stable over time, at least at the level accessible by non-invasive neuroimaging (at the cellular level, we know that quite rapid reconfiguration of synapses, dendrites, and even axons can occur with experience). Thus simply assessing the size of a particular brain area, or its cortical thickness, or connectivity patterns, can tell us little about how a person performs a transient cognitive activity such as producing a word or remembering a spatial location. On the other hand, there are profound changes in neuroanatomy over the lifespan that certainly do relate to concomitant changes in cognitive function. As well, even at a similar point in development, individuals' neuroanatomy may vary in systematic ways with respect to factors such as their intelligence, personality traits, and disease states. On yet shorter time scales, research has suggested that measurable anatomical changes can occur over days or weeks. Such changes have been related to experience – particularly learning – and thus exemplify a type of dynamic change that can be measured by structural imaging.

A second important facet of structural imaging is the recent upsurge of interest in mapping the human **connectome** – how different brain areas are connected to each other, which can be imaged using an MRI technique known as diffusion tensor imaging (DTI). Drawing on parallels with how advances in our understanding of the genome have revolutionized science and medicine, the notion of the connectome has gained significant traction in both the scientific and popular media. DTI and connectomics are the topic of the next chapter, so we will set aside further discussion of this topic for the time being.

Thirdly, an accurate and detailed understanding of both the constants, and inter-individual variation, in neuroanatomy is a vital foundation for other functional imaging techniques: having a maximally (ideally, microscopically) detailed anatomical 'frame' on which to map the results of functional imaging studies can help to resolve many important questions and provide a level of understanding that temporal dynamics alone could not support. Indeed, influenced by early lesion-deficit case reports by Broca and Wernicke, neuroanatomists working in the early part of the twentieth century used structural evidence to support the notion of a highly modular, functionally specialized organization of the cortex. For example, in 1904 Korbinian Brodmann – who spent his life studying the comparative neuroanatomy of different animals – wrote:

> The specific histological differentiation of cortical areas provides irrefutable proof of their specific functional differentiation ... The large number of distinct structural zones suggests a spatial specialization of various individual functions, and finally the all-round sharp demarcation of many areas indicates inexorably a strictly circumscribed localization of their corresponding physiological function. (Brodmann, 1999)

This underscores the importance of understanding the structural organization of the brain to discerning how it functions. In many cases, imaging techniques like fMRI or MEG reveal large, extended areas of activation which may either comprise a single, functionally specialized area, or multiple areas subserving different aspects of function for the process under investigation. Anatomical mapping can provide a framework on which to map functional data that allows for richer and better-informed interpretation of the functional data.

In this chapter we discuss several different approaches to structural imaging. We will start with efforts to link structural imaging at the level of resolution possible using non-invasive techniques with humans, to microscopic-level imaging that is only possible postmortem. We then turn to **morphometry**, the study of the size and shape of brain regions, which involves manual or semi-automated tracing of brain structures. Finally, the majority of the chapter focuses on **computational neuroanatomy** – morphometric approaches that use automated algorithms to derive a variety of measures from structural MRI in a less subjective, and more efficient way than traditional morphometric methods.

LINKING MICRO- AND MESO-SCALES OF CORTICAL ORGANIZATION

As we saw in Chapter 1, the brain is organized into many distinct regions with sizes on the order of centimetres. Structurally, these regions are defined – and differentiated from each other – by the types, densities, and distribution of cells across cortical layers (**cytoarchitecture**), local connectivity patterns (**myeloarchitecture**), receptor types and densities, and gene expression patterns. This level of organization was characterized by various neuroanatomists over the twentieth century, most notably by Brodmann whose numbered 'areas' are still widely used as a reference system in functional imaging. A number of different maps are shown in Figure 9.1. The anatomical distinctions between these regions strongly imply that they support different functions and have different connectivity patterns with other areas. Indeed, the spatial scale of these **meso-maps** is in the order of millimetres to centimetres, which is comparable to the scale of regional organization that the results of functional imaging studies (for example, fMRI, PET, and MEG) suggest. At the same time, defining these meso-level areas based on their cyto- or myeloarchitectonic properties is impossible using any non-invasive imaging technique currently available. Although we are able to obtain structural MR images at well below the 1 mm level using high-field scanners (especially in postmortem brains where extremely long scan times are possible), this is far from detailed enough to characterize any of the cellular- or subcellular-level properties that define these areas; moreover, most of the micro-anatomical techniques used in such mapping require the use of stains or other invasive biochemical agents that are only suitable for non-living tissue. Indeed, high-resolution structural MRI scans appear to predominantly reflect myelin density (since contrast is driven primarily by differences between fat and water; myelin is composed predominantly of fat whereas cell bodies and inter-cellular space are more predominantly water). Thus even if spatial resolution were not an issue, this technique would not be sufficient to fully characterize a brain region in terms of all of the anatomical features that define it.

We are thus left with a very significant gap: although non-invasive functional imaging techniques are capable of resolving activity at the level of these meso-maps – which appears to be a critical level for understanding brain organization – we cannot actually define these maps cyto- or meylo-architectonically in a living individual. Although many neuroanatomists have defined cytoarchitectural maps of the human brain (such as the examples shown in Figure 9.1), there are fundamental barriers to the usefulness of these maps in interpreting neuroimaging data. For one, most of these maps were created before the advent of neuroimaging, and there is no reliable way to directly map them onto a structural MR image – the maps simply exist as pictures, typically drawn by hand onto a schematic representation of a brain. Even Brodmann areas, which are widely used as a reference system in neuroimaging papers, are typically assigned based on a gross approximation – the assignment of areas to a 3D coordinate system for use in brain imaging was originally done by Talairach and Tournoux (1988) for their atlas 'by hand', working to

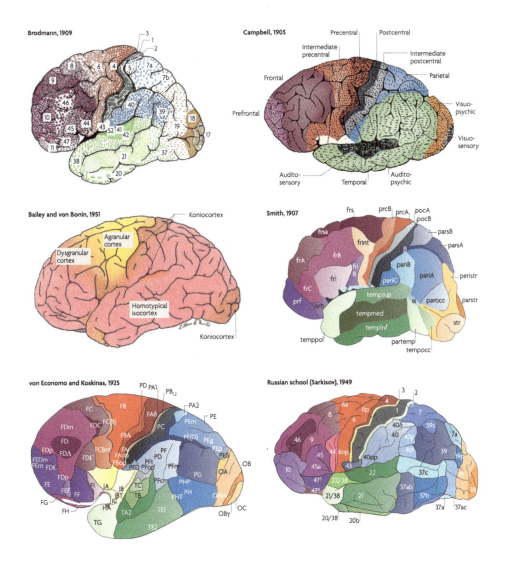

Figure 9.1 Examples of cytoarchitectural maps produced by different neuroanatomists over the course of the twentieth century. Reprinted from Zilles and Amunts, 2010 with permission of Springer Nature

approximately map Brodmann's original drawing to the sulcal and gyral patterns of their reference brain. In other words, no cytoarchitectural information from the reference brain was actually used to make the assignment of these areas. A second problem with these historical maps is that there are many of them, and they differ in the number of regions, their locations, the boundaries between them, and the types of information used to make these assignments. This is due both to differing approaches to fixing and staining the brains, and differing criteria as to how to define regions. Moreover, for these historical maps the only way the definition of regions could be done was by eye, and so there is a significant element of subjectivity – and potentially bias – in these maps. A final limitation is that none of these maps provide any characterization of the extent to which the cytoarchitecturally defined regions vary between individuals – either generally or more specifically with respect to easily observed, gross anatomical landmarks such as sulci and gyri.

In an effort to address these problems, neuroanatomists have been working to develop a **probabilistic atlas** relating micro- to meso-scale neuroanatomy, using postmortem tissue from a set of ten human brains. This is called the JuBrain project (Mohlberg, Eickhoff, Schleicher, Zilles, & Amunts, 2012) – based in Jülich and Düsseldorf, Germany – working as part of the **Human Brain Project**. This work involves scanning the brains with very high-resolution structural MRI, and then fixing the brains, staining them to highlight cell bodies, slicing them very finely (20 µm), and then photographing the slices using computer-controlled microscopy (Amunts, Schleicher, & Zilles, 2007; Amunts, Schleicher, Bürgel, Mohlberg, Uylings, & Zilles, 1999; Zilles & Amunts, 2010). The slice images are then processed using computer algorithms to characterize the cytoarchitecture automatically. These algorithms define a **grey level index (GLI)**, which reflects cell density. Systematic variation in GLI across different cortical layers is used to define cytoarchitectural regions and their boundaries, as shown in Figure 9.2. These cytoarchitectural maps can be directly mapped onto each individual's structural MRI, and all ten individuals' MRIs have been spatially normalized to the MNI152 template. This allows JuBrain to provide a probabilistic cytoarchitectural atlas, which tells the user, for any given point in the MNI152 space, what the probability is (across those ten postmortem brains) that the location is part of one or another cytoarchitectural region. Due to the painstaking nature of this work, the entire brain has not yet been mapped out – although that is the ultimate goal. Parallel efforts are under way to develop similar probabilistic atlases of myeloarchitecture, receptor mapping, and gene expression patterns. It is hoped that technological advances will help make these efforts more automated, and thus speed the progress of these efforts; as of this writing, the available JuBrain atlas represents over 20 years of work by a large team of scientists, and even the cytoarchitectonic component of the mapping is not yet completed – so the scale of this ambitious enterprise is clearly enormous.

An important early finding of this work was that the cytoarchitectonic boundaries vary with respect to gross sulcal and gyral anatomy across individuals. In other words, although there is an intuitive appeal when looking at the cortical surface to consider each gyrus a functional area, separated from other areas by sulci, this is not a reliable approach. In reality, cytoarchitectonic boundaries may well occur somewhere on the surface of a gyrus or midway down the bank of a sulcus, and do not consistently respect the large-scale folding patterns of the cortex. This is not universally true: in some cases the folding patterns do line up with cytoarchitectonic boundaries fairly consistently. This is particularly true of primary sensory and motor cortices, but for 'secondary' or higher-level 'associative' cortical areas the relationship between gross anatomy and cytoarchitecture is less consistent. The bottom panel of Figure 9.2 shows examples of variability for a primary sensory

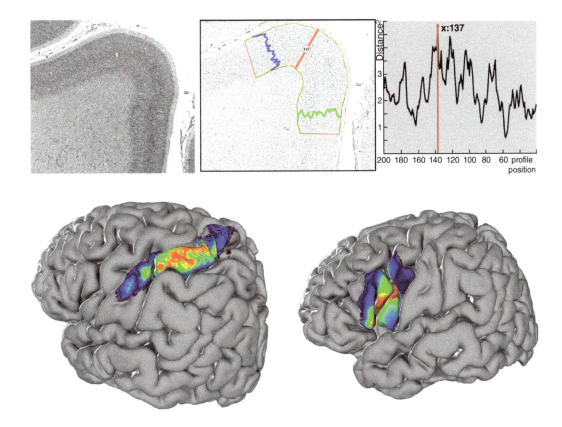

Figure 9.2 Examples of how the probabilistic cytoarchitectonic maps contributing to the JuBrain project are created. The top three panels show slices of stained tissue from the occipital cortex of a single postmortem human brain. The top left panel shows the border (red line) between two visual areas, V2 and hOc3d. The top middle panel shows the grey level index (GLI) profiles for each of these areas: V2 in blue, and hOc3d in green. The top right panel shows how the border between these areas was identified automatically on the basis of GLI profiles. In this panel, the y axis shows Mahalanobis distance, a multivariate statistical method used to quantify how different the GLI is for adjacent profiles along the cortical surface. The border between areas is identified as where the Mahalanobis distance of GLI profiles is maximal. The bottom panels show the probabilistic maps from the JuBrain atlas for two other cytoarchitectonic areas: primary somatosensory cortex (Brodmann area – BA – 1) on the left, and Broca's area (BA 44) on the right. Areas in red represent the greatest overlap between individuals (100%), while dark-blue areas represent the least overlap. Note that while both areas show inter-individual variablity, the primary sensory area shows less variablity, and virtually all of this variability is restricted to a single gyrus (the postcentral gyrus), bordered by sulci. In contrast, Broca's area (an example of higher-order associative cortex) shows greater spatial extent of variability between individuals, and this variability crosses several sulci and overlaps with different additional gyri in different individuals (the dark blue areas). Top panel from Amunts and Zilles (2015); bottom panel generated the JuBrain online viewer (jubrain.fz-juelich.de, retrieved 15 September 2016)

and higher-order associative region. This is not to say there is no consistency – even for higher-level cortical regions such as Broca's area (Brodmann's areas 44 and 45), researchers were able to identify a 'core' region that showed 100 overlap between all ten postmortem brains. However, it is important to recognize that there is variability among individuals, and with respect to sulcal and gyral folding patterns. Thus although neuroanatomists have traditionally used the sulci and gyri as anatomical landmarks for defining cortical areas (for example, Broca's area is defined as the left inferior frontal gyrus of the left hemisphere) – and neuroimagers have followed this practice – this was largely for the sake of convenience: these were easily observed landmarks that appear relatively consistent across individuals. This has important implications for the preprocessing and interpretation of neuroimaging data, as we discuss below.

Recently, a parallel effort has been made to identify consistent meso-level maps across individuals based solely on multimodal, in vivo MR imaging. This effort is based on the premise that if there is indeed a meso-level of brain organization that is consistent across humans, then it should emerge from meso-scale imaging methods. However, any one imaging technique (or experimental paradigm in functional imaging) is unlikely to be sufficient to reliably delineate this level of organization. Thus Glasser and colleagues (2016) combined data from multiple structural and functional MR imaging modalities. The data were obtained from 449 individuals as part of the **Human Connectome Project** – a massive, multi-site neuroimaging project. These included T1- and T2-weighted anatomical images (the ratio of which was used to compute myelin density), diffusion-weighted images (see next chapter), fMRI data from seven cognitive tasks (which allowed for 86 distinct contrasts), and functional connectivity derived from rs-fMRI data.

The data preprocessing involved several innovations over the more 'traditional' steps described in the Chapter 6. Firstly, only data from the cortical surface were used. This involved segmenting the grey matter from other tissue types (in the structural images) and then flattening this to a cortical surface representation, which was further tessellated to a mesh of approximately 30,000 vertices (an important data reduction step – compare this to the more than 200,000 voxels in the 2 mm MNI template image). Images from each individual were then coregistered by matching first the major sulcal patterns – a coarse-grained approach that relies on the high degree of similarity across individuals in major anatomical landmarks such as the central sulcus and Sylvian fissure, similar to the spherical surface-based approach described in Chapter 6. This was followed by a step using more complex features of the data, including the myelin density and rs-fMRI connectivity maps. The motivation for performing registration this way, rather than the traditional approach based solely on matching anatomical shape or features (that is, the linear affine and non-linear methods described in the fMRI chapter), comes from the cytoarchitectural work described above: cytoarchitecturally defined areas (and by extension, areas defined by functional and connectomic data) do not always match well with gross sulcal/gyral anatomy. Thus if functional data are used to help inform the registration, greater accuracy is likely to result. Glasser and colleagues reported that their approach of registering images based on features from myelin density and rs-fMRI maps led to 30–50% less spatial distortion of the images than traditional registration, and ultimately resulted in much higher overlap of activation in task-based fMRI data.

The researchers took a conceptually similar approach to that used in the JuBrain project for identifying borders between areas. Borders are sharp changes in relevant properties of the cortex (for example, cell density in cytoarchitecture; myelin density or connectivity patterns in human neuroimaging data). In cytoarchitecture, the borders are identified by finding points along the cortical surface of maximum 'dissimilarity' between cell-density profiles. For the in vivo human data, the researchers computed the **spatial derivatives** of each imaging modality map. The spatial derivative is a mathematical computation that represents the slope, or rate of change, in each map. In other words, a voxel in a spatial derivative map does not reflect the data at that point in the brain, but rather how much the data change *between* points adjacent to that location. Contours in the spatial derivative map are thus likely to represent borders between areas, since they represent the areas of greatest change in the maps. This is illustrated in Figure 9.3: panels (a) and (b) show myelin density and fMRI maps, respectively, and panels (e) and (f) show their corresponding gradient maps. Identification of the area borders was performed in a semi-automated way by two expert neuroanatomists, based on data averaged across 210 subjects. The neuroanatomists defined borders based on gradient contours that occurred in at least two distinct imaging modality maps and were consistent in their approximate location between cerebral hemispheres, along with several other criteria. The borders were then refined by an automated algorithm that identified the most probable shape of each border, based on features in the data. The validity of these areas was confirmed in several ways, including assessing how well the maps from the original set of 210 subjects matched those from a separate group of 210 subjects, and using machine-learning algorithms to determine how reliably the set of brain regions could be identified in individual subjects. Ultimately, this work identified a set of 180 distinct cortical areas in each cerebral hemisphere – a number quite consistent with those estimated on the basis of cytoarchitectonic data by early twentieth-century neuroanatomists such as von Economo and Koskinas (1925), and Vogt and Vogt (1919). This parcellation is shown in Figure 9.4, and it is interesting to compare this to the historical maps shown above in Figure 9.1.

MORPHOMETRY

Morphometry is the study of shape, in this case the shape of the brain and its component structures. Although most of this chapter is devoted to methods aimed at automating this process – and thus making it more objective and less observer-dependent – here we will briefly discuss more 'traditional', manual approaches to morphology. This approach involves obtaining high-resolution (typically 1 mm^3) anatomical MR images (typically T1-weighted). A trained neuroanatomist then traces the outline of the neuroanatomical structure of interest (for example, the hippocampus) on each slice of the MR image, using software designed for this

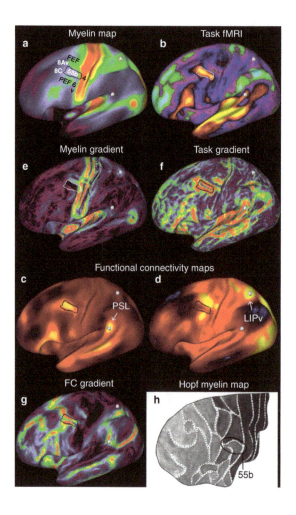

Figure 9.3 Identifying putative cortical area borders based on spatial gradients of multimodal neuroimaging data. Reprinted from Glasser et al., 2016 with permission of Springer Nature

purpose. While some software packages allow the user to trace on a subset of images (such as every third slice) – and then interpolates the tracings for the intervening slices – this can result in reduced accuracy due to the complex 3D structure of the brain. Once the structure has been traced through all the slices of the image in which it can be identified, the software can compute quantitative measures, such as the volume and surface area of the structure. These measures can then be compared between groups of subjects, or tracked within individuals over time (for example, in studies of progressive disease).

Manual tracing has some important limitations, which is why researchers have developed alternative techniques. For one, it is a very time-consuming, labour-intensive process. Accurately tracing a structure that may appear on dozens of 1 mm

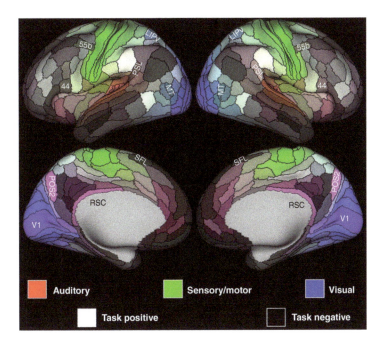

Figure 9.4 The 180 cortical areas defined in the meso-map created by Glasser and colleagues (2016) on the basis of multimodal in vivo MRI data. Colours represent how the individual areas relate to rs-fMRI data, as shown in the legend at the bottom of the figure. Reprinted from Glasser et al., 2016 with permission of Springer Nature

slices of brain is slow and tedious. Moreover, it requires extensive knowledge of neuroanatomy, including an appreciation of the range of variability that a particular structure can take across individuals. Further, it is often rather subjective. Some structures, such as the hippocampus, are reasonably well-delineated anatomically; however, others are less so. In particular, there are relatively few definite boundaries between areas of the cerebral cortex, and many of these depend on triangulating on the basis of other anatomical landmarks. Since these landmarks in turn are likely to vary between individuals, this can make the entire process difficult to accurately replicate. Indeed, it is common practice to have multiple anatomists trace each brain structure of interest in each subject in a study, and use either average measures derived from this, or some other process of resolving inconsistencies. This process, however, dramatically increases the time and cost of doing the research, and reduces its accuracy while still not guaranteeing that the same results would be obtained from the same data using a new group of anatomists. Moreover, many of the changes detected by the automated methods we will discuss later are so small (for example, in the early stages of neurodegeneration) that they could be missed (or lost in the variance) in manual tracing. As well, a significant investment of time is required to train people to do this work, but it is extremely boring. As a result, very intelligent, highly trained people must spend long hours performing menial work, and relatively few people are likely to want to perform this work for long periods of time, which in turn necessitates training new workers. This method is also very limited in what it can tell us – essentially only the volume of a structure and its surface area. It cannot tell us, for example, what proportion of a structure is grey versus white matter. Since each structure has to be traced individually, it is uncommon for more than one or two structures to be traced at all, meaning that much information might be missed (if anatomical changes occurred in brain areas other than those traced). As well, it is conceivable that a structure might change shape without changing volume, or that the ratio of grey to white matter might change without the volume changing.

Fortunately, semi-automated methods of identifying and tracing anatomical structures have been developed that overcome some of the issues of subjectivity and labour intensiveness. These approaches generally rely on template MR images on which the target structure(s) have been identified. One example of this is **diffeomorphic mapping**, which can be used on the hippocampus and other 'closed' structures (that is, those with clearly defined boundaries; this would not be applicable to regions of the cerebral cortex because they are 'open' and do not have clear macroscopic boundaries). The MRIs of individual participants in a study are registered to the template, using a rigid-body linear transformation that does not alter the size or shape of the individual's brain (similar to co-registration of functional and structural images within an individual, as described for fMRI studies in Chapter 6). A second step then identifies the target structure, and defines the outer surface of the structure. Thousands of points are then defined on the surface (using tessellation), and the distance of each point on the individual's brain structure to that of the template is computed (where the template represents an average of many healthy people). An advantage of this method is that it can provide more complex metrics than simply volume and surface area; for example, shape changes and relationships between volume and shape can be quantified. While such semi-automated processes are less subjective and error-prone than purely manual methods, they still have limitations. Firstly, the anatomical structures of interest must be accurately identified and labelled (by hand) on each image contributing to the template (although this one-time investment of effort pays far greater dividends than manual tracing of every person in every study a lab conducts). Secondly, the process is referred to as 'semi-automated' because identification of the target structures still relies on anatomical landmarks being manually identified on each study participant's brain. While these are generally fairly objective and easy to identify, this step is time consuming and makes replicability more difficult. The limitations of manual and semi-automated approaches to morphometry have led to the development of numerous automated approaches to computational neuroanatomy, which we turn to next.

COMPUTATIONAL NEUROANATOMY

Computational neuroanatomy is a broad range of techniques that employ automated algorithms for quantifying morphological changes in brain structures. Because they are automated, they avoid the issues of subjectivity and labour intensiveness that limit manual and semi-automated methods. Moreover, they operate across the entire brain simultaneously, and so they provide a comprehensive view of the brain rather than being limited to certain anatomical structures. The primary approaches to computational neuroanatomy are **voxel-based morphometry (VBM)**, **deformation-based morphometry (DBM)**, and **tensor-based morphometry (TBM)**, as well as cortical thickness measures such as **voxel-based cortical thickness (VBCT)** and **surface-based cortical thickness (SBCT)**. Although each of these methods produces a different metric, they have in common the fact that they rely on automated spatial normalization methods not only to align individual brains with each other and/or a template, but also to compute the quantification itself. Conceptually, this makes sense – since spatial normalization involves computing the transformations that change the size and shape of one brain (typically that of an individual) to another (typically a template), the spatial transformation necessarily encodes the information about how the individual's brain differs in size and shape from that of the template. The various approaches to computational neuroanatomy vary in the normalization algorithms they use, and what measures are derived from these, but at their core they all rely on quantifying the spatial normalization process.

All of the approaches to computational neuroanatomy involve similar preprocessing steps. First is **brain extraction**, in which the brain is identified and extracted from the surrounding tissue (for example, the skull) in the image. The second step, **tissue segmentation**, is required for some techniques (including VBM and VBCT); in this step the grey matter, white matter, and CSF are identified and separated from each other, yielding separate output images for each. There are different algorithms for this, but they generally rely on a combination of templates and the inherent contrast between tissue types in the T1-weighted image. Tissue segmentation is followed by **spatial normalization** (often called registration), and then statistical comparison. The type of spatial normalization, and what measures are derived from this for statistical comparison, are largely what distinguishes the different approaches, as we will see below.

Experimental Design

From a cognitive neuroscience perspective, experimental design for computational neuroanatomy studies is relatively straightforward – one does not need to worry about things like the optimal control condition, task difficulty, numbers of stimuli, etc. However, there are nonetheless several important factors to consider. First off, broadly speaking there are two types of studies that can be performed: longitudinal and cross-sectional. **Longitudinal** studies involve tracking the same individuals over time, to quantify within-individual changes in anatomy. Thus multiple MRI scans are obtained from each individual. This approach is common in studies of learning, development, aging, and neurodegenerative diseases. **Cross-sectional** studies involve comparing different groups of individuals, at a single point in time. For example, a group of people with a particular disease such as Alzheimer's may be compared to a group of age-matched, healthy controls. The two types of design can be combined: two different groups might be studied longitudinally, with cross-sectional comparisons made at different time points. In general, longitudinal designs are more sensitive and powerful because each individual acts as their own control. In a cross-sectional design, any differences between groups could be due to factors that differ between the groups other than the main difference of experimental interest (for example, one group might have a disease and the other be healthy controls, but they might also differ in education levels, how active they are, etc.). In a longitudinal design, we have measures from the same individual over time, so any changes in anatomy should be attributable to changes that individual has experienced (for example, progression of the disease). However, longitudinal designs should still employ control groups, to ensure that any changes that are seen over time in the group of interest are specific to that group and not simply changes that could be seen in any random sample of individuals. For example, in an older population diagnosed with dementia, we would want to know that the changes observed over time were specific to people with dementia and not just the result of normal aging.

Although longitudinal studies are more sensitive, they take longer to conduct (since they necessarily involve gaps of time between the multiple scans), and cost proportionally more (since they require multiple scans per participant). The duration of the study can also create other problems. For instance, any longitudinal study suffers from attrition – people dropping out of the study – which can be hard to predict but requires starting with a greater number of participants than are ultimately expected to be needed to have sufficient statistical power. Even for people who do not drop out of the study, there is a risk that some people will miss a scan at one of the time points, either resulting in missing data, or data acquired at a different point in time (relative to their other scans) than other participants. Outside of participant issues, another issue with long-term studies is that computational neuroanatomy – perhaps more than other methods – is very sensitive to MRI scanning parameters. Thus the scanner should not have its software or hardware changed or upgraded over the duration of the study. Because MRIs are multi-user resources, often controlled by entities who have priorities other than a particular individual research study, it can be difficult for a researcher to prevent (or sometimes even predict) such changes – especially for studies that last a year or longer. At the very least, the researcher should maintain a close working relationship with whoever manages the MRI facility.

While the most common use of computational neuroanatomical methods is to compare groups of people and/or map changes in structure over time, it is also possible to use these methods in correlational studies. For example, in a training study a simple (longitudinal) question might be whether, as a group, people who received a particular type of training show localized changes in cortical thickness. A more nuanced question – which would also increase our confidence in there being a causal link between the training and observed structural changes in the brain – would be to correlate changes in cortical thickness with performance on a learning task. This would allow us to determine whether, for example, people who showed greater learning also experienced greater changes in cortical thickness. Even outside of a longitudinal design, correlations with behaviour can be interesting.

For example, one could investigate whether reaction time in a visual attention task correlated with cortical thickness in regions of the brain known to be involved in visual attention.

Another issue of experimental design is which MRI pulse sequence to use. For most morphometry methods, T1-weighted structural MR images are employed. This is a very routine type of scan that any MRI machine is capable of; however, for quantitative neuroanatomy the quality of these images needs to be higher than for other purposes (such as fMRI, or even clinical diagnosis). The images need to have very good SNR, and excellent contrast. That is, the grey matter, white matter, and CSF should all be very distinguishable from each other. While T1 weighting inherently creates contrast between these tissue types, with some scanning parameters the borders – especially between grey and white matter – may be vague and difficult to distinguish. This is problematic because, as we will see, an important step in any computational neuroanatomical approach is automatic segmentation of these tissue types, based on contrast. If the grey–white matter boundary is not clear in the image, this segmentation will fail and further analysis cannot be performed. An important point to note here is that methods that rely on such segmentation generally perform well with data from the cerebral cortex, but less well (often quite poorly) with subcortical data, because segmentation of grey from white matter in subcortical structures can be more difficult. If subcortical structures are of interest, then scanning parameters should be optimized for that purpose. Likewise, lesions and other types of neuropathology create odd intensity values in the T1-weighted MR images and pose significant problems for segmentation. Special steps need to be taken if data with such pathology is to be used, usually involving acquiring different MR images with different contrast weighting (for example, both T1 and T2). Another important consideration is image homogeneity: on many scanners some areas of the image tend to be brighter than others (irrespective of grey–white matter contrast). For example, unless the individual has a very large head, the back of their head will tend to be closer to the head coil of the MRI scanner than the front of their head (since the back of the head rests on the head coil), and this proximity can make the image brighter at the back of the head. Proper tuning of the head coil and scan parameters can account for this, but this is dependent on the technical expertise available at each MRI centre. Such inhomogeneities can sometimes be compensated for in post-processing of the images, but it is incumbent on the researcher to know what to look for and correct such inhomogeneities as needed.

A final consideration is the data-processing pipeline. In any experiment, the same processing and analysis steps should be applied to every dataset. This is, hopefully, obvious as good experimental practice in any situation – inconsistent treatment of the data can lead to variability in the results that could be misattributed to experimental factors (such as differences between groups). However, even for a study as a whole, there are many options in terms of algorithms and parameters that the researcher needs to make informed decisions about. In the context of computational neuroanatomy, perhaps the most significant is the choice of normalization algorithm – since the results in many cases are derived directly from the type and amount of change in the brain images that occur in the normalization step. Thus it is critical for a researcher working in this field to understand the choices that are available (and, indeed, spatial normalization is an ongoing area of research with new algorithms constantly under development), and recognize that these choices may impact the outcome of their studies.

Voxel-Based Morphometry (VBM)

Voxel-based morphometry (VBM) is probably the most well-known and widely used approach to computational neuroanatomy. This is not because it is necessarily the 'best' approach (indeed, this really depends on the research question), but it is easy to perform in the widely available SPM software package, which makes the method quite accessible. VBM, as typically used, is a measure of the local grey matter 'concentration' in the area around a given voxel (although white matter or CSF data can be used instead of grey matter). VBM operates by segmenting the brain image into different tissue types and then applying spatial normalization. Normalization proceeds through two steps. The first is a linear affine step that matches each individual's brain to a standard template (such as the MNI152 average brain), getting the best approximate match by adjusting the size and global shape of the brain. This is followed by a non-linear step, which induces more local (finer-grained) 'warps' in the individual's brain image to make it better match the shape of the template brain. Non-linear warping is essential in computational neuroanatomical methods such as VBM, because linear methods are not precise enough to match an individual's brain to a template at the level of accuracy needed; this differs from fMRI where many studies use only linear normalization methods (though even for fMRI, non-linear methods generally yield better accuracy). A key step in the registration process in VBM is that after the non-linear warping is applied, a correction is applied to each voxel to account for the amount of expansion or contraction that voxel experienced during registration. This is done by multiplying the voxel's intensity value by its relative volume before versus after warping. So, if a voxel is doubled in size, its intensity in the normalized image will be half of what it was in the original image. This step is critical to VBM (and the interpretation of the results), because the computation of grey matter concentration is based on voxel intensities relative to their volume. Thus, this step effectively preserves the original amount of grey matter in each individual's brain after normalization.

Of course, as discussed in Chapter 7, even non-linear registration is not perfect, and there will always be some residual differences in shape between any individual brain and the template. This is a limitation of VBM that is important to keep in mind – although any MRI-based technique is limited by the spatial resolution of the original image, the effective resolution of VBM is somewhat lower than that due to limitations in the registration accuracy. However, VBM accommodates this through an additional step: spatial smoothing. This is done in the same way as was described in the fMRI chapter, using a kernel in the range of 4–16 mm. As in fMRI, the choice of kernel is driven by the **matched filter theorem**, which states that the optimal filter kernel size matches the spatial extent of the expected differences. In practice it is unlikely that the researcher will know this (unless the study is a replication of previous work), but prior literature can be used to guide the choice; changing the kernel size by a couple of millimetres is unlikely to significantly impact the outcome of the study, although kernels of 4 and 16 mm might well identify different patterns of differences. As in fMRI, spatial smoothing serves several functions: blurring the images slightly helps account for small inaccuracies in the registration; as well, it serves to make the distribution of the data more statistically normal (Gaussian), which improves the reliability of the subsequent statistics; finally, it also reduces spatial noise in the image (again by the matched filter theorem – not only do we optimize identifying effects at the spatial scale of our kernel, but we minimize interference from noise at a finer spatial scale). A very important consequence of smoothing to keep in mind is that once smoothed, the data value (image intensity) at each voxel does not represent the grey matter concentration at that voxel – it represents the local grey matter concentration in a *region* around the voxel, with the size of the region dependent on the size of the smoothing kernel. Again, the effective resolution of the VBM map will be lower than the actual resolution of the image, but the explicit application of a spatial smoothing kernel will help quantify and standardize the level of effective resolution across the brain, and across subjects.

Statistical comparison of images between groups is performed after smoothing. Similar to how fMRI data is typically analysed, in VBM 'mass univariate' statistics are used in which the same statistical test is performed separately at each voxel in the image, with corrections for multiple comparisons typically implemented using Gaussian random field theory. The statistics are commonly t-tests, since VBM studies are typically designed to compare between two groups (for example, a clinical group and healthy controls), although ANOVA could be used if there are more than two groups in the study. While VBM was originally developed for cross-sectional designs, it can be readily applied to longitudinal designs as well. For example, a t-test could be used to compare the VBM maps of a group of people at two different time points (for example, in a learning study), or more complex statistical methods (such as regression) could be used to compare changes over time between different groups.

As noted above, VBM is a measure of **grey matter concentration** (or concentration of another tissue type such as white matter). However, the term 'concentration' has a very specific meaning in the context of VBM, which may at first seem non-intuitive. It is not the same as grey matter density as might be measured in a cytoarchitectonic study, where the microscopic spatial resolution allows the number of individual cell bodies in a given volume to be accurately quantified. The MR images used in VBM do not have anywhere near the resolution or sensitivity for us to be able to measure cell-packing density. In a T1-weighted MR image, the original intensity value of each voxel (prior to normalization) is related to the proportion of the voxel actually containing grey matter; even after segmentation some voxels overlap both grey matter and another tissue type, such as CSF or white matter (this is called a partial volume effect), and so these would have lower proportions – or 'concentrations' – of grey matter. Importantly, however, in VBM 'concentration' also refers to the fact that the data are adjusted by the amount of expansion or contraction each voxel experienced during spatial normalization. A voxel in the normalized image that corresponds to an area of the brain that shrank relative to its original size and shape, would have greater concentration because that voxel represents data from a larger area of grey matter in the un-normalized brain. Likewise, a voxel that is expanded during the normalization process will have its intensity (concentration) value reduced proportionately. Thus, after normalization the intensity value at each voxel reflects a combination of its original intensity and the amount of size change it underwent.

Understanding this is critical to interpreting VBM data, and to recognizing the limitations of the technique. In a pragmatic sense, since VBM is always focused on differences (either between groups, or within individuals over time), obtaining statistically significant differences is meaningful because it reflects differences in grey matter concentration. If one group shows localized reduction in the VBM metric relative to another group, we could conclude that there was less grey matter measured in that region. However, because of the limitations of what a T1-weighted MR image is sensitive to, it may be challenging to interpret such changes further. For example, a reduction in the thickness of the cortex in a given region would result in a decrease in grey matter concentration in a VBM study. However, since VBM does not measure cortical thickness directly (see below for techniques that do), this would be only one possible inference. Since T1-weighted MR images are primarily sensitive to concentrations of myelin, changes in myelin density could also impact VBM results (although myelin concentration is relatively low in grey matter). There are a number of other possible reasons that differences could occur in a VBM study and importantly, some of these could reflect technical errors rather than neurophysiologically interesting reasons. Some of these are depicted in Figure 9.5. Most importantly, errors in registration of the images could result in erroneous results. This is why highly accurate, non-linear normalization methods are required. Ideally, any such errors would occur randomly across datasets, rather than following systematic patterns that differ between groups. However, systematic differences are possible; for example, if a patient group is characterized by systematically different brain shapes, or if one group was positioned differently in the scanner (for example, to accommodate a clinical need), or if one group tended to move in the scanner more than the other (note that motion correction is not possible for structural MR images because – unlike fMRI images – the entire scan comprises a single time point and brain volume). Differences in cortical folding can also result in VBM differences, since a fold occurring in a voxel will result in a higher concentration of grey matter than a non-folded segment of cortex. Other technical errors, such as errors in the tissue segmentation step (resulting either in grey matter not being correctly recognized as such, or white matter or CSF being mis-categorized as grey matter) can also impact the results.

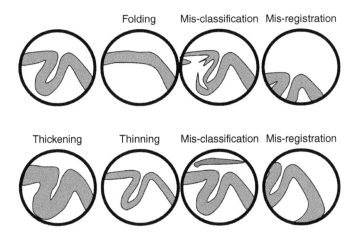

Figure 9.5 Several different factors could result in measured changes in a VBM study. Some of these might be neurophysiologically interesting, whereas others reflect technical errors. Reprinted from Ashburner and Friston (2007) with permission of Elsevier

Deformation-Based Morphometry (DBM)

As with VBM, **deformation-based morphometry (DBM)** is a measure based on quantifying the changes that occur to a brain image when it is spatially normalized. However, while VBM reflects differences in grey matter concentration, DBM reflects differences in the relative *positions* of a brain structure between different groups, or within individuals over time. In other words, DBM is sensitive to changes or differences in the shape of the brain. DBM is based on the parameters calculated by the spatial normalization algorithm that reflect the magnitude and direction of movement of each voxel from its position in the original (un-normalized) image to the normalized (template) image. DBM results can be quantified either at the whole-brain level, or at the individual voxel level. At the whole-brain level, values from every voxel in the grey matter are combined and reduced to a single number that reflects the amount of shape change the brain underwent during normalization. This can be useful in providing an overall sense of how much the shapes of different groups' brains differ (for example, at different ages during development). Alternatively, voxel-level data can be analysed to identify more localized changes in shape.

Figure 9.6 shows a schematic example of DBM data from a slice of the brain. Each voxel is represented as a vector (a pair of numbers reflecting the magnitude and direction) which can be visualized as an arrow representing the direction and amount of movement that each voxel experienced during the normalization process. Note that these vectors represent local changes, after removing any global changes (in brain size, shape, and/or rotation) that were applied to the image in the first stage of the registration. This figure is schematic in the sense that we are only visualizing the deformation vectors in one dimension; in fact, the deformation information at each voxel is a complex 'vector field' that contains three vector elements representing the shape change (size and direction) in three dimensions. These are called **3D deformation fields**. Understanding this is important because this representation of the data is more complex than in other methods we have previously discussed, such as fMRI or VBM. In those methods, we have a single value at each voxel (representing intensity). Having three values at each voxel necessitates the use of different statistical techniques, as discussed below, as well as presenting challenges for visualization. As well, further data processing is required prior to statistical analysis, because in DBM we are interested specifically in the direction and distance of the change in *position* of each voxel, but not in the change in size of the voxel, or

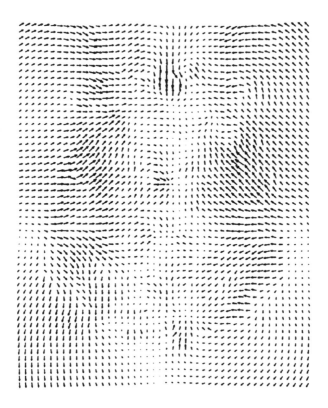

Figure 9.6 An example of a single slice of a DBM map, showing the amount and direction of movement that was applied to each voxel by spatial normalization. Note that while normalization induces three-dimensional changes in brain shape, this 2D image shows only the component of this movement that occurred in the axial (horizontal) plane. Reprinted from Ashburner and Friston (2004) with permission of Elsevier

other transformations that were applied during normalization such as global scaling and rotation of the image. Thus after obtaining the 3D deformation fields additional steps are required to derive the desired directional information from the fields. This is relatively straightforward mathematically, and is routinely performed in DBM software.

As noted, the 3D vectors at each voxel in a DBM image necessitate that different statistics be used, because instead of a single data value per location we have several. Thus multivariate statistics are employed, which involve computing the parameters that best fit the entire set of 3D vectors, rather than fitting a single (intensity) value as we do in univariate statistics. Commonly, this is done using MANOVA or MANCOVA (multivariate analysis of variance/covariance), which are well-established methods in statistics for dealing with multivariate data. The critical statistics produced by these methods are known as Hotelling's $T2$ and Wilks' lambda, and these can be used to summarize the degree of shape change between two sets of data (groups or time points) across the whole brain. Alternatively, Hotelling's $T2$ can be applied on a voxel-by-voxel basis to provide more precise information as to the location of the changes in brain shape. However, it is critical to understand that the voxel locations resulting from such an analysis do not represent the locations of shape changes themselves. Rather, given that we are comparing different groups (or time points), any statistical differences tell us that the brain structure at that voxel location is in relatively different positions in the two groups (or time points, for a longitudinal design). Another limitation of DBM is that the multivariate methods – by design – reduce very complex information to a simpler form that captures the most prominent features of the differences between groups but at the cost of a more thorough characterization. As we will see in the next section, tensor-based morphometry (TBM) builds on DBM to provide more detailed information concerning the nature of shape changes in the brain.

Tensor-Based Morphometry (TBM)

Tensor-based morphometry (TBM), like VBM and DBM, is based on measurements derived from the spatial normalization of brain images. Whereas VBM provides a measure of tissue concentration, and DBM a measure of the differences in position of brain structures, TBM is a measure of changes in the *volume* of brain structures (although it can be extended to other aspects of shape change as well). The ability to capture localized volume changes makes TBM particularly useful in longitudinal designs (for example, of brain growth during childhood, or atrophy in old age), although it can be applied in cross-sectional experiments as well. TBM starts from the same data as DBM: the deformation fields that mathematically describe the mapping from the original brain image to the normalized one, after accounting for global changes in brain volume, shape, and position. However, whereas DBM uses the deformation fields themselves, TBM is based on measures derived from the deformation fields, known as the Jacobian matrix. This matrix captures local information from the normalization for each voxel, including volume changes, rotation, and shearing (changes in the shape of a voxel independent of changes in its volume). Figure 9.7 illustrates how the shapes of individual voxels are changed by the normalization process, and the corresponding Jacobian matrix values.

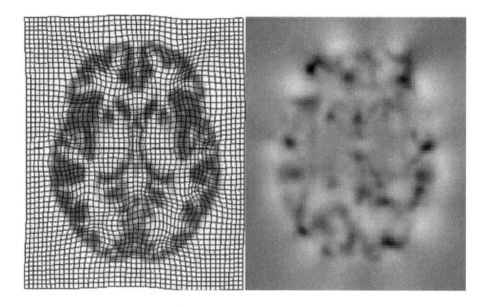

Figure 9.7 The left panel shows a slice of a normalized image, overlaid with a grid showing how each original (square) voxel's shape was modified by the normalization. Note how individual voxels may have changed in size and shape, but may also have experienced rotation or shearing (non-uniform shape changes). The right panel shows the Jacobian determinants; bright areas represent locations in which the gridlines moved farther apart as a result of normalization, while darker areas represent gridlines moving closer together. Reprinted from Ashburner and Friston (2007) with permission of Elsevier

The most common application of TBM uses the **Jacobian determinant**, a measure derived from the Jacobian matrix that specifically captures the volume changes. While this discards other, shape-related changes (for example, rotation, shearing), it can be very useful because often volumetric changes are of primary interest in a study. This simplification facilitates both data analysis and interpretation. For example, studies of brain growth in development, and atrophy in various neurodegenerative disorders, may be primarily focused on characterizing where in the brain, and to what degree, volume changes occur. Moreover, the volume changes implicitly capture the effects of rotation and translation, even if they do not quantify them directly. This can be seen in Figure 9.7: because the number of voxels in the image do not change during normalization, translation and rotation both effect changes in the volumes of voxels, and likewise volume changes necessarily induce translation, rotation, and shearing. Volume changes are also intuitively easy to understand. Thus by basing TBM on these changes, the researcher can report the data in a way that is readily interpretable by people who are not as well versed in the field, yet still implicitly captures the complex 3D changes in shape that exist. Alternatively, the researcher may choose to adopt a more complex approach that integrates additional measures from the Jacobian matrix, since all of these metrics are amenable to the general TBM method.

An additional attraction of TBM, relative to DBM, is that taking the Jacobian determinant results in a single value per voxel, and so familiar univariate statistical methods can be used (like in fMRI or VBM), rather than multivariate statistics. Although multivariate statistics are entirely valid analytical techniques, as we saw in the discussion of DBM they typically require some simplification prior to interpretation, which can result in a loss of information. As well, multivariate statistics require greater statistical understanding both on the part of the researcher and, ultimately, the reader of the scientific paper, which means the results may be less broadly accessible, or more open to misinterpretation. The interpretation of TBM using the Jacobian determinant is also relatively straightforward, even relative to the other computational neuroanatomy methods we have discussed: whereas VBM reflects a somewhat abstract metric of grey matter concentration, and DBM tells us that certain voxels may be in relatively different positions between groups/time points, TBM tells us how much size change has occurred. Note, however, that VBM and TBM can be seen to lie along a continuum: since VBM's calculation of grey matter concentrations is multiplied by the change in volume that each voxel experienced during normalization (and in fact, this is done using the Jacobian determinant), VBM maps will contain information that overlaps with TBM. However, TBM is a more 'pure' measure of volume changes because this is specifically what the Jacobian determinant encodes. VBM, on the other hand, combines volumetric changes with any other changes that may have occurred in grey matter that affect intensity in a T1-weighted MR image. While this makes VBM somewhat more complicated to interpret, it also means that VBM may be sensitive to differences that TBM is not.

Cortical Thickness Measures

All of the computational neuroanatomical methods discussed so far are voxel-based analysis methods that operate on 3D brain-imaging data. While they can all be informative, any voxel-based method is limited by **partial volume effects** – the fact that a voxel may contain a mixture of different tissue types (such as grey matter and white matter). Moreover, even changes that have a straightforward interpretation (like volume changes in TBM) are somewhat general in that the same magnitude of volume change could be caused by growth in one direction (for example, the cortex becoming thicker), or along multiple dimensions (for example, a local area of the brain growing). Given that the cortex comprises a sheet covering the outer surface of the brain, and that it is organized into layers, it is desirable to be able to quantify cortical thickness directly. Here we will discuss two methods for doing this.

The first method is **voxel-based cortical thickness** (**VBCT**) mapping (Hutton, De Vita, Ashburner, Deichmann, & Turner, 2008; Hutton, Draganski, Ashburner, & Weiskopf, 2009). VBCT was developed as an extension of VBM, and is based on very similar methods. The critical difference is that in VBM, after the T1-weighted MR image is segmented (into grey matter, white matter, and CSF), the data analysis focuses solely on a single tissue type (typically grey matter). In contrast, in VBCT the CSF and white matter images are not discarded but used to define the inner and outer boundaries, respectively, of the cortex. A mathematical approach known as the Laplace equation is then used to calculate the distance from every point on the outer surface of the grey matter to its corresponding point on the inner surface. Since the cortex is a complex, curved 3D shape and its thickness varies, finding the 'corresponding points' on the outer and inner surfaces of the cortex is not as simple as drawing a straight line through the cortex, as Figure 9.8 shows. Instead, a formula known as the Laplace equation is applied in the following manner: for each voxel on the outer surface, the straight line that is exactly perpendicular to the outer surface of the cortex at that point is found. This connects the outer surface to the next voxel layer below it, where the procedure is then repeated: finding the straight line from the outer surface of that voxel layer to the next voxel layer. This process is repeated until the inner surface is reached. Then, the process is repeated going from the inner surface to the outer surface, and the average of the outer-to-inner and inner-to-outer distance values is computed to arrive at a thickness measurement. Additional steps are performed to identify small sulci which, at the resolution of the MR image, might appear as unusually thick sections of cortex as illustrated in Figure 9.8. This is done by starting with the white matter image, finding its outer surface, and then adding a single layer of voxels (representing grey matter) to the image. After each layer is added, the Laplace equation is computed to characterize the thickness of the newly added cortical layer. This thickness should be relatively consistent across the cortex but, as panel (c) of Figure 9.8 illustrates, for small sulci this process will result in estimated thicknesses that are exceptionally large (since the two banks of the sulci will be 'merged'). When such abnormally large thickness values are identified, the algorithm labels these as sulci and treats these differently to calculate the true cortical thickness within the sulcus. This entire procedure results in a 3D image in which the intensity values of voxels within the cortex are the estimates of the thickness of the cortex at that point. Thus, travelling through the cortex from a point on the outer surface to its corresponding point on the inner surface, all voxels will have the same value. As a result, although the images can be treated as 3D volumes for statistical analysis and visualization, it is also sufficient to analyse only the values from the outer surface of the cortex. This can be visualized on an inflated or flat-mapped brain as shown in Figure 9.9.

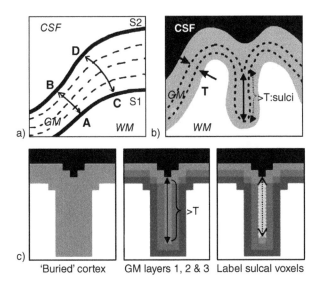

Figure 9.8 Procedure for calculating cortical thickness using the VBCT method. Panel (a) shows how the Laplace equation is used to identify corresponding points on the inner and outer surfaces of the cortex, without being constrained to straight lines. Panel (b) shows an example of a small sulcus which, in the MR image, has no identifiable CSF between its opposite banks. To the VBCT algorithm, this will likely end up being treated as an exceptionally thick portion of cortex, rather than a fold. To account for this VBCT includes a correction method as shown in panel (c). Successive layers, each one voxel thick, are added starting from the inner surface (white matter), and the Laplacian is calculated after the addition of each layer. In this way, small sulci can be identified as locations in which the thickness increases by significantly more than the size of a single voxel. Reprinted from Hutton and colleagues (2008) under the Creative Commons Attribution License (CC BY)

An alternative to the voxel-based approach described above is **surface-based cortical thickness (SBCT)** calculation (Fischl & Dale, 2000). This approach relies on a rather different method of representing the inner and outer layers of the cortex, prior to calculating thickness. Voxel-based methods, as the name suggests, operate at the voxel level, meaning that they represent the brain image data in a 3D Cartesian coordinate system (that is, a grid). Because this leverages computational methods developed for other brain-imaging applications, including fMRI and VBM, this approach may have intuitive appeal for users, and is also computationally relatively simple and efficient. SBCT approaches, in contrast, require an additional and computationally intensive step to create a model of the cortical surface. This is based on

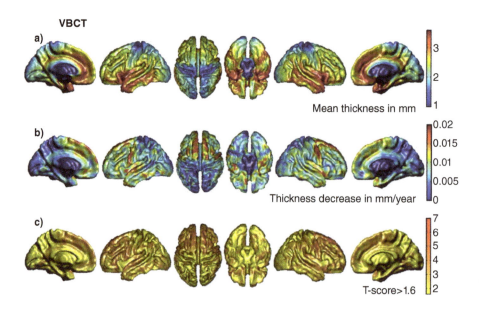

Figure 9.9 Example of VBCT results from a study investigating changes in cortical thickness with age, across a group of 48 people ranging in age from 22 to 60 years. Reprinted from Hutton and colleagues (2009) under the Creative Commons Attribution License (CC BY)

the same methods described for spherical surface-based normalization in Chapter 6. The approach begins with the segmentation of the T1-weighted MR image into grey matter, white matter, and CSF, just like VBCT or VBM. However, rather than focusing on the grey matter component, SBCT starts with the white matter segment. It creates a tessellated representation of the outer surface of the white matter. Thus the key difference in algorithms at this point is that VBCT represents the surface as a set of voxels in a 3D image, whereas SBCT represents the surface as a smooth, connected set of triangles of varying size and shape, connected by points at their vertices. This tessellation is initially very jagged, because it is based on cube-shaped voxels, and so in the next step it is smoothed using techniques from computer vision known as deformable surface algorithms. This creates an interpolated surface that has a higher resolution than the original MR image, and faithfully represents the smooth, complex shape of the outer surface of the white matter – which is also the inner surface of the grey matter. The outer surface of the grey matter is created by taking a copy of the white matter surface, and inflating it in 3D (again using deformable surface algorithms) until the vertices reach the boundary of the CSF identified by the initial tissue segmentation step. In other words, the grey matter (and its thickness) is not computed directly from the grey matter component of the tissue segmentation, but is interpolated as the space between the white matter and CSF. Algorithms for creating surface-based representations are quite complex and time-consuming to run, both

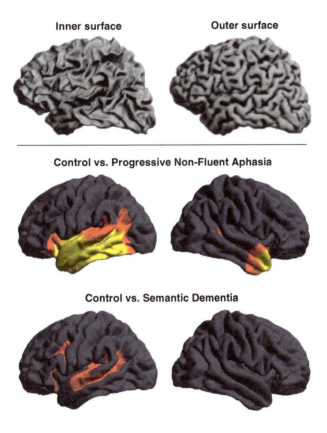

Figure 9.10 Surface-based cortical thickness (SBCT) calculation and results. The top left panel shows the inner cortical surface (which is the outer surface of the white matter) while the top right panel shows the outer cortical surface (the grey matter–CSF boundary). The grey matter thickness is computed as the difference between these two surfaces, after they have been converted to tessellated meshes. The bottom panels show this an example of applying this method to comparisons between two groups of people with different types of dementia, each compared with healthy controls. Coloured regions represent statistically significant differences in cortical thickness, with yellow representing greater statistical significance. Top panel reprinted from Dale, Fischl, and Sereno (1999) with permission from Elsevier; bottom images reprinted from Clarkson and colleagues (2011) with permission from Elsevier

because of the complexity of the mathematics involved, and more so because they are prone to various types of errors, such as 'holes' and 'tears' in the surface, and erroneous connections (for example, two points on opposite sides of a sulcus might end up connected – similar to the issue of small sulci described above for VBCT). Automated methods for identifying and correcting these issues have been developed, but add to the computation time. Once the surfaces are computed, thickness is estimated in a manner similar to that described for VBCT, performing point-to-point mapping between the inner and outer surfaces. Figure 9.10 shows examples of the inner and outer surfaces of the grey matter, and how the thickness is calculated as the space between them.

Thus the difference between voxel- and surface-based methods lies not so much in how thickness is calculated, but rather on how the MR images are processed prior to the thickness calculations. VBCT is more computationally efficient and may fit better within the context of data-processing steps – and software – that a researcher is familiar with if they have previous experience with VBM or fMRI. However, although at some stages of processing VBCT interpolates the MR images to higher resolution than the original MR images (from 1 mm down to 0.5 or even 0.25 mm), it ultimately has lower inherent spatial resolution than SBCT, and may have less accuracy due to partial volume effects. The greater computational complexity employed in SBCT results in greater spatial resolution due to the change from voxel- to surface-based (tessellated) representation of the data and the use of deformable surface algorithms that are able to represent the complex curvature of the cortical surface more precisely than cube-shaped voxels ever can. A comparison of these methods found that while both performed similarly in detecting between-group (patient versus control) differences and classifying individuals as patients or controls, the SBCT method was most sensitive to changes over time in longitudinal data (Clarkson et al., 2011).

SUMMARY

Structural neuroimaging provides complementary information to functional imaging. While structural measures cannot tell us about the computations performed by a brain area, or the cognitive operations it supports, structural methods such as cytoarchitectonics can help shape and constrain our understanding of the brain's functional organization because areas that are micro-anatomically distinct are likely to function differently. Viewing the brain as a set of functionally and anatomically distinct regions as the meso-scale can aid in the interpretation of functional imaging data by receding hundreds of thousands of individual voxels to a more tractable set of regions whose activation and connectivity can be compared. While historical approaches to structural neuroanatomy used either invasive methods (such as postmortem histological examination), or labour-intensive, difficult-to-reproduce tracing methods on structural MR images, modern approaches have provided automated solutions.

Computational neuroanatomy refers to the class of automated techniques for characterizing morphometry – the size, shape, and (in some cases) composition of brain areas. These techniques typically employ a common pipeline involving brain extraction, segmentation of different tissue types (grey matter, white matter, CSF), spatial normalization, and statistical comparison. Statistical comparison typically involves contrasts between different groups of participants (for example, people with a disease relative to healthy controls), or between the same individuals over time in longitudinal studies (for example, in development or with disease progression or treatment). Cross-sectional studies can be used to compare different age groups without the need for obtaining scans from the same individuals over long periods of time.

Computational neuroanatomical techniques differ primarily in the dependent measure that is derived for statistical analysis. Voxel-based morphometry (VBM) is one widely used method that characterizes the 'concentration' of grey matter (or other tissue types) in a measure that is sensitive both to the intensity of MR signal in each voxel, and its size. Deformation-based morphometry (DBM) measures the amount of change in shape experienced by each brain (or voxel) during spatial normalization, while tensor-based morphometry (TBM) provides measures of the change in volume of brains/voxels during spatial normalization. Another class of techniques measure critical thickness. While this does not represent shape information the way morphometric techniques do, it has a relatively intuitive and straightforward interpretation. Cortical thickness can be measured either using surface-based or voxel-based techniques. Surface-based techniques are generally considered to be more accurate, but are much more computationally complex and intensive.

THINGS YOU SHOULD KNOW

- Cytoarchitecture refers to the types, densities, and distributions of cells across cortical layers, while myeloarchitecture refers to the types, densities, and distributions of local connectivity patterns across layers. Both can be used to define meso-scale anatomical regions, but do not necessarily yield the same patterns of organization.

- Cytoarchitecture and myeloarchitecture cannot be determined from MRI images because they require microscopic examination of tissue. However, by combining structural MR imaging with histological examination of postmortem brain tissue, probabilistic maps can be created that predict the cytoarchitecture of a given brain region in living humans.

- Recent work has defined and identified meso-scale cortical regions based on a combination of anatomical and functional features, based entirely on MRI scans, that show correspondence with other parcellation schemes based on cytoarchitecture and myeloarchitecture.

- Morphology is study of shape; in structural brain imaging it refers to the study of the size and shape of brain regions and how these are influenced by factors such as development, experience, and disease. Traditional approaches to morphology required manual tracing and measurement of individual brain regions, which is labour-intensive and challenging to reproduce. Automated methods have thus been developed to obtain morphometric measurements more quickly and reliably; these are referred to as computational neuroanatomy.

- In general, computational neuroanatomy involves obtaining structural MR images, extracting the brain from non-brain tissue, segmenting the brain tissue into different types, spatial normalization, and statistical comparison.

- Voxel-based morphometry is a measurement of the concentration of grey matter (or another tissue type) on a voxel-by-voxel basis in the brain. This measure combines information regarding the intensity of each voxel and its size relative to other brains.

- Deformation-based morphometry describes the amount of movement different voxels in the brain undergo during spatial normalization. As such, the measure reflects how different a given brain is in size and shape from a reference brain. This can be computed either as a single value for the whole brain, or as values at each location (voxel) in the brain. DBM can identify differences in shape between groups (or over time), but is somewhat nonspecific regarding the nature of those differences.

- Tensor-based morphometry measures the amount of change in volume that each voxel (or the whole brain) undergoes during spatial normalization. Compared to VBM, TBM is a more straightforward measure of brain volume, but VBM may capture information that TBM does not.

- Cortical thickness is the distance between the outer and inner surfaces of the cortex, but is often operationalized as the distance between CSF and white matter. This can be calculated either from surface-based representations of the cortex, or from 3D, voxel-based representations. Voxel-based measures are more straightforward to compute, but may have lower spatial resolution and be more subject to imaging artifacts.

FURTHER READINGS

Chung, M.K. (2012). *Computational Neuroanatomy: The Methods*. Singapore: World Scientific.

Penny, W.D., Friston, K.J., Ashburner, J.T., Kiebel, S.J., and Nichols, T.E. (Eds.) (2006). *Statistical Parametric Mapping: The Analysis of Functional Brain Images*. New York: Academic Press.

10 Connectomics: Diffusion Tensor Imaging (DTI) and Tractography

LEARNING OBJECTIVES

After reading this chapter, you should be able to:

- Explain how the diffusion of water provides an indirect means of imaging white matter tracts.
- Describe the pulse sequence used for DTI.
- Describe the preprocessing steps involved in DTI analysis, and explain the rationale for each.
- Explain the measure of fractional anisotropy and how it can be used.
- Explain the difference between diffusion tensor calculations and tractography.
- Contrast voxel-based and tract-based approaches to analysing diffusion MRI data.
- List several ways in which tractography analyses can be used in research and clinical settings.
- Identify limitations of diffusion imaging-based approaches to tractography.

INTRODUCTION

Connectomics is the term applied to the study of brain connectivity. This term is quite new, with the first uses of the term 'connectome' appearing in the literature in 2005 (Sporns, Tononi, & Kötter, 2005). However, the study of anatomical connections within the brain precedes the development of this term by roughly 200 years, when it was commonly known as **hodology** (Catani, 2011). In 1809 Johann Reil first published a report of a method of soaking the brain in alcohol that made it more amenable to dissection, thus allowing him to identify white matter fibres running between different parts of the brain (Reil, 1809). Reil's findings were greatly extended by Karl Burdach, who published a three-volume textbook of anatomy between 1819 and 1826, which included Latin names for many major white matter tracts in the brain that are still in use today, such as the arcuate fasciculus and cingulum (Burdach, 1819). While Reil's and Burdach's work focused on anatomical description, in the late nineteenth century Theodor Meynert developed a 'hodological' theory of brain function that integrated brain connectivity into a model of how learning, memory, movement, and language depended on convergence – or association – of information from multiple brain areas (Meynert, 1885). Indeed, the work of Meynert and his students is today termed the 'associationist school'. Meynert was a Viennese psychiatrist whose primary interest was in elucidating the physiological bases of mental illness, and who mentored such luminaries as Sigmund Freud and Carl Wernicke. Meynert also developed a taxonomy in which connections within the brain were divided into three categories: projection (in and out of the cortex to other parts of the brain), commissural (connections between hemispheres), and association (connections between cortical areas). Building on Meynert's work, Wernicke published in 1874 the first proposal of a 'disconnection' syndrome in which a neurocognitive function (in this case, language) could be disrupted not only by damage to a cortical region, but also by damage to white matter connections *between* cortical regions.

A limitation of early work in hodology was that methods were limited to post-mortem dissections of the brain, which relied on significant skill, could only identify the largest fibre bundles in the brain, and did not afford means of fine-grained examination or quantification. However, at the same time as interest in the practical implications of white matter connections was developing, novel staining techniques were being pioneered that allowed microscopic visualization of both cell bodies and connections. This led to significant work into the twentieth century in characterizing brain connectivity at micro-, meso-, and macro-anatomical scales, the description of many circuits within the brain, and an understanding of the roles of these circuits in specific behaviours and diseases. A direct consequence of this work was the development of frontal lobotomy as a technique for treating psychiatric patients: based on animal work showing reduced aggression in monkeys after connections between the thalamus and frontal lobes were severed, it was posited that a similar treatment could be applied to people suffering from psychosis (Moniz, 2006). This approach was found to create more manageable patients and was widely popularized in America by neurologist Walter Freeman and neurosurgeon James Watts from the late 1940s through the 1960s, when the many negative consequences of the technique became widely appreciated. The notion of surgical disconnection also led to the development of the technique of severing the corpus callosum as a treatment for intractable epilepsy, which led to research by Roger Sperry, Michael Gazzaniga, and others characterizing the unique cognitive capabilities of the two cerebral hemispheres.

In spite of the advances to our knowledge provided by hodology, through most of the twentieth century there were still only limited ways of studying brain connectivity, and none that were useful in vivo or non-invasively. Continued advances in staining techniques allowed for approaches such as injecting a tracer into a brain region and allowing it to diffuse down axons from neurons in that region to the areas that the axons projected to, allowing for in vivo and, in some cases, activity-dependent mapping in animals. However, these techniques still involved toxic traces and required sacrifice of the animal at the end, making them unsuitable for use with humans. In 1994 however, Basser, Mattiello, and LeBihan published the first report on an MRI technique known as **diffusion tensor imaging** (DTI; Basser, Mattiello, & LeBihan, 1994), which quickly led to the development of non-invasive, in vivo MRI-based tracing of white matter tracts in humans through the close of the twentieth century and up to the present.

WHAT ARE WE MEASURING?

The **connectome** is the complete set, or matrix, of connections in a brain – although in practice the connectome is the subset of those connections that we are able to map out given the available technology. The connectome is composed of two types of elements: brain regions and the connections between them. In its simplest form, the connectome can be conceptualized as a square matrix, as shown in Figure 10.1, with the complete set of brain regions along both axes, and the presence or absence of a connection between each pair of areas coded as 1 or 0, respectively. For each connection defined in the matrix, however, a full description of the connectome would include properties such as the direction of the connection (sometimes distinguished from the connectome as the **projectome**), connection strength, whether it is excitatory or inhibitory, and even features such as the conduction delay, myelination, etc. The goal of such a rich and detailed description of the human connectome is far from being achieved, however ambitious large-scale, multi-centre research projects such as the **Human Connectome Project** have been developed to pursue these goals.

As outlined in Chapter 1, connections in the brain involve projections extending from neurons: axons carry the spiking output of neurons when they generate action potentials, and dendrites receive input from axons and summate all of their inputs to modulate postsynaptic potentials and possibly trigger action potentials in the receiving neurons. Most neurons' axons are coated in a **myelin sheath**, which is composed of oligodendrocytes (a type of glial cell) and high in fat content. The myelin serves to electrically insulate the axons, allowing faster and longer-distance propagation of action potentials. Since the brain is organized on multiple scales, connectivity can likewise be characterized this way: there are very short-range connections between neurons (micro-scale; for example, between cells within a region), then there are connections within a region (for example, between cortical columns; meso-scale), and finally there are long-range connections between different brain areas (macro-scale) – and this over-simplifies what is really a continuum of connectivity distances and types. The **white matter** of the brain is composed primarily of axonal projections, which is why in T1-weighted anatomical MR images it appears bright relative to the grey matter of the cortex – the high fat concentration in the myelin causes relatively slower relaxation than in the grey matter, which is composed largely of cell bodies and has relatively little fat.

At present, our ability to resolve structural connections using in vivo neuroimaging methods is limited to the longer-range connections (although as with all areas of neuroimaging, these limits are constantly being pushed through technique development). Our ability to identify these connections based on MR imaging is based almost entirely on a technique known as **diffusion-weighted imaging (DWI)**, which has a number of derivative techniques including diffusion tensor imaging (DTI) and diffusion MRI tractography (terms which we will explain later). DWI goes a step beyond typical structural imaging, in which contrast is largely driven by the relative proportions of water and fat in each voxel. These 'static' imaging techniques allow us to identify white matter and distinguish it from grey matter or CSF, and even to identify white matter lesions (such as occur in multiple sclerosis). However, the resolution of these structural techniques is far from high enough for us to be able to resolve individual axons in order to identify their orientations and the paths that they follow.

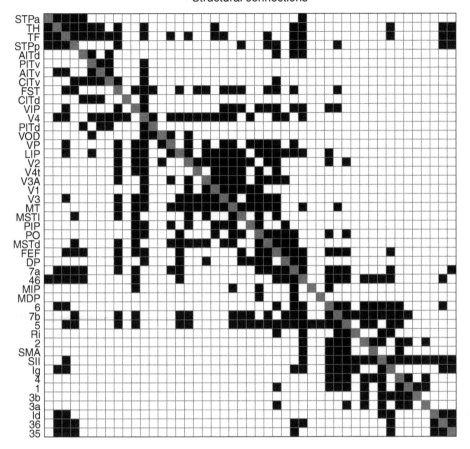

Figure 10.1 An example of a connectome matrix, showing the presence or absence of white-matter pathways between a set of 47 sensory and motor areas of macaque cortex. The area labels are provided only on the y axis, but the same areas, in the same order, are plotted along the x axis as well. Because the connectivity matrix does not encode information concerning the direction of the connections, the matrix is symmetrical across the diagonal (grey squares). Although this example was based on 505 pathways identified using invasive tracing studies, the same type of matrix can be derived from diffusion MRI data. From Honey, Kötter, Breakspear, & Sporns, 2007, copyright 2007, National Academy of Sciences USA; used with permission

DWI allows us to infer information about the orientation of fibres within a voxel through a specific MRI pulse sequence. Like virtually all MR imaging, the principle of diffusion MRI is based on hydrogen atoms, and more specifically water. Although white matter has a high fat content, the inside of the axons is filled largely with water (along with electrolytes such as sodium and potassium). Regardless of whether an action potential is propagating along the axon or not, the water molecules inside of axons have relatively stable positions – that is to say, there is no flow of water within an axon from one end to the other. However, simply due to the inherent heat energy in the brain, all molecules – including water – move randomly over very small distances. This random movement is known as **Brownian motion** and is not a unique property of axons – essentially all atoms and molecules experience Brownian motion unless there is no heat energy (that is, if they were frozen to absolute zero). This motion is very slight; within the living brain over the course of 50 ms (about the time of a DWI measurement), a water molecule will diffuse about 10 µm. What is special about the Brownian motion of water molecules inside axons, however, is that it is **anisotropic** – that is, because the fatty myelin sheath is hydrophobic (resists water), the water molecules inside axons tend to diffuse preferentially along the direction of the axons, rather than across their cell walls. In contrast, diffusion in other parts of the brain, such as grey matter and CSF, is **isotropic** – it occurs in every direction with basically equal probability since there are no barriers to the molecules' diffusion. This is an oversimplification, because in grey matter there are axons as well as cell bodies, and cell walls as well as intracellular structures can act as barriers to diffusion. However, in white matter the amount of myelin is very high due to the dense packing of axons. More importantly, white matter is largely composed of fibre bundles – large numbers of axons running in parallel and connecting the same or nearby brain regions – so that within a white-matter voxel there will be a high proportion of axons within which water is diffusing preferentially along the same direction.

There are a couple of important points to note about DWI. Firstly, although myelinated axons are a significant reason for anisotropic diffusion in the brain, this is not the only mechanism causing anisotropic diffusion. Axons themselves – even if not myelinated – can cause anisotropic diffusion along their length due to the relatively low permeability of their cell walls to water. This has been demonstrated, for example, in mouse embryos at a developmental stage when axons exist, but are not yet myelinated. Based on comparisons between immature and adult brains, it has been estimated that 60% of anisotropic diffusion in adult white matter is attributable to the axons themselves, with the other 40% to myelin (Mori, 2007). However, this estimate may be inaccurate because of changes in the density of axons that occur with development; other data suggest that myelin may account for only 20% of the anisotropy of diffusion. Another caveat is that if a voxel in a DWI image contains a mixture of axonal fibres oriented in different directions, the net diffusion from that voxel may have relatively low anisotropy even though the voxel is densely packed with oriented fibres, because diffusion does not preferentially occur in a single direction (the measurement from the voxel simply averages all of the diffusion directions). These caveats are particularly important to keep in mind when comparing DWI data between different research groups: although decreased anisotropy may indicate a reduction of myelin, it could also be caused by increased crossing fibres, or even other cellular-level processes that affect water diffusion.

Thus although DWI is commonly used as a measure of white-matter integrity and orientation, it must always be remembered that we are not imaging white-matter tracts directly – we are inferring them from water diffusion. Another important point to realize is that DWI measurements cannot inform us about the direction that information flows along a tract. The random diffusion of water occurs equally in both directions along a fibre, and is not influenced by the propagation of electrical potentials along the axon. Finally, always remember that this diffusion is not a biological process – it is a physical one that requires only ambient heat energy. Thus DWI works similarly in living and cadaver brains. This is an important point and one that is often misunderstood – for instance, people sometimes have a misunderstanding that the movement of water molecules is related to the conduction of action potentials. Always remember that DWI is a structural imaging method.

HOW DO WE MEASURE IT?

A DWI pulse sequence is one that is sensitive to the Brownian motion of water molecules. As in much of MR imaging, the specifics of diffusion weighting are obtained through manipulation of the gradient magnetic fields (gradients). Recall that in addition to the strong standing magnetic field of the MRI scanner (for example, 1.5, 3.0, or 7.0 T), additional magnetic fields that change along a particular direction can be induced transiently. This is how slice selection and phase and frequency encoding are performed in structural imaging. In diffusion imaging, slice selection is performed in the same way as in conventional structural imaging described earlier in this book. However, after this, things happen quite differently.

The principle of diffusion imaging is that we can use a magnetic field gradient to 'tag' water molecules according to their location along a particular axis. This phase encoding is achieved through a **dephasing gradient** applied soon after the RF excitation pulse. Recall that RF excitation provides energy at the resonant (Larmor) frequency of the molecules, causing the net magnetization vector to tip from the longitudinal to the transverse plane. Applying the dephasing gradient after RF excitation increases the magnetic field at one end of the axis of the gradient, and decreases it at the other end. Since the molecules' precessional frequency is directly related to the magnetic field strength, the effect of the gradient is to speed up precession at one end and slow it down at the other. This in turn induces a phase roll when the gradient is turned off: all the molecules return to precessing at the same speed (frequency), but due to their transient acceleration/deceleration along the gradient axis, they have different phases. This is illustrated in Figure 10.2. This phase roll serves to 'tag' the water molecules according to their position along the gradient. Then, a certain amount of time is allowed to pass. During this time, as diffusion occurs the water molecules will travel along random paths, thus changing their locations. As a result, the smooth phase roll induced by the dephasing gradient will be disrupted as molecules precessing with a given phase move to other locations. Following this diffusion time, a second, **rephasing gradient** is applied. This gradient works to 'unwind' the phase roll induced by the dephasing gradient. At this point, if no diffusion had occurred and all water molecules were in the same locations as when the dephasing gradient was turned off, the rephasing gradient would reset all phases along the gradient axis to be the same. However, since water molecules in fact diffused, the rephasing gradient is only partially effective at resetting the phases – the more a molecule has moved, the more its 'reset' phase will differ from the original phase associated with its ending position. Immediately after the dephasing gradient, the signal is read out (the echo time, or TE). At this point, if no diffusion had occurred along the gradient direction, signal would be strong all along this direction (though it would still vary according to the density of water molecules in each voxel). In contrast, the more diffusion that occurred along the direction of the gradient, the less effective the rephasing will be and the more signal loss that will occur. In other words, signal intensity in a diffusion-weighted image is high when little diffusion occurred, and low when more diffusion occurred.

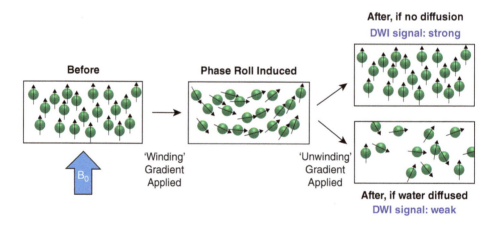

Figure 10.2 Schematic diagram of the effects of a diffusion MRI pulse sequence. The left panel shows that, initially, all hydrogen atoms precess in synchrony, with their axes aligned with the main magnetic field (B_o). A magnetic field 'winding' gradient is then applied across the slice, leading to a 'phase roll' whereby precession rates vary across the slice (middle panel). This serves to 'tag' protons according to their position in the slice. Then, a rephasing ('unwinding') gradient is applied. The top right panel shows what would happen if no water diffusion occurred: rephasing would cause the phase of all molecules to come back into alignment. However, if the molecules diffused randomly between the winding and unwinding pulses, we end up with the state shown in the bottom right panel, where few protons have the original phase. Moreover, because some of the original protons in the excited slice diffused outside of the slice, we have fewer total excited protons contributing to the signal in the slice. As a result, greater diffusion leads to a reduced diffusion-weighted signal

Note that throughout the above description the term, 'along the gradient direction' was used repeatedly. This is an important point: a single diffusion-weighted acquisition is sensitive only to diffusion along a single direction. Thus a number of acquisitions are required, using gradients along different directions, in order to determine primary directions of diffusion in each voxel in the image. In principle, a minimum of three directions are required for a three-dimensional image. It is not necessary to obtain as many gradient directions as there are possible directions of diffusion in the brain, because a direction of diffusion that is intermediate between two measured directions will show some evidence of diffusion along each of the measured directions, so the true direction of diffusion can be inferred by combining the images. Even so, obtaining only three directions of diffusion would provide very limited information and so the estimation of true diffusion directions would be prone to significant inaccuracy. As well, a single voxel may contain diffusion in multiple directions, and resolving these require obtaining diffusion measurements in more directions. Finally, computation of the diffusion tensor (described later in this chapter) is necessary for many of the uses of DWI in cognitive neuroscience, and mathematically this requires a minimum of seven directions of diffusion to be measured.

In practice, a large number of diffusion gradient directions (typically in the range of 55–90) are obtained in a typical DWI scan for connectomics research. Note that although MRI scanners typically only have three sets of gradient coils, aligned with the primary spatial dimensions of the scanner bore, a gradient field along any direction can be created by combining these gradient coils in different ways. Offline processing (discussed below) serves to combine these images to derive a number of measures such as the primary direction of diffusion within each voxel. In addition to acquiring multiple directions, it is critical to obtain one or more 'baseline' images using the same pulse sequence, but without diffusion weighting along any direction (this is often called a $b = 0$ image, because b is a measure of diffusion weighting). This unweighted image is essential because the signal at each voxel is primarily determined by its tissue composition, with the diffusion due to Brownian motion causing relatively small changes in the strength of this signal. Therefore, analogously with fMRI, we can only compute the amount of diffusion that occurred along a particular direction by subtracting the image measuring diffusion along that direction from the baseline scan.

Having described the basics of DWI, there are some details that are worth discussing. Firstly, although DWI is sensitive to the very small, Brownian motion of water molecules, other movements of liquid occur in the brain as well. These movements, such as blood flow and CSF circulation, generally occur on a larger scale (recall that Brownian motion amounts to only about 10 μm in the time used to acquire a diffusion-weighted image). These larger-scale, 'bulk' movements of molecules look very different to a DWI sequence than Brownian motion. This is because of both the higher speed at which such flow occurs, and the fact that in general such flow will be coherent in its speed and direction across all nearby molecules (as opposed to random for Brownian motion). Thus if blood is flowing through a vessel in a DWI voxel, the refocusing pulse will cause 'perfect' rephasing – all the protons will be precessing in phase with each other and thus no signal loss will occur (there will be an overall phase shift relative to the case when absolutely no movement of molecules occurred, but this doesn't matter at readout time). In practice, the situation is more complex because it is likely that the direction of such bulk flow will not be perfectly parallel to the direction of the diffusion being measured, and there may be bends in the blood vessel or a number of capillaries captured within the voxel, with flow occurring in different directions. Thus such bulk flow may have some impact on reducing signal in the voxel. However, because rates of blood and CSF flow are much higher than the speed of Brownian motion, a pulse sequence tuned to detect Brownian motion will be largely insensitive to such flow.

It is also worth noting that there are a variety of DWI pulse sequences that vary to differing degrees from the basic one described above. Both spin echo and gradient echo sequences can be used; however, the one that is almost universally used at present is echoplanar imaging (EPI) – the same type of sequence used in fMRI. EPI sequences for DWI are quite different in their specific parameters from those used in fMRI, but the benefits and costs of EPI are similar. EPI allows for fast imaging, which reduces artifacts due to blood and CSF flow as well as head movement (including pulsations of the brain with each heartbeat), as well as yielding reasonable scan times for whole-brain acquisitions. A typical whole-brain DWI scan with approximately 50 directions and a spatial resolution of 2 × 2 × 2 mm may take 10–15 min using EPI, which feels long enough to a person having to hold still in an MRI scanner! Another parameter that varies between sequences is whether the sequence uses a refocusing gradient pulse that is in the opposite direction to the dephasing pulse, or in the same direction. This may seem counterintuitive – a refocusing pulse in the opposite direction will cause phase unwinding as described above, whereas one in the same direction as the original pulse will create even more dephasing. However, in the case where the same direction is used for both pulses, they are separated by a 180° RF pulse which serves to invert (flip) the NMV such that the refocusing pulse has the desired effect.

In practice, there are a few parameters that the researcher performing DWI must decide on. One is the spatial resolution. As with all MR imaging, SNR decreases nonlinearly with voxel size, and so there is always a trade-off between getting the best spatial resolution, and obtaining a strong enough signal. Currently voxel sizes on the order of 1–2 mm isotropic are standard, although the lower bounds of this are being pushed using very high field (7 T+) scanners; indeed, the greatest demand for such high-powered magnets is for doing DWI much more than for fMRI. The number of directions obtained is limited by the hardware and scan time, but in practice numbers in the range of 50–100 are feasible; for basic DTI there is not necessarily a large benefit to increasing the number of directions from 50 to 100, but for more advanced analysis techniques that can be applied in tractography; more directions provide a significant improvement. The other parameter that has a strong influence on the image quality is known as the **b-factor**. This number reflects both the strength of the gradient along the diffusion direction, and the duration that it is on for. Increasing either of these factors increases sensitivity to diffusion, and so b is a convenient way to summarize these two related parameters. In practice $b = 1000$ is a good minimum for DTI, with some approaches using much higher (for example, 5000–8000) values. A critical limitation on the parameters chosen for DWI is the fact that applying a large number of RF pulses and cycling high-amplitude gradient magnetic fields on and off can actually heat the tissue of the person being scanned. All MRI scanners have built-in safety mechanisms that calculate the SAR (specific absorption rate – a measure of how much RF energy the body can safely absorb without heating) of a sequence and prevent the use of settings that would endanger the participant. However, these safety settings (combined with the specific hardware and pulse sequences available) may place limits on the parameters of the DWI sequence. In some cases, using too-ambitious parameters can actually cause the MRI system to stop mid-scan and not allow scanning to start again until the machine has cooled down.

Cardiac artifacts are also problematic in DWI. With every heartbeat, the brain pulses with the force of blood being pumped into it. This pulsation is large enough that it can often be observed by the naked eye when the brain is exposed, for example during neurosurgery. This pulsation causes changes in the size and shape of the brain, particularly around the ventricles and outside edges of the brain. In DWI, these have the effect of increasing the amount of phase dispersion across the brain (that is, creating greater phase roll than was induced by the MR gradients alone), which in turn artificially inflate measures of diffusion. The best way to deal with this problem is **cardiac gating**. This involves measuring the heartbeat (EKG, or electrocardiogram) of the person being scanned, using a chest strap which is connected to the MR scanner. The scanner can then time the acquisition of each image to occur at the same point in the person's cardiac cycle, thus eliminating any artifacts caused by the brain being in different phases of pulsation on different acquisitions.

DATA ANALYSIS

Preprocessing

Like fMRI data, DWI data requires preprocessing prior to analysis to remove artifacts and optimize our sensitivity to effects in the data. Most of these steps are fairly straightforward and uncontroversial, and are easily performed in any mainstream DTI analysis software. These steps can be broadly broken down into three stages: artifact correction, alignment to a standardized template (normalization), and derivation of diffusion tensor parameters. A DWI dataset comprises a set of brain volumes that each have a different diffusion direction, as well as the unweighted baseline ($b = 0$) image or images. These images are typically all saved in a single data file for export from the MRI scanner. In addition, two other pieces of information are required for analysis: the set of gradient (diffusion) directions corresponding to each brain volume in the file, and the associated b value for that volume. These are typically stored in the header (meta-data) portion of the raw image files, but many analysis packages require them to be extracted to separate files.

Artifact Correction

As with fMRI, small head motions can cause significant distortions to DWI data, and these can be corrected using the same motion correction algorithms used for fMRI data. As well – and more importantly – **Eddy currents** are an artifact induced by the gradients during DWI data collection that cause spatial distortions, particularly along the phase encoding direction. Eddy currents are loops of electrical current induced in conductive pieces of the MRI hardware, such as the cryostat containing the liquid helium needed to cool the coils that maintain the standing, strong magnetic field of the MRI scanner. These currents are created through Faraday's laws of induction (the right-hand rule), and induce their own magnetic fields that are opposite to those that induced them in the first place. Thus, Eddy currents resist the electromagnetic fields that are intentionally produced by the MRI pulse sequence, which can cause lags and other distortions in the fields. This is a problem since MR imaging is so dependent on the precise timing and spatial gradients specified in the pulse sequence. Eddy currents can cause geometric distortions of images, misregistrations between different diffusion weighting directions, and ultimately miscalculations of the directions of diffusion in individual voxels. Both Eddy currents and motion can be corrected in a single step; indeed, in some software there is only an 'Eddy current correction' step – but this also accomplishes motion correction. Although historically the same motion correction algorithms used on fMRI data were applied to DWI data for this purpose, these were shown to have some shortcomings, especially for data collected with very high b values. More accurate methods have been developed specifically for DWI data, and are included in analysis software packages.

In addition to Eddy current and motion correction, another step that is often applied is to correct for magnetic field inhomogeneities. Because DWI data are typically acquired using a fast pulse sequence like EPI, they are subject to the geometric image distortions caused by such sequences that were described in the fMRI chapter. If the researcher acquires a 'field map' scan in addition to the DWI data, this can be used to correct for these distortions. The effects of this step will be to improve the accuracy of both the registration of the DWI data to the anatomical image, and of the diffusion computations in areas where geometric distortion is present.

Spatial Smoothing

Spatial smoothing is typically performed on DWI data, as with fMRI and VBM data, and for similar reasons. That is, smoothing helps to reduce spatially random noise and small errors in misregistration between subjects, while at the same time enhancing true differences – assuming that the spatial extent of the differences is roughly the same as the smoothing kernel (the matched filter theorem). However, there are some drawbacks to smoothing. Firstly, as with other types of MRI data, it may not be known in advance what the spatial extent of a difference will be, and this may vary across different parts of the brain. This makes it difficult to choose an optimized kernel size. Indeed, differences in the choice of smoothing kernel size have been shown to lead to different conclusions from the same DWI dataset (Jones, Symms, Cercignani, & Howard, 2005). Secondly, although smoothing can reduce the effects of imperfect spatial registration, it does so in a rather blunt way, smoothing equally in a sphere around each voxel. Misregistrations may have more complex spatial patterns that are not properly corrected simply by smoothing. Finally, smoothing can amplify partial volume effects that occur when a voxel contains a mixture of different tissue types (such as both grey and white matter), or a mixture of fibre orientations (such as when two tracts are close to each other). This is because the blurring will tend to spread partial volume effects from the voxels where they occur, to adjacent voxels that may not have contained partial volume effects prior to smoothing. Thus in general – especially since voxel sizes for DWI are generally much smaller than for fMRI – relatively conservative (small) smoothing kernels should be used.

Diffusion Tensor Calculations

Computing the diffusion tensor is the key first step in getting useful information out of DWI data. Indeed, diffusion MR imaging is commonly referred to as diffusion tensor imaging (DTI) because this step is so central to any of the analysis approaches that may be applied to the data. The purpose of calculating the **diffusion tensor** is to reduce the raw image, with its many different diffusion-weighted directions, to a single image that reflects the primary direction of diffusion of water in each voxel. This process starts with the preprocessed raw data, which are the set of brain volumes with different diffusion weightings, each with the $b = 0$ (unweighted) image subtracted. These are called **apparent diffusion coefficient (ADC)** images. These ADC values for the different directions are combined mathematically to compute the diffusion tensor matrix at each voxel. In turn, from this matrix we can derive six parameters that define an ellipsoid (a 3D oval), which is a visual representation of the primary direction of diffusion in each voxel, as well as the degree of anisotropy of the diffusion. Figure 10.3 shows examples of different ellipsoid shapes, and their interpretations.

Interpreting these ellipsoids is somewhat intuitive, but does require some deeper understanding. If the voxel has isotropic diffusion, the ellipsoid will be a perfect sphere. Conversely, if the voxel has highly anisotropic diffusion, the ellipsoid will resemble the shape of a cigar, with its long axis following the strongest (principal) direction of diffusion. The six parameters calculated from the diffusion tensor matrix include three values encoding the shape of the ellipsoid; these are the principal **eigenvalues**, (labelled λ_1, λ_2, and λ_3) which encode the relative amount (strength) of diffusion along the primary direction of diffusion and the two directions orthogonal to the first. The other three parameters are the **eigenvectors** (v_1, v_2, and v_3), which encode the direction of diffusion for each of these eigenvalues. An important point to note here is that – while v_1 and λ_1 encode the primary direction and strength of diffusion, respectively, in that direction – the second and third eigenvectors and eigenvalues (λ_2, λ_3, v_2, and v_3) do not represent the second- and third-strongest directions

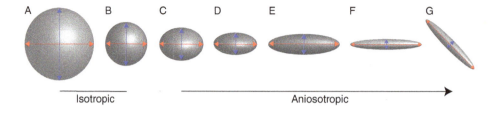

Figure 10.3 Examples of different ellipsoids that could be derived from DTI data. Each ellipsoid represents the direction and strength of diffusion in three dimensions. For simplicity, only the two strongest directions of diffusion are indicated with lines and arrows; the strongest direction of diffusion (first eigenvector) is shown in red, and the second-strongest direction orthogonal to the first direction (second eigenvector) is shown in blue. Arrowheads are drawn at both ends of these lines to emphasize the fact that DTI does not provide information as to the direction of diffusion. The first two spheres on the left (A and B) represent isotropic diffusion; however, the strength of diffusion is twice as great in the leftmost example. The remaining ellipsoids represent increasingly anisotropic diffusion, moving C to F. The two rightmost ellipsoids (F and G) represent the same strengths of diffusion, but in different primary directions

of diffusion. This is because the second and third eigenvectors are required mathematically to be orthogonal to the first. In general, if a voxel contains only fibres running in a single direction, this is not an issue since the primary eigenvector will represent the direction of those fibres, and the ellipsoid will be quite elongated in that direction. However, voxels may contain a mixture of fibres oriented in different directions (crossing fibres). In this case, the ellipsoid will have a more complex shape. For example, a 'pancake'-shaped ellipsoid would indicate that there is not one, but two strong directions of diffusion. However, since the second eigenvector is mathematically required to be orthogonal to the first, the orientation of the two 'flat' axes of the pancake may not reflect the true directions of diffusion. This is illustrated for the simpler 2D case in Figure 10.4. We will return to the issue of crossing fibres later, as more complex mathematical approaches are needed to distinguish voxels containing crossing fibres from those that lack strongly oriented fibres in any direction, and to estimate the directions of those crossing fibres. For the time being, keep in mind that cigar-shaped ellipsoids likely represent the presence (and direction) of fibre bundles, whereas voxels whose ellipsoids look like pancakes, spheres, or other shapes may either not contain white matter tracts, or contain a mixture of fibres of different orientations.

Because the interpretation of ellipsoid maps is not entirely intuitive, and is somewhat removed from our primary goal in connectomics (characterizing fibre tracts), a more common way to show DTI data is to plot coloured maps of the direction of the principal eigenvector at each voxel. An example of this is shown in Figure 10.5. Diffusion along the principal axes (x = left–right; y = anterior–posterior; z = inferior–superior) are

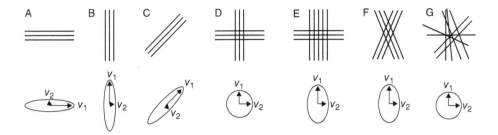

Figure 10.4 Schematic examples illustrating how varying compositions of fibre orientations within a single voxel (top row) influence the diffusion tensor ellipsoid (bottom row). Within the ellipsoid, the first and second eigenvectors are drawn. Although DTI is performed in three dimensions, this 2D example serves to illustrate the key points more simply. (A) shows a voxel containing fibres of a single orientation; its tensor ellipsoid shows a clear direction of diffusion. Likewise, (B) and (C) show voxels containing fibres of single orientations; the angle of the first eigenvector reflects the orientation of the fibres. (D) shows a voxel that contains equal numbers of fibres of two orthogonal orientations (crossing fibres); its primary and secondary eigenvectors are of equal length, indicating that the voxel does not reflect orientations of a single direction. In (E), we again have orthogonal crossing fibres, but there are more fibres in one direction than the other. As a result, the tensor ellipsoid is not round - as in the case of equal numbers of crossing fibres - but nor is it as oval as in (A), (B), or (C). Moreover, this case is indistinguishable from (F), in which there are equal numbers of fibres in two directions, but the directions are not orthogonal to each other. Finally, (G) shows a case of randomly oriented fibres. The tensor ellipsoid in this case is indistinguishable from (D). Overall, this figure emphasizes that DTI is an imperfect means of estimating white-matter tract orientation, especially when a voxel contains crossing fibres

represented by primary colours (red, blue, and green, respectively), and angles off of these principal directions are represented by blends of the primary colours in proportion to the angle. These maps are useful for visualizing three-dimensional fibre tract orientations in two-dimensional images. However, they are of limited use in performing quantitative, statistical analyses of DTI data – in part because each voxel is represented as a 3 × 3 matrix rather than a single value. For quantitative analysis, we turn to other measures.

The most common metric derived from DTI data is **fractional anisotropy (FA)**. FA is computed as a fraction of the difference in the size of each of the three principal eigenvectors, relative to their summed length (mathematically, FA is a measure of normalized variance along the principal eigenvectors). In other words, FA represents the anisotropy of the voxel, regardless of its orientation. FA values can range from 0 to 1, with 1 representing diffusion along a single direction only, and 0 representing perfectly isotropic diffusion. Overall, white-matter voxels will tend to have higher

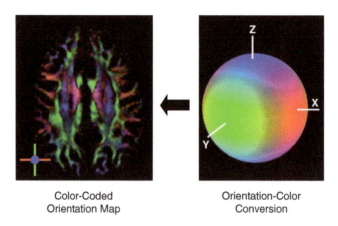

Color-Coded
Orientation Map

Orientation-Color
Conversion

Figure 10.5 Directionally encoded fibre orientation maps of an axial slice of a human brain, using colour to represent the primary direction of diffusion for anisotropic voxels. The colour wheel on the right indicates how colour is used to represent fibre orientations in 3D. Adapted with permission from Elsevier from Mori and Zhang (2006)

FA values than grey-matter voxels, and within the white matter high FA values will be found in voxels through which pass a relatively large number of fibres running in a single direction. FA is often interpreted as a measure of 'white-matter integrity' since if white matter were to break down in a particular location, diffusion would become less anisotropic and FA would consequently decrease. However, FA is an imperfect measure of white-matter integrity; voxels that contain a mixture of fibres running in two or more different directions will have a lower FA value than voxels with fibres all running in the same direction, even though both contain high proportions of strongly oriented fibres. FA is also susceptible to **partial volume effects**, which occur if a voxel contains a mixture of white matter tracts and other tissue (such as blood vessels, CSF, or grey matter). Nonetheless, FA remains a popular metric in DTI studies because it is easy and quick to compute and can be (cautiously) interpreted in terms of white matter integrity. As well, because we have reduced the tensor from a 3 × 3 matrix to a single number, FA lends itself readily to voxel-by-voxel (mass univariate) statistical analysis, which is readily available in most software packages and makes for straightforward statistical comparisons – for example between groups of people, or within groups over time. Several other metrics can be calculated from the diffusion tensor, including mean diffusivity (MD; the average of the three eigenvalues), relative anisotropy (RA; the standard deviation in eigenvalues divided by MD), and volume ratio (VR; the sum of the eigenvalues divided by MD). However, the interpretation of these measures is often less clear or relevant than FA, so FA is the most commonly used.

While FA measures have value, they do not tell us anything about the orientation of the fibres in each voxel. As noted above, although visual examination of directionally encoded fibre orientation maps such as those in Figure 10.5 can be informative, it is not immediately intuitive how those could be quantified. Although we could compare orientation along the primary diffusion direction between groups of people, there are likely to be few cases where we would expect actual changes in the orientation of a fibre bundle, rather than the strength of diffusion. Furthermore, perhaps the greatest appeal of DTI to cognitive neuroscience is its ability to inform us about connectomics – how brain areas are connected to each other. This is, by definition, not something that can be studied at the level of individual voxels. Rather, we need to identify fibre tracts running through the brain, ideally identifying the areas in cortex and/or midbrain that are connected by these fibres. Even if we are interested in measures of tract integrity, we may wish to quantify the integrity of a tract as a whole, rather than on a voxel-by-voxel basis. To address such questions, we need to perform tractography.

Tractography

Tractography is the process of mapping white-matter tracts that connect different brain regions. When we view a coloured image of primary diffusion directions, such as Figure 10.5, we perform a sort of tractography 'by eye' – we can follow the apparent pathways over space by mentally 'connecting the dots' of similarly coloured voxels. A similar process can be performed computationally, using one of a variety of methods. The simplest of these is **streamlining**, which involves starting from a particular voxel and identifying which surrounding voxel's principal eigenvector is best aligned with the principal eigenvector (the strongest direction of diffusion) of this voxel. Conceptually, we can think of drawing a line through the voxel along the principal eigenvector direction and identifying the voxels adjacent to the starting voxel that the line passes through. This is shown in Figure 10.6. Depending on the research question, one can either start with a single 'seed' voxel and follow a streamline in both directions from there, or identify two regions of interest (ROIs) and find tracts that connect them (one can go even further and specify 'waypoints' between the starting and ending ROIs that tracts must pass through). In the latter case, it is normal to run the tracking twice: once starting from each ROI. Either way, the process of 'connecting the dots' by following the principal eigenvectors is continued through adjacent voxels until some termination point is reached. Several stopping criteria can be defined. One is FA value: low FA suggests a lack of oriented fibres (or a mixture of orientations), and so it is logical to stop when the streamline reaches a voxel whose FA value is below a threshold that reflects certainty in the orientation of the voxel. Another criterion is the degree of bend from one voxel to the next: although there are some fibres in the brain that bend at fairly sharp angles (including the descriptively named 'U-fibres'), in general when performing tractography we expect that the fibres we are tracking will bend only slightly from voxel to voxel. A third option is, if one is performing point-to-point tracking (to identify tracts that run from one location through a second location), then when the streamline from the starting point reaches the second point, the tracking stops. Alternatively, however, one could allow the streamlining to continue until an FA or angular threshold is reached.

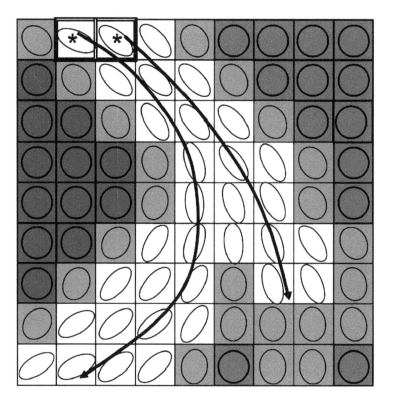

Figure 10.6 Schematic 2D illustration of streamlining to identify voxels connected in a tract. The shading of each square (voxel) represents its degree of anisotropy, as does the shape of the ellipse. Two streamlines (black arrows) are shown, originating from two adjacent voxels (stars). A streamline follows the principal direction of diffusion through each voxel to identify the adjacent voxel that is most likely part of the same tract. This is subject to several constraints, including the maximum amount a streamline can bend over a particular distance. Another constraint, shown in the right-hand tract, is that the streamlining process terminates when an isotropic voxel is encountered. Adapted with permission of Elsevier from Mori and Zhang (2006)

The streamlining approach has a number of limitations. Firstly, it is quite sensitive to noise. Although noise is a problem in any neuroimaging, in streamlining the issue is magnified by the fact that we are dealing with a single voxel at a time; this has several consequences. For one, the streamline is dependent on the particular voxel chosen as the starting point. If the particular voxel chosen is noisier or has a less accurate representation of the true orientation of fibres in that general area, the streamline may be inaccurate. Likewise, greater noise or inaccuracy in any voxel along the streamline will cause a misestimation of the true orientation of the fibre, and any such errors will be magnified as the streamlining process continues. As an analogy, if you fail to make a necessary left turn in Albuquerque, then many miles later you may find yourself in Denver rather than Los Angeles! As well, if noise results in an FA value below the stopping threshold, tracking may stop entirely.

Other limitations of streamlining stem from true anatomical features. As mentioned earlier, streamlining methods have a threshold constraining the amount that a tract can bend within a certain length; if the fibre being tracked truly bends at an angle greater than this threshold, the tracking will fail. However, the angular thresholds used are generally based on anatomical knowledge so this is typically only a concern if one is attempting to track U-fibres. Other anatomical features include branching and crossing fibres. If a tract branches, a streamline may have equal probability of following one of the two branches, and will either fail or reveal only one of the branches. If two fibre pathways cross in a particular voxel, the situation becomes more difficult. If a voxel has equal numbers of fibres running in two perpendicular directions, the FA ellipsoid will have a pancake shape (with the first and second eigenvectors being of equal length) and so the primary direction of diffusion will be indeterminate. In this case, angular constraints on the path of the tract may help the streamline pass through this voxel rather than bending sharply; alternatively tracking may break down. A breakdown is more likely if a larger proportion of fibres cross the voxel perpendicular to the streamline because then the primary direction of diffusion will be perpendicular to the streamline entering the voxel. In other cases, the fibres may cross at angles less than 90 degrees. These cases are even more problematic because the tensor calculations work by defining a primary direction of diffusion in the voxel, then define the second and third eigenvectors as being orthogonal to that direction. In other words, rather than the first eigenvector representing the direction of one of the two tracts, and the second eigenvector representing the other tract, the primary eigenvector will follow the average of the two fibre pathways – a direction midway between them that doesn't accurately reflect the direction of either true pathway. These limitations were illustrated earlier in Figure 10.4.

A number of approaches have been developed to deal with the limitations of streamlining, which may be used singly or in combination. One approach is smoothing (sometimes called **regularization**). Just as with fMRI, the idea behind smoothing is that adjacent voxels are likely to have similar orientations, whereas noise is random across voxels. Therefore averaging the information from each voxel with that from adjacent voxels should reinforce the true directionality, while reducing noise. Another approach is called 'fitting', in which – rather than simply aligning the streamline with the principal eigenvector of each voxel – the streamline incorporates information from previous voxels such that it forms a smoother line. This is essentially a variant of the 'maximum angle' constraint; rather than providing a stopping criterion, however, it simply smooths the line running across multiple voxels. Conceptually related to fitting is the **tensor line approach**, which carries the 'momentum' of the streamline from high-FA voxels through those with lower FA. Thus rather than breaking down, streamlining can continue through voxels with higher noise or uncertainty – as long as the region of low FA is surrounded by areas of higher FA.

A rather different strategy is incorporated in **probabilistic tractography**. Although there are several variants of this approach, in general they all run the streamlining multiple times. Each time, a slightly different orientation is used for each voxel. These orientations deviate from the principal eigenvector pseudo-randomly, within certain limits. The range of these limits is determined by the DTI ellipsoid, and is related to the estimated probability of the principal direction of diffusion. Thus in areas of high certainty the range of variation is small, whereas in areas of high uncertainty (such as low FA or high probability of crossing fibres) a wider range of possible directions of the streamline are fitted. Repeating this process many times allows one to estimate the reliability of the streamlining and determine where the highest areas of uncertainty are. Other approaches, such as first marching and simulated annealing are particularly good at differentiating voxels where FA is low due to noise or a lack of oriented fibres, from voxels that contain crossing fibres. For example, simulated annealing does this by fitting an equation with two terms representing two different orientation directions and finding a solution that fits both directions as well as possible. Often such algorithms operate in a two-stage fashion, such that the subset of voxels that have high uncertainty (and thus being likely to contain crossing fibres) are first identified, and then multiple directions are estimated only in this subset of voxels. This is important because attempting to optimize a two-direction solution at voxels containing only one direction of fibres would work poorly and could cause errors.

Other constraints can be imposed by the user based on prior anatomical knowledge. One of the most simple and obvious ones is the **brute force** approach. This involves simply tracking from (or through) multiple adjacent seed/ROI voxels rather than picking a single seed voxel or a start/end pair of voxels. The brute force approach reduces the dependency of the solution on the particular choice of seed voxel and makes it more robust to noise; this can be combined with any of the solutions described above. However, it is important that the user be confident that all of the voxels within the seed/ROI are truly part of the same tract, or else the streamlines may deviate at some point, resulting in a more confusing solution. Using the two-ROI, point-to-point tracking approach can also help minimize propagation-of-error issues because tracks that go far 'off the mark' will not reach the endpoint ROI. As well, running the tracking in both directions between ROIs and averaging the solutions will tend to be more robust than tracking in a single direction, especially if using curve-fitting or tensor line approaches since tracking into a noise region may be more robust from one direction than another. For both single-point and point-to-point tracking, another option is to include masks. These are areas of the brain that the user is very certain should not contain any fibres from the tract of interest; streamlines that enter these areas either stop or are removed entirely from the solution.

Spatial Registration and Normalization

Because DWI scans are optimized for sensitivity to water diffusion, and are subject to geometric distortion, they do not show anatomy as clearly as a typical T1-weighted structural MR image. Therefore a high-resolution T1 image is typically collected and used both to map an individual's diffusion data to their anatomy, and also to warp the individual's brain to a standard template (such as the MNI152 average brain) for group analysis. The process of doing this is the same as was described for other types of MRI data (including fMRI and computational neuroanatomy), and benefits from using non-linear, rather than linear affine, registration. However, since non-linear registration approaches generally work by attempting to match the overall shape of an individual's brain to a template, this does not guarantee that the actual tracts have been aligned – getting one individual's brain shape to match the template may force voxels from a particular tract into locations that, in the template, belong to another tract. This concern can be ameliorated in part by using less severe forms of nonlinear registration (typically the software has options such as the degrees of freedom that control the amount of warping that can occur). Non-linear registration can also compound the partial volume effects mentioned in the previous section: in warping and then resampling the voxels, data from two distinct tracts could be combined in some voxels. Another issue with non-linear registration is that if the brains involved have gross structural differences (for example, due to pathology), spatial normalization will correct for these but in doing so may introduce other differences. This is particularly true if these differences are systematic, as in the comparison between a patient group and healthy controls (such as enlarged ventricles in one group, or atrophy). In this case, the process of matching the brains' shapes may introduce systematic differences at the individual voxel level that are difficult to detect.

One way of addressing this, at least in part, is to perform all of the analysis of an individual's DWI data (for example, calculation of diffusion tensors, fractional anisotropy, and tractography) in the individual's 'native' space, not in the spatially transformed space. Because spatial normalization necessarily changes the voxel values in the image, it is always preferable to perform as much of the analysis as possible on the data prior to applying any transformations; the spatial transformations are then applied to the results of the individual-level analyses. However, this practice alone does not eliminate the issues described in the previous paragraph, because data from a particular tract can still become misaligned, or merged with another tract, during normalization. However, it is standard practice to perform DTI calculations in an individual's native space.

An additional approach is to perform analysis on FA values averaged over entire, anatomically defined tracts, rather than performing voxel-wise analysis. A limitation of this approach is that it requires the user to work with pre-defined tracts; however, at this point in time there are established atlases and models of major white-matter tracts to use as the basis for such definitions. Alternatively, one can define the tract(s) based on tractography performed on the subjects in the experiment under analysis; for example, using an ROI-based approach as described in the previous section. A more advanced approach, which helps control for errors in streamlining in individual subjects' data as well as registration errors, is **model-based tract segmentation**. In this approach, pre-defined models of major white-matter tracts are used as a starting point, based on a white-matter atlas. However, rather than simply using the tracts as defined in the atlas – which assumes both perfect registration of each individual to the standard template, and that there is no inter-individual variability in tract shape or size – the algorithm uses these as a starting point but estimates the true shape and centre of each individual's tract based on models of the normal range of variation in shape of the tract. A limitation of this approach is that prior anatomical models of the tract(s) to be analysed are required, although these can be created if they do not already exist.

Rather than performing tract-based segmentation, another approach that can reduce the issues caused by spatial normalization is **skeletonization**. This reduces the normalized data to a white-matter 'skeleton' derived from the averaged, normalized FA maps of all of the participants in a particular analysis. This is in some ways similar to the tract-based segmentation approach described in the previous paragraph; however, it is 'tract-agnostic' in that it does not require any prior information concerning the location or shapes of tracts. Rather, the centres of major tracts are identified by an algorithm that finds the maximum local FA values throughout the averaged FA map (since FA will presumably be highest at the centre of a tract). This results in a map consisting of thin (single-voxel) lines representing the centres of the major tracts. To address the issue of imperfect alignment between subjects (that is, the centre of the tract in the average may not represent the exact centre in every individual), for each subject the algorithm searches the FA values close to each voxel in the FA skeleton, to find the maximum local FA value for that subject (assuming this to be the tract centre for that individual). The algorithm then projects (copies) this value to the corresponding voxel within the FA skeleton for that subject. This procedure can be thought of as a more intelligent or principled non-linear warping process, based on assumptions about the local microstructure of tracts rather than trying to match the overall shape of the brain. It also helps reduce the influence of partial volume effects, because centres of tracts with local maximum FA values are the least likely to contain crossing fibres or other tissue types (since high FA indicates strong diffusion primarily along one direction). A limitation of this approach is that because it is based around local maximum FA values, it is insensitive to smaller white matter pathways and smaller branches. As well, it is insensitive to differences in the size of white-matter tracts, which might occur between groups or over time (for example, with disease progression or learning). It is also important to note that this process is typically applied on FA, not tractography data. However, once the skeleton is obtained from the FA data, it can be used to mask other types of data, including tractography data in which voxel values contain orientation information.

Statistics

Voxel-Wise Analysis

As noted earlier, maps of voxel-wise measures such as FA can be analysed essentially the same way as fMRI or VBM data. First, the FA (or MD, or other metrics; for the present discussion we will use FA for simplicity) maps of each individual subject in the study are registered to a common template (such as the MNI152). Following spatial normalization, ideally accompanied by additional techniques such as tract identification or skeletonization as discussed in the previous section, values are compared at each voxel – either between groups of people (for example, healthy controls versus a patient group) or within a group, at different time points (for instance, to study progression of a disease, or effects of a treatment). Correction for multiple comparisons should be performed as for fMRI and VBM.

An important consideration in analysing DTI data, however, is that the statistical methods typically employed in such mass univariate analyses – such as ANOVA or linear mixed effects modelling – are not appropriate. These methods assume a normal distribution of data values (and of noise), but this has been shown not to be true for DTI data, at least not consistently throughout the brain (Ellingson, Groisser, Osborne, Patrangenaru, & Schwartzman, 2016; Jones et al., 2005; Marenco et al., 2006). Therefore nonparametric statistical techniques are more appropriate. Nonparametric statistical techniques were introduced in the MEG chapter, where more details can be found.

Tract-Based Analysis

A significant limitation of voxel-based analyses is that they provide no information about tracts or connectivity. It is possible, just as with fMRI or VBM data, to look up the locations of significant voxels in an atlas in order to determine which tracts any observed effects are in. However, atlases are approximations and so some voxels may be misidentified as being part of the wrong tract in a particular dataset. Performing tractography and/or skeletonization can help minimize the risk of mislabelling a tract, but voxel-wise analyses do not tell us about the tract as a whole. Further, as noted above approaches such as skeletonization may prevent us from detecting differences in the periphery of tracts – the core of a tract may be similar across groups, but the overall size/volume may differ or tract integrity may be lower only in the more peripheral aspects of the tract (although in practice this would likely appear identical to a difference in tract volume). One approach to overcoming this is to compute mean FA within each tract, and use this as the basis for statistics. However, averaging over many voxels along the length of a tract can cause an appreciable loss of information – subtle differences may not come out in the average, and if differences do emerge, it will be unclear whether they characterize the tract as a whole or some sub-part of it.

One approach that integrates streamlining into a voxel-based analysis is probabilistic tracking, which was described above. From a statistical standpoint, what is interesting about probabilistic tracking is that, given a particular seed ROI (or pair of ROIs in point-to-point tracking), the values at any voxel are not simply binary values (indicating that a voxel is either part of the tract, or not). Instead, the value at each voxel in the image represents the estimated probability that the voxel is part of the tract. Having continuously varying values means that, across subjects, we can perform statistics whose results reflect these probabilities.

As this discussion of DTI computation and analysis has likely made apparent, there is no single 'right' way to analyse DTI data, and indeed far less agreement within the field as to what the best approach to preprocessing and analysis is compared to some other methods, such as fMRI (though even there, there are considerable differences of opinion). It is also worth noting that there are some cases where quantification of tracts is not required. For example, one might perform a voxel-wise analysis and then use tractography only to identify which tract(s) pass through areas identified as having significant differences. In clinical applications, a neurologist or surgeon may wish to visualize tracts to determine whether and how they have been altered in an individual patient, for example by a brain tumour. Such visualization could help understand a pattern of symptoms, or plan a surgical approach. However, for the most part all humans have largely similar tractography patterns; in research applications typically the differences that are looked for are relatively subtle and require quantification and statistical analysis for interpretation.

APPLICATIONS AND LIMITATIONS

Applications

A common use of DTI is to compare people with a specific disease or condition with healthy controls, using voxel-wise analysis of FA. One disease that has been studied extensively is schizophrenia, which we will use as a case study here. A meta-analysis of studies comparing people with schizophrenia with control subjects combined data from 15 publications, representing a total of 407 patients and 383 controls (Ellison-Wright & Bullmore, 2009). The analysis revealed two clusters of lower FA in the left-hemisphere white matter of the patient group: one in the frontal lobe and one in the temporal lobe. Each cluster was about 2 cm^3. To identify which tract(s) each significant cluster involved, the authors performed tractography on a single healthy person's data (someone who was not part of any of the studies in the meta-analysis). Based on this, the authors identified five distinct tracts passing through the frontal lobe cluster, and four passing through the temporal lobe cluster. These are shown in Figure 10.7. While this study is important in identifying consistencies across studies, it nevertheless has limitations, as its authors note. Firstly, since the tractography was based on a single individual, it is possible that one or more of the tracts identified were not actually affected by schizophrenia but rather were implicated due to misregistration. As well, it is interesting that the areas of lower FA were relatively small, focal clusters overlapping a number of tracts rather than more elongated effects that followed a particular tract. This may in part be due to the fact that the meta-analysis took as its input the coordinates of the peak between-group differences in each study; however, such clusters are not atypical in individual DTI studies. It is possible that the voxel-based approach, particularly combined with spatial smoothing, creates patterns that appear more 'blob-like' than naturally occur in the white matter itself. This underscores the importance of understanding the preprocessing and analysis steps used when interpreting neuroimaging data.

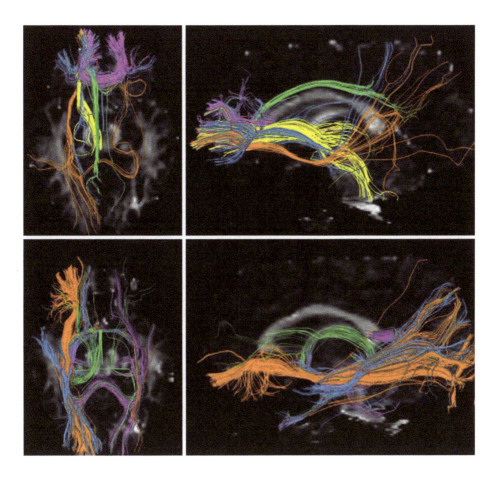

Figure 10.7 Fibre tracts passing through two regions of interest identified as having abnormal FA values in a meta-analysis of DTI studies of schizophrenia. The top panels show fibres passing through a region of the left frontal lobe, and the bottom panels show fibres passing through a region of the left temporal lobe. Reprinted with permission from Elsevier from Ellison-Wright and Bullmore (2009)

Another example shows an extension of probabilistic tractography: using DTI for anatomical segmentation. This was elegantly demonstrated in a paper by Behrens and colleagues (Behrens, Johansen-Berg, & Woolrich, 2003) in which they used each voxel in the thalamus as a seed point, and used probabilistic tracking to determine where that thalamus location connected to in the cortex. The resulting map, shown in Figure 10.8 is quite compelling: adjacent voxels in the thalamus connected to adjacent regions in the cortex, and these patterns reflected what was previously known about the organization of thalamic nuclei and their projections to the cortex, from invasive and postmortem tracer studies. More broadly, this demonstrated a connectivity-based approach to anatomical segmentation that can be used to complement the cytoarchitectonic and micro-scale myeloarchitectonic maps described elsewhere in this book. Like those other anatomical maps, connectivity-based maps could be used to help interpret the results of fMRI or other localization-based functional imaging techniques like MEG. For example, one could determine whether an area of activation represented a single connectivity-defined region, or multiple regions. As well, such connectivity maps could be combined with effective connectivity analysis to help constrain the set of possible effective connectivity models being compared to those that were anatomically plausible. As described in the previous chapter, recent multimodal MR imaging has used DTI in combination with other structural and functional measures to derive a consistent parcellation scheme for the cerebral cortex.

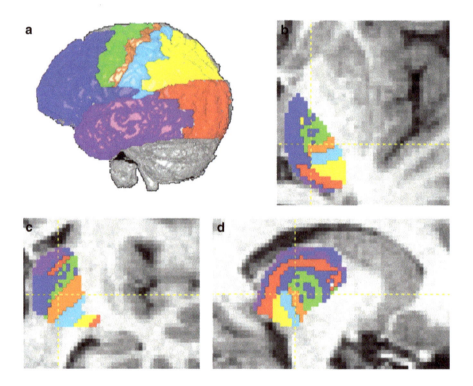

Figure 10.8 Connectivity-based parcellation of the thalamus. Tracts were computed from each voxel in the thalamus to the cerebral cortex, and then each thalamic voxel was assigned a colour based on which region of the cortex it was most likely to be connected to. Panel (a) shows the colour coding of major cortical regions, and (b)–(d) show different views of the thalamus, with colours reflecting the cortical area each voxel was shown to be connected to. The results reflect the known organization of thalamic projections to the cortex. Reprinted from Behrens and colleagues (2003) with permission of Nature Publishing Group

Limitations

DTI is a powerful technique and provides essentially the only non-invasive way to study the white-matter pathways of the brain in living organisms. As such they provide an exciting complement to functional and other structural techniques, which can enrich our understanding of how the brain works. There are, however, numerous limitations of DTI that should always be kept in mind. These include questions concerning the validity of the technique, the relationship between structural and functional connectivity measures, and the diversity of ways in which the data can be analysed.

A first way of assessing the validity of DTI is not using tissue at all, but 'phantoms' – objects designed with specific properties to validate imaging protocols. The validity of DTI for tracing specific pathway shapes has been demonstrated both using software models of tracts, and phantoms made of non-biological tissues such as rayon or dialysis fibres (Hubbard & Parker, 2009). Other studies have used biological samples with highly oriented fibres such as muscle, spinal cord, and the optic chiasm. The optic chiasm is a particularly interesting test case because it has a very characteristic and well-understood shape, is composed of axons, and a significant number of these cross each other. The validation work has consistently demonstrated the validity of DTI in tracking white matter fibres (Hubbard & Parker, 2009). These approaches are also valuable in testing new pulse sequences or analysis techniques, as they provide a 'gold standard' for comparison.

Aside from DTI, the primary methods for performing tractography in brain tissue are through postmortem fixation and dissection of the brain, and chemical tracer methods. Postmortem dissection is really useful only for visualizing major white-matter bundles, and suffers from the limitation that major tracts that can be characterized this way (such as the longitudinal fasiculi and corona radiata) are defined purely on visual inspection of the gross anatomy; at a finer-grained level these tracts probably contain numerous terminations and branches that connect many different brain areas. However, it is certainly possible to test whether the major tracts identifiable through postmortem dissection match what is seen with DTI. Lawes and colleagues compared postmortem dissections with in vivo DTI tractography from different individuals (Lawes et al., 2008), using detailed qualitative analysis of the overall morphology of major tracts (such as where tracts constricted, where they fanned out, and so on). The correspondence between DTI and dissection was found to be very high; an example of this can be seen in Figure 10.9.

Another approach to validation in both humans and animals is to determine whether DTI shows the predicated effects in disease states or development. For example, multiple sclerosis (MS) is associated with demyelination, and people with MS show reduced FA in white matter that corresponds with other markers of the location of focal demyelination (plaques) such as T2-weighted MR imaging. Similarly, since myelination occurs over the course of development, FA is expected to be lower in juvenile brains and this has been repeatedly demonstrated.

Since it is possible to perform DTI on animals, and indeed on animals postmortem (since Brownian motion of water molecules occurs similarly in living and

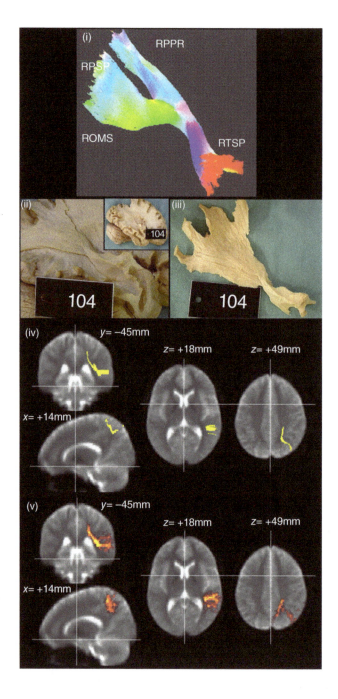

Figure 10.9 Comparison of DTI reconstruction of a white-matter fibre tract (the right temporo-parieto-occipital pathway) with postmortem dissection of that tract from the same individual. Panel (i) shows the isolated tract as reconstructed using DTI; (ii) shows the dissected tract exposed in the fixed, postmortem brain; (iii) shows the tract after removal from the brain, highlighting its similarity with the DTI-reconstructed version; (iv) shows the average location of the tract across 15 individuals; and (v) shows the inter-subject variability in tract location (with yellow representing lower variability, and red representing higher variability). Reproduced with permission of Elsevier from Lawes et al., 2008

dead tissue, assuming the temperature is the same), correspondence between chemical tracer and DTI measures can be made. Chemical tracer methods are considered the 'gold standard' for tractography, and they are far more precise than DTI because they involve injecting a chemical in specific cell bodies and then allowing it to diffuse throughout those cells (the tracer typically does not exit the cell as it is designed not to cross the cell membrane). The tracer will diffuse down the axons and thus identify the projection targets of the injected cells. This technique is not applicable to humans as it involves injection of potentially toxic chemicals, and requires postmortem dissection to identify the projection targets of the cells. Nevertheless, many studies have validated DTI using chemical tracer studies (Hubbard & Parker, 2009). A particularly interesting development is the use of MR-visible tracers. For example, a manganese isotope, Mn^{2+}, is an effective chemical tracer that can be injected into cells, and is visible in MR imaging because it is paramagnetic. Thus Mn^{2+}-injected animals can be scanned with both DTI and Mn^{2+}-sensitive pulse sequences and the results compared directly, within individual animals. Because of the invasiveness of chemical tracer methods (even MR-compatible tracers are not safe to administer in humans), they are only applicable to animal models. Thus an important limitation is that while they support the validity of DTI in general, one can question how such information can be extrapolated to humans. One recent study, however, addressed this issue by comparing chemical and DTI tracing in macaque (monkey) brains with DTI tractography in humans, using projections to the ventral prefrontal cortex (Jbabdi, Lehman, Haber, & Behrens, 2013). These projections were of interest because they are well documented in monkeys, and have complex trajectories. Overall, the researchers found high correspondence between gold-standard chemical tracing and DTI in both macaques and humans. Where there was a lack of correspondence, it was not between chemical tracing and DTI within monkeys, but between monkeys and humans. Because of the high correspondence between methods within monkeys, the authors concluded that this likely represents a true between-species difference rather than an error or limitation of the DTI technique – which indeed emphasizes the value of DTI in humans, as well as the limitations of extrapolating from animal to human data.

Several other issues are not as well resolved. While DTI is a valuable technique for performing tractography, streamlining breaks down near the grey matter due to the decreasing FA values. Thus while we can extrapolate streamlines to make guesses as to where the fibre tracts enter the cortex, we cannot actually visualize this directly. Therefore it is difficult, if not impossible, to determine for certain whether a tract terminates in a particular cortical (or subcortical) area, or simply passes by it. Relatedly, tracts that pass perpendicular to a given region of cortex – that is, the tracts seem to pass by the area, rather than pointing towards or terminating in it – may in fact have branches that infiltrate that area of cortex. There is hope that novel imaging protocols and analysis techniques can reduce this uncertainty, by allowing more reliable tracking into areas of low FA, but at present this is a critical limitation to keep in mind: not only can we merely infer the white-matter tracts from DTI based on water diffusion, but even if we accept the validity of such tracking we can never be entirely sure that the fibres connect to specific grey-matter regions. That said, for tracts that are well understood and have been mapped in postmortem brains, we have a very good idea of their termination points in the cortex and so can use this information to validate the inferences we make about the same tracts as identified by DTI.

Related to this, another question is how DTI measures of structural connectivity compare to estimates of functional or effective connectivity, such as those provided by fMRI or source-localized MEG or EEG. Recall that functional connectivity refers simply to correlations in activity between brain regions, while effective connectivity makes inferences as to the direction of information flow. Because DTI measures (random) Brownian motion, we cannot infer the directionality of information flow from DTI data. Thus DTI cannot help constrain functional or effective connectivity estimates regarding directionality. However, DTI can help restrict the range of connectivity models one is willing to entertain in an effective connectivity analysis – if there is no structural evidence for a connection between brain areas, then one might best avoid positing such a connection in an effective connectivity model. The danger in this is that DTI might not have the resolution to identify a tract that does exist, especially if it is small, crosses other tracts, or bends to a greater degree than allowed by the streamlining algorithm. Another consideration – especially for functional connectivity – is that two brain areas may be functionally connected without being structurally connected. For example, one brain region (A) may project to two other regions (B and C), and so those areas (B and C) may show correlated activity – functional connectivity – in the absence of a direct structural connection due to their common influence by A. With these caveats in mind however, the combination of tractography with functional imaging is an exciting area that holds great promise for the future.

Finally, it is worth noting – as has likely been apparent in this section – that perhaps more than any other application of MRI in cognitive neuroscience, there are many possible (and valid) approaches to data preprocessing and analysis. While fMRI yields essentially a single type of value (BOLD signal), a wide range of measures can be obtained from a DTI scan, and different scanning parameters (particularly b value and field strength) can yield different measurements and levels of resolution that can provide qualitatively different information. Even with a given dataset, one can ask many different questions, look at a variety of measures, and use different algorithms that make different assumptions about the underlying data. Thus doing DTI well involves a deep and extensive understanding of the technique, its limitations and trade-offs, and the many ways in which data can be analysed. While this is true of any cognitive neuroscience technique, it is perhaps amplified in the case of connectomics.

SUMMARY

Connectomics is the study of connections between the brain, with the ultimate goal being to describe the projectome – the complete set of connections in the brain and their directions. While brain connectivity can be studied down to the microscopic level using invasive techniques, at present our ability to characterize connectivity non-invasively in humans is limited to techniques based on diffusion

MR imaging. This is an indirect approach in which the natural, random Brownian motion (diffusion) of water molecules is measured; because the fatty myelin sheath prevents water diffusion, water molecules inside axons tend to diffuse along the length of axons rather than in any other direction. By using a sequence of dephasing and then rephasing magnetic field gradients, systematically applied along many different directions, one can infer the existence and orientation of major white matter tracts from the diffusion directions of water.

After a series of preprocessing steps, including correcting for motion artifacts and Eddy currents, the diffusion tensor is calculated to identify the primary direction of diffusion (eigenvector) in each voxel, as well as the two directions orthogonal to that direction (which are not necessarily the second or third strongest directions of diffusion). From here, a number of different measures can be computed, allowing many possible dependent measures from a single scan. Some of these analyses are performed voxel-wise in a mass univariate approach. A common measure that can be derived from the diffusion tensor is fractional anisotropy (FA), which reflects the degree to which diffusion in a given voxel is anisotropic (preferential in one direction) rather than isotropic. FA within known white-matter tracts is often described as a measure of 'white-matter integrity', since lower FA reflects less anisotropic diffusion, which could be caused by thinner or degraded white matter. However, because there are many possible reasons why FA could change, interpretations should be cautious and consider alternative explanations as well as seeking support through converging evidence from other sources. One important consideration is that FA will be lower in voxels that contain fibres oriented in more than one direction, such as locations of crossing fibres. Advanced analysis techniques have been developed to identify possible crossing fibre locations and distinguish these from other causes of low FA. Tract-based approaches involve performing some form of streamlining to trace paths across multiple voxels, to determine the start and end points of tracts. These generally involve defining seed points, either at one or both ends of a tract, or somewhere along the middle. While tractographic analysis can provide useful descriptions and visualisations, a current challenge is in identifying quantitative ways of characterising and analysing fibre tracts based on these data. Another challenge in tractography is that, because diffusion becomes more isotropic in grey matter, it can be challenging to determine the actual endpoints of white-matter tracts in the cortex.

While DTI is a powerful technique, as with all cognitive neuroscience techniques it has some significant limitations. Chief among these are that it is an indirect measure in which we infer the existence and direction of fibre tracts from the diffusion of water – we are not imaging the white matter itself. While there exists clear validation of the technique in that diffusion MR tractography reveals tracts that are highly anatomically consistent with those identified through 'gold standard' methods such as dissection, our interpretation of changes in DTI measures such as FA is more speculative. Further work is needed in order to be able to draw stronger associations between DTI-based measures and parameters relevant to understanding brain anatomy and function, such as intactness of white matter, the size and number of connectivity fibres, or the information-carrying capacity of a tract. It is also important to always remember that DTI is an anatomical technique, and does not reveal anything about the activity or information carried along a fibre tract.

THINGS YOU SHOULD KNOW

- Water molecules naturally move randomly due to the influence of heat energy, which is known as Brownian motion. The fatty myelin sheath of the axons that carry action potentials from one neuron to another block water diffusion, meaning that water diffuses preferentially along the length of axons (anisotropically).

- Diffusion tensor imaging (DTI) uses a specialized EPI pulse sequence to characterize the direction of water diffusion. This involves applying dephasing, and then rephasing magnetic field gradients along a particular direction after RF excitation. If water molecules stay in the same location, their signal will cancel out between the dephasing and rephasing gradients; however, diffusion will cause imperfect rephasing, resulting in measurable signal change. By repeating this along many different directions, and comparing to a scan without diffusion gradients, the amount and direction of diffusion can be computed.

- After correction for head motion and Eddy currents, diffusion-weighted MRI data can be subjected to diffusion tensor analysis to determine the principle direction of water diffusion in each voxel of the image. Spatial registration and normalization are commonly applied, as in fMRI, to normalize the size and shape of individuals' brains to a standard template. This is normally performed after computing the diffusion tensor.

- Fractional anisotropy (FA) is a common measure derived from the diffusion tensor. It reflects the proportion of diffusion in the primary direction relative to diffusion in the two directions orthogonal to this direction. FA is a common measure used in mass univariate, voxel-wise analyses of DTI data. It is often interpreted as a measure of white-matter integrity, although other interpretations are possible.

- Beyond voxel-wise measures, DTI data may also be analysed through tractography, to characterize tracts that pass through many voxels in the image. These rely on streamlining to determine the most likely direction of a tract from one voxel to the next, given the primary direction of diffusion in each voxel. Tractographic approaches can involve one or more seed regions, which can serve as starting, ending, and/or middle points of a hypothesized tract. These approaches can be informed and constrained by prior knowledge regarding the locations and end points of different tracts. The streamlines provided by tractography are more descriptive than quantitative, but can be used to help characterize the locations of changes in FA as well as to understand connectivity patterns.

- Tractography analyses can be used in a variety of ways. In research usually the focus is on comparing different groups of individuals; for instance, to identify regions of white matter differences between people with a particular disease and healthy controls, or over time (for example, in studies of development, ageing, or learning). Another use is in deriving connectivity-based parcellations of the brain. These may aid in the functional and anatomical characterization of different brain areas, based on their unique connectivity patterns. Tractography maps may also help in the development, testing, and interpretation of models from functional connectivity analysis, to constrain the range of models to those that are anatomically plausible.

- While the anatomical characterization of white matter tracts by DTI is highly consistent with the results of 'gold standard' postmortem mapping techniques, much remains poorly understood about the nature of the DTI signal and, in particular, how to relate quantitative measures of water diffusion to neurally relevant parameters such as the intactness of white matter, and the size, density, and number of axons within a tract. As well, DTI cannot provide information regarding the direction of the white-matter projections it identifies.

FURTHER READINGS

Johansen-Berg, H., and Behrens, T.E.J. (Eds.) (2013). *Diffusion MRI: From Quantitative Measurement to In vivo Neuroanatomy*. New York: Academic Press.

Jones, D.K. (Ed.) (2010). *Diffusion MRI: Theory, Methods, and Applications*. Oxford: Oxford University Press.

Mori, S., and Tournier, J.-D. (2013). *Introduction to Diffusion Tensor Imaging and Higher Order Models*. New York: Academic Press.

Sporns, O., Tononi, G., & Kötter, R. (2005). The human connectome: A structural description of the human brain. *PLoS Computational Biology*, *1*(4), e42–47.

11 Positron Emission Tomography (PET)

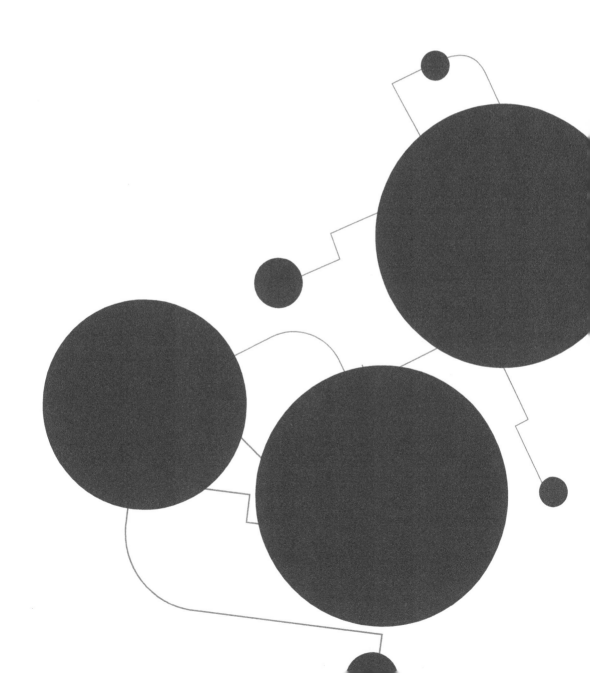

LEARNING OBJECTIVES

After reading this chapter, you should be able to:

- Explain the origins of the PET signal at the subatomic level.
- Explain how PET data is acquired and reconstructed.
- Define PERs and list the names and uses of several.
- Describe the potential risks of PET and how they are mitigated.
- Explain the constraints that PET imposes on experimental design in cognitive neuroscience.
- List several use cases for PET over fMRI in cognitive neuroscience research.
- Discuss the value of multimodal PET.

INTRODUCTION

Positron emission tomography (PET) is a unique imaging modality in several ways. Firstly, although it is very safe, PET is nominally more invasive than other imaging techniques because it involves introducing radioactive tracers into the body. Secondly, although – like fMRI – PET allows indirect identification of neural activity levels through measurements of blood flow and tracking the uptake of oxygen, PET can also be used to map the distribution of many other molecules in the brain, including receptors and neuromodulators, as well as disease markers such as amyloid (a hallmark of Alzheimer's disease).

PET was first developed in the 1970s and has steadily evolved as a technique over time. The basis of PET imaging is introducing a radioactive tracer with a very short half-life into the body (through injection or inhalation), and then recording how it gets distributed in the tissue of interest. Because the radioactivity is very short-lived and used in low concentrations, PET is a safe technique to use – although precautions need to be followed concerning the handling of the radioactive materials, and the number of scans that an individual can undergo in a specified period of time. As such, whether PET is truly a 'non-invasive' technique can be debated, but at worst it is minimally invasive and it is certainly safe.

PET imaging was really the first technique that was able to localize activation in the living human brain non-invasively (that is, without surgery), with pioneering work done at Washington University in St. Louis, USA, in the 1980s. This work was a landmark in creating the field of cognitive neuroscience, and required collaboration between radiologists, physicists, and cognitive psychologists to jointly develop both the imaging technique itself, and appropriate ways of designing experiments to isolate and localize particular cognitive functions. Indeed, it was a report on this work published in *Discover* magazine in the late 1980s that prompted me, the author of the book you are reading, to pursue studying cognitive neuroscience as a career.

Clinically, PET has a number of uses. Its primary application is in oncology where it is used for diagnosis, and to assess the extent and nature of different cancers, document their progress, and track the effects of treatment on different types of cancer. PET is also used in cardiology to assess perfusion and the viability of heart muscle. In neurology it can be used in the diagnosis and characterization of epilepsy as well as brain cancers. Most recently PET has found a role in the diagnosis of dementias, including Alzheimer's disease, and in tracking the effects of treatment. Experimentally, PET can be used as a functional imaging technique as well as to assess the distribution of drugs in the brain and their actions. We will discuss these applications below, but first we will describe the fundamentals of how PET works.

WHAT ARE WE MEASURING?

PET uses ionizing radiation – radiation that has sufficient energy to liberate subatomic particles (such as electrons) from atoms. This is in contrast to non-ionizing radiation such as light, heat, radio, and microwaves. The radioactive materials used in PET imaging are called **positron-emitting radioligands** (**PERs**). These are variants of common atoms such as oxygen (O), fluorine (F), and iodine (I) that are chemically unstable because they have one more proton than they have neutrons in their nucleus (recall that an atom is composed of a nucleus of protons and neutrons – usually in equal numbers – along with a surrounding cloud of electrons). These atoms do not remain unstable for long after they are created; the imbalance in charge is resolved by one of the protons being converted to a neutron. To do this, the positive charge of the proton is released; this positively charged particle is called, quite logically, a **positron**. There are two possible fates for a positron. As it moves, it gradually loses energy through interactions with other subatomic particles, including electrons, protons, and neutrons. Ultimately, it may lose virtually all of its energy and combine with a negatively charged electron to form a particle called positronium. This is the fate of approximately one-third of positrons in the body. The other two thirds combine with an electron prior to losing all of their energy. In this case, the result of the positron–electron collision is **annihilation**, which causes a release of electromagnetic radiation in the form of a pair of **photons** (light particles), which travel in approximately 180° directions from one another. This process is shown in Figure 11.1. It is these photons that are detected and measured in PET imaging, using **coincidence detectors** that produce output when two photons are detected arriving at detectors 180° opposite each other within a very short time window (effectively, simultaneously). The proton in the original atom's nucleus, whose positive charge was ejected, becomes a neutron (since it now has zero charge), thus creating a stable nucleus; as part of this process an electron is ejected as well, to balance the overall charge of the atom.

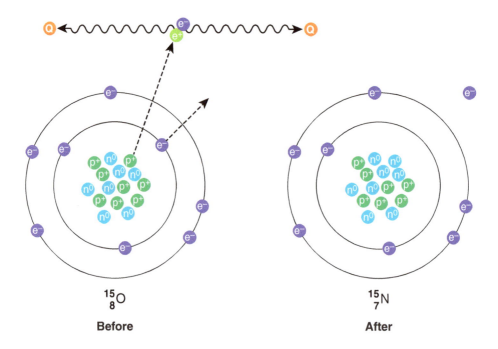

Figure 11.1 Schematic example of positron emission and subsequent annihilation. In the left panel, the atom is unstable because it has one more proton (positive charge; p⁺) than neutrons (n⁰). The instability results in the loss of one positive charge (proton), which is emitted from the nucleus as a positron (e⁺). Upon leaving the atom, the positron collides with an electron (e⁻), and both are annihilated, resulting in the formation of two photons (Q), which travel in approximately 180° directions (wiggly lines). To balance the charge of the atom, an electron is ejected as well (although this has no direct relevance to PET imaging). The right panel shows that after positron emission, the atom is converted from unstable oxygen to stable nitrogen, with one less proton and electron, and one more neutron. In the notation for oxygen (O) and nitrogen (N), the top number (mass number) indicates the total number of particles in the nucleus, while the bottom number (atomic number) indicates the number of protons

It is important to understand that while the process described above is the most common fate of a positron, other fates are possible; a number of factors contribute to uncertainty and thus limit the spatial accuracy of PET imaging. Firstly, three rather than two photons may be produced, although this occurs in less than 1% of cases. Secondly, the paths of the two photons relative to one another may vary from strictly 180°, often by half a degree or so. Thirdly, a photon may be deflected by a nearby electron – a phenomenon known as **Compton scattering** – resulting in the photon pair travelling in directions quite different from 180°. The photon may also be converted to a pair of electrons – known as **pair production** – and thus never reach a coincidence detector. A large proportion of photons are also absorbed by tissue and thus never reach a coincidence detector. Thus not all annihilation events are actually detected, and of those that are, some may be inaccurately localized because the photons do not reach rings exactly 180° opposite each other. This mislocalization is shown in Figure 11.2. Another issue limiting the accuracy of PET is that positrons travel some distance from their originating nucleus prior to annihilation. This distance varies depending on the PER, as a function of the energy inherent in the atom; atoms with higher atomic numbers (that is, more neutrons and protons) have higher energy and thus their photons typically travel farther prior to annihilation. On average, these travel distances range from approximately 1 to 6 mm, though at the maximum this can reach over 14 mm. Modern PET scanners have ways of coping with these issues to increase their accuracy; nevertheless, the physics of positron generation and photon travel impose limits on the ultimate spatial resolution and accuracy of the scanners.

HOW DO WE MEASURE IT?

Physics and Instrumentation

The basic components of a PET scanner are a bed for the subject to lie on, a set of rings of coincidence detectors, and the instrumentation involved in recording and storing the coincidence events. A contemporary commercial PET scanner is shown in Figure 11.3. In addition to the scanner, an essential part of any PET imaging centre is a **cyclotron** – a facility for making the PERs necessary for imaging. PERs necessarily have a very short half-life (the time it takes for 50% of a radioactive substance to decay), because they need to decay significantly within a short period of time once they are introduced in to the body, to ensure reasonably short-duration scans and safety of the recipient. Because of this, they cannot be stored for any significant length of time. Thus most PET scanning facilities consist of both a scanner and cyclotron facility, although in some cases PERs are shipped to the imaging centre from a cyclotron in another location, on a daily basis. An example of a cyclotron facility is shown in Figure 11.4. These requirements mean that a PET facility is very expensive to build and to maintain, and PET scans may cost two to three times more than MRI scans.

A PET scanner consists of a set of **detector rings**, each of which is composed of a number of **scintillation detectors**, arranged in a circle as shown in Figure 11.5. A typical scanner will have on the order of 40–50 detector rings; in the simplest acquisition mode each detector ring corresponds to a single slice in a PET image, although more sophisticated 3D acquisition methods allow for increased numbers of slices by combining data across rings. Because the particles emitted by positron decay are photons – light particles – the scintillation detectors are necessarily devices that are sensitive to light. They are made of crystals composed of materials that have specific properties in terms of how they react to light; in particular, they react to photons

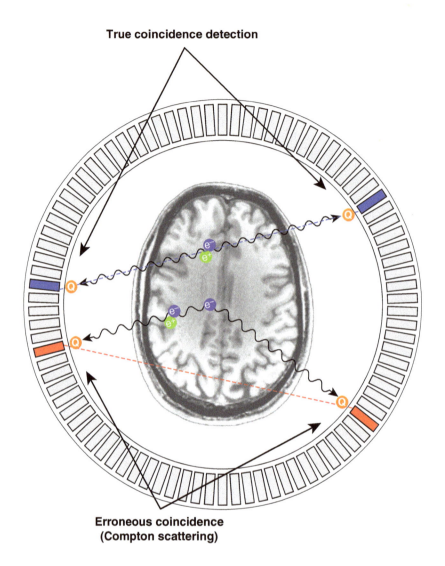

Figure 11.2 Example of how coincidence detection works, and how mislocalization can occur. Two different annihilation events are shown. In the top one, the photons are emitted at 180° angles to each other, and reach coincidence detectors along the straight line defined by their path (shown in blue). This is an accurate coincidence detection. In the bottom example, one of the photons encounters an electron along its path, and this intersection causes the path of the photon to change. Thus when the two photons from this annihilation event reach the coincidence detectors, the straight line between them (shown in red) does not intersect with the origin of the photons. This coincidence event would be mislocalized to a location along the red line

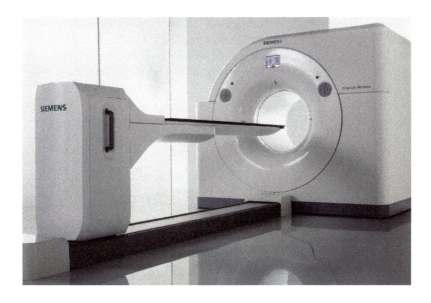

Figure 11.3 A commercial PET scanner. Like many current offerings, this model combines PET and CT imaging in one unit. The benefits of combined PET-CT imaging are discussed later in this chapter. Image copyright Siemens AG, Munich/Berlin; used with permission

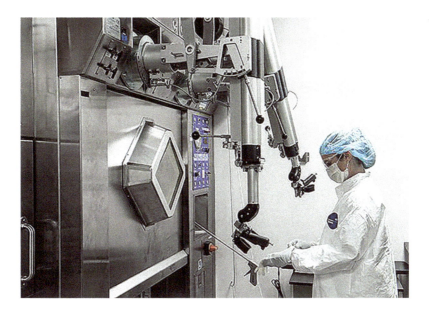

Figure 11.4 A cyclotron facility used to produce positron emitting radioligands (PERs) used in PET scanning. Radioactive materials are kept inside the heavily shielded container on the left, with the necessary apparatus for the technician to manipulate and view the process safely outside the shielding on the mechanical arms in the centre of the picture. Image used with permission of Lawson Health Research Institute, London, Ontario, Canada

having the specific energy generated by positron decay, 511 keV (kiloelectron Volts), rather than reaching to light more generally (so that PET scans do not have to be conducted in total darkness). When a scintillation detector absorbs the photons emitted by positron decay, it reacts by producing light of its own – a phenomenon known as **luminescence**.

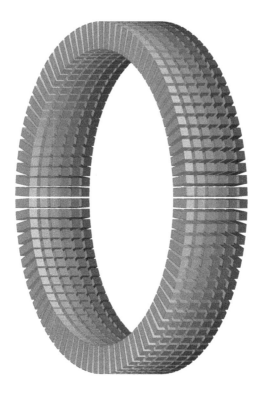

Figure 11.5 Schematic diagram of a set of six PET detector rings, each consisting of a large number of scintillation detectors (shown as small rectangles) arranged in a circle. The head of the person being scanned would be placed in the centre of these rings

Since the output of scintillation detector crystals is light, they must be connected to devices that turn light into electricity so that the data can be recorded. The devices that do this are called **photodetectors** and in PET scanners these can be one of two types: **photomultiplier tubes** (**PMTs**) or semiconductor-based **photodiodes**. Photodiodes have lower SNR and are sensitive to temperature, so generally PMTs are used, although newer generations of photodiodes are replacing these. PMTs are devices containing a series of photocathodes in a vacuum. **Photocathodes** are materials with a property that when a photon of sufficient energy reaches them, they absorb that energy and use it to release **photoelectrons**. An important property of photocathodes is that, as term 'photomultiplier' suggests, they can release more than one photoelectron for each photon received, and when a set of photocathodes are arranged in series (like a set of mirrors angled to reflect light back and forth along a path), a single photon can result in the production of a large number of photoelectrons, thus amplifying the signal before it is recorded at the end of the photomultiplier tube. A more recent alternative to PMTs are **avalanche photodiodes (APDs)**. Unlike conventional photodiodes, APDs inherently multiply the input light signal (the 'avalanche') – similar to the action of PMTs – by virtue of the photoelectric effect whereby an electron excited by the arriving photon excites other electrons. The advantages of APDs are both that they are much smaller than PMTs, and that they are not influenced by magnetic fields, while PMTs are. The latter property is important in new combined PET–MRI scanners that have been developed and released commercially in recent years (discussed later in this chapter). APDs are subject to heating, however, and therefore require additional engineering to keep them cool.

Each scintillation detector, or channel, in a PET scanner typically consists of several crystals, typically connected to a number of photodiodes. While a one-to-one coupling of crystals to PMTs is possible, in a system capable of 3D scanning of a human this would involve a very large number of electronic channels, which would make the scanner prohibitively expensive. As well, PMTs are very large so reducing their number reduces the overall size of the scanner. Clever systems have therefore been developed to allow high spatial resolution in a reduced number of channels, called **block detectors**. Each block detector consists of a grid of scintillation detector crystals (for example, 8 x 8 crystals, each approximately 4–14 mm in size) connected to a smaller number of PMTs (for example, 4) or a somewhat larger number of APDs (for example, 9, owing to their smaller size). The input from each crystal (that is, unique sensor location) is directed to all photodetectors in a uniquely weighted fashion, such that the location of the individual crystal that was excited can be recovered in post-processing. The array of photomultipliers is connected to electronics that encode and transmit the signals separately for each scintillation detector, allowing spatial resolution in each channel equivalent to the number of crystals in the array. An example of an APD-based block detector is shown in Figure 11.6.

A number of materials are available for use as the crystals in scintillation detectors; development and testing of new crystal materials is also an active area of research and development. The choice of crystal is based on a trade-off between a number of factors. These include the stopping power of the material for photons specifically of 511 keV; decay time of the luminescence; the amount of light output; and the energy resolution (how sensitive the material is to variations in photon energy level). **Stopping power** is important because greater stopping power means a greater proportion of emitted photons are detected, and thus higher signal-to-noise. **Decay time** is a critical parameter because it places limits on the temporal resolution of the scintillation detectors. This is not related to the temporal resolution of PET scanning (for example, how quickly whole-brain images can be obtained); rather it is important because the coincidence events that PET scanners are designed to detect are on the order of a few nanoseconds (ns) and a material with long decay times will be more

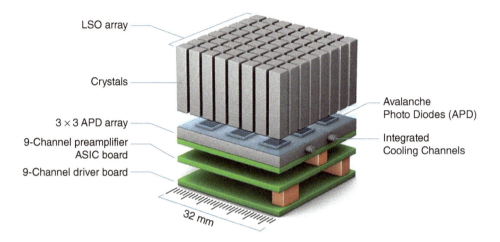

Figure 11.6 Diagram of a block detector used in PET imaging. At the top is an 8 × 8 array of detector crystals, in this example made from $Lu_2SiO_5{:}Ce$ (LSO). Below this is the array of photodetectors; this example uses APDs. Many older models use PMTs which are much larger than APDs, so this layer would be a few centimetres thick with PMTs. Note the cooling channels that are required to dissipate the heat generated by the APDs. A typical scanner might contain 128 such block detector modules in total, or 8192 individual detector elements. Image copyright Siemens AG, Munich/Berlin; used with permission

likely to record false coincidences. In contrast, a short decay time not only increases the proportion of true coincidences detected, but allows the system to record more coincidences per unit time, resulting in higher signal-to-noise ratio (SNR). **Light output** is important because this is the signal that is recorded; higher light output increases both spatial and energy resolution of the scanner. **Energy resolution** refers to how sensitive the crystal is to the energy level of the photons detected; Compton-scattered photons lose energy and so better energy resolution means that the scanner is better able to reject Compton-scattered photons and record a greater proportion of coincidence events caused by photons that travelled 180° relative to each other. A common material used in scintillation detectors is bismuth germanate, $Bi_4Ge_3O_{12}$ (BGO), due to its combination of good ability to stop photons generated by positron decay, its relatively short decay time, and good energy resolution. Other common options include lutetium oxyorthosilicate doped with cerium $Lu_2SiO_5{:}Ce$ (LSO), sodium iodide doped with thallium (NaI(Tl)), and barium fluoride (BaF_2).

Data Acquisition and Image Reconstruction

Data acquisition in PET involves detecting true coincidence events while at the same time minimizing the number of 'false alarms' caused by random events. Coincidence detection is a conceptually simple process: pairs of scintillation detectors are linked by a circuit that generates an output if, within a short time after one photon is recorded by one detector, a second photon is registered in the opposite detector. For each detector in a ring, a range of detectors opposite to it in the ring – for which a straight line between the two detectors passes through the imaging field of view – are connected by coincidence detectors. This is shown in Figure 11.7; the paths between pairs of coincidence detectors are called **lines of response**. The time window for allowable coincidence events is very short, as low as 3–4 ns. Since the bore of a PET scanner is typically about 1 m (100 cm) in diameter, and photons travel at the speed of light (3×10^8 m/s), a photon travels the entire diameter of the scanner in 3.3 ns. Depending on the timing properties of the crystals used in the scintillation detectors, the size of the coincidence window may be somewhat larger than 4 ns, but because of the time it takes for photons to travel, even crystals with more precise timing resolution cannot have coincidence windows below 3 ns.

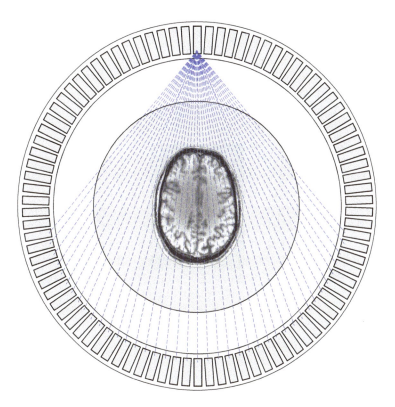

Figure 11.7 A diagram showing valid lines of response between a single block detector and other detectors in the same ring. Each blue line between a pair of detectors is a line of response. Note that not all possible pairs of detectors form valid lines of response, because lines connecting pairs that are too close together would fall outside the scanner's field of view (grey shaded area)

A coincidence detection is considered a true event if the two photons are collected within the timing window between a pair of detectors that are considered to have valid geometry (see Figure 11.7), as long as both photons have energy levels within the acceptable range. This is related to the energy resolution of the crystal material and is designed to reduce the number of false alarms triggered by Compton-scattered photons. However, random events are nevertheless prevalent in PET imaging; on average in water a photon travels 7 cm before encountering and being deflected by an electron. Since the head is somewhat denser than water, and more than 7 cm in diameter, it follows that many of the photons emitted by positron decay are Compton-scattered prior to reaching a coincidence detector. The rate of random coincidences increases as the square of the activity level of the PER in the tissue, multiplied by the coincidence window – that is, non-linearly – whereas the rate of true detections only increases linearly with activity level. This means that as activity increases, the rate of random coincidence detections goes up much faster than the rate of true detections.

Because of the high proportion of false coincidence events, measures must be taken to optimize the proportion of true events detected, while minimizing random event detections. Using a relatively narrow range of acceptable energy for detected photons (centred on 511 keV) is one step that is taken to do this, although this is in part limited by the choice of crystal material in the scintillation detectors. Another important means of improving accuracy is to estimate the rate of random-scattered events. This is typically done 'offline' (not when a person is in the scanner), using a water-filled cylinder into which the PER can be introduced to a specific location (such as a small tube through the centre of the cylinder) in a controlled fashion. Since the actual location of the PER is restricted, and known, it is easy to estimate the proportion of randomly scattered photons in the reconstructed image because these are all the photons that are localized outside of the PER-containing part of the cylinder.

One of the more interesting – and perhaps initially non-intuitive – aspects of PET imaging is how images are reconstructed. PET imaging is typically done in 2D; although the reconstructed images are three-dimensional, the 3D images are constructed from a set of 2D slices, with each slice corresponding to one detector ring. It is also possible to do 'true' 3D PET imaging, but this technique is used to improve sensitivity to activation, rather than to improve spatial resolution. We will discuss 3D PET later, but first we will describe 2D image reconstruction. Perhaps the most surprising thing about PET imaging is that the location of any individual positron decay event – the origin point of the photons that are recorded – cannot be known. All we know is that an event occurred along a particular line between two coincidence detectors, but not where along that line the event occurred. Although in principle it is possible to know this, using what is called **time of flight imaging** with a scintillation crystal that has very high temporal resolution, this is not typically done. Instead, the location of activity is estimated from the total photon counts along each line defined by pairs of coincidence detectors.

The process of reconstructing the image from lines defined by coincidence detector pairs is called **back-projection**, because lines of response are drawn back across the imaging space (field of view of the PET scanner) between coincidence detectors that detected valid photon pairs. The initial process of detecting photons is called 'projection'; back-projection image reconstruction mathematically reverses this process. One can imagine that these lines of response are drawn darker the more coincidence events were detected along that line. Since a photon pair emitted from a particular location is equally likely to reach any pair of coincidence detectors whose connecting line passes through the location of the positron decay, the back-projected image should be darker in areas where more photon emissions occurred, because more lines will cross there. This is illustrated in Figure 11.8.

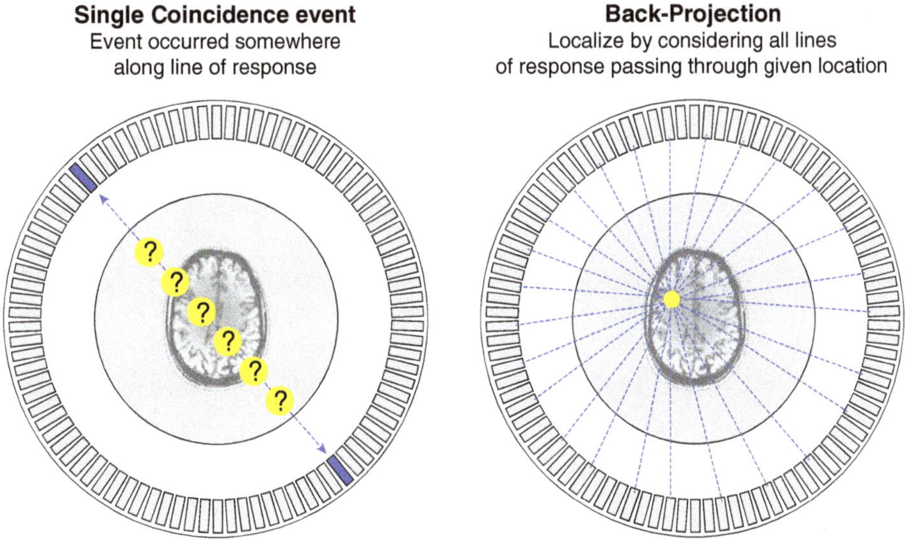

Figure 11.8 Back-projection in PET image reconstruction. A single coincidence event (left) tells us only that an annihilation event occurred somewhere along the line of response, but not where along that line. However, during image reconstruction the data from each point in the image is derived from the sum of all coincidence events that were detected along any line of response passing through that location. This is called back-projection, as the data are projected back from all of the coincidence detector pairs to the image space. This is illustrated in the right panel for a target location shown in yellow; note that, for simplicity, not all lines of response passing through the target location are shown

Because there are a limited number of coincidence detectors, a back-projected image contains blurring artifacts that would make a circular source look more like a multi-pointed star. This is because the back-projected image will be blurred along the lines of response, but not along lines that fall in between pairs of detectors. This artifact is less pronounced as the number of coincidence detectors in the scanner increases, but is nevertheless a source of artifact. To correct for this, PET images are spatially filtered during reconstruction (typically using specific types of filters such as ramp or Hanning filters). For this reason, the reconstruction process for PET images is commonly called **filtered back-projection**. Filtering prior to back-projection also corrects for another issue in image reconstruction. This is the fact that more lines of response cross through the centre of the imaging field of view than through more peripheral areas. Appropriate filtering prior to back-projection compensates for this oversampling of the centre of image space.

As noted earlier, although 2D PET imaging is sufficient to generate a 3D image by assembling a series of slices derived from each detector ring, true 3D imaging can increase sensitivity. Due to scattering and absorption of photons, PET is an inherently insensitive technique, with only approximately 0.5% of emitted photons being recorded by a detector ring in 2D imaging. Since photons are equally likely to travel in any direction, limiting acquisition to photons that travel within the plane of a single detector ring grossly undersamples the number of positron emission events that occur in the body, even ignoring all the Compton-scattered and observed photons. Thus in 3D imaging we increase the sensitivity of the PET scan by also registering coincidence events between detectors located in different detector rings. The geometry of this is shown in Figure 11.9. By allowing 3D data acquisition, sensitivity of PET imaging can be increased five- to seven-fold. However, as with 2D imaging, some parts of the 3D imaging space are oversampled relative to others; it can be seen in Figure 11.9 that more between-ring lines of response pass through the centre of the imaging space defined by the set of slices, than through parts of the head located closer to one or the other end of the set of slices. Thus a correction factor must be applied during 3D imaging reconstruction, but ultimately the gains in sensitivity are greater in the centre of the imaging volume than at its periphery.

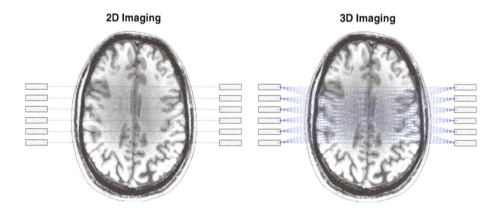

Figure 11.9 Comparison of 2D and 3D image acquisition schemes for PET. In 2D imaging, coincidence events are only detected within a single detector ring/image slice. In 3D imaging, coincidence events are detected both within a ring, and also across different rings. This increases both the spatial resolution, and the overall SNR since a much larger number of coincidence events can be detected

Positron-Emitting Radioligands (PERs)

One of the biggest strengths of PET for cognitive neuroscience is the wide range of PERs available; more than 50 PERs have been used in human brain imaging, and more are in constant development (Jones & Rabiner, 2012; Matthews, Rabiner, Passchier, & Gunn, 2012). Two of these are perhaps most familiar to cognitive neuroscientists, due to their extensive use in functional imaging, especially prior to the advent of functional MRI. The two PERs commonly used to map 'brain activation' are radio-labelled oxygen (^{15}O; note that for radioactive isotopes, the superscript number before the element name is the 'mass number', and indicates the total number of neutrons and protons in the nucleus. By convention, this mass number is specified for radioactive isotopes, and/or when distinguishing different isotopes. By this convention, 'regular', non-radioactive oxygen would be written as ^{16}O and fluorodeoxyglucose as ^{18}F or FDG). However, as we discuss below, a much wider range of PERs are available that specifically map particular receptor types or subtypes – allowing mapping of specific neuromodulator systems and activity – as well as to map other physiological markers such as β-amyloid in Alzheimer's disease.

^{15}O is the most commonly used PER for functional PET imaging because, as a form of oxygen, it is carried by the blood, crosses the blood–brain barrier, and is taken up in neural tissues in proportion to their levels of activity. Different measures can be derived using ^{15}O PET; the most common are quantifying the cerebral metabolic rate of oxygen ($CMRO_2$) and measuring rates of regional cerebral blood flow (CBF). An attraction of ^{15}O is that its half-life is only about two minutes. This means that if a person performs a particular task or experiences a particular type of sensation over the two-minute period of peak activity, after ^{15}O is administered, the distribution of positron emissions in the brain can be attributed to the effects of that task/stimulation. After a relatively short wash-out period, another dose of ^{15}O tracer can be administered under a different task/stimulation condition, without contamination of that image with residual radioactivity from the preceding scan. Further details of PET experimental design using ^{15}O are discussed later in the chapter.

In contrast, if a tracer with a longer half-life is used, then either the participant has to perform the task for longer, or a long wash-out period is required after each condition. FDG has a much longer half-life than ^{15}O (110 minutes) and so is not feasible for use in most task-related functional imaging studies. However, since it is radioactively labelled glucose – which is converted to a primary energy source in the brain – FDG can be used to examine the rates of cellular metabolism in different brain regions. This can be performed in people while they are resting, in particular to compare healthy people with different clinical populations, and to map changes that occur with development and ageing.

As noted above, PET offers many imaging possibilities beyond simply identifying areas that change in neural activity. A wide range of PERs (also known as PET tracers, ligands, or radiopharmaceuticals) are available that allow researchers and clinicians to map sites of the synthesis of different neuromodulators, as well as their receptor-binding activity. A number of PERs have been developed for imaging the dopamine system, including a dopamine precursor (^{18}F-DOPA) to track dopamine synthesis, a dopamine transporter label, and labels specific to different types of dopamine receptors, including D_1 and D_2 receptors. These have been very useful in studying diseases that affect the dopaminergic system. For example, Parkinson's disease involves the degeneration of dopamine-producing neurons, and radio-labelled dopamine tracers can reveal both rates of dopamine synthesis in the brain (indicative of the stage of the disease) as well as activity at dopamine receptors before and after treatment (which can show the efficacy of a drug in reaching its targets). An example is shown in Figure 11.10. Similarly, for serotonin there are PERs for specific serotonin receptor subtypes and serotonin transporter. PERs also exist to label opioid, nicotinic, benzodiazepine, and cannabinoid receptors, as well as enzymes that break down neuromodulators, including monoamine oxidase (MAO) and acetylcholinesterase.

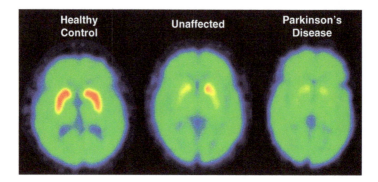

Figure 11.10 Comparison of dopamine transporter (^{18}F-DOPA) imaging in three groups. Healthy controls show high levels of dopamine in the basal ganglia (red areas). In contrast, people with Parkinson's disease (PD; right panel) show much lower levels of dopamine in the basal ganglia. In this study the PD group were carriers of a mutation of the gene LRRK2 which causes dominant inheritance of PD. The middle panel shows clinically unaffected carriers of the same LRRK2 mutation; these people had intermediate levels of dopamine transporter. Reprinted with permission of Elsevier from Stoessi, Martin, McKeown, and Sossi (2011)

PERs have also been developed to bind to particular proteins. A particularly successful example of this is Pittsburgh Compound B (PIB) which binds to β-amyloid, a protein that forms plaques in the brains of people with Alzheimer's disease and is considered one of the hallmarks of the disease. PIB has been used in many studies to map the extent of β-amyloid plaque development in people with Alzheimer's, as well as to image the effects of candidate drugs designed to reduce β-amyloid. An example of this is shown in Figure 11.11. More recently, a PER that binds to the tau protein (present in neurofibrillary tangles; the other hallmark of Alzheimer's disease) has been developed, allowing researchers to better understand the progression of Alzheimer's disease, and how it differs from healthy aging and other forms of cognitive impairment. Other clinical areas where PET imaging has been extensively used include epilepsy, schizophrenia, depression, anxiety, and cerebrovascular disease.

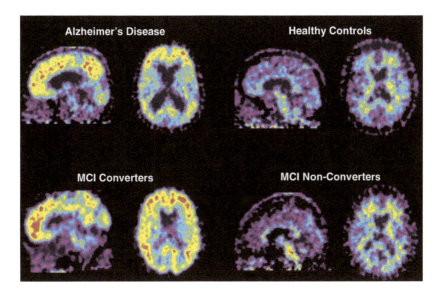

Figure 11.11 PIB (Pittsburgh Compound B) imaging of β-amyloid density in four groups of older adults. Comparing the top two groups, it is clear that there is much greater PIB binding throughout the brain in people with Alzheimer's disease (AD) than healthy, age-matched controls (red and yellow indicate the highest binding). The bottom two rows show the comparison of two groups of adults with mild cognitive impairment (MCI) who were at high risk of developing AD but did not have that diagnosis at the time of imaging. The 'MCI converters' group later developed AD (an average of eight months later) whereas the non-converters did not. The data demonstrate that those people who later developed AD had much higher levels of PIB months prior to developing AD, indicating that PIB could serve as an early marker to identify those who will develop AD. Reprinted with permission of Elsevier from Forsberg and colleagues (2008)

The development of PERs is an active area of research in drug development, because PERs can be used to image drug activity in vivo. This includes mapping whether a drug is actually taken up in its target areas; assessing the relationship between drug dosage and the amount of the drug actually taken up in tissue (since levels measured through blood draws may not reflect actual uptake); the effects of a drug on a target other than a receptor (for example using PIB to map β-amyloid levels); and downstream effects of a drug, such as glucose metabolism or neuromodulator release. The ideal characteristics of a PER include being selective for the target of interest, and having a molecular structure that allows labelling with radioisotopes that have appropriate properties (including a short half-life, and being otherwise safe for use in the human body). Selection of the PER must be made with the target in mind as well; the target should have a high affinity for binding the PER (so that the PER 'sticks' to the right places), combined with a limited capacity for binding the PER (so that binding is in proportion to the density of the target, as opposed to taking up large amounts of the PER everywhere). Extensive research is done in developing PERs, to characterize these properties along with the pharmacodynamics of the compound – such as how long it takes to reach peak concentrations in target tissue, how those concentrations relate to the dose administered, how long it takes for the PER to wash out, how it is metabolized, and so on. For neuroimaging, an additional important criterion is that the PER needs to cross the blood–brain barrier.

Radiation Safety

An obvious concern to anyone when they first learn about PET imaging is the safety of introducing radioactive compounds into the human body. Terms such as 'nuclear' and 'radiation' commonly have a negative connotation and indeed, high doses of radiation can be dangerous – the most common consequence being cancer – and even fatal. At the same time, our bodies are capable of handling small doses of radiation, and in fact we are exposed to low doses of radiation in our daily lives, including from the sun and from the Earth. Many common medical procedures other than PET involve low doses of radiation, including X-rays and CT scans. As well, certain treatments, particularly for cancer, involve higher doses of radiation directed at the cancerous tissue. In a clinical context, the exposure to radiation is considered safe and any possibility of increased risk of cancer is outweighed by the benefits of accurate diagnosis and effective treatment of serious medical conditions. However, in the context of basic research and even early-stage clinical research – when the participants are unlikely to derive any direct benefit from the exposure to radiation – the question of safety requires even more careful consideration.

As a starting point, we must be able to quantify a dose of radiation. Radiation itself is commonly measured in becquerel (Bq), where 1 Bq = 1 event of radiation emission per second. Another, related unit is the curie (Ci). The becquerel is a very small unit, whereas the curie is a very large one; 1 Ci = 3.7×10^7 Bq. However, these are rates of emission rather than strictly quantities of energy. In physics, energy quantity is typically measured in joules (J). However, the effects of radiation on the human body depend on the amount of energy absorbed by the body and by the mass of the body, and are measured in units of **gray (Gy)**, where 1 Gy = 1 J absorbed per kilogram of body weight. A further refinement of this measurement is required because different types of radiation are not equally harmful. Thus to accurately quantify the effective dose of radiation an animal is exposed to, the amount of radiation in gray must be weighted by a factor corresponding to the harmfulness of the radiation. For example, the types of radiation commonly used in medical imaging, including X-rays and gamma rays, have a weighting factor of 1, while alpha particles have a weighting of 20 because they are much more harmful to the body. Multiplying radiation dose in gray by the appropriate weighting factor results in a measurement in units of **sievert (Sv)** – which is the unit commonly used in safety guidelines.

One sievert is a substantial dose of radiation – exposure to 1 Sv in a single dose creates a risk of later developing cancer of approximately 5%, and a 10 Sv exposure is likely to lead to death within days or weeks. Safe levels of exposure are thus measured in fractions of a sievert. Although official safety guidelines vary by country and industry, a commonly used guideline developed by the American Conference of Governmental Industrial Hygienists specifies 20 mSv (thousandths of a sievert) as the **threshold limit value (TLV)** per year for people who work around radiation (including X-ray technicians, people in labs where radiation is used, nuclear power plants, etc.), with a further restriction of a total cumulative exposure of 50 mSv over a five-year period. The recommended TLV for the general public specified by the International Commission on Radiological Protection is 1 mSv; however, many people are exposed to higher levels than this simply from the radioactive 'background' of their daily lives, including the sun (especially during air travel, where the thinner atmosphere at higher altitudes provides less protection from radiation from outer space), and the earth (for example, radon gas is common in many homes). Average background exposure may be in the order of 2.5 mSv per year.

In medical imaging, two important concepts related to radiation exposure are the equivalent dose and the effective dose. **Equivalent dose** reflects the fact that not all tissues in the body are equally affected by radiation; **effective dose** is the sum of the equivalent doses of the various organs of the body. For example, the testes and ovaries are most affected (accounting for 20% of the effects of radiation), with the lungs, colon, bone marrow, and stomach being the next-most affected tissue types (12% each). The limits specified in the previous paragraph are the effective dose limits; separate limits can be specified for different parts of the body depending on their susceptibility. For example, the limit for the lens of the eye is lower than for the hands or feet. In assessing the effects of a PER administered during a PET scan, it is thus important to be able to quantify the distribution of the PER in the body, as well as knowing its half-life so that the total dose over time can be estimated. Recognition of the uneven effects of radiation on the body can inform administration strategies. For example, since the lungs are particularly susceptible, injecting ^{15}O may be preferable to inhaling it; the effects of PERs on the bladder (where ultimately the PERs are concentrated to void from the body as urine) can be reduced by having people drink lots of water and urinate frequently.

In adult PET scans, effective doses of radiation can range from 5 to 30 mSv, while in paediatric studies the effective doses may be much higher due to the lower mass of a child – in some cases coming close to 100 mSv even though the actual quantity of PER may be lower than for an adult. While these levels are well in excess of what is considered safe for occupational exposure, the risks in these cases are considered to outweigh the harms since the people receiving these doses typically have cancer and would most likely die (or die sooner) without the PET scans. In research studies where the participant will not benefit from the PET scan, more conservative limits are imposed. A typical research PET scan involves an exposure of 7–8 mSv which, while still above the recommendation for the general public, is well below what is considered safe for people working around radiation. However, a person should undergo at most only two to three such scans per year so as to keep the cumulative dose within safe limits.

It is also important to recognize that the radiation used in PET imaging poses a potential risk to the researchers and staff conducting the imaging, and so appropriate safety protocols must be in place at the PET facility. These include how the PERs are handled and how materials such as syringes are disposed of, as well as how long anyone stands near a participant following PER administration, as radioactivity from an injected person can affect those standing within 1 m of that person. While these incidental levels of exposure are comparatively low (on the order of µSv, or thousandths of a mSv), over time their cumulative effects on people working routinely in these environments should not be overlooked. In summary, it is important to recognize that PET scanning, when done in the context of appropriate safety guidelines, is very safe and does not pose significantly increased health risks to either the person being scanned, nor the staff involved in the scanning. At the same time, understanding radiation safety is critical and anyone engaging in PET research should be properly trained.

EXPERIMENTAL DESIGN

Designs for functional PET imaging should follow the general guidelines for good experimental design discussed in previous chapters. A significant limitation of PET, however, is that it has such poor temporal resolution. Using ^{15}O imaging, a single scan takes approximately 90 s to acquire. During this period, the participant should be 'on task' the entire time, and should only be performing a single task or seeing a particular kind of stimuli or experimental condition, since the scan results will reflect cumulative brain activity over this entire 90 s period of time. This creates challenges because in many experimental designs, alternating conditions and unpredictability of the stimuli are essential. For example, in a typical 'oddball' paradigm that would elicit a P3 ERP component, a series of standard stimuli are punctuated at unpredictable intervals by an occasional deviant stimulus, which evokes the P3. Brain activity summed over a 90 s scan in this paradigm would not allow us to distinguish activity between standard and deviant trials. In many other paradigms – even if occasional, unpredictable stimuli are not central to the task – we are interested in comparing the brain responses between different conditions and some level of unpredictability is necessary. This is because virtually any stimulus that is repeated multiple times or in a predictable pattern will lead to behavioural habituation and neural adaptation. 'Habituation' is defined as a decrease in response to a stimulus with repetition; more pertinent to a discussion of measuring brain activity is **adaptation**, which is a decrease in neural response with repeated/predictable stimuli. Adaptation is an inherent property of the brain that allows neurons to code information – news of differences in the environment – by not responding strongly to things that are constant. However, in neuroimaging experiments, adaptation is typically something to be avoided as it makes the target neural responses more difficult to detect.

The temporal constraint on PET is one of several reasons why fMRI replaced it as the dominant, high spatial resolution imaging technique in cognitive neuroscience (along with lower cost and no concerns about radiation). However, several clever designs were developed as attempts to overcome the temporal limitations of PET. For example, one can employ a parametric factorial design in which the level of a certain variable is systematically varied over scans, and then areas whose activity is correspondingly modulated with this variation are looked for. For example, in an oddball paradigm, during each scan a series of standard stimuli could be presented, alternating with deviant stimuli. Critically however, the number of deviant stimuli would be varied across the scans: in one scan, perhaps 10% of stimuli would be deviants, in another 20%, and in another 30%. Control scans containing no deviants could also be included. The expectation would be that areas of the brain that specifically responded to deviant stimuli would show a systematic increase in activation from the 0% to the 30% deviant scans. A similar design was employed in an influential, early PET study on language processing, which examined the effects of speech rate on brain activity in different regions of the temporal lobe (Price et al., 1992). Superior temporal lobe regions in and around primary auditory cortex showed a linear increase in activity as the rate of speech (words per minute) was increased. In contrast, activity in the temporal-parietal junction (classically termed Wernicke's area, and thought to be associated with accessing word meanings) remained constant across speech rates, though it showed greater activity to all speech conditions than to a non-linguistic control condition. The authors were thus able to demonstrate a distinction between sensory regions that were sensitive to physical features of the stimuli, and 'cognitive' regions sensitive to the content irrespective of irrelevant physical properties.

In many other applications of PET, experimental design is much simpler. Often the goal of the study is to compare activity of a particular neuromodulator system between groups. For example, contrasting people with a particular clinical diagnosis versus healthy controls, or examining a patient group over time to study disease progression or the effects of a treatment. In these cases, scans are typically done while the participants are simply lying awake in the scanner with no particular task (that is, resting state scans, similar to rs-fMRI). In other cases it might be of interest to examine neuromodulator activity between different experimental conditions. However, many PERs have sufficiently long half-lives that each scan is necessarily tens of minutes in duration – and with long washout periods required between scans – which precludes including multiple experimental conditions in a scanning session.

On the other hand, depending on the experimental design this may not be a problem. For example, Koepp and colleagues (Koepp, Gunn, Lawrence, & Cunningham, 1998) compared two, 50 min PET scans – one during which subjects played a simple but challenging video game, and the other in which they simply rested quietly. Participants were informed that after the scans they would be paid an amount based on their score in the video game, thus increasing the stakes and expected reward derived from playing. The PER used was raclopride ([^{11}C]RAC), which binds dopamine type-2 (D_2) receptors. This was chosen because dopamine is known to be involved in neuronal reward systems. As shown in Figure 11.12 [¹¹C]RAC binding was reduced in the striatum (basal ganglia – an area known to be involved in reward processing and learning) during video-game playing compared to rest, and was lower in people who scored highest in the video game. This demonstrated that video-game playing – and indeed, performance in the game – was related to endogenous dopamine release; greater levels of self-produced dopamine resulted in fewer available receptors for the externally administered dopamine marker to bind to. (This may seem counter-intuitive at first, but the [¹¹C]RAC competes with endogenous dopamine at the receptors, so uptake levels of the PER are inversely proportional to endogenous dopamine levels.) Each scan had to be 50 min long due to the half-life of [¹¹C]RAC, although during each 50 min scan the researchers were able to obtain multiple measurements of PER levels, as seen in Figure 11.12. This experimental design worked around the necessity of these long scans for each condition by using a single task that was engaging for participants for that period of time (playing a video game), and a research question that centred around relatively long-duration states rather than brain activity associated with transient events. Nevertheless, because the within-subjects experimental design required scanning each person under both rest and video game conditions, each participant had to undergo two separate scans on separate days.

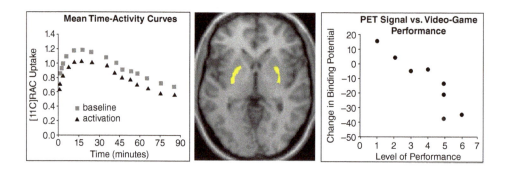

Figure 11.12 Data from Koepp and colleagues (Koepp et al., 1998) comparing raclopride ([¹¹C]RAC) uptake in the left ventral striatum in two 50 min experimental conditions: a baseline condition during which participants performed no task, and a condition in which participants played a video game in which a higher score resulted in a higher cash payment at the end of the study. [¹¹C]RAC binds to dopamine D_2 receptors, which are involved in reward processing. Decreased [¹¹C]RAC binding reflects higher levels of intrinsic dopamine, so the left panel of the figure demonstrates greater dopamine release during video game playing. The right panel shows that the video-game–baseline difference in [¹¹C]RAC binding was greatest in people who scored highest on the video game. The middle panel shows the location of the changes in [¹¹C]RAC binding in the basal ganglia - an area known to be involved in reward processing and learning. Centre image copyright Nature Publishing Group and reproduced with permission; data plots adapted from Koepp and colleagues (1998)

Another interesting recent application of PET to cognitive neuroscience involves comparing neuromodulator activity between healthy individuals who vary along a continuum of some trait, such as personality traits. For example – again investigating the dopaminergic reward system – multiple studies have shown an association between dopamine levels and traits such as impulsivity and novelty-seeking (Bernow et al., 2011; Leyton, 2002; Oswald et al., 2007; Zald et al., 2008).

Improving Temporal Resolution

Multimodal neuroimaging involving PET is an emerging area of research. One interesting example of this builds on the field of resting state fMRI (rs-fMRI), discussed earlier in this book. This paradigm has garnered great interest over the past decade and more, because it allows comparison of brain activity in the absence of any stimuli or task, which allows researchers to avoid confounds present in task-related fMRI when comparing between groups of people who may perform the task differently, or with different levels of difficulty or success. It also allows us to investigate interactions between brain areas – functional connectivity – to gain a better understanding of neural networks rather than the neb-phrenological approach of looking at activity within individual regions. Although functional connectivity can be examined under task conditions as well, rs-fMRI is where much of this approach was developed and remains an active area of research.

However, rs-fMRI has also generated controversy precisely because no task is involved. Thus we cannot be certain what people are doing during these scans, though there is inevitably a high degree of individual variability. Moreover, because we do not fully understand the physiological mechanisms relating the BOLD fMRI response to neuronal activity, we do not really understand what changes, neurophysiologically, when the strength of a correlation between two brain areas as measured by fMRI changes. Passow and colleagues (Passow et al., 2015) sought to understand better the nature of the resting state by using fMRI and FDG PET with the same group of participants, to relate BOLD fMRI measures with rates of glucose metabolism. Although numerous previous studies had compared fMRI and functional PET scans within the same groups of individuals, what was most interesting about this study is that the authors developed a novel approach to PET that allowed for greater temporal resolution using FDG than had previously been obtained. Participants underwent an MRI scan, including a 7.5 min resting state fMRI scan, followed immediately on the same day by a PET scan, which included a 60 min resting state FDG scan. Critically however, the authors developed a novel technique in which the PET images were reconstructed as a set of 12 separate images, each 5 min in duration – rather than as a single 60 minute scan. This allowed the authors to examine correlations in the fluctuations in FDG activity over time, between different brain regions – comparable to a typical rs-fMRI analysis, albeit over a time scale roughly ten times as long. The results of this analysis demonstrated that the activity of a very similar set of brain areas showed correlated BOLD fMRI and FDG PET signals. This in turn supported the contention that the correlations observed in rs-fMRI reflect changes in cerebral metabolism, allaying concerns that rs-fMRI might merely reflect correlated changes in blood flow unrelated to actual brain activity.

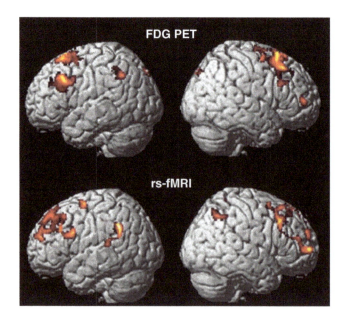

Figure 11.13 Functional connectivity maps obtained from the same group of people, scanned with FDG PET and resting state fMRI (rs-fMRI). Red/yellow areas are those showing significant correlations in signal over time with a 'seed' location in the posterior cingulate cortex. The data show highly similar spatial patterns from the two imaging modalities, suggesting that rs-fMRI reflects correlations in metabolic activity between brain areas. Excerpted from Passow and colleagues (2015), licensed under Creative Commons CC BY-NC-ND 4.0

DATA ANALYSIS

Data analysis of functional PET images shares many similarities with fMRI analysis, but is in some ways less complex. Functional PET data are not time series (the study described in the previous section being a notable exception). Rather, each scan integrates measurements over a specific period of time (for example, 90 s for ^{15}O PET or 20–60 min for ^{18}F fluorodeoxyglucose PET) and in ^{15}O PET typically multiple scans are acquired in each of several conditions – at least, a baseline and an experimental condition).

As with fMRI, data need to be motion-corrected, although again because the scans are not time series, this is simpler. An average of all the individual scans can be created, and each individual scan realigned to that using the same linear registration methods used for fMRI. Since PET scans are not sensitive to contrast in the brain that is relevant to anatomical description (such as between grey matter, white matter, and CSF), on their own PET scans cannot be very accurately aligned to a standard template such as the MNI152 average brain. Ideally, a structural MR image from each individual will be obtained and this would be used in registration – the PET images can be registered to the structural MR image, and the MRI can be used for spatial normalization to allow warping of each individual's functional data to a standard MRI template. Failing this, many modern PET systems are actually combined PET–CT scanners and so a CT scan can be obtained in the same session as the PET scans. While CT does not offer the same level of resolution or grey–white-matter contrast as structural MRI, it yields good quality anatomical images that can improve the quality of the registration. Spatial smoothing is also applied to PET images, typically using a Gaussian kernel as with fMRI; however, since the inherent spatial resolution of PET is somewhat lower than for fMRI, the smoothing kernel will in general be larger (perhaps 10–12 mm).

One preprocessing step that is recommended for PET (but not fMRI) is grand mean scaling, where the values in each image are normalized by dividing them by the mean values for that image, then multiplied by 100. This results in the mean activity in each scan having the same value of 100. This is done because the overall tracer levels may vary from scan to scan; for example, typically all the PER used in a scanning session is prepared at one time, and so over the course of the session the radioactivity is continuously degrading. Thus the level of PER activity in the sample injected in the last scan of the session will be lower than that injected in the first scan. In comparing a set of scans from one experimental condition with those of another, if there happened to be overall higher tracer levels in the scans from one condition, this could bias the results. Grand mean scaling (or 'global normalization') serves to counter this potential bias. Statistical analysis of PET images typically involves a repeated-measures ANOVA design, since multiple measurements (scans) are typically made for each experimental condition.

MULTIMODAL PET

While PET scanning on its own can be valuable, the unique properties of PET can also be combined with other imaging techniques to increase its power. In particular, it is now quite standard for scanners to be combined PET/CT scanners, rather than solely PET. This is a natural fit, because CT involves the use of X-rays and the two technologies not only co-exist without technical interference, but CT actually improves the quality of PET scans. More recently, combined PET–MRI scanners have been developed. Although these are not widely available at this time, they represent an important step forward and are likely to become the clinical standard in the future, enabling both improved clinical applications and a new range of research applications combining the strengths of each of these techniques.

PET-CT

Computerized tomography (CT, also known as computerized axiom tomography, or 'CAT scans') is an imaging modality based on X-rays. While conventional X-ray images produce only a single two-dimensional image taken from a single perspective, CT scanners incorporate an X-ray device that rotates around the person being scanned, acquiring many images from different angles and then using computer algorithms to create higher-resolution, 2D or 3D images from these. Clinical CT was developed beginning in the 1960s and first became available in the 1970s, and has since become a mainstay of diagnostic imaging for the head as well as other organs. Contrast in CT images is based on the ability of different types of tissue to block X-rays. It is sensitive to contrast between bone, fat, and water; however, its soft tissue contrast (for example, between grey and white matter and CSF) and spatial resolution are inferior to that of MRI. Therefore, a CT scan of the head does not allow visualization of gyral and sulcal anatomy with the same precision as structural MRI. It is, however, very useful in diagnosing different types of stroke (for example, haemorrhagic – bleeding – vs. ischaemic – caused by clotting), tumours, and other pathologies in the brain, and provides much more anatomical precision than PET alone.

Combining CT with PET was a natural and logical technical development, as both rely on radiation detection (albeit different types of radiation), and there are clinical advantages to doing both scans at the same time. For one, accurate PET scanning requires **attenuation correction**, which compensates for the fact that different tissues absorb PERs differently (especially bone). CT scans provide ideal information for PET attenuation correction, especially if the scans are obtained without the patient moving (that is, in the same scanner). In a PET-only scanner, a 'transmission scan' is required to perform attenuation correction, which takes much longer than a CT scan, and so PET–CT scanners shorten the overall required duration of a PET scan.

The second advantage of combined PET–CT is for spatial registration of the images. If the PET scan is performed alone, and an anatomical CT or MRI scan is performed in a different scanner at different times, there is greater potential for inaccuracies when later registering the images. A CT scan obtained at the same time as the PET scan, with the person in the same position, facilitates anatomical registration. Combined PET–CT also saves time and money, because a CT scan only takes a few minutes to perform, and so it is far more efficient to do this at the same time as the PET scan, rather than scheduling a separate appointment for a CT scan on a different scanner. Since PET scans are sensitive to PER distribution rather than contrast that is relevant to anatomical localization, they provide poor anatomical information. For example, if the PER is hardly taken up around the outside edges of the brain, then it can be hard to even determine the shape or spatial extent of the brain in a PET scan – which obviously makes localization of activity more challenging. A CT scan can facilitate more accurate localization of PET data. Although an anatomical MRI can provide much better anatomical localization, this could add significantly to the cost of the study, whereas including a CT scan within the PET protocol adds very little cost. Even if an MRI scan is obtained, registering the MRI to the PET scan is facilitated if there is an anatomical CT scan available that was acquired with the person in the same position as when the PET scans were obtained.

PET-MRI

One of the most exciting developments in functional imaging is the emergence of combined PET–MRI scanners, such as the one shown in Figure 11.14. While PET–CT offers some advantages over PET alone, MRI offers many advantages over CT. For one, MRI produces much higher-resolution anatomical images and can be tuned to a variety of different contrasts. Thus a combined PET–MRI scan can yield (in addition to the functional PET data) high-resolution T1-weighted anatomical images, images with other weighting such as T2 that may be useful in localizing pathology (for example, tumours), MR spectroscopy, diffusion-weighted images, and even fMRI. Also, unlike PET–CT, where the two types of images must be acquired sequentially, PET–MRI scanners can obtain both types of image simultaneously. This is obviously very efficient, and means that during a PET scan (which can be quite lengthy, on the order of 30–90 minutes for some PERs) a whole range of MRI scans can also be obtained. Clearly this is both a good use of time and money, and also facilitates anatomical localization of the PET images. As with combined PET–CT, PET–MRI also facilitates attenuation correction, although the process is less straightforward

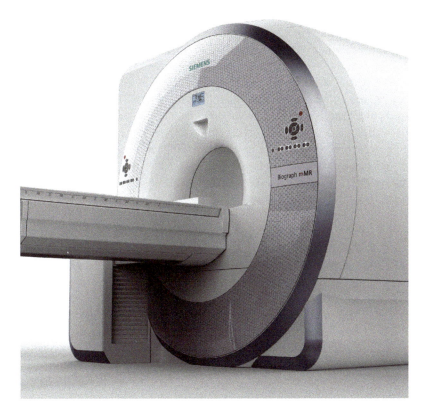

Figure 11.14 A PET-MRI scanner that allows PET and 3T MRI imaging in a single unit. Image copyright Siemens AG, Munich/Berlin; used with permission

and (at least at present) less accurate. It is nonetheless possible and this technology is an active area of research and development.

Combined PET–MRI has several other advantages that can improve the quality of both the PET and MRI scans. One limitation of PET is the **partial volume effect**, which is caused by its limited spatial resolution. Some anatomical structures are smaller than the resolution of a PET scan (which is on the order of 3–5 mm), and as well the grid of PET voxels usually does not align perfectly with the borders between anatomical structures. Thus data from PET voxels often contains a heterogeneous combination of tissue types or anatomical structures, which limits the precision with which PET signals can be localized or assigned to a particular anatomical region. MRI scans can be used to segment the tissue into different types, and improve the spatial precision of PET. Another feature of combined PET–MRI that improves the quality of PET scans is motion correction. PET scans take extended periods of time, during which some motion on the part of the participant is inevitable. If an MRI scan is conducted at the same time that has relatively high temporal resolution (for example, an EPI scan), then conventional MRI motion correction techniques can be applied to the MRI data, and the motion vectors derived from this (that is, the amount and direction of motion estimated over time) can be applied to the PET data. This improves both the spatial precision of the PET scans, and the quality of the attenuation correction.

PET–MRI can improve the quality of PET scans by aiding in quantification. Accurate reconstruction of PET scans depends on time-activity curves that are based both on the pharmacokinetics of the PERs (that is, how the PERs are absorbed and how they break down), but also on the rate and volume of blood flow through the tissues that are being scanned. In conventional PET this can be done by invasive methods such as cannulating the participant (placing a measurement tube in an artery or vein); however, with MRI, non-invasive techniques are available, including time-of-flight MRI angiography to map the blood vessels and to measure actual rates of blood flow through the vessels. Another means of improving the accuracy of PET quantification is by including a combined PET–MRI scan of the trunk of the body, prior to the brain scan. Although this adds time to the scan, it improves the estimation of PER uptake. This is because while uptake is generally estimated based on body mass alone, uptake in fat is considerably less than in other tissue types. The PET–MRI body scan allows estimation of lean body mass – as distinct from the mass of fat in the body – and thus more accurate uptake estimates.

PET–MRI can also be used to test and validate new imaging techniques. For example, new MRI methods have recently been developed to measure iron in the brain as a proxy for β-amyloid deposits, which can be validated using a PER such as PIB which is sensitive to β-amyloid density (recall that β-amyloid is a hallmark of Alzheimer's disease). PET–MRI also has a larger role in the imaging of dementia, as each technique on its own offers some unique diagnostic abilities. For example, recent studies have combined resting state fMRI and DTI with PIB PET to gain a better understanding of how β-amyloid deposits relate to functional changes seen in AD, showing a decrease in functional connectivity for areas with β-amyloid deposits (Myers et al., 2014).

PET–MRI offers great potential for new insights and clinical applications in many areas, including oncology, epilepsy, vascular disorders, as well as in basic research. The ability to simultaneously obtain fMRI data and measure activity of particular neuromodulator systems will allow us greater insight into the functioning of the healthy brain, disease mechanisms, and the effects of pharmaceutical agents. While the advent of fMRI largely displaced PET as a routine functional imaging technique, combined PET–MRI opens the door to using fMRI for localizing changes in neural activity with high spatial and relatively high temporal resolution, while simultaneously leveraging the unique capabilities of PET for molecular imaging of physiological markers that MRI is incapable of detecting.

At the same time, it must be realized that combined PET–MRI is a much more expensive and technically challenging enterprise than using either technique on its own. Firstly, the cost of a combined PET–MRI scanner is very high since each is distinct and expensive technology on its own and combining the two presents additional engineering challenges. Secondly, running PET and MRI scans rely on almost entirely different sets of skills and knowledge. PET technicians must be trained to safely handle and administer radioactive materials, and understand how to work with the critical time constraints imposed by the rapid breakdown of PERs. In contrast, MRI technicians must be educated in MRI safety, as well as having a detailed understanding of MRI physics, the applications of the many different types of MRI pulse sequences, and how to adjust the parameters of each of these sequences to the needs of the scan. As a consequence, at least at the present time few people have the proper training to act as combined PET–MRI technicians, and so a pair of technicians is required to run simultaneous scans. In clinical settings, PET and MRI scans are interpreted by different medical specialties – nuclear medicine and radiology respectively – and so combined scans require additional professional expertise and collaboration as well. Likewise, the technical demands of processing and analysing PET and MRI data are very different so not only do researchers need far more training than if they were to use only one type of imaging modality, but they may need to have additional expertise to figure out how best to combine the data types. At present, no mainstream software is available that is designed to combine PET and MRI data for research applications. Thus while PET–MRI holds immense promise, it is also one of the most advanced and technically challenging areas of research at this time.

SUMMARY

PET imaging is unique among the neuroimaging techniques covered in this book, both in that it is mildly invasive (to the extent that radiation is used, albeit at safe levels), and in that it offers the ability to image a wide range of biochemical markers beyond those indexing neuronal activity. PET requires PERs, which are characterized by chemical instability that results in radioactive emission of positrons. Positrons are annihilated when they meet electrons, resulting in creation of a pair of photons that are detected by scintillation detectors arranged in

rings around the person being scanned. The vast majority of annihilation events do not result in both photons of a pair reaching the detector rings, for reasons including that they disperse in other directions, or are scattered, or absorbed by tissue. For these reasons, to gain sufficient signal-to-noise ratio PET scans involve accumulating photon coincidence events over time, typically several minutes to an hour. Accumulating coincidence events over time is also necessary for accurately estimating the PER concentration in any given brain region (or voxel in the image), because a coincidence event along a particular line of response does not tell us where along that line the positron originated. To reconstruct a PET image, a method called filtered back-projection is used. This considers, for each voxel in the image, all the coincidence events along lines of response passing through that voxel; filtering is used to account for the inherent spacing between individual lines of response that is imposed by the spacing of the scintillation detector crystals in the detector ring.

As well as the need to accumulate sufficient coincidence events to obtain good SNR, an additional limitation on the temporal resolution of PET is that the PER takes time to be flushed from the body, limiting how quickly one scan can follow another. This, along with safety limits on radioactive exposure, limits how many scans an individual can have in a given session, or in a year. For this reason cognitive neuroscience experiments involving PET must block conditions into relatively long time periods, rating from 90 s (for ^{15}O measures of cerebral blood flow) to an hour (for ^{18}FDG measures of glucose metabolism). PERs can be developed for a wide range of biochemical targets. These include indirect markers of neural activity like cerebral blood flow or glucose metabolism, neuromodulators like dopamine and serotonin, and disease markers like β-amyloid.

Although PET has some significant limitations relative to fMRI – including much lower temporal resolution, moderately lower spatial resolution, and the need to use radioactivity – it has some advantages as well. These include the ability to image neuromodulator concentrations and disease markers, as well as the fact that there is no magnetic field or RF energy that, in MRI, precludes scanning people with some implanted devices such as cochlear implants. An exciting recent technical advance is scanners that combine PET and MRI in a single unit. These open up possibilities of simultaneous multimodal neuroimaging that could provide greater insight into functional brain activation, as well as enhanced understanding of the physiological processes underlying the fMRI BOLD response.

THINGS YOU SHOULD KNOW

- The PET signal is created by radioactive decay of atoms that are unstable due to having one more proton than neutrons. Such atoms stabilize by converting one proton to a neutron, emitting a positron in the process. Positrons travel a short distance before encountering an electron and being annihilated, resulting in the formation of a pair of photons which travel in opposite directions at the speed of light.

- PET scanners detect and localize these positrons through scintillation detectors tuned to the photons emitted by positron annihilation. PET scanners consist of a number of detector rings; the number of these determines the number of slices the PET image can contain. Coincidence detectors are used to identify pairs of photons that arrive simultaneously at two detectors along a line of response passing through the tissue. Since the origin of the photon could be anywhere along that line of response, PET data must be reconstructed through back-projection. This involves computing, for each location in the image volume, the number of detections occurring along lines of response passing through that location. This can be done exclusively within each detector ring, for 2D imaging, or across rings for 3D imaging.

- The radioactive substances introduced into the body for PET imaging are called positron-emitting radioligands (PERs). These generally involve a chemically unstable atom bound to a molecule of physiological interest, such as oxygen or glucose. PERs have a short half-life and therefore must be synthesized in a cyclotron shortly before use. Common PERs for functional imaging include oxygen (^{15}O, for measuring cerebral blow flow or oxygen metabolism) and fluorodeoxyglucose (^{18}FDG, for measuring glucose metabolism). As well, a number of PERs are used to trace specific neuromodulator systems, including ^{18}F-DOPA for dopamine, or markers of specific diseases, such as Pittsburgh Compound B (PIB) which binds to β-amyloid, a hallmark of Alzheimer's disease.

- Because PET uses radioactive tracers, there is the potential for harmful levels of radiation exposure when working with PET or having a PET scan. The amount of radiation exposure associated with an adult receiving an individual PET scan is higher than recommended for incidental exposure by the general public, but well within the ranges considered safe for people who work around radiation. The risks of PET are mitigated by safety standards that ensure safe handling of PERs, and limit the number of PET scans that a person can receive in a year.

- The time required for a single PET scan is determined by the PER being used – both by how long it takes to accumulate in the tissue of interest, and how long it takes to degrade or be flushed out by the body. Studies using ^{15}O require approximately 90 s per scan, while ^{18}FDG studies take approximately 20–60 min. This limits the types of cognitive neuroscience experiments that can be performed with PET, since participants must perform a single task/experimental condition for the duration of a scan. Recent technical advances have allowed researchers to obtain measurements at multiple time points during long scans, allowing for some improvement in temporal resolution.

- While fMRI has largely supplanted PET in cognitive neuroscience research, PET nevertheless has some unique capabilities. Most notably, the ability to synthesize PERs for many different physiologically relevant compounds allows for direct imaging of different neuromodulator systems and disease markers, which is not possible with fMRI. Because PET does not use radio waves or magnetic fields, it is also safe and feasible for use with people who would typically be excluded from fMRI, such as cochlear implant users. As well, PET is completely silent, whereas fMRI creates very loud acoustic noise, so some studies of auditory processing may benefit from PET.

- PET scanners often integrate CT scanners, which are based on X-rays. This combination allows for improved quality and accuracy of the PET scans through attenuation correction, as well as improved spatial registration and anatomical localization. A recent advance is combined PET–MRI scanners, which have several advantages. These include improved spatial localization, accuracy in quantifying PER concentrations, and simultaneous acquisition of fMRI and PET-based neuromodulator concentration measures – creating the ability to relate fMRI BOLD signal to more direct and specific indices of neural activity.

FURTHER READINGS

Bailey, D.L., Townsend, D.W., Valk, P.E., & Maisey, M.N. (Eds.) (2005). *Positron Emission Tomography: Basic Sciences*. London: Springer-Verlag.

Granov, A., Tiutin, L., & Schwarz, T. (2013). *Positron Emission Tomography*. Berlin: Springer Science & Business Media.

12 Near-Infrared Optical Imaging (fNIRI)

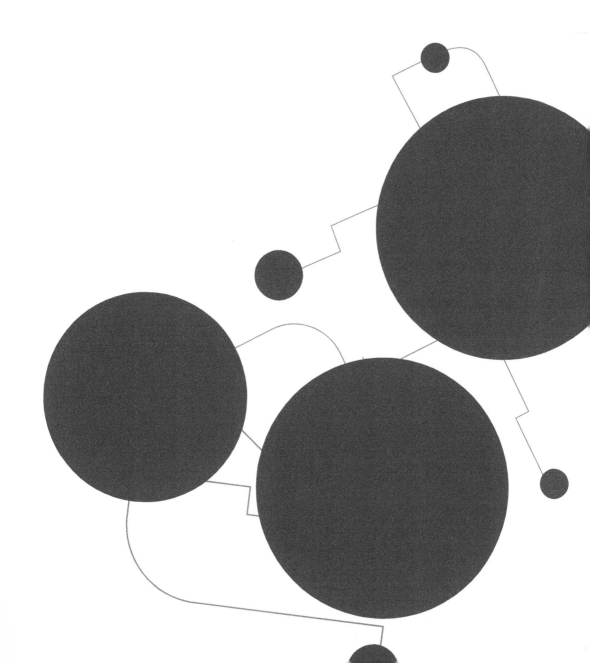

LEARNING OBJECTIVES

After reading this chapter, you should be able to:

- Explain how the concentration of a substance can be determined using spectrophotometry, and how this principle is applied in fNIRI.
- Distinguish between the fast and slow optical signals, and what each measures.
- Describe the basic hardware necessary for fNIRI.
- Explain why multiple wavelengths of light are required for fNIRI, and the costs and benefits of using more than two wavelengths.
- Describe common sources of noise in fNIRI.
- Explain the limitations on spatial and temporal resolution in fNIRI.
- Compare and contrast the three ways of measuring fNIRI signal.
- Describe the preprocessing steps typically employed for fNIRI data.
- Discuss how fNIRI can be combined with other imaging techniques.

INTRODUCTION

Optical imaging involves shining light on biological tissue and measuring what is reflected back. For neuroimaging there are invasive forms of optical imaging, which require exposing the surface of the cortex, as well as non-invasive forms which involve shining light through the skull. The invasive approach is commonly used in animal studies, although it has been used in human neurosurgical settings as well (Pouratian, Sheth, Martin, & Toga, 2003). This chapter will focus exclusively on the non-invasive techniques. The origins of optical imaging are in the field of analytical chemistry, where **spectrophotometry** was developed as a way of measuring the concentration of a compound in a solution. Its application to biological tissue can be traced back to World War II, when Glen Millikan first demonstrated that quantitative measurements of light transmission were sensitive to the oxygenation of blood and muscle (Chance, 1991). This discovery led to ongoing development of the technique, which has many modern applications. A very common one is pulse oximeters used in hospitals, which clip on to the finger and use light to measure pulse and oxygen levels in the blood; some modern 'smart watches' likewise use light to measure heart rate. Non-invasive optical imaging of the brain was first demonstrated by Frans Jöbsis, who reported measurements of haemoglobin oxygenation in the brain using near-infrared (NIR) light in 1977 (Jöbsis, 1977). Jöbsis determined that the skull was quite transparent to light in the NIR range, allowing for non-invasive measurements of the brain. This work stimulated further research on the topic, and the development of novel technologies for neural NIR measurements throughout the 1980s and early 1990s. Throughout the 1980s, the research was largely focused on developing and validating NIR imaging (NIRI) as a method of measuring blood oxygenation in the brain. In the early 1990s, the first functional (fNIRI) studies were published, attracting the interest of cognitive neuroscientists interested in non-invasive functional brain imaging techniques. Much like the early development of fMRI – in which three independent research groups published the first papers demonstrating the technique in the same year – the first fNIRI were published in 1993 by four different groups (Chance, Zhuang, UnAh, Alter, & Lipton, 1993; Kato, Kamei, Takashima, & Ozaki, 1993; Okada, Tokumitsu, Hoshi, & Tamura, 1993; Villringer, Planck, Hock, Schleinkofer, & Dirnagl, 1993). (An interesting note is that Britton Chance, who led one of these studies, was 80 at the time of that publication and had been publishing in the area of biological spectrophotometry since before World War II; he continued to be an active leader in the development of optical brain-imaging techniques until his death in 2010 at the age of 97!)

Although non-invasive optical brain imaging has existed for approximately the same amount of time as fMRI, it is not nearly as prevalent. That is to say, there are far fewer research groups using the technique and there are far fewer publications using fNIRI than fMRI. There are several reasons for this. Firstly, while fMRI uses equipment that is widely available (due to its ubiquity in hospitals), optical imaging relies on specialized equipment that, while available from serval manufacturers, is research-dedicated. Related to this, fMRI built on a large, established knowledge and technological base concerning MRI; this technical development has been driven by the economic forces supporting mainstream clinical care. In contrast, fNIRI was a new technique built on a novel technology (though spectroscopy had been around for a long time prior, its application to non-invasive imaging of the brain was a unique technical challenge) that has not found widespread clinical utility. The fact that fNIRI relies on novel technology also means that in the early stages each research group was largely developing its own technology. Although a number of commercial systems are now available, there is a high degree of heterogeneity among the commercial offerings, along with many groups continuing to use 'homebrewed' systems. This in turn affects generalizability, and also creates dilemmas for potential new adopters of this imaging approach. Another limitation of optical imaging compared to fMRI is that light only penetrates about 1–3 cm through the skull, meaning that there is much brain activity that occurs too deep inside the head for fNIRI to measure. With the superficial cortical regions that fNIRI can measure, the spatial resolution is limited by the scattering of light to about 10 mm, which is much lower than fMRI. As well, localization of optical signals in the brain is an ill-posed problem and thus carries inherent ambiguities and uncertainty. In contrast, MRI provides high spatial resolution, highly accurate localization, better SNR, and requires less technical knowledge and skill to use for cognitive neuroscience research (assuming the MRI centre has specialized technicians and physicists, as is common).

One might wonder, then, why anyone would pursue optical imaging at all. The answer is that it holds great promise on several fronts. Firstly, the cost of purchasing and maintaining the equipment is far less than an MRI (and comparable to EEG), and does not involve the specialized siting requirements or constraints of MRI (such as a shielded room, and eliminating ferromagnetic materials and electromagnetic fields). Optical-imaging set-ups can be very lightweight and portable, and relatively insensitive to head motion, making them suitable to situations where MRI would not be feasible. For example, optical imaging is quite appropriate for studies of infants, people with cochlear implants, or experiments involving head or body motion – none of which are practical for fMRI. At the same time, fNIRI can measure essentially the same signal as fMRI – blood oxygenation – and in fact permits a wider variety of measurements, since the technique allows separate measurements of oxygenated and deoxygenated haemoglobin, as well as total blood volume and oxygen saturation. In addition to haemodynamic signals, optical imaging can detect much faster signals that are in the order of temporal resolution afforded by EEG and MEG. As such, optical imaging likely has the most as-yet-unrealized potential of any imaging technique in this book. Indeed, it is an area of high growth, with the number of published papers using the technique doubling every three and a half years (Boas, Elwell, Ferrari, & Taga, 2014).

As a final note, the current heterogeneity in the field in terms of approaches to using the technique is reflected in the diversity of terms used by different researchers to refer to this technique. These include fNIRI, (f)NIRS (near-infrared spectroscopy), DOI (diffuse optical imaging), DOT (diffuse optical tomography), NIT (near-infrared tomography), NIN (near-infrared neuroimaging), and EROS (event-related optical signals). In general these largely refer to the same thing, although with some subtleties that we will touch on later in the chapter; in this chapter we will use 'fNIRI' to refer to all types of non-invasive optical imaging.

WHAT ARE WE MEASURING?

Slow Optical Signals

Detection of **slow optical signals** – the haemodynamic response – is by far the most prevalent form of optical imaging. It has a SNR that is close to that of fMRI and so is relatively easy to detect, compared to the fast signal (which is discussed in the following section). The BOLD response was discussed in the fMRI chapter; recall that it typically takes 2–3 s to begin to rise after a stimulus, peaks after roughly 6–8 s, and returns to baseline after 12–20 s. A feature of fNIRI compared to fMRI is that we can separately measure concentrations of oxygenated haemoglobin (oxy-Hb) and deoxyhaemoglobin (deoxy-Hb), as well as combining these to derive a measure of total blood volume (tHb). In contrast, the BOLD fMRI signal reflects the ratio of oxy-Hb to deoxy-Hb, but is largely dominated by oxy-Hb. This is because oxy-Hb is present in much higher concentrations than deoxy-Hb, especially in activated tissue (refer to the fMRI chapter for more details on the BOLD response). A point to note here is that fNIRI publications sometimes refer to the measured response as 'BOLD signal'; however, it should be kept in mind that this is not identical to the fMRI

BOLD signal; tHb is probably closest to fMRI BOLD signal but is derived in fNIRI from the combination of two measured signals – oxy-Hb and deoxy-Hb – whereas in fMRI BOLD it is directly measured. An interesting consequence of this is that whereas BOLD fMRI provides a signal in arbitrary units (which are not interpretable on their own), fNIRI's separate measurements of oxy-Hb and deoxy-Hb can provide quantitative measurements of the concentration of each of these components, in standard units (though this requires calibration that is not possible with all fNIRI systems). Figure 12.1 shows an example of the three measures obtained using fNIRI. As expected, oxy-Hb and deoxy-Hb have opposite time courses, and the tHb signal largely follows the shape of oxy-Hb, but somewhat attenuated. Akin to the 'brain versus vein' debate discussed in the context of fMRI, a concern in optical imaging is the extent to which the recorded signal originates from the small vessels directly feeding neurons (capillaries), as opposed to larger vessels; fortunately, blood vessels larger than about 1 mm in diameter tend to completely absorb light, so only smaller vessels scatter light and contribute to the fNIRI signal.

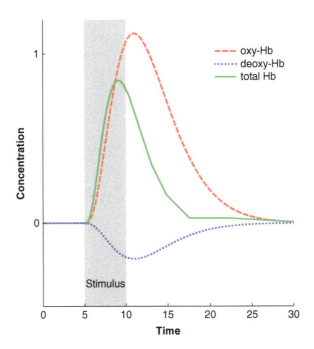

Figure 12.1 Example time course of response measured using fNIRI to a 5 s long stimulus. oxy-Hb = oxyhaemoglobin; deoxy-Hb = deoxyhaemoglobin; tHb = total haemoglobin

Although we are estimating haemoglobin-based signals, fundamentally what we are measuring in fNIRI is light transmitted through the head. Light is transmitted from an **emitter** (sometimes called 'source') into the head, and measured by a **detector** located some distance (typically 3–4 cm) away; collectively the emitters and detectors are called **optodes**. As they travel through the head, the individual photons of light will be scattered as they encounter different molecules; as well, some will be absorbed. As a result, the light received at the detector contains a small proportion of the total light emitted, and from photons that travelled a variety of different paths through the head. Studies of how light is scattered in tissue have shown that the majority of photons' paths that pass through the cortex and reach the detector fall within a crescent- or banana-shaped path between emitter and detector, as shown in Figure 12.2. The intensities of light used in fNIRI are limited by safety considerations; with intensities at the source being in the range of milliwatts to microwatts. Combined with the scattering properties of the tissue, this limits the penetration depth to a maximum of 2–3 cm through the adult skull (although deeper penetration can be achieved at the same intensity through the thinner skulls of infants). This is an important factor because, as shown in Figure 12.2, it means that fNIRI is only sensitive to activation in the superficial parts of the cerebral cortex, not even the depths of cortical sulci. As well, the distance between the scalp and brain differs across the head, being typically closest at the front of the head and farthest at the midline parietal area, and so fNIRI's sensitivity to brain activation is not uniform across the head. Another important thing to note is that not all of the photons that comprise the recorded fNIRI signal actually pass through the cortex at all – in fact, the majority of photons only pass through the superficial layers. Furthermore, only a small percentage of the photons from an emitter reach a given detector (regardless of whether they passed through cortex or only superficial layers), both because many are absorbed and – although Figure 12.2 shows the optical path in two dimensions – the

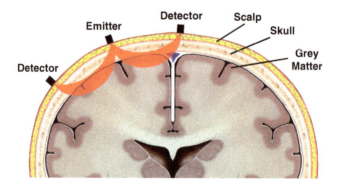

Figure 12.2 The range of most probable paths of NIR light through the cerebral cortex forms a crescent- or banana-shaped path between the emitter and detector, typically separated by 3-4 cm. Note that this does not reflect the entire range of possible paths of photons from the emitter through the head, but rather those that pass through the cortex and reach a particular detector. Permission obtained via iStock.com

light source is aimed perpendicular to the scalp, so the light is equally likely to travel in any direction through the head. Ultimately, it is estimated that fully three-quarters of the light energy is absorbed by non-brain tissues, and only about 3% reaches the cerebral cortex (Scholkmann et al., 2014).

NIR light has wavelengths in the 650–950 nm range; for reference, the visible spectrum of light ranges from approximately 400 nm (violet) to 700 nm (red), so NIR imaging uses some wavelengths that are in the red range of the visible spectrum, and some that are truly infra-red and invisible to the naked eye. Intuitively, this choice of wavelengths makes sense: firstly, blood is red, and changes hue depending on how oxygenated it is; secondly, if you hold your hand up on a sunny day, you will see a reddish tinge around the edges of your fingers because light at this end of the spectrum passes through tissues relatively easily, compared to shorter wavelengths. Indeed, for non-invasive imaging a key requirement is that the skin and skull be relatively transparent to the wavelengths used, so that the light can pass into the brain and back out again.

Typically, two wavelengths of light are used in NIRI, shining either simultaneously or in a rapidly alternating fashion. Two wavelengths are used because a primary goal is to discriminate oxy-Hb from deoxy-Hb, and these have different profiles of light absorption. Thus the two wavelengths of light are chosen to optimize discrimination of oxy-Hb from deoxy-Hb. Figure 12.3 shows the absorption profiles of oxy-Hb and deoxy-Hb, along with other biological constituents that are present in high concentrations and absorb light; these light-absorbing compounds are collectively termed **chromophores**. From this figure it is evident why the NIR range is used: not only do oxy-Hb and deoxy-Hb have distinct profiles in this range (in comparison to their overlap in most of the visible spectrum), but water (the most ubiquitous compound in the body) has virtually no absorbance in this range, meaning it will not confound the measurements.

The data shown in Figure 12.3 suggest that certain wavelengths are optimal for optical imaging, based on where the maximal separation between oxy-Hb and deoxy-Hb occurs. However, different systems use different pairings of wavelengths, based on different assumptions and goals. A common pairing is 690 and 830 nm, although using something in the range of 760–780 nm for the lower wavelength is also common. A significant amount of theoretical work has gone into determining what the optimal wavelengths are, but these are all based on sets of assumptions and necessary simplifications. Wavelength choice is ultimately a mathematical optimization problem that needs to account for not only the absorption spectra of oxy-Hb and deoxy-Hb, but also other chromophores and the intervening tissues, including scalp, skull, and hair. Because of the number of chromophores in the head, and their range of concentrations within and between individuals, there is no single, obvious correct answer. Several studies have also considered including more than two wavelengths of light (up to 5), or even a continuous spectrum over the NIR range in order to optimize distinguishing the haemodynamic signal from other chromophores. However, there are safety limits on the amount of light (power) that can be transmitted through the head, and this total power needs to be divided by the number of wavelengths used. The intensity of the light source directly impacts SNR, so using only

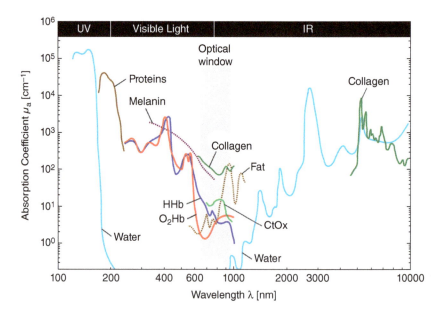

Figure 12.3 Light absorption profiles of oxy-Hb, deoxy-Hb, and other prevalent chromophores in human tissue. Spectra are given with respect to the specific concentration in mM. CtOx = cytochrome oxidase. Reprinted with permission of Elsevier from Scholkmann and colleagues (2014)

two wavelengths is in principle the best way to maximize detection of a functionally relevant signal.

Although fNIRI is sensitive to changes in oxy-Hb and deoxy-Hb, it is also sensitive to a number of other physiological and non-physiological factors that contribute noise to the measurements. A significant contributor to noise is the extra-cerebral (non-brain) tissues that the light passes through which, as noted above, absorb most of the light energy transmitted. Among these, a particular source of noise is non-brain blood flow, especially through vessels in the scalp and meninges (the layers covering the surface of the brain). In principle, in an experiment contrasting fNIRI signals under different experimental conditions, non-cerebral blood flow might be considered irrelevant since it would not be expected to be modulated by the experimental manipulations. However, this is not strictly true. For example, body movements – including hand movements as might be produced during motor responses, as well as speaking or other movement – cause changes in cerebral blood flow and pressure that will affect both the oxygenation and dilation of scalp blood vessels. As well, blood flow is affected by autonomic nervous system arousal, which can change depending on a person's state, including the affective or arousing value of stimuli. Head movements can also dramatically affect the optical signal, if the optode moves with respect to the scalp. This issue varies depending on the type of system used (see below), but at the very least a good system for fixing the optodes to the scalp is important, and excessive motion should be avoided when possible. Another contributor to noise is the hair: dark hair especially absorbs a significant amount of light. Thus it is important to carefully comb the hair away from each optode; nonetheless data from people with darker hair may have lower SNR than from fairer-haired or bald individuals.

Fast Optical Signals

In addition to slow, haemodynamic signals, NIR optical imaging is capable of detecting neural signals that change much more rapidly. These so-called **fast optical signals (FOS)** vary on the same time scale as EEG and MEG (that is, at the millisecond level) and can be measured using essentially the same equipment as the slow signals (though not all hardware capable of recording slow signals is capable of recording fast signals, as discussed in detail later). However, when the technique is focused on the fast signals it is typically given a separate name (and, naturally, an associated acronym): this is often **EROS**, for **'event-related optical signal'**. This is useful insofar as the nature of the measurements is rather different, but it is important to remember that EROS/FOS is really a different approach to using fNIRI technology, rather than an entirely different technology.

The fast optical signals arise from activity-dependent changes in how light is scattered by the cerebral cortex (Gratton, 2010). This phenomenon was first reported in vitro, in isolated neurons and brain tissue slices, and appears to be dependent on the opening and closing of neuronal ion channels. It is thought that the fast signal in non-invasive optical imaging is driven by changes in the size of neurons: as ion channels open during neuronal depolarization (pushing the cell towards an action potential), the cells swell, especially around the dendrites where the majority of receptors are located. Conversely, if a cell is hyperpolarized (making it less likely to fire), the cell shrinks. The changing proportion of intracellular versus extracellular fluid appears to affect light scattering and drive the fast optical signal. Data suggest that fast optical signals are generated by both pyramidal cells and interneurons (cells that largely form local connections within a brain area). Conversely, EEG/MEG signals are largely driven by pyramidal cells with little or no contribution from interneurons. As such, we can expect that although fast optical signals will have similar temporal patterns to EEG/MEG measurements, the signals from these different techniques are not expected to be identical, and EROS can be a complement to EEG/MEG rather than a replacement.

The fast optical signal has been somewhat more controversial in the literature than the slow signal. Several lines of evidence support the existence of the fast signal and its neural origin (Gratton, 2010). Firstly, as noted above, a fast optical signal based on cell swelling has been reported in numerous in vitro studies where the cells can be observed directly, eliminating the ambiguity that comes from relying on non-invasive in vivo measurements alone. Secondly, the temporal dynamics of the fast signal match what would be predicted from EEG/MEG studies. Thirdly, numerous studies have compared fast optical signals between different experimental conditions using appropriately controlled tasks and stimuli, and shown not only statistically reliable differences in experimental comparisons, but a lack of such differences in control comparisons. It is worth noting that some published studies have either failed to find reliable effects, or questioned whether they were of neural origin or artifactual (Radhakrishnan, Vanduffel, Deng, Ekstrom, Boas, & Franceschini, 2009; Steinbrink, Kempf, Villringer, & Obrig, 2005). However, methodological questions limit the interpretability of these studies, and subsequent work seems to have addressed the concerns and further confirmed the existence of the fast signal (Chiarelli, Di Vacri, Romani, & Merla, 2013). An example of the fast signal and its correspondence to simultaneously recorded ERPs is shown in Figure 12.4. Nevertheless, the vast majority of non-invasive optical imaging studies have focused on the slow signal. One primary reason for this is likely the fact that the slow signal has higher SNR and thus is easier to detect and obtain significant results for, thus increasing the likelihood of success of an experiment, and reducing the number of trials needed per condition. As well, measuring the fast signal requires specifications that not all fNIRI systems possess.

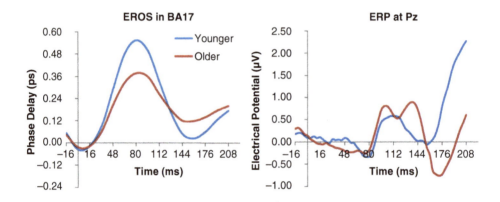

Figure 12.4 An example fast optical signal (EROS) time course (left), and comparison with simultaneously recorded ERPs (right), during visual stimulation (a chequerboard pattern in which the squares rapidly changed between black and white), averaged over two groups of participants (older and younger adults). Note that the peak of the EROS time course, at approximately 80 ms, corresponds to the peak of the earliest visual component, C1 (appearing as a negativity at electrode Pz); the C1 component is known to be generated in primary visual cortex (Brodmann's area 17). Reprinted with permission of Elsevier from Fabiani and colleagues (2014)

In principle, a unique advantage of optical imaging is that one can obtain both 'fMRI-like' and 'EEG/MEG-like' signals using the same imaging device (MEG is probably the better analogy here, given the depth limitations of fNIRI). Indeed, some studies have analysed both fast and slow signals from the same data (Chiarelli, Romani, & Merla, 2014). In practice, things are more complicated for a few reasons. First off, there are differences in how the data are preprocessed and analysed (for example, artifact removal) which requires a thorough understanding of the differences between the two signals, and likely distinct processing streams. As well, the temporal nature of the fast versus slow signals influences how experiments should be designed in the first place, along the lines of differences between ERP and fMRI experiments. For example, for fast signals one might wish to have randomly intermixed trials from different conditions with relatively short inter-stimulus intervals, whereas for slow signals one might want to block multiple trials of the same condition together to improve SNR, or provide longer and/or jittered inter-stimulus intervals to allow sufficient baseline periods in event-related designs. Secondly, although the techniques broadly rely on the same technology, not all hardware that is capable of measuring slow signals can record fast signals. Thus an experimental set-up and data-processing stream that is optimal for measuring one signal may not be optimal for the other.

Since measuring fast signals relies on similar technology to slow signals, we will generally discuss these together in the remainder of the chapter, noting differences as relevant. However, there are a few notable differences that bear mention here. For one, we noted in the previous section that at least two wavelengths of light are necessary for measuring the slow signal, because we wish to distinguish oxy-Hb and deoxy-Hb signals. With fast EROS measurement, there is only one signal to measure, and so a single wavelength is sufficient; often, 830 nm is used. Secondly, current optical imaging technology imposes a limit on the temporal resolution of measurements; while sampling rates of up to 1000 Hz are possible from a single optode, increasing the number of sensors necessitates a decrease in sampling rate for reasons discussed in the next section. Thus the effective sampling rate for a multi-optode system may be limited to 50 Hz or less, meaning that samples are separated by 20 ms or even longer. This is not a limit that is specific to fast signal measurements; however, it is more of a limitation for these since, by definition, we wish to record a rapidly changing signal. In contrast, the slow nature of the BOLD signal means that low sampling rates are less of a concern. Not only does this limit the highest temporal frequencies that can be measured (recall that the Nyquist theorem states that the highest frequency we can accurately capture is a half to a third the sampling rate), but it also affects the SNR of the recordings. This is because the more time points we have, the more information we have to be able to separate true signal from noise. As well, although many sources of noise such as head movements and dark hair are equally relevant for fast and slow signal measurement, other noise sources are more of an issue for fast signals. In particular, artifacts associated with heartbeat (which has a frequency of about 1 Hz) need to be removed via filtering, ICA, or some other mechanism.

HOW DO WE MEASURE IT?

Overview

Broadly speaking, all fNIRI systems involve optodes (emitters and detectors); some way of affixing the optodes to the scalp; hardware that generates the light; photodetectors that detect the transmitted light; and software that records the data. There are a wide range of options, however, for each of these components, leading to perhaps greater heterogeneity among fNIRI systems than any other technique discussed in this book. Beyond the specific component choices (but also related to these), a key differentiator between different fNIRI recording systems – and experiments – is how the measurements are obtained. There are three different technologies to do this, as illustrated in Figure 12.5. The first and most common, **continuous wave (CW)**, simply shines light of a particular wavelength (or wavelengths) and measures absorption of the light at the detectors. The other two methods, which are collectively called 'time-resolved techniques', are more complex, but offer advantages in terms of sensitivity and precision. **Frequency-domain (FD)** measurements involve varying the intensity of the light at a particular frequency. This allows for the measurement not only of absorption, but also the timing of light arriving at the detector; for this reason, FD systems are used for measuring fast signals. In contrast to these other two techniques, which both involve continuous light (either intensity-modulated or not), **time-domain (TD)** measurements involve rapid pulses of light and offer even greater temporal sensitivity than FD systems. FD and TD approaches are capable of quantitative measurements of oxy-Hb to deoxy-Hb concentrations; CW can only provide relative measurements of these concentrations between different experimental conditions. We will discuss each of these technologies later in the chapter.

Regardless of the choice between CW, FD, and TD systems, many considerations and design features are common to all of these technologies. First of all, any fNIRI system needs to be able to generate light with very specific properties, transmit that light to specific locations on the head (via emitters), and record what is emitted at one or more locations on the head (via detectors). The light is typically generated within a hardware 'box' and transmitted to the head via optical fibres, rather than placing the light sources directly on the scalp. There are two types of lights sources currently in use for optical imaging systems: **light-emitting diodes (LEDs)** and **laser diodes (LDs)**. LEDs have several benefits, in that they are lower-cost and it is very easy to adjust their output intensities. However, a disadvantage is that they have a relatively wide bandwidth, typically on the order of 25–50 nm – so specifying a pair of light sources of 690 and 830 nm could actually result in sources of 665–715 and 805–855 nm. This would result in less accurate measurement and separation of the chromophores. LDs, on the other hand, have very precise, narrow bandwidths of less than 1 nm, and also perform well at high frequencies – essential for FD and TD systems. However, they are only available in a limited set of wavelengths, so the desired wavelengths for a particular system may not be achievable. LDs are also larger than LEDs and thus impose limits on how small a system can be. Because they are lasers, LDs also carry additional safety considerations. Firstly, they should not be shone directly into the eyes – an issue which simply requires proper training of system users and safe handling of the equipment, and can also be mitigated by design of the optodes. The other is that in principle, lasers could generate pulses strong enough to cause heating of the tissue and discomfort or even burns. However, these concerns are easily addressed in the design of the instruments to ensure they follow established international safety guidelines. Thus the amount of radiation the head is exposed to during fNIRI is much lower than would be experienced simply being outside on a sunny day.

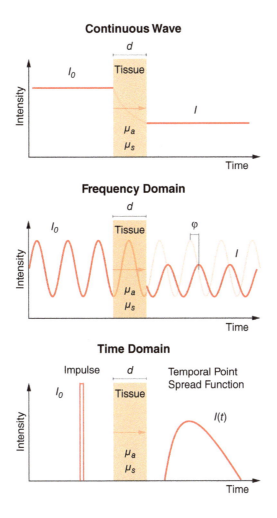

Figure 12.5 Comparison of continuous wave, frequency domain, and time domain fNIRI approaches. In each panel, the intensity of light from the emitter is represented as I_o and the light recorded by the detector (after passing through tissue) as I; the distance of the optical path through the tissue is quantified as d. In all cases, the intensity of the light is attenuated after passing through the tissue, due to both absorption (quantified as the absorption coefficient, μ_a) and scattering (μ_s). Note that in frequency domain imaging, not only is the light attenuated, but there is a phase delay, quantified by φ. In time domain imaging, the photons contained in a brief pulse of transmitted light arrive at the detector over a range of times, creating a distribution (point spread function) of intensity values over time, $I(t)$. Reprinted with permission of Elsevier from Scholkmann and colleagues (2014)

Different technologies are available for the light detectors as well. One of these, photomultiplier tubes (PMTs), will be familiar from the chapter on PET imaging. These involve a material that releases an electron when a photon touches it, combined with a tube that allows the electron to trigger the release of additional electrons, amplifying (multiplying) the signal. These are extremely sensitive and allow the system to count individual photons, which is the highest level of precision obtainable. They also allow for very fast measurements, which is an important consideration in FD and TD systems. However, photomultiplier tubes are sensitive to magnetic fields and ambient light, and are also comparatively large in size and have high electricity demands. The sensitivity to magnetic fields is a particular consideration because with other technologies, fNIRI can be done inside an MRI scanner. One alternative is photodiodes, in which photons are absorbed by a semiconductor, resulting in a change in voltage that is then recorded. Photodiodes are simpler to use as they have lower electricity requirements, are smaller, and are not sensitive to magnetic fields or ambient light. However, photodiodes do not internally amplify the signal as photomultiplier tubes do, meaning that additional engineering (for example, preamplifiers) is required to obtain good SNR. A third technology is the avalanche photodiode, which works by light changing internal voltage, like photodiodes, but has an internal amplifying characteristic (the 'avalanche') more like photomultiplier tubes, overcoming the issue of weak signals noted for photodiodes. Avalanche photodiodes, like photodiodes, are small, insensitive to magnetic fields and ambient light, and allow even faster sampling than photodiodes. Their major disadvantages are that they have high, specialized voltage requirements, and are sensitive to temperature and thus typically require some sort of internal cooling. The use of a fourth technology, **silicon photomultipliers**, is currently under investigation as these offer the advantages of avalanche photodiodes combined with the single-photon counting abilities of photomultiplier tubes. However, this technology has not yet found its way into any commercial imaging devices.

The optodes must be held in place against the head in some way, and several considerations are important here. First of all, optical fibres are typically made of glass and are quite fragile, so the system needs to protect the fibres from breaking, ensuring they do not bend much. Secondly, the fibres need to be held perpendicular to the head to ensure full and even distribution of the light; as well, some sort of optical insulation needs to be provided around the tips of the optodes to prevent interference from ambient light, which can wash out the desired signal otherwise. Thirdly, the fibres need to be placed in a specific arrangement, both relative to the head/brain of the subject, and relative to each other. Emitter and detector fibres need to be located in specific positions relative to each other, and with spacing that provides optimal signal as discussed above. Most systems have source and detector optodes at distinct locations; however some have a source and emitter at each optode location. Different systems fix optode position in different ways. The majority of these use a stretchable cap such as is used in EEG; others use a band that can be placed over different parts of the head, or a hard-shell helmet. An example is shown in Figure 12.6. One current limitation of all fNIRI systems is that due to the per-channel expense, the fact that there is an optimal emitter–detector separation distance, and the fact that increasing the number of channels decreases sampling rate, most systems do not provide full-head coverage. Commercial systems typically have in the range of 1–50 each of emitters and detectors. Many systems are designed in a modular fashion: either the optodes can be plugged into various different locations in the cap/helmet, or the array of optodes are held in a fixed position relative to each other on a flexible pad that can be positioned over different parts of the head. Thus the researcher can place the optode array over the part of the brain that is of interest in a particular study. Some systems, however, are less flexible; for example, there are systems specifically designed to be placed over the forehead that are designed only to record frontal lobe activity.

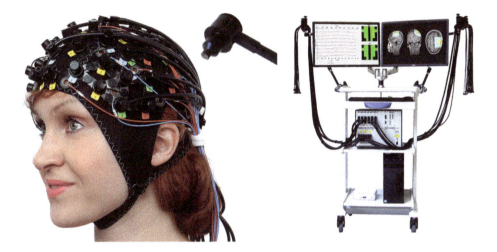

Figure 12.6 An example fNIRI system. The left panel shows optodes secured to the scalp by an elastic cap, much like that used in EEG systems. The optodes are the black cylinders; this example also includes EEG electrodes (discs connected to coloured wires). The middle panel shows a close-up of one optode, which would plug into a circular holder in the cap. The right panel shows the complete hardware system; on the middle shelf is the hardware box that generates the light and records the signals. Images courtesy of NIRx Medical Technologies LLC

The number of channels and their positioning is another consideration. One important consequence of the banana-shaped path that light travels through the brain is that there is an optimal range of distances between emitter and detector optodes. The lower limit of this range is imposed by the fact that photons that penetrate into the brain must necessarily travel a certain distance from the emitter before re-emerging from the head; photons that re-emerge close to the emitter very likely only penetrated the surface layers of the head and did not reach the brain. The maximum distance between emitter and detector, on the other hand, is limited by several factors. One is the fact that, because the majority of photons that pass through the brain do follow the banana-shaped path, they tend to emerge from the head within a relatively narrow range of distances; some photons travel further through the cortex, but longer paths increase the likelihood that the photon will be absorbed or scattered away from the scalp, reducing SNR at greater separation distances. The other consideration is that in general, researchers wish to achieve the best spatial resolution possible; greater emitter–detector distances reduce spatial resolution since the signal can originate from anywhere between the two optodes. The majority of fNIRI systems use separations of 2–4 cm, as this has been determined to be optimal to capture the majority of photons passing through the brain. In some cases (primarily for fast signals), separations up to 6–7 cm may be used. In this latter case, usually closer separations are used as well, so signals from a given emitter are recorded from multiple detectors at different distances. If possible, it is also ideal to have multiple emitter–detector pairs sampling the same brain tissue (that is, different paths cross through the same brain region), as this will increase SNR. Figure 12.7 shows how emitter–detector separation distance affects the depth and extent of cortex that the light passes through, demonstrating why 3-4 cm is a commonly used separation distance.

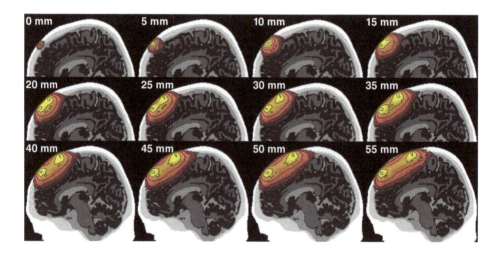

Figure 12.7 Simulation data showing photon sensitivity profiles at a range of emitter-detector separation distances. Colours represent the intensity of light reaching any given point in the tissue, and contour lines show each order of magnitude loss in sensitivity from peak, truncated after 5 orders of magnitude. In this simulation, sensitivity to the cerebral cortex is best at separations of 30 mm or more. Note that at separations greater than approximately 35 mm there is no increased sensitivity to deeper regions of cortex; however, due to the greater lateral separation there is increased ambiguity as to where along the optical path a particular activation signal originates from. Reprinted from Strangman, Li, and Zhang (2013), licensed under Creative Commons BY 4.0

A related topic is how we conceptualize the number of 'channels' in an fNIRI system, and how the spatial arrangement (montage) of optodes is determined. Obviously, this depends significantly on the number of emitters and detectors the system has, which is a significant differentiator between systems – both in terms of the overall number of optodes, and the balance between emitters and detectors. Some systems have more emitters than detectors, while others have the opposite. In general, though, we can call a path between a single emitter and detector a **channel**, since this represents the light transmitted through one particular part of the brain. Because the emitted light travels in all directions through the head from each emitter, the light from a given emitter can be received by multiple detectors – creating multiple channels – and conversely a detector can receive light from multiple emitters. Thus, a system with four emitters and one detector would be considered a four-channel system. The number of channels is not always as simple as multiplying the number of emitters by the number of detectors, however, because this depends on the arrangement of the optodes and their distances. Systems with a large number of optodes are likely to include many possible emitter–detector pairs that are too far away from each other to be combined as a channel. As well, in systems with many channels, there will likely be some optodes that are completely surrounded by other optodes (making all possible pairings feasible), and others on the edge of the array that have optodes only on some sides. Sensor numbers notwithstanding, the scattering of light in the head itself imposes a lower limit on the spatial resolution of fNIRI to about 10 mm.

An important issue in optical imaging is how to determine, at a given detector, which emitter generated the photons that are received. As can be seen in Figure 12.6, in a multi-channel system the emitters and detectors are interspersed and so a given detector will inevitably sense light from multiple emitters (likewise, an single emitter's light may be picked up by multiple detectors). Accurately localizing the signal depends on knowing which emitter–detector pair that signal is coming from. The solution to this problem is called **multiplexing**. This is a generic term that refers to different ways of combining multiple, distinct signals and separating them later, as is done with technologies such as cellular phones and computer networking. Optical imaging systems typically use one of three types of multiplexing. In **time multiplexing**, only one emitter is turned on and transmitting light at any given time. The system cycles through turning each emitter on and off in turn, and once each has been on once, the cycle begins again. In this way, the system knows at any given time to associate the data received at the detector with a particular emitter. A disadvantage of this approach is that it imposes a limit on the temporal resolution of such systems, since increasing the number of channels increases the amount of time required to cycle through all the channels. Each emitter only needs to be on for 1–2 ms, so with a low number of channels (for example, four emitters), this is not much of a problem, as the sampling rate can be in the order of 100–200 Hz. However, with a larger number of emitters the sampling rate can drop to 50 Hz or lower. As noted earlier, this is less of a concern for haemodynamic (slow) signal imaging, but does impose limitations on the temporal resolution when performing fast imaging. Another option is **frequency multiplexing**. This is achieved by modulating the intensity of the light at different frequencies for each emitter. These frequencies are very high – typically in the kHz range – and allow for separation of the signals at the detector by applying a fast Fourier transform to isolate the amount of light received at the distinct frequency associated with each emitter. Alternatively, the hardware in the amplifier that receives the signals may have separate channels that are tuned to the frequencies of individual emitters. An advantage of frequency multiplexing is that all emitters are on continuously, so data can be received simultaneously across all channels. Thus there is no limitation on sampling rate or temporal resolution imposed by frequency multiplexing, because the rates of frequency modulation are very high. The third – and least-common – approach is **code multiplexing**. All emitters are active simultaneously; however, they are each switched on and off (very rapidly) according to different sequences or 'codes'. Conceptually this is similar to frequency multiplexing in that the data from all emitters are mixed together at the receiver, and then decoded because each emitter has a different 'signature'. The difference is that frequency multiplexing uses regular, sinusoidal frequencies as the signatures, whereas code multiplexing uses non-periodic, on–off pulses as the signatures.

Continuous Wave Imaging

Continuous wave (CW) imaging is the most common form of fNIRI. Light of a specific frequency and intensity is continuously transmitted from the emitter, and the attenuation (absorption) of the light is calculated as the reduction in intensity of light received by the detector. This process of quantifying the concentration of a compound via light absorption was originally demonstrated in ex vivo conditions, by chemists. The basic relationship between light absorption and concentration of a solution is described by an equation known as the **Beer–Lambert law**. Absorbance is defined as the ratio of the intensity of the input light, to the intensity of the output light after it passes through the solution. Mathematically, this is described as:

$$A = \log_{10}(I_0/I)$$

where I_0 is the original intensity and I is the transmitted intensity. The Beer–Lambert law describes how this relates to the concentration of the material the light passed through:

$$A = \log_{10}(I_0/I) = \varepsilon l c$$

where l is the length of the transmission path, c is the concentration of the solution, and ε is the **absorption coefficient**, a constant specific to the particular compound being studied. Obviously things get much more complicated in biological tissue with so many different compounds in the 'sample' (the head), but here we're starting from a simple case of measuring the concentration of a single, pure compound in a solution.

The Beer–Lambert law is easy to understand intuitively if we think of a test tube full of clear water. In this case, light will pass easily through it, so there will be little absorption. If we add a drop of food dye to the water, the colour will change slightly. The molecules in the food dye absorb some of the light passing through the test tube, reducing the amount of light that reaches the receiver. As we increase the amount (concentration) of dye in the test tube, the solution will get darker, and thus absorption will increase, and the brightness of the transmitted light will decrease. The Beer–Lambert law specifies a direct mathematical relationship that allows us to quantitatively determine the concentration of the dye in the solution by measuring the amount of light absorption, as long as we know the absorption coefficient of the dye.

In CW fNIRI, a **modified Beer–Lambert law (MBLL)** is applied that takes into account the scattering of light in biological tissue, and uses the absorption coefficients of oxy-Hb and deoxy-Hb, allowing us to measure the concentrations of oxy- and deoxy-haemoglobin. Of course, there are many compounds other than oxy-Hb and deoxy-Hb in the head that will affect light transmittance, but in fNIRI the simplifying assumption is made that the concentrations of all these other compounds remain constant during the measurement, and only oxy-Hb and deoxy-Hb change. Although this may not be exactly true, it is not unreasonable to expect that the concentration of other compounds with significant absorbance at the chosen wavelength(s) of light will not change systematically with an experimental manipulation.

Another limitation of the MBLL is that it assumes that the medium that the light passes through is homogeneous. This assumption is violated in the brain, because haemoglobin is only present within the blood vessels, and not any of the other tissue that the light passes through. However, the impact of this assumption being violated is only that fNIRI significantly underestimates the true concentrations of oxy-Hb and deoxy-Hb in the small vessels; the measurements of their relative concentrations – and, critically, changes in these – are still proportional to the true values.

A more significant limitation of the MBLL is that it includes a constant called the **differential path length (DPL)** factor, which accounts for the scattering of light that occurs in biological tissue but not in test tubes. This factor varies considerably between individuals – by as much as 15% – and so using an incorrect value can yield a significant degree of error in measurement. The DPL can be measured using FD or TD fNIRI, but not with CW imaging – leading to greater inaccuracy when using CW in particular. However, the factors known to affect DPL include age, sex, and wavelength, so in a typical study with a relatively restricted age range and an even balance of participants of each sex, using a particular wavelength, the true amount of error is likely to be much less than 15%, and is further mitigated by the mere fact of averaging data across individuals (some of whom will have larger error, and others smaller).

Frequency-Domain Imaging

While CW fNIRI is the most commonly used technology – due to its relative technical simplicity, ability to perform haemodynamic imaging reliably, and its use in the majority of commercially available imaging devices – its major limitation is that it can only measure the intensity of light received, but not timing information. While CW devices transmit light at a constant intensity, frequency domain (FD) devices modulate the intensity of the emitted light at a very high rate (100–500 MHz). Using this technology, three measures can be obtained. The first is average intensity, comparable to a CW measurement; the second is intensity changes at the frequency the light is modulated at; and the third (and most interesting) is **phase delay**. Phase delay allows for estimation of the average arrival time of photons at the detector. This is possible because the light intensity is modulated at a high sinusoidal frequency: phase refers to the timing of the peaks of intensity. The farther a photon travels between the emitter and detector, the more phase lag it will demonstrate relative to the original source light. Thus in a FD system, the phase of the light received at the detector is compared with a 'reference' phase, which is determined by passing the same light transmitted from the emitter through a vacuum tube with known light transmission properties, to a detector.

This phase delay information is useful because the time it takes for photons to travel from the emitter to the detector is proportional to the distance they travel: light that passes through the superficial tissues but not the brain will have faster transmission times than light that passes more deeply, through the brain. As a result, the light received at the detector will contain a mixture of phase delays, which effectively average together so that what is measured is the mean phase delay. The timing information obtained from phase delay measurements improves SNR, relative to CW imaging, for several reasons. Firstly, phase delay is more sensitive to signals from deeper tissues, because the photons passing deeper take longer to arrive at the detector, and these longer times (large values) have a greater influence on the mean phase delay than the smaller values generated by peripherally travelling photons. Secondly, since the phase delay signal is sensitive to path length, it can offer enhanced spatial resolution because changes in brain activity at different depths are in principle distinguishable, given the right analysis algorithms. Finally, because the measurements relate to time and not absolute intensity, phase delay measurements are much less sensitive than CW to artifactual changes in light intensity. These changes can be caused by ambient light, but especially by movement of the optodes relative to the head, which commonly occurs with head movement. Phase delay measurements are therefore especially advantageous with infants or in studies that involve movement. The benefits of phase delay measurements are applicable to measuring both slow and fast optical signals. However, due to the intrinsically lower SNR of fast signals, FD imaging is particularly valuable for fast optical imaging.

Time-Domain Imaging

Time-domain (TD) fNIRI builds on the principles of FD imaging, in the sense of looking at the timing of the optical signal rather than its intensity. However, TD fNIRI has much greater temporal sensitivity than FD. In TD imaging, a pulsed laser is used as the light source, rather than a continuously-on light source that varies in intensity, as in FD. The timing of the pulses in TD imaging is extremely fast, with each pulse lasting only tens of picoseconds (10^{-12} s, or quadrillionths of a second). Combined with a very fast detector capable of counting single photons, a TD system is able to precisely quantify the temporal distribution of when the photons from each pulse are received at the detector. The resulting measurement is the **distribution of time-of-flight (DTOF)** of the individual photons originating from a single pulse of light. This is shown in Figure 12.8. A TD fNIRI time series thus comprises a series of DTOF measurements. The value of the exquisite temporal resolution of TD fNIRI is not in the sampling rate it affords to the fNIRI signal per se, but rather to the ability of each TDOF measurement to differentiate between photons arriving at the sensor at different times. Because the time it takes a photon

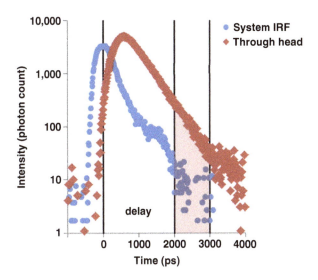

Figure 12.8 Distribution of time-of-flight (DTOF) values obtained in time-domain (TD) fNIRI. Each point represents the number of individual photons recorded at a detector at a given time after transmission from the emitter, summed over a large number of transmitted pulses of light. Blue circles are the system impulse response function, representing light transmitted over a known distance through a vacuum tube rather than through the head. Red diamonds are the data from light transmitted through the head. Note that the overall DTOF of the light transmitted through the head is shifted to the right, reflecting the additional time taken by photons to pass through the tissue. Since the majority of photons do not pass through the brain but follow shorter paths through superficial tissues, the peak of the measured DTOF primarily represents those superficially travelling photons, while later time periods reflect light that passed through the cortex. The shaded area from 2000–3000 ps represents a probable period during which the data primarily reflect cortical activity. Thus, intensity data can be analysed only from this time window to avoid confounds from superficial tissues. Adapted with permission of Elsevier from Torricelli and colleagues (2014)

to travel from the emitter to detector is proportional to the distance it travels, the early portion of the DTOF represents photons that travelled shorter paths (more peripheral, non-brain paths), whereas the later portion of the DTOF represents farther-travelling photons – those that most likely passed through the cortex. This allows improved sensitivity to true neural signals by focusing analysis on the later portion of the DTOF (for example, only those photons received later than the mean or peak of the distribution, or only those within a selected time window). This is a significant technological advantage, since CW and FD fNIRI signals are inherently dominated by the light that passes through peripheral tissues.

Besides its better ability to isolate neural from nuisance signals, TD fNIRI has other advantages as well. One is the ability to easily measure the necessary optical properties of each head that is imaged. Recall that accurately calculating concentration of oxy-Hb and deoxy-Hb using the MBLL relies on knowing the absorption coefficient, and also that one important source of error in CW fNIRI measurements is the differential path length (DPL) factor. Both of these parameters vary between individuals, but in CW and FD imaging either default, assumed values have to be used for these, or time-consuming and sometimes awkward calibration steps have to be performed for each individual (such as measuring optical signals at a number of different emitter–detector distances); DPL cannot be obtained from CW measurements. TD imaging, in contrast, allows relatively rapid calculation of these parameters for each individual without relying on multiple emitter–detector distances. Beyond the increase in accuracy provided by this ability to calibrate for each individual, this calibration also means that measurements provided by TD fNIRI can be truly quantitative measures of concentration, rather than relative measurements – which are all CW or FD can provide. This also allows TD imaging to estimate a quantitative value of another parameter – oxygen saturation in tissue – which is of importance in some clinical applications.

Another advantage of TD fNIRI is that its sensitivity is not affected by emitter–detector distance. Recall that with CW and FD imaging, there is an optimal range of emitter–detector distances that maximize the detection of photons that passed through the brain. Too short distances result in detecting primarily photons that travelled through superficial (non-brain) paths, while at too long a distance the amount of detected light is reduced; the depth of penetration is also dependent on emitter–detector distance. At the same time, however, greater emitter–detector separation results in reduced SNR due to fewer photons that travel that far. In TD imaging, because we separate photons based on their time of arrival, a single sensor can distinguish between deeper and shallower travelling photons. Signals from deeper tissue can be obtained without increasing emitter–detector distance and the concomitant reduction in signal strength. Signals from deeper tissues will nonetheless be weaker in TD imaging, simply because the odds of a photon being absorbed or scattered away from the detector increase with depth. However, the advantage is that TD offers good depth resolution with single emitter–detector separation. Indeed, TD fNIRI can even be performed with zero (null) emitter–detector separation (Torricelli et al., 2005), again based on the principle that we can exclude earlier arriving (superficial) photons and focus on the later arriving (deep) ones. Using null emitter–detector separation holds significant promise in terms of improving spatial resolution of fNIRI. First of all, the zero separation means that all detected photons can be localized to a very narrow vertical column directly under the optode. Secondly, the lack of separation between emitter and detector optodes allows for potentially very dense placement of the optodes on the head. This overcomes the limitation that, although the theoretical limit of fNIRI's spatial resolution is ~1 cm, the requirement of placing optodes 3–4 cm apart enforces a reduction in spatial resolution.

TD fNIRI requires specialized equipment, even compared to other types of fNIRI. Firstly, the light source itself is different, because rather than constant illumination, the source has to produce very short, precise pulses. This is done using pulsed lasers, which can generate short bursts of light (100 ps or less) at high frequencies (up to 100 MHz). There are a few technologies available for this, including solid state lasers, pulsed diode lasers, and supercontinuum fibre lasers. Solid state lasers are the most commonly used, as they have good power and a range of available wavelengths of light. However, they are comparatively large, and switching them between wavelengths can be slow. Pulsed diode lasers are more compact, but are less powerful (resulting in lower SNR) and need extended warm-up time (one hour) before they can be used. Supercontinuum lasers are a relatively new technology with good power and other favourable optical properties. However, as a new technology there are still issues related to power and robustness that need to be addressed before they can enter widespread use. The detectors used in TD imaging likewise have higher demands than other types of fNIRI, as they need to have both very high sensitivity to light (in order to count individual photons), and to be very fast. The most common approach is known as **time-correlated single photon counting**. This can use a variety of light detectors, including photomultiplier tubes (PMTs), micro-channel plate PMTs, single-photon avalanche photodiodes, and hybrid detectors that combine a PMT and avalanche photodiode. Time-correlated single photon counting works on the principle that in the narrow time windows used for detection (a few thousand ps), the odds of detecting even a single photon are quite low. Thus to determine the DTOF a relatively large number of sampling cycles are required to detect enough photons to reliably estimate the DTOF. This does not significantly impact the temporal resolution of the fNIRI measurements because the individual samples in TCSPC are so fast, so tens or even hundreds of thousands of measurements can be taken in a second. The technology required to detect single photons is, necessarily, extremely sensitive to light. This imposes an upper limit on the intensity of the light coming from the emitter, so as not to saturate or even damage the detector. This is why the odds of detecting a single photon in a narrow time window are so low, but also imposes limits on the SNR of these systems.

In spite of its many advantages, TD fNIRI is still quite obscure, and has a number of limitations. First of all, the technology required for this type of imaging is larger, more fragile, and more expensive than for CW or FD fNIRI. In fact, there are virtually no commercial systems available; the majority of research using TD fNIRI has been conducted using systems designed and built by individual research groups. The lack of commercial availability largely limits the technique to research aimed at further developing the technique, or to people with access to those labs conducting technique development. This is because building, using, and maintaining such 'one-off' systems is not feasible for the typical cognitive neuroscience lab whose efforts are focused on using the technique to do research on functional brain organization, rather than making a particular technology work. However, as research advances and new technical innovations make smaller and lower-cost systems feasible, the advantages of TD imaging will likely result in its becoming a more mainstream technique. Another important limitation is that TD systems typically have lower contrast-to-noise ratios (CNR) than CW systems. This is due in part to the fact that the specifications for TD imaging are different and more specific than for CW, limiting the choice of components, and thus in some cases the performance of those components. As well, as noted above the high sensitivity of the single-photon detectors limits the intensity of light used, and thus imposes a limit on SNR that is not present for CW or FD systems.

DATA ANALYSIS

Although we have seen that there are several ways of acquiring fNIRI data, ultimately all of these methods generate time series data from a set of channels. In this sense, the data, and how they are processed, share commonalities with other time series methods we have examined, including EEG, MEG, and fMRI. Many of the preprocessing and analysis steps will thus be familiar, although the nature of optical data imposes some differences. Most notably, the raw time series data need to be converted; for example, in CW data from intensity values to haemoglobin concentrations using the MBLL. Another step unique to optical imaging is attempting to separate signals or neural origin from light that passed only through superficial layers of the head. As well, much like EEG or MEG data the researcher has the choice of simply analysing the data from each channel, or performing source localization (often called **tomographic imaging** in the fNIRI context) and reporting data in terms of 3D spatial coordinates in the brain. This in turn will affect the type of statistical analyses that are performed. Another important consideration is whether the interest is in the fast or the slow optical signal – some preprocessing steps are generic to all forms of the data, whereas others (such as filter settings) are dependent on the signal of interest.

As with other imaging modalities, there are a variety of software packages available for fNIRI preprocessing and analysis, including both commercial and open source offerings. Because of the many types of optical imaging, and – as we will see – different ideas about the ideal processing pipeline, these packages vary considerably in the types of tools they offer, and are under active development. As always, for someone interested in starting to do optical imaging, the best approach is to read widely, and take a course, or spend time in a lab that already has expertise in analysing similar data. As a critical consumer of the fNIRI literature, it is important to recognize that there is much less standardization or even agreement on the best procedures, so it is important to pay close attention to the steps performed on the data, especially in trying to compare data between labs.

Data Conversion

The first step in the optical-imaging pipeline is to convert the raw time series data into the signal of interest. For CW data, this typically involves applying the MBLL to convert intensity values into concentrations of each chromophore of interest (that is, oxy-Hb and deoxy-Hb). This simple statement belies a fair amount of underlying complexity and subtlety though, because in general the MBLL as applied to optical imaging is a grossly over-simplified model of how light is actually transmitted through the many-layered and highly heterogeneous medium of the head. As a result, ongoing work is directed at improving the MBLL for the specific use case of fNIRI, and different software packages may implement this in different ways. Regardless of the particular implementation used, the resulting time series data represent concentration values; typically two time series are generated per channel: one for oxy-Hb and one for deoxy-Hb. As noted earlier, the haemoglobin concentration values may be specified in relative terms (arbitrary units), or in absolute terms. CW data can generally only be specified in relative terms, whereas FD and TD data can yield absolute values if appropriate calibration is done.

For FD data, a fast Fourier transform is typically used to isolate the signal at the frequency that the light intensity was modulated at, and the phase delay at this frequency is compared to the reference phase. Thus the resulting data are a time series of photon time-of-flight values, which can be used in this form if analysing the fast signal. If the interest is in the slow signal, the phase shift data can be converted to haemoglobin concentrations using the MBLL.

For TD data, the raw data are time series of DTOFs, which can be converted to haemoglobin concentrations according to the MBLL. However, since the key advantage of TD imaging is the fact that the DTOF separates early/superficial from late/neural signals, typically the intensity values from the DTOF are first separated by time. There are several different approaches to doing this. The simplest is to designate a particular time window, or a set of time windows, and extract mean intensity values from each. Using multiple time windows can be especially valuable if there is an interest in 3D imaging and obtaining good depth resolution within the cortex. Other approaches use changes in variance (since variance increases with time within the DTOF) or other more complex statistical models. In all cases, with TD data the measured DTOFs are compared with a reference distribution (the instrument response function, or IRF) that is obtained by placing the emitter and detector optodes directly against each other to determine the DTOF of the system itself.

Quality Assurance

As with any data, the first step that should always be performed is quality assurance. This involves – at least – visual examination of the raw data time series to ensure that they look as expected. Because optical imaging relies on contact of sensors with the scalp, one common source of poor-quality data is poor contact here – either throughout the scan due to a poorly placed (or damaged) optode, or transiently due to movements. It is not uncommon for some channels to be removed completely for some participants due to optode problems.

Motion Correction

Although motion artifacts are an issue in both fMRI and fNIRI, the sources of these artifacts in fNIRI are very different: in fMRI the problem is the movement of the head within the magnetic field, whereas motion artifacts in optical imaging data generally are the result of the optodes moving relative to the scalp. With fNIRI, such gross overall movements of the head through space are not necessarily a problem and, indeed, one oft-touted advantage of fNIRI is its ability to be used in freely moving participants. However, sudden shaking of the head, touching the optodes, and even some types of contractions of facial muscles can cause movement of the optodes relative to the head, resulting in artifacts because the amount of light transmitted and/or received will be drastically reduced when the contact between optode and skin is reduced. For this reason it is best practice to consider and try to minimize such movements during the experiment. As well, movement is less likely if the optodes are firmly attached to the head; thinner (or no) hair tends to result in less optode movement, whereas thick hair can be more problematic. The manifestations of motion artifacts in the data tend to look like either transient 'spikes' (large changes that return to/close to baseline), shifts that do not return to baseline, or low-frequency fluctuations. As in fMRI, a particularly problematic type of motion is that which is correlated with the effects of interest in some way – for example, movements created by participants' responding to the task.

Identification of motion artifacts can be done on the time series data using a simple threshold-based method. This looks for periods where the change in amplitude and/or standard deviation of the signal exceeds a pre-defined threshold within a relatively narrow period of time. The simplest approach is to then simply mark those segments of time and remove them or otherwise ignore them in data analysis. However, in general it is preferable to correct the motion artifacts rather than lose data. Having identified motion-containing segments of the data as described above, one approach to correction is spline interpolation, which creates a mathematical model of the shape of the motion artifact. Once the best fit of this model is identified, it is subtracted from the data. Another approach uses a **Kalman filter**, which is an algorithm that is more often used in predicting the trajectories of spaceships, missiles, and controlling the movement of robots. Kalman filters are particularly suited for making predictions concerning the future values of some measurement, based on past values, in the presence of noise. The Kalman filter compares the variance of the time series during periods marked as containing motion with variance during motion-free periods, and uses this information to predict what the data would have looked like without the motion artifact. This is analogous to predicting the true trajectory of a rocket when it passes behind a cloud, based on visual observation of its trajectory up until it disappeared.

Other motion correction approaches take a more complex approach to identifying the artifacts than simply looking at amplitude or variance. **Principal components analysis (PCA)** breaks the data into a set of uncorrelated component time series. Components with high variance tend to be artifactual (since artifacts tend to be large relative to physiological data), so the components that explain the most variance in the data can be removed. This can be effective, but PCA runs the risk of removing real data along with artifacts in cases where the motion is correlated with the task. A preferable alternative is independent components analysis (ICA), which we discussed in the context of EEG artifact correction. ICA uses more complex, higher-order statistical properties of the data than PCA to separate the signal into independent components. As a result, the components are not necessarily uncorrelated from each other, but are more likely to originate from different sources. Another approach is **discrete wavelet filtering**, in which a **wavelet** – a short 'snippet' of a waveform with a particular shape – is fit to a time series by shifting, stretching, and/or scaling it to best represent features in the data. This relies on the fact that motion artifacts will occur relatively rarely and have a different shape than the physiological data of interest, and so outliers in the fitted wavelet distribution can be assumed to be artifacts, and removed. Another approach is **correlation-based signal improvement**. This is based on the assumption that true oxy-Hb and deoxy-Hb signals are, in general, strongly negatively correlated. Since head motion affects the optode – and thus measurements of both oxy-Hb and deoxy-Hb similarly – during head motion the two chromophores' signals will be strongly positively correlated. The algorithm thus simply corrects for motion by removing the correlated component of the signal. A limitation is that the correlation between oxy-Hb and deoxy-Hb is in practice variable and so the approach relies on an assumption that is not met. A comparison of several of these methods (not including ICA) found that all significantly improved the data quality relative to not performing motion correction (Brigadoi et al., 2014). Of them, discrete wavelet filtering was the most robust and reliable. Another study (Robertson, Douglas, & Meintjes, 2010) compared wavelet filtering with ICA and found that while wavelets were effective at removing 'spike'-type artifacts, ICA was more effective overall, including dealing with slower-changing artifacts. A limitation of any study comparing motion correction techniques, however, is that it is hard to know if the results will generalize to other datasets. In general, any approach to motion correction is preferable to not performing this step, but the optimal algorithm may have to be determined in each lab based on the nature of the data being collected.

Short-Distance Correction

Depending on the optode array, some channels may have relatively short emitter–detector separation distances (2 cm or less). For CW and FD systems, these short-distance channels provide little, if any, usable information about brain activity because few photons will have travelled deeply enough over this separation to penetrate the cortex. One option in this case is to simply discard data from any such short-distance channels. However, another option is to use these short-distance channels to model the noise: since they are expected to be dominated by blood flow in the scalp and other non-brain tissues, they can be used to estimate and subtract these noise signals from other channels that also contain neural signals. In the simplest approach, one can simply use linear regression to subtract the short-distance channel signal from the data from long-distance channels. Other approaches improve on this using adaptive or Kalman filtering. These approaches can reduce noise by anywhere from 3–60%, with somewhat better noise reduction for oxy-Hb than deoxy-Hb. Many implementations of short-distance correction have involved deliberate design of the optode configuration for this purpose, by adding detectors very close (for example, 5 mm) to each emitter explicitly for the purpose of using these for correction. More generally, it is recommended that distances of 15 mm or less be used for short-distance correction, to ensure sensitivity only to superficial haemodynamic signals.

Separating Signals from Noise

As with other types of time series data, temporal filtering is an important step in fNIRI preprocessing to enhance signal detection and reduce noise. The type of filtering, and particularly the cut-offs, naturally depend on whether the researcher's interest is in the fast or the slow signal, since these occur on very different time scales. For slow haemodynamic signals, the filtering needs are similar to fMRI studies: low frequencies are high-pass filtered to reduce effects of drift in the signal, as well as low-frequency aliasing of signals such as pulse and breathing that occur at frequencies higher than the sampling rate of the system, while high frequencies are low-pass filtered – typically with a cut-off twice as high as the frequency of stimulation – since modulation of the haemodynamic response at these higher rates would not be experimentally relevant, and thus would only contribute noise. The actual filter settings chosen need to consider the nature of the acquisition system (in particular the sampling rate, which determines the highest frequency that can actually be sampled without aliasing), as well as the frequency of stimulation. For slow signals, the high-pass cut-off is typically around 0.01 Hz, while low-pass cut-offs range from 0.1–0.8 Hz. For fast signals, a similar high-pass cut-off (0.01 Hz) can be used, since low-frequency artifacts are unwanted; however, since the fast signal is (by definition) rapidly changing, a higher low-pass cut-off (for example, 10–30 Hz) must be used to ensure that the fast neural signal is not filtered out.

Other approaches may be used, however. For example, if one is using regression to identify a stimulus-locked HRF that lasts for about 10 s – or perhaps 30 s in the case of a block design – the presence or absence of, say, 30 Hz noise will likely have little effect on identifying the HRF unless the 30 Hz noise is very large. Therefore, some researchers may choose not to apply low-pass filtering at all, beyond what is needed during recording to prevent aliasing. Removing low frequencies is more important because these can manifest as slow drift that affects estimation of the baseline, or the overall ability to detect experimental effects. However, instead of filtering other approaches can be used. One involves using linear regression, with simple polynomials modelling the low-frequency drift, such as linear, quadratic, and cubic trends. A more sophisticated approach is wavelet-based detrending – essentially, modelling short periods of fluctuation at particular frequencies and with particular shapes. An advantage of wavelet-based detrending is that it can be applied in a regression framework that also includes the predicted HRF. Compared with an approach that attempts to remove low-frequency signals prior to statistical analysis, wavelet-based detrending allows for greater similarity between the wavelets modelling low-frequency noise, and the expected haemodynamic response. In contrast, the cut-offs used in conventional filtering need to be conservative to ensure that the haemodynamic response is not filtered out along with the noise.

Another approach, touched on earlier in the context of motion correction, is **ICA**. In principle, ICA is able to separate components of the signal that are statistically independent of each other, and therefore different noise signals should emerge as separate components from task-related physiological signals. ICA has been demonstrated to be effective in this regard for fNIRI. However, as with other applications of ICA, there are a few caveats to consider. Firstly, the number of components is constrained by the number of independent sources of information, which in this case is the number of channels. Thus in low-channel systems it may not be possible to derive as many independent components as are needed to model all of the different sources in the signal. Applying other artifact correction or removal techniques – such as filtering – prior to ICA can also improve the results by limiting the number of different sources of information that ICA has to separate. Finally, ICA does not always perfectly separate signal from noise, and is dependent on the operator to decide which components to keep or discard. Thus while is it a very useful tool, ICA should not be the sole approach to artifact removal.

Source Localization: Optical Tomography

The issues faced in localizing fNIRI signals have many parallels with other imaging techniques we have covered already. Like EEG and MEG, fNIRI uses measurements made from a set of sensors located around the head. Source localization is thus an **inverse problem**, which is by definition mathematically ill-posed, meaning it has an infinite number of possible solutions. However, unlike EEG but more like MEG, source localization is somewhat simplified by the fact that the range of possible origins of the measured signal is quite constrained. In MEG, the constraint comes from the limited propagation of magnetic fields; in fNIRI, the constraint arises from the limited penetration depth of the NIR light used. Source localization in fNIRI also has some conceptual overlap with PET, where back-propagation is used to infer the sources of photons based on the multiple lines of response passing through a given point in the head; in fNIRI, more than one channel (emitter–detector pair) may involve a path through the same section of the brain (especially when a large number of channels and/or multi-distance measurements are used), which can both increase SNR and reduce uncertainty concerning localization.

The simplest way of analysing fNIRI data, as with EEG/MEG, is to simply analyse the time series data from each channel and not worry about where, exactly, in the brain the signals come from. In some cases, this may be sufficient to answer the research question. For instance, in a study relating motor cortex activity to hand movements, it might be sufficient to place a small array of optodes over the general region of the motor cortex (using the International 10–10 System as a guide) and assume that any task-related signal changes originated in the hand area of the motor cortex. On the other hand, in spite of its limited depth penetration and spatial resolution, fNIRI can provide relatively fine-grained spatial information – indeed, one of the most appealing features of the technique is its ability to provide cortical localization of the BOLD signal with lower cost, and fewer (or at least different) constraints, than fMRI. At the same time, given variability in head size and brain anatomy, even if the optodes are placed on each participant's scalp systematically (for example, using the International 10–10 System) one can expect individual variability in which brain areas each optical channel captures. Thus simply averaging the same channels together across subjects without consideration of individual anatomy may lead to far less accurate results than could be obtained using more sophisticated methods.

Many approaches are available for localizing fNIRI signals, which vary in their complexity, assumptions, and requirements. In general, source localization of fNIRI data is referred to as **optical tomography** (including a range of names and acronyms such as diffuse optical tomography or DOT). One key differentiator among techniques is whether an anatomical MRI scan is required or not. In general, having an MRI scan from each participant will yield the most accurate localization results. At the same time, this requirement adds complexity, time, and cost to the study. Thus several approaches have been developed to co-register fNIRI data to a standard brain template. In large part the process works similarly regardless of whether an individual's own MRI or a standard one is used. First of all, the locations of the optodes need to be registered to the MR image, which can be done either with reference to the International 10–10 System (if optodes are placed according to such a system), or more accurately by using a digitizer that creates a 3D representation of the location of each optode as well as the shape of the head. The optode location information is then co-registered with the structural MR image using algorithms similar to those described in the fMRI and MEG chapters. The next step is to segment the different relevant tissue types (for example, skull, CSF, grey matter) and represent each as a tessellated surface individually, from the MRI scan. This is essentially the same process as described for source localization in the MEG chapter. However, relative to MEG and EEG, optical signals are more dramatically affected by the thickness of the scalp (that is, the tissue outside of the skull) so the thickness of this needs to be modelled accurately, whereas with M/EEG it is at best a minor consideration. Thus whereas M/EEG source localization often uses boundary element models (BEMs), which represent each tissue type as a 2D surface, fNIRI source localization uses **finite element models (FEMs)**, in which layers are represented in 3D, as surfaces with varying thickness.

Having co-registered the optode locations with the cortical surface and intervening tissues, the next step is to identify, for each subject, the brain region that each optical channel is sensitive to. This is a variant of the forward solution introduced earlier for MEG/EEG source localization. In this case, we need a computational model that defines the range of possible paths a photon may take between each emitter–detector pair, and the probability that a photon will take each of those possible paths. The simplest approach to this problem actually ignores the possible range of paths and projects the location of each optode from the scalp to the surface of the brain (for example, by taking the cortical surface point with the shortest distance to the optode or projecting a line from the optode to the scalp, tangential to the surface of the scalp), and then defines the channel at the cortical level as the space in between the projected emitter and detector locations. However, this ignores much of what is known about the complexity of light propagation through the head, and is subject to a fairly high degree of error. As well, it is not amenable to multi-distance measurements.

A variety of more sophisticated approaches have thus been developed. One uses the MBLL; if the data is analysed at the channel level, then a single MBLL formula is used with generic values for the absorption and scattering coefficients. In the tomographic application of this approach, different values of these coefficients are assigned to each voxel in the image (or vertex on each surface) depending on the tissue type and its measured thickness. A more sophisticated approach to the forward problem uses a model known as the Boltzman radiative transfer equation (or photon diffusion equation), which provides increased complexity in modelling light scattering in tissue.

The forward solutions model how light is predicted to pass through the brain, given the set of optodes and the anatomy and optical properties of the tissue. However, as with M/EEG, localizing the origin of the measured fNIRI signals involves solving the more-complex inverse problem. This involves using the forward solution that was computed, to determine from a measurement which among the infinite range of possible distributions of paths is most likely given the data. As well, some form of **regularization** (mathematical compensation) must be made for the fact that there are far fewer independent measurements (channels) than there are possible locations in the brain contributing to that measurement. Common approaches to this include the Tikhonov regularization, spatially variant regularization (SVR), and depth-compensated DOT (DC-DOT).

Statistical Analysis

As with other areas of fNIRI, there are many options available for statistical analysis of the data. Fortunately, these should all be familiar from previous chapters and techniques covered in this book. Since fNIRI data are fundamentally time series data, analysis methods used in M/EEG and fMRI are generally applicable here. For the slow optical signal, studies generally use block designs. Because these offer better SNR than event-related designs – and fNIRI generally suffers from lower SNR than fMRI – this is an ideal situation when the experimental question is amenable to it. On the other hand, event-related designs are readily implementable when the experimental situation demands, and can be quite robust, as shown in Figure 12.9. Many early studies took a relatively simple approach to analysing block designs, by simply averaging the signal across all blocks of the same condition and performing either *t*-tests between pairs of conditions, or ANOVA for more complex designs. However, as with fMRI this 'sledgehammer' approach discards much useful information from the time series, and may be overly susceptible to noise. Thus more recent studies tend to use the **general linear model (GLM)** to perform a multiple regression analysis. This offers advantages over averaging in that the GLM can include nuisance variables to model out expected effects that are not of interest; for example, linear drift could adversely affect the estimation of averages for each block in a simpler analysis, whereas a linear drift term could be explicitly modelled in a GLM analysis.

The approach to GLM analysis is much the same as in fMRI: the stimulus time series is convolved with a model of the haemodynamic response function (HRF) and then this is regressed against the data. This can be done either with the data from each channel, or from each voxel if source localization has been performed. There are several nuances that differentiate fNIRI from fMRI analysis, however. For one, whereas fMRI yields a single measure (BOLD signal), fNIRI typically provides at least three signals: oxy-Hb, deoxy-Hb, and tHb; as well some systems allow for other measurements such as oxygen saturation. It is not uncommon to perform analysis on at least oxy-Hb and deoxy-Hb, and report the results of each separately. Studies that have compared these measurements generally find similar results for each (Hassanpour et al., 2014), although because the magnitude of oxy-Hb tends to be larger than deoxy-Hb or tHb, this may show the greatest sensitivity to experimental effects. Alternatively, some papers simply analyse the signals from each wavelength of light used in the fNIRI system rather than converting to haemoglobin measurements, although this approach makes the data somewhat less interpretable than measurements that reflect more easily understood quantities such as haemoglobin concentration. One also has a choice of which model of the HRF to use, as in fMRI. Given that deoxy-Hb changes tend to be more transient than those in oxy-Hb, it may be the case that different models are more appropriate for the different signals. As with fMRI, subject-specific HRFs derived from separate reference scans (for example, simple finger-tapping) tend to yield more robust results than using a generic HRF, but with the same caveats as in fMRI: the HRF may vary from location to location in the brain, and also this procedure adds time to the overall experimental protocol. An example of the results of this approach to analysis are shown for source-localized data in Figure 12.9.

Another important difference between fMRI and fNIRI analysis concerns multiple comparison correction. In fMRI, we typically have tens or hundreds of thousands of voxels, and thus statistical tests, and so we must properly account for the high likelihood of finding false positives. Likewise in fNIRI, we have some number of channels or, if performing source localization, some number of voxels in the brain; source localization typically generates voxels of approximately the same size as in fMRI, although these are limited to the surface of the brain. However, a key

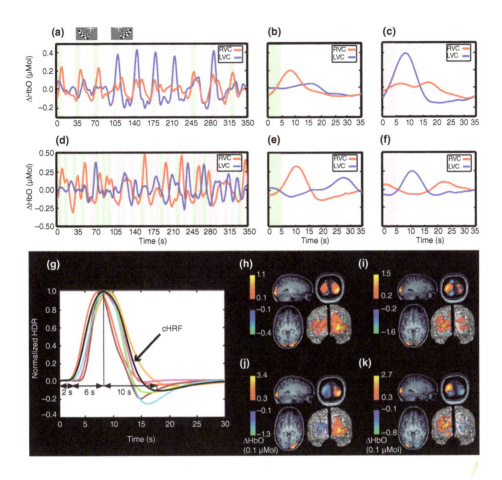

Figure 12.9 An example of GLM-based analysis of source-localized fNIRI data. In this study (which included both blocked and event-related stimulus runs), participants viewed a rotating chequerboard stimulus (a, top) that alternately stimulated the left and right visual fields. Due to the crossed nature of the visual system, this should yield activity in right and left occipital lobes, respectively. Data from the oxy-Hb signal were source-localized and the resulting time courses for each voxel in the brain were analysed using the GLM. Panel (a) shows the time course for an individual participant during the blocked run, for individual voxels in the right (red) and left (blue) primary visual cortex. Panels (b) and (c) show the HRFs from the block design run, obtained by averaging across blocks. Panels (d) through (f) show the equivalent data from the event-related (randomized stimulus order) runs. Panel (g) shows the fitted HRFs for individual ten participants/runs from the block design runs, as well as the average of these (cHRF, black) which was used as the model HRF for analysing the event-related data. Panels (h) and (i) show the thresholded statistical parametric maps for one individual from the blocked runs for left and right hemifield stimulation, respectively, while (j) and (k) show the comparable results from the event-related runs for that individual. Image reproduced with permission of Elsevier from Hassanpour, White, Eggebrecht, Ferradal, Snyder, & Culver (2014)

difference is that the degree of spatial correlation between voxels is quite different in the two techniques. In fMRI, it can be approximated by a Gaussian (normal) distribution. However, in fNIRI the spatial correlations between voxels are much higher: the data from many voxels are estimated by a much lower number of optical channels – potentially as low as 1, and even if a high-density, multi-distance set-up is used there are far more voxels than channels. Thus in fMRI, nearby voxels are correlated primarily because both BOLD signals and physiological noise extend over larger distances than the size of a single voxel; however, the measurements of each voxel are independent due to the nature of fMRI's spatial sampling. By contrast, in optical imaging the data contain both physiological- and measurement-related correlations because the same channel is being used to estimate the data at multiple voxels. For this reason, the most common approach to multiple comparison correction in fMRI, Gaussian random field theory, is inappropriate for fNIRI. However, alternative methods have been developed, including use of a 'tube' formula that considers both physiological and measurement-related correlations (Ye, Tak, Jang, Jung, & Jang, 2009). Alternatively, the false discovery rate (FDR) method – which is also used in some fMRI and other neuroimaging studies – can be used as it makes no assumptions about the nature of spatial correlations.

For the fast optical signal, the approach to analysis is necessarily different because the target signals are not related to blood oxygenation and are thus not expected to have the shape of the HRF. As well, such studies typically use event-related designs since the fast signal is amenable to this. Different research groups have approached this problem either more like er-fMRI analysis, or more like ERP analysis. In the former, the GLM is used to analyse the continuous time series, with the difference being that rather than an HRF a simpler model of the expected activation is used, such as a short-duration (for example, 30 ms) square wave (often called an impulse response function, or IRF). In such cases, multiple lags of this IRF may be included since the delay of the onset of the experimental effects, and their duration, are not known in advance (Chiarelli et al., 2014). In the more ERP-like approach, the continuous time series is segmented into short epochs around the onset of each stimulus (for example, from 100 ms prior to 1000 ms post-onset), baseline-corrected (by subtracting the mean of the post-stimulus period from each time point), and averaged across trials. Then, as in ERP analyses, mean intensities can be analysed within time windows of interest using t-tests or ANOVAs.

MULTIMODAL IMAGING

Optical imaging is perhaps the technique that is most amenable to combination with other neuroimaging and neurostimulation techniques. This is because the parts of the fNIRI system that come into contact with the participant (the optodes) can easily be manufactured without any metal or electronic components. Light is transmitted between the fNIRI hardware and the head using optical fibres, which are made of glass or plastic, and the equipment for affixing these to the scalp can be made from plastic, rubber, and fabric. Thus there is no electromagnetic interference generated by fNIRI that would contaminate EEG, MEG, or MRI measurements, nor will the fields generated by TMS or TES affect the optical measurements. (Although some types of photodetectors are affected by magnetic fields, these can be located outside the shielded MRI room.) Furthermore, light can travel for very long distances in optical fibres with very little effect on the signal quality (optical fibres are commonly used to transport signals over tens or even thousands of kilometres), so in situations such as MRI where the fNIRI hardware needs to be kept well away from the participant (for example, in another room), it is easy to adapt the system to using long optical fibres running from the participant in the scanner to the hardware in another room, through a **waveguide** in the MRI room's shielding.

There are two general reasons why one would want to combine fNIRI with another imaging method. One is to gain a richer understanding of a particular neurocognitive process; the other is to further our understanding of what fNIRI actually measures. For example, Cui and colleagues (Cui, Bray, Bryant, Glover, & Reiss, 2011) performed simultaneous fMRI and CW fNIRI on a group of participants under several different task conditions, to better understand how fNIRI measurements relate to underlying activity. This treated fMRI as a 'gold standard' for localization. The results yielded several interesting insights. For one, scalp–brain distance was negatively correlated with the fMRI–fNIRI correlation; in other words, for areas of the brain that are farther from the scalp (and thus the fNIRI sensors), SNR is poorer and so the ability to detect brain-related signals is weaker. In this study (which used somewhat limited coverage of the head), brain–scalp distance was found to be greatest

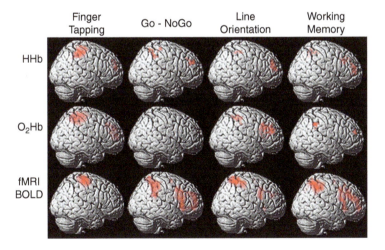

Figure 12.10 Comparison of localization of haemodynamic signals obtained from several task contrasts using simultaneous CW fNIRI (deoxy-Hb and oxy-Hb signals) and fMRI BOLD in a study by Cui and colleagues (2011). Reprinted with permission of Elsevier

over the parietal lobe, and smallest over the frontal lobes. As well, although fMRI and fNIRI signals were significantly correlated when activation was present, the contrast-to-noise ratio (CNR) was consistently higher for the fMRI signal than either oxy-Hb or deoxy-hB fNIRI signals. Finally, the authors identified the voxels within the path of each fNIRI channel that correlated best with the fMRI signal, in order to determine what point along the optical path fNIRI is most sensitive to. The results showed that the strongest contributions came from regions 2–2.5 cm under the scalp, but were fairly evenly distributed along the banana-shaped path between emitter and detector. Overall, the results of this study showed good agreement between the localization of fNIRI and fMRI signals, as shown in Figure 12.10.

Other studies have used fast optical signals to aid in localizing the sources of EEG signals (Mathewson et al., 2014; Medvedev, Kainerstorfer, Borisov, & VanMeter, 2010), and also to localize and characterize changes in motor cortex activity induced by TMS (Parks, Maclin, Low, Beck, Fabiani, & Gratton, 2012). A number of commercially available systems have been developed to facilitate multimodal imaging involving fNIRI, such as caps that allow interleaved placement of optodes and EEG electrodes, as shown in Figure 12.6.

SUMMARY

Functional NIRI employs the principles of spectrophotometry, which is a technique for calculating the concentration of a material in a liquid by passing light through the substance. In the case of brain imaging fNIRI involves shining near-infrared light into the head and measuring the amount of light transmitted at a location a few centimetres away from the source, to measure the concentrations of oxygenated haemoglobin and deoxyhaemoglobin. As such, fNIRI is an indirect measure of neural activity, based on a physiological marker very similar to what is measured in fMRI, and the shape and time course of the fNIRI HRF is very similar to that of BOLD fMRI. However, whereas the fMRI BOLD response is sensitive to the ratio of oxy-Hb to deoxy-Hb, fNIRI provides separate measurements of the concentrations of each of these, as well as combining them for a measure of total blood volume. In addition, fNIRI can measure a 'fast signal' that has timing more similar to EEG/MEG measures and is thought to reflect changes in intra/extra-cellular volume (cell swelling) that occur with ion flux across cell membranes.

Broadly speaking, there are three ways to obtain fNIRI measurements. Continuous wave (CW) systems shine light of a specific frequency and intensity continuously during recording, and measurements are based on the drop in light intensity at the detector relative to the emitter. Frequency-domain (FD) systems also shine light continuously, but modulate the intensity of the light at a specific frequency, which allows for measurement of both light absorption (as in CW fNIRI) and timing. The timing information provided by FD systems allows them to measure both slow and fast signals, whereas CW systems can only measure slow signals. Time-domain (TD) systems send a series of rapid pulses of light, which allow for enhanced temporal sensitivity relative to FD. Beyond simply improving the temporal resolution of fNIRI, the temporal information provided by FD and TD can improve sensitivity to true brain activation. This is because light that does not pass through the brain, but only superficial tissues of the head, will arrive at the detector sooner than light that passes through the brain, and indeed signals from deeper in the brain will arrive later than those from more shallow brain regions. Time-based measurements are also less sensitive to head movements than CW data.

Regardless of the types of measurement, all fNIRI systems depend on sources of light (LEDs or lasers), optical fibres to transmit the light to and from the head, optodes to interface with the head, and light detectors such as photodiodes or photomultipliers. Although fNIRI has existed for as long as fMRI, it is used much less widely, and the hardware and data-analysis technologies employed are quite variable. While a number of commercial fNIRI systems exist, many other systems are purpose-built in individual labs – especially the most technically advanced systems. Due to cost and other constraints, few fNIRI systems provide full head coverage, but instead consist of a small array of emitters and detectors that are placed over the brain region of interest for a given study. Like MEG data, fNIRI data can be analysed either at the sensor level, or by performing source localization – often called optical tomography in this context.

As a neuroimaging technique, fNIRI has several strong points. It is wearable, and relatively lightweight and insensitive to head movement, making it a good technique to use with infants, children, and other people who might not do well in an fMRI or MEG scanner. As well, it is silent (unlike fMRI), has low operating costs (unlike fMRI or MEG), and few contraindications (so, for example, people who could not have an MRI scan due to implanted metal or devices could participate in an fNIRI study). The spatial resolution of fNIRI is limited in that light only penetrates a few centimetres into the head, and with most approaches there is a minimum separation distance between light emitters and detectors that limits spatial resolution laterally to approximately 2–3 cm. At the same time, this spatial resolution is sufficient to resolve localized brain activity at the meso-anatomical scale, and activity measured with fNIRI aligns closely with what is obtained with fMRI, within cortical regions that are accessible to fNIRI.

THINGS YOU SHOULD KNOW

- Spectrophotometry is a technique for determining the concentration of a substance by shining light through the substance and measuring the amount of light absorbed. Absorbance is related to concentration through the Beer–Lambert law. In fNIRI, light of specific wavelengths is shined through the head in order to measure the concentrations of oxygenated and deoxygenated haemoglobin.

- The slow optical signal refers to that generated by oxy-Hb and deoxy-Hb. This is an indirect measure of neural activity very similar to the BOLD response measured by fMRI. In contrast, the fast signal changes on a time scale similar to EEG and MEG signals, and is thought to be directly related to cell swelling and shrinkage that occurs as activity-dependent ion channels open and close.

- Performing fNIRI requires sources of light that have specific, narrow-band wavelengths and controllable intensity; a means of transmitting the light to the head (fibre optics and optodes); and light detectors (photodiodes or photomultipliers). It is important that the optodes touching the head hold the fibres securely (to resist motion-related artifacts) and protect the measurements from ambient light.

- The wavelengths of light used in fNIRI are chosen to maximize sensitivity to oxy-Hb and deoxy-Hb, while minimizing the interference from other chromophores (light-absorbing compounds) including water. Because oxy-Hb and deoxy-Hb have different light absorption profiles across the near-infrared spectrum, a minimum of two wavelengths must be used in fNIRI in order to distinguish these two chromophores. Commonly, one wavelength shows greater absorption by oxy-Hb while the other shows greater absorption by deoxy-Hb. Using additional wavelengths could help reduce contamination of the signal by other (non-haemoglobin) chromophores, but there is a limitation on the total amount of light energy that can safely be transmitted into the head, which must be divided by the number of wavelengths used. Thus increasing the number of wavelengths decreases the strength of the signal obtained from each.

- A major impediment to fNIRI signals is the hair, especially when it is dark and/or thick, as this can block light transmission. Although fNIRI is less sensitive to head movement than is fMRI, movement of the optodes can create large artifacts, especially if the movement allows ambient light to reach the optodes. Another source of noise arises from the fact that most of the light coming from the emitter does not pass through the brain, but only through more superficial tissues. As well as reducing the signal overall, this can contaminate the signal since blood vessels outside the brain will also contribute to the haemodynamic signal measured.

- The spatial resolution of fNIRI is limited both by the fact that safe levels of light energy only penetrate a few centimetres into the head, and that the light emitters and detectors must be placed 2–4 cm apart to allow light to reach the brain. The fact that the brain is variable in its distance from the outer surface of the head also creates variable depth resolution across the head. Time-domain fNIRI holds the promise of improved spatial resolution by more accurately estimating the signal from deep sources, and allowing for reduced emitter–detector distance. Most fNIRI systems also limit coverage to one part of the head, meaning that whole-brain imaging is not usually possible. The temporal resolution of fNIRI is limited by the fact that light from multiple emitters will reach each detector, requiring some form of multiplexing that can reduce the time between measurements for each channel. Thus there is commonly a trade-off between number of channels and sampling rate.

- The fNIRI signal can be measured in three ways. Continuous wave (CW) imaging involves shining a light of constant intensity and wavelength, whereas frequency domain (FD) imaging involves modulating intensity sinusoidally at a specific frequency. FD imaging is less sensitive to head movement than CW, and also provides information regarding the timing of light transmission through the head, whereas CW only provides intensity (absorption) information. FD is thus required for measuring the fast signal. Time-domain imaging has greater temporal precision than FD imaging, by using very brief pulses rather than continuous transmission of light. This allows for measuring the distribution of travel times of individual photons, which allows researchers to filter out signals whose transmission times are too short to have passed through the brain, as well as resolving signals from different depths of penetration.

- Preprocessing of fNIRI data requires steps similar to M/EEG and fMRI, including temporal filtering, and removal or correction of head-movement artifacts. ICA may also be used to isolate signals from various noise sources. Unique to fNIRI is the need for short-distance correction, which attempts to remove signal from photons that passed through superficial, rather than brain, tissues. Source localization of fNIRI signals is in principle similar to the approach used in M/EEG: forward solutions are determined based on models of brain anatomy and the physics of signal transmission, and then the combination of activation strengths at different sources that best matches the observed data is determined through an iterative process. However, because in fNIRI the signal is optical, the principles of signal transmission employed are very different. For instance, the thickness of the skull should be determined at each location rather than assuming a constant value, because this impacts the transmission of light far more than magnetic or even electrical signals.

- The fNIRI technique naturally lends itself to pairing with other imaging modalities. For instance, fNIRI systems are generally safe to use in MRI environments as the hardware placed on the participant's head is generally non-metallic and does not interfere with electromagnetic fields. Likewise, fNIRI produces no electromagnetic noise that would interfere with M/EEG recordings, and so can be used with these devices. Indeed, a number of systems allow for fNIRI optodes and EEG electrodes to be fitted into the same caps, allowing for simultaneous recording. For these same reasons, fNIRI is also compatible with neurostimulation techniques discussed in the next two chapters.

FURTHER READINGS

Boas, D.A., Elwell, C.E., Ferrari, M., & Taga, G. (2014). Twenty years of functional near-infrared spectroscopy: Introduction for the special issue. *NeuroImage*, *85*(P1), 1–5.

Chen, Y., and Kateb, B. (Eds.) (2017). *Neurophotonics and Brain Mapping*. Boca Raton, FL: CRC Press.

Ferrari, M., & Quaresima, V. (2012). A brief review on the history of human functional near-infrared spectroscopy (fNIRS) development and fields of application. *NeuroImage*, *63*(2), 921–935.

Scholkmann, F., Kleiser, S., Metz, A.J., Zimmermann, R., Pavia, J.M., Wolf, U., & Wolf, M. (2014). A review on continuous wave functional near-infrared spectroscopy and imaging instrumentation and methodology. *NeuroImage*, *85*(P1), 6–27.

13 Transcranial Magnetic Stimulation (TMS)

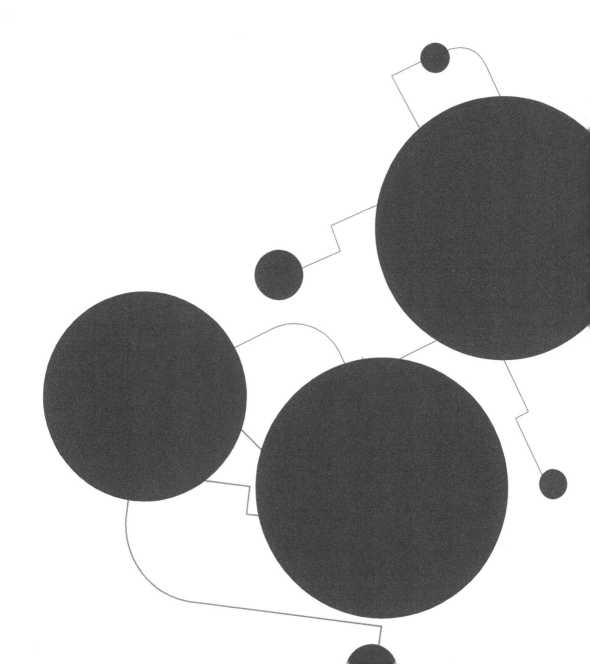

LEARNING OBJECTIVES

After reading this chapter, you should be able to:

- Describe how TMS stimulates the brain.
- Describe common ways of determining the location of TMS stimulation in the brain.
- Describe several different protocols for delivering TMS, including their temporal patterns and effects.
- Describe the primary neurochemical means by which TMS is thought to operate.
- List the types of controls necessary for ensuring the causal relationship between TMS and observed results.
- Identify important risks and safety considerations in performing TMS.

INTRODUCTION

The next two chapters focus on **non-invasive brain stimulation** (**NIBS**) techniques (sometimes abbreviated NTBS for non-invasive transcranial brain stimulation). These include transcranial magnetic stimulation (TMS) and transcranial electrical stimulation (tES). TMS involves inducing a transient electrical current in the cortex via the right-hand rule, using a strong magnetic field. In contrast, tES involves direct application of a weak electrical current to the scalp, which is conducted to the brain. Each of these methods actually comprises a set of techniques, as we will discuss in detail in this chapter and the next. It is worth noting that cognitive neuroscience research can also be done using invasive stimulation methods, although these are beyond the scope of this book. These include direct electrical stimulation of the cortex during neurosurgery (often used clinically to identify motor or language cortex so that critical areas can be avoided during resection), using electrodes implanted for the purposes of epilepsy monitoring (recording electrodes placed on the surface of the cortex can sometimes also be used for stimulation), and using implanted brain stimulators such as deep brain stimulators (DBS).

The techniques in this chapter differ fundamentally from those described in previous chapters, in that they necessarily involve an intervention – applying electrical or magnetic stimulation to the brain – rather than recording brain activity. At the same time, however, the use of these techniques falls squarely within the paradigms of cognitive neuroscience that should by now be familiar to the reader. Most cognitive neuroscience involves the application of some sort of stimulus – be it visual, auditory, or via another sensory modality – and then measuring some sort of response – either a behavioural one or using a neuroimaging technique (or both). In brain stimulation studies, the stimulus is electromagnetic (though this may be combined with sensory stimulation and/or a task), but the results are assessed using the same methods we are now familiar with: behavioural responses and/or neuroimaging techniques.

Brain stimulation has a colourful history, to say the least. Brunoni and colleagues (2012) note that a physician of the Roman Emperor Claudius, Scribonius Largus, described how headache could be relieved by delivering an electrical shock by placing a live stingray on the head – a practice also recommended by later physicians including Galen and Pliny the Elder; electric fish were also recommended as a treatment for epilepsy by Muslim physician Ibn-Sidah. Much later, in the eighteenth century, came Galvani's original experiments with frogs suggesting that the nervous system relied on electrical impulses. Galvani's nephew Aldini took a more dramatic approach to investigating this phenomenon, by performing electrical stimulation experiments on the freshly decapitated corpses of executed convicts at the turn of the nineteenth century. Aldini reported that electrical stimulation to various parts of the brain elicited facial grimaces (on the corpses, though perhaps this triggered similar responses in onlookers as well). While it is unclear whether his primitive techniques elicited muscle contractions due to stimulation of the brain, or of the facial muscles directly, Aldini's work provided some of the first evidence supporting the contention that the human brain and nervous system relied on electrical signalling. Approximately 100 years later, several physicians reported on experiments with patients whose brains were exposed due to disease or injury, providing the opportunity for direct electrical stimulation and again providing strong evidence for the role of electricity in neural signalling in humans, this time in vivo – though it should be noted that similar experiments had already been performed throughout the nineteenth century in other animals. This work eventually led to the seminal work of Wilder Penfield, Herbert Jasper, and colleagues in the early to mid-twentieth century, who developed the method of electrical stimulation mapping during awake neurosurgery in humans that is still the gold standard to this day in neurosurgery. Although many early attempts at stimulating the brain via magnetism were made, it was not until the 1980s that TMS as we now know it was invented – specifically, the ability to deliver a brief and focal pulse via electromagnetic induction.

A final introductory note to this chapter is that the sections are laid out somewhat differently than for previous chapters. This is because the question 'What are we measuring?' is a bit different for NTBS techniques than for neuroimaging methods. NTBS is not a measurement, and so measuring the effects of NTBS employs the behavioural and/or neuroimaging methods described previously in this book. In general, however, in using NTBS what we are measuring is the effect of modulating the activity of a particular brain region on behaviour and/or brain activity. NTBS can be used to increase (facilitate) or decrease (inhibit) the activity of a focal brain region (typically a few square centimetres), and in doing so can provide information as to the causal role of that brain region in a particular cognitive function. Indeed, this is perhaps the greatest unique contribution of NTBS: whereas brain imaging can indicate or suggest that a particular brain area may be involved in a particular task, NTBS can potentially prove or disprove the role of that area, and reveal its functional contribution. For example, the mere fact that the inferior frontal gyrus (IFG, or Broca's area) 'lights up' in fMRI studies of speech production does not prove that Broca's area is necessary, or causally involved, in speech production. Neuropsychological lesion-deficit studies can provide causal evidence, in that damage to the IFG leads to speech production difficulties in a majority of patients. However, such evidence is not optimal because lesions vary in their cause, location, size, and comorbidities, creating numerous confounds to interpretation. On the other hand, TMS can induce transient 'virtual lesions' by disrupting activity to a targeted part of the brain. Thus by administering virtual lesion TMS to the IFG of a group of otherwise healthy people during a speech production task, we can determine with much greater confidence whether this brain area is necessary for speech production (which indeed, it is).

HOW DO WE DO IT?

TMS involves inducing an electrical current in the brain, using a strong magnetic field. Faraday's laws of induction (the right-hand rule) specify that a current is induced by flux, or change, in a magnetic field. Thus TMS works using pulses: brief, but strong, fluctuations in electrical current through a conductive coil. The coil (insulated in plastic) is held directly over the scalp of the person being stimulated, and the pulse induces a strong, time-varying magnetic field which in turn induces an electrical current in the brain of the person stimulated. The coil is connected to the main TMS device, which includes a capacitor, a device which can store electrical potential. This is charged to a high voltage, which is then released as a strong current (in the order of 8000 A) when the operator presses the switch on the TMS coil. A pulse is very short – it typically has a rise time of 100–200 μs and lasts for only 1 ms – but induces a magnetic field strength in the order of 1.5–3 T, which is comparable to an MRI scanner. However, the effects of this field are very different from the static magnetic field of an MRI, for several reasons. For one thing, since – according to the right-hand rule – current is induced by magnetic *flux* (that is, a changing field), the constant magnetic field of an MRI will not induce a current the way a 1 ms fluctuation of the same magnetic field strength does. As well, the strength of an induced magnetic field drops off exponentially with distance, and the overall size of an induced magnetic field is proportional to the size of the coil of wire that is inducing it. Thus an MRI, which has to have a coil large enough for a human body to fit in, has a very large surrounding magnetic field which requires housing it in a shielded room with very specific 'safe' distances to ensure that ferromagnetic items are not pulled into the scanner with great speed and force. In contrast, the field induced by the small TMS coil drops off over distances of a few centimetres. This is advantageous in two regards. Firstly, a TMS device does not need a specially shielded room, and electrical and ferromagnetic equipment can safely be kept quite close to the device. Secondly, this means that the neural stimulation provided by TMS is very focal. Even with the coil pushed firmly against the scalp, it is estimated that TMS stimulation only penetrates 1.5–2 cm below the scalp, meaning it only directly affects the cerebral cortex (or cerebellum, depending on placement), and possibly not even the deepest sulci of the cortex. The spread of the stimulation laterally is also quite focal, estimated at about 12 cm² at a depth of 2 cm below the scalp, or a patch about 3.5 x 3.5 cm. The depth and spread of the stimulation vary with the design of the stimulation coil.

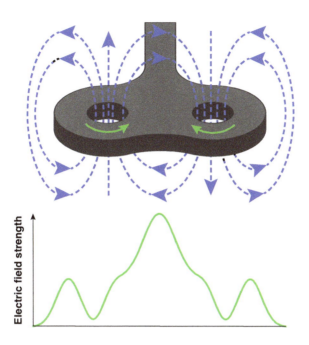

Figure 13.1 Schematic diagram of a TMS coil and the magnetic and electric fields it induces. The coil shown (grey) is a figure-8 design, which is one of the most commonly used designs in cognitive neuroscience research. Inside the plastic housing, conductive wire is wound in a figure-8 design around the two holes shown, such that current flowing through the wire (shown by green curved arrows) runs clockwise in one 'lobe' of the coil, and counter-clockwise in the other lobe. By the right-hand rule, these currents induce magnetic fields (shown as blue dashed lines) flowing in opposite directions in each lobe of the coil, such that they summate at the centre. The bottom panel shows the strength of electric field induced under the coil, in the two-dimensional plane running from one side of the coil to the other

The most common types of TMS coil are the circular and the figure-8 shapes, as shown in Figure 13.2. Although the circular coil is the simplest design, the current distribution that it induces in the brain is actually somewhat complex, as shown in Figure 13.3. This is because of the right-hand rule: if you hold your right hand with thumb extended and fingers curled, you can imagine that the current in the coil flows in the direction of your thumb and the magnetic field wraps around it with the curl of your fingers. While this is relatively straightforward for a straight conductor, with a small coil such as a circular TMS coil, the current moves in a small circle and thus induces a magnetic field whose orientation changes quite quickly over a small amount of space. Consequently, direction of the current induced in the brain under one side of the coil will be opposite to the direction of the current induced on the other side of the coil, and very little current will actually be induced directly under the centre of the coil – which is somewhat counterintuitive since one might expect the centre of the loop to be the focus of the stimulation. For this reason, **figure-8 coils** (also called **'figure-of-eight' coil**) are generally preferred for many TMS applications. These contain two conducing loops positioned side-by-side, in which current flows in opposite directions (that is, clockwise in one loop, counterclockwise in the other). Where the two loops touch, at the centre of the coil (the middle of the '8'), the magnetic fields induced by the two conductors will summate, because the current is flowing in the same direction in both loops. Slightly farther away, the opposite windings of the two conductors will cause the induced magnetic fields to cancel out, helping to make the stimulation more focal under the centre of the coil. At either end of the coil (the top and bottom of the '8'), weaker, electric fields will be induced, in the opposite direction from the induced field at the centre of the coil. This is illustrated in Figure 13.1. However, these have a much weaker impact on the brain, both because they don't benefit from the summation of two coils, and because the coil is held such that the centre is touching the scalp. Due to the curvature of the head, the ends of the coil do not touch the scalp and are consequently farther away from the brain; since magnetic field drops off exponentially with distance, this means a much weaker induced current under these areas (which is treated as negligible in most studies). In recent years, more complex coil designs have been developed that combine many different shapes and orientations of windings. One notable design is the 'H coil', which involves several different windings covering a substantial part of the head, all encased in a helmet-like enclosure. The H coil can stimulate to a depth of approximately 6 cm below the scalp, allowing stimulation to be targeted at deep structures such as the cingulate gyrus and orbitofrontal cortex.

Because TMS delivers such focal stimulation, positioning of the coil is very important. In the early days of TMS, it was typical to start by estimating the location of the stimulation target using measurements, such as the International 10–10 System used for EEG electrode placements. Using this system, one can estimate the location of a brain area with reference to an atlas, and anterior–posterior and left–right measurements of the head. This can be done simply by measuring, or by using an EEG-style cap that has 10-10 system locations marked on it (but no actual EEG electrodes). Such a method is necessarily approximate, since individual neuroanatomy is highly variable. However, this can form a starting point from which the experimenter stimulates at different locations until obtaining a 'positive' response. For example, when the motor cortex area corresponding to a particular finger is stimulated, the finger muscles will twitch (which is measurable using electromyography – EMG) and if the stimulation is strong enough the finger will visibly move. Thus systematically stimulating over a grid of locations corresponding to the general location of the motor cortex will allow the experimenter to determine the precise location to target a particular body part when doing TMS in the motor system.

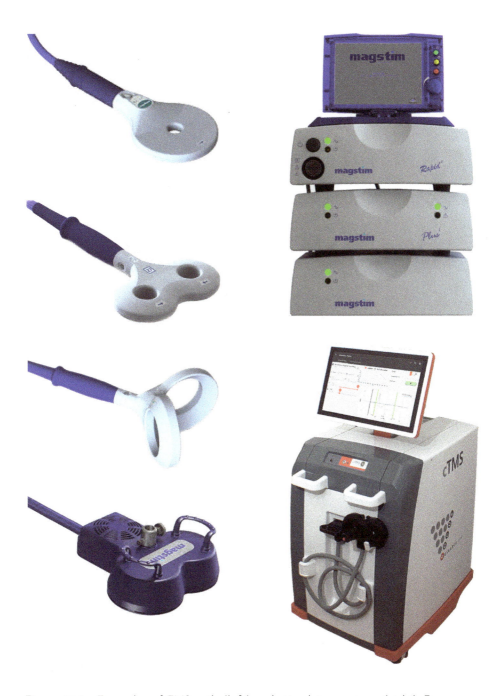

Figure 13.2 Examples of TMS coils (left) and stimulator systems (right). From top to bottom, the coils are a single-ring, figure-8, double cone, and an air-cooled figure-8 (with a built-in fan to reduce overheating). The bottom right system shows a figure-8 coil (black) plugged into the front of the stimulator unit. Images courtesy Magstim Inc. (coils and top right) and Rogue Research Inc. (bottom right)

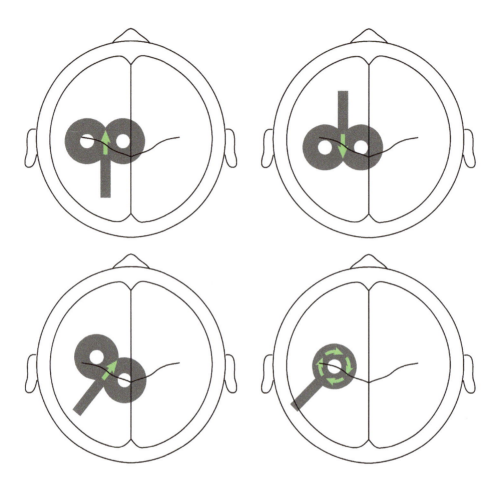

Figure 13.3 Effects of coil orientation on induced electrical current field. With a figure-8 coil (left and top right), the electrical current induced is largest directly under the centre of the '8' portion of the coil, oriented parallel to the handle of the coil. With a circular coil (bottom right), the induced current flows in a circular direction under the coil; note that the current is strongest under the actual loop of the coil, and not in the centre of the loop

Perhaps unsurprisingly, the majority of TMS research has been done on the motor system because it is so easy to know when the right target has been stimulated. The visual system also provides some clear markers: for example, when area V5/MT (which processes visual motion) is stimulated, moving **phosphenes** (illusory points of light – colloquially called 'seeing stars' when they are induced by a bump to the head) are perceived. When colour-sensitive V4 is stimulated, coloured phosphenes are seen, and stimulation of retinotopically organized primary visual cortex can result in phosphenes located in the corresponding quadrant of the visual field.

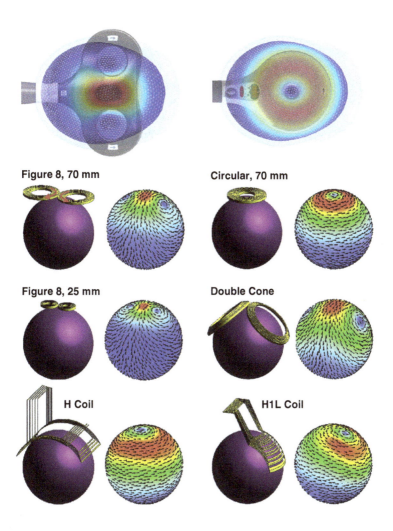

Figure 13.4 Top row shows the strength (colour, ranging from red, maximum, to blue, minimum) of the electrical currents induced by 70 mm figure-8 (left) and 50 mm circular (right) coils on the surface of the brain as viewed from above the coil. The bottom three rows show both the strength and direction (small arrows) of the electrical currents induced by different coil designs, estimated using a spherical model of the head. Images in the top row provided by Dr Matthew Biginton of the Magstim Company and used with permission. Bottom rows adapted from Deng, Lisanby, & Peterchev, 2013 with permission of Elsevier

Although this approach may sound a bit crude, it is highly effective because the procedures provide concrete proof that a functionally specific area of the brain is being stimulated. However, both the precise position and orientation of the coil determine the location that is stimulated most focally, and so a hand-held approach is at best approximate, and at worst not replicable. Much greater anatomical precision can be obtained using **neuro-navigation**, as shown in Figure 13.5. This involves a 3D motion tracking system, typically using an infrared camera that detects markers placed on specific locations on the subject's head, and on the TMS coil. The markers on the head are registered to the corresponding locations on a 3D anatomical MRI of the subject (or, if their MRI is not available, a standard atlas such as the MNI152 can be used; naturally this reduces anatomical accuracy), and then the neuro-navigation system shows the location of the TMS coil relative to the subject's brain, in real time on a computer screen. This allows the experimenter to target anatomical areas with essentially millimetre-level precision. Moreover, if fMRI data is available, this can be co-registered with the neuro-navigation system and superimposed on the anatomical MRI. In this way, TMS stimulation can be directed towards areas that fMRI has identified as being relevant to a particular task.

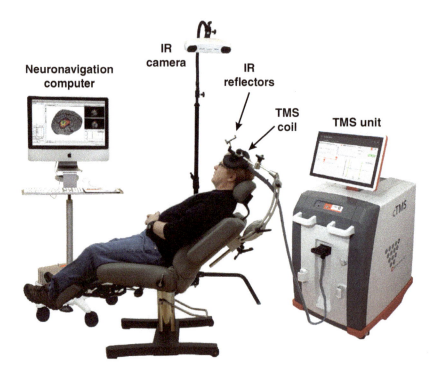

Figure 13.5 A neuro-navigation system for TMS. The system uses an infrared (IR) camera to detect markers that reflect IR light. The TMS coil is held in place with a mechanical arm, and has IR markers on it. The position of the coil relative to the head is determined by digitizing certain fiducial markers (reference points on the head, like the bridge of the nose and the ears). The computer screen shows a structural MR scan of the person receiving TMS; the fiducial markers are also located on that scan. This allows the software to show the position of the TMS coil relative to the brain, in real time, to precisely target a brain area for stimulation. Image used with permission of Rogue Research Inc.

While neuro-navigation on its own is of great assistance, another useful tool is a way to hold the TMS coil in a fixed position. The operator can hold the coil in their hand, however relatively small movements can have relatively dramatic effects on the location of stimulation. This means that over any period of stimulation, the operator's hand may move, and if repeated periods of stimulation are applied – either within an experiment or across sessions – replicability may be an issue due to variation in the position of the coil. Thus one can use an articulated mechanical arm that allows the coil to be positioned and fixed in place, often combined with an apparatus that holds the subject's head in a fixed position so that it doesn't move relative to the coil. Such set-ups are essential for reliable, replicable results. Another option is robotic TMS systems, wherein the mechanical arm is attached to motors that can move it automatically. Robotic systems can be programmed to move to a desired stimulation position simply by indicating it in the neuro-navigation software, and can also adapt 'on the fly' to movements of the subject's head.

A final technical aspect we will touch on here is the shape of the stimulation pulse. A pulse involves the time required to reach maximum intensity (rise time), duration of the pulse, and the time required for intensity to drop to baseline. As well, pulses can be monophasic, biphasic, or polyphasic, as shown in Figure 13.6. A **monophasic pulse** reaches its intensity peak and then returns to baseline (zero voltage). Although this is the simplest type of pulse conceptually, it actually requires a more complex electrical circuit to produce than a biphasic pulse, because the natural effect of passing a current through the coil is oscillatory: the initial rise and fall would be followed by an equal and opposite negative voltage. This is in fact the shape of a **biphasic pulse**, which forms one complete cycle of a sine wave. A **polyphasic pulse** is a more general case of the biphasic pulse, involving one or more full positive–negative cycles. Although TMS initially relied primarily on monophasic pulses, biphasic pulses became more widely used when it was realized that these actually allow 'recycling' of the electrical energy in the circuit, which allows the capacitor (the part of the stimulator that builds up and stores the large amount of energy needed for each pulse) to recharge more quickly between pulses, as well as less heating of the coil. Other advantages of biphasic and polyphasic pulses is that they are less affected by the direction of the current within the coil (since there are equal and opposite currents over time), and they tend to produce stronger neural responses than monophasic pulses.

Stimulation Protocols

The important parameters to set for TMS include the type, duration, frequency, and strength of the magnetic pulses. Different sets of parameters can yield dramatically different effects, all using the same TMS machine. Most fundamentally, depending on the frequency of stimulation, TMS can have either an excitatory (facilitatory) or inhibitory effect on brain activity and task performance. The most simple usage is **single-pulse TMS** which, as the name suggests, involves applying one isolated pulse (recall that a pulse lasts about 1 ms). This causes immediate excitation of the stimulated cortex, followed by a 'silent' period when neural activity and excitability are reduced.

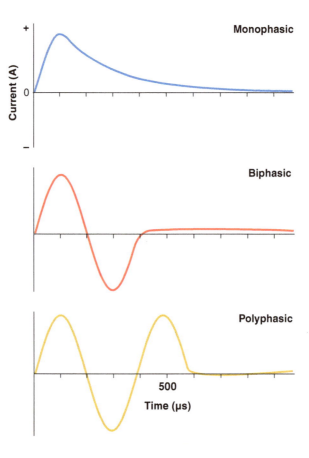

Figure 13.6 Different pulse shapes used in single-pulse TMS, represented as the strength of the electrical current that is passed through the TMS coil as a function of time

Another common protocol is **repetitive TMS (rTMS)**, in which a series of pulses are administered, typically at a fixed frequency. Here, the frequency of stimulation determines the effects: stimulation frequencies of 1 Hz or less cause decreased excitability (cortical inhibition), whereas frequencies higher than 1 Hz (commonly used frequencies include 4-9 Hz, 10 Hz, and 20 Hz) typically cause increased excitability (facilitation). More complex protocols include **theta burst stimulation (TBS)**, which involves a series of brief triplets of stimulation (3 pulses at 50 Hz) interspersed with slightly longer rest periods (which can be milliseconds up to seconds long), **quadripulse stimulation (QPS)**, which involves bursts of four pulses in rapid succession separated by longer (for example, 5 s) periods, and **paired-pulse stimulation** which involves a pair of single pulses that can either be delivered to the same location with a fixed interval, or to two different brain regions to investigate inter-regional connectivity (and requiring two TMS machines and coils). In what follows we will delve deeper into the uses and effects of these different protocols.

Single-Pulse Stimulation

Single-pulse protocols are commonly used in studies of the motor system. In fact, even studies that use other stimulation protocols almost always start with a single-pulse motor mapping paradigm to determine the intensity of stimulation that will be used in the main experiment. This is because individuals' thresholds for stimulation with TMS vary quite widely, and for safety reasons (see later in this chapter) it is important to find the weakest level of stimulation that will yield the desired effects. The motor system is ideal for determining stimulation intensity because the threshold required to obtain a response can easily be measured: one simply attaches **EMG (electromyograph**; measurements of neuromuscular activity) electrodes to the arm or finger, performs systematic stimulation mapping across a gird placed over the motor cortex to identify the location corresponding to the muscle target with EMG, and then determines what level of stimulation intensity is required to obtain a **motor evoked potential** (**MEP** – the EMG response elicited when a muscle contracts) on 50% of trials. This intensity is defined as the **resting motor threshold (rMT)** and stimulation intensity in the main part of the experiment is typically expressed as a percentage of rMT (for example, 100% or 50%). Because the intensity of stimulation can vary widely among individuals, the standard in the field is to specify the stimulation intensity to be used in a study as a percentage of rMT, and use the rMT determined for each individual participant to determine the intensity for that individual. This allows for a standardization of stimulation intensity in terms of 'functional' levels tailored to the individual. The motor mapping procedure is shown in Figure 13.7.

The reliability of rMTs has been shown to be quite high across repeated TMS sessions on the same person, although an individual's threshold can vary with their state, including whether or not they recently exercised, and whether they are fatigued or well rested. It is also possible to measure the **active motor threshold (aMT)**, by having the subject contract the target muscle during stimulation; aMT is typically lower than rMT because of the 'assistance' provided by the subject's voluntarily activating their motor cortex, in addition to the stimulation provided by TMS. In addition to rMT and aMT, another measure that is commonly obtained in single-pulse TMS studies is the **silent period (SP)**: immediately after an MEP is evoked by a TMS pulse to the motor cortex, noise in EMG recordings from the targeted muscle is suppressed. This suppression lasts for hundreds of milliseconds, and the duration of the SP can vary depending on the state of the subject and the experimental conditions, making SP duration a variable of interest in many studies. Distinct SPs can be measured from a muscle contralateral (cSP) and ipsilateral (iSP) to the stimulated motor cortex, and these two SPs are thought to reflect different pathways. The first 50 ms of the cSP seem to reflect spinal mechanisms, with the later period reflecting cortical inhibition. In contrast, the iSP is thought to reflect inhibition across the corpus callosum from the ipsilateral to contralateral motor cortex.

Single-pulse TMS has a number of experimental applications, in addition to its use in simply mapping the motor cortex locations of specific muscles, and determining optimal stimulation levels. For example, imagined movements have been shown to lower rMT, similar to overtly contracting a muscle as when determining aMT.

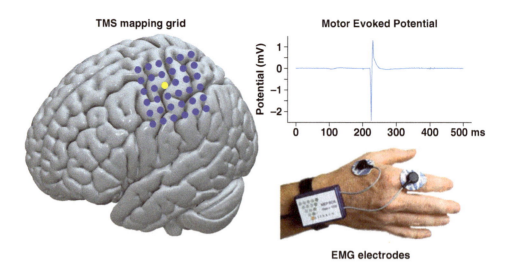

Figure 13.7 Motor mapping with TMS. The left panel shows a grid of stimulation sites centred over the central sulcus. Each site would be stimulated in turn to identify the site that evokes the maximum motor evoked potential (MEP), shown here in yellow. The bottom right panel shows the two electromyogram (EMG) electrodes placed on the hand that would be used to record the MEP from the targeted muscle. The top right panel shows an example MEP. MEP courtesy of Dr Shaun Boe; photo of EMG electrodes courtesy of Rogue Research Inc.

Single-pulse TMS has the advantage over the other protocols discussed below of high temporal precision, since a single pulse is so brief in duration. This makes it ideal for studying the temporal dynamics of processing. In a seminal early study, Amassian and colleagues (1989) examined the effects of TMS on visual perception. Single pulse TMS applied over the primary visual cortex (V1) caused masking effects – that is, the subject's not perceiving a visual stimulus – when the TMS pulse occurred 80–100 ms after visual stimulus onset. However, if the TMS pulse occurred between 40–60, or 120–140 ms after stimulus onset, no masking occurred and the stimulus was reported accurately by the participant. In a later study (Amassian et al., 1993), the researchers used a backward masking procedure in which a high-contrast stimulus (the visual mask) was displayed 100 ms after the target stimulus. This mask normally prevented participants from accurately reporting the target stimulus presented before the mask; however single-pulse TMS 80–100 ms after the mask 'unmasked' the target stimulus, leading to accurate perception. In this way, the researchers were able to identify that processing in V1 between 80–100 ms is critical (necessary) for visual perception. Notably, this time period is also when the P1–N1 ERP complex occurs.

Single-pulse TMS is also used in clinical research. A common use of single-pulse protocols is in the study of recovery from stroke, in which the primary motor

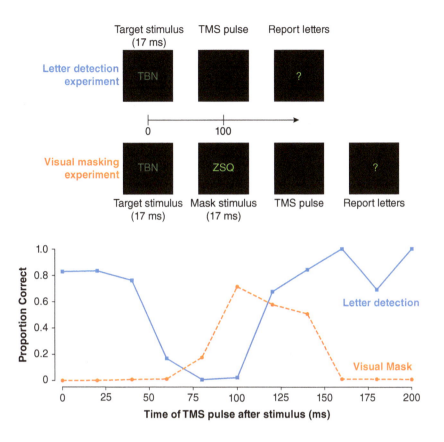

Figure 13.8 Paradigm and data from two experiments by Amassian and colleagues examining the effects of TMS on visual perception. In the first experiment (letter detection; Amassian, R.Q. Cracco, Maccabee, J.B. Cracco, Rudell, & Eberle, 1989), participants were asked to report the identity of three randomly chosen letters that were presented very briefly (17 ms). A single TMS pulse was delivered some time between the onset of the letters and the prompt to report them, ranging from 0–200 ms after the stimulus, in 25 ms increments. The blue line in the bottom panel shows that a TMS pulse delivered 80–100 ms after the target stimulus maximally disrupted people's ability to detect the letters. This is in line with the timing of the earliest cortical visual evoked potentials. In the second experiment (visual masking; Amassian et al., 1993), the letter detection task was again used, but the three letters that participants were asked to report were followed 100 ms later by a visual mask (three different random letters, brighter than the target letters). Normally, a visual mask at this latency is effective in preventing detection of the target letters. However, as shown by the orange line in the bottom panel, a TMS pulse 80–150 ms after the visual mask disrupted the effects of the mask, making it possible for participants to accurately report the target letters that had preceded the mask. Adapted with permission of Elsevier from Amassian and colleagues (1989, 1993)

cortex is often affected, leading to movement problems (apraxia). Stroke can reduce MEPs contralateral to the side of the stroke (that is, in the motor cortex controlling the affected limb), and at the same time increase ipsilateral MEPs, and so tracking changes in these – as well as in rMT – can be used to assess whether changes are occurring in the brain, even when these are small and not necessarily accompanied by observable improvements in the person's ability to move the affected limb. Single-pulse TMS can also be used in the assessment of different neurological conditions.

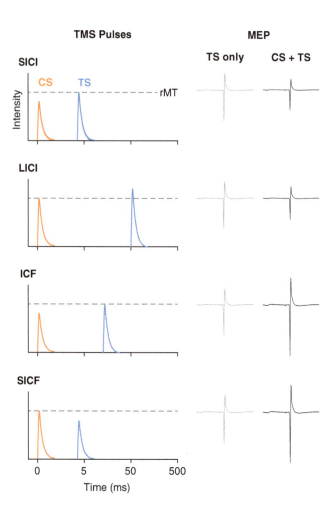

Figure 13.9 Examples of the four standard paired-pulse TMS (ppTMS) protocols, showing the relative timing and magnitude (relative to resting motor threshold, rMT, dashed line) of the conditioning stimulus (CS, orange) and test stimulus (TS, blue), and the resulting effects on the size of the resulting MEP (dark grey) relative to a control, single-pulse condition in which only the TS is administered (light grey). Note that time is plotted on a log scale. Refer to Table 13.1 for details of each ppTMS protocol

For example, people with Parkinson's disease show a reduced-duration cSP, whereas people with concussions show a prolonged cSP.

Paired-Pulse Protocols

Paired-pulse TMS (ppTMS), as the name suggests, involves administering two TMS pulses in rapid succession. Using a pair of pulses opens up a wide range of possibilities, because the two pulses can be to the same or different cortical regions, and – depending on the strength and timing of each pulse – the effects can be inhibitory or facilitatory. Paired-pulse TMS is more technically demanding than single-pulse or rTMS (see next section) because the short intervals between pulses (as little as 1 ms) necessitate two stimulator hardware units, since the stimulation intensity of the two pulses is rarely the same, and a stimulator unit requires more time to recharge after each pulse than the inter-pulse intervals typically used in such studies. The two stimulator units can be connected to different coils, if two different brain sites are to be stimulated, or to a single coil if the same site is to be stimulated by both pulses.

The advantage of ppTMS is that it allows investigation of cortical circuits and connectivity. This is a very flexible technique because of the different effects that different parameters can produce. Within a ppTMS protocol, the first pulse is called the initial **conditioning stimulus (CS)**, and the second pulse is labelled the subsequent **test stimulus (TS)**. This technique has been studied most extensively in the motor system, where four primary types of ppTMS can be defined, based on how and when they affect MEPs. These are summarized in Table 13.1. Typically in the

Table 13.1 Different ppTMS protocols used in studying the motor system

Protocol name	Inter-Pulse Interval (IPI)	CS intensity (relative to rMT)	TS intensity (relative to rMT)	Effects
SICI (Short-interval intracortical inhibition)	1–6 ms	Sub-threshold	Threshold or supra-threshold	Axonal refractoriness; $GABA_A$-mediated inhibition
LICI (Long-interval intracortical inhibition)	50–200 ms	Threshold	Supra-threshold	Postsynaptic $GABA_B$-mediated inhibition
ICF (Intracortical facilitation)	8–30 ms	Sub-threshold	Threshold or supra-threshold	Facilitation; possibly mediated by NMDA
SICF (Short-interval intracortical facilitation)	1–5 ms	Threshold or supra-threshold	Sub-threshold	Facilitation; mediated by glutamate

motor system, the TS is targeted at the M1 representation of the effector muscle of interest, while the site of the CS varies depending on the aim of the study. The most common CS site is the motor cortex ipsilateral to the target effector (that is, the motor representation in the hemisphere opposite to that receiving the TS). Stimulating the mirror-image sites in ipsilateral and contralateral M1 allows the investigation of inter-hemispheric inhibition and facilitation, and this combination of stimulation sites yields the strongest effects. Other common sites for the CS are the cerebellum or peripheral nerves (such as the median nerve running to the hand).

The investigation of cortical circuits using ppTMS can be enhanced by simultaneous EEG recording. ERPs evoked in TMS protocols are generally called TEPs (TMS-evoked potentials). In the simplest case, the effects of ppTMS are measured in the motor system simply by examining MEPs (the output of the motor system). However, it is also possible to use ppTMS on pairs of regions outside the motor system – but if one wishes to investigate connectivity between non-motor regions, MEPs are of no use, and so other markers of activity are needed. EEG provides a direct index of the electrical activity of other brain regions, and so can be used in this way. While we have learned that the scalp-recorded maximum of an EEG/ERP potential may be distant from its source in the brain, in the case of ppTMS the experimenter knows which two brain areas were stimulated, and so any effects on the EEG can be associated with the connectivity between these two brain regions, regardless of where the EEG effects are maximal. It is nonetheless important to consider that any TMS protocol – including ppTMS – may have more widespread or 'downstream' effects on brain areas other than the area or areas directly stimulated: the effects measured with EEG may in fact be generated by other brain areas that are connected to those stimulated. This does not really undermine the value of ppTMS, however, as any effects obtained (relative to an appropriate control condition) can be interpreted as relating to the connectivity of the two brain regions involved. We will consider this issue in more depth in the section on combining TMS with neuroimaging later in this chapter.

An initial example of combined ppTMS–EEG was a study by Fitzgerald and colleagues (2008), who compared the effects of ppTMS where both the CS and TS were delivered to the same brain location. In three different experiments, the motor cortex, middle frontal gyrus (dorsolateral prefrontal cortex, or DLPC), and parietal lobe were targeted. In each experiment, the researchers compared TEPs time-locked to the onset of a supra-threshold TS when the TS was either preceded 100 ms earlier by a CS or not, in an LICI protocol. TEP amplitude was reduced by an average of about 40% when preceded by a CS, in any of the brain areas studied. This demonstrated that LICI operates similarly in motor and non-motor brain areas. A more recent study demonstrated effects of DLPC stimulation on the TEP using both SICI and ICF protocols, with reduced TEPs for SICI and enhanced TEPs for ICF (Cash et al., 2016).

These combined ppTMS–EEG studies demonstrate another use of the technique: in these studies, both pulses were delivered to the same brain area, so they were not studies of cortical connectivity. However, since previous studies involving different neurotransmitter agonists and antagonists have associated the different ppTMS protocols with distinct inhibitory and excitatory neurotransmitter systems (see Table 13.1), these paradigms allow the interrogation of the function of different neurotransmitter systems. For example, schizophrenia is associated with changes in DLPC function, and ppTMS to the DLPC has shown changes in people with schizophrenia relative to healthy controls using an LICI paradigm, thus associating changes in DLPC with $GABA_B$-related inhibition. An extension of this approach involves combining ppTMS and EEG with administration of different drugs, in what is called pharmaco–TMS–EEG (Ziemann, 2016).

Repetitive TMS (rTMS)

Repetitive TMS (rTMS) comprises a wide range of TMS stimulation protocols that can have facilitatory or inhibitory effects, depending on their parameters. They are distinguished from single-pulse or paired-pulse TMS by the fact that multiple (more than two) stimulation pulses are delivered at a pre-determined and specific frequency. The simplest rTMS protocols involve stimulation at a fixed frequency; rates of 1 Hz (that is, 1 pulse per second) or less, termed **low-frequency rTMS**, have inhibitory effects, whereas **high-frequency rTMS**, with rates > 1 Hz (typically ranging from 1–50 Hz), generally have excitatory effects (with some exceptions). In the motor system, low-frequency rTMS results in reduced MEPs and decreased cortical activity (as measured, for example, by EEG), whereas high-frequency rTMS leads to increased MEP amplitude and cortical activation. Like single-pulse TMS, low-frequency rTMS can be used in 'virtual lesion' studies to explore the effects of disrupting activity in a particular brain region; it is particularly useful in studies where the task to be performed (and possibly disrupted) takes place over a relatively extended amount of time. With single-pulse TMS, the pulse has to be very carefully timed to coincide with the predicted timing of the neural event under study; with rTMS one has much greater flexibility. Thus while single-pulse TMS is valuable for chronometric studies due to its precise timing, rTMS can be useful in situations such as disrupting speech production or working memory, which take some time to perform. Another feature of rTMS is that for many stimulation protocols, the effects on cognition last longer than the duration of stimulation – sometimes up to an hour or more after a single session, or for weeks or months after a series of sessions (a protocol of 20 minutes of rTMS every day for ten days is used, for example, in treating depression).

As well, rTMS can be used in ways similar to ppTMS to investigate cortico-cortical connectivity between pairs of regions. For example, Romei and colleagues (Romei, Chiappini, Hibbard, & Avenanti, 2016) investigated connections between primary visual cortex (V1), and the temporal-occipital brain region tuned to visual motion (V5). Although visual information initially travels from V1 to V5, there are also 're-entrant' connections in the opposite direction, by which V5 modulates V1. Evidence suggests that these are important for conscious awareness of motion and 'top-down' control of motion perception. The researchers hypothesized that they could enhance the sensitivity to visual motion in a challenging detection task by using TMS to strengthen the re-entrant inputs from V5 to V1. To do this, they developed a paradigm in which participants received low-frequency (0.1 Hz) rTMS to both V1 and V5 (using two TMS coils, one over each area). This was a combination of rTMS and ppTMS, in that rTMS was delivered to both areas, but the relative timing of the pulses to each area was manipulated. Specifically, V5 could be stimulated either 20 ms before, 20 ms after, or at the same time as V1 – each delay was used with a different group of participants, and a fourth group received sham stimulation. The 20 ms delay was chosen based on prior research suggesting that this was the time required for V5 input to modulate V1. All subjects performed a challenging motion discrimination task, and performance was tested before, immediately after, and then at half-hour intervals after the stimulation. The paradigm and results are illustrated in Figure 13.10. Only the group that received V5 followed by V1 stimulation showed significant improvement on the motion discrimination task, and the enhancement was found to last for at least 60 minutes. The authors concluded that stimulating V5 followed 20 ms later by stimulating V1 induced short-term strengthening of the re-entrant connections between them, via Hebbian mechanisms ('cells that fire together, wire together').

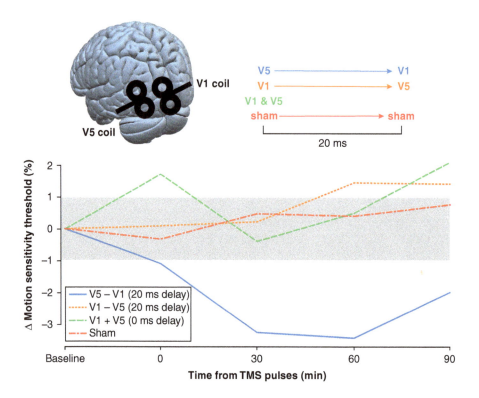

Figure 13.10 Illustration of the paradigm and resulting data of the study Romei and colleagues described in the text. Participants' task was to view a field of moving dots, in which some proportion moved in a coherent direction (either left or right) and the remainder of the dots moved in random directions, and indicate the direction of coherent motion. Thresholds were determined prior to TMS by varying the proportion of coherently moving dots. Behavioural performance on

Figure 13.10 (Continued)
the motion direction discrimination task are plotted in the bottom panel; note that negative values indicate better performance relative to the pre-TMS baseline measurements (fewer dots had to be moving coherently for accurate detection). Adapted with permission of Elsevierfrom Romei and colleagues (2016)

Protocols using rTMS can be broadly divided into 'online' and 'offline', as well as inhibitory or facilitatory. The online/offline distinction refers to the task performed by the rTMS recipient: online protocols involve a task performed during rTMS (for example, instructing someone to try to say the days of the week while stimulating the left prefrontal cortex), whereas offline protocols involve rTMS followed by task performance, and utilize the fact that the rTMS effects last for some time after stimulation. Most online protocols use inhibitory rTMS, following the virtual lesion approach, whereas offline protocols may be inhibitory or facilitatory. **Online inhibitory protocols** typically deliver rTMS in relatively short bursts; for example, in speech mapping (which involves stimulating different areas of the frontal lobe to determine where interruption of normal speech occurs, and can be used clinically for determining language lateralization), a typical protocol involves ten pulses at 5 Hz (2 s total duration), repeated every 5 s. The timing of each burst is time-locked to the presentation of a picture that the subject is asked to name; the 2 s duration ensures that stimulation occurs during the entire time that the person is viewing and attempting to retrieve and articulate the name of the picture. Note that although the 5 Hz stimulation is in the range typically considered 'facilitatory', this has been found to be effective at disrupting speech production; stimulation frequencies in the 5–10 Hz range are often used in online inhibitory studies.

In contrast, offline protocols typically use longer trains of stimulation, which seem to be required to have effects that last beyond the period of stimulation. True low-frequency rTMS (≤ 1 Hz) is the norm in **offline inhibitory protocols**, where the stimulation duration may be as long as 15–30 min. A more recent stimulation protocol for inhibitory rTMS is **continuous theta burst stimulation (cTBS)**. This protocol involves three pulses at 50 Hz, with 5 Hz spacing (that is, three pulses 20 ms apart, repeated every 200 ms), typically delivered for 20 or 40 s (resulting in a total of 300 or 600 pulses), at 80% AMT. This is illustrated in Figure 13.11. This protocol was inspired by work showing both that theta bursts are a common pattern of activity in the hippocampi of rats during exploratory behaviour, and in vitro work showing that this pattern of stimulation is effective in inducing neuroplasticity in brain slices. The resulting suppression in brain activity has been shown to last for 30–40 min or more. The major advantage of this technique over low-frequency rTMS is that it takes less than 1 minute (as opposed to 15 min or more with 1 Hz rTMS) to induce long-lasting inhibitory effects. This makes it much more efficient, and reduces both the discomfort of the recipient (depending on the site of stimulation – especially near the face – rTMS may induce unpleasant, strong muscle contractions) and the chance of the person moving their head and thus changing the location of stimulation during the protocol.

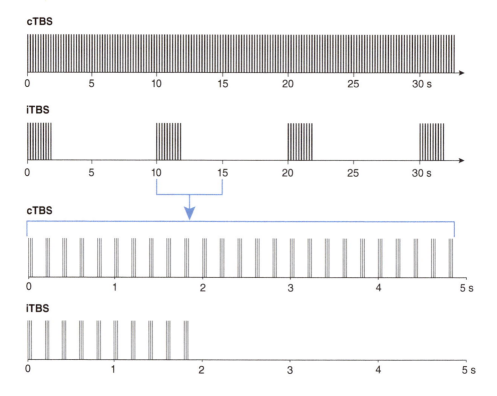

Figure 13.11 Theta burst stimulation (TBS) protocols. The top two rows show timelines of the continuous (cTBS) and intermittent (iTBS) variants of this protocol. In cTBS, triplets of pulses 20 ms apart are delivered every 200 ms; in iTBS, ten such triplets are delivered followed by an 8 s gap before the next set of ten triplets are delivered. The cTBS protocol typically results in inhibition of activity in the stimulated area, lasting 30-60 min, whereas the iTBS protocol typically results in facilitation of activity in the targeted brain area, lasting upwards of 30 min

Offline facilitatory protocols are quite varied in their parameters. Common ones include 10 Hz stimulation delivered in five or six pulse trains lasting approximately 500 ms and spaced 3 s apart; 20–25 Hz stimulation delivered in trains of 10–100 over 500 ms, spaced 15–20 ms apart; and 4–9 Hz (with highly variable parameters across studies). Choice of protocol depends on the brain area to be stimulated and the experimental goals, and should be guided by prior literature as well as experimentation in the lab. A variant of theta-burst stimulation has also been developed as an offline facilitatory protocol: **intermittent TBS (iTBS)** involves the same pattern of three pulses at 50 Hz with 5 Hz spacing that is used in cTBS, but rather than delivering this continuously, 2 s bursts (30 pulses) are delivered separated by 10 s intervals, over a total duration of approximately 200 s (see Figure 13.11). Like cTBS, the iTBS protocol has effects that last upwards of 30 minutes (but facilitatory rather than inhibitory), with a very time-efficient period of stimulation; however, the effects of iTBS have been reported to be weaker and less consistent than cTBS (Huang et al., 2009).

WHAT ARE THE EFFECTS ON THE BRAIN?

Consideration of how TMS affects brain activity is important to understand and interpret the results of TMS experiments. We have already learned that a TMS pulse introduces a strong electrical current in brain tissue directly under the stimulating coil, which disrupts brain activity during the pulse. However, this does not explain the lasting (offline) effects of TMS – which can last for up to an hour after a single session – nor why different stimulation protocols have radically different effects (for example, inhibition versus facilitation) or different durations of effects. One approach to understanding this has been to examine neurotransmitter systems by administering drugs that up- or down-regulate particular neurotransmitters. This literature has also been informed by the literature on long-term potentiation and depression in animal and in vitro electrophysiological studies. Another perspective on this question comes from a consideration of how the electrical currents induced by TMS conduct through the brain, and what long-range effects TMS might have. Although up until now we have focused on the 'direct' impacts of TMS on the small area under the coil that is directly stimulated, the brain is a densely interconnected network and so it is reasonable to expect that TMS will also have effects on other brain areas that are connected to the one stimulated. This may include conduction of the actual TMS-induced current, but also effects induced in distant brain regions by changes in activity that occur in the directly stimulated area.

Because the current induced by TMS occurs parallel to the orientation of the coil, the direct effects of TMS occur primarily on axons that lie in a plane parallel to the cortical surface. TMS effects are induced primarily in axons, rather than cell bodies, since the induction of current requires a conductor of some length. These are largely excitatory (glutamatergic) inputs to the cortex, and horizontal interneuron connections which are primarily inhibitory (GABAergic). Pyramidal neurons (which comprise the primary outputs of cortical regions, and are the primary source of signals in many neuroimaging techniques including EEG, MEG, and fMRI) are oriented with their axons running perpendicular to the cortical surface, and so the effects of TMS on these neurons is thought to be primarily indirect, through connections to the horizontally running cell types. Of course, this is a relatively simplistic and schematic view of cortical microanatomy; the reality is that there are many types of axons with varying orientations and bends, and the cortex itself is folded and so pyramidal neurons on the bank (side) of a sulcus may be oriented the same way, relative to the TMS coil, as horizontal neurons on the top of a gyrus – modelling the exact effects of TMS on any brain region would be an extremely complex task. Nonetheless, it works as a simple, tractable model of TMS effects. Studies of the motor system have found that TMS induces a series of waves through the corticospinal network (CSN). The initial effect of stimulation is the **direct (D-) wave**, a large wave thought to be caused directly by the stimulation pulse. This is followed by a series of smaller, **indirect (I-) waves**, which are thought to reflect reverberating activation within the CSN and other neural circuits connected to it. In other words, as the initial D-wave travels through the circuit and across synapses, it induces changes in activation that continue, and feed back into the CSN, as I-waves. Not all stimulation protocols induce both D- and I-waves; the effects depend on the intensity of stimulation and the circuit stimulated. Even within the motor system, only I-waves are seen at lower levels of stimulation in slower-conducting circuits, whereas D-waves are seen at lower intensities than I-waves in faster-conducting circuits.

Pharmacological studies have allowed a greater understanding of the mechanisms by which TMS works (Ziemann et al., 2015). The effects of different drugs have been examined on a number of different measures. One common measure is MT, which is taken as a measure of cortical excitability. MT is raised (that is, inducing an effect with TMS requires a stronger pulse) by drugs that block voltage-gated sodium channels (for example, anti-epileptic drugs such as carbamazepine or lamotrigine), while MT is lowered by ketamine, a drug that facilitates glutamatergic (excitatory) neurotransmission. This tells us that induction of TMS effects depends on voltage-gated sodium channels (which are a primary mechanism of action potentials and their propagation along axons); the role of glutamate is thought to be that the axons stimulated by TMS terminate at synapses that rely on glutamatergic neurotransmission. Other classes of drugs – including those that modulate calcium ion channels, GABA (the primary inhibitory neurotransmitter in the brain), dopamine, noradrenaline, acetylcholine, and serotonin – have not been shown to consistently modulate MT. Another measure investigated is the **MEP input–output curve**: the relationship between stimulation intensity and MEP amplitude. This measure reflects neurotransmission through the corticospinal circuit, including D- and I-waves, by a supra-threshold pulse. As such, it reflects the propagation of TMS effects across a series of synapses and reverberating through the network. This involves both excitatory and inhibitory synapses, and thus it is not surprising that it is modulated by both GABA and glutamate. In addition, noradrenaline and serotonin appear to be involved, whereas drugs affecting other neurotransmitters do not. A third measure is the duration of the cortical silent period (SP), described above under single-pulse protocols. This measure reflects postsynaptic inhibition in cortical motor neurons, and may be related to the 'transient lesion' effects of TMS. The CSP is mediated primarily by GABAergic neurotransmission, with both $GABA_A$ and $GABA_B$ receptors playing a role.

The mechanisms underlying the effects of rTMS are not well understood. Pharmacological intervention studies with humans have indicated that both $GABA_A$ agonists and NMDA antagonists block the long-lasting inhibitory effects of rTMS, suggesting a role of both inhibitory (GABA) and excitatory (glutamate) neurotransmitters in modulating these effects. However, other studies have suggested that only GABA is affected by cTBS, suggesting that the particular stimulation protocol may affect which neurotransmitter systems are influenced.

CONSIDERATIONS IN EXPERIMENTAL DESIGN

A number of things need to be considered in designing a TMS experiment. One crucial consideration is experimental control: we can only assess what effects TMS has by comparing it to a condition where the participant experiences the same stimuli and performs the same task, without TMS – or perhaps with TMS to a different brain region. Several problems arise when considering a no-TMS control condition. Firstly, TMS creates a sensory experience for the recipient: there is a very loud 'click' during each pulse, and the coil itself can move, creating a tapping sensation on the scalp at the site of stimulation. Thus at a minimum, TMS and no-TMS conditions would differ in these experiences. Moreover, depending on the site and strength of stimulation, TMS can also cause peripheral nerve stimulation, resulting in anything from minor 'twitching' sensations to painful contractions of muscles in the face or neck. These sensory effects can potentially influence individuals' behaviour in two general ways. On the one hand, these sensory side effects may be distracting, and interfere with task performance. For example, in a study designed to investigate these effects, 'sham' TMS stimulation – which mimicked the peripheral sensations of TMS without delivering stimulation to the cortex – to one side of the head cause automatic shifts of spatial attention to the side of stimulation, resulting in better detection of visual targets on the corresponding side of visual space (Duecker & Sack, 2015). On the other hand, the sensory side effects provide cues that stimulation is occurring, which could lead to **placebo effects** or **demand characteristics** – biases (either conscious or unconscious) on the part of the recipient that cause them to perform in ways that are consistent with what they expect from the TMS. Thus the effects of TMS could partially or wholly reflect placebo effects rather than true effects of brain stimulation. Placebo effects of TMS are not merely theoretical either: they have been reported in several clinical treatment studies (Duecker & Sack, 2015). The solution that most researchers adopt is to use a **sham stimulation** condition as a control, rather than a no-stimulation condition. However, this term is used broadly to describe a number of rather different approaches, each of which has some disadvantages.

Sham Stimulation

One approach to sham stimulation is to compare TMS delivered to the desired 'target' brain area (**verum**, or true, stimulation), with TMS delivered to a different area that is expected not to influence behaviour on the experimental task. The preferred alternative site is the vertex (top centre) of the head, on the assumption that directly below this is the central fissure that divides the two cerebral hemispheres, and thus no area of the brain should receive stimulation (at least not using a figure-of-eight coil). One issue with this approach is that if the recipient knows anything about functional neuroanatomy (and certainly if they know much about TMS), they are likely to realize that vertex stimulation is the control condition. In this case, the use of this technique to eliminate potential bias on the part of the recipient is invalidated. Another issue is that this approach is based on a largely untested assumption that sham stimulation does not affect brain activity. Jung and colleagues (Jung, Bungert, Bowtell, & Jackson, 2016) performed an fMRI study to test this directly, performing resting-state fMRI scans both before and after vertex stimulation. They found that vertex stimulation did not increase BOLD signal anywhere in the brain, but did *decrease* BOLD signal in several parts of the default mode network. However, vertex stimulation did not lead to changes in functional connectivity between different brain regions in the default mode network, leading the authors to conclude that vertex stimulation is a valid control site for TMS. Since vertex stimulation did influence BOLD signal across the brain, it nonetheless seems prudent to consider this effect in combined TMS–fMRI studies.

Another approach to sham stimulation is to hold the stimulating coil so that its outer edge touches the scalp, rather than the centre, or to reverse the coil, placing its back against the scalp rather than its front. Because TMS coils are designed to deliver very focal stimulation, and the induced magnetic field drops off so sharply with distance, moving the focal point of the stimulator several centimetres from the head in this fashion reduces or prevents any stimulation from reaching the brain. At the same time, this provides both the auditory and at least some of the tactile sensations that accompany verum stimulation. However, depending on the angle of the coil, some level of stimulation may reach the brain. As well, the TMS-savvy participant may be able to tell the difference by feel since the way the coil touches the scalp, and the 'tap' of the pulse itself, will feel different. As well, the peripheral nerve or muscle stimulation that accompanies TMS over many parts of the scalp (particularly near the face) is typically not induced by these approaches.

A final approach is to use a sham TMS coil. These are sold by TMS manufacturers and look just like real coils, and are designed to simulate the sound and feel of real TMS pulses. Typically sham coils are built much like real coils, but have magnetic shielding, or reduced amounts of wire in the coils, to reduce the strength of the magnetic field while producing a weak magnetic pulse that is strong enough to stimulate peripheral nerves but not the cortex. Alternatively, they may have electrodes on their surface that create weak electrical stimulation that simulates the peripheral nerve effects of TMS. In this way, it is harder to tell the difference between real and sham stimulation, although people who have more experience with TMS (for example, people working in a TMS lab) are still frequently able to discriminate real from sham stimulation. The biggest disadvantage of sham coils is that they add significantly to the cost of the TMS system. As well, they need to be switched with real coils, meaning that it may be difficult to randomly intermix verum and sham stimulation, rather than administering these in different blocks of trials. On the other hand, they provide a level of control that may be essential to provide confidence in the results of the study.

Regardless of the approach to sham stimulation that is used, it is advisable (though unfortunately, rarely done) for researchers to actually assess the efficacy of their attempts at blinding subjects to when real TMS is actually being delivered. As well, any well-designed TMS experiment should include both a sham stimulation condition, and conditions where stimulation is delivered to brain areas and/or at time points that are not expected to affect performance on the task. This is critical to demonstrate that any effects obtained during stimulation of the target region of cortex are truly specific to that brain area and/or time point, as opposed to being due to either peripheral stimulation, or simply cortical stimulation in general.

Stimulation Intensity

A separate consideration in experimental design is how the stimulation level is determined for an individual. As noted, this is typically done as a percentage of resting or active motor threshold. However, an individual's threshold is not constant, and can be changed quite quickly by activity. For example, recent muscle contractions – ranging from exercising at the gym prior to a TMS session, to much simpler things such as contracting the hand muscles just before TMS – can significantly raise rMT, as well as the motor effects that result from supra-threshold TMS. Thus careful control of the participant's behaviour prior to and during the determination of motor threshold is important, as is inquiring about their level of activity prior to the session. This is not only an issue in the motor system either: it has been shown that spatial attention can modulate the threshold for TMS to induce phosphenes during occipital lobe stimulation (Bestmann, Ruff, Blakemore, Driver, & Thilo, 2007). Thus researchers should consider how the manipulations inherent in their experimental design might also influence the excitability of the cortical regions they plan on stimulating.

TMS COMBINED WITH NEUROIMAGING

TMS allows systematic modulation of neural activity; however, the technique itself does not provide any means of directly measuring this modulation. Historically, the conclusions made from TMS studies regarding neural mechanisms were largely inferential, based on knowledge (or educated guesses, depending on whether neuro-navigation was used or not) of what brain area was stimulated, and measurements of the resulting behaviour on the part of the subject; in the case of the motor system, EMG could be used as well. Neuroimaging, however, provides an excellent complement to TMS because it can show us more directly how brain activity is modulated by the stimulation. This is particularly important because the brain is a network of interconnected areas, so it would be naïve to think that any and all effects resulting from TMS were attributable to only the brain area that was directly stimulated. The modulation of one brain area is virtually guaranteed to have 'downstream' effects on other areas that it is connected to, which likely mediate some of the behavioural effects seen after stimulation. Combining neuroimaging with TMS can help us to understand the effects of TMS better. Given the strengths of the different imaging techniques covered in previous chapters, one can see that they all offer different potential insights into the mechanisms of TMS. PET can inform us as to the effects of TMS on different neurotransmitter systems, while EEG can be used to assess the timing and duration of TMS-induced effects; fMRI can show which regions' activity is modulated by stimulation. As with behavioural studies, combined TMS–neuroimaging studies can be classified as offline or online depending on whether the stimulation occurs prior to the imaging, or during. Online protocols create many more technical considerations than offline ones, because the TMS-evoked electromagnetic fields can cause interference with the neuroimaging hardware and measurements; on the other hand, online experiments generally provide stronger data because of the ability to associate stimulation with changes in activity in real time, rather than many minutes after the fact. Furthermore, the technical hurdles are tractable (though often at significant financial and logistical cost), and many groups have successfully published data from such experiments. In the remainder of this section we will discuss each of these techniques in turn, considering the technical issues inherent in combining TMS with each imaging technique, as well as examples of some of the benefits.

TMS–PET

Combining PET with TMS is relatively easy, because PET measurement does not rely on electrical potentials or magnetic fields. Because TMS does generate an electromagnetic field, it is important to consider the placement of the TMS equipment relative to the PET scanner to prevent interference with the PET system's electronics. However, because the TMS-evoked fields drop off so sharply with distance, this is relatively easy to accomplish – especially because the slow time course of PET acquisitions largely precludes the use of online protocols. Thus one could employ an offline approach in which participants first receive TMS, and then receive a PET scan. A control scan prior to the TMS might also be considered if there is a need to establish a baseline; however, the half-life of the PER used in the PET scan needs to be considered as some require a relatively long wash-out time; in such cases the control scan could be done on a separate group of participants, or on a different day.

An example is an early study by Strafella and colleagues (2001), who performed 10 Hz rTMS over the left dorsolateral prefrontal cortex (DLPC) for 30 min outside of the PET scanner. Within 5 min of the completion of the stimulation, [^{11}C]raclopride (which binds to D2 receptors and is sensitive to extracellular dopamine concentration; see Chapter 11) was injected and the PET scan began, which lasted for 60 min. The results showed that [^{11}C]raclopride binding decreased specifically in the left caudate nucleus of the basal ganglia, reflecting an increase in endogenous dopamine. No changes in [^{11}C]raclopride binding were observed in other areas of the basal ganglia, nor were any changes observed after a control condition in which the occipital cortex, rather than DLPC, was stimulated. These results are consistent with known anatomical connections between the caudate and DLPC, and indeed knowledge of anatomical connectivity patterns was helpful to the authors in interpreting their results: DLPC has direct connections to the ipsilateral caudate nucleus and indirect connections to other basal ganglia areas; the fact that dopamine was modulated only in the left caudate indicates that TMS affected direct projections but did have wider-ranging effects on dopamine levels.

TMS-fMRI

Offline designs combining TMS with fMRI are relatively straightforward, because the TMS system can be placed in a location near the MRI scanner – but far enough away that interference does not occur – and the subject simply moved from the TMS room to the MRI scanner between phases of the experiment. However, the strong magnetic field of the MRI scanner makes online stimulation protocols more challenging, as three types of artifacts may occur. The first are **static artifacts** associated with the presence of metal in and near the MRI scanner. The primary material in TMS coils is copper, which is not ferromagnetic and so in itself is not a major problem. However, other components of the coil (such as switches) may have ferromagnetic components, so re-engineering the coils may be necessary; many companies now produce TMS coils specifically designed for use in MR environments. The main TMS unit, however – which houses the capacitor and other hardware that generate and control the stimulation pulses – cannot be near the scanner and should really not be in the same room as the MRI. Fortunately, TMS systems work fine with a relatively long cable running from the main hardware unit to the coil, and so the hardware can be placed outside the MRI room and the wire to the coil run through a waveguide (a shielded tube through the MRI wall shielding). A special consideration of such a set-up is that the longer cable running to the coil will have greater resistance than the shorter cables typically used in non-fMRI TMS experiments, which will reduce the actual level of stimulation delivered at the coil, for a given output setting on the TMS unit. A second challenge is **dynamic artifacts** created by the magnetic pulse of the TMS coil when stimulation occurs. Since MRI relies on very accurate mapping of the magnetic field inside the bore of the scanner, a TMS pulse (which, at 1–2 T, is in the order of magnitude as the field strength of the scanner itself, and far larger than the gradient fields induced to perform spatial encoding) will inevitably disrupt this and make imaging impossible during a pulse. Fortunately, TMS pulses are very short (milliseconds) in duration, and the fields drop off sharply with distance. Thus it is possible to synchronize MRI acquisition with TMS stimulation (by linking the devices via a computer) in such a way that the MRI scans are acquired outside the 70–100 ms time window immediately after TMS, during which the MRI data would be affected (this can be done by slightly lengthening the repetition time – TR – of the fMRI pulse sequence). Since the delay between any stimulus/neural event and the associated MRI-measured BOLD response is in the order of several seconds, this short delay in data acquisition does not interfere with accurate fMRI scanning. A final consideration are **sensory artifacts** that arise from the fact that a TMS pulse produces an audible noise as well as a tactile 'tapping' sensation on the head, and possibly muscle contractions as well. This is not unique to fMRI but is a consideration for any neuroimaging study (and for that matter, behavioural studies as well, as discussed earlier). It is best addressed through an experimental design that includes appropriate control conditions.

An important use of combined TMS–fMRI is that it is possible to determine how TMS modulates the activity both of the area directly stimulated, and other areas of the brain as well. These interactions can be quite complex, which is an important consideration in interpreting the results of any TMS experiment. Indeed, while this does not undermine the use of TMS to create 'virtual lesions', it underscores the fact that, just as with real brain lesions, the effects of virtual lesions cannot simply be attributed to disruption of function in the targeted brain area, but are wide-ranging effects across the network of brain regions connected to the lesioned area. As an example, in one online TMS–fMRI study, Ruff and colleagues (Ruff, Blankenburg, & Bioertomt, 2009) stimulated four different brain areas using bursts of five stimulation pulses at 9 Hz, alternating with fMRI acquisitions. This was done by using an **interleaved** EPI acquisition sequence with a TR of 3 s, of which approximately 2400 ms was used to acquire fMRI data, and the remaining 'silent' period was used to deliver the TMS. On each trial, subjects would randomly either see a visual stimulus designed to strongly drive peripheral visual areas (rapidly changing colour and movement, presented to the visual periphery but not the foveal area around a fixation point), or no stimulus, and then receive TMS on each of three subsequent TRs (so, three bursts of five pulses each, over 9 s). The TMS was delivered to one of four brain areas (frontal eye fields – FEF – or intraparietal sulcus – IPS – in each hemisphere), at one of four randomly varied intensity levels (between 40–80% rMT); as a control condition, on 20% of trials no TMS was administered. This experimental design is shown in Figure 13.12. Analysis of the fMRI data focused not on the stimulated areas, but on retinotopically organized areas of the occipital lobe, including areas V1, V2, V3, V4, and V5. The results demonstrated the wide-ranging effects of TMS, and the complexity of relationships between site of stimulation and changes in BOLD activity in remote locations. After FEF stimulation to either hemisphere, activity in occipital regions representing the central (foveal) visual field decreased. However, after right frontal stimulation only, activity in occipital areas representing the peripheral visual field increased. The differences in left versus right hemisphere stimulation were even more pronounced in the parietal lobe, where right IPS stimulation modulated V5 (motion-sensitive cortex) responses to moving stimuli in proportion to the intensity of stimulation, while left IPS stimulation did not affect V5 BOLD signal levels. These findings are in accord with the previously known right hemisphere dominance for visual–spatial processing, and the roles of the FEF and IPS in spatial cognition.

TMS–EEG

Performing TMS while recording EEG presents some unique challenges. The high temporal resolution of EEG makes it an attractive complement to TMS, especially because EEG offers the potential to measure the near-immediate effects of TMS on electrical activity itself, rather than indirect effects on BOLD or neurotransmitter activity. On the other hand, because TMS involves creating a large electromagnetic pulse, a massive artifact will be recorded in the EEG data, creating several problems. Combining EEG with TMS in an offline design is much more straightforward,

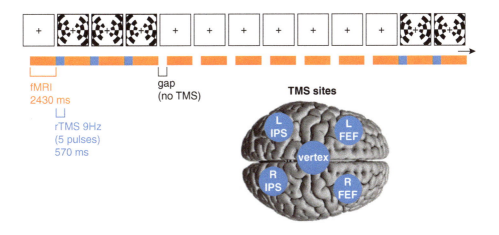

Figure 13.12 Schematic of the combined TMS-fMRI experiment conducted by Ruff and colleagues and described in the text. To avoid interference between TMS pulses and fMRI data collection, an interleaved fMRI pulse sequence was used, in which MR data acquisition (one brain volume) occurred for 2430 ms followed by a 570 ms gap prior to the start of the next MR acquisition. Thus the TR of the fMRI sequence was 3000 ms. During the MR acquisition gaps, rTMS was delivered in some experimental blocks. The area targeted by TMS was varied between fMRI runs, as shown in the bottom panel. During the experimental blocks, a patterned visual stimulus (involving movement and colour changes) was presented to the peripheral visual fields of the participant. Experimental blocks alternated with rest blocks in which no TMS or visual stimulation were delivered; these rest blocks were longer to allow the effects of TMS to wear off prior to the next experimental block. Adapted from Ruff and colleagues (2009)

except that if one is interested in EEG responses soon after TMS, the EEG electrode cap should be applied prior to TMS. This in turn requires some consideration around the type of electrodes used in the cap; however, this is an issue with online studies as well, which is the primary focus of this section.

The first set of problems arise from the electrodes and how they are applied to the scalp. The materials used in the electrodes and wires should be non-ferromagnetic, so that they do not move during the TMS pulses. This is typically not a problem, because passive EEG electrodes and wires are commonly made of non-ferromagnetic materials such as tin, silver, and copper; however, it is wise to ensure that all materials meet these specifications, and to test the set-up extensively – even non-ferromagnetic materials may move or heat up during stimulation. Heating of electrodes is a significant concern: medical safety guidelines state that materials above 41°C should not come in contact with human skin due to the risk of burns; however, a single TMS pulse can cause up to 5°C of heating, and so repeated pulses could quickly create a problem. The amount of heating depends on the size, shape, and conductivity of the electrode, however. It has been found that small, pellet-type electrodes heat far less than more conventional disc-shaped electrodes, and conductance can be reduced by making electrodes out of plastic or other non-conductive material, rather than metal, and coating them with silver–silver chloride. As well, TMS will induce currents in any loops in a conductive wire, so it is important to ensure that all wires run as straight as possible; twisted or coaxial wires can also help reduce artifacts. It is also important to ensure that the TMS coil does not touch any EEG electrode, because movement of electrodes during each TMS pulse would occur, creating electrode movement artifacts. Finally, it is recommended that electrode impedances be kept very low (< 5 kΩ). This is much lower than is typically required for contemporary EEG systems; however, TMS pulses can result in polarization (a strong difference in potential) across the electrode–electrolyte–skin interface and this is minimized by minimizing the impedance to current flow across this interface. Secondly, the electronics of the EEG system must be robust enough not to suffer long-term damage from the TMS pulses, and kept a safe distance away from the stimulating coil. Most modern EEG systems are robust enough to handle the TMS pulses without damage, although this is a point that should be confirmed with the amplifier manufacturer prior to attempting this.

The larger concern, however, is the artifacts that are induced in the EEG data by TMS, due to the fact that the electrical current induced by the pulse is several orders of magnitude larger than EEG itself. An example of this artifact is shown in Figure 13.13. One issue is that the TMS pulse may cause **saturation** of the amplifier, which happens when an electrical potential in the electrodes exceeds the range that the amplifier is able to measure. This results in **blocking**, during which time the amplifier measures a flat line, and no signal can be recovered. While this does not damage the amplifier, it can take seconds or even tens of seconds for the amplifier to recover to the point where it can accurately measure EEG again. Thus TMS-compatible EEG amplifiers either need to have a very large dynamic range (that is, the range of potentials they are able to measure is greater than the size of the TMS artifacts), or some sort of gating device that prevents signals from reaching the amplifier if they exceed a particular threshold. Several amplifier designs have been used that involve 'sample-and-attenuate' or 'sample-and-hold' circuits that measure the voltage coming in before the signal reaches the amplification stage. If the input exceeds a certain voltage, it will be attenuated, or blocked altogether from reaching the amplifier, for a certain amount of time. While no usable data is recorded during this period, such an approach eliminates saturation, meaning that good EEG data can be recorded again much sooner than if the amplifier had to recover from saturation. Alternatively, using a wide-dynamic range amplifier that doesn't saturate with the TMS pulse, one can simply record the artifacts and remove them afterward in post-processing. Artifact removal can be performed using several methods, including independent components analysis (ICA), signal-space projection (SSP), and regression (Mutanen, Kukkonen, Nieminen, Stenroos, Sarvas, & Ilmoniemi, 2016). It is recommended to acquire the EEG data with a much higher sampling rate than would typically be used (1000–5000 Hz, rather than 200–500 Hz). This allows the recording system to record the artifacts more accurately and recover more quickly, at the expense of dramatically increasing the size of the data files.

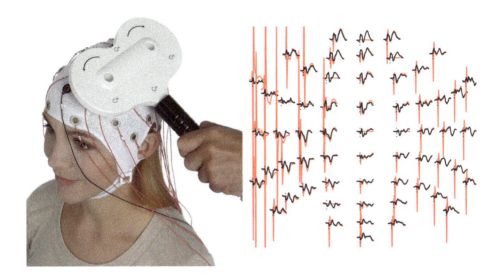

Figure 13.13 Combined EEG and TMS. The left panel shows a participant wearing a TMS-compatible EEG cap, while being stimulated with a figure-8 coil. Note that the wires from each EEG electrode are very straight to prevent TMS inducing any current in the wires. The right panel shows an example of EEG data with the TMS-induced muscle artifact (red) and after (black) artifact removal using an algorithm developed by Mutanen and colleagues (2016). The EEG data were collected using a sample-and-hold EEG amplifier that removed the electrical artifact created by the TMS pulse itself; however, the muscle artifact remained and thus required post-processing for removal. Left panel image courtesy of Brain Products GmbH; right panel reprinted from Mutanen and colleagues (2016) with permission of Elsevier

A number of artifacts are likely to be recorded in the EEG during TMS. The pulse itself will create an artifact; this is unavoidable and the period during the pulse should be considered unusable for EEG. Following the pulse, continued artifact is likely to be present. Firstly, if the amplifier saturates there will be a period of blocking, but either way there will be 'ringing' artifacts caused by the dropoff (gradient) of the induced magnetic field. As well, TMS often induces contractions of scalp muscles, typically in a period about 10 ms after stimulation, and blinks may be induced as well; both of these create EEG artifacts. Finally, there is commonly a **decay artifact** which is thought to have a number of causes, including current induction, electrode–skin polarization, and electrode movement. In addition, the recharging circuit in the TMS system will induce an artifact in the EEG recordings as the stimulator gets ready for the next pulse. Many TMS systems now have the ability to control the timing of this recharging, so that the user can ensure that it occurs after the time window during which EEG will be analysed (for example, 500–1000 ms after the TMS pulse). In post-processing, segments of the data containing pulse, saturation, and ringing artifacts are normally identified (either manually or by an automated algorithm) and excluded from the data. Decay and muscle artifacts are comparatively smaller, and can be removed from the data using an approach such as independent components analysis (ICA; discussed in the EEG chapter), allowing analysis of the EEG during the time periods that these artifacts occurred in.

As discussed earlier, combined TMS–EEG can be useful in studying the effects of TMS both on the stimulated site, and on more distant brain regions – and thus cortical connectivity. TMS induces unique patterns of EEG activity, called **TMS-evoked potentials (TEPs)**, as shown in Figure 13.14, and so it is important to characterize and understand these. The TEPs induced are highly dependent on the site of stimulation, the orientation of the coil, and the stimulation protocol and – like TMS in general – on the cognitive state of the person being stimulated. Thus it is important to characterize the baseline TEPs for a particular stimulation protocol in addition to investigating the effects of any experimental manipulation or investigating a special (for example, clinical) population. For example, TMS to the primary motor cortex induces a series of TEP components, including the N15, P30, N45, P55, N100, and P180. The earlier components are thought to reflect the direct effects of stimulation, while later occurring ones likely reflect activity conducted from stimulated areas to other regions, and/or reverberant or re-entrant activity back to the stimulated area from other areas. TMS also affects the frequency spectrum of EEG data, and so frequency-domain analyses can also be of interest.

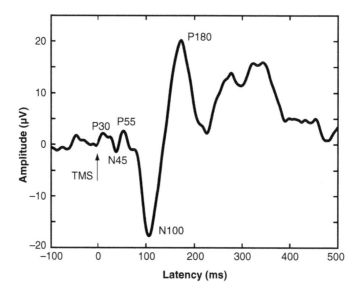

Figure 13.14 An example of a TMS-evoked potential (TEP). This was evoked by single-pulse TMS delivered to primary motor cortex (arrow; time 0). The component peaks labelled in the figure are all characteristic of TMS stimulation rather than being evoked by endogenous (self-generated) movements. Reprinted from Ilmoniemi and Kičić (2009) under CC BY-NC 3.0

SAFETY

Safety is an important consideration with TMS, since we are inducing electrical currents in the brain. Although the technique has an excellent overall safety record, in the early days of TMS experimentation there were a number of reports of cases in which people had seizures following TMS. This sparked careful and systematic investigation of the causes of these incidents, examining both the stimulation protocols and the selection of participants. This resulted in the publication of safety guidelines by a consensus group in 1998 (Wassermann, 1998), which were subsequently updated based on new information (Rossi, Hallett, Rossini, & Pascual-Leone, 2009). These guidelines are detailed and extensive, and we will only touch on the more significant points here; anyone considering using TMS should seek out the most current safety guidelines and read them in detail.

Perhaps the most alarming risk of TMS is an epileptic seizure. Rossi and colleagues (2009) surveyed the literature and found 16 reported cases of seizure associated with rTMS (none associated with single-pulse TMS), seven of which occurred prior to the publication of the original safety guidelines (and thus whose causes were considered addressed by those safety guidelines). Of the new cases, four were deemed to have happened in studies that used rTMS outside of the published safety guidelines. Furthermore, of the four seizures reported to have occurred in studies operating within safety guidelines, three cases involved people who were taking epileptogenic medications (that is, known to increase the risk of seizure), and in two cases careful examination called into question whether the reported events were truly seizures caused by the TMS, as opposed to other clinical events and/or occurring many hours post-TMS. Even among those studies operating outside the published safety guidelines, the majority of seizures occurred in people taking epileptogenic medications. One additional case of seizure was reported, this one being the only case associated with cTBS. The cause in this case was not clear, but the authors reviewing the case emphasized the need for further investigation into dose-response relationships specifically for cTBS. Given the fact that thousands of people have received rTMS in studies and clinical settings over more than 20 years, and that reporting of adverse events such as seizures is mandatory, the low number of cases of seizure should be taken to reflect a very good safety profile for TMS – particularly when safety guidelines are followed. Notably, many TMS studies are performed on people with epilepsy, and the risk of TMS-induced seizure in people who are already prone to seizures is only 1.4% (Rossi et al., 2009).

While seizures are the most dramatic possible side effect of TMS, there are a number of other safety concerns that should be understood. Firstly, heating and burns are a possibility. As noted earlier, electrodes such as those used in EEG can heat up, and so those designed specifically for TMS should be used and the guidelines for their use followed. Implanted metal in the head can also heat up; this includes implanted stimulation electrodes (for example, deep brain stimulators), aneurysm clips, and metal plates. Heating above 43°C can cause irreversible brain damage. Thus proper and thorough screening for implants is necessary. Although titanium, which is a primary metal used in medical implants, has low conductivity and may have design features (for example, notches) that minimize heating, movement is another concern for implanted metals, including plates and clips. The amount of movement in many cases might be so minimal as to not cause concern, but the onus is on the TMS operator to carefully consider the risk–benefit ratio in such situations. Any metal that can be removed (especially externally, such as jewellery, glasses, etc.) should be done prior to TMS.

TMS can also induce currents in implanted electrodes. Such electrodes might be in the brain, in devices such as deep brain stimulators, vagal nerve stimulators, or cochlear implants, as well as elsewhere in the body such as cardiac pacemakers. Several studies have investigated the safety of TMS with such devices, both ex vivo (in simulated bodies) and in vivo. Although TMS may induce current in these systems, the currents are generally small and within the range of those normally generated by the devices. However, the ex vivo studies did indicate that stimulating too close to the internal pulse generator of the stimulator (the part of the device that generates pulses) could damage the device, and several other limitations of the studies leave open the possibility of dangerous currents being generated that were not detectable given the methodology of the studies. At the same time, several in vivo studies have been performed on people with implanted devices with no negative effects. In general, caution is recommended and TMS should only be performed on people with implanted stimulators where it is medically warranted and the safety concerns have been fully considered. TMS should never be performed near the pulse generator of any such device, nor in people with cochlear implants; the design of cochlear implants poses significant safety risks for TMS.

While long-term effects of strong magnetic fields have received some attention in the media, there is no evidence that these fields pose a risk in TMS, either to the recipient or the TMS operator. A more immediate concern is hearing damage due to the loud noise produced with each pulse, which may exceed 140 dB (comparable to a gunshot, or jet engine at a distance of 30 m) and is well in excess of hearing safety guidelines. Thus it is important that both the TMS operator and recipient, as well as anyone else in the vicinity, wear proper hearing protection during stimulation. TMS can also cause physical discomfort due to muscle contractions, which can both be painful during stimulation, and result in a lasting headache. It is estimated that nearly 40% of TMS recipients experience pain and 30% have lasting headache (Rossi et al., 2009). The amount of muscle contraction varies significantly depending on where stimulation is targeted (near the face – such as over the frontal lobes – being particularly unpleasant). Participants should be warned of possible discomfort; bite guards (such as are used in contact sports) may be advisable if stimulation causes jaw contractions, and over-the-counter analgesics may be used if a headache results.

Another category of TMS effects to be considered are on brain activity and cognition. On the one hand, these are often the expected and even desired consequences of TMS, given that the goal of applying stimulation is to modulate brain activity and cognition. On the other hand, these effects need to be considered as possible side effects as well, particularly if they are of long duration or have a negative impact on the recipient. However, by and large these effects are of relatively small magnitude and short duration, rarely lasting longer than the experimental session.

Participants should be monitored by the experimenter though, and if they appear dizzy or otherwise compromised, it is advisable to ensure that the participant remains in the lab and under observation until the side effects pass. Longer-term changes have been reported after repeated rTMS sessions; again, this is typically a desired effect of administering multiple sessions. For instance, rTMS is used in the treatment of depression, obsessive-compulsive disorder, and other psychiatric conditions. There have been no reports of negative consequences of such treatments, however. On the other hand, in psychiatric populations TMS has occasionally been reported to induce psychiatric symptoms, including mania, psychosis, agitation, anxiety, and suicidal ideation. These have not, however, been reported in otherwise healthy people without a prior psychiatric diagnosis, and it is often unclear whether the reported symptoms are attributable to the TMS, since they are symptoms of pre-existing conditions.

SUMMARY

TMS is a form of NIBS that stimulates the brain by passing a strong electrical current through a conductor, held near the head. The current induces a magnetic field via the right-hand rule, which in turn induces a brief electrical current in the brain of the person stimulated. TMS is quite focal, though the distribution of current in the brain depends on the shape and size of the stimulating coil. The optimal way to determine how to position the TMS coil to target a specific brain region is using neuro-navigation, which combines real-time tracking of the head and coil position with a structural MR image of the person's head and brain. In the absence of this, scalp landmarks or measurements (like the International 10–10 System) can be used; however, these will increase the variance in brain locations stimulated relative to using an individual's own anatomy. An alternative approach is to systematically apply TMS stimulation to a number of locations on a grid over the general targeted area, and choose the stimulation location as that which yields the strongest response (for example, a muscle twitch, or visual phosphenes).

A number of different stimulation protocols are commonly used in TMS research, depending on the aims of the experiment. These vary in the type and duration of the effects. Single-pulse TMS involves delivering isolated pulses, which causes immediate excitation followed by a period of reduced activity in the area stimulated. Single-pulse motor mapping is also commonly used as part of many different TMS protocols, in order to define an individual's resting motor threshold, which is then used to set the level of stimulation in the experimental protocol. Paired-pulse protocols use a pair of pulses with specific relative timing and strength, to the same or different areas; these are useful in characterizing relationships between activity in different brain regions. An alternative to delivering individual or paired pulses is delivering a long series of pulses at fixed intervals, known as repetitive TMS (rTMS). Low-frequency rTMS (1 Hz or less) tends to have inhibitory effects on the targeted brain area, while high-frequency rTMS (> 1 Hz) tends to have excitatory effects. Low-frequency TMS is often used to induce 'transient lesions' in a brain area; during inhibitory stimulation impaired performance on a task suggests that the stimulated brain region plays a critical role in task performance. A variant of rTMS is theta burst stimulation (TBS), which involves bursts of three pulses separated by longer silent periods. This can be applied continuously or intermittently, resulting in inhibition or facilitation, respectively.

TMS exerts effects both through the current induced in the target cortex (direct effects) and through propagation of either the stimulation current, or induced changes in neural activity, to more distant brain regions. Pharmacologically, the immediate effects of single-pulse TMS are most strongly modulated by affecting the activity of sodium ion channels or glutamate; however, inhibitory and longer-lasting effects are also modulated by GABA and neuromodulators such as noradrenaline and serotonin. Overall, relatively little is understood about the precise mechanisms mediating the effects of TMS, but they are likely quite complex and widespread.

Because TMS is a form of stimulation and not a measurement, experiments using TMS rely on behavioural and/or neuroimaging measures to quantify the effects of stimulation. A critical consideration in behavioural measurements particularly is distinguishing true effects of brain stimulation from placebo or 'demand' effects caused (consciously or unconsciously) by participants' awareness that they are being stimulated. To control for this, TMS to the targeted brain area should be compared with some form of sham stimulation. Several approaches to sham stimulation are available, each with some limitations.

Neuroimaging can be combined with TMS to assess the effects of stimulation on brain activity as well as behaviour. MR-compatible TMS systems can be used in an MRI scanner; although large artifacts will occur during stimulation, the delayed timing of the BOLD HRF means that the effects of TMS on BOLD signal will occur after the period of artifacts. TMS can induce large currents in the EEG electrodes which not only create artifacts that overwhelm the EEG signal, but also damage the EEG hardware. TMS compatible EEG systems either block currents that exceed a certain level (in which case EEG data is lost for the artifact period), or have an exceptionally large dynamic range so as to be able to record the TMS-induced currents (and later remove them using signal processing techniques). As well, conductive coils such as loops of wire or circular electrodes can heat significantly during TMS, creating risks to the participant; electrodes that protrude from the scalp may also prevent the TMS coil from being held close enough to the scalp. Special electrode designs can avoid these issues.

When used according to published safety guidelines, TMS is generally safe. However, there are a number of important considerations to ensure the safety and comfort of participants. Firstly, people should be screened for risk factors such as epilepsy, if the risk factor is not the focus of the study, and for implanted metal or devices in the head that could heat, move, or malfunction as a result of stimulation. Because TMS is very loud, hearing protection should always be used by operator and participant. Some people report headache after TMS (and TMS can cause unpleasant muscle contractions depending on the site of stimulation), which can be treated with over-the-counter analgesics. Participants should also be monitored for dizziness, disorientation, or other symptoms, but these generally dissipate with time.

THINGS YOU SHOULD KNOW

- TMS uses the principle of the right-hand rule to induce a transient electrical current in the brain via a magnetic field created by passing a strong electrical current through a conductive coil.

- TMS is quite focal (approximately 12 cm^2) and so precise targeting of the intended brain region is important. This is ideally done using a neuro-navigation system with the individual's anatomical MRI scan, but can also be achieved using scalp-based landmarks or functional mapping.

- TMS can be delivered as individual, paired, or longer trains of regularly spaced pluses. Single pulses can be used in mapping and in studying the timing of brain activity. Paired pulses can be used to examine interactions between brain areas or timing within a brain area. Repetitive TMS can have inhibitory or facilitative effects depending on whether stimulation is low or high frequency, respectively, and its effects can be assessed online as a person is performing a task, or offline after stimulation has ended. A variant of rTMS is theta burst stimulation, which can have longer-lasting effects following a shorter period of stimulation.

- The effects of TMS are mediated by sodium ion channels, glutamate, GABA, and several neuromodulators. The effects depend on the stimulation protocol and are overall not well understood.

- Because TMS makes a loud noise and a 'tapping' sensation on the head, it is possible that observed effects of stimulation could be attributable to placebo or demand characteristics on the part of the participant (either consciously or unconsciously), rather than the brain stimulation itself. To control this, 'true' stimulation should be compared with one or more control conditions. Sham stimulation can be delivered in several ways, including by tipping the coil so it does not stimulate the brain, stimulating an area not expected to influence the task, or using a special sham coil. Each has limitations and these should be considered in designing and interpreting TMS experiments.

- Neuroimaging can be used to assess the effects of TMS on brain activity.

- While TMS is generally safe when used according to published safety guidelines, there are a number of risks that should be considered. Unless a specific patient group is the focus of the study, people with neurological conditions (especially seizure disorders) should not participate in TMS studies as there is a risk of seizure. As well, due to the electromagnetic fields involved, people with implanted metal or devices should not normally receive TMS. Due to the acoustic noise, hearing protection should always be used. Participants may experience headaches, pain, unpleasant muscle contractions, dizziness, or other symptoms, although these are typically of short duration.

FURTHER READINGS

Rossi, S., Hallett, M., Rossini, P.M., & Pascual-Leone, A. (2009). Safety, ethical considerations, and application guidelines for the use of transcranial magnetic stimulation in clinical practice and research. *Clinical Neurophysiology, 120*(12), 2008–2039.

Rotenberg, A., Horvath, J.C., & Pascual-Leone, A. (Eds.) (2014). *Transcranial Magnetic Stimulation*. New York: Springer.

Walsh, V., Pascual-Leone, A., & Kosslyn, S.M.. (2005). *Transcranial Magnetic Stimulation: A Neurochronometrics of Mind*. Cambridge, MA: MIT Press.

Wasserman, E., Epstein, C., Ziemann, U., Walsh, V., & Paus, T. (Eds.) (2008). *Oxford Handbook of Transcranial Stimulation*. Oxford: Oxford University Press.

14 Transcranial Electrical Stimulation (tES: tDCS, tACS, tRNS)

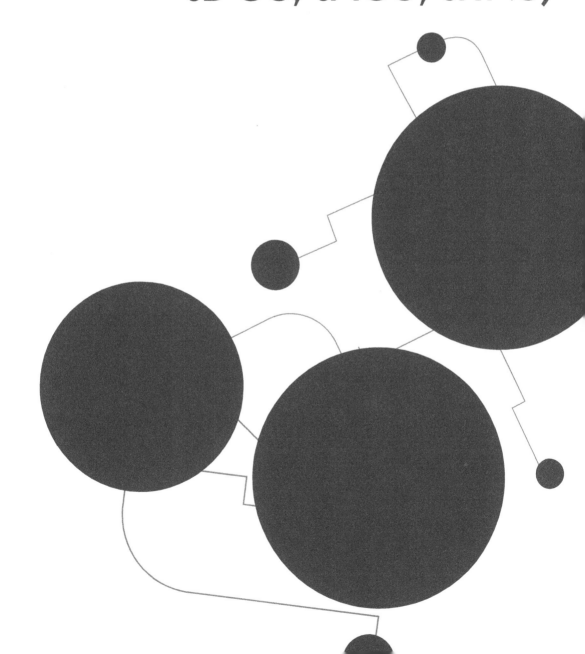

LEARNING OBJECTIVES

After reading this chapter, you should be able to:

- Describe how tES is administered, including types of hardware and current levels.
- Describe the advantages of high-definition tES.
- Compare and contrast the three primary tES stimulation protocols.
- Describe the known pharmacology of tES action.
- Describe different models of how tES affects brain activity.
- Discuss important considerations of participant selection for tES.
- Explain how tES studies can be blinded to control for placebo and demand effects.
- Discuss safety considerations in administering tES.

INTRODUCTION

Transcranial electrical stimulation (tES) refers to a broad class of NTBS techniques that involve passing relatively weak currents through the skull for the purpose of stimulating the brain. Although both TMS and tES are non-invasive stimulation techniques, they are quite distinct in both how they affect the brain, and how the stimulation is delivered. The head is highly transparent to magnetic fields, meaning that TMS pulses reach the brain with approximately the same strength that they are generated. In contrast, the tissues of the head – most notably the skull, but also the scalp and to a weaker degree, CSF – are electrically insulating. This means that in tES, the electrical current that reaches the brain is much weaker than the current that was applied to the outside of the head. At the same time, applying strong electrical currents to the skin can create discomfort and even burning of the tissue, which means that there is an upper limit to the amount of electrical stimulation that can be delivered non-invasively and safely. This limit means that the strength of the effects of tES are far less than those of TMS: rather than overwhelming and driving action potentials in the stimulated cortex as TMS does, tES merely 'nudges' neuronal cell membrane potentials towards greater or lesser polarization, making the neurons more or less likely to fire in response to other stimulation (which could be provided by other neurons, or by TMS in the case of combined tES–TMS studies that we discuss later). As such, the effects of tES are generally described as **neuromodulation**. It should be noted that, contrary to the convention in TMS, in electrical stimulation the 't' for 'transcranial' is typically written in lower case, as in tES. In fact, 'TES' with a capital 'T' refers specifically to a distinct technique, involving the use of stronger but much more transient electrical currents, that elicits responses more like TMS.

While we touched on some of the earliest recorded uses of brain stimulation in the introduction to the previous chapter, some additional highlights are notable in the history of electrical stimulation. The systematic use of non-invasive electrical brain stimulation began early in the twentieth century, with attempts to induce general anaesthesia (at that time, nitrous oxide and ether were the only real alternatives, and were fraught with risks and limitations) (Guleyupoglu, Schestatsky, Edwards, Fregni, & Bikson, 2013). Electrosleep was developed, initially in Russia, by delivering current through electrodes placed over the eyes. Later research determined that the electrical stimulation did not induce sleep directly, but rather created a very relaxed state that led to sleep, prompting a change in terminology to cranial electrotherapy stimulation (CES). CES has been fairly widely used since the 1960s and 1970s, and has seen a resurgence in the twenty-first century as a non-pharmacological treatment that is approved by the US Food and Drug Administration (FDA) for conditions such as insomnia, anxiety, and depression. Another, more widely known form of electrical stimulation is electroshock or electroconvulsive therapy (ECT). This involves application of repeated, high-intensity pulses to deliberately induce generalized seizures. ECT was first used in 1938 and was quite widely used in the treatment of serious psychiatric disorders (such as psychosis and major depression). Serious side effects of ECT, including severe memory loss (to the point that some patients had to re-learn to walk and perform basic bodily functions), combined with the development of pharmacological treatments for psychiatric conditions in the 1950s and 1960s, led to a decline in the use of ECT. However, in recent decades it has seen a resurgence and is currently an accepted treatment in many countries; in the US it is estimated that approximately 100,000 people per year receive ECT (Hermann, Dorwart, Hoover, & Brody, 1995), primarily in cases that are not responsive to drugs and/or when a rapid response is required (for example, when the near-term likelihood of suicide is high). It is important to recognize that the currents used in tES are far weaker than those used in ECT, and carry none of the risks or side effects of ECT.

The use of tES in cognitive neuroscience has a much shorter history, with the first contemporary studies published at the turn of the twenty-first century (Nitsche & Paulus, 2000; Priori, Berardelli, Rona, Accornero, & Manfredi, 1998). These studies were founded on prior work in animals that had shown modulation of neuronal membrane potentials via electrical stimulation of the scalp, as well as a few behavioural studies with humans in the 1970s and 1980s suggesting modulation of reaction times. The reason the 1998 and 2000 studies are considered the origins of modern tES, in spite of earlier work, is that they systematically demonstrated relationships between electrical stimulation and both behaviour and physiological responses, thus elucidating possible mechanisms of action and motivating further research. Both studies investigated the motor system, which is – as we learned in the TMS chapter – an ideal system for studying neurostimulation because it produces easily quantifiable muscle responses (MEPs). As well, both studies used TMS in combination with tES. In this way, they were able to show that administering tES prior to TMS altered the size of the TMS-evoked MEP. Specifically, if the anode (sending current) was placed over the motor cortex, MEP amplitudes were increased, suggesting that the input current made the stimulated neurons more likely to fire. Conversely, if the cathode (electrode where current flows out of the head, back to the device) was placed over motor cortex, MEP amplitude decreased, suggesting that cathodal stimulation made neurons less likely to fire. Since then, the technique has been used in many different ways to investigate many different neurocognitive systems (totalling well over 1000 published journal articles; Bikson et al., 2016), though the motor cortex continues to be the most widely studied of these. The applications that have received the most attention, however, are those that have found evidence that tES might affect neuroplasticity and thus facilitate learning, memory, and neurorehabilitation.

There are a number of tES approaches that differ in how the stimulation is delivered over time, as shown in Figure 14.1. The most common is **transcranial direct current stimulation (tDCS)**, in which a current of a fixed magnitude is passed from one electrode to another, through the head, for some amount of time (ranging from a few to tens of minutes). Another option is to vary the strength of the current sinusoidally at a particular frequency (typically ranging from a few Hz to over 100 Hz); there are two variants of this, one called **transcranial alternating current stimulation (tACS)** and the other called **oscillatory tDCS (o-tDCS)**. Finally, there is **transcranial random noise stimulation (tRNS**, sometimes called tRCS with the 'C' standing for 'current'), in which the intensity is varied randomly over time rather than being constant or varying at a set frequency. We will explore all of these in the following sections.

HOW DO WE DO IT?

The minimal equipment necessary for tES (at least tDCS) is quite simple: some devices are little more than a 9 V battery connected to two electrodes. However, to perform systematic investigations some additional technology is required, because at a minimum we would like to be able to quantify and control the electrical current flowing into the head. Thus devices typically have a voltmeter built in to measure current flow, and a knob to adjust the current level. Research-grade instruments typically also measure the impedance and adjust the electrical potential accordingly. This is because what is ultimately important is the current flowing through the head, and (as discussed in Chapter 3), by Ohm's law, for a given voltage current decreases as impedance increases. Two electrodes are placed on the head (or elsewhere on the body), and the electrical current flows from one to the other through the body. In tDCS, the 'sending' electrode is called the **anode**, and the 'receiving' electrode is called the **cathode** (in other tES variants, the labelling is more complicated, as discussed later). In most applications, these electrodes are much larger than those used in EEG; typically they are made from conductive rubber held inside large (for example, 5 × 7 cm) sponges that are soaked in saline (an electrically conductive solution, that is, electrolyte). The reason for using large electrodes is that the current that is

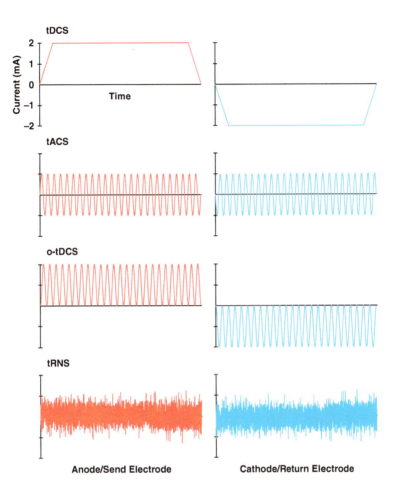

Figure 14.1 Schematic diagram of the different types of stimulation protocols commonly used in tES, plotted as variation in current over time. Typical stimulation protocols last approximately 5–13 min; however, for illustration purposes, time is not to scale in this figure (although current is on the same scale for all plots). The left column shows the current at the anode, or 'send' electrode (since in tACS and tRNS, the terms anode and cathode are not appropriate), while the right column shows current at the cathode/'return' electrode. In tDCS, the current is ramped up at the start, and down at the end of the stimulation period, typically for 10–45 s. In tACS and o-tDCS, sinusoidal variation of the current is used, typically in the range of human EEG (that is, 3–30 Hz). The difference between tACS and o-tDCS is that with tACS the current is centred on zero, so that each electrode acts as anode half the time and cathode half the time; in o-tDCS, the current is centred on half the maximum value, so that one electrode is always the anode (with current varying between zero and the maximum desired intensity) and the other electrode is always the cathode (ranging from zero to the negative of the maximum intensity). In tRNS, current is random at each time point. Note that the variation in current magnitude in all three stimulation protocols shown is effectively equivalent: in tDCS, the current has a continuous positive value for the duration of the stimulation at the anode, and a continuous negative value at the cathode (of equal magnitude to the anode). Similarly, in o-tDCS, the current ranges from 0 to 2 at the anode and 0 to −2 at the cathode. In the tACS and tRNS examples, the current range (between maximum and minimum values) at each electrode is equivalent to the range in the tDCS example (2 mA), but ranges from +1 to −1 rather than from 0 to +2 at the tDCS anode, and 0 to −2 at the cathode

used creates tingling or itching sensations, and these are reduced by increasing the surface area of the electrode. As well, just as with EEG the impedance of the scalp provides an impediment to current flow, so it is important to clean the skin where the electrodes will be placed, and measure impedance regularly during the experiment. Since the sponges can dry out – which will increase impedance, possibly causing burning or discomfort – regular checking and re-wetting of the electrodes may be necessary. Higher-end tES devices intended for research may have other features as well, such as the ability to deliver sham stimulation (discussed later in the context of experimental design), and to 'blind' the operator as to whether real or sham stimulation is being delivered on a given trial to prevent any possible bias (the device would record what stimulation was actually delivered to the participant for later analysis, of course). An example TES system is shown in Figure 14.2.

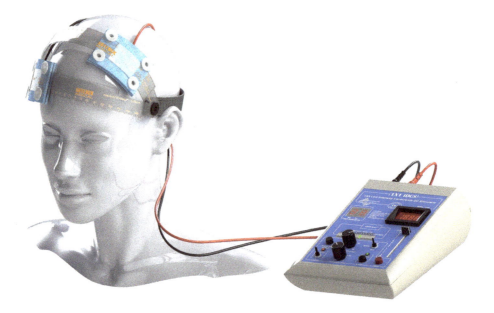

Figure 14.2 An example of a transcranial electrical stimulation (tES) system. On the model head are two sponge electrodes, each measuring 6 x 9 cm. The positions of these electrodes are similar to some studies that targeted the left dorsolateral prefrontal cortex (DLPC), with the anode over the left DPC and the cathode over the right supraorbital region. The stimulator unit is shown on the right. It is battery-powered and has controls to adjust stimulus current strength and duration, as well as the ability to deliver sham stimulation and a brief 'tickle' stimulus that helps familiarize the person being stimulated to the sensation of current onset and offset. Courtesy of Soterix Medical Inc.

The current delivered to the scalp is measured in milliamperes (mA), and is typically in the range of 1–2 mA (less than 0.5 mA is generally considered insufficient to generate neural effects, but may be used for sham stimulation). This is within the same range as the current that would pass through your tongue if you touched it to the terminals of a 9 V battery – enough to create a tingling sensation, but not dangerous. By comparison, a current in the 5–10 mA range is perceived as painful, so the currents used in tES are well below that threshold (and the instruments sold for research in this area restrict the current flow to ensure safety). However, the sudden onset of even a 0.5 mA current induces a tingling sensation that can feel unpleasant, especially to people who are not used to it and/or anxious, and so it is common for tDCS protocols to involve a short ramp-up time for the current at the start of stimulation and ramp-down at the end.

An advance over the traditional, large pad electrodes is 'high definition' or **HD-tES**. This uses smaller electrodes (typically EEG electrodes), with the anode and cathode placed much closer together (2–4 cm) than with larger sponge electrodes. One of the first, and widely used, approaches to this is known as the '4 × 1 ring' configuration (Datta, Bansal, Diaz, Patel, Reato, & Bikson, 2009), in which the anode is surrounded by four cathodes, each 3 cm from the central anode. The goal of HD-tES is to stimulate a much more focal area of the brain. The issues of participant comfort that led to the use of larger pads in the first place is addressed by using different electrode designs and conductive materials (such as electrolyte gel, as in EEG studies), and even in some cases topical anaesthetic; in general the 4 × 1 approach seems to be well tolerated by participants (Richardson, Fillmore, Datta, Truong, Bikson, & Fridriksson, 2014; Villamar, Volz, Bikson, Datta, DaSilva, & Fregni, 2013). More recent developments in HD-tES include the addition of more electrodes, and the design of complex stimulation montages (electrode positions) using modelling software that aim to optimize current delivery to a targeted brain area. An example of this is shown in Figure 14.3.

Transcranial Direct Current Stimulation (tDCS)

The mostly common form of tES is tDCS, which uses a constant current flowing from the anode, through the brain to the cathode over the entire stimulation period, as shown in Figure 14.4. In general, the brain area under the anode is depolarized (neurons become more sensitive to input and more likely to fire) while under the cathode it is hyperpolarized (less sensitive to input/less likely to fire). In most cases, the focus of the study is on delivering anodal stimulation to a particular brain area, and so anode placement is driven by the research question. The cathode may be placed elsewhere on the head, but is often placed somewhere away from the brain, such as near the eye, on the chin, or even on the clavicle (collarbone) or arm. This can help isolate the locus of effects because if the cathode is placed over a brain area, it may be hard to distinguish whether any observed effects are due to the anodal excitation or cathodal inhibition effects. However, as we will see later in this chapter, the location of the cathode can significantly affect the current path and, consequently, the brain area(s) that are actually stimulated.

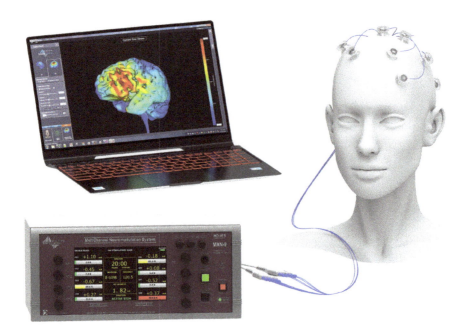

Figure 14.3 HD-tES system. This figure shows an HD-tES stimulator unit (bottom left) that allows the design and control of complex stimulation protocols, with the ability to control the current at each electrode independently. The return or ground electrode automatically adjusts to balance the current out of the head with the combination of all input electrodes. Top left shows the anatomical targeting software that allows researchers to design current distribution across the electrodes to optimally focus stimulation on a desired brain area. On the right is a model head with a complex array of electrodes. Courtesy of Soterix Medical Inc.

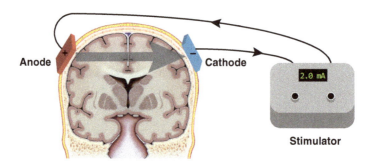

Figure 14.4 Diagram of tDCS, showing the anode and cathode (in this case placed on either side of the head), and the direction of current flow. Note that the grey arrow indicating current flow through the head is approximate – as discussed later in the chapter, current flow is dependent on head shape, neuroanatomy, and other factors; as well, much current is shunted along the scalp rather than entering the head

The protocols used in tDCS studies vary widely, depending on the goals of the experiment. The main parameters to set in tDCS are the current strength, the duration of stimulation, and where the anode and cathode are located. Current strength and duration of stimulation are not independent, either; together they determine the total amount of current passed through the brain. However, total current alone is not sufficient to predict the effects of tDCS, and in fact the effects of time and intensity, as well as their interaction, are non-linear. For example, studies have shown that with anodal stimulation, cortical excitability increases as duration of stimulation increases from 5–13 min (with a fixed current intensity), but longer durations (for example, 26 min) may end up causing a reversed effect (that is, suppression). Thus duration and intensity need to be chosen based on a solid understanding of the relevant literature. We discuss these and related concerns (such as electrode location) in greater detail in the section on experimental design. Another important parameter is whether stimulation is delivered 'online' or 'offline'; these terms have similar usage with tES as with rTMS. **Online** tES refers to designs in which stimulation is delivered during a task of interest, such as when performing a task that the participant is supposed to learn, or simply performing a task on which performance (for example, RT, accuracy) is the primary outcome variable. **Offline** tES involves applying stimulation for a period of time (typically 10–20 min) prior to learning or other task performance, then measuring the longer-term effects of the stimulation. After-effects of tES depend on the intensity, duration, location, and type (tDCS, tACS, etc.) of stimulation but may last for an hour or more after a single session, or much longer with repeated sessions.

Since tES is a stimulation technique, it does not yield any measurements directly – similarly to the case with TMS. Instead, research using tES examines its effects on behaviour, cognition, emotion, and/or brain activity using additional methods such as MEPs, reaction times, and neuroimaging. As noted earlier, the first demonstrations of the efficacy of tDCS were based on MEP recordings; however, it was recognized that in modulating neuronal membrane potentials, tDCS could potentially modulate neuroplasticity. Since at the neuronal level learning is largely dependent on long-term potentiation (LTP) and depression (LTD) – and these are in turn based on increasing (LTP) or decreasing (LTD) the likelihood of one neuron firing when one of its inputs does – depolarizing neurons using anodal tDCS should increase the likelihood of LTP whereas cathodal stimulation should increase the likelihood of LTD. Nitsche and colleagues (2003) found initial, partial support for this in that anodal tDCS over motor cortex improved RTs during a motor learning task. Subsequent studies have also shown improvements in learning with tDCS applied either before or during learning, during REM sleep after learning (when memories are consolidated), and also when it is applied across a series of learning trials on multiple days.

In addition to the motor cortex, the application of tDCS to other brain regions, and in non-motor tasks, has been studied. Because this is a relatively new field, there are a wide range of stimulation protocols being used, as well as a range of brain areas and cognitive functions. As such, it is valuable to look to meta-analyses of the literature to get a better sense of the overall trends. One brain area that has been heavily investigated is the dorsolateral prefrontal cortex (DLPC), the area around the middle frontal gyrus. The DLPC plays important roles in numerous cognitive functions, including working memory, executive control, and emotional regulation. A meta-analysis of 61 tDCS studies of DLPC (Dedoncker, Brunoni, Baeken, & Vanderhasselt, 2016) found that anodal stimulation led to significant performance increases (faster RT and greater accuracy) across a range of cognitive tasks, while cathodal tDCS had no consistent effects. Two other meta-analyses looked specifically at memory (Hill, Fitzgerald, & Hoy, 2016; Mancuso, Ilieva, Hamilton, & Farah, 2016); together these suggest that offline tDCS, especially to left DLPC, may improve memory accuracy, with the effects being more prominent in studies that combined tDCS with cognitive training aimed at improving working memory (compared to cognitive training plus sham tDCS). There is also evidence that repeated, offline tDCS sessions can be beneficial as treatment for psychiatric conditions including major depression, schizophrenia, and substance abuse (Kekic, Boysen, Campbell, & Schmidt, 2016).

Transcranial Alternating Current Stimulation (tACS)

Whereas tDCS uses a current of constant amplitude and polarity for the entire duration of stimulation (aside from the ramping at the start and end of stimulation), tACS uses sinusoidally varying amplitude and polarity. This was illustrated in Figure 14.1. The goal of tACS is to influence intrinsic oscillatory (frequency-domain) neural activity; recall from the EEG chapters that there are characteristic frequency bands of neural activity (listed in Table 3.1) associated with different brain areas, types of activity, cognitive activity, and levels of consciousness. Thus in tACS, the choice of stimulation frequency is based on the frequency of naturally occurring neural oscillations. For example, if one wanted to influence alpha power, one would use a frequency in the EEG alpha band (8–14 Hz). The desired effect of applying tACS is typically **entrainment** (that is, synchronization) of neural oscillations, which is technically two effects. One is inducing oscillations in the brain at the stimulation frequency (or boosting the amplitude of oscillations that are already occurring). The other effect is **phase locking**, in which the phase of neural oscillations synchronizes with that of the stimulation (recall from the MRI chapter that phase locking is when the peaks and troughs of two sine waves line up with each other; see Figure 6.7). Because neural oscillations are detectable with EEG, it is typical in tACS experiments to record EEG before and after stimulation to quantify the effects on brain activity (because the stimulation is electrical, and at the same frequency as the expected EEG activity, it is impossible to isolate the neural EEG signal during stimulation itself). Some studies have simply measured behavioural responses before and after, however. The effects of tACS-induced entrainment can last for at least 30 min, following 10 min of stimulation (Antal & Herrmann, 2016).

Neural oscillations in particular frequency bands have been associated with numerous functions – especially in communication between different brain areas, including cortico-cortical interactions (typically in the gamma band, 30–100 Hz) and thalamo-cortical interactions (alpha band, 8–14 Hz). As well, changes in alpha band power are associated with attention (for example, alpha oscillations generated in the occipital lobe increase when the eyes are closed, or when people are tired or bored), and with movement (generated in the motor cortex). Using tACS can inform us as to the causal role of these oscillations in cognition: while observing changes in power in a particular frequency band (using EEG) associated with state or task performance can be suggestive, our inference of causality is stronger if we can also show that directly manipulating the amplitude and phase of oscillations affects behaviour. Indeed, this has been shown in numerous studies, with effects such as boosting memory performance and enhancing motor learning, and inducing or altering sensory perceptions (Feurra, Paulus, Walsh, & Kanai, 2011; Paulus, 2011; Thut, Schyns, & Gross, 2011). These effects are frequency-specific, in that they are induced by certain frequencies (usually those associated with the same tasks based on EEG measurements). As well, studies have shown that the effects are maximal if the stimulation frequency is tuned to the individual's brain rhythms. For example, while the alpha band is typically defined as 8–14 Hz, a given individual's EEG will typically show maximal alpha power at one specific frequency within that range (for example, 10 Hz), and using this empirically measured frequency for tACS will have stronger effects than using a different frequency within the alpha band (Thut et al., 2011). In addition to frequencies in the sub-100 Hz range that typically characterizes human EEG, some tACS studies have used higher frequencies, in the range of 100–250 Hz. This is known as the **ripple frequency** range, based on short bursts recorded in this range in the hippocampus in animal studies, and associated with memory encoding. In an initial study, Moliadze and colleagues (Moliadze, Antal, & Paulus, 2010a) found that 10 min of stimulation at 140 Hz (but not 80 Hz, and more weakly at 250 Hz) increased excitability of primary motor cortex (as measured by TMS) for up to an hour after stimulation.

An important point of note about tACS is that the labels 'anode' and cathode' for the two electrodes lose their meaning. This is because the alternation of the current is between the maximum positive and maximum negative value of the stimulating current, so each electrode switches between being the anode and the cathode at the frequency of stimulation. As a result, the net change in the polarization of the neuronal cell membranes as a direct consequence of the stimulation should be zero. This also means that tACS will modulate the brain areas under *both* electrodes similarly, at the frequency of stimulation (although the phases at the two electrodes are always opposite – so a peak at one electrode corresponds to the trough at the other; see Figure 14.1). This means that the location of each electrode can have effects, which is an important consideration in designing the experiment. In some cases, the stimulation frequency may have no effects at one electrode location, if that brain area does not operate at, and is not sensitive to, that frequency. In other cases however, a focus on the location of one electrode over a target brain region, without considering the possible effects of the location of the other electrode, could complicate interpretation of the results.

The opposite phases at the two electrodes in tACS can be undesirable, for example if researchers wish to examine what happens when oscillations are synchronized between two brain areas. If phase-locked stimulation at two different scalp locations is desired, an additional electrode can be used, and stimulation would be delivered in-phase to two of the electrodes, with the third acting as the return path for the current. In a first demonstration of this approach, Polanía and colleagues (Polanía, Nitsche, Korman, Batsikadze, & Paulus, 2012) studied verbal working memory. They first conducted an EEG study demonstrating (as had prior research) that electrodes over left frontal (DLPC) and parietal cortices show a significant increase in phase synchronization in the theta band (4–8 Hz) while people perform a verbal working memory task. These findings suggest that synchronized activity between these two brain areas is important in maintaining items in working memory. Polanía and colleagues delivered theta band (6 Hz) alternating current through two 'target' electrodes (one over DLPC, one over parietal cortex), with one return electrode to balance the current, placed over the vertex of the head (presumed to be a neutral location for the task and stimulation frequency). The researchers were able to control the frequency and phase of the tACS signal at each stimulating electrode, and compared performance on the working memory task when the theta stimulation was phase-synchronized over frontal and parietal regions, and when it was perfectly out of phase (so a peak at the frontal electrode corresponded to a trough at the parietal electrode). This is illustrated in Figure 14.5. In-phase tACS during the task increased memory performance, while out-of-phase stimulation actually led to significantly worse memory performance than sham stimulation. As an additional control, the researchers performed the same manipulations using 35 Hz tACS and found that neither synchronized or desynchronized stimulation at this frequency affected performance on the memory task relative to sham stimulation.

In an elaboration of Polanía and colleagues' study, Alekseichuk and colleagues (Alekseichuk, Turi, de Lara, Antal, & Paulus, 2016) examined **cross-frequency coupling**. This is a phenomenon observed in hippocampus and cortico-cortical connectivity, in which bursts of a high frequency (gamma band, 30–100 Hz) synchronously occur on the peaks of a lower, 'carrier' frequency (theta band). Cross-frequency coupling has been associated with memory and attention, and in this study the researchers again used a working memory task. Since the focus of this study was on cross-frequency coupling (rather than interactions between brain regions, as in the previous study) they stimulated at only one cortical site (left DLPC), using a 4 × 1 configuration as described earlier. They compared simple theta-band tACS with theta tACS in which 50 ms bursts of gamma occurred either synchronized with the peaks or troughs of the theta stimulation waves, as well as a condition in which bursts of gamma were delivered without concurrent theta modulation. This is illustrated in Figure 14.6. Note that the theta peaks can be thought of as brief periods of anodal tDCS stimulation (when neuronal membrane excitability is particularly high), whereas the troughs are when that electrode is acting as the cathode (decreasing membrane excitability). The results showed that memory performance (measured with both speed and accuracy) was highest when 80–100 Hz gamma bursts co-occurred with the peaks of theta stimulation, while gamma bursts co-occurring with the theta troughs actually led to worse memory performance than theta stimulation alone. These two studies demonstrate both how tACS can be used to modulate brain activity in very sophisticated ways, and also how TES can be used to go beyond the correlations between brain rhythms and behaviour that can be shown

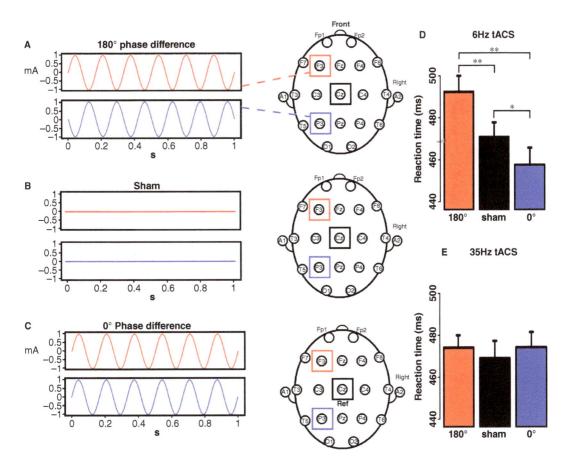

Figure 14.5 The three-electrode tACS experiment performed by Polanía and colleagues (2012). (A) shows the 'desynchronized' condition in which 6 Hz stimulation was delivered to electrodes over F3 and P3 (according to the International 10-10 System) perfectly out of phase; that is, when the current strength was at its peak positive value at one site, it was at its peak negative value at the other. Formally, this is known as a 180° phase difference. Stimulation was delivered in this manner continuously for the entire ~15 min that participants performed the working memory task. (B) shows the sham condition in which no current was delivered. (C) shows the 'synchronized' condition, in which tACS was delivered at 6 Hz as in the desynchronized condition, but in-phase (0° phase difference) between the frontal and parietal stimulating electrodes. (D) shows reaction times in the memory task for the three conditions, demonstrating slowed reaction times relative to sham in the desynchronized condition but speeded reactions in the in-phase condition. (E) shows the reaction time results from a control experiment using 35 Hz tACS with the same three conditions, demonstrating that the effects of (de)synchronization were specific to theta-band stimulation. Reprinted from Polanía and colleagues (2012) with permission of Elsevier

with recording techniques like EEG, and actually test for causality – that is, whether manipulating brain rhythms manipulates behaviour.

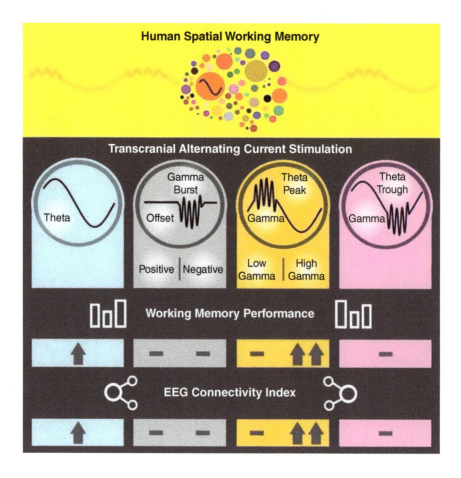

Figure 14.6 Schematic description of the methods and findings from Alekseichuk and colleagues' (2016) study of cross-frequency coupling using tACS. Participants performed a spatial working memory task while tACS was applied over the left frontal cortex (top row). In different sessions, participants received either theta stimulation, gamma-burst stimulation, or a combination of the two (second row from top). The combination involved either gamma bursts coinciding with the peaks of the theta stimulation (orange), or the troughs (pink). The third row shows that working memory performance was better in the theta-only condition than gamma-only or gamma bursts in the theta troughs, but performance was best when gamma bursts coincided with theta peaks. Resting-state EEG was also recorded before and after tACS; the bottom row of the figure shows that the measure of EEG connectivity used (phase-locking in the theta band) was increased proportionately to the changes in working memory performance. Reprinted from Alekseichuk and colleagues (2016), with permission of Elsevier

Oscillatory tDCS (o-tDCS)

There is also a variant of tACS known as oscillatory tDCS, or o-tDCS. This is conceptually similar to tACS in that the current is modulated at a specific frequency. The difference is that whereas in tACS the current alternates between the maximum positive and negative current strengths at each electrode, in o-tDCS the current alternates around a constant positive (at the anode) or negative (at the cathode) baseline level of current. This is illustrated in Figure 14.1. For example, with tACS if we use 1 mA as the stimulation strength, the current at each electrode will vary from +1 to -1 mA. However, using o-tDCS the baseline (average over time) current at the anode might be +1 mA but vary between +0.5 and +1.5 mA, while the current at the cathode would vary from -0.5 to -1.5 mA. Little direct comparison has been done between the effects of tACS and o-tDCS and so the differences between them – and relative merits of each – are not well understood.

Random Noise Stimulation (tRNS)

A final type of tES protocol involves stimulating the brain with current whose strength varies randomly from one time point to the next (typically with approximately 1000 time points delivered per second). This is done by choosing the amplitude values at random from a normal distribution, centred on zero and with maximum positive and negative values being half the total maximum current to be used (in other words, if the stimulation current is set to 1 mA, the random values will vary between -0.5 and +0.5 mA). Stimulation typically lasts for around 10 min, meaning that the stimulation contains well over half a million random values. An example time course of tRNS is shown in Figure 14.1. When a tRNS time series is viewed in the frequency domain, the normal distribution of values produces an essentially flat frequency distribution in the range of zero to half of the stimulation rate. So for example, tES devices often deliver 1280 pulses per second; because of the Nyquist theorem the maximum possible alternating current that can be produced is 640 Hz (half of 1280). Therefore, when delivering tRNS the frequencies between 0.1–640 Hz will be equally present, which is effectively white noise. However, in some cases researchers have used 'coloured noise', meaning that the tRNS frequency spectrum is limited to a narrower range, such as 0.1–100 or 100–640 Hz.

The first report of tRNS was by Terney and colleagues (Terney, Chaieb, Moliadze, Antal, & Paulus, 2008). As is typical of pioneering tES work, they started by using tRNS in conjunction with TMS delivered to primary motor cortex, and measured TMS-evoked MEPs. MEP amplitude increased by 20–50% after 10 min of tRNS (0–640 Hz, -0.5–0.5 mA), indicating that tRNS has significantly increased motor cortex excitability. These effects lasted for more than 60 min after tRNS ended, but had returned to baseline by 90 min. Terney and colleagues also investigated the effects of tRNS on implicit learning in a serial reaction time study. Here they found that tRNS over motor cortex during the learning blocks led to significantly better learning (faster reaction times) than sham stimulation. Interestingly, when Terney and colleagues compared low-frequency tRNS (lf-tRNS; 0.1–100 Hz) and high-frequency tRNS (hf-tRNS; 101–640 Hz), they found that only high-frequency tRNS was effective in increasing MEP amplitude; MEPs after low-frequency tRNS were no different than in a sham stimulation condition. Since most relevant human EEG frequencies are below 100 Hz, this suggests that tRNS operates on the brain in a different way than tACS. In other words, tRNS does not work simply as 'broad-band tACS' because the signal happens to contain modulation at particular frequencies that are effective in tACS (for example, theta, alpha, or gamma bands). Instead, the higher frequencies have been hypothesized to act via different mechanisms. We will discuss this in more detail in the next section.

Other studies have extended Terney and colleagues' findings to other domains, and compared tRNS with other forms of tES. In one study, Fertorani and colleagues (Fertonani, Pirulli, & Miniussi, 2011) compared hf-tRNS, lf-tRNS, anodal tDCS, cathodal tDCS, and sham stimulation over the primary visual cortex (Oz in the International 10–10 System) while people performed a challenging learning task in which they had to discriminate between the orientation of two lines that differed only minimally from each other. Both tRNS conditions were associated with significantly better learning than either tDCS condition, with hf-tRNS yielding the best learning performance. Another study demonstrated longer-term effects of tRNS: Snowball and colleagues (2013) applied hf-tRNS bilaterally over DLPC for 20 min periods on five consecutive days, while people performed two arithmetic learning tasks (rote memorization of facts, and calculations). Not only were the people who received hf-tRNS faster and more accurate after five days of practice, but when asked to come back to the lab six months later, they still showed significantly faster RTs, demonstrating that the tRNS-facilitated learning was maintained over a long period of time.

Although tRNS is a very promising technique, the number of published studies using it is still much lower than either tDCS or tACS – in spite of the fact that the first published studies using tRNS and tACS appeared in the same year. It seems likely that, if the effects of tRNS are found to be reliable through replication and additional studies, it will gain greater prevalence in the field – and possibly surpass tDCS. Firstly, tRNS seems to induce stronger effects than tDCS, which is clearly advantageous. As well, most participants do not report any tactile sensation during tRNS, whereas tDCS induces a distinct tingling sensation. Beyond the fact that some people find the tDCS sensation unpleasant, it makes blinding participants to whether they are in the stimulation or sham conditions difficult, which may in turn lead to biased results due to demand characteristics or placebo effects. While sham stimulation typically involves briefly ramping up the current and then bringing it back to zero (over the course of 30 s – not long enough to induce effects on brain activity but enough to induce tingling), experienced participants in particular may still be able to tell the difference between tDCS and sham simply by feel (Richardson et al., 2014). Thus tRNS may provide both stronger effects, and better experimental control.

WHAT ARE THE EFFECTS ON THE BRAIN?

As already noted, tES does not directly induce action potentials. Rather, its mechanism of action is thought to be modulation of neural membrane potentials. At rest, neurons are polarized; that is, the electrical potential inside the neuron is negative relative to the surrounding extracellular fluid. Since tES was first used, it has been speculated that anodal tDCS depolarizes neurons (that is, makes the electrical potential inside the cell closer to zero) – increasing their likelihood to fire – while cathodal stimulation hyperpolarizes them. As such, tDCS can make neurons more or less sensitive to input from other brain areas (or from other external stimulation, such as TMS). This suggests a fairly obvious mechanism by which tDCS can affect learning: at the cellular level, learning can be defined as a change in the strength of synaptic connections, and is supported by two primary mechanisms. **Long-term potentiation (LTP)** is a process whereby a neuron becomes more likely to fire in response to input from another neuron; **long-term depression (LTD)** is the reverse, with the neuron becoming less likely to fire in response to a specific input. By depolarizing neurons in a brain area – thus making them more likely to fire in response to input – anodal tDCS can induce LTP. Conversely, cathodal tDCS can induce LTD since it decreases the likelihood that the stimulated neurons will fire in response to input. This model is known as the **anodal excitation–cathodal inhibition (AECI)** model. Since LTP is a critical mechanism for learning, the widespread findings that tDCS enhances learning are easily interpreted in the context of the AECI model. However, while this description provides a straightforward explanatory mechanism, the effects are actually somewhat more nuanced. For example, as we have already noted, anodal stimulation can result in hyperpolarization/inhibition if it is sustained for too long. As well, while the AECI model explains the effects of tDCS, it is not appropriate for tACS or tRNS – since in both cases 'anode' and 'cathode' lose their meaning, and the net offset voltage over the course of stimulation is zero (as opposed to net depolarization or hyperpolarization for tDCS). We therefore need to dig a bit deeper to better understand how tES works more broadly.

Pharmacology

The pharmacology of tDCS has been studied in humans by administering a variety of receptor agonists and antagonists, as well as through inference from the results of paired-pulse TMS protocols known to rely on specific neurotransmitters (for example, ICF and SICI; see the chapter on TMS). However, this knowledge is at present quite limited due to the small number of studies, the narrow range of drugs used, and the fact that any drug may have effects either directly on the neurons receiving tES, or more systemically via network effects (such as modulation of neural activity either upstream or downstream from the stimulated area). The concentrations of positively charged calcium and sodium ions across neuronal membranes are critical to maintaining (and changing) electrical potentials, and so several studies have investigated the effects of drugs that block these ion channels (Stagg & Nitsche, 2011).

Blocking calcium channels causes a reduction in the effects of anodal tDCS during stimulation, and blocking sodium channels eliminates the effects altogether. This suggests that the depolarizing effects of anodal stimulation are caused by increased positively charged ions entering neurons. Both calcium and sodium channel blockers also eliminated the after-effects of anodal tDCS, indicating that ion flux is critical to both the online and offline effects of tDCS. Calcium ions seem particularly important, and one predominant calcium ion channel is controlled by NMDA receptors, which are activated by the excitatory neurotransmitter glutamate. Interestingly, blocking NMDA receptors does not affect the online effects of anodal tDCS, but does reduce the (offline) after-effects. Relatedly, an NMDA agonist increases the duration of anodal tDCS after-effects. This suggests that the offline effects of tDCS are dependent on changes in glutamate activity induced by the stimulation, but that glutamate is not directly relevant in modulating effects during stimulation. Activity of the inhibitory neurotransmitter GABA is also modulated by anodal tDCS. As with glutamate, GABA-modulating drugs do not influence the effects of online tES, but rather the after-effects. Specifically, GABA agonists (which stimulate GABA receptors) decrease the offline effects of anodal tDCS for approximately the first 10 min after stimulation; however, subsequently neural excitability is actually higher with a GABA agonist. Neuromodulators, including acetylcholine, dopamine, and serotonin, have also been shown to modulate the effects of tDCS, although these have been less extensively studied.

Effects at the cathode during tDCS seem to be modulated by slightly different mechanisms. Specifically, calcium and sodium channel blockers do not modulate the effects at the cathode during stimulation, even though they do at the anode. This may be because, when membranes are hyperpolarized, these ion channels become deactivated – so blocking them pharmacologically has no additional effect. The offline effects of cathodal tDCS are abolished by an NMDA antagonist, but are not affected by GABA-modulating drugs. However, other evidence (using SICI with paired-pulse TMS, which is GABA-dependent) suggests that GABA levels are decreased under the cathode after tDCS. Offline effects of cathodal tDCS appear to again relate to activity of NMDA, GABA, glutamate, dopamine, serotonin, and acetylcholine receptors.

The effects of tDCS on neurotransmission are also affected by the strength and duration of stimulation, as noted earlier. This has been attributed to differences in calcium flux. Specifically, low influx of calcium into neurons is known to cause LTD, while moderate influx has no effects, and larger influx causes LTP. However, very dramatic calcium influx will actually reduce LTP, because at some point the high intracellular levels of calcium trigger homeostatic mechanisms to balance the ion levels and membrane potential. This complex relationship between calcium levels and synaptic modulation has been used to explain the effects noted earlier whereby the normally enhancing effects of anodal tDCS on motor learning are reversed when stimulation is extended from 13 to 26 minutes – it is speculated that the longer duration leads to high calcium levels that trigger homeostatic regulation. Such homeostatic regulation – that is, the body's ability to keep the operation of physiological processes within an acceptable range for normal function – is an important consideration in tES. Generally speaking, tDCS works by pushing neuronal membrane potentials away from the levels that they are normally regulated at. The body's natural response will tend to be to attempt to compensate for any tDCS-induced changes – for example, through changes in neurotransmitter levels, receptor and/or ion channel activation – and so the longer stimulation is sustained for, the more these compensatory mechanisms can be expected to complicate the predicted effects of tES.

The pharmacological mechanisms of tACS and tRNS have been far less studied than tDCS. In general, tACS is thought to operate primarily through entrainment of intrinsic neural oscillations (that is, enhancing naturally occurring processes that control these oscillations). Also, since the current is constantly fluctuating between positive (anodal) and negative (cathodal) values, it is not expected that there will be any net effect of tACS on ion levels. The case of tRNS is interesting because, although it has similar (though apparently stronger) effects on learning than tDCS, its after-effects are not affected by NMDA-modulating drugs the way offline tDCS effects are. However, the after-effects of tRNS are reduced by both a sodium channel blocker and a GABA agonist. This suggests that while both tDCS and tRNS reduce inhibitory GABA levels (which in turn facilitate learning), tRNS is not dependent on NMDA receptors but is dependent on modulation of sodium channel activity. These differing pharmacological effects may help explain why tRNS has more powerful effects on learning than tRNS. It has also been suggested that tRNS disrupts the normal homeostatic regulation systems mentioned above, which tend to counteract the effects of tDCS (Fertonani et al., 2011). The constant changes in membrane potential induced by tRNS, in contrast to the sustained de- or hyper-polarization caused by tDCS, may 'confuse' homeostatic mechanisms, which may in part explain the stronger effects of tRNS.

Activity Dependence

Earlier the AECI (anodal excitation–cathodal inhibition) model was introduced as a basic explanation of how tDCS works. This model provides a straightforward framework for understanding many of the basic findings in the tES (especially tDCS) literature. However, it is very likely overly simplistic, especially when we consider stimulation of areas other than primary motor cortex, and modes of stimulation other than tDCS. Two important refinements to the AECI model consider activity levels within the stimulated region, and within the larger network of connected brain areas (Fertonani & Miniussi, 2017). The **activity-dependent model** builds on the AECI by integrating the observation that the effects of tES are dependent on the state, or activity level, of the brain area immediately prior to stimulation. If neurons within a brain area are already generally depolarized – for example due to high levels of input from another brain area – then anodal tDCS is likely to have stronger effects than if the brain area is generally more hyperpolarized. Consider as an example the motor or premotor cortex: if someone is already planning a motor movement, tDCS may have stronger effects than if a movement was not planned, because planning a movement increases activity within these brain areas. Conversely, if a brain area is particularly hyperpolarized (for example, due to high levels of inhibition) then anodal tDCS is likely to have weaker effects. Activity-dependent effects have been demonstrated in many studies. For example, Tseng and colleagues (2012) found that anodal tDCS to the right parietal cortex improved visual working memory performance, but only in people whose working memory span was low to begin with – people with high spans did not show any effects of stimulation. Similarly, Bortoletto and colleagues (Bortoletto, Pellicciari, Rodella, & Minussi, 2015) found that during a motor task that normally shows practice effects (involving fast movements), anodal tDCS actually impaired learning, whereas the same stimulation during a task that normally does not show practice effects (involving slow movements) led to improvements in performance. The authors interpreted this as indicating that there is an optimal level of excitability in motor cortex to facilitate learning – one which is normally achieved during the 'fast' task but not the 'slow' one. By using tDCS, the combined excitation level in the 'fast' condition exceeded this optimum, whereas tDCS combined with the 'slow' task achieved this optimum level.

Thinking a bit more deeply about the activity-dependent model, we know that any brain area comprises a large number of different types of neurons, and often different populations of neurons. For example, within primary motor cortex different cells are tuned to movements in different directions. Thus if a movement is planned in a particular direction, the activity-dependent model would predict that tDCS would affect the neurons tuned to that movement direction differently from neurons tuned to other directions, because the neurons tuned to the relevant direction would have higher activation levels than those tuned to directions of movements that were not being executed. This principle was demonstrated by Antal and colleagues (Antal, Nitsche, Kruse, Kincses, Hoffman, & Paulus, 2004) in area V5 of the visual cortex (within which neurons are tuned to specific directions of motion), across two tasks. In one task, participants saw an array of moving dots on a screen, and had to identify the direction that the majority of dots were moving in. The researchers first determined the minimum number of dots that had to be moving in the same direction for each individual to accurately perform this detection (their psychophysical threshold), then applied anodal or cathodal tDCS. Cathodal tDCS actually *improved* performance on the task (reduced the threshold for detection), which Antal and colleagues attributed to reduced competition between the neurons tuned to the primary direction of motion, and neurons tuned to other directions. That is, cathodal tDCS reduced the likelihood of V5 neurons firing, but since more dots were moving in the target direction than any other direction, the neurons tuned to the target direction retained a level of activity that facilitated behavioural detection. In contrast, the activity of neurons stimulated by the 'noise' dots (moving in random directions) was suppressed. In other words, cathodal tDCS improved the signal-to-noise ratio in V5, facilitating detection. In another task, however, anodal tDCS improved performance while cathodal tDCS reduced it. The difference was that, in this second task, all of the dots were moving in the same direction (participants just had to say if they were moving upward or downward). Since there was no competing noise from other movement directions, cathodal stimulation merely reduced activity levels overall (rather than reducing noise levels), whereas anodal tDCS increased the likelihood that neurons tuned to the direction of motion would fire, creating a stronger neural signal on which to base the decision.

The **network activity-dependent model** extends this line of thinking even further. First of all, it recognizes that tES to a particular brain region is likely to affect not only that area, but other (remote) areas that are connected to the stimulated area. 'Downstream' regions (those receiving input from the stimulated area) will obviously see changes in input if the stimulated area's activity changes; 'upstream' areas (providing input to the stimulated area) may also be modulated by the increased sensitivity of the stimulated area to input, if there is any sort of feedback from the stimulated area to the input area. Moreover, it is well known that some brain areas participate in multiple neural networks, in task-dependent ways, especially in higher-order **'association' cortices**. Thus the same brain area may be active in a number of distinct tasks, but between tasks the other areas that are co-activated with this one area will differ. The network activity-dependent model would predict that the effects of stimulation to such a 'multi-purpose' brain area would depend on the task being performed before/during stimulation, such that if other tasks were tested after stimulation, only the task performed before/during stimulation would be affected. An extension of this line of thinking is that if tES is performed when people are at rest (rather than performing a task, that is, 'offline' tES), then the network(s) most affected by this stimulation will be those functionally connected with the stimulated area during rest (such as observed in resting-state functional connectivity studies).

Stochastic Resonance

Building on the network activity-dependent model, one principle that has been proposed to explain the effects of tES is **stochastic resonance**. This concept comes from physics, and applies to many complex, non-linear systems such as lasers, chemical reactions, semiconductors, and biology (Gammaitoni, Hänggi, Jung, & Marchesoni, 1998). We are already familiar with the concept of resonance, in which an input signal whose frequency matches the resonant frequency (or frequency of ongoing activation) of a system allows transfer of energy to the system or, thought of another way, amplification of the system's activity. Indeed, this is the mechanism thought to underlie the effects of tACS. Stochastic resonance can be thought of as a non-specific form of resonance, in which noise is input to the system (in this case, the brain) rather than any one specific frequency. If the system itself is noisy – for example, a brain region whose neurons have different baseline levels of activity, and different sensitivities to the task or stimuli at hand – the input noise can nudge the overall activity levels of the system upward. Assuming that some neurons are closer to their firing threshold to begin with (because they are sensitive to the task/stimuli), then the right amount of input noise should boost the activity of the 'target' (task-relevant) neurons above threshold, while the activity of irrelevant neurons will also increase, but stay below threshold. This was seen in the results of the first experiment by Antal and colleagues (2004).

The notion of stochastic resonance is in line with other evidence about how neurobiological and neurocognitive systems function. Specifically, many phenomena – including the probability of a neuron firing given an input, and psychophysical thresholds for detecting stimuli – are governed by non-linear **sigmoidal** (s-shaped) functions, as shown in Figure 14.7. The hallmark of a sigmoidal function is that at the low end of input intensity, there is little response, but in the 'optimal range' for the function, small changes in input strength produce disproportionately larger changes in the response. Then at some point, the response saturates and increased input strength produces little change in response. For example, if we consider a simple psychophysical task in which a person needs to detect a flash of light, we would start with no flash, and gradually increase the intensity of the flash. At first, the stimulus will be so dim that the person can never detect it, and so slight increases in brightness would not result in an increased probability of detection. However, at some point the stimulus becomes barely bright enough to detect, so the probability of detecting it starts to increase (that is, on some trials the person would detect it, on others they would miss). The detection probability will continue to increase as the stimulus gets brighter, but at some point the stimulus will be so bright that it is reliably detectable on every trial – this is the top, flat portion of the sigmoid. Returning to tES, the idea of stochastic resonance is that increasing the overall activity level of the system (that is, using tES to make neurons more likely to fire) can 'shift' the sigmoid function leftward, such that less external input is needed for the brain system to reach its threshold level of firing in the case of weak signals – but stronger signals may be less affected, if they were already eliciting responses close to the upper 'saturation' region of the sigmoid.

The left column shows a condition in which approximately equal proportions of dots are moving in each of eight directions. Neural firing rates are generally sufficient for each direction of motion to influence the behavioural response, which results in an inability to identify a coherent direction of motion. Because neurons tuned to all motion directions are already excited above threshold, tES has a non-specific effect of increasing neural responsiveness, but does not affect detection.

In the middle column, a small majority of dots are moving in one direction (partial coherence), but there is still sufficient competition from 'noise' dots moving in other directions that the participant is unable to detect the coherent motion (that is, activation of the neurons tuned to the majority direction is below threshold). In this case, tES increases the responsiveness of all subpopulations of neurons, but raises activity above threshold only for those tuned to the direction of coherent motion.

In the right column, a larger proportion of dots are moving in the target direction, and as a result neurons tuned to this direction fire strongly and the participant is able to detect the coherent direction without tES. Here, a stronger dose of tES is applied (for example, 2 mA rather than 1 mA). Because the neurons tuned to the primary direction of motion are already close to their maximal firing rates (that is, near the plateau of the sigmoid function), tES has relatively little effect on this subpopulation. However, the stronger dose of tES increases the responsiveness neurons tuned to other directions sufficiently that after tES, their firing rates increase above the detection threshold. As a result, in this case tES actually makes the detection task more

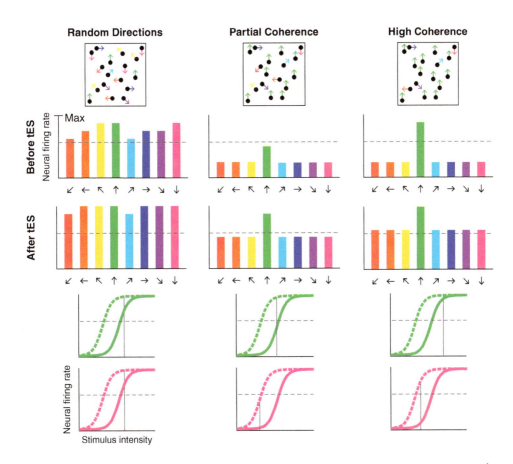

Figure 14.7 An illustration of the concept of stochastic resonance in tES, using a visual psychophysics paradigm in which participants must detect the direction of coherently moving dots. Of interest is the activity in visual motion-sensitive area V5 of the cortex, which has subpopulations of neurons tuned to different directions of motion. In each column, the top panel illustrates the proportion of dots moving in different directions; the coloured arrows represent directions of motion and typically many more dots would be presented than shown here. The middle panels (bar plots) show neural firing rates induced by the stimulus, for the subpopulations of neurons tuned to each direction (indicated by arrows under each plot). The lighter shaded area of each bar indicates the increase in firing rate after tES is applied, and the dashed line represents the minimum activity threshold for each subpopulation of neurons to influence the person's judgement of motion direction. The bottom panels show the sigmoid response functions of two of these neural populations: those tuned to upward motion (green) and those tuned to downward motion (pink). The sigmoid plots demonstrate the nonlinear response typical of neurons, described in the text. The solid sigmoids represent the response properties of the neurons prior to tES, and the dashed sigmoid shows how tES shifts the response curve leftward. The effect of tES is to make neurons more prone to fire given a weaker input. Adapted from Minuissi, Harris, & Ruzzoli, 2013

difficult, because it increases the 'noise' from neurons tuned to other directions. These results demonstrate the complex relationship between tES intensity, pre-stimulus activity, and the response properties of neurons.

Conduction through the Brain

In this section we consider two factors. The first is how, and how much, electricity actually reaches the brain during tES. The second, related question is where the current flows, and how precise we can be about which brain areas are stimulated. As discussed throughout this book, every person's brain is different in many ways, including its size, shape, and cortical folding patterns. This is a limitation in interpreting scalp-based recordings like EEG and MEG, and why it is so valuable to have anatomical MRI scans from individual participants when performing source localization, averaging across people in an fMRI study, or using neuro-navigation with TMS. The case with tES is no different. In most published tES studies to date, electrode placement has been based on very generalized assumptions about the location of brain areas under the skull, often based on the International 10–10 System. For example, studies targeting primary motor cortex might centre an electrode over C3 or C4, because these are the 10–10 System positions that generally lie over the central sulcus, where the primary motor cortex is located. Likewise, studies targeting the DLPC typically place electrodes over F3 or F4. Individual differences in the underlying neuroanatomy can, to some degree, be considered negligible because the size of the pads in traditional tES (typically in the order of 35 cm^2) are so large that they are rather non-specific in the brain areas they target. On the other hand, modelling studies have shown that current distribution over large electrode pads in tES is not uniform; instead, current is actually concentrated at the edges of the pads. Questions of precision also become more important as HD-tES becomes more common. Another consideration is that the folding of the cortex means that different neurons and cortical areas will experience different polarities of stimulation from the same electrode, simply based on where the electrode is placed and how that part of the cortex is oriented relative to the scalp. Given the different folding patterns among individuals, and the fact that the same functional or mesostructural (cytoarchitectonic, myeloarchitectonic, etc.) area may be on the gyrus of one individual, but the bank or depth of a sulcus in another, it seems reasonable to expect that a stimulating electrode placed at a given 10–10 System location might well affect different individuals differently. Indeed, this may be one of the important reasons why several meta-analyses of the tES literature have to this point produced results ranging from weak to discouraging (Antal, Keeser, Priori, Padberg, & Nitsche, 2015; Hill et al., 2016; Horvath, Forte, & Carter, 2015; Kekic et al., 2016; Summers, Kang, & Cauraugh, 2015).

To address these concerns, a number of studies have been conducted to, on the one hand, empirically measure the intra-cerebral currents induced by tES and, on the other hand, to create individualized computational models of current flow using approaches closely related to those used in M/EEG source localization. One important question is how much current delivered by tES actually reaches the brain. Given that the skull is a poor conductor of electricity, and much poorer than the scalp, it is expected that a significant amount of the tES current is shunted along the scalp surface, rather than reaching the brain. Of the current that does pass through the skull, a significant additional amount is shunted by the highly conducting CSF. These factors affect both the amount of current reaching the brain, and also their focality, because the high conductivity of the scalp and CSF, combined with the low conductivity of the skull, will tend to smear the current out over a larger space than the surface of the electrode – just as was described for EEG, but in reverse.

To determine how much current actually reaches the brain, Opitz and colleagues (2016) measured intracranial electrical potentials in two people with epilepsy, who had strips of electrodes surgically implanted on the surface of their brain. This is a common procedure in neurology to help localize the source of seizures, and the electrodes are typically left in the head for many days to allow for continuous monitoring. This provides interesting opportunities for research, although the placement of electrodes is driven solely by clinical considerations and so is not always optimal for a particular research question, and provides limited coverage of the cortex in any given individual. Opitz and colleagues applied tACS at a low frequency (1 Hz) and a range of current strengths up to 1 mA (a value commonly used in tES studies), with one electrode over the forehead and one at the base of the skull or, in other conditions, with the electrodes over the left and right temples. These electrode configurations allowed for measurements across the brain, with the maximum possible separation of stimulating electrodes on the head. They found that intracranial electrical potentials were largest directly under the two stimulating electrodes, and tapered off with distance from the electrodes. This was unsurprising, since all current flows in through the anode and out through the cathode (so must be concentrated at those locations) whereas, in between, the current can be broadly distributed throughout the scalp and brain. In a study published around the same time, Huang and colleagues (2017) used a similar procedure in ten people with epilepsy. Both studies observed that intracortical potentials varied across individuals, and that the measured intracortical potentials were on the low end of what has been found to be effective in inducing physiological effects (such as entrainment of cortical rhythms) in vitro, in animal studies. Thus while numerous studies have reported significant effects using 1 mA currents, it is possible that some of the variability in results across the literature are due to the use of currents that are barely strong enough to induce measurable effects. When this consideration is combined with individual variability in brain shape and conduction properties, it may be that some studies show weak, or null, effects due to low current combined with bad luck in selection of participants.

Other studies have used advanced computational modelling, called finite element modelling (FEM), to estimate current strengths and distributions in individual brains, as well as the effects of different electrode sizes and positions. Recall that in the MEG chapter, when discussing source localization we introduced boundary element models (BEMs), which model each relevant tissue type as a tessellated layer with a specific electrical conductivity (or magnetic permeability) value. FEMs are essentially a three-dimensional extension of BEMs: rather than treating each tissue type as a 2D layer, each is modelled as a 3D structure. In other words, FEMs consider the conductivity of each tissue layer as a function of its thickness, rather than assuming a uniform conductivity value for a given tissue type (FEMs are also used in fNIRI source localization, as mentioned in Chapter 12, because light transmission is affected by skull thickness). This makes them more precise, because for example the skull varies in thickness between individuals and even across the head within individuals, and conductivity is proportional to thickness. The primary disadvantage of FEMs is that they are significantly more computationally intensive both to produce (since there is an added dimension), and especially to use in modelling electrical fields in the head, since rather than a single conductivity value across the surface of a particular tissue, the conductivity now varies at each point on the surface. In general such FEMs rely on specialized supercomputing facilities.

Using FEM, Datta and colleagues (2009) modelled the distribution of electrical potentials in a single human subject, based on a high-resolution structural MRI scan. They compared current strength and distribution in a simulated tDCS study, between 7 × 5 cm electrode pads, and a 4 × 1 ring configuration (HD-tES), with the anode in both cases positioned over motor cortex (C3) and the cathode for the pad configuration over the contralateral forehead (as is common in motor cortex tES studies). The current strength was adjusted for the electrode type, using 1 mA for the pads and 2 mA for the 4 × 1 array, as required by the smaller electrode sizes. For both electrode configurations, the peak intracortical potentials from the model were comparable to those obtained empirically in the intracortical recording studies mentioned above. Critically, however, the distribution of current in the models differed quite drastically between the two electrode configurations, as shown in Figure 14.8. For the large pad electrodes, the current was maximal not under either electrode, but in the frontal lobe contralateral to the anode, closer to the cathode. Indeed, current was generally stronger over the frontal lobes than over the motor cortex, in spite of the fact that tES studies using this electrode configuration typically assume that they are stimulating the motor cortex. Moreover, the distribution of current was not uniform across the cortex between the electrodes, but varied with the folding pattern of the cortex and the thickness of the skull; the authors noted that fields were largest on the tops of certain gyri and that the distribution of CSF likely played a role in this – with the greater volume of CSF in the sulci surrounding the gyri acting as current sinks that funnelled the current to the tops of the gyri, where CSF is thinner. By comparison, the 4 × 1 ring configuration produced much more focal electrical potentials in primary motor cortex directly under the anode, although they still varied with the folding pattern of the cortex. These results suggest significant caution is necessary in basing inferences about what brain areas are stimulated, simply on electrode position with traditional tES. They also emphasize the advantages of HD-tES, while underscoring the fact that even with this more focal stimulation method, individual differences in cortical folding patterns relative to electrode position will influence the results. The authors also observed that studies in children and older adults should consider the significant anatomical differences in these groups from younger adults: young children have thinner skulls, and infants have fontanelles where the skull has yet to fuse and which thus provide low-resistance paths

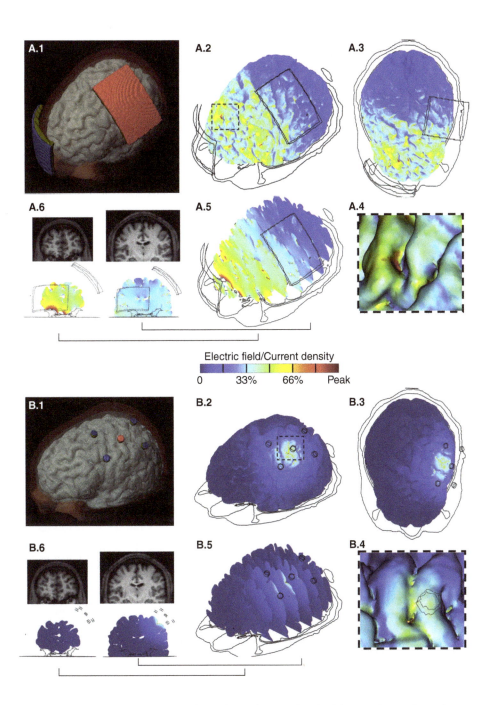

Figure 14.8 Models of current flow through an individual human brain, based on a finite element model (FEM) derived from the individual's structural MRI scan, for conventional large, rectangular sponge electrodes (A) and a 4 · 1 HD-tES ring configuration (B). In both A and B, (1) shows the anode (red) and cathode (blue) positions; (2), (3), and (5) show estimated electric field magnitude on the surface

Figure 14.8 (Continued)

of the brain from three different views; (4) shows a zoomed-in view of the area bordered by dashed lines in (2). (6) shows electric fields in two slices in the coronal plane, corresponding to the T1-weighted MR images directly above them. These results demonstrate that conventional tES electrodes create very broadly distributed, and uneven, voltage distributions in the brain, whereas HD-tES induces much more focal effects which nonetheless vary with sulcal/gyral anatomy. Reprinted from Datta et al. (2009) with permission of Elsevier

for current to travel. In contrast, the cortex atrophies with age, meaning that older adults will in general have greater volume of CSF – and some clinical populations such as people with dementia may respond differently from healthy adults due to greater cortical atrophy.

Other work has considered the relative positions of the anode and cathode in 'traditional' tES studies using large sponge pad electrodes (Bikson, Datta, Rahman, & Scaturro, 2010; Moliadze, Antal, & Paulus, 2010b). These have shown that the location of the cathode plays a significant role in determining current path, and thus where stimulation is focused. While this should not seem entirely surprising, given that current flows between the two electrodes, it is an important consideration because, although many tDCS studies of motor cortex have used the 'standard' cathode placement on the contralateral forehead, many other studies (especially outside the motor system) have placed the cathode elsewhere on the body (such as the arm or clavicle) to ensure that any observed effects are due to the placement of the anode, and not the cathode. However, these studies have generally assumed that cathode placement did not affect the intensity or distribution of current at the anode location. Modelling and empirical data indicate that when placing the cathode on these 'extracephalic' (non-head) locations, first of all the intensity of the current must be increased to result in the same level of intracerebral potential (because the farther the current has to travel, the weaker it becomes), and secondly modelling should be performed to understand how the current will be distributed in the brain.

Together these studies both confirm that tES does indeed result in increased electrical potentials in the cerebral cortex, and suggest that in the future the field needs to become much more sophisticated in its approach to choosing stimulation parameters, including current strength, electrode configuration, and electrode positioning. The practice of using a single current strength for all participants, and consistent electrode placement based on 10–10 System locations or other assumptions about the underlying anatomy, appear to create the appearance of standardization of procedures that actually results in widely varying intensity and distribution of currents inside the head across individuals. Indeed, Bestmann and Ward (2017) likened current practice in the field to 'posting a letter without a stamp or address, and hoping it will arrive at its destination' (p. 865). Ideally, FEM would be used to optimally target the desired brain region, and to equate actual intracerebral current delivered to that area on a per-individual basis. However, significant technical development remains to be done in this area due to the complexity and computational demands of FEM.

CONSIDERATIONS IN EXPERIMENTAL DESIGN

We have already touched on several considerations in tES experiment design in this chapter, including the different stimulation protocols available (that is, tDCS, tACS, tRNS), and parameters such as current strength, duration, electrode size, and electrode placement. These, along with the other factors we consider in this section – participant selection and the role of individual differences; and experimental control – are essential to understand for anyone wishing to work in this field, or even interpret data from tES studies. Although tES has been used as a research technique for almost two decades now, there is still a high degree of heterogeneity in the parameters used, and the quality of the studies. As noted earlier, meta-analyses have often reported no or weak effects of tES, even though many individual studies produce compelling results. One issue in the field is that tES equipment is relatively inexpensive to purchase, compared to TMS or virtually any of the neuroimaging techniques covered in this book. The relatively simple technology and low cost involved may mean that it is easier to obtain and start using such a device, than it is to gain the background knowledge to use it correctly. As well, it has naturally taken time for enough experimentation to be conducted, and reported in the peer-reviewed literature, for real consensus to develop around what appropriate parameters might be – and this is still an evolving area of research. Only recently have evidence-based guidelines for tES been published (Bikson et al., 2016; Lefaucheur et al., 2016; Woods et al., 2016); with this information available it seems likely that increasing numbers of high-quality studies will be published, with further systematic exploration of the effects of different parameters and detailed reporting of the relevant parameters. In addition, greater understanding of the important effects of electrode size and placement should also help to reduce the variance within and between studies.

Participant Selection

One important finding in the literature is that there is significant variability between individuals in their response to tES. For example, López-Alonso and colleagues (López-Alonso, Cheeran, Río-Rodríguez, & Fernández-del-Olmo, 2014) investigated the effect of 13 min of 1 mA nodal stimulation to the motor cortex of 56 young adults (aged 19–24 years). They found that only 45% of participants showed the predicted increase in MEP amplitude, whereas the other 55% of participants showed decreased MEP amplitude. When the data from all participants were pooled, no significant effect of stimulation was obtained, but when separated into a 'responder' and 'non-responder' groups, the responders showed statistically significant increases in MEPs at every 5 min interval for the hour after stimulation, while the non-responders showed significant decreases at some, but not all, time points. Several variables, such as age, were examined but none predicted who would be a tES responder. In a similar study, again using motor cortex tDCS with MEPs as the outcome measure but also comparing three levels of stimulation intensity (0, 1, and 2 mA) found that, out of 12 young adults, 52% showed a significant response to 2 mA stimulation but only 33% showed a response at 1 mA (Ammann, Lindquist, & Celnik, 2017).

There are many reasons why individuals may vary in their response to tES. Firstly, individual differences in anatomy, including skull thickness and cortical folding patterns, likely influence how much current reaches the intended area of the brain. As noted earlier, using individualized FEMs based on high-resolution anatomical MRI scans may help to improve consistency by suggesting optimal positioning of electrodes to target a region in an individual. Related to this, such modelling can also be used to adjust the current delivered to ensure consistent electrical potential at the targeted brain region, rather than a consistent input current level, which will lead to widely varying intra-cerebral potentials. Secondly, since the effects of tES seem to depend on GABA and glutamate levels – or more generally on the excitation–inhibition balance in a given brain region – individual differences in neurotransmitter levels will likely influence tES effects. While it is standard practice in tES studies (as in all cognitive neuroscience) to exclude people with known neurological or psychiatric conditions, as well as those taking psychoactive or neuromodulatory medications, excitation–inhibition balance may still vary widely between, and even within, individuals. For example, recent use of recreational drugs such as nicotine, alcohol, and cannabis may influence excitation–inhibition balance. Another intra-individual variable is fatigue: excitability, at least in the motor cortex, increases with time awake and especially with sleep deprivation. For this reason it is good practice to conduct tES studies at a consistent time of day and certainly, if repeated sessions are performed, to conduct all sessions for an individual at the same time of day. Assessing individuals' recent sleep history may also be worthwhile. Cortical excitability can also vary with age, as can the specific neural networks engaged by a particular task. For this reason, tES studies should be conducted on relatively narrow age ranges, and/or age should be considered as a variable in the analysis.

There is also evidence that, in women, GABA levels vary over the menstrual cycle, being highest when progesterone levels peak (which occurs in the luteal phase, approximately one week after ovulation). Other neurotransmitter levels are also influenced by hormone levels, further suggesting that excitation–inhibition balance may vary systematically across the menstrual cycle. For this reason, some tES studies have excluded women, while others have ensured that women participated only during the follicular phase of their cycle on the assumption that cortical inhibition would be lower. However, there is little empirical evidence to support these practices; a few studies have reported that TMS-evoked MEP amplitudes varied with menstrual phase (Smith, Adams, Schmidt, Rubinow, & Wassermann, 2002; Smith et al., 1999), but no tES studies have directly examined this question – nor have any studies investigated the relative influence of menstrual cycle relative to other sources of inter-individual variability in response to stimulation. Nevertheless, there seems to be some justification for at least noting the stage of menstrual cycle for female participants, and considering it as a factor in data analysis.

Blinding and Sham Stimulation

As with any intervention study, and as we discussed in the chapter on TMS, it is important to include a sham stimulation (placebo) condition in tES studies to ensure that any observed effects are attributable to the electrical stimulation and not **demand characteristics** (conscious or unconscious changes in behaviour driven simply by the belief on the part of the participant that 'something' should change due to the intervention). Sham stimulation is somewhat easier in tES than in TMS, because tES does not create acoustic noise or physical movement of the stimulator. However, the onset and offset of tDCS currents in particular can induce sensations including a tingling or itching (which in some individuals can be unpleasant or even painful); the sustained period of stimulation does not result in any sensation at the 1–2 mA current levels typically employed. For this reason, rather than the control or sham condition being a complete lack of stimulation, it is common to ramp the current up to the same intensity as used in the **verum** (real stimulation) condition, then ramp it down again over the course of a few seconds (typically 10–45 s). Stimulation of this duration is insufficient to induce changes in cortical excitability, but induces sensations similar to real stimulation. Another approach that has been used, either alone or in combination with sham stimulation, is the use of a topical anaesthetic cream to minimize the sensations induced by stimulation.

Although the ramping and topical anaesthetic approaches have been widely used, some data suggests they may not be sufficient. Richardson and colleagues (2014) compared several different sham protocols with verum 2 mA stimulation, including a 45 s ramp down from 2 mA to either 1 or 0 mA using a 4 × 1 ring configuration, and a novel 1 x 1 configuration in which the anode and cathode were placed immediately next to each other (as opposed to the 2.5 cm spacing used in the 4 × 1 array), but 2 mA current was still used. This 1 x 1 configuration was thought to shunt most of the current across the scalp, rather than into the brain. Topical anaesthetic was used in all cases. Participants were asked to rate 'overall sensation' on an analogue scale at 1 min intervals during 5 min of stimulation in each condition. None of the sham conditions were found to be entirely statistically equivalent to the verum stimulation in sensation ratings – even with topical anaesthetic applied. However, the 1 x 1 configuration with 2 mA of current was most similar to the verum. This suggests that further development should be done in the area of sham protocols. In particular, the investigators only obtained sensation ratings, but took no measures of the effects of the different conditions on cortical excitability or behaviour, so it is not guaranteed that the 1 x 1, 2 mA 'sham' condition had no effect on the brain.

Another effect of tES is skin **erythema**, or reddening of the skin under the electrode due to dilation of surface blood vessels. Since participants cannot see their own heads during stimulation, this is less of an issue for participants, although if an extracephalic location such as the arm is chosen for the cathode in tDCS studies, this may be visible. As well, erythema can provide an indication to the experimenter as to what condition is being delivered, which invalidates any blinding procedures that may be in place. A solution to this problem is to use an anti-inflammatory drug such as aspirin, or topical ketoprofen.

The issue of experimenter blinding is an important one, especially in clinical trials. Research-grade tES systems often include a feature to allow for blinding, in which the device is programmed in advance with the experimentally randomized settings for a particular participant and session. Thus the operator of the device has only to enter the participant ID and session number, and the intended stimulation will be delivered without cueing the operator as to the settings.

SAFETY

Any technique that involves delivering electrical stimulation to the brain must necessarily consider safety. There are several possible risks to consider here: discomfort, skin damage, brain damage, and seizure induction. A recent review of the literature by Bikson and colleagues, covering 488 peer-reviewed publications, over 33,000 sessions, and over 1,000 participants (including some individuals who have each received over 100 tDCS sessions) concluded that, 'there is no evidence for irreversible injury produced by conventional tDCS protocols within a wide range of stimulation parameters' (Bikson et al., 2016: 657). Moreover, tES devices are generally unregulated, which implies a lack of concern about their safety by the federal and other agencies that typically regulate medical devices.

The levels of current delivered in tES studies are rarely above 2 mA, though a few studies have gone as far as 4 mA. Recall from the start of the chapter that 5 mA is at the lower end of what the average person reports as painful. The large numbers of tES studies that have been reported without serious adverse events suggest that current in this range is safe for humans, and this is backed up by empirical and modelling data. Animal studies have been conducted in which relatively strong currents were used (and systematically varied across animals) to stimulate the brain transcranially, and then the animals were sacrificed to assess tissue damage. The results were then translated to human equivalents by first building FEMs of the animals (rats) to compute the peak electrical fields created by the applied stimulation levels, and then determining what level of tES current would be required in humans to create the same intracranial electrical field. These studies suggest that current in the range of 60–170 mA would be required to cause brain damage in humans using tES (Bikson et al., 2016), meaning that the levels used in human studies are ten or more times smaller than those considered dangerous. It is important to consider that these are estimates based on a number of assumptions about how the currents are conducted in rats versus humans – and so should not be taken as definitive guidelines – but they are reassuring in suggesting that the levels used in human studies are far below those that might be dangerous.

As discussed in the previous section, tES and especially tDCS induces sensations under the electrodes that range from tingling to painful, and increase in intensity with current strength. Some individuals, especially those who may be anxious about the procedure or otherwise sensitized, may react more negatively to these sensations, and so it is important during the informed consent process to clearly explain to potential participants what they may experience. It can also be helpful to apply the electrodes and then, prior to the start of the experiment proper, to deliver short duration (10–30 s) periods of 'tickle' stimulation, starting at low intensities and increasing to the maximum level planned for the experiment. This serves to familiarize people with the sensations they can expect. Topical anaesthetic can also help reduce, if not eliminate, these sensations. Skin burns are also a risk with tES. These result from high impedance between the electrode and the skin, and can be avoided by properly lowering impedance. In practice this means that lab protocols should ensure that the skin is properly prepared (for example, cleaned) and that sufficient conductive material is used between the electrode and the skin. For sponge electrodes, the sponges should be well saturated with electrolyte solution, monitored for drying during the study, and re-wetted as necessary. For HD-tES and other protocols using small electrodes, electrode holders (as used in EEG) should be used to keep the electrode a fixed distance from the scalp, with conductive gel or paste bridging the scalp-electrode gap. Some cases of skin burns have been reported in the literature, but were always associated with failure to follow these safety protocols.

Naturally, people with a history of neurological disorders should be excluded from tES studies targeting healthy individuals, and there have been no reported cases of seizures triggered by tES. Careful screening is essential since increasing cortical excitability could increase seizure risk in predisposed individuals. At the same time, a number of studies have investigated the use of tDCS in people with epilepsy. In particular, interest has focused on whether cathodal stimulation – since it reduces neural excitability – can reduce symptoms of epilepsy. Several studies have indeed reported a reduction in both EEG discharges symptomatic of epilepsy and incidence of seizures after cathodal stimulation (Bikson et al., 2016). Various forms of tES have been used in clinical trials with dozens of other conditions, including stroke, tinnitus, depression, chronic pain, and schizophrenia, again without any cases of serious adverse events. Children and older adults are generally considered especially vulnerable populations, and there is reason to proceed with particular caution when using tES because electrical conduction may be different. In particular, children's smaller head sizes and thinner skulls mean that more current will reach the brain at a given stimulation level. Nevertheless, in their review Bikson and colleagues found that tES had been used in over 2800 sessions across nearly 500 children without incident. Likewise, although healthy aging and especially dementia are associated with increased CSF volume (and thus greater conductivity), dozens of studies comprising hundreds of older adults have been conducted without any serious adverse events. Another possible concern is with implanted electrical devices, such as pacemakers and deep brain stimulators. People with such devices are generally excluded from tES studies on principle, both for the protection of the person and the implanted device. However, modelling studies suggest that there are very large impedances between these implanted devices and the body, which would prevent any appreciable tES from reaching the device and causing ill effects.

A final safety note concerns the fact that a number of tES devices are available for sale to the general public, often at very low prices that make them highly accessible (at the time of writing, systems were available from online marketplaces and vendor websites in the US$75–300 range, compared with thousands of dollars for a research-grade system). This has raised a number of concerns in the scientific and medical community (Hogenboom, 2014; Wurzman, Hamilton, Pascual-Leone, & Fox, 2016) around safety, for a few reasons. First of all, the consumer-grade devices are generally unregulated and so the levels of current delivery may be unknown, and/or higher than the levels generally used in human research studies. Secondly, at-home users may have little or no knowledge of the tES research literature, and so have little guidance concerning appropriate use or safety. This can create risks such as skin burns caused by not knowing how to properly lower and maintain impedance between the electrode and skin, or over-stimulation if a user thought 'more is better' and decided to attach a larger battery. There are other, more theoretical risks as well; for example, although the available data suggest that even hundreds of tES sessions are safe, there is little data concerning multiple sessions per day, or sessions lasting more than 30–40 min. Moreover, in research settings all experimental parameters are recorded, procedures are reviewed by ethics boards, and any serious adverse events must be reported. Thus any situations that do cause concern will rapidly reach the scientific community, whereas these standards do not apply to at-home users. A further concern is that without a proper understanding of functional neuroanatomy, the role of the anode versus cathode, and other technical considerations, at-home users could inadvertently cause effects other than (or even opposite to) those desired, for example by reversing the cathode and anode, or delivering anodal stimulation for a period long enough for its effects to reverse. The available tES literature, while constantly growing, is still quite narrow in terms of the combinations of electrode placement, current level, and tasks performed during stimulation that have been studied. Other combinations of these and other parameters may have rather different effects – and as noted earlier, sometimes the effects of changing a parameter have non-linear or even reversed effects. For these reasons, people attempting at-home brain stimulation may well end up with null effects, or even very different effects from what they hoped for.

SUMMARY

Transcranial electrical stimulation (tES) is a neuromodulation technique comprising a variety of different stimulation protocols that can variously make cortex more or less excitable, or entrain cortical oscillations at specific frequencies. The levels of current delivered to the brain are much lower than with TMS, and the effects are less dramatic. While conventional tES uses large sponge electrodes with relatively large anode–cathode separation, HD-tES aims for more focal stimulation through the use of smaller electrons and reduced anode–cathode separation. The accuracy of tES in targeting a specific brain region can be quite variable using conventional approaches, but can be significantly improved with HD-tES combined with software that models the distribution of current based on individual anatomy.

Different stimulation protocols can be used to achieve different effects. With tDCS, a constant level of current is delivered for several minutes, typically leading to increased cortical excitability at the anode and reduced excitability at the cathode, although the anodal effect may reverse if stimulation extends beyond 15–20 min. The effects of tDCS can include faster response times and improved learning and memory, although these vary with stimulation level and task. Random noise stimulation (tRNS) involves delivering current levels that vary randomly at each time point, and has effects that are similar to tDCS, but may be stronger and/or longer lasting. In contrast to tDCS and tRNS, tACS delivers current that alternates sinusoidally between positive and negative at each electrode. The focus of tACS studies is usually on entraining intrinsic cortical rhythms, such as alpha, theta, or gamma. This can be used to demonstrate causal links between power changes in specific frequency bands, and cognitive or behavioural effects.

The effects of tES seem to be modulated by sodium and calcium ion channels, glutamate and GABA, and neuromodulators. A number of models of how tES affects neural activity have been proposed. A common theme within these is that by increasing cortical excitability, neuronal activity at or just below threshold may be pushed above threshold. In studies of learning, this may facilitate strengthening of synaptic connections via long-term potentiation (LTP) if neurons are made more likely to generate action potentials in response to input. In experiments where behaviour depends on differences in activity between different populations of neurons within a cortical area (such as determining the direction of a coherent population of moving dots from 'noise' dots moving in random directions), this can improve performance by raising the activity of 'relevant' neurons above threshold while that of 'non-relevant' neurons remains below threshold. However, in cases where only one population of neurons is active to begin with (such as when only dots moving in one direction are presented), tES can decrease performance by raising the level of noise (activity of task-irrelevant neurons).

Although a large number of positive findings have been reported in the literature, both meta-analyses and studies of individual differences have suggested that the effects of tES can be quite variable. One reason for this is differences in experimental protocols, such as levels and duration of stimulation, as well as the locations of anode and cathode. As well, individual differences can significantly affect outcomes. Individual differences in cortical anatomy can drastically affect the current reaching the brain, even with consistent placement of electrodes relative to scalp-based landmarks. Electrode placement using individual MRI-based anatomy and finite element modelling can significantly improve the accuracy of the brain area stimulated, and the level of stimulation delivered. As well, response to tES can be affected by individual differences in age, fatigue, time of day, drug usage, and, in women, stage of menstrual cycle. It is important to consider, track, and standardize these variables to achieve reproducible results. Another factor to consider in tES studies is proper blinding to ensure the participant, and ideally the experimenter, do not know at a given time whether a person is receiving real or sham stimulation. This is challenging because tES can cause itching or tingling sensations as well as erythema (scalp reddening). These may be mitigated, but not always eliminated, by topical medicines. Development of optimal sham stimulation conditions is an active area of research; current approaches include turning on stimulation only transiently (in the case of tDCS), delivering low levels of stimulation, or placing anode and cathode next to each other (with small HD-tES electrodes) to prevent current from reaching the brain.

Overall, tES is a promising technique both for cognitive neuroscience research and applications in cognitive enhancement and treatment of neurological and psychiatric conditions. Although it is generally safe, there are minor risks of discomfort or burning that can be mitigated by following safety guidelines; however, the relative simplicity of the technology – combined with its potential benefits to users – has led to the availability of unregulated, consumer-grade systems to the general public. This has raised concerns about the safety and advisability of such unregulated use, as individual users may not have the expertise to achieve the desired effects (especially since the research community has yet to converge on how to do this), and the consumer systems may not provide the same levels of control and safety used in experimental settings.

THINGS YOU SHOULD KNOW

- tES is the delivery of low levels of electrical current to the brain to modulate brain activity. At least two electrodes are required: one anode, at which current enters the body, and one cathode, where it exits. Research-grade tES devices involve a device that generates the current at a specified level, and measures impedance continuously to ensure that current flow is kept at the desired level. Current levels rating from 1 to 2 mA are typical in tES, although higher levels may be used in some cases.

- While in conventional tES, the anode and cathode are positioned relatively far apart, in HD-tES they are placed more closely together to provide more focal stimulation. As well, a larger number of electrodes are used, such as four cathodes surrounding a single anode. HD-tES may be performed in conjunction with finite element modelling, which allows prediction of current flow through the head and enables more accurate targeting of particular brain regions for stimulation.

- The three most common stimulation protocols for tES are tDCS, tACS, and tRNS. tDCS involves administering current of a fixed level for the entire duration of stimulation. This tends to make cortex under the anode more excitable, but less excitable under the cathode. tACS involves current alternating at a fixed, sinusoidal frequency; usually the frequency is chosen to entrain a particular frequency emanating from the brain, as measured by EEG. tACS has similar effects at both electrodes, because current constantly alternates between positive and negative, but in some cases effects may be different depending on whether the current is phase-locked or out of phase at two electrode locations. tRNS involves current that randomly changes in strength from moment to moment (approximately every millisecond), and causes increases in cortical excitability that are similar, but in some cases stronger, than tDCS.

- The online (during stimulation) effects of anodal tES depend on sodium and calcium ion channel activity, while offline (lasting) effects seem to also rely on glutamate, GABA, and neuromodulators. The online effects of cathodal stimulation are less affected by pharmacological manipulations; however, the offline effects depend on glutamate and possibly GABA, as well as neuromodulators.

- The anodal excitation–cathodal inhibition (AECI) model proposes that anodal stimulation increases cortical excitability (making neurons more likely to fire in response to a given level of input), while cathodal stimulation reduces it. The activity-dependent model extends the AECI model by suggesting that tES' effects are modulated by the current state of activity in the brain, and thus may vary between and even within individuals, depending on factors like the task being performed, fatigue, and any drugs consumed. The network activity model further recognizes the fact that a brain area targeted by tES is wired to other brain areas, whose activity might influence the effects of tES (as well as being modulated by tES). Finally, the stochastic resonance model suggests that tES increases the level of noise (nonspecific neural excitation) in stimulated areas, which can result in either improved or decreased task performance depending on the relative activation levels of task-relevant and task-irrelevant neurons within the region.

- Both meta-analyses of published literature and empirical studies of individual differences suggest that tES can have quite varied effects across individuals and studies. In some cases, only approximately half of participants receiving tES showed the expected effects. Factors that can significantly influence the effects of tES include cortical anatomy, age, pharmacology, disease states, time of day, and, in women, menstrual cycle. At a minimum, care should be taken with participant selection and consistency should be applied in the timing and other conditions of an experiment. As well, HD-tES systems used in conjunction with current modelling software and FEMs based on each individual's cortical anatomy will likely provide much more consistent targeting of desired brain regions, and levels of current delivered to those areas.

- Side effects of tES include tingling sensations under the electrodes and reddening of the skin (erythema). Since the effects of tES should be validated relative to no-stimulation conditions in, ideally, a double-blind fashion, this creates challenges for experimental design. Topical treatments such as anaesthetic and anti-inflammatory medications can help mitigate these effects, though they may not be fully effective in all cases. Sham stimulation can be applied by either ramping current up and then immediately down again at the start and end of the sham stimulation period, administering low levels of current that are not expected to modulate brain activity, or placing the anode and cathode right next to each other. However, each method has shortcomings and further work is needed to develop ideal sham conditions.

- tES is generally very safe at the range of stimulation levels that can be administered by research-grade systems, as long as safety guidelines are followed (such as ensuring low impedance between scalp and electrodes). Skin burns can result if these guidelines are not followed. Even following guidelines,

unpleasant tingling or itching sensations may occur, though these can be reduced by topical anaesthetic.

FURTHER READINGS

Bikson, M., Grossman, P., Thomas, C., Zannou, A.L., Jiang, J., Adnan, T., et al. (2016). Safety of transcranial direct current stimulation: Evidence based update 2016. *Brain Stimulation*, *9*(5), 641–661.

Fertonani, A., & Miniussi, C. (2017). Transcranial electrical stimulation. *The Neuroscientist*, *23*(2), 109–123.

Knotkova, H., & Rasche, D. (Eds.) (2015). *Textbook of Neuromodulation*. New York: Springer.

Polanía, R., Nitsche, M.A., & Ruff, C.C. (2018). Studying and modifying brain function with non-invasive brain stimulation. *Nature Neuroscience*, *21*(2), 1–14.

Woods, A.J., Antal, A., Bikson, M., Boggio, P.S., Brunoni, A.R., Celnik, P., et al. (2016). A technical guide to tDCS, and related non-invasive brain stimulation tools. *Clinical Neurophysiology*, *127*(2), 1031–1048.

Glossary

3D deformation fields A matrix representation of size and shape changes that occur when a brain image is spatially normalized. Each location in the image contains three vector elements representing the shape change (size and direction) in three dimensions. Used in deformation-based morphometry and tensor-based morphometry.

A priori Latin for 'from what is before'. This term is typically used to refer to experimental predictions (hypotheses) that are made in advance of running the experiment, or statistical tests planned in advance to test these hypotheses.

Abductive reasoning Inferring the most likely cause of an event, based on an informed understanding of possible causes of the event. Forms the basis for reverse inference.

Absorption coefficient A constant, specific to a substance that relates its concentration to the amount of light it absorbs. A key term in the Beer–Lambert law.

Accuracy In behavioural research, accuracy refers to whether an individual makes a correct response on a given experimental trial or, more generally, to the proportion of correct responses made in each experimental condition.

Action potential The transmission of electrical potential from the soma of a neuron, down its axon, triggering release of neurotransmitters at the neuron's synapses. Also known as 'firing' of a neuron.

Active electrode In EEG, the active electrode is the electrode located over the scalp region of interest. Typically EEG recording involves multiple active electrodes distributed across the scalp.

Active electromagnetic shielding An alternative approach from passive shielding to reduce electromagnetic interference in a room, such as one containing an MEG scanner. Typically involves some passive shielding, combined with sensors that measure the impinging external magnetic fields. The recordings from these sensors are then used to cancel out the external noise from the recorded signal. Active shielding reduces the weight of the shielding required for an MEG system, which can make siting requirements more feasible.

Active motor threshold (aMT) The intensity of a TMS pulse that elicits an MEP on 50% of trials, when the muscle is contracting.

Activity-dependent model A model of the mechanism by which tDCS affects brain activity, which builds on the AECI by integrating the observation that the effects of tES are dependent on the state, or activity level, of the brain area immediately prior to stimulation. This model suggests that anodal tDCS is likely to have stronger effects when neurons in a brain area are already relatively depolarized due to activity, than if the brain area is generally more hyperpolarized.

Adaptation See 'neural adaptation'.

Adaptive mean amplitude The average electrical potential over a specified time period, centred around the maximum positive or negative potential value in a time window. Often used as a dependent measure in ERP research rather than peak amplitude, because it is less sensitive to noise.

ADC See 'apparent diffusion coefficient'.

Additive factors design A generalized form of the subtraction method, involving several experimental conditions in which a variable of interest is systematically manipulated.

Adenosine triphosphate (ATP) A molecule that is the primary source of energy for cells in the body, including the source of energy supporting neural activity.

AECI See 'anodal excitation–cathodal inhibition model'.

Aerobic metabolism A sequence of biochemical reactions that transform glucose into adenosine triphosphate (ATP) through the consumption of oxygen. Compared to anaerobic metabolism, aerobic metabolism is more efficient, but requires oxygen.

Affine linear registration An algorithm used in spatial normalization and motion correction to adjust the position and/or size and shape of the brain, using mathematically linear transformations.

Agonist A chemical that binds to, and stimulates, a specific type of neuronal receptor.

Aliasing An artifact that can be caused when the frequencies contained in a signal are more than a half to a third of the sampling rate. Because the sampling rate is insufficient to capture the timepoint-to-timepoint fluctuation in the signal, the aliased signal is recorded as a low-frequency artifact. See also 'Nyquist frequency'.

Ampère's circuital law A mathematical description of the relationship between electrical current flow and associated magnetic fields. When a current flows through a conductor, a magnetic field is generated around the conductor. Often called the 'right-hand rule' because if one visualizes the current as flowing in the direction of the thumb of the right hand, the magnetic field flows in the direction of the curled fingers of the right hand.

Amplifier (EEG) An essential part of any EEG system's hardware, which serves to increase the amplitude of the measured signals prior to recording. Amplification is necessary due to the small size of the electrical potentials recorded from the scalp.

aMT See 'active motor threshold'.

Anaerobic metabolism A sequence of biochemical reactions that transform glucose into adenosine triphosphate (ATP) without the use of oxygen. Compared to aerobic metabolism, anaerobic metabolism is less efficient, and generates lactate as a by-product, but does not require oxygen.

Analogue scale A scale, such as a rating scale, in which a response is made along a continuous dimension. Contrasts with ordinal scales.

Anatomically defined ROI See 'region of interest'.

Angular momentum A fundamental characteristic of a spinning object (such as a proton), proportional to its inertia and speed.

Anisotropic Not equal in all directions or dimensions. In diffusion tensor imaging, refers to preferential diffusion of water in one direction, which is used to infer the presence and orientation of white-matter tracts.

Annihilation In subatomic physics, the result of a collision between a positron and an electron, causing the release of a pair of photons.

Anodal excitation–cathodal inhibition (AECI) model A model of the mechanism by which tDCS affects brain activity, suggesting that by depolarizing neurons in a brain area – thus making them more likely to fire in response to input – anodal tDCS can induce LTP. Conversely, cathodal tDCS can induce LTD since it decreases the likelihood that the stimulated neurons will fire in response to input.

Anode An electrode that injects current into a substance.

Antagonist A chemical that binds to a specific type of neuronal receptor and blocks the action of that receptor. The function of antagonists is thus opposite to that of agonists.

APD See 'avalanche photodiode'.

Apparent diffusion coefficient (ADC) A type of image produced in diffusion tensor imaging analysis, by subtracting the $b = 0$ (unweighted) image from each direction-weighted image. ADC maps are combined to compute the diffusion tensor.

Artifact In neuroimaging data, an artifact is any feature caused by non-neural sources that impairs the ability to view or interpret the data. Artifacts can come from physiological sources such as blinks or muscle contractions, or from non-physiological sources such as electromagnetic interference from nearby devices.

Artifact correction Mathematical removal of an artifact from EEG or other neuroimaging data, while preserving the data in the same time period originating from the brain.

Association cortex A general term for areas of the cerebral cortex that receive and integrate inputs from multiple other cortical regions. Generally thought to support multi-sensory integration and higher-level cognition.

Astrocyte A type of glial cell with a star-shaped configuration in the brain and spinal cord. Astrocytes take glutamate up from the synaptic cleft after it has served in excitatory neurotransmission. Among other functions, astrocytes are involved in regulating local blood flow through processes that wrap around capillaries and influence vasodilation. Glutamate levels influence astrocytes' control of vasodilation, and so astrocytes appear to serve as a critical component in how the BOLD response is related to neural activity.

Astrocyte-neuron lactate shuttle hypothesis A theory of how the BOLD response is related to neural activity, via the use of anaerobic metabolism in astrocytes to recycle glutamate, producing lactate as a by-product.

ATP See 'adenosine triphosphate'.

Attenuation correction A step in PET image reconstruction that compensates for the fact that different tissues absorb PERs differently (especially bone).

Avalanche photodiode (APD) A type of photodiode that produces output that is greater than its input. APDs thus amplify their input, resulting in better signal-to-noise ratio than conventional photodiodes.

Axial gradiometer A gradiometer constructed from two conducting loops wound in opposite directions. In MEG, one loop is close to the head while the other is farther away. Both coils thus sample environmental magnetic fields, while only one samples fields from the head. As a result, the opposite windings cancel out environmental noise while preserving neural signals. Sensitive to the perpendicular component of the MEG signal.

Axial plane In neuroimaging, the axial plane is defined by the anterior–posterior and left–right dimensions, and is perpendicular to the inferior–superior dimension.

Axon The process extending from a neuron that carries its electrical output to synaptic terminals.

b-factor A parameter in diffusion weighted imaging (DWI) that reflects both the strength of the gradient along the diffusion direction, and the duration that it is on for. Increasing either of these factors increases sensitivity to diffusion, and so b is a convenient way to summarize these two related parameters.

Back-projection An approach to image reconstruction, used in PET imaging. Allows localization of concentrations of PERs in the imaged volume by summing the coincidence detections from all lines of response that pass through a particular location in the volume.

Band-pass filter A combination of low- and high-pass filters, resulting in attenuating both high and low frequencies while passing a band of frequencies between these. Opposite to a notch filter.

Bandwidth A continuous range of frequencies (or wavelengths) measured as the difference between high and low frequency cutoffs, in Hertz (Hz).

Baseline condition In a neuroimaging experiment, a baseline condition is a theoretically 'neutral' condition that is not expected to elicit any specific neural activity related to stimulus processing, task performance, or externally driven cognitive activity. This serves as a reference against which to compare brain activation measurements in experimental conditions. See also 'resting state'.

Beamformer A spatial filter used in source localization. A set of weights (multipliers) are applied to the data from each sensor, such that the signal from every location in the brain volume other than the region of interest is suppressed.

Beer–Lambert law A mathematical formula relating the concentration of a substance to the amount of light it absorbs. A modified form of the Beer–Lambert law is used in fNIRI; see 'Modified Beer–Lambert law'.

Between-subjects design An experimental design in which results are compared between different groups of participants. This includes designs in which the groups are inherently different (for example, patients versus healthy controls), and designs in which people are sampled from a single population and randomly assigned to different groups to receive different levels of one or more independent variables.

Biphasic pulse A shape of TMS pulse in which an initial rise and fall in intensity is followed by an equal and opposite negative voltage before returning to baseline.

Block detector A grid of scintillation detector crystals, used in PET imaging, connected to a smaller number of photodetectors. The input from each crystal (that is, unique sensor location) is directed to all photodetectors in a uniquely weighted fashion, such that the location of the individual crystal that was excited can be recovered in post-processing. This serves to increase the spatial resolution of the PET scanner relative to the number of individual photodetectors.

Blocked design A type of experimental design in which multiple trials of a particular condition occur together (in a 'block'), not interspersed with trials of other conditions. Contrast with randomized or event-related designs. Commonly used in fMRI, PET, and fNIRI to increase SNR.

Blocking An effect in EEG amplifiers (and associated, recorded data) that results in recording of a 'flat line' rather than time-varying signal. Caused by saturation of the amplifier.

Blood oxygenation level dependent (BOLD) The name of the physiological response to brain activation that forms the basis of the fMRI signal. Increased glutamate levels associated with increased neural activity trigger vasodilation, leading to a net increase in oxygenated haemoglobin around the active neurons.

BOLD See 'blood oxygenation level dependent'.

Bootstrapping A technique in nonparametric statistics to estimate the true distribution of values in a population, from a sample of the population. Data are randomly sampled with replacement, meaning that the same data point (subject or trial, depending on the level of the analysis) could be represented multiple times whereas other data points could not be present at all in a particular sample.

Boundary element model (BEM) In neuroimaging, a model of the different tissues of the head that is used in source localization. Each tissue type is represented as a surface (thin layer) with specific properties relevant to the technique, such as electrical conductivity for EEG. Contrast with finite element models.

Boxcar design A simple type of blocked design, alternating between experimental and control conditions.

Brain extraction A preprocessing step applied to MRI data in which the brain is isolated from the skull and other surrounding, non-brain tissues.

Brownian motion The random motion of molecules caused by heat energy. Forms the basis of the DWI signal.

Brute force approach In tractography, an approach that involves tracking from (or through) multiple adjacent seed/ROI voxels rather than picking a single seed voxel or a start/end pair of voxels. Reduces the dependency of the solution on the particular choice of seed voxel and makes it more robust to noise.

Calibrated BOLD fMRI Methods in which both physiological and neural activation factors are systematically manipulated, to yield quantitative measurements of the rate of oxygen metabolism in the brain ($CMRO_2$).

Cardiac gating A technique used in MR imaging to synchronize image acquisition with the cardiac cycle (heartbeat) of the person being scanned. Can reduce artifacts in MR images such as EPI and DWI.

Categorical variable A variable that has discrete levels, rather than values that vary along a continuum. Distinct categories or groups are common examples of categorical variable levels. In some cases, particular levels of a continuous variable may be used as levels of a categorical variable. Also called a 'factor'.

Cathode An electrode through which current flows out of a substance.

Central sulcus The deep sulcus (fissure) separating the frontal and parietal lobes of the cerebral cortex.

Cerebral cortex The outer surface of the brain, composed largely of cell bodies as well as local and long-range connections between cells. Most areas of human cerebral cortex have six distinctive layers, sometimes with sub-layers. Supports most cognitive activity in humans and other mammals. From the Latin word for 'bark'.

Cerebrospinal fluid (CSF) A clear liquid that the brain and spine are suspended in. CSF serves to physically and chemically protect and buffer the brain.

Cerebrovascular reserve (CVR) A measure of the amount of change in BOLD signal that different brain areas undergo as a function of carbon dioxide levels.

Channel In neuroimaging techniques such as EEG and fNIRI, a channel typically refers to a single source of data. In EEG, the active electrodes are the channels. In fNIRI, each valid emitter–detector pair is a channel, meaning that typically the number of channels is a multiple of the number of emitters and detectors.

Chromophore A light-absorbing compound. In the context of fNIRI, oxyhaemoglobin and deoxyhaemoglobin are chromophores of interest, whereas other compounds such as melanin and fat are chromophores that can contribute noise to the signal.

Closed field A theoretical construct used to describe generators of EEG signal. A closed field is any configuration of neurons that cannot generate a measurable EEG signal at a distance. This may be due to the arrangement of the neurons, and/or a lack of synchronous electrical potential oscillations.

Code multiplexing An approach to multiplexing in which each source (such as an emitter in fNIRI) is switched on and off rapidly according to different sequences or 'codes'.

Cognitive conjunction See 'conjunction analysis'.

Cognitive neuroscience The field of study aimed at understanding how the brain produces thoughts, emotions, and behaviour.

Coherence See 'phase synchronization'.

Coincidence detector A device that detects when two events occur simultaneously. Used in PET imaging to detect photon pairs produced by positron annihilation.

Component In ERP, a peak or trough in the waveform that is defined by characteristic timing, scalp distribution, polarity, and eliciting conditions. In general, the term 'component' is used to refer to peaks or troughs in measurements at scalp electrodes, and may reflect the activity of multiple, distinct brain regions overlapping in time. See also 'latent component'

Compton scattering Deflection of a photon by an electron. Creates noise in PET images because it causes a pair of photons to travel in directions that are not 180° opposed to each other.

Computational neuroanatomy Morphometric approaches that use automated algorithms to derive a variety of measures from structural MRI in a less subjective, and more efficient way than traditional morphometric methods.

Computerized tomography (CT) An imaging modality based on X-rays. While conventional X-ray images produce only a single two-dimensional image taken from a single perspective, CT scanners incorporate an X-ray device that rotates around the person being scanned, acquiring many images from different angles and then using computer algorithms to create higher-resolution, 2D or 3D images from these.

Condition-rich design An experimental design that employs relatively large numbers of experimental conditions – often treating individual stimuli as conditions, rather than grouping these into categories (for example, for face stimuli, each individual is treated as a separate condition, rather than averaging across all faces). Used in neuroimaging studies for which multivariate analysis is planned.

Conditioning stimulus (CS) In paired-pulse TMS, the first stimulation pulse.

Conjunction analysis A type of analysis, sometimes performed on fMRI data, in which the overlap between two (or more) different activation maps (derived from different experimental contrasts) is visualized and interpreted. Sometimes called 'cognitive conjunction' because the goal is usually to identify brain regions that are commonly activated across different tasks or conditions that share an underlying cognitive operation.

Connectivity In the context of brain organization, connectivity refers to how different brain areas communicate and work together.

Connectome A complete description of the structural connections between neurons in the brain. In practice, the term may be used to refer to the complete set of connections that are resolvable at a certain level of resolution, or by a particular technique. See also 'projectome'.

Connectomics The study of the connectome, or more generally of brain connectivity.

Continuous theta burst stimulation (cTBS) A type of repetitive TMS protocol in which triplets of pulses are delivered at 50 Hz, with 5 Hz spacing (that is, three pulses 20 ms apart, repeated every 200 ms), typically delivered for 20 or 40 s (resulting in a total of 300 or 600 pulses). Typically has long-lasting (up to one hour) inhibitory effects.

Continuous variable A variable whose possible values vary along a continuum, rather than discrete levels. For example, brightness and loudness are continuous variables.

Continuous wave (CW) An approach to fNIRI in which light of a particular wavelength(s) is emitted continuously, with constant intensity, and the intensity of light at detectors is quantified.

Contrast The difference in intensity values in an image. In MRI, contrast refers to the ability to resolve different tissue types (such as grey versus white matter) by intensity (brightness) values in the image.

Contrast weighting In MRI, the relative intensities of different tissue types, determined by the parameters of the pulse sequence.

Control group In a between-subjects experimental design, a control group is a group of participants whose data serve as a reference for comparison to the 'experimental group'. For example, if a study examines a group of people with a specific disease, the control group might be people without the disease. Or, the experimental group might receive a treatment or intervention, while the control group does not.

Convolution A mathematical operation commonly used in signal processing, whose result describes how one shape is modified by another. For example, in fMRI data analysis, the predicted signal produced by the brain for an experiment can be derived by convolving the time course of events in the experiment with a model of the HRF.

Coronal plane In neuroimaging, the axial plane is defined by the inferior–superior and left–right dimensions, and is perpendicular to the anterior–posterior dimension.

Correlation-based signal improvement A motion correction technique for fNIRI, based on the assumption that true oxy-Hb and deoxy-Hb signals are, in general, strongly negatively correlated. Since head motion affects the optode – and thus measurements of both oxy-Hb and deoxy-Hb – similarly during head motion the two chromophores' signals will be strongly positively correlated. The algorithm thus simply corrects for motion by removing the correlated component of the signal.

Cortical columns Clusters of neurons typically tens of microns in size, with distinct patterns of local connectivity running through the layers of the cerebral cortex, perpendicular to the outer surface of the brain. Columns have particular, repeating arrangements in a cortical area, which act as functional units.

Counter-balancing An approach in experimental design in which each possible permutation of levels is tested. For example, in an experiment with two conditions (1 and 2) counter-balancing stimuli may involve grouping stimuli into two sets (A and B), and ensuring that half of the participants experience stimulus set A in condition 1, and the other half of participants experience stimulus set A in condition 2, and vice-versa.

Cross-frequency coupling Synchronization of changes in the amplitude of oscillations at different frequencies. For example, bursts of gamma-band EEG have been observed to occur time-locked to the peaks of theta oscillations when items are held in working memory.

Cross-sectional design An experimental design in which data are compared between different groups. Critically, the groups are assumed to be samples from the same larger population, but at the time of testing represent different temporal stages of development or disease progression. Contrasted with longitudinal designs, cross-sectional designs are typically used in an attempt to characterize changes that occur over time, by using a between-subjects rather than a within-subjects (longitudinal) design.

CS See 'conditioning stimulus'.

CT See 'computerized tomography'.

cTBS See 'continuous theta burst stimulation'.

Current (electrical) Movement of electrical charge from one location to another, through a conductor.

CVR See 'cerebrovascular reserve'.

CW See 'continuous wave'.

Cyclotron A facility for creating radioactive substances, such as positron-emitting radioligands used in PET imaging.

Cytoarchitecture A description of the structure of the cerebral cortex (typically consistent within a region of the cortex) based on the types of cells present, and their densities across different layers of the cortex.

D-wave See 'direct wave'.

DBM See 'deformation-based morphometry'.

DCM See 'dynamic causal modelling'.

Decay artifact An relatively long-duration EEG artifact caused by TMS, thought to have a number of causes, including current induction, electrode–skin polarization, and electrode movement.

Decay time A property of crystals used in scintillation detectors that sets the temporal resolution of coincidence detectors. Influences the signal-to-noise ratio of a PET scanner.

Deformation-based morphometry (DBM) A computational neuroanatomy method aimed at quantifying the changes in the relative positions of a brain, or brain structure, that occur when a brain image is spatially normalized, after accounting for global changes in brain volume, shape, and position.

Demand characteristics Biases (either conscious or unconscious) on the part of the recipient that cause them to perform in ways that are consistent with what they expect from a treatment.

Dendrite Processes on neurons that receive input from other neurons, via synapses.

Dependent variable A variable that is measured in an experiment, whose value is expected to vary depending on the level(s) of independent variables manipulated in the experiment. Dependent variables may be called 'outcome measures' and are measured, rather than directly manipulated, in an experiment.

Dephasing gradient In DWI, a magnetic field gradient that applies a phase roll to water molecules along a particular direction. Used early in the pulse sequence to 'tag' water molecules as to their position along the gradient direction.

Depolarization The elimination of electrical polarization, resulting in a balance of electrical charge between two locations.

Detector In fNIRI, a device that detects light used to obtain the imaging signal.

Detector ring In PET imaging, a ring of scintillation coincidence detectors used to count photons emitted from the body.

Diffeomorphic mapping A morphometric approach that can be applied to 'closed' brain structures (those having defined borders in three dimensions), which involves tessellating the outer surface of the structure, and measuring the distance of each point on the structure to that of a reference structure.

Difference waveform An ERP waveform derived by subtracting the waveform in one experimental condition from another. Typically used in subtraction methodology to isolate the effects of an experimental manipulation from irrelevant factors.

Differential amplifier The type of amplifier typically used in EEG data collection, which measures the difference in electrical potential between active and reference electrodes, each relative to the ground electrode.

Differential path length (DPL) factor A constant in the modified Beer–Lambert law that accounts for the scattering of light that occurs in biological tissue but not in test tubes. This factor varies considerably between individuals – by as much as 15% – and so using an incorrect value can yield a significant degree of error in measurement. Can be measured using FD or TD fNIRI, but not with CW imaging – leading to greater inaccuracy when using CW in particular.

Diffusion tensor A mathematical object representing diffusion along its primary direction, and the two directions orthogonal to that.

Diffusion tensor imaging A technique used to infer properties of the white matter of the brain, such as integrity and orientation of fibre tracts, using diffusion weighted MR imaging.

Diffusion weighted imaging (DWI) An approach to MRI scanning that measures the amount of diffusion (movement) of water. Commonly used as the basis for studies investigating brain connectivity, because water within axons tends to diffuse parallel to their direction of orientation.

Dipole An object that has two ends (poles) with opposite values or charges. An electrical dipole has positive and negative charges at its two poles. Formally, a dipole is a point source of infinitely small size.

Direct wave (D-wave) The initial effect of TMS, measured (using EEG) as electrical activity and thought to be directly caused by the TMS pulse.

Discrete scale See 'ordinal scale'.

Discrete wavelet filtering A signal processing technique in which a wavelet is fit to a time series by shifting, stretching, and/or scaling it to best represent features in the data. Used for motion correction of fNIRI data.

Disjunction analysis The reverse of a conjunction analysis, to determine which areas of activation do not overlap between two (or more) experimental contrasts.

Distribution of time-of-flight (DTOF) The distribution of the times that individual photons were received by a photodetector in time-domain fNIRI. Because the time it takes a photon to travel from the emitter to detector is proportional to the distance it travels, the early portion of the DTOF represents photons that travelled shorter paths (more peripheral, non-brain paths), whereas the later portion of the DTOF represents farther-travelling photons – those that most likely passed through the cortex.

DPL See 'differential path length factor'.

DTOF See 'distribution of time-of-flight'.

Dynamic artifacts When performing TMS in or near an MRI scanner, artifacts in the MR image associated with the transient magnetic field pulse(s) created by the TMS pulse(s).

Dynamic causal modelling (DCM) An approach to effective connectivity analysis that uses an explicit model of the relationship between how neural activity is modulated by external input (the experimental manipulation), combined with a second model of how that neural activity relates to the observable BOLD signal. Also involves comparison between different possible models of information flow between brain regions.

Dynamic statistical parametric mapping (dSPM) An approach to source localization that uses noise normalization.

Echo planar imaging (EPI) An MRI pulse sequence commonly used in fMRI and diffusion weighted imaging (DWI). A defining feature of EPI is that k space is completely filled with every excitation, in contrast to conventional pulse sequences that require many excitation steps with different phase encoding gradient weightings to fill k space. This is achieved by traversing k space in a 'zig-zag' fashion. EPI enables the very fast imaging required for fMRI.

Echo time (TE) The time between excitation and signal readout (the echo) in an MRI pulse sequence.

Eddy current Electrical current induced by changing magnetic fields in a conductor. A common type of artifact in DWI caused by rapidly switching magnetic field gradients.

Effective connectivity An approach to data analysis applied to time-resolved neuroimaging data aimed at characterizing interactions between different brain regions. Whereas functional connectivity involves computing correlations but cannot determine the directionality of such relationships (that is, which area influences the activity of another), effective connectivity provides such 'directional' information.

Effective dose A measurement of the amount of radioactivity absorbed by the body, computed by summing the equivalent doses for all organs in the body.

Efficiency (experimental) A measure of the optimality of different experimental designs, in terms of the number, timing, and experimental conditions of each experimental trial or event, that is a function of the variance in the predicted neuroimaging time series.

Eigenvalue In diffusion tensor imaging, eigenvalues reflect the strength of diffusion in the principal direction and in the two directions orthogonal to that.

Eigenvector In diffusion tensor imaging, eigenvectors reflect the principal direction of water diffusion (first eigenvector) and in the two directions orthogonal to that.

Electrical current See 'Current (electrical)'.

Electrical ground See 'Ground (electrical)'.

Electrical potential See 'Potential (electrical)'.

Electroencephalography (EEG) A technique that measures the summed electrical potentials of neurons in the brain, through electrodes placed on the outside of the head (invasive EEG can also be performed using implanted electrodes).

Electromyography (EMG) Measurements of neuromuscular activity, typically by electrodes placed over specific muscles.

Electrooculogram (EOG) A measurement of the electrical potential across one or both eyes, typically by electrodes placed above and below the eyes (vertical EOG), or lateral to either eye (horizontal EOG).

EMG See 'electromyography'.

Emitter In fNIRI, a device that emits light used to obtain the imaging signal.

Endogenous component An ERP component elicited by cognitive or other psychological (endogenous) factors.

Endophenotype Where phenotypes are directly observable manifestations of an individual's genetic makeup (genotype), endophenotypes are phenotypes that are not directly observable, but must be determined through biological test or imaging technique. This can include things such as enzyme activity, personality type, or activation patterns in a particular neuroimaging paradigm.

Energy resolution A property of crystals used in scintillation detectors that refers to how sensitive the crystal is to the energy level of the photons detected. Photons from sources other than positron annihilation, as well as Compton-scattered photons, have distinct energy levels from unscattered, annihilation-generated photons. Better energy resolution yields better signal-to-noise ratio of a PET scanner by recording a greater proportion of true coincidence events.

Entrainment A phenomenon in which oscillations in one system become synchronized, with enhanced amplitude, by oscillations of the same frequency in another system. For example, tACS uses electrical stimulation at a specific frequency to increase the amplitude of EEG rhythms in the individual at that frequency.

EPI See 'echo planar imaging'.

Epoching In EEG, the process of breaking continuous EEG data into short segments time-locked to the onset of events of experimental interest. Typically used to derive ERPs from EEG data. Also called 'segmentation'.

Equivalent current dipole (ECD) A term used in EEG and related fields to refer to a simplification whereby an area of some size (such as a patch of neurons) and containing many electrical dipoles is treated as a single dipole.

Equivalent dose A measurement of the amount of radioactivity absorbed by the body, that is specific to the organ in question. Accounts for the fact that different organs have different levels of sensitivity to radiation.

EROS See 'event-related optical signal'.

Erythema Reddening of the skin. One cause is stimulation with tES.

Event-related desynchronization (ERD) A term used in reference to oscillatory brain activity measurements such as EEG or MEG, to describe an decrease in power within some frequency band time-locked to an event of experimental interest.

Event-related optical signal (EROS) A name used for the technique of using fNIRI to measure the fast optical signal.

Event-related potentials (ERP) EEG measurements time-locked to the onset of events of experimental interest, and generally averaged over many trials of a particular experimental condition to improve signal-to-noise ratio.

Event-related synchronization (ERS) A term used in reference to oscillatory brain activity measurements such as EEG or MEG, to describe an increase in power within some frequency band time-locked to an event of experimental interest.

Evoked potentials (EPs) See 'event-related potentials'.

Excitation In MRI, the process of tipping the net magnetization vector out of the longitudinal plane, towards the transverse plane. Opposite to relaxation.

Exogenous component An ERP component elicited by external, sensory factors.

Eye tracking A technique in which the position of the eyes is monitored and recorded. Generally this is used to detect where a person's gaze is directed.

FA See 'fractional anisotropy'.

Factor See 'categorical variable'.

Factorial design An experimental design involving the systematic manipulation of two or more experimental factors. Typically factorial designs are fully crossed, meaning each possible combination of variables is tested.

False discovery rate (FDR) An approach to multiple comparison correction that works by controlling the proportion of discoveries (p values that exceed the desired threshold) that are false positives, based on a ranking of the p values. This approach is adaptive depending on characteristics of the data, in particular the total number of discoveries but also the total number of tests and the desired level of significance.

Faraday cage An enclosure made of conductive material, that attenuates external electromagnetic fields. Commonly used to insulate neuroimaging equipment from noise caused by other electronic devices and/or magnetic fields.

Fast optical signal (FOS) In fNIRI, a signal that shows rapid changes related to stimulation or task performance, thought to be caused by changes in cell swelling that occur with changes in neural activity. See also 'event-related optical signal (EROS)'.

fcMRI Functional connectivity analysis of fMRI data.

FD See 'frequency domain fNIRI'.

FDR See 'false discovery rate'.

FEM See 'finite element model'.

Figure-8 coil The most common shape of stimulation coil used in TMS, involving copper wire wound in a figure-8 shape. This design yields the most concentrated stimulation strength directly under the centre of the coil.

Figure-of-eight coil See 'figure-8 coil'.

Filter response A description of the effects of a filter. Often visualized as a plot of frequency versus amplitude, to show which frequency range(s) a filter attenuates.

Filtered back-projection The process of spatially filtering PET data prior to back-projection, to minimize artifacts caused by the back-projection process.

Filtering The mathematical process of attenuating the power of a signal in a specific frequency range.

Finite element model (FEM) In neuroimaging, a model of the different tissues of the head that is used in source localization. Each tissue type is represented as a 3D surface with varying thickness and associated variations across the surface in specific properties relevant to the technique, such as electrical conductivity for EEG. Contrast with boundary element models, which model surfaces as having constant properties across the surface.

Flip angle The angle of the net magnetization vector relative to the longitudinal plane. Proportional to the amount of RF energy used in excitation.

Flux transformer In MEG, a superconducting device that transmits magnetic flux from near the head, where it occurs, to the SQUID. The shape of the flux transformer determines its sensitivity properties.

fMRI-a See 'fMRI adaptation'.

fMRI adaptation (fMRI-a) A type of experimental design designed to characterize different populations of neurons within a specific brain region, that respond to different stimulus characteristics or other properties. Stimuli that are identical, or share particular features, are presented repeatedly, leading to a reduced fMRI response due to neural adaptation in the brain region of interest. Then, stimuli predicted to have distinct features are presented, which will elicit an increased fMRI response if different (non-adapted) neurons within the brain region are sensitive to the changed stimulus features.

Forward solution The mathematical process of determining – given the number, location, orientation, and strength of the generators of a signal – how the signal would appear at sensors recording it from a distance. The opposite of the inverse problem, but mathematically well-posed because there is a single solution to any forward problem. Forward solutions are used as the basis for attempts to solve the inverse problem.

Fourier series A combination of waveforms of different frequencies, that are combined to form a complex waveform, or derived from a complex waveform by a Fourier transform.

Fourier transform A mathematical operation by which a complex time-varying waveform is decomposed into power (amplitude) over a continuous range of frequencies. This is based on the principle that any complex time-varying waveform can be represented as a weighted set of sinusoidal waveforms of different frequencies. Applying a Fourier transform to time-domain data results in frequency-domain representation.

Fractional anisotropy (FA) A measure derived from diffusion tensor imaging data, computed as the fraction of the difference in the size of each of the three principal eigenvectors, relative to their summed length. Often interpreted as a measure of 'white matter integrity'.

Fractional area latency In ERP research, a dependent measure calculated by first calculating the mean amplitude of the waveform in a specified time window, and then determining the time from the start of the window at which the mean amplitude reaches a specified percentage of the total. For example, 50% fractional area latency is the time required to reach 50% of the total mean amplitude within the window.

Frequency In physics and mathematics, frequency refers to the number of cycles per unit time of a sinusoidally oscillating wave. Typically measured in units of Hertz (Hz), or cycles per second.

Frequency bands (EEG) In EEG measurements, oscillatory signals are commonly seen in different ranges, associated with different states of consciousness and brain activity. These ranges are referred to as bands, and include delta, theta, alpha, beta, gamma, and mu.

Frequency domain Representation and/or analysis of data as it varies over frequency. If the data vary over time (for example EEG data), the frequency-domain representation necessarily collapses over time (or periods of time), and are visualized with frequency on the x axis (abscissa) and amplitude of the measured brain activity signal on the y axis (ordinal). If data vary over space (for example, MRI data), the frequency-domain representation collapses across space and are represented in k space.

Frequency encoding gradient In MRI, the gradient applied along one of two spatial dimensions within a slice, perpendicular to the slice and phase encoding gradient directions. Determines the readout along the x axis in k space.

Frequency multiplexing An approach to multiplexing in which each source (such as an emitter in fNIRI) is modulated at a different frequency. Allows simultaneous transmission of multiple signals.

Frequency-domain (FD) fNIRI An approach to fNIRI in which light of a particular wavelength(s) is emitted continuously, with intensity that varies sinusoidally. Both the intensity and timing (phase) of the light arriving at the detector are quantified.

Full-width at half-maximum (FWHM) A measure commonly used to describe the amount of spatial smoothing (filtering) applied to an image such as an fMRI scan. Given a shape (or kernel) such as a Gaussian function, the FWHM reflects the width of this shape at half of its maximum amplitude. See also 'spatial smoothing'.

Fully crossed design A factorial experimental design in which each possible combination of variables is tested.

Functional connectivity An approach to data analysis used with fMRI, MEG, and other forms of time-resolved neuroimaging data. The time course of activity is correlated between different voxels or brain regions to identify areas whose activity is significantly correlated. This can be applied even to data that do not have multiple experimental conditions, such as resting state data. Compared to effective connectivity, functional connectivity does not provide information about the directionality of influence.

Functional integration An approach to understanding brain organization that combines segregation and connectivity to provide a more complete understanding of brain function.

Functional MRI (fMRI) A technique that provides an indirect measure of neuronal activity via localized changes in the ratio of oxygenated and deoxygenated blood.

Functional near-infrared optical imaging (fNIRI) A technique that uses near-infrared light to provide a measure of brain activity. FNIRI can be used to measure both a 'slow' signal that is sensitive to the concentrations of oxyhaemoglobin and deoxyhaemoglobin, and a 'fast' signal related to cell swelling.

Functionally defined ROI See 'region of interest'.

FWHM See 'full-width at half-maximum'.

GABA Gamma-aminobutyric acid, the primary inhibitory neurotransmitter in the brain. Its primary action is to adjust the permeability of neuronal membranes to increase polarization, making the neuron less likely to generate an action potential.

Gaussian random field theory (GRFT) A branch of mathematics describing noise that has a Gaussian (multivariate normal) distribution in multiple dimensions. Used in fMRI analysis as one approach to multiple comparison correction, in which the noise in fMRI data is assumed to have a Gaussian distribution. GRFT is used to predict the probability of observing a cluster of voxels above the statistical threshold, given the spatial extent of the cluster and its magnitude of activation.

GCA See 'Granger causality analysis'.

General linear model (GLM) A parametric statistical model that relates independent variables to dependent variables using linear terms. Commonly used in statistics, GLMs for the basis of ANOVA, regression, and other common types of analysis.

GLI See 'grey level index'.

Glia Cells of the nervous system that do not conduct electrical signals, but perform functions such as recycling neurotransmitters, modulating neural activity, controlling development and neural plasticity, and modulating local blood flow.

GLM See 'general linear model'.

Glutamate The primary excitatory neurotransmitter in the brain. Once released from neurons, glutamate is largely taken up and recycled by glia.

Gradient (magnetic field) A continuous variation in magnetic field strength over space. Used in MRI for spatial encoding.

Gradiometer A magnetic field sensor that measures differences in magnetic field strength over space (gradients).

Grand average In ERP, the average of measurements across trials and participants.

Granger causality analysis (GCA) An approach to effective connectivity analysis in which two time series are correlated at multiple time lags relative to each other. Part of a larger class of models known as cross-correlation, or more generally multivariate autoregressive models.

Graph theory A branch of mathematics devoted to the study of graphs. Applied to neuroimaging data, graph theory provides a set of tools for representing and analysing the activity of networks of brain regions in terms of how they are physically connected, and/or how they functionally interact.

Gray (Gy) A unit for quantifying radioactivity absorbed by the body, where 1 Gy = 1 Joule absorbed per kilogram of body weight.

Grey level index (GLI) A measure of cell density across cortical layers, used in characterizing the cytoarchitecture of brain regions.

Grey matter Generally refers to the cerebral cortex, but more generally to any region of the brain with a high concentration of cell bodies, relative to axons. So called because when stained with formalin, or viewed in a T1-weighted MR image, this tissue appears grey in colour.

Grey-matter concentration In voxel-based morphometry of grey matter, a dependent measure that reflects a combination of the original intensity of a voxel, and the amount of size change it underwent during spatial normalization.

GRFT See 'Gaussian random field theory'.

Ground (electrical) A reference point that electrical potential is measured relative to. The term can also refer to a return path for electrical current. While the Earth is commonly used as ground in electrical systems, this is unsafe in contexts such as EEG. For this reason, a virtual ground is typically created within the EEG amplifier circuitry.

Ground electrode In EEG, the ground electrode serves as the reference for measuring electrical potential at both the active and reference electrodes.

Gy See 'Gray'.

Gyro-magnetic ratio A fixed property of any MR-active nucleus, relating its magnetic moment to its angular momentum.

Gyrus A 'bump' or convex fold on the surface of the cerebral cortex. See also 'sulcus'.

Haemodynamic response function (HRF) The shape of the BOLD fMRI response over time. Has a generally characteristic shape involving onset 2–3 s after stimulus onset, peaking at 6–8 s, and a return to baseline between 10–12 s. May have a subsequent period of 'undershoot' up to 18–20 s. All times are approximate, and the shape and timing of the HRF shows considerable variation both within individuals, between brain areas, and between individuals.

Haemoglobin (Hb) The molecule in the blood that transports oxygen from the lungs to other tissues, including the brain. Contains iron (heme). Changes in haemoglobin's molecular structure, depending on the amount of oxygen bound to it, is the basis of the BOLD signal measured by fMRI and fNIRI.

Hb See 'haemoglobin'.

HCP See 'Human Connectome Project'.

HD-tES See 'high definition tES'.

Head position indicators (HPIs) In MEG, sensors placed at landmark positions on the head that generate high-frequency electrical signals. These are detected by the MEG system and used to track the position of the head, and may be used to later correct the data for head movement.

High definition tES (HD-tES) An approach to tES that aims to improve the spatial resolution and specificity with which tES is delivered to a target brain region. Rather than using two large electrodes as in conventional tES, a larger number of smaller electrodes are used, typically placed close together over the target brain region. One common configuration is the 4 × 1 ring montage, which consists of one anode surrounded by four cathodes, each 3 cm from the anode.

High-frequency rTMS Repetitive TMS with stimulation rates of greater than 1 Hz, which typically has excitatory (facilitatory) effects on brain activity and behaviour.

High-pass filter A filter that attenuates low frequencies, while passing high frequencies without attenuation.

Hillyard Principle An approach to experimental design in cognitive neuroscience, in which the physical stimuli are held constant across experimental conditions, and only the psychological conditions are manipulated. The motivation for the Hillyard Principle is to avoid confounds in neuroimaging measures that can be caused by unintended differences in brain responses caused by physical characteristics of the stimuli that are not of experimental interest. Originally coined by Steven Luck (2005/2014).

Hodology A term historically used for connectomics.

HRF See 'haemodynamic response function'.

Hub In graph theory, a node that shows a disproportionate number of connections with other nodes.

Human Brain Project A large-scale, multi-site European neuroimaging initiative that aims to develop computational tools for neuroimaging.

Human Connectome Project (HCP) A large-scale, multi-site USA-based neuroimaging initiative that aims to characterize brain structure, organization, and function, using MRI, behavioural, and genetic methods, across 1000 individuals.

Hypercapnia Elevated blood carbon dioxide levels.

Hyperoxia Elevated blood oxygen levels.

Hypothesis A prediction as to the outcome of an experiment, or more generally about the nature of reality. In experimentation, hypotheses should be generated prior to running the study and the statistics employed should be planned to test the hypothesis.

I-wave See 'indirect wave'.

Impedance The amount of opposition to current flow. Also known as 'resistance' in some (alternating current) electrical systems. In EEG, impedance between the scalp and each electrode usually represents the greatest opposition to current flow, and so lowering scalp impedance is critical to obtaining good quality EEG data.

Incidental finding An unexpected finding in an experiment, not intended as part of the study. Typically used in MRI to refer to identifying neuropathology that was not expected (and usually previously unknown by the participant).

Independent components analysis (ICA) A form of mathematical blind source separation, that breaks a signal into a number of components that are statistically independent of each other. Can be used for artifact correction and for identifying distinct signals from within the brain.

Independent variable A variable that is explicitly and intentionally manipulated by a researcher in an experiment. Typically independent variables are manipulated to determine their influence on the dependent variable.

Indirect wave (I-wave) Effects of TMS that follow the D-wave, measured (using EEG) as electrical activity and thought to reflect reverberating activation within the CSN and other neural circuits connected to it.

Informed consent The practice of informing people prior to the start of an experiment that they will participate in, as to the procedures, risks, and options for terminating participation in the study. Informed consent is a key pillar of research ethics.

Inion A scalp landmark point located at the base of the skull, along the midline of the head from left to right.

Inter-stimulus interval (ISI) The time between the end of one stimulus, and the onset of the next stimulus. See also 'stimulus onset asynchrony'.

Interaction In experimental design and statistics, the influence of one independent variable on the effects of another independent variable.

Interleaved MRI acquisition A technique used in fMRI in which image acquisition is alternated with periods in which no data are acquired. Contrasts with conventional MRI scanning in which data are acquired continuously. Interleaved protocols are typically used to avoid effects that can occur during MRI acquisition, such as acoustic noise (which could interfere with perception of auditory stimuli), or artifacts from TMS pulses.

Intermittent TBS (iTBS) A type of repetitive TMS protocol in which triplets of pulses are delivered at 50 Hz, with 5 Hz spacing (that is, 3 pulses 20 ms apart, repeated every 200 ms), typically delivered separated by 10 s intervals, over a total duration of approximately 200 s. Generally has facilitative effects that last for approximately 30 min.

International 10–10 System An internationally standardized system for placing EEG electrodes on the human head. Electrode positions are determined as 10% increments of measurements made between scalp landmarks along the anterior–posterior and left–right dimensions of the head, allowing the positions to scale according to the size and shape of an individual's head.

Inverse problem The mathematical process of determining the number, location, orientation, and strength of the generators of a signal recorded from a distance. In neuroimaging, this is typically the problem of determining the origin in the brain of signals recorded from the scalp, such as with EEG or fNIRI data – known as source localization. The inverse problem is mathematically ill-posed, in that there are a virtually infinite number of possible solutions given a particular pattern of scalp-recorded data.

Inverse solution See 'inverse problem'.

Isotropic Equal in all directions or dimensions. In diffusion tensor imaging, refers to equal diffusion of water in all directions. Can also be used to refer to voxels that have the same size in all three dimensions; thus a 3 mm isotropic voxel would measure 3 × 3 × 3 mm.

iTBS See 'intermittent TBS'.

Jacobian determinant A measure derived from the Jacobian matrix that specifically captures the volume changes, used in tensor-based morphometry.

Josephson junction Two superconductors connected by a weak link, used to measure magnetic field flux.

k space The frequency-domain representation of a 2D image, obtained by a 2D Fourier transform. Typically shown with zero frequency in the centre.

Kalman filter An algorithm particularly suited for making predictions concerning the future values of some measurement, based on past values, in the presence of noise. Commonly used in predicting flight trajectories of missiles and other objects, but can be used to correct for motion artifacts in fNIRI data.

Kernel The shape of a function used for smoothing or filtering.

Larmor equation An equation relating precessional speed to magnetic field strength.

Larmor frequency The speed of precession of an MR-active nucleus.

Laser diode (LD) A type of light source, used in fNIRI emitters. Advantages are that they have narrow bandwidths (yielding high accuracy) and have excellent temporal properties. Disadvantages are that they are relatively expensive, bulky, and are available only in certain wavelengths.

Latency The time between two points. Used as a dependent measure in ERP research, latency refers to the time between the event of interest and a feature of the ERP waveform, such as a peak.

Latent component A construct used in ERP research to describe the underlying generators of scalp-recorded components. In ERP research 'component' typically refers to scalp-recorded component; however, these can have multiple underlying sources in the brain that have different locations and time courses. Latent components are the time courses of these underlying components. Typically these are not visible, except possibly through source localization. See also 'component'.

Lateralized readiness potential (LRP) An ERP waveform derived from the subtraction of data from equivalent electrode locations over the motor cortex in each cerebral hemisphere, in the period preceding an overt motor response. Reflects brain activity related to the planning of motor movements.

Lead field The sensitivity patterns of magnetometers and gradiometers.

Least squares estimation A mathematical technique, commonly used in statistics and image processing, to minimize the differences between two values. Different guesses as to an ideal value are tested iteratively, and the one that yields the smallest squared difference is chosen.

Lesion-deficit method A method of understanding the function of particular brain areas by studying the effects of damage to that area. This method has commonly been used clinically and experimentally in neuropsychology. See also voxel-based lesion-symptom mapping (VLSM).

Light-emitting diode (LED) A type of light source, used in fNIRI emitters. Advantages are that they are low cost and it is easy to adjust light intensity. Disadvantages are that they have relatively wide bandwidth, which can result in lower accuracy of measurements.

Light output A property of crystals used in scintillation detectors that determines the strength of the output signal. Influences the spatial and energy resolution of a PET scanner.

Line of response In PET imaging, the lines between detector pairs which pass through the imaging space. Valid lines of response are those that pass through the object being imaged (such as the head).

Local minimum In least squares estimation and other iterative mathematical processes, a local minimum is the smallest value in a restricted (local) range of values, but not the smallest value in the entire range.

Long-term depression (LTD) Weakening of a synaptic connection, making a receiving neuron less likely to generate an action potential in response to input from the sending neuron. Opposite of LTP.

Long-term potentiation (LTP) The strengthening of a synaptic connection between two neurons, resulting in the receiving neuron being more likely to fire in response to input from the sending neuron. LTP occurs when the output of the sending neuron is followed within a short period of time by an action potential in the receiving neuron. LTP is often described by the phrase 'neurons that fire together, wire together'.

Longitudinal design A type of within-subjects experimental design in which the same individuals are tested at multiple points in time, typically using the same assessments at each time point.

Longitudinal plane In MRI, the plane defined by the strong magnetic field of an MRI scanner.

Low-frequency rTMS Repetitive TMS with stimulation rates of 1 Hz or less, which typically has inhibitory effects on brain activity and behaviour.

Low-pass filter A filter that attenuates high frequencies, while passing low frequencies without attenuation.

Luminescence Light emission by a substance, not caused by heating.

Magnetic field map A MRI image acquired through a specialized pulse sequence, to map how the magnetic field of the MRI scanner is altered by the presence of a particular object, such as a head. Can be used to correct for distortions in EPI images.

Magnetic flux Change in magnetic field strength.

Magnetic moment A quantity representing the strength and orientation of a magnet or magnetic field, or a magnetic dipole.

Magnetic resonance imaging (MRI) A technique for imaging the structure or function of a part of the body through the use of a strong magnetic field, additional magnetic field gradients, and radio frequency (RF) energy.

Magnetic susceptibility A measure of a material's magnetic properties, which is positive if the material is paramagnetic. Because paramagnetic materials create magnetic fields, magnetic susceptibility is the basis of the T2* contrast in fMRI BOLD imaging. As well, magnetic susceptibility artifacts can be created in some types of imaging, such as EPI, if a voxel contains a mixture of materials with very different magnetic susceptibility, such as occurs between the sagittal sinuses and the orbitofrontal part of the brain, and between the ear canals and the inferior temporal lobes.

Magnetically permeable A property of a material that allows magnetic fields to flow through it. Magnetically permeable metals are used in passive shielding of MEG systems, to deflect external magnetic fields around, rather than into, the room.

Magnetoencephalography (MEG) A technique that measures the flux (change) in magnetic fields generated by the flow of electrical current in the brain.

Magnetometer A device used to measure magnetic field flux.

Main effect The effect of manipulating a single independent variable, independent of the effects of manipulating any other variable.

Masking (fMRI analysis) An operation in which a portion of an image, such as an fMRI activation map, is included in, or excluded from, further analysis. For example, a mask defined by the shape of the brain can be used to exclude voxels outside the brain from further analysis.

Mass univariate analysis An approach to statistical analysis typically used with neuroimaging data, such as EEG or fMRI, that involve large numbers of measurements at each time point, from multiple locations. The data from each location are analysed in the same way, but independently of each other. Contrast with multivariate analyses, in which data from multiple locations are analysed simultaneously in a single model, or ROI analyses in which data are collapsed over spatially defined regions.

Matched filter theorem A theorem in signal processing stating that the signal-to-noise ratio of data can be improved by processing the data with a filter that matches the signal in the data. In other words, correlating the data with the shape of the expected signal will help isolate that signal. Informs the choice of a kernel size for spatial smoothing in fMRI preprocessing.

MBLL See 'modified Beer–Lambert law'.

Mean amplitude The average electrical potential over a specified time period. A common dependent measure in ERP research.

Mental chronometry The practice of measuring reaction times (RTs) to understand cognition.

MEP See 'motor evoked potential'.

MEP input–output curve A plot of the relationship between stimulation intensity and MEP amplitude.

Meso-maps Maps of the brain at the 'meso' scale, typically on the order of centimetres, based around distinct brain regions that may be defined functionally, anatomically based on cytoarchitecture or myeloarchitecture, or some combination of these sources of information.

Minimum norm estimation (MNE) A distributed source solution for the inverse problem in source localization, which assumes that the correct solution is the one that minimizes the overall difference between the data and the model, while keeping the average amplitudes of the entire set of dipoles to a minimum. Modern implementations of MNE thus employ an additional regularization, a parameter which 'penalizes' shallow sources in favour of deeper ones.

Mixed designs Experimental designs that contain both between- and within-subjects manipulations.

Model-based tract segmentation An approach to tractography in which pre-defined models of white matter tracts are used as a starting point to estimate the true shape and centre of an individual's tract.

Modified Beer–Lambert law (MBLL) A modification to the Beer–Lambert law required for its application to fNIRI. The MBLL takes into account the scattering of light in biological tissue, and uses the absorption coefficients of oxy-Hb and deoxy-Hb, allowing measurement of the concentrations of oxyhaemoglobin and deoxyhaemoglobin.

Modularity (graph theory) In graph theory, a property whereby groups of brain areas that show high correlations with each other are largely separated from other such densely interconnected networks.

Molecular lattice The molecular environment surrounding an atom or molecule. In MRI, affects T1 recovery and T2 decay times.

Monophasic pulse A shape of TMS pulse that quickly reaches its intensity peak and then returns to baseline (zero voltage).

Morphometry The study of the size and shape of brain regions.

Motion correction A preprocessing step that can be applied to various forms of neuroimaging data that may contain artifacts caused by head motion, with the aim of reducing these artifacts.

Motor evoked potential (MEP) The EMG response elicited when a muscle contracts.

MR-active nucleus Any atom that has a magnetic moment and angular momentum, and could therefore be detected using MRI.

Mu metal A special blend of metals specifically designed to deflect magnetic fields, composed primarily of nickel and iron, with copper and chromium or molybdenum. Used as a form of passive shielding for MEG systems.

Multimodal The use of more than one neuroimaging and/or neurostimulation technique (modality) to address a particular experimental question. Multimodal studies may use the techniques simultaneously (for example, recording EEG in an MRI scanner, while fMRI data is also acquired), or asynchronously (for example, having the same participants perform the same task in two separate sessions, one while EEG is recorded and another while fMRI is performed).

Multiple comparison correction Any statistical approach aimed at controlling for Type I error (false positives) that might occur due to performing a large number of statistical tests, as in mass univariate analysis.

Multiplexing A technique in signal transmission that allows decoding of multiple, independent signals from a single data stream. See also, 'time multiplexing', 'frequency multiplexing', and 'code multiplexing'.

Multivariate analysis A statistical analysis that models the effect of independent variables on multiple dependent variables simultaneously. In fMRI analysis, multivariate approaches are often contrasted with mass univariate approaches to analysis, in that multivariate analyses simultaneously consider the activation levels at all voxels within an ROI (or the whole brain) rather than analysing the time course of each voxel individually.

Myelin A sheath surrounding the axons of neurons that is high in fat content, and serves to electrically insulate the axons. This speeds electrical conduction along the axon and increases the distance that a signal can be carried. In the central nervous system, myelin is formed by oligodendrocytes, a type of glial cell. In the peripheral nervous system it is formed by Schwann cells.

Myeloarchitecture An description of the structure of the cerebral cortex (typically consistent within a region of the cortex) based on the type, density, and distribution across cortical layers of local and long-range connections between neurons.

Nasion A scalp landmark point located at the bridge of the nose (where the top of the nose meets the forehead).

Net magnetization vector (NMV) The net magnitude and orientation of all the protons in a particular sample.

Network activity-dependent model An extension of the activity-dependent model of tDCS, suggesting that the effects of tDCS to a brain area may be influenced by activity in other brain areas, and may also influence activity levels in distant brain areas.

Network-based correlation An approach to functional connectivity analysis where the time course from each voxel (or more commonly, each ROI) in the image is correlated with the time course from every other voxel or ROI. Often subsequently analysed with graph-theoretical approaches. Contrast with 'seed-based correlation'.

Network discovery Any analytical approach aimed at identifying and characterizing networks without explicit prior knowledge or hypotheses regarding which areas are connected.

Neural adaptation The phenomenon that neurons tend to show reduced firing rates upon repeated presentation of stimuli that they are sensitive to. See also, 'fMRI adaptation'.

Neuroethics The study and application of ethical principles in neuroscience. This includes research ethics pertaining to neuroscience studies, as well as the ethical implications of neuroscience research and its applications.

Neurohormone A type of hormone that has effects on the nervous system. Neurohormones are generally produced by neuroendocrine cells at some distance from the cells that they influence, and are transmitted to their targets through the blood.

Neuromodulator A type of chemical that serves a signalling function in the nervous system. Neuromodulators work similarly to neurotransmitters in that they bind to specific receptors to modulate cellular membrane potential or other functions. However, the action of neuromodulators is generally slower and longer lasting than neurotransmitters, and may have less localized effects.

Neuro-navigation In NIBS, the technique of targeting stimulation to a particular brain area based on relating an anatomical image of the brain to the position of the stimulation device.

Neurons The cells of the nervous system that receive electro-chemical input, conduct electrical signals, and generate action potentials as output.

Neuroprivacy The branch of neuroethics concerned with safeguards and limitations of privacy related to an individual's brain activity and other neuroscientific measures.

Neuropsychology The study of brain–behaviour relationships. As commonly used, neuropsychology refers specifically to work with people who have suffered brain damage (through injury or disease), and the process of relating patterns of damage to behavioural and cognitive deficits. The term may also refer to clinical practice in which people with brain damage are assessed and/or treated for functional deficits.

Neurostimulation A technique that stimulates neural activity. Non-invasive forms include transcranial magnetic stimulation (TMS) and transcranial electrical stimulation (tES).

Neurotransmitter A chemical that is used by neurons to communicate with other neurons. Neurotransmitters are released from synaptic vesicles on 'sending' neurons, typically in response to an action potential, and form temporary bonds with receptors located on 'receiving' neurons (typically on the dendrites).

NIBS See 'non-invasive brain stimulation'.

NMV See 'net magnetization vector'.

Node In graph-theoretical analysis of neuroimaging data, a node corresponds to a brain region, which is assumed to have a distinct functional role.

Noise A generic term used to refer to any features of recorded data that are not of experimental interest, or are otherwise undesirable.

Noise normalization A regularization used in source localization which recognizes that noise levels may not be the same at every dipole across the surface of the brain, and converts the data to z statistics by dividing the estimated strength by the variance of that estimate, at each dipole individually.

Non-invasive brain stimulation (NIBS) Techniques for stimulating the brain non-invasively, including transcranial magnetic stimulation and transcranial electrical stimulation.

Non-linear registration Algorithms used in spatial normalization that involve mathematically nonlinear functions, such as 2D sine wave gratings. Generally result in a better fit than linear methods, and thus less inter-individual variability in the residual difference between shapes of the individual and reference (template) brains.

Nonparametric statistics A general approach to statistics in which, rather than assuming a specific distribution of data values a priori, the distribution is estimated from the data themselves. See also 'bootstrapping' and 'randomization'.

Notch filter A filter that attenuates a narrow range of frequencies, while passing lower and higher frequencies without attenuation. The opposite of a band-pass filter.

Nyquist frequency The maximum frequency that can be recorded without aliasing, given the sampling rate. Formally the Nyquist frequency is half the sampling rate, but in practice it is advisable to filter out frequencies higher than one-third of the sampling rate.

Ocular artifacts Artifacts in neuroimaging data (such as EEG or MEG) caused by the eyes. These include eye movements and blinks.

Offline inhibitory protocol A type of repetitive TMS protocol in which inhibitory rTMS is delivered for a period of time, typically while the participant is not performing a task, and then the effects of TMS on task performance are assessed some period of time after stimulation.

Offline In the context of neuroimaging, 'offline' typically refers to tasks or measurements performed after something else has happened. For example, in NIBS, offline protocols involve delivering stimulation while the participant is not performing any task, and then later measuring task performance after stimulation has ended.

Offline facilitatory protocol A type of repetitive TMS protocol in which facilitative rTMS (such as high-frequency rTMS, or iTBS) is delivered for a period of time, typically while the participant is not performing a task, and then the effects of TMS on task performance are assessed some period of time after stimulation.

Online In the context of neuroimaging, 'online' typically refers to tasks or measurements performed while something else is happening. For example, in NIBS, online protocols involve stimulation while the participant is performing a task.

Online inhibitory protocol A type of repetitive TMS protocol in which inhibitory rTMS is delivered in short bursts while the receiver is performing some task, to assess the immediate effects of TMS on task performance.

Open field A theoretical construct used to describe generators of EEG signal. An open field comprises many neurons aligned in parallel, whose cellular membrane potentials are fluctuating synchronously. Open field configurations of neurons are necessary to generate a measurable EEG signal at a distance.

Operational definition A definition of a term for a particular purpose.

Optical tomography Source localization approaches to fNIRI. See 'tomographic imaging'.

Optically pumped magnetometers (OPMs) An alternative to SQUIDs for measuring magnetic fields. OPMs use a laser beam to polarize ions, which are depolarized by magnetic fields. Have been used in prototype MEG systems and have the advantage of not requiring supercooling, resulting in a wearable MEG device.

Optodes In fNIRI, the sensors placed on the head, including both emitters and detectors.

Ordinal scale A scale, such as a rating scale, in which a fixed and pre-determined set of response options, which vary along a single dimension, are available.

Oscillatory tDCS (o-tDCS) A form of tES in which a sinusoidally oscillating current is used. In contrast to tACS, where the current oscillates between positive and negative intensities at both electrodes, in o-tDCS the current oscillates between zero and its maximum positive value at the anode, and between zero and its maximum negative value at the cathode.

Outcome measure See 'dependent variable'.

Oxygen extraction fraction The proportion of oxygen extracted from blood when the brain is in a resting state.

Pair production Conversion of a photon to a pair of electrons. In PET imaging, results in reduced signal as the photon is not detected by the scanner.

Paired-pulse TMS (ppTMS) A TMS protocol involving a pair of single pulses that can either be delivered to the same location with a fixed interval, or to two different brain regions to investigate inter-regional connectivity.

Parallel component (of magnetic field) In MEG, the component of the magnetic field emanating from the head that is oriented parallel to the scalp.

Parallel imaging A form of MRI acquisition in which multiple RF receiving coils are used simultaneously to acquire the data. Can decrease the required time for a scan, and/or increase image quality.

Paramagnetic Material having magnetic properties, in that it is weakly attracted to an external magnetic field, and forms its own weak, local magnetic field aligned with the external field. This causes small changes in the local magnetic field strength. The fact that deoxyhaemoglobin is paramagnetic, while oxyhaemoglobin is not, leads to the BOLD effect that is the basis of the fMRI signal.

Parametric design An experimental design that investigates how the dependent variable is influenced by changes across a range of levels of some independent variable. The independent variable in such designs is typically continuous, rather than factorial.

Partial volume effects In brain imaging, artifacts or errors that can occur when a voxel contains more than one type of tissue or other material, such as grey and white matter, or grey matter and CSF.

Passive electromagnetic shielding A form of electromagnetic shielding, such as a Faraday cage, that works solely due to its shape and material composition. Contrast with 'active shielding'.

Peak amplitude The maximum amplitude of a signal within a specified time window. A common dependent measure in ERP research.

Peak latency In ERP research, the time between the onset of an event, and the peak positive or negative value in a particular time range. The time range is typically specified to capture a particular component, such as the P1.

Peak-to-peak amplitude The difference between the maximum positive and negative electrical potentials within a specified time range, typically two temporally adjacent peaks in an ERP waveform. Sometimes used as a dependent measure in ERP research.

PER See 'positron-emitting radioligand'.

Peri-auricular points Comparable scalp landmark points on the left and right sides of the head, in or around the ears. Commonly used in measurements for the International 10–10 System.

Permutation distribution In nonparametric statistics, bootstrapping and/or randomization are used repeatedly to generate hundreds or thousands of samples (permutations) of the data. The permutation distribution is the resulting distribution of values from all of these permutations, and is used to determine the threshold values for statistical significance.

Perpendicular component (of magnetic field) In MEG, the component of the magnetic field emanating from the head that is oriented perpendicular to the scalp. Also called the radial component.

Phase The position in time of a particular point within an oscillating waveform. For example, the location of the positive peaks in a waveform. Often used to describe the relative offset of peaks of waves of the same frequency.

Phase delay In frequency-domain fNIRI, the time delay between the phase of the light received at a detector after passing through the head, and the phase of a reference beam of light that was transmitted from the emitter through a vacuum tube with known light transmission properties, to a detector.

Phase encoding gradient In MRI, the gradient applied along one of two spatial dimensions within a slice, perpendicular to the slice and frequency encoding gradient directions. Determines the location of the readout along the y axis in k space.

Phase locking See 'phase synchronization'.

Phase roll In MRI, the effect of applying a magnetic field gradient on the precessional phase of protons, resulting in a sinusoidal variation in phase over space along the gradient direction.

Phase synchronization Alignment of the phase of different waveforms or other oscillation patterns, such as the precession of protons.

Phosphene A form of visual hallucination in which one experiences the visual perception of light, without that light entering the eye. Often takes the form of small, bright spots that may move. Colloquially referred to as 'seeing stars'. Can be induced by TMS delivered to parts of the visual cortex.

Photocathode A material that absorbs photons of specific energy, and produces photoelectrons as a result.

Photodetector A device used for measuring light, typically by turning light into electrical current.

Photodiode A type of photodetector based on semiconductor diodes.

Photoelectron An electron produced when light shines on a material.

Photomultiplier tube (PMT) A type of photodetector that amplifies the amount of light it receives via a series of photocathodes.

Photon A particle of light. Pairs of photons produced by annihilation of a positron are what is detected to form the PET imaging signal.

Physiological measures In cognitive science and related fields, physiological measurements refer to measurements of non-neural physiological parameters that are influenced by psychological states. These include heart rate, respiration, and skin conductance, and generally reflect the level of arousal of the individual.

Placebo effect An effect caused by a treatment that is due to the individual's perception that they received the treatment, rather than being caused by the chemical or physical effects of the treatment itself.

Planar gradiometer A gradiometer constructed from two conducting loops wound in opposite directions and equidistant from the scalp. In MEG, planar gradiometers measure magnetic flux laterally across the scalp (the parallel component).

PMT See 'photomultiplier tube'.

Polarization A state in which the amount of electrical charge differs between two locations, such as between the inside and outside of a neuron, or between the body and axon of a neuron.

Polyphasic pulse A shape of TMS pulse that has multiple peaks (phases).

Positron A subatomic particle with a positive charge, created when a proton converts to a neutron.

Positron emission tomography (PET) A technique that measures the concentration of radioactive substances (positron-emitting radioligands, or PERs) in the brain. PERs can be made for a variety of markers, including blood oxygenation, glucose metabolism, or neurotransmitter distribution.

Positron-emitting radioligand (PER) A radioactive tracer used in positron emission tomography, composed of a molecule that binds to a desired target receptor or is consumed in a target physiological process, combined with a radioisotope that has a short half-life and is otherwise safe to use.

Post hoc Latin for 'after the fact'. In experimentation, the term is typically used to refer to procedures done after the data have been collected and partially analysed, and which may therefore be biased by the researcher's observations or interpretations of the data. Often contrasted with the term 'a priori'.

Post hoc test In statistics, a test that is performed 'after the fact' or as a follow-up to further investigate or break down a significant main effect or interaction.

Potential (electrical) The amount of electrical charge that could flow from one location to another.

Power (signal processing) In frequency-domain representations, power is the amplitude of the signal at a given frequency.

Power (statistical) See 'statistical power'.

PPI See 'psychophysiological interactions'.

ppTMS See 'paired-pulse TMS'.

Precession The changing orientation of the axis of a spinning object, such as a proton. The 'wobble' of a spinning top is an example of precession.

Preprocessing Steps performed on data to improve the signal-to-noise ratio and thus make it more likely to detect any significant effect of interest that is in the data.

Primary auditory cortex (A1) The area of the superior temporal gyrus that receives primary auditory input. Cells primarily respond to basic auditory features such as frequency. Has a tonotopic organization, with cells tuned to similar frequencies being located close to each other.

Primary motor cortex (M1) The area of the cerebral cortex, located on the post-central gyrus, that serves as the primary site for controlling voluntary motor output.

Primary visual cortex (V1) The area of the occipital lobe of the cerebral cortex that receives visual input from the retina, via the thalamus. Contains cells that respond to largely simple features such as line orientation and brightness. Has a retinotopic organization. The organization of V1 is 'crossed', such that the right hemisphere receives input from the left visual field, and vice-versa.

Principal components analysis A mathematical technique used to decompose data into components that are maximally uncorrelated from each other.

Probabilistic atlas In brain imaging, an atlas or definition of discrete brain regions in which each voxel of the brain is not assigned a single label, but rather is associated with a number of probability values defining the likelihood, across individuals, that the voxel is part of a particular brain region. Developed to account for inter-individual variability in relationships between cytoarchitecture and gross sulcal/gyral anatomy.

Probabilistic tractography An approach to tractography that involves running streamlining multiple times using different pseudo-random variants of the direction of the principal eigenvector, in an attempt to compensate for noise in estimating the true principal direction of diffusion in that voxel.

Projectome Similar to the connectome, the projectome is a complete description of the structural connections between neurons in the brain. The projectome is distinguished from the connectome by describing not only the endpoints of each connection, but also the direction that information flows along the connection. In practice, the term may be used to refer to the complete set of projections that are resolvable at a certain level of resolution, or by a particular technique.

Prospective design See 'longitudinal design'.

Psychophysics A special class of behavioural research dealing with sensation and perception, focused on measuring people's sensitivities to variations along stimulus dimensions (such as brightness or loudness). A common approach in psychophysics is to determine an individual's threshold for detection of some stimulus or property.

Psychophysiological interactions (PPI) An approach to effective connectivity analysis that involves determining whether the correlation in BOLD activity between two regions (or more generally, between one region and the rest of the brain) changes with an experimental manipulation.

Psychophysiological measures See 'physiological measures'.

Publication bias The observation that experiments resulting in statistically significant results are more likely to be accepted for publication in peer-reviewed journals than non-significant ones. The result of publication bias is that valid experimental results that do not yield statistically significant results are less likely to be published, resulting in an uneven reporting of data in the literature. This is one factor proposed to have resulted in the replicability crisis, because even if the result of an experimental manipulation does not yield statistically significant results in the majority of experiments, only the significant results may be reported.

Pulse sequence In MRI, the sequence of events used to generate and record a signal. This typically includes the timing and amplitude of the RF pulse, gradients, and echo (readout).

Pupillometry A technique in which the diameter of the pupil (the centre of the eye that lets light into the retina) is measured. Pupil diameter is influenced by arousal, and so pupillometry may be considered a type of psychophysiological measure.

Pure insertion The assumption that variables do not interact, and thus if one variable is manipulated, any effect of the manipulation can be attributed to that variable.

Pyramidal cell A highly abundant type of neuron in the cerebral cortex that supports advanced cognitive functions. Pyramidal cells are considered a predominant source of signal measured by many non-invasive neuroimaging techniques, including EEG and fMRI.

Quadripulse stimulation A TMS protocol that involves bursts of four pulses in rapid succession separated by longer (for example, 5 s) periods.

Radio frequency The frequency of waves in the radio range (20 KHz–30 GHz).

Randomization (statistics) A technique in nonparametric statistics to estimate the true distribution of values in a population, from a sample of the population. Unlike bootstrapping, all the data are used, but are randomly reassigned to different conditions to estimate the distribution of values if there was no true effect of experimental condition.

Rating scale A type of behavioural measure in which an individual selects one response from a range of options that scale along a particular dimension. Can be analogue or ordinal.

Reaction time (RT) A measure of the amount of time it takes a human (or other animal) to generate an overt motor response to some stimulus. Also called response time. The practice of measuring RTs to understand cognition is often called mental chronometry.

Receptor A chemical structure on a cell membrane that causes a change in cellular function when a neurotransmitter binds to it. Receptors are specific to particular neurotransmitters.

Reference electrode In EEG, the reference electrode serves as the basis for determining the electrical potential at the active electrode, by determining the potential difference between the active and reference electrodes. Thus the location of the reference electrode in part determines the magnitude of the potential recorded at the active electrode. After data collection, EEG data can be re-referenced to a different electrode from that used as the reference during recording.

Refresh rate The frequency with which information is updated. Commonly used with reference to computer displays (monitors) to describe how rapidly the screen image can be changed. The refresh rate of the monitor determines the shortest possible duration of a visual stimulus in an experiment.

Region of interest (ROI) A defined area of space, commonly used to group or simplify measurements in neuroimaging data. This is often useful in reducing the total number of statistical tests performed. For example, an EEG montage of 64 electrodes covering the scalp might be clustered into nine ROIs along anterior–posterior and left–right dimensions. In fMRI, ROIs may be defined based on anatomical structures, or functionally based on activation in a 'functional localizer' task.

Regularization In mathematics, the application of constraints to help solve an ill-posed problem (such as the inverse problem) or to prevent over-fitting.

Relaxation In MRI, the process by which the net magnetization vector returns to alignment with the longitudinal plane, and precessional phase desynchronizes. Occurs following excitation.

Repetition time (TR) The time between subsequent RF pulses in an MRI scan.

Repetitive TMS (rTMS) A TMS protocol in which a series of pulses are delivered in rapid succession, at a pre-determined frequency. The effects of the series of pulses, rather than of any individual pulse, are of experimental interest.

Rephasing gradient In DWI, a magnetic field gradient that is applied some time after a dephasing gradient, with equal slope but opposite direction to the dephasing gradient. If water molecules have not diffused, this should result in perfect cancellation of the phase roll caused by the dephasing gradient. When water molecules diffuse, however, a reduction in the DWI signal results.

Replicability crisis A term used to refer to the observation that many research findings published in peer-reviewed scientific journals cannot be replicated by other researchers (or even the same researchers) using the methods described in the publication. See also 'publication bias'.

Replicable Repeatable. In experimentation, careful and accurate documentation and reporting of all procedures is necessary to ensure that results can be replicated.

Representational similarity analysis (RSA) A form of multivariate analysis often applied to fMRI or other types of neuroimaging data. Uses condition-rich or time-continuous designs combined with explicit models of how information in the stimuli or tasks might be represented by the brain, and examines the degree of similarity in multivariate activation patterns across stimuli as a function of stimulus or model properties.

Resonance The transfer of energy from one material to another when they oscillate at the same frequency, resulting in greater amplitude of oscillation of the receiving material.

Response contingency A situation, such as in behavioural research, where individuals are required to make different responses to different stimuli.

Resting motor threshold (rMT) The intensity of a TMS pulse that elicits an MEP on 50% of trials, when the muscle is not contracting. Often used to determine stimulation levels for TMS delivered to other brain areas.

Resting state A state often used as a baseline condition in neuroimaging studies, or which is studied in its own right to understand physiological processes that occur when people lie still without performing any specific task, or experiencing stimuli other than that provided by the ambient environment of the neuroimaging device.

Resting state fMRI (rs-fMRI) A type of fMRI design in which no experimental tasks or stimuli are used, but rather participants are simply instructed to lie still, either with their eyes open or closed. See also 'resting state'.

Retinotopic An organizational property of numerous cortical regions, by which spatial locations in the cortical region map to locations on the retina (and thus in the visual world) in a spatially consistent way. Thus nearby locations in the retina would map to nearby locations in the cortical region.

Reverse inference In neuroimaging, the practice of interpreting the activation of a particular brain area as reflecting the operation of a particular cognitive process, based on prior literature describing the cognitive processes associated with activation of that brain region. Reverse inference can be useful, but may be problematic if the past literature is not systematically surveyed, or if the brain region in question is associated with a wide variety of cognitive operations.

RF See 'radio frequency'.

Right-hand rule See 'Ampère's circuital law'.

Ripple frequency Frequencies in the range of 100–250 Hz which have been recorded from hippocampus associated with memory encoding.

rMT See 'resting motor threshold'.

Rolloff See 'transition band'.

rs-fcMRI See 'Resting state fMRI'.

rs-fMRI See 'Resting state fMRI'.

RSA See 'representational similarity analysis'.

rTMS See 'repetitive TMS'.

Sagittal plane In neuroimaging, the sagittal plane is defined by the anterior–posterior and inferior–superior dimensions, and is perpendicular to the left–right dimension.

Sampling rate In data acquisition, the frequency with which the data are read by the data acquisition device and stored. Typically reported in samples per second (Hertz).

Saturation In EEG, a situation where the signal entering the amplifier is greater than the range of electrical potentials it can handle. This may occur due to artifacts such as from TMS pulses, and results in blocking.

SBCT See 'surface-based cortical thickness'.

Scintillation detector A specialized type of light detector used in PET imaging. Made of crystals whose properties determine factors such as sensitivity and temporal resolution.

Seed-based correlation An approach to functional connectivity analysis where the time course from each voxel in the image is correlated with the time course from a single 'seed' voxel or ROI. Contrast with 'network-based correlation'.

Segregation In brain mapping, segregation is the delineation of distinct areas of the brain on the basis of their structure and/or function.

Sensory artifacts When performing TMS in or near an MRI scanner, artifacts in the MR image associated with the individual's sensory perceptions of the TMS pulse, including the sound and 'tapping' sensation, as well as possible involuntary muscle contractions.

Sham stimulation In NIBS, an activity designed to make the receiver (and possibly experimenter) think that stimulation is being delivered, when in fact it is not. Used to control for placebo and demand characteristic effects.

Shimming The process of adjusting the magnetic field around an object, such as the head, to make the magnetic field homogenous at the start of an MRI scan. Can be used to correct for magnetic susceptibility artifacts.

Sievert (Sv) A unit for quantifying radioactivity absorbed by the body that includes a weighting factor that accounts for differences in biological risk between different types of radiation (such as X-rays versus gamma rays). The sievert is commonly used in safety guidelines for radioactive exposure.

Sigmoid A s-shaped function that describes various phenomena, such as the probability of a neuron firing given an input, and psychophysical thresholds for detecting stimuli. The hallmark of a sigmoidal function is that at the low end of input intensity, there is little response, but in the 'optimal range' for the function, small changes in input strength produce disproportionately larger changes in the response. Then at some point, the response saturates and increased input strength produces little change in response.

Signal-to-noise ratio (SNR) The relative amounts of signal and noise in a measurement. In general, 'signal' refers to the quantity whose measurement is desired (such as brain activity related to an experimental manipulation) and 'noise' refers to any other source of variance in the measurements (including, in neuroimaging, both brain activity not relevant to the experimental manipulation, and other sources).

Silent period (SP) The period immediately after an MEP is evoked by a TMS pulse to the motor cortex, when noise in EMG recordings from the targeted muscle is suppressed. This suppression lasts for hundreds of milliseconds, and the duration of the SP can vary depending on the state of the subject and the experimental conditions, making SP duration a variable of interest in many studies.

Silicon photomultiplier A relatively recent innovation in photodetector technology, combining advantages of avalanche photodiodes with the single-photon counting abilities of photomultiplier tubes.

Sine wave grating A 2D version of a sine wave, which appears as greyscale stripes.

Single-pulse TMS A TMS protocol in which a single isolated pulse is delivered, typically separated by many seconds, or longer, from any subsequent pulse, and in which the effects of each single pulse are of experimental interest.

Skeletonization A technique used in tractography that reduces the normalized data to a white matter 'skeleton' derived from the averaged, normalized FA maps of all of the participants in a particular analysis.

Skin potential A slowly changing electrical potential caused by changes in the conductivity of the skin. Commonly observed in EEG data when scalp impedance is not sufficiently low, or when electrical conductivity along the skin increases, for example due to sweat.

Slice (MRI) A 2D matrix of voxels representing MRI data in a specific plane through the body.

Slice selection A step in an MRI pulse sequence in which a gradient is applied to vary the Larmor frequencies of protons along the slice direction of the intended image.

Slice selection gradient In MRI, the gradient along the plane defining the slices of the image. Typically turned on during excitation.

Slow optical signal In fNIRI, a signal that shows relatively slow changes related to stimulation or task performance, and reflects the BOLD response.

Small-world properties In graph theory, a type of organizational structure that consists of a number of densely interconnected modules (sub-networks) which are connected globally through a set of short paths (that is, any given node is linked to any other one through a relatively low number of intervening nodes).

Soma The body of a neuron.

SP See 'silent period'.

Spatial derivative A mathematical computation that represents the slope, or rate of change, over space. Also called a spatial gradient.

Spatial frequency Frequency in two dimensions, such as of a sine wave grating.

Spatial normalization The process of changing the shape of an individual brain to match the shape of another. Commonly applied to MRI scans, and other spatially defined neuroimaging data, to adjust the shapes and sizes of all the individual brains in a dataset to match a standard template brain's shape, allowing averaging of the data across individuals.

Spatial resolution In the context of brain imaging or behavioural techniques, spatial resolution refers to the sensitivity of the technique to differences across space. Higher spatial resolution means that information can be obtained from smaller units of space.

Spatial smoothing Applying a spatial filter to an image. Typically performed as an fMRI preprocessing step, using a Gaussian kernel, to improve the signal-to-noise ratio of the data. See also 'matched filter theorem'.

Spectrophotometry A technique for determining measuring the amount of light reflected by, or transmitted through, a material. Used in biochemistry to determine the concentration of a substance.

Spherical surface-based normalization An algorithm used in spatial normalization in which the cerebral cortex is represented mathematically as a continuous 2D surface, inflated into a spherical shape, and then aligned with a reference (template) brain by matching the size, location, and orientation of major sulci and other gross anatomical features.

Spiral imaging An MRI pulse sequence sometimes used in fMRI, in which k space is completely sampled with every excitation. This is done by traversing a spiral path through k space. Compared to EPI, spiral imaging is less physically demanding on magnetic gradient hardware because the orientation of the gradients change slowly and continuously in a sinusoidal fashion, compared with the rapid switching of directions of the phase encoding gradient in EPI.

Staircase method A method in psychophysics in which some stimulus property is systematically varied in order to determine the person's psychophysical threshold. In the staircase method, intensity is initially set below the expected threshold (making it undetectable), and then raised on subsequent trials until the participant can reliably detect it. Then, the staircase direction is reversed and the stimulus intensity is systematically lowered again until the participant can no longer detect it. This reversal process is repeated several times, and the threshold value is typically set to be the intensity level at which the person is able to accurately make the detection/discrimination 50% of the time.

Standardized low-resolution brain electromagnetic tomography (sLORETA) An approach to source localization that uses noise normalization.

Static artifacts When performing TMS in or near an MRI scanner, artifacts in the MR image associated with the presence of metal in and near the MRI scanner.

Statistical power The likelihood of detecting a statistically significant difference, given a particular experimental effect size, variance, and sample size, if the difference actually exists.

Stimulus onset asynchrony (SOA) The time between the onset of one stimulus, and the onset of the next stimulus. See also 'inter-stimulus interval'.

Stochastic resonance A phenomenon used to describe the effects of tES. It is a non-specific form of resonance, in which noise is input to the system resulting in increases in activity within the system that are proportionate to pre-stimulation levels of activity. Thus in a case where some neural populations are firing relatively strongly compared to other populations (such as when many dots are moving coherently in one direction, while others move randomly), neurons that were near threshold may be 'nudged' above threshold, whereas the activity of competing neurons will remain below threshold. However, in a situation where only one population of neurons is active (such as when dots are all moving in one direction), stochastic resonance can increase the level of activity of task-irrelevant neurons.

Stopping power A property of crystals used in scintillation detectors that describes what proportion of photons trigger a response. Influences the signal-to-noise ratio of a PET scanner.

Streamlining A process used in tractography that involves starting from a particular voxel and identifying which surrounding voxel's principal eigenvector is best aligned with the principal eigenvector (the strongest direction of diffusion) of this voxel. This is repeated at the next voxel, effectively 'connecting the dots' to determine the most likely path of a fibre tract given the data.

Subtraction method An experimental approach based on the premise that if all possible variables are held constant, except for one which is manipulated, then the difference in the dependent measure represents the effect of the experimental manipulation. Depends on the assumption of pure insertion.

Sulcus A fissure or concave fold on the surface of the cerebral cortex. See also 'gyrus'.

Superconducting quantum interference device (SQUID) A very sensitive magnetometer, made superconducting through cooling to a very low temperature, and involving Josephson junctions.

Surface-based cortical thickness (SBCT) A morphometric method aimed at characterizing cortical thickness. Analysis is performed using data in surface-based format, where the thickness of the grey matter is derived as the distance from the outer surface of the white matter to the CSF. Contrast with voxel-based cortical thickness.

Sv See 'sievert'.

Sylvian fissure The deep fissure separating the temporal lobe from the frontal and parietal lobes.

Synapse The junction between two neurons, where communication can occur between the neurons via chemical messengers, including neurotransmitters and neuromodulators.

T1 recovery In MRI, the component of relaxation describing the return of the net magnetization vector to the longitudinal plane.

T1 relaxation time In MRI, a property of a material, given a particular magnetic field strength, describing the time it takes for 63% of the longitudinal relaxation to recover following excitation.

T2 decay In MRI, the component of relaxation describing the loss of phase coherence.

T2 relaxation time In MRI, a property of a material, given a particular magnetic field strength, describing the time it takes for a 63% reduction of the NMV in the transverse plane following excitation.

T2* decay Rapid dephasing following MR excitation, caused by small, local inhomogeneities in the magnetic field, which can be caused by magnetic properties of some molecules as well as by the fact that magnetic field inhomogeneities are caused near the boundaries of different tissue type. Deoxyhaemoglobin causes T2* decay, which forms the basis for the BOLD fMRI signal.

TBM See 'tensor-based morphometry'.

TBS See 'theta burst stimulation'.

TD fNIRI See 'time-domain (TD) fNIRI'.

TE See 'echo time'.

Temporal resolution In the context of brain imaging or behavioural techniques, temporal resolution refers to the sensitivity of a technique to variations in the measured signal over time. Higher temporal resolution means that more information is obtained per unit time, or that there is greater sensitivity to changes over shorter periods of time.

Tensor-based morphometry (TBM) A computational neuroanatomy method that measures changes in the volume of brain structures and which can be extended to other aspects of shape change as well. Based on measures derived from the deformation fields, known as the Jacobian matrix. This matrix captures local information from the normalization for each voxel, including volume changes, rotation, and shearing.

Tensor line approach A strategy for improving the accuracy of streamlining in tractography, which carries the 'momentum' of the streamline from high-FA voxels through those with lower FA.

TEPs See 'TMS-evoked potentials'

Tessellation The process of representing a surface mathematically as a set of triangles.

Test stimulus (TS) In paired-pulse TMS, the second stimulation pulse.

Theta burst stimulation (TBS) An rTMS protocol in which short triplets of stimulation are delivered at regular intervals.

Threshold limit value (TLV) The safety limit for radioactive exposure, as defined by a governing body.

Time-continuous design A variant of condition-rich experimental designs, using stimuli that vary continuously over time, such as movies. Each time point in the data is treated as a separate experimental condition.

Time-correlated single photon counting A technique used in time-domain fNIRI, that works on the principle that in the narrow time windows used for detection (a few thousand ps), the odds of detecting even a single photon are quite low. Thus to determine the DTOF a relatively large number of sampling cycles are required to detect enough photons to reliably estimate the DTOF.

Time domain Representation and/or analysis of data as it varies over time. In visualization of neuroimaging data in the time domain, typically time is plotted on the x axis (abscissa) and amplitude of the measured brain activity signal on the y axis (ordinate).

Time-domain (TD) fNIRI An approach to fNIRI in which light of a particular wavelength(s) is emitted in brief pulses, rather than continuously. This allows quantification of the time of arrival of photons at the detector.

Time-frequency analysis A frequency-domain analysis of time-varying signals (such as EEG or MEG) in which the power over a range of frequencies is analysed as a function of time. This involves obtaining frequency-domain representations for short, sequential periods of time (often with each time window overlapping partially with those before and after it).

Time multiplexing An approach to multiplexing in which each source (such as an emitter in fNIRI) is on at a given time; sources alternate sending signals in rapid succession. Temporal resolution thus decreases with the number of signals being multiplexed.

Time of flight imaging A form of PET imaging in which the relative timing of arrival of a pair of photons from a coincidence event is measured.

Tissue segmentation A preprocessing step applied to MRI data in which different tissue types (typically grey matter, white matter, and CSF) are separated into separate images so that each can be analysed separately.

TLV See 'threshold limit value'.

TMS-evoked potentials (TEPs) Unique patterns of EEG activity elicited by TMS. Note that these are not TMS artifacts, but signals of neural origin that are triggered by TMS.

Tomographic imaging Imaging by sections (such as slices or voxels) using some form of penetrating wave. MRI, fNIRI, and CT scans are all examples of tomography. In fNIRI, the term is used to refer to source-localized, rather than channel-based, approaches to data analysis and visualization.

TR See 'repetition time'.

Tractography The process of mapping white matter tracts that connect different brain regions.

Transcranial alternating current stimulation (tACS) A tES method that involves passing an alternating current between electrodes. At each electrode, the current alternates sinusoidally between the maximum positive and negative amplitude values. Typically used to entrain cortical oscillations at a frequency of intrinsic cortical oscillations, as measured by EEG.

Transcranial direct current stimulation (tDCS) A tES method that involves passing a current of a fixed amplitude between electrodes for a set duration of time, typically 5–15 minutes.

Transcranial electrical stimulation (tES) A neurostimulation technique that involves passing a relatively weak electrical current between two or more electrodes placed on the scalp. Can make stimulated neurons more or less excitable. Often referred to as 'neuromodulation' rather than 'neurostimulation' to reflect the relatively weaker effects of tES relative to TMS.

Transcranial magnetic stimulation (TMS) A neurostimulation technique that creates a large and very brief electrical current in the brain via electromagnetic induction.

Transcranial random noise stimulation (tRNS) A tES method that involves passing a current whose amplitude varies randomly from time point to time point, typically 1000 or more times per second, for a period of several minutes. Effects are generally similar to tCDS, but may be stronger and/or longer-lasting.

Transition band In describing a filter response, the transition band is the range of frequencies that are partially attenuated, in between frequencies that are not attenuated, and those that are maximally attenuated. Also called 'roll-off'.

Transverse component In MRI, the size of the NMV in the transverse plane. Because the readout coil of an MRI system is in the transverse plane, the transverse component determines the magnitude of the recorded MRI signal.

Transverse plane In MRI, the plane perpendicular to the longitudinal plane.

TS See 'test stimulus'.

Tuft A dense area of dendrites on a neuron

Variable In experimentation, a specific, well-defined dimension or property that can have different values.

Variance Difference, or variability. Typically used to refer to the fact that measurements of a dependent variable are not all the same. Experimental variance generally refers to variance that is attributable to experimental manipulations (such as different levels of an independent variable). 'Random' variance usually refers to variance that can be attributed to random selection of samples from a population. 'Unexplained' variance refers to variance that is not explained by experimental manipulations or other known causes.

Vasoconstriction A decrease in the diameter of blood vessels, resulting in reduced blood flow.

Vasodilation An increase in the diameter of blood vessels, increasing blood flow. Opposite to vasoconstriction.

VBCT See 'voxel-based cortical thickness'.

VBM See 'voxel-based morphometry'.

Verbal response A response, such as in behavioural research, consisting of one or more words.

Vertex (graph theory) See 'node'.

Vertex (of head) The point at the top of the head that is half-way between the nasion and inion along the anterior–posterior dimension, and between the peri-auricular points along the left–right dimension. In the International 10–10 System, this is electrode location Cz.

Vertex (tessellation) A tessellated surface is represented as a set of triangles, whose corners (meeting points of edges) are called vertices.

Verum A term used in NIBS to refer to real, or 'true' stimulation, as contrasted with sham (fake) stimulation.

Virtual electrode A theoretical construct used to describe the data derived for a specific spatial location in the brain, from source localization such as beamforming.

Voxel Volume element – the three-dimensional equivalent to pixels. Voxels are the units of data in volumetric neuroimaging data such as MRI, and source-localized EEG and MEG.

Voxel-based cortical thickness (VBCT) A morphometric method aimed at characterizing cortical thickness. Analysis is performed using data in 3D volumetric (voxel-based) format. Contrast with surface-based cortical thickness.

Voxel-based lesion-symptom mapping (VLSM) A technique for relating patterns of brain damage to cognitive or behavioural deficits. Structural MRI scans are used to delineate the extent of a lesion (brain damage) in each of a sample of patients, and the areas where lesions most consistently correlate with scores on a particular cognitive or behavioural test are identified.

Voxel-based morphometry (VBM) A computational neuroanatomy approach aimed at detecting differences in the intensity of structural MR images on a voxel-by-voxel basis. Most commonly applied to grey matter, where it is referred to as a measure of 'grey-matter concentration'.

Waveguide A metal tube whose diameter-to-length ratio is designed to prevent electromagnetic fields from passing through it. Commonly used as a way of passing cables and the beam from a video projector into a magnetically shielded room.

Wavelet A short-duration oscillating waveform with a specific frequency, and an amplitude that varies over time, starting and ending with zero amplitude. Often used in time-frequency analysis.

White matter Areas of the brain composed primarily of myelinated axons. The term is often applied specifically to the part of the brain between the cerebral cortex and midbrain structures, which contains fibres connecting different cortical areas as well as fibres connecting the cortex to other brain regions such as the thalamus and basal ganglia. However, white matter exists in other brain structures such as the cerebellum. So called because when stained with formalin, or viewed in a T1-weighted MR image, this tissue appears white in colour.

Within-subjects design An experimental design in which results are compared between different experimental conditions, within the same individuals. Put another way, each individual in the study experiences each level of a variable that is manipulated within-subjects.

References

Adrian, E.D., & Matthews, B.H.C. (1934). The interpretation of potential waves in the cortex. *The Journal of Physiology*, *81*(4), 440–471. http://doi.org/10.1113/jphysiol.1934.sp003147

Aguirre, G.K., Zarahn, E., & D'esposito, M. (1998). The variability of human, BOLD hemodynamic responses. *NeuroImage*, *8*(4), 360–369. http://doi.org/10.1006/nimg.1998.0369

Alekseichuk, I., Turi, Z., de Lara, G.A., Antal, A., & Paulus, W. (2016). Spatial working memory in humans depends on theta and high gamma synchronization in the prefrontal cortex. *Current Biology*, *26*(12), 1513–1521. http://doi.org/10.1016/j.cub.2016.04.035

Amassian, V.E., Cracco, R.Q., Maccabee, P.J., Cracco, J.B., Rudell, A., & Eberle, L. (1989). Suppression of visual perception by magnetic coil stimulation of human occipital cortex. *Electroencephalography and Clinical Neurophysiology/Evoked Potentials Section*, *74*(6), 458–462. http://doi.org/10.1016/0168-5597(89)90036-1

Amassian, V.E., Cracco, R.Q., Maccabee, P.J., Cracco, J.B., Rudell, A.P., & Eberle, L. (1993). Unmasking human visual perception with the magnetic coil and its relationship to hemispheric asymmetry. *Brain Research*, *605*(2), 312–316.

American Clinical Neurophysiology Society (2006). Guideline 5: Guidelines for standard electrode position nomenclature. *American Journal of Electroneurodiagnostic Technology*, *46*(3), 222–225.

Ammann, C., Lindquist, M.A., & Celnik, P.A. (2017). Response variability of different anodal transcranial direct current stimulation intensities across multiple sessions. *Brain Stimulation*, *10*(4), 757–763. http://doi.org/10.1016/j.brs.2017.04.003

Amunts, K., & Zilles, K. (2015). Architectonic mapping of the human brain beyond Brodmann. *Neuron*, *88*(6), 1086–1107. http://doi.org/10.1016/j.neuron.2015.12.001

Amunts, K., Schleicher, A., Bürgel, U., Mohlberg, H., Uylings, H.B.M., & Zilles, K. (1999). Broca's region revisited: Cytoarchitecture and intersubject variability. *Journal of Comparative Neurology*, *412*(2), 319–341. http://doi.org/10.1002/(SICI)1096-9861(19990920)412:2<319::AID-CNE10>3.0.CO;2-7

Amunts, K., Schleicher, A., & Zilles, K. (2007). Cytoarchitecture of the cerebral cortex – more than localization. *NeuroImage*, *37*(4), 1061–1065. http://doi.org/10.1016/j.neuroimage.2007.02.037

Anderson, S.F., Kelley, K., & Maxwell, S.E. (2017). Sample-size planning for more accurate statistical power: A method adjusting sample effect sizes for publication bias and uncertainty. *Psychological Science*, *28*(11), 1547–1562. http://doi.org/10.1177/0956797617723724

Andersson, J.L.R., Jenkinson, M., & Smith, S. (2007). *Non-linear registration aka Spatial normalisation*, FMRIB Technical Report TR07JA2 (pp. 1–22). Oxford: FMRIB.

Anonymous (2005). How volunteering for an MRI scan changed my life. *Nature, 434*(7029), 17. http://doi.org/10.1038/434017a

Antal, A., & Herrmann, C.S. (2016). Transcranial alternating current and random noise stimulation: Possible mechanisms. *Neural Plasticity, 2016*(19), 1–12. http://doi.org/10.1155/2016/3616807

Antal, A., Nitsche, M.A., Kruse, W., Kincses, T.Z., Hoffmann, K.-P., & Paulus, W. (2004). Direct current stimulation over V5 enhances visuomotor coordination by improving motion perception in humans. *Journal of Cognitive Neuroscience, 16*(4), 521–527. http://doi.org/10.1162/089892904323057263

Antal, A., Keeser, D., Priori, A., Padberg, F., & Nitsche, M.A. (2015). Conceptual and procedural shortcomings of the systematic review 'Evidence that Transcranial Direct Current Stimulation (tDCS) generates little-to-no reliable neurophysiologic effect beyond MEP amplitude modulation in healthy human subjects: A systematic review' by Horvath and Co-workers. *Brain Stimulation, 8*(4), 846–849. http://doi.org/10.1016/j.brs.2015.05.010

Ashburner, J.T., & Friston, K.J. (2004). Morphometry. In R.S.J. Frackowiak, K.J. Friston, C.D. Frith, R.J. Dolan, C.J. Price, S. Zeki, J. Ashburner, & W. Penny (Eds.), *Human Brain Function* (pp. 707–722). London: Elsevier Academic Press.

Ashburner, J., & Friston, K. (2007). Voxel-based morphometry. In K. Friston, J. Ashburner, S. Kiebel, T. Nichols, & W. Penny (Eds.), *Statistical Parametric Mapping: The Methods* (pp. 92–98). Amsterdam: Elsevier. http://doi.org/10.1016/b978-012372560-8/50007-3

Attwell, D., & Iadecola, C. (2002). The neural basis of functional brain imaging signals. *Trends in Neurosciences, 25*(12), 621–625. http://doi.org/10.1016/S0166-2236(02)02264-6

Aubert-Broche, B., Evans, A.C., & Collins, L. (2006). A new improved version of the realistic digital brain phantom. *NeuroImage, 32*(1), 138–145. http://doi.org/10.1016/j.neuroimage.2006.03.052

Baillet, S. (2011). Electromagnetic brain mapping using MEG and EEG. *Oxford Handbooks Online*. Oxford University Press. http://doi.org/10.1093/oxfordhb/9780195342161.013.0007

Bandettini, P.A., Wong, E.C., Hinks, R.S., Tikofsky, R.S., & Hyde, J.S. (1992). Time course EPI of human brain function during task activation. *Magnetic Resonance in Medicine, 25*(2), 390–397. http://doi.org/10.1002/mrm.1910250220

Barnes, G.R., Hillebrand, A., Fawcett, I.P., & Singh, K.D. (2004). Realistic spatial sampling for MEG beamformer images. *Human Brain Mapping, 23*(2), 120–127. http://doi.org/10.1002/hbm.20047

Basser, P.J., Mattiello, J., & LeBihan, D. (1994). MR diffusion tensor spectroscopy and imaging. *Biophysical Journal, 66*(1), 259–267. http://doi.org/10.1016/S0006-3495(94)80775-1

Bates, E., Wilson, S.M., Saygin, A.P., Dick, F., Sereno, M.I., Knight, R.T., & Dronkers, N.F. (2003). Voxel-based lesion–symptom mapping. *Nature Neuroscience, 6*(5), 448–450. http://doi.org/10.1038/nn1050

Behrens, T., Johansen-Berg, H., & Woolrich, M.W. (2003). Non-invasive mapping of connections between human thalamus and cortex using diffusion imaging. *Nature Neuroscience, 6*(7), 750–757. http://doi.org/10.1038/nn1075

Benjamini, Y., & Hochberg, Y. (1995). Controlling the false discovery rate: A practical and powerful approach to multiple testing. *Journal of the Royal Statistical Society. Series*

B (Methodological), 57(1), 289–300. http://doi.org/10.2307/2346101?ref=search-gateway:f7cedf277de8a670ff5bf1859ff89ffb

Berger, H. (1929). Über das Elektrenkephalogramm des Menschen. *Archiv Für Psychiatrie Und Nervenkrankheiten*, 87(1), 527–570. http://doi.org/10.1007/BF01797193

Bernow, N., Yakushev, I., Landvogt, C., Buchholz, H.-G., Smolka, M.N., Bartenstein, P., Lieb, K., Gründer, G., Vernaleken, I., Schreckenberger, M., & Fehr, C. (2011). Dopamine D2/D3 receptor availability and venturesomeness. *Psychiatry Research: Neuroimaging*, 193(2), 80–84. http://doi.org/10.1016/j.pscychresns.2011.01.011

Bestmann, S., & Ward, N. (2017). Are current flow models for transcranial electrical stimulation fit for purpose? *Brain Stimulation*, 10(4), 865–866. http://doi.org/10.1016/j.brs.2017.04.002

Bestmann, S., Ruff, C.C., Blakemore, C., Driver, J., & Thilo, K.V. (2007). Spatial attention changes excitability of human visual cortex to direct stimulation. *Current Biology*, 17(2), 134–139. http://doi.org/10.1016/j.cub.2006.11.063

Bikson, M., Datta, A., Rahman, A., & Scaturro, J. (2010). Electrode montages for tDCS and weak transcranial electrical stimulation: Role of 'return' electrode's position and size. *Clinical Neurophysiology*, 121(12), 1976–1978. http://doi.org/10.1016/j.clinph.2010.05.020

Bikson, M., Grossman, P., Thomas, C., Zannou, A.L., Jiang, J., Adnan, T., et al. (2016). Safety of transcranial direct current stimulation: Evidence based update 2016. *Brain Stimulation*, 9(5), 641–661. http://doi.org/10.1016/j.brs.2016.06.004

Binder, J.R., Frost, J.A., Hammeke, T.A., Bellgowan, P.S.F., Rao, S.M., & Cox, R.W. (1999). Conceptual processing during the conscious resting state: A functional MRI study. *Journal of Cognitive Neuroscience*, 11(1), 80–93. http://doi.org/10.1162/089892999563265

Birn, R.M., Saad, Z.S., & Bandettini, P.A. (2001). Spatial heterogeneity of the nonlinear dynamics in the FMRI BOLD response. *NeuroImage*, 14(4), 817–826. http://doi.org/10.1006/nimg.2001.0873

Biswal, B., Yetkin, F.Z., Haughton, V.M., & Hyde, J.S. (1995). Functional connectivity in the motor cortex of resting human brain using echo-planar MRI. *Magnetic Resonance in Medicine*, 34(4), 537–541.

Boas, D.A., Elwell, C.E., Ferrari, M., & Taga, G. (2014). Twenty years of functional near-infrared spectroscopy: Introduction for the special issue. *NeuroImage*, 85(P1), 1–5. http://doi.org/10.1016/j.neuroimage.2013.11.033

Bode, S., Bennett, D., Sewell, D.K., Paton, B., Egan, G.F., Smith, P.L., & Murawski, C. (2018). Dissociating neural variability related to stimulus quality and response times in perceptual decision-making. *Neuropsychologia*, 111, 190–200. http://doi.org/10.1016/j.neuropsychologia.2018.01.040

Bortoletto, M., Pellicciari, M.C., Rodella, C., & Miniussi, C. (2015). The interaction with task-induced activity is more important than polarization: A tDCS study. *Brain Stimulation*, 8(2), 269–276. http://doi.org/10.1016/j.brs.2014.11.006

Boto, E., Holmes, N., Leggett, J., Roberts, G., Shah, V., Meyer, S.S., et al. (2018). Moving magnetoencephalography towards real-world applications with a wearable system. *Nature*, 555(7698), 1–20. http://doi.org/10.1038/nature26147

Boynton, G., Engel, S., Glover, G., & Heeger, D. (1996). Linear systems analysis of functional magnetic resonance imaging in human V1. *The Journal of Neuroscience, 16*(13).

Brigadoi, S., Ceccherini, L., Cutini, S., Scarpa, F., Scatturin, P., Selb, J., Gagnon, L., Boas, D.A., & Cooper, R.J. (2014). Motion artifacts in functional near-infrared spectroscopy: A comparison of motion correction techniques applied to real cognitive data. *NeuroImage, 85*(P1), 181–191. http://doi.org/10.1016/j.neuroimage.2013.04.082

Broca, P. (1865). Sur le faculté du langage articlué. *Bulletin De La Société d'Anthropologie, 6*, 337–393.

Brodmann, K. (1999). *Localization in the Cerebral Cortex* (*Vergleichende Lokalisationslehre der Grothirnrinde*) (L.J. Garey, Trans.). London: Imperial College Press.

Brookes, M.J., Vrba, J., Robinson, S.E., Stevenson, C.M., Peters, A.M., Barnes, G.R., Hillebrand, A., & Morris, P.G. (2008). Optimising experimental design for MEG beamformer imaging. *NeuroImage, 39*(4), 1788–1802. http://doi.org/10.1016/j.neuroimage.2007.09.050

Brookes, M.J., Zumer, J.M., Stevenson, C.M., Hale, J.R., Barnes, G.R., Vrba, J., & Morris, P.G. (2010). Investigating spatial specificity and data averaging in MEG. *NeuroImage, 49*(1), 525–538. http://doi.org/10.1016/j.neuroimage.2009.07.043

Brunoni, A.R., Nitsche, M.A., Bolognini, N., Bikson, M., Wagner, T., Merabet, L., et al. (2012). Clinical research with transcranial direct current stimulation (tDCS): Challenges and future directions. *Brain Stimulation, 5*(3), 175–195. http://doi.org/10.1016/j.brs.2011.03.002

Buckner, R.L., Koutstaal, W., Schacter, D.L., Dale, A.M., Rotte, M., & Rosen, B.R. (1998). Functional-anatomic study of episodic retrieval. II. Selective averaging of event-related fMRI trials to test the retrieval success hypothesis. *NeuroImage, 7*(3), 163–175. http://doi.org/10.1006/nimg.1998.0328

Burdach, K.F. (1819). *Vom Baue und Leben des Gehirns* (Vol. 1). Leipzig: Dyk'sche Buchhdl.

Button, K.S., Ioannidis, J.P.A., Mokrysz, C., Nosek, B.A., Flint, J., Robinson, E.S.J., & Munafò, M.R. (2013a). Confidence and precision increase with high statistical power. *Nature Reviews Neuroscience, 14*(8), 585–585. http://doi.org/10.1038/nrn3475-c4

Button, K.S., Ioannidis, J.P.A., Mokrysz, C., Nosek, B.A., Flint, J., Robinson, E.S.J., & Munafò, M.R. (2013b). Power failure: Why small sample size undermines the reliability of neuroscience. *Nature Reviews Neuroscience, 14*(5), 365–376. http://doi.org/10.1038/nrn3475

Buxton, R.B., Griffeth, V.E., Simon, A.B., Moradi, F., & Shmuel, A. (2014). Variability of the coupling of blood flow and oxygen metabolism responses in the brain: A problem for interpreting BOLD studies but potentially a new window on the underlying neural activity. *Frontiers in Neuroscience, 8*(8), 1510. http://doi.org/10.3389/fnins.2014.00139

Canadian Institutes of Health Research, Natural Sciences and Engineering Research Council of Canada, and Social Sciences and Humanities Research Council of Canada (2014). *Tri-Council Policy Statement: Ethical Conduct for Research Involving Humans* (TCPS). Ottawa, ON: Government of Canada.

Cash, R.F.H., Noda, Y., Zomorrodi, R., Radhu, N., Farzan, F., Rajji, T.K., Fitzgerald, P.B., Chen, R., Daskalakis, Z.J., & Blumberger, D.M. (2016). Characterization of glutamatergic and GABAA-mediated neurotransmission in motor and dorsolateral prefrontal cortex using paired-pulse TMS–EEG. *Neuropsychopharmacology, 42*(2), 502–511. http://doi.org/10.1038/npp.2016.133

Catani, M. (2011). The functional anatomy of white matter: From postmortem dissections to in vivo virtual tractography. In D.K. Jones (Ed.), *Diffusion MRI* (pp. 5–18). Oxford: Oxford University Press. http://doi.org/10.1093/med/9780195369779.003.0001

Chance, B. (1991). Optical method. *Annual Review of Biophysics and Biomolecular Structure*, *20*(1), 1–28. http://doi.org/10.1146/annurev.biophys.20.1.1

Chance, B., Zhuang, Z., UnAh, C., Alter, C., & Lipton, L. (1993). Cognition-activated low-frequency modulation of light absorption in human brain. *Proceedings of the National Academy of Sciences of the United States of America*, *90*(8), 3770–3774. http://doi.org/10.2307/2361827?refreqid=search-gateway:007b3734a243cd053969ba290e99e129

Chiarelli, A.M., Di Vacri, A., Romani, G.L., & Merla, A. (2013). Fast optical signal in visual cortex: Improving detection by General Linear Convolution Model. *NeuroImage*, *66*, 194–202. http://doi.org/10.1016/j.neuroimage.2012.10.047

Chiarelli, A.M., Romani, G.L., & Merla, A. (2014). Fast optical signals in the sensorimotor cortex: General Linear Convolution Model applied to multiple source–detector distance-based data. *NeuroImage*, *85*(P1), 245–254. http://doi.org/10.1016/j.neuroimage.2013.07.021

Cichy, R.M., Pantazis, D., & Oliva, A. (2014). Resolving human object recognition in space and time. *Nature Neuroscience*, *17*(3), 455–462. http://doi.org/10.1038/nn.3635

Clarkson, M.J., Cardoso, M.J., Ridgway, G.R., Modat, M., Leung, K.K., Rohrer, J.D., Fox, N.C., & Ourselin, S. (2011). A comparison of voxel and surface based cortical thickness estimation methods. *NeuroImage*, *57*(3), 856–865. http://doi.org/10.1016/j.neuroimage.2011.05.053

Cremers, H.R., Wager, T.D., & Yarkoni, T. (2017). The relation between statistical power and inference in fMRI. *PloS One*, *12*(11), e0184923–20. http://doi.org/10.1371/journal.pone.0184923

Cui, X., Bray, S., Bryant, D.M., Glover, G.H., & Reiss, A.L. (2011). A quantitative comparison of NIRS and fMRI across multiple cognitive tasks. *NeuroImage*, *54*(4), 2808–2821. http://doi.org/10.1016/j.neuroimage.2010.10.069

Dale, A.M., & Buckner, R.L. (1997). Selective averaging of rapidly presented individual trials using fMRI. *Human Brain Mapping*, *5*(5), 329–340. http://doi.org/10.1002/(SICI)1097-0193(1997)5:5<329::AID-HBM1>3.0.CO;2-5

Dale, A.M., Fischl, B., & Sereno, M.I. (1999). Cortical surface-based analysis. *NeuroImage*, *9*(2), 179–194. http://doi.org/10.1006/nimg.1998.0395

Dale, A.M., Liu, A.K., Fischl, B.R., Buckner, R.L., Belliveau, J.W., Lewine, J.D., & Halgren, E. (2000). Dynamic statistical parametric mapping: Combining fMRI and MEG for high-resolution imaging of cortical activity. *Neuron*, *26*(1), 55–67. http://doi.org/10.1016/S0896-6273(00)81138-1

Damoiseaux, J.S., Rombouts, S.A.R.B., Barkhof, F., Scheltens, P., Stam, C.J., Smith, S.M., & Beckmann, C.F. (2006). Consistent resting-state networks across healthy subjects. *Proceedings of the National Academy of Sciences of the United States of America*, *103*(37), 13848–13853. http://doi.org/10.2307/30050344?refreqid=search-gateway:be5a2a38816cbfea4df067a1749e8747

Datta, A., Bansal, V., Diaz, J., Patel, J., Reato, D., & Bikson, M. (2009). Gyri-precise head model of transcranial direct current stimulation: Improved spatial focality using a ring electrode versus conventional rectangular pad. *Brain Stimulation*, *2*(4), 201–207.e1. http://doi.org/10.1016/j.brs.2009.03.005

Davidson, D.J., & Indefrey, P. (2007). An inverse relation between event-related and time-frequency violation responses in sentence processing. *Brain Research*, *1158*, 81–92. http://doi.org/10.1016/j.brainres.2007.04.082

Davis, H., Davis, P.A., Loomis, A.L., Harvey, E.N., & Hobart, G. (1939). Electrical reactions of the human brain to auditory stimulation during sleep. *Journal of Neurophysiology*, *2*(6), 500–514. http://doi.org/10.1152/jn.1939.2.6.500

Davis, P.A. (1939). Effects of acoustic stimuli on the waking human brain. *Journal of Neurophysiology*, *2*(6), 494–499. http://doi.org/10.1152/jn.1939.2.6.494

De Luca, M., Beckmann, C.F., De Stefano, N., Matthews, P.M., & Smith, S.M. (2006). fMRI resting state networks define distinct modes of long-distance interactions in the human brain. *NeuroImage*, *29*(4), 1359–1367. http://doi.org/10.1016/j.neuroimage.2005.08.035

Dedoncker, J., Brunoni, A.R., Baeken, C., & Vanderhasselt, M.-A. (2016). A systematic review and meta-analysis of the effects of transcranial direct current stimulation (tDCS) over the dorsolateral prefrontal cortex in healthy and neuropsychiatric samples: Influence of stimulation parameters. *Brain Stimulation*, *9*(4), 501–517. http://doi.org/10.1016/j.brs.2016.04.006

Delorme, A., Sejnowski, T., & Makeig, S. (2007). Enhanced detection of artifacts in EEG data using higher-order statistics and independent component analysis. *NeuroImage*, *34*(4), 1443–1449. http://doi.org/10.1016/j.neuroimage.2006.11.004

Deng, Z.-D., Lisanby, S.H., & Peterchev, A.V. (2013). Electric field depth–focality tradeoff in transcranial magnetic stimulation: Simulation comparison of 50 coil designs. *Brain Stimulation*, *6*(1), 1–13. http://doi.org/10.1016/j.brs.2012.02.005

Dronkers, N.F., Plaisant, O., Iba-Zizen, M.T., & Cabanis, E.A. (2007). Paul Broca's historic cases: High resolution MR imaging of the brains of Leborgne and Lelong. *Brain*, *130*(5), 1432–1441. http://doi.org/10.1093/brain/awm042

Duecker, F., & Sack, A.T. (2015). Rethinking the role of sham TMS. *Frontiers in Psychology*, *6*. http://doi.org/10.3389/fpsyg.2015.00210

Economo, von, C., & Koskinas, G.N. (1925). *Die Cytoarchitektonik der Hirn- rinde des erwachsenen Menschen*. Vienna and Berlin: Julius Springer.

Eklund, A., Nichols, T.E., & Knutsson, H. (2016). Cluster failure: Why fMRI inferences for spatial extent have inflated false-positive rates. *Proceedings of the National Academy of Sciences*, *113*(28), 7900–7905. http://doi.org/10.1073/pnas.1602413113

Ellingson, L., Groisser, D., Osborne, D., Patrangenaru, V., & Schwartzman, A. (2016). Nonparametric bootstrap of sample means of positive-definite matrices with an application to diffusion-tensor-imaging data analysis. *Communications in Statistics – Simulation and Computation*, 0–0. http://doi.org/10.1080/03610918.2015.1136413

Ellison-Wright, I., & Bullmore, E. (2009). Meta-analysis of diffusion tensor imaging studies in schizophrenia. *Schizophrenia Research*, *108*(1–3), 3–10. http://doi.org/10.1016/j.schres.2008.11.021

Fabiani, M., Gordon, B.A., Maclin, E.L., Pearson, M.A., Brumback-Peltz, C.R., Low, K.A., McAuley, E., Sutton, B.P., Kramer, A.F., & Gratton, G. (2014). Neurovascular coupling in normal aging: A combined optical, ERP and fMRI study. *NeuroImage*, *85*, 592–607. http://doi.org/10.1016/j.neuroimage.2013.04.113

Farwell, L.A., & Donchin, E. (1991). The truth will out: Interrogative polygraphy ('lie detection') with event-related brain potentials. *Psychophysiology*, *28*(5), 531–547. http://doi.org/10.1111/j.1469-8986.1991.tb01990.x

Fechner, G. (1966). *Elements of Psychophysics* (D.H. Howes & E.G. Boring, Eds.; H.E. Adler, Trans.). New York: Holt, Rinehart & Winston.

Fertonani, A., & Miniussi, C. (2017). Transcranial electrical stimulation. *The Neuroscientist*, *23*(2), 109–123. http://doi.org/10.1177/1073858416631966

Fertonani, A., Pirulli, C., & Miniussi, C. (2011). Random noise stimulation improves neuroplasticity in perceptual learning. *The Journal of Neuroscience*, *31*(43), 15416–15423. http://doi.org/10.1523/JNEUROSCI.2002-11.2011

Feurra, M., Paulus, W., Walsh, V., & Kanai, R. (2011). Frequency specific modulation of human somatosensory cortex. *Frontiers in Psychology*, *2*, 1–6. http://doi.org/10.3389/fpsyg.2011.00013

Fischl, B., & Dale, A.M. (2000). Measuring the thickness of the human cerebral cortex from magnetic resonance images. *Proceedings of the National Academy of Sciences*, *97*(20), 11050–11055. http://doi.org/10.1073/pnas.200033797

Fischl, B., Sereno, M.I., Tootell, R.B.H., & Dale, A.M. (1999). High-resolution intersubject averaging and a coordinate system for the cortical surface. *Human Brain Mapping*, *8*(4), 272–284. http://doi.org/10.1002/(SICI)1097-0193(1999)8:4<272::AID-HBM10>3.0.CO;2-4

Fitzgerald, P.P.B., Daskalakis, Z.J., Hoy, K., Farzan, F., Upton, D.J., Cooper, N.R., & Maller, J.J. (2008). Cortical inhibition in motor and non-motor regions: A combined TMS-EEG study. *Clinical EEG and Neuroscience*, *39*(3), 112–117. http://doi.org/10.1177/155005940803900304

Formisano, E., De Martino, F., Bonte, M., & Goebel, R. (2008). 'Who' is saying 'what?': Brain-based decoding of human voice and speech. *Science*, *322*(5903), 970–973. http://doi.org/10.1126/science.1164318

Forsberg, A., Engler, H., Almkvist, O., Blomquist, G., Hagman, G., Wall, A., Ringheim, A., Langstrom, B., & Nordberg, A. (2008). PET imaging of amyloid deposition in patients with mild cognitive impairment. *Neurobiology of Aging*, *29*(10), 1456–1465. http://doi.org/10.1016/j.neurobiolaging.2007.03.029

Fox, M.D., Vincent, J.L., Van Essen, D.C., & Raichle, M.E. (2005). The human brain is intrinsically organized into dynamic, anticorrelated functional networks. *Proceedings of the National Academy of Sciences of the United States of America*, *102*(27), 9673–9678. http://doi.org/10.1073/pnas.0504136102

Fox, P.T., Raichle, M.E., Mintun, M.A., & Dence, C. (1988). Nonoxidative glucose consumption during focal physiologic neural activity. *Science*, *241*(4864), 462–464.

Friston, K.J. (2011). Functional and effective connectivity: A review. *Brain Connectivity*, *1*(1), 13–36. http://doi.org/10.1089/brain.2011.0008

Friston, K.J., Frith, C.D., Liddle, P.F., & Frackowiak, R.S.J. (1991). Comparing functional (PET) images: The assessment of significant change. *Journal of Cerebral Blood Flow & Metabolism*, *11*(4), 690–699. http://doi.org/10.1038/jcbfm.1991.122

Friston, K.J., Zarahn, E., Josephs, O., Henson, R.N.A., & Dale, A.M. (1999). Stochastic designs in event-related fMRI. *NeuroImage*, *10*(5), 607–619. http://doi.org/10.1006/nimg.1999.0498

Friston, K.J., Harrison, L., & Penny, W. (2003). Dynamic causal modelling. *NeuroImage*, *19*(4), 1273–1302. http://doi.org/10.1016/S1053-8119(03)00202-7

Gammaitoni, L., Hänggi, P., Jung, P., & Marchesoni, F. (1998). Stochastic resonance. *Reviews of Modern Physics*, *70*(1), 223–287.

Gazzaniga, M.S. (1989). Editor's note. *Journal of Cognitive Neuroscience*, *1*(1), 2.

Gazzaniga, M.S. (2018). The consciousness instinct. *Cognitive Neuroscience Society Annual Meeting*, 24 March, Boston, MA.

Genovese, C.R., Lazar, N., & Nichols, T. (2002). Thresholding of statistical maps in functional neuroimaging using the false discovery rate. *NeuroImage, 15*(4), 870–878. http://doi.org/10.1006/nimg.2001.1037

Glasser, M.F., Coalson, T.S., Robinson, E.C., Hacker, C.D., Harwell, J., Yacoub, E., et al. (2016). A multi-modal parcellation of human cerebral cortex. *Nature, 536*(7615), 171–178. http://doi.org/10.1038/nature18933

Gowen, E., & Miall, R.C. (2007). Differentiation between external and internal cuing: An fMRI study comparing tracing with drawing. *NeuroImage, 36*(2), 396–410. http://doi.org/10.1016/j.neuroimage.2007.03.005

Gramfort, A. (2013). MEG and EEG data analysis with MNE-Python. *Frontiers in Neuroscience, 7*, 267. http://doi.org/10.3389/fnins.2013.00267

Grant, S., Aitchison, T., Henderson, E., Christie, J., Zare, S., Murray, J.M., & Dargie, H. (1999). A comparison of the reproducibility and the sensitivity to change of visual analogue scales, Borg scales, and Likert scales in normal subjects during submaximal exercise. *Chest, 116*(5), 1208–1217. http://doi.org/10.1378/chest.116.5.1208

Gratton, G. (2010). Fast optical imaging of human brain function. *Frontiers in Human Neuroscience*, 1–9. http://doi.org/10.3389/fnhum.2010.00052

Gratton, G., Coles, M.G.H., & Donchin, E. (1983). A new method for off-line removal of ocular artifact. *Electroencephalography and Clinical Neurophysiology, 55*(4), 468–484.

Grill-Spector, K., Kushnir, T., Edelman, S., Avidan, G., Itzchak, Y., & Malach, R. (1999). Differential processing of objects under various viewing conditions in the human lateral occipital complex. *Neuron, 24*(1), 187–203. http://doi.org/10.1016/s0896-6273(00)80832-6

Groppe, D.M., Urbach, T.P., & Kutas, M. (2011). Mass univariate analysis of event-related brain potentials/fields I: A critical tutorial review. *Psychophysiology, 48*(12), 1711–1725. http://doi.org/10.1111/j.1469-8986.2011.01273.x

Gross, J., Kujala, J., Hamalainen, M., Timmermann, L., Schnitzler, A., & Salmelin, R. (2001). Dynamic imaging of coherent sources: Studying neural interactions in the human brain. *Proceedings of the National Academy of Sciences, 98*(2), 694–699. http://doi.org/10.1073/pnas.98.2.694

Guleyupoglu, B., Schestatsky, P., Edwards, D., Fregni, F., & Bikson, M. (2013). Classification of methods in transcranial electrical stimulation (tES) and evolving strategy from historical approaches to contemporary innovations. *Journal of Neuroscience Methods, 219*(2), 297–311. http://doi.org/10.1016/j.jneumeth.2013.07.016

Hagler, D. J., Jr., Halgren, E., Martinez, A., Huang, M., Hillyard, S. A., & Dale, A. M. (2009). Source estimates for MEG/EEG visual evoked responses constrained by multiple, retinotopically-mapped stimulus locations. *Human Brain Mapping, 30*(4), 1290–1309. http://doi.org/10.1002/hbm.20597

Hallinan, D., Friedewald, M., Shutz, P., & de Hert, P. (2014). Neurodata and neuroprivacy: Data protection outdated? *Surveillance and Society, 12*(1), 55–72.

Handwerker, D.A., Ollinger, J.M., & D'Esposito, M. (2004). Variation of BOLD hemodynamic responses across subjects and brain regions and their effects on statistical analyses. *NeuroImage, 21*(4), 1639–1651. http://doi.org/10.1016/j.neuroimage.2003.11.029

Handwerker, D.A., Gonzalez-Castillo, J., D'Esposito, M., & Bandettini, P.A. (2012). The continuing challenge of understanding and modeling hemodynamic variation in fMRI. *NeuroImage, 62*(2), 1017–1023. http://doi.org/10.1016/j.neuroimage.2012.02.015

Hansen, P.C., Kringelbach, M., & Salmelin, R. (2010). *MEG: An Introduction to Methods*. Oxford: Oxford University Press.

Hanson, L.G. (2008). Is quantum mechanics necessary for understanding magnetic resonance? *Concepts in Magnetic Resonance Part A, 32A*(5), 329–340. http://doi.org/10.1002/cmr.a.20123

Hassanpour, M.S., White, B.R., Eggebrecht, A.T., Ferradal, S.L., Snyder, A.Z., & Culver, J.P. (2014). Statistical analysis of high density diffuse optical tomography. *NeuroImage, 85*(P1), 104–116. http://doi.org/10.1016/j.neuroimage.2013.05.105

Hasson, U., Furman, O., Clark, D., Dudai, Y., & Davachi, L. (2008). Enhanced intersubject correlations during movie viewing correlate with successful episodic encoding. *Neuron, 57*(3), 452–462. http://doi.org/10.1016/j.neuron.2007.12.009

Haxby, J.V., Gobbini, M.I., Furey, M.L., Ishai, A., Schouten, J.L., & Pietrini, P. (2001). Distributed and overlapping representations of faces and objects in ventral temporal cortex. *Science, 293*(5539), 2425–2430. http://doi.org/10.2307/3084889?refreqid=-search-gateway:fc9d250aa6567c01598b2f4e7abf24d5

Haxby, J.V., Guntupalli, J.S., Connolly, A.C., Halchenko, Y.O., Conroy, B.R., Gobbini, M.I., Hanke, M., & Ramadge, P.J. (2011). A common, high-dimensional model of the representational space in human ventral temporal cortex. *Neuron, 72*(2), 404–416. http://doi.org/10.1016/j.neuron.2011.08.026

Hebb, D.O. (1949). *The Organization of Behavior*. New York: John Wiley & Sons.

Heckman, G.M., Bouvier, S.E., Carr, V.A., Harley, E.M., Cardinal, K.S., & Engel, S.A. (2007). Nonlinearities in rapid event-related fMRI explained by stimulus scaling. *NeuroImage, 34*(2), 651–660. http://doi.org/10.1016/j.neuroimage.2006.09.038

Henson, R. (2006). Efficient experimental design for fMRI. In W.D. Penny, K. Friston, J. Ashburner, S. Kiebel, & T. Nichols (Eds.), *Statistical Parametric Mapping* (pp. 193–210). Amsterdam: Elsevier. http://doi.org/10.1016/b978-012372560-8/50015-2

Herculano-Houzel, S. (2009). The human brain in numbers: A linearly scaled-up primate brain. *Frontiers in Human Neuroscience, 3*, 1–11. http://doi.org/10.3389/neuro.09.031.2009

Herdman, A.T., Wollbrink, A., Chau, W., Ishii, R., Ross, B., & Pantev, C. (2003). Determination of activation areas in the human auditory cortex by means of synthetic aperture magnetometry. *NeuroImage, 20*(2), 995–1005. http://doi.org/10.1016/s1053-8119(03)00403-8

Hermann, R.C., Dorwart, R.A., Hoover, C.W., & Brody, J. (1995). Variation in ECT use in the United States. *American Journal of Psychiatry, 152*(6), 869–875. http://doi.org/10.1176/ajp.152.6.869

Hill, A.T., Fitzgerald, P.B., & Hoy, K.E. (2016). Effects of anodal transcranial direct current stimulation on working memory: A systematic review and meta-analysis of findings from healthy and neuropsychiatric populations. *Brain Stimulation, 9*(2), 197–208. http://doi.org/10.1016/j.brs.2015.10.006

Hillebrand, A., & Barnes, G.R. (2002). A quantitative assessment of the sensitivity of whole-head MEG to activity in the adult human cortex. *NeuroImage, 16*(3), 638–650. http://doi.org/10.1006/nimg.2002.1102

Hillebrand, A., & Barnes, G.R. (2003). The use of anatomical constraints with MEG beamformers. *NeuroImage*, *20*(4), 2302–2313. http://doi.org/10.1016/j.neuroimage.2003.07.031

Hillebrand, A., & Barnes, G.R. (2005). Beamformer analysis of MEG Data. *International Review of Neurobiology*, *68*, 149–171. http://doi.org/10.1016/S0074-7742(05)68006-3

Hillyard, S.A., & Anllo-Vento, L. (1998). Event-related brain potentials in the study of visual selective attention. *Proceedings of the National Academy of Sciences of the United States of America*, *95*(3), 781–787. http://doi.org/10.2307/44189?refreqid=search-gateway:118e8442b34d4cc7704dd70d61f8ba10

Hillyard, S.A., Hink, R.F., Schwent, V.L., & Picton, T.W. (1973). Electrical signs of selective attention in the human Brain. *Science*, *182*(4108), 177–180. http://doi.org/10.1126/science.182.4108.177

Hoge, R.D., Atkinson, J., Gill, B., Crelier, G.R., Marrett, S., & Pike, G.B. (1999). Linear coupling between cerebral blood flow and oxygen consumption in activated human cortex. *Proceedings of the National Academy of Sciences of the United States of America*, *96*(16), 9403–9408.

Hogenboom, M. (2014, August 24). Warning over electrical brain stimulation. *BBC News*, 24 August. Available at: www.bbc.com/news/health-27343047 (accessed 11 December 2017).

Holmes, C.J., Hoge, R., Collins, L., Woods, R., Toga, A.W., & Evans, A.C. (1998). Enhancement of MR images using registration for signal averaging. *Journal of Computer Assisted Tomography*, *22*(2), 324–333. http://doi.org/10.1097/00004728-199803000-00032

Honey, C.J., Kötter, R., Breakspear, M., & Sporns, O. (2007). Network structure of cerebral cortex shapes functional connectivity on multiple time scales. *Proceedings of the National Academy of Sciences*, *104*(24), 10240–10245. http://doi.org/10.1073/pnas.0701519104

Horner, A.J., & Andrews, T.J. (2009). Linearity of the fMRI response in category-selective regions of human visual cortex. *Human Brain Mapping*, *30*(8), 2628–2640. http://doi.org/10.1002/hbm.20694

Horvath, J.C., Forte, J.D., & Carter, O. (2015). Quantitative review finds no evidence of cognitive effects in healthy populations from single-session transcranial direct current stimulation (tDCS). *Brain Stimulation*, *8*(3), 535–550. http://doi.org/10.1016/j.brs.2015.01.400

Huang, Y., Liu, A.A., Lafon, B., Friedman, D., Dayan, M., Wang, X., Bikson, M., Doyle, W.K., Devinsky, O. & Parra, L.C. (2017). Measurements and models of electric fields in the in vivo human brain during transcranial electric stimulation. *eLife*, *6*(e18834), 1–27. http://doi.org/10.7554/eLife.18834.001

Huang, Y.-Z., Sommer, M., Thickbroom, G., Hamada, M., Pascual-Leonne, A., Paulus, W., Classen, J., Peterchev, A.V., Zangen, A., & Ugawa, Y. (2009). Consensus: New methodologies for brain stimulation. *Brain Stimulation*, *2*(1), 2–13. http://doi.org/10.1016/j.brs.2008.09.007

Hubbard, P.L., & Parker, G.J.M. (2009). Validation of tractography. In H. Johansen-Berg & T.E.J. Behrens (Eds.), *Diffusion MRI* (pp. 353–375). Amsterdam: Elsevier Inc. http://doi.org/10.1016/B978-0-12-374709-9.00016-X

Huettel, S.A., Obembe, O.O., Song, A.W., & Woldorff, M.G. (2004). The BOLD fMRI refractory effect is specific to stimulus attributes: Evidence from a visual motion paradigm. *NeuroImage*, *23*(1), 402–408. http://doi.org/10.1016/j.neuroimage.2004.04.031

Huettel, S., Song, A., & McCarthy, G. (2014). *Functional Magnetic Resonance Imaging*, 3rd Edition. Sinauer Associates.

Hutton, C., De Vita, E., Ashburner, J.T., Deichmann, R., & Turner, R. (2008). Voxel-based cortical thickness measurements in MRI. *NeuroImage*, *40*(4), 1701–1710. http://doi.org/10.1016/j.neuroimage.2008.01.027

Hutton, C., Draganski, B., Ashburner, J.T., & Weiskopf, N. (2009). A comparison between voxel-based cortical thickness and voxel-based morphometry in normal aging. *NeuroImage*, *48*(2), 371–380. http://doi.org/10.1016/j.neuroimage.2009.06.043

Hyman, S.E. (2011). Cognitive enhancement: Promises and perils. *Neuron*, *69*(4), 595–598. http://doi.org/10.1016/j.neuron.2011.02.012

Ienca, M. (2015). Neuroprivacy, neurosecurity and brain-hacking: Emerging issues in neural engineering. *Bioethica Forum*, *8*(2), 51–53.

Illes, J., & Borgelt, E. (2009). Brain imaging: Incidental findings – in practice and in person. *Nature Reviews Neurology*, *5*(12), 643–644. http://doi.org/10.1038/nrneurol.2009.192

Illes, J., Desmond, J.E., Huang, L.F., Raffin, T.A., & Atlas, S.W. (2002). Ethical and practical considerations in managing incidental findings in functional magnetic resonance imaging. *Brain and Cognition*, *50*(3), 358–365. http://doi.org/10.1016/s0278-2626(02)00532-8

Ilmoniemi, R.J., & Kičić, D. (2009). Methodology for combined TMS and EEG. *Brain Topography*, *22*(4), 233–248. http://doi.org/10.1007/s10548-009-0123-4

Ioannidis, J.P.A. (2005). Why most published research findings are false. *PLoS Medicine*, *2*(8), e124–6. http://doi.org/10.1371/journal.pmed.0020124

Jbabdi, S., Lehman, J.F., Haber, S.N., & Behrens, T.E. (2013). Human and monkey ventral prefrontal fibers use the same organizational principles to reach their targets: Tracing versus tractography. *The Journal of Neuroscience*, *33*(7), 3190–3201. http://doi.org/10.1523/JNEUROSCI.2457-12.2013

Jöbsis, F.F. (1977). Noninvasive, infrared monitoring of cerebral and myocardial oxygen sufficiency and circulatory parameters. *Science*, *198*(4323), 1264–1267. http://doi.org/10.2307/1745848?ref=search-gateway:e61f0faec10c61a1be626b4b32aed82c

Jones, D., Symms, M., Cercignani, M., & Howard, R. (2005). The effect of filter size on VBM analyses of DT-MRI data. *NeuroImage*, *26*(2), 546–554. http://doi.org/10.1016/j.neuroimage.2005.02.013

Jones, T., & Rabiner, E.A. (2012). The development, past achievements, and future directions of brain PET. *Journal of Cerebral Blood Flow & Metabolism*, *32*(7), 1426–1454. http://doi.org/10.1038/jcbfm.2012.20

Jung, J., Bungert, A., Bowtell, R., & Jackson, S.R. (2016). Vertex stimulation as a control site for transcranial magnetic stimulation: A concurrent TMS/fMRI study. *Brain Stimulation*, *9*(1), 58–64. http://doi.org/10.1016/j.brs.2015.09.008

Jung, T.P., Humphries, C., Lee, T.W., Makeig, S., McKeown, M.J., Iragui, V., & Sejnowski, T.J. (1998). Removing electroencephalographic artifacts: Comparison between ICA and PCA (pp. 63–72). Presented at the Neural Networks for Signal Processing VIII. Proceedings of the 1998 IEEE Signal Processing Society Workshop (Cat. No.98TH8378), IEEE. http://doi.org/10.1109/nnsp.1998.710633

Kanwisher, N., McDermott, J., & Chun, M.M. (1997). The fusiform face area: A module in human extrastriate cortex specialized for face perception. *The Journal of Neuroscience*, *17*(11), 4302–4311. http://doi.org/10.1523/jneurosci.17-11-04302.1997

Kato, T., Kamei, A., Takashima, S., & Ozaki, T. (1993). Human visual cortical function during photic stimulation monitoring by means of near-infrared spectroscopy. *Journal of Cerebral Blood Flow & Metabolism*, *13*(3), 516–520. http://doi.org/10.1038/jcbfm.1993.66

Kay, K.N., Naselaris, T., Prenger, R.J., & Gallant, J.L. (2008). Identifying natural images from human brain activity. *Nature*, *452*(7185), 352–355. http://doi.org/10.1038/nature06713

Kekic, M., Boysen, E., Campbell, I.C., & Schmidt, U. (2016). A systematic review of the clinical efficacy of transcranial direct current stimulation (tDCS) in psychiatric disorders. *Journal of Psychiatric Research*, *74*(C), 70–86. http://doi.org/10.1016/j.jpsychires.2015.12.018

Koepp, M.J., Gunn, R.N., Lawrence, A.D., & Cunningham, V.J. (1998). Evidence for striatal dopamine release during a video game. *Nature*, *393*, 266–268.

Kriegeskorte, N., Mur, M., & Bandettini, P. (2008). Representational similarity analysis – connecting the branches of systems neuroscience. *Frontiers in Systems Neuroscience*, *2*, 1–28. http://doi.org/10.3389/neuro.06.004.2008

Kutas, M., & Hillyard, S.A. (1980). Reading senseless sentences: Brain potentials reflect semantic incongruity. *Science*, *207*(4427), 203–205. http://doi.org/10.1126/science.7350657

Kwong, K.K., Belliveau, J.W., Chesler, D.A., Goldberg, I.E., Weisskoff, R.M., Poncelet, B.P., Kennedy, D.N., Hoppel, B.E., Cohen, M.S., Turner, R., et al. (1992). Dynamic magnetic resonance imaging of human brain activity during primary sensory stimulation. *Proceedings of the National Academy of Sciences of the United States of America*, *89*(12), 5675–5679. http://doi.org/10.2307/2359716?ref=search-gateway:8d542f9dc13d8ab9657f4631b8217b82

Lalancette, M., Quraan, M., & Cheyne, D. (2011). Evaluation of multiple-sphere head models for MEG source localization. *Phys Med Biol*, *56*(17), 5621–5635. http://doi.org/10.1088/0031-9155/56/17/010

Lashley, K.S. (1929). *Brain Mechanisms and Intelligence: A Quantitative Study of Injuries to the Brain*. Chicago: University of Chicago Press.

Lawes, I.N.C., Barrick, T.R., Murugam, V., Spierings, N., Evans, D.R., Song, M., & Clark, C.A. (2008). Atlas-based segmentation of white matter tracts of the human brain using diffusion tensor tractography and comparison with classical dissection. *NeuroImage*, *39*(1), 62–79. http://doi.org/10.1016/j.neuroimage.2007.06.041

Lefaucheur, J.-P., Antal, A., Ayache, S.S., Benninger, D.H., Brunelin, J., Cogiamanian, F., et al. (2016). Evidence-based guidelines on the therapeutic use of transcranial direct current stimulation (tDCS). *Clinical Neurophysiology*, *128*(1), 56–92. http://doi.org/10.1016/j.clinph.2016.10.087

Leyton, M. (2002). Amphetamine-induced increases in extracellular dopamine, drug wanting, and novelty seeking: A PET/[11C]Raclopride study in healthy men. *Neuropsychopharmacology*, *27*(6), 1027–1035. http://doi.org/10.1016/S0893-133X(02)00366-4

Limb, C.J., & Braun, A.R. (2008). Neural substrates of spontaneous musical performance: An fMRI study of jazz improvisation. *PloS One*, *3*(2), e1679. http://doi.org/10.1371/journal.pone.0001679

Lin, A.-L.L., Fox, P.T., Hardies, J., Duong, T.Q., & Gao, J.-H.H. (2010). Nonlinear coupling between cerebral blood flow, oxygen consumption, and ATP production in human visual cortex. *Proceedings of the National Academy of Sciences of the United States of America*, *107*(18), 8446–8451. http://doi.org/10.1073/pnas.0909711107

Lin, F.-H.H., Witzel, T., Ahlfors, S.P., Stufflebeam, S.M., Belliveau, J.W., & Hämäläinen, M.S. (2006). Assessing and improving the spatial accuracy in MEG source localization by depth-weighted minimum-norm estimates. *NeuroImage*, *31*(1), 160–171. http://doi.org/10.1016/j.neuroimage.2005.11.054

Logothetis, N.K., Pauls, J., Augath, M., Trinath, T., & Oeltermann, A. (2001). Neurophysiological investigation of the basis of the fMRI signal. *Nature*, *412*(6843), 150–157. http://doi.org/10.1038/35084005

López-Alonso, V., Cheeran, B., Río-Rodríguez, D., & Fernández-del-Olmo, M. (2014). Inter-individual variability in response to non-invasive brain stimulation paradigms. *Brain Stimulation*, *7*(3), 372–380. http://doi.org/10.1016/j.brs.2014.02.004

Luck, S.J. (2014). *An Introduction to the Event-Related Potential Technique* (2nd ed.). Cambridge, MA: MIT Press.

Luck, S.J., & Gaspelin, N. (2016). How to get statistically significant effects in any ERP experiment (and why you shouldn't). *Psychophysiology*, *54*(1), 146–157. http://doi.org/10.1111/psyp.12639

Mackay, C.E., Filippini, N., & Smith, S.M. (2009). Group comparison of resting-state FMRI data using multi-subject ICA and dual regression. *NeuroImage*, *47*(Suppl. 1), S148.

MacLeod, J., Stewart, B.M., Newman, A.J., & Arnell, K.M. (2017). Do emotion-induced blindness and the attentional blink share underlying mechanisms? An event-related potential study of emotionally arousing words. *Cognitive, Affective, and Behavioral Neuroscience*, *17*(3), 1–20. http://doi.org/10.3758/s13415-017-0499-7

Magaki, S.D., Williams, C.K., & Vinters, H.V. (2017). Glial function (and dysfunction) in the normal & ischemic brain. *Neuropharmacology*, *134*, 1–8. http://doi.org/10.1016/j.neuropharm.2017.11.009

Makeig, S., Bell, A.J., & Jung, T. (1996). Independent component analysis of electroencephalographic data. Presented at the Advances in Neural Information Processing Systems, Cambridge, MA: MIT Press.

Malonek, D., & Grinvald, A. (1996). Interactions between electrical activity and cortical microcirculation revealed by imaging spectroscopy: Implications for functional brain mapping. *Science*, *272*(5261), 551–554. http://doi.org/10.1126/science.272.5261.551

Mancuso, L.E., Ilieva, I.P., Hamilton, R.H., & Farah, M.J. (2016). Does transcranial direct current stimulation improve healthy working memory? A meta-analytic review. *Journal of Cognitive Neuroscience*, *28*(8), 1063–1089. http://doi.org/10.1162/jocn_a_00956

Mangun, G.R. (2013). *Cognitive Electrophysiology of Attention*. New York: Academic Press.

Mansfield, P. (2001). Multi-planar image formation using NMR spin echoes. *Journal of Physics C: Solid State Physics*, *10*(3), L55–L58. http://doi.org/10.1088/0022-3719/10/3/004

Marenco, S., Rawlings, R., Rohde, G.K., Barnett, A.S., Honea, R.A., Pierpaoli, C., & Weinberger, D. R. (2006). Regional distribution of measurement error in diffusion tensor imaging. *Psychiatry Research: Neuroimaging*, *147*(1), 69–78. http://doi.org/10.1016/j.pscychresns.2006.01.008

Mark, C.I., Mazerolle, E.L., & Chen, J.J. (2015). Metabolic and vascular origins of the BOLD effect: Implications for imaging pathology and resting-state brain function. *Journal of Magnetic Resonance Imaging*, *42*(2), 231–246. http://doi.org/10.1002/jmri.24786

Matheson, H., & Newman, A.J. (2008). *Race and structural encoding of faces* (Vol. 49). Presented at the Psychonomic Society annual meeting, Chicago.

Mathewson, K.E., Beck, D.M., Ro, T., Maclin, E.L., Low, K.A., Fabiani, M., & Gratton, G. (2014). Dynamics of alpha control: Preparatory suppression of posterior alpha oscillations by frontal modulators revealed with combined EEG and event-related optical signal. *Journal of Cognitive Neuroscience*, *26*(10), 2400–2415. http://doi.org/10.1162/jocn_a_00637

Matthews, P., Rabiner, E., Passchier, J., & Gunn, R. (2012). Positron emission tomography molecular imaging for drug development. *British Journal of Clinical Pharmacology*, *73*(2), 175–186. http://doi.org/10.1111/j.1365-2125.2011.04085.x

McCarthy, G., Luby, M., Gore, J., & Goldman-Rakic, P. (1997). Infrequent events transiently activate human prefrontal and parietal cortex as measured by functional MRI. *Journal of Neurophysiology*, *77*(3), 1630–1634. http://doi.org/10.1152/jn.1997.77.3.1630

McClure, S.M., Li, J., Tomlin, D., Cypert, K.S., Montague, L.M., & Montague, P.R. (2004). Neural correlates of behavioral preference for culturally familiar drinks. *Neuron*, *44*(2), 379–387. http://doi.org/10.1016/j.neuron.2004.09.019

Medvedev, A.V., Kainerstorfer, J.M., Borisov, S.V., & VanMeter, J. (2010). Fast optical signal in the prefrontal cortex correlates with EEG. In *XII Mediterranean Conference on Medical and Biological Engineering and Computing 2010*, 29, 631–634. Berlin, Heidelberg: Springer Berlin Heidelberg. http://doi.org/10.1007/978-3-642-13039-7_159

Menon, R.S. (2012). The great brain versus vein debate. *NeuroImage*, *62*(2), 970–974. http://doi.org/10.1016/j.neuroimage.2011.09.005

Menon, V., & Dougherty, R.F. (2009). Resting-state functional connectivity reflects structural connectivity in the default mode network. *Cerebral Cortex*, *19*(1), 72–78. http://doi.org/10.1093/cercor/bhn059

Meynert, T. (1885). *Psychiatrie. Klinik der Erkrankungen des Vorderhirns, begründet auf dessen Bau Leistungen und Ernährung*. Wien: Wilhelm Braumüller.

Miniussi, C., Harris, J.A., & Ruzzoli, M. (2013). Modelling non-invasive brain stimulation in cognitive neuroscience. *Neuroscience and Biobehavioral Reviews*, *37*(8), 1702–1712. http://doi.org/10.1016/j.neubiorev.2013.06.014

Mohlberg, H., Eickhoff, S.B., Schleicher, A., Zilles, K., & Amunts, K. (2012). *A New Processing Pipeline and Release of Cytoarchitectonic Probabilistic Maps – Jubrain*. Peking: Organization for Human Brain Mapping.

Moliadze, V., Antal, A., & Paulus, W. (2010a). Boosting brain excitability by transcranial high frequency stimulation in the ripple range. *The Journal of Physiology*, *588*(24), 4891–4904. http://doi.org/10.1113/jphysiol.2010.196998

Moliadze, V., Antal, A., & Paulus, W. (2010b). Electrode-distance dependent after-effects of transcranial direct and random noise stimulation with extracephalic reference electrodes. *Clinical Neurophysiology*, *121*(12), 2165–2171. http://doi.org/10.1016/j.clinph.2010.04.033

Moniz, E. (2006). Prefrontal leucotomy in the treatment of mental disorders. *American Journal of Psychiatry*, *93*(6), 1379–1385. http://doi.org/10.1176/ajp.93.6.1379

Mori, S. (2007). *Introduction to Diffusion Tensor Imaging*. Amsterdam: Elsevier.

Mori, S., & Zhang, J. (2006). Principles of diffusion tensor imaging and its applications to basic neuroscience research. *Neuron*, *51*(5), 527–539. http://doi.org/10.1016/j.neuron.2006.08.012

Morris, Z., Whiteley, W.N., Longstreth, W.T., Weber, F., Lee, Y.-C., Tsushima, Y., et al. (2009). Incidental findings on brain magnetic resonance imaging: Systematic review and meta-analysis. *British Medical Journal*, *339*, b3016. http://doi.org/10.1136/bmj.b3016

Mumford, J.A. (2012). A power calculation guide for fMRI studies. *Social Cognitive and Affective Neuroscience*, *7*(6), 738–742. http://doi.org/10.1093/scan/nss059

Mumford, J.A., & Nichols, T.E. (2008). Power calculation for group fMRI studies accounting for arbitrary design and temporal autocorrelation. *NeuroImage*, *39*(1), 261–268. http://doi.org/10.1016/j.neuroimage.2007.07.061

Mutanen, T.P., Kukkonen, M., Nieminen, J.O., Stenroos, M., Sarvas, J., & Ilmoniemi, R.J. (2016). Recovering TMS-evoked EEG responses masked by muscle artifacts. *NeuroImage*, *139*, 157–166. http://doi.org/10.1016/j.neuroimage.2016.05.028

Myers, N., Pasquini, L., Göttler, J., Grimmer, T., Koch, K., Ortner, M., et al. (2014). Within-patient correspondence of amyloid-β and intrinsic network connectivity in Alzheimer's disease. *Brain*, *137*(7), 2052–2064. http://doi.org/10.1093/brain/awu103

Newman, A.J., Ullman, M.T., Pancheva, R., Waligura, D.L., & Neville, H.J. (2007). An ERP study of regular and irregular English past tense inflection. *NeuroImage*, *34*(1), 435–445. http://doi.org/10.1016/j.neuroimage.2006.09.007

Newman, A.J., Supalla, T., Hauser, P.C., Newport, E.L., & Bavelier, D. (2010a). Prosodic and narrative processing in American Sign Language: An fMRI study. *NeuroImage*, *52*(2), 669–676. http://doi.org/10.1016/j.neuroimage.2010.03.055

Newman, A.J., Supalla, T., Hauser, P., Newport, E.L., & Bavelier, D. (2010b). Dissociating neural subsystems for grammar by contrasting word order and inflection. *Proceedings of the National Academy of Sciences of the United States of America*, *107*(16), 7539–7544. http://doi.org/10.1073/pnas.1003174107

Newman, A.J., Supalla, T., Fernandez, N., Newport, E.L., & Bavelier, D. (2015). Neural systems supporting linguistic structure, linguistic experience, and symbolic communication in sign language and gesture. *Proceedings of the National Academy of Sciences*, *112*(37), 201510527–11689. http://doi.org/10.1073/pnas.1510527112

Newman, A., Fawcett, J.M., Bodner, G.E., Stewart, B.M., Roddick, K., Lambert, A., & Krigolson, O. (2018). *Neural Correlates of the Production Effect: An fMRI Study* (p. 121). Presented at the Canadian Society for Brain, Behaviour, and Cognitive Science Annual Meeting, St. John's, NL.

Nichols, T.E., & Holmes, A.P. (2001). Nonparametric permutation tests for functional neuroimaging: A primer with examples. *Human Brain Mapping*, *15*, 1–25.

Nitsche, M.A., & Paulus, W. (2000). Excitability changes induced in the human motor cortex by weak transcranial direct current stimulation. *The Journal of Physiology*, *527*(3), 633–639. http://doi.org/10.1111/j.1469-7793.2000.t01-1-00633.x

Ogawa, S., Lee, T.M., Kay, A.R., & Tank, D.W. (1990a). Brain magnetic resonance imaging with contrast dependent on blood oxygenation. *Proceedings of the National Academy of Sciences of the United States of America*, *87*(24), 9868–9872. http://doi.org/10.2307/2356515?ref=search-gateway:f209f334f750128f094732bc2154bc7f

Ogawa, S., Lee, T.M., Nayak, A.S., & Glynn, P. (1990b). Oxygenation-sensitive contrast in magnetic resonance image of rodent brain at high magnetic fields. *Magnetic Resonance in Medicine*, *14*(1), 68–78. http://doi.org/10.1002/mrm.1910140108

Ogawa, S., Tank, D.W., Menon, R., Ellermann, J.M., Kim, S.-G., Merkle, H., & Ugurbil, K. (1992). Intrinsic signal changes accompanying sensory stimulation: Functional brain mapping with magnetic resonance imaging. *Proceedings of the National Academy of Sciences of the United States of America*, *89*(13), 5951–5955. http://doi.org/10.2307/2359470?ref=-search-gateway:af3e1ee65b7b1ad5403a0309232bbea7

Okada, F., Tokumitsu, Y., Hoshi, Y., & Tamura, M. (1993). Gender- and handedness-related differences of forebrain oxygenation and hemodynamics. *Brain Research, 601*(1), 337–342.

Opitz, A., Falchier, A., Yan, C.-G., Yeagle, E.M., Linn, G.S., Megevand, P., Theilscher, A., Ross, D.A., Milha., M.P., Mehta, A.D., & Schroeder, C.E. (2016). Spatiotemporal structure of intracranial electric fields induced by transcranial electric stimulation in humans and nonhuman primates. *Nature Reviews Neuroscience, 6*(1), 1–11. http://doi.org/10.1038/srep31236

Osterhout, L., & Holcomb, P.J. (1992). Event-related brain potentials elicited by syntactic anomaly. *Journal of Memory and Language, 31*(6), 785–806.

O'Reilly, J.X., Woolrich, M.W., Behrens, T.E.J., Smith, S.M., & Johansen-Berg, H. (2012). Tools of the trade: Psychophysiological interactions and functional connectivity. *Social Cognitive and Affective Neuroscience, 7*(5), 604–609. http://doi.org/10.1093/scan/nss055

Oswald, L.M., Wong, D.F., Zhou, Y., Kumar, A., Brasic, J., Alexander, M., Ye, W., Kuwabara, H., Hilton, J., & Wand, G.S. (2007). Impulsivity and chronic stress are associated with amphetamine-induced striatal dopamine release. *NeuroImage, 36*(1), 153–166. http://doi.org/10.1016/j.neuroimage.2007.01.055

Parkkonen, L., Fujiki, N., & Makela, J.P. (2009). Sources of auditory brainstem responses revisited: Contribution by magnetoencephalography. *Human Brain Mapping, 30*(6), 1772–1782. http://doi.org/10.1002/hbm.20788

Parks, N.A., Maclin, E.L., Low, K.A., Beck, D.M., Fabiani, M., & Gratton, G. (2012). Examining cortical dynamics and connectivity with simultaneous single-pulse transcranial magnetic stimulation and fast optical imaging. *NeuroImage, 59*(3), 2504–2510. http://doi.org/10.1016/j.neuroimage.2011.08.097

Pascual-Marqui, R.D. (2002). Standardized low-resolution brain electromagnetic tomography (sLORETA): Technical details. *Methods and Findings in Experimental and Clinical Pharmacology, 24*(Suppl D), 5–12.

Passow, S., Specht, K., Adamsen, T., Biermann, M., Brekke, N.A L., Craven, A., et al. (2015). Default-mode network functional connectivity is closely related to metabolic activity. *Human Brain Mapping, 36*(6), 2027–2038. http://doi.org/10.1002/hbm.22753

Paulus, W. (2011). Transcranial electrical stimulation (tES–tDCS; tRNS, tACS) methods. *Neuropsychological Rehabilitation, 21*(5), 602–617. http://doi.org/10.1080/09602011.2011.557292

Pellerin, L., & Magistretti, P.J. (1994). Glutamate uptake into astrocytes stimulates aerobic glycolysis: A mechanism coupling neuronal activity to glucose utilization. *Proceedings of the National Academy of Sciences of the United States of America, 91*(22), 10625–10629. http://doi.org/10.2307/2366082?ref=search-gateway:9fd62ef685c4bb946c5c9693ec54d33a

Peres, M.F.P., & Valena, M.M. (2011). Headache: Endocrinological aspects. In G. Nappi & M.A. Moscowitz (Eds.), *Handbook of Clinical Neurology* (1st ed., Vol. 97, pp. 717–737). Amsterdam: Elsevier B.V. http://doi.org/10.1016/S0072-9752(10)97060-7

Perry, G., Adjamian, P., Thai, N.J., Holliday, I.E., Hillebrand, A., & Barnes, G.R. (2011). Retinotopic mapping of the primary visual cortex – a challenge for MEG imaging of the human cortex. *European Journal of Neuroscience, 34*(4), 652–661. http://doi.org/10.1111/j.1460-9568.2011.07777.x

Petersen, S.E., Fox, P.T., Posner, M.I., Mintun, M., & Raichle, M.E. (1988). Positron emission tomographic studies of the cortical anatomy of single-word processing. *Nature*, *331*(6157), 585–589. http://doi.org/10.1038/331585a0

Polanía, R., Nitsche, M.A., Korman, C., Batsikadze, G., & Paulus, W. (2012). The importance of timing in segregated theta phase-coupling for cognitive performance. *Current Biology*, *22*(14), 1314–1318. http://doi.org/10.1016/j.cub.2012.05.021

Poldrack, R. (2006). Can cognitive processes be inferred from neuroimaging data? *Trends in Cognitive Sciences*, *10*(2), 59–63. http://doi.org/10.1016/j.tics.2005.12.004

Poldrack, R.A. (2011). Inferring mental states from neuroimaging data: From reverse inference to large-scale decoding. *Neuron*, *72*(5), 692–697. http://doi.org/10.1016/j.neuron.2011.11.001

Poldrack, R.A., Baker, C.I., Durnez, J., Gorgolewski, K.J., Matthews, P.M., Munafò, M.R., Nichols, T.E., Poline, J.-B., Vul, E., & Yarkoni, T. (2017). Scanning the horizon: Towards transparent and reproducible neuroimaging research. *Nature Reviews Neuroscience*, *18*(2), 1–12. http://doi.org/10.1038/nrn.2016.167

Posner, M.I., & Raichle, M.E. (1994). *Images of Mind*. New York: Scientific American Library.

Posner, M.I., Petersen, S.E., Fox, P.T., & Raichle, M.E. (1988). Localization of cognitive operations in the human brain. *Science*, *240*(4859), 1627–1631. http://doi.org/10.2307/1701013?ref=search-gateway:2e6f325b611909b9f966b8c686473023

Pouratian, N., Sheth, S.A., Martin, N.A., & Toga, A.W. (2003). Shedding light on brain mapping: Advances in human optical imaging. *Trends in Neurosciences*, *26*(5), 277–282. http://doi.org/10.1016/S0166-2236(03)00070-5

Price, C.J., & Friston, K.J. (1997). Cognitive conjunction: A new approach to brain activation experiments. *NeuroImage*, *5*(4), 261–270. http://doi.org/10.1006/nimg.1997.0269

Price, C., Wise, R., Ramsay, S., Friston, K., Howard, D., Patterson, K., & Frackowiak, R. (1992). Regional response differences within the human auditory cortex when listening to words. *Neuroscience Letters*, *146*(2), 179–182. http://doi.org/10.1016/0304-3940(92)90072-F

Prichard, J., Rothman, D., Novotny, E., Petroff, O., Kuwabara, T., Avison, M., Howseman, A., Hanstock, C., & Shulman, R. (1991). Lactate rise detected by 1H NMR in human visual cortex during physiologic stimulation. *Proceedings of the National Academy of Sciences of the United States of America*, *88*(13), 5829–5831. http://doi.org/10.2307/2357272?ref=search-gateway:a47b8e8f1136b7bc3e313cbc2a2c1de0

Priori, A., Berardelli, A., Rona, S., Accornero, N., & Manfredi, M. (1998). Polarization of the human motor cortex through the scalp. *Neuroreport*, *9*(10), 2257–2260. http://doi.org/10.1097/00001756-199807130-00020

Purves, D., Augustine, G.J., Fitzpatrick, D., Hall, W.C., LaMantia, A.-S., Mooney, R.D., Platt, M.L., & White, L.E. (2017). *Neuroscience* (6 ed.). Oxford: Oxford University Press.

Radhakrishnan, H., Vanduffel, W., Deng, H.P., Ekstrom, L., Boas, D.A., & Franceschini, M.A. (2009). Fast optical signal not detected in awake behaving monkeys. *NeuroImage*, *45*(2), 410–419.

Reil, J.C. (1809). Das balken-system oder die hirnschenkel-organisation im großen Gehrin. *Archiv Fur Die Physiologie*, *9*, 172–195.

Richardson, J.D., Fillmore, P., Datta, A., Truong, D., Bikson, M., & Fridriksson, J. (2014). Toward development of sham protocols for high-definition transcranial direct current stimulation (HD-tDCS). *NeuroRegulation*, *1*(1), 62–72. http://doi.org/10.15540/nr.1.1.62

Riggs, L., Moses, S.N., Bardouille, T., Herdman, A.T., Ross, B., & Ryan, J.D. (2009). A complementary analytic approach to examining medial temporal lobe sources using magnetoencephalography. *NeuroImage*, *45*(2), 627–642. http://doi.org/10.1016/j.neuroimage.2008.11.018

Robertson, F.C., Douglas, T.S., & Meintjes, E.M. (2010). Motion artifact removal for functional near infrared spectroscopy: A comparison of methods. *IEEE Transactions on Biomedical Engineering*, *57*(6), 1377–1387. http://doi.org/10.1109/TBME.2009.2038667

Romei, V., Chiappini, E., Hibbard, P.B., & Avenanti, A. (2016). Empowering reentrant projections from v5 to v1 boosts sensitivity to motion. *Current Biology*, *26*(16), 2155–2160. http://doi.org/10.1016/j.cub.2016.06.009

Rossi, S., Hallett, M., Rossini, P.M., & Pascual-Leone, A. (2009). Safety, ethical considerations, and application guidelines for the use of transcranial magnetic stimulation in clinical practice and research. *Clinical Neurophysiology*, *120*(12), 2008–2039. http://doi.org/10.1016/j.clinph.2009.08.016

Ruff, C.C., Blankenburg, F., & Bjoertomt, O. (2009). Hemispheric differences in frontal and parietal influences on human occipital cortex: Direct confirmation with concurrent TMS–fMRI. *Journal of Cognitive Neuroscience*, *21*(6), 1146–1161. http://doi.org/10.1162/jocn.2009.21097

Saggar, M., Quintin, E.-M., Kienitz, E., Bott, N.T., Sun, Z., Hong, W.-C., et al. (2015). Pictionary-based fMRI paradigm to study the neural correlates of spontaneous improvisation and figural creativity. *Nature Reviews Neuroscience*, *5*(1), 1–11. http://doi.org/10.1038/srep10894

Scholkmann, F., Kleiser, S., Metz, A.J., Zimmermann, R., Pavia, J.M., Wolf, U., & Wolf, M. (2014). A review on continuous wave functional near-infrared spectroscopy and imaging instrumentation and methodology. *NeuroImage*, *85*(P1), 6–27. http://doi.org/10.1016/j.neuroimage.2013.05.004

Simpson, W.A., Newman, A.J., & Aasland, W. (1997). Equivalent background speed in recovery from motion adaptation. *Journal of the Optical Society of America A*, *14*(1), 13–22.

Simpson, W.A., Braun, W.J., Bargen, C., & Newman, A.J. (2000). Identification of the eye–brain–hand system with point processes: A new approach to simple reaction time. *Journal of Experimental Psychology, Human Perception and Performance*, *26*(6), 1675–1690. http://doi.org/10.1037/0096-1523.26.6.1675

Smith, M.J., Keel, J.C., Greenberg, B.D., Adams, L.F., Schmidt, P.J., Rubinow, D.A., & Wassermann, E.M. (1999). Menstrual cycle effects on cortical excitability. *Neurology*, *53*(9), 2069.

Smith, M.J., Adams, L.F., Schmidt, P.J., Rubinow, D.R., & Wassermann, E.M. (2002). Effects of ovarian hormones on human cortical excitability. *Annals of Neurology*, *51*(5), 599–603. http://doi.org/10.1002/ana.10180

Snowball, A., Tachtsidis, I., Popescu, T., Thompson, J., Delazer, M., Zamarian, L., Zhu, T., & Cohen Kadosh, R. (2013). Long-term enhancement of brain function and cognition using cognitive training and brain stimulation. *Current Biology*, *23*(11), 987–992. http://doi.org/10.1016/j.cub.2013.04.045

Sporns, O., Tononi, G., & Kötter, R. (2005). The human connectome: A structural description of the human brain. *PLoS Computational Biology*, *1*(4), e42–7. http://doi.org/10.1371/journal.pcbi.0010042

Spruston, N. (2008). Pyramidal neurons: Dendritic structure and synaptic integration. *Nature Reviews Neuroscience*, *9*(3), 206–221. http://doi.org/10.1038/nrn2286

Stagg, C.J., & Nitsche, M.A. (2011). Physiological basis of transcranial direct current stimulation. *The Neuroscientist*, *17*(1), 37–53. http://doi.org/10.1177/1073858410386614

Stehling, M.K., Turner, R., & Mansfield, P. (1991). Echo-planar imaging: Magnetic resonance imaging in a fraction of a second. *Science*, *254*(5028), 43–50. http://doi.org/10.2307/2879537?ref=search-gateway:4742ead356ab8c1e8ea21e723b81e053

Steinbrink, J., Kempf, F.C.D., Villringer, A., & Obrig, H. (2005). The fast optical signal – robust or elusive when non-invasively measured in the human adult? *NeuroImage*, *26*(4), 996–1008. http://doi.org/10.1016/j.neuroimage.2005.03.006

Stoessi, A.J., Martin, W.W., McKeown, M.J., & Sossi, V. (2011). Advances in imaging in Parkinson's disease. *The Lancet Neurology*, *10*(11), 987–1001. http://doi.org/10.1016/S1474-4422(11)70214-9

Strafella, A.P., Paus, T., Barrett, J., & Dagher, A. (2001). Repetitive transcranial magnetic stimulation of the human prefrontal cortex induces dopamine release in the caudate nucleus. *The Journal of Neuroscience, 21*(RC157), 1–4.

Strangman, G.E., Li, Z., & Zhang, Q. (2013). Depth sensitivity and source-detector separations for near infrared spectroscopy based on the Colin27 brain template. *PloS One*, *8*(8), e66319–13. http://doi.org/10.1371/journal.pone.0066319

Summers, J.J., Kang, N., & Cauraugh, J.H. (2015). Does transcranial direct current stimulation enhance cognitive and motor functions in the ageing brain? A systematic review and meta- analysis. *Ageing Research Reviews*, *25*, 1–13. http://doi.org/10.1016/j.arr.2015.11.004

Takano, T., Tian, G.-F., Peng, W., Lou, N., Libionka, W., Han, X., & Nedergaard, M. (2006). Astrocyte-mediated control of cerebral blood flow. *Nature Neuroscience*, *9*(2), 260–267. http://doi.org/10.1038/nn1623

Talairach, J., & Tournoux, P. (1988). *Co-planar Stereotaxic Atlas of the Human Brain. Stuttgart*. New York: G. Thieme.

Tanner, D., Morgan-Short, K., & Luck, S.J. (2015). How inappropriate high-pass filters can produce artifactual effects and incorrect conclusions in ERP studies of language and cognition. *Psychophysiology*, *52*(8), 997–1009. http://doi.org/10.1111/psyp.12437

Tarkiainen, A., Liljeström, M., Seppä, M., & Salmelin, R. (2003). The 3D topography of MEG source localization accuracy: Effects of conductor model and noise. *Clinical Neurophysiology*, *114*(10), 1977–1992. http://doi.org/10.1016/s1388-2457(03)00195-0

Terney, D., Chaieb, L., Moliadze, V., Antal, A., & Paulus, W. (2008). Increasing human brain excitability by transcranial high-frequency random noise stimulation. *The Journal of Neuroscience*, *28*(52), 14147–14155. http://doi.org/10.1523/JNEUROSCI.4248-08.2008

The Committee on Science and Law (2005). Are your thoughts your own? 'Neuroprivacy' and the legal implications of brain imaging. *The Record*, *60*(2), 407–437.

Thulborn, K.R., Waterton, J.C., Matthews, P.M., & Radda, G.K. (1982). Oxygenation dependence of the transverse relaxation time of water protons in whole blood at high field. *Biochimica Et Biophysica Acta (BBA) – General Subjects*, *714*(2), 265–270.

Thut, G., Schyns, P.G., & Gross, J. (2011). Entrainment of perceptually relevant brain oscillations by non-invasive rhythmic stimulation of the human brain. *Frontiers in Psychology*, *2*(170), 1–10. http://doi.org/10.3389/fpsyg.2011.00170

Torricelli, A., Pifferi, A., Spinelli, L., Cubeddu, R., Martelli, F., Del Bianco, S., & Zaccanti, G. (2005). Time-resolved reflectance at null source-detector separation: Improving contrast and resolution in diffuse optical imaging. *Physical Review Letters*, *95*(7), 34. http://doi.org/10.1103/PhysRevLett.95.078101

Torricelli, A., Contini, D., Pifferi, A., Caffini, M., Re, R., Zucchelli, L., & Spinelli, L. (2014). Time domain functional NIRS imaging for human brain mapping. *NeuroImage*, *85*(P1), 28–50. http://doi.org/10.1016/j.neuroimage.2013.05.106

Tseng, P., Hsu, T.-Y., Chang, C.-F., Tzeng, O.J.L., Hung, D.L., Muggleton, N.G., Walsh, V., Liang, W.-K., Cheng, S.K., & Juan, C.-H. (2012). Unleashing potential: Transcranial direct current stimulation over the right posterior parietal cortex improves change detection in low-performing individuals. *The Journal of Neuroscience*, *32*(31), 10554–10561. http://doi.org/10.1523/JNEUROSCI.0362-12.2012

Verkhratsky, A., & Kirchhoff, F. (2007). Glutamate-mediated neuronal-glial transmission. *Journal of Anatomy*, *210*(6), 651–660. http://doi.org/10.1111/j.1469-7580.2007.00734.x

Villamar, M.F., Volz, M.S., Bikson, M., Datta, A., DaSilva, A.F., & Fregni, F. (2013). Technique and considerations in the use of 4x1 ring high-definition transcranial direct current stimulation (HD-tDCS). *Journal of Visualized Experiments*, (77), 1–15. http://doi.org/10.3791/50309

Villringer, A., Planck, J., Hock, C., Schleinkofer, L., & Dirnagl, U. (1993). Near infrared spectroscopy (NIRS): A new tool to study hemodynamic changes during activation of brain function in human adults. *Neuroscience Letters*, *154*(1), 101–104.

Vogt, C., & Vogt, O. (1919). *Allgemeinere Ergebnisse unserer Hirnforschung* (Results of our brain research in a broader context). Leipzig: J.A. Barth.

Vu, A.T., Jamison, K., Glasser, M.F., Smith, S.M., Coalson, T., Moeller, S., Auerbach, E.J., Uğurbil, K., & Yacoub, E. (2017). Tradeoffs in pushing the spatial resolution of fMRI for the 7T Human Connectome Project. *NeuroImage*, *154*, 23–32. http://doi.org/10.1016/j.neuroimage.2016.11.049

Wagner, A.D., Schacter, D.L., Rotte, M., Koutstaal, W., Maril, A., Dale, A.M., Rosen, B.R., & Buckner, R.L. (1998). Building memories: Remembering and forgetting of verbal experiences as predicted by brain activity. *Science*, *281*(5380), 1188–1191. http://doi.org/10.1126/science.281.5380.1188

Wassermann, E.M. (1998). Risk and safety of repetitive transcranial magnetic stimulation: Report and suggested guidelines from the International Workshop on the Safety of Repetitive Transcranial Magnetic Stimulation, 5–7 June 1996. *Electroencephalography and Clinical Neurophysiology/Evoked Potentials Section*, *108*(1), 1–16. http://doi.org/10.1016/S0168-5597(97)00096-8

White, N.C., Fawcett, J.M., & Newman, A.J. (2014). Electrophysiological markers of biological motion and human form recognition. *NeuroImage*, *84*, 854–867. http://doi.org/10.1016/j.neuroimage.2013.09.026

Woods, A.J., Antal, A., Bikson, M., Boggio, P.S., Brunoni, A.R., Celnik, P., et al. (2016). A technical guide to tDCS, and related non-invasive brain stimulation tools. *Clinical Neurophysiology*, *127*(2), 1031–1048. http://doi.org/10.1016/j.clinph.2015.11.012

Worsley, K.J. (2001). Statistical analysis of activation images. In P. Jezzard, P.M. Matthews, & S.M. Smith (Eds.), *Functional Magnetic Resonance Imaging: An Introduction to the Methods* (pp. 251–270). New York: Oxford University Press. http://doi.org/10.1093/acprof:oso/9780192630711.003.0014

Worsley, K J., Evans, A.C., Marrett, S., & Neelin, P. (1992). A three-dimensional statistical analysis for CBF activation studies in human brain. *Journal of Cerebral Blood Flow & Metabolism*, *12*(6), 900–918. http://doi.org/10.1038/jcbfm.1992.127

Wurzman, R., Hamilton, R.H., Pascual-Leone, A., & Fox, M.D. (2016). An open letter concerning do-it-yourself users of transcranial direct current stimulation. *Annals of Neurology*, *80*(1), 1–4. http://doi.org/10.1002/ana.24689

Yarkoni, T., Poldrack, R.A., Nichols, T.E., Van Essen, D.C., & Wager, T.D. (2011). Large-scale automated synthesis of human functional neuroimaging data. *Nature Methods*, *8*(8), 665–670. http://doi.org/10.1038/nmeth.1635

Ye, J.C., Tak, S., Jang, K.E., Jung, J., & Jang, J. (2009). NIRS-SPM: Statistical parametric mapping for near-infrared spectroscopy. *NeuroImage*, *44*(2), 428–447. http://doi.org/10.1016/j.neuroimage.2008.08.036

Zald, D.H., Cowan, R.L., Riccardi, P., Baldwin, R.M., Ansari, M.S., Li, R., Shelby, E.S., Smith, C.E., McHugo, M., & Kessle, R.M. (2008). Midbrain dopamine receptor availability is inversely associated with novelty-seeking traits in humans. *The Journal of Neuroscience*, *28*(53), 14372–14378. http://doi.org/10.1523/JNEUROSCI.2423-08.2008

Ziemann, U. (2016). Pharmaco-TMS-EEG for testing brain excitability and connectivity. *Clinical Neurophysiology*, *127*(3), e21–e22. http://doi.org/10.1016/j.clinph.2015.11.058

Ziemann, U., Reis, J., Schwenkreis, P., Rosanova, M., Strafella, A., Badawy, R., & Müller-Dahlhaus, F. (2015). TMS and drugs revisited 2014. *Clinical Neurophysiology*, *126*(10), 1–23. http://doi.org/10.1016/j.clinph.2014.08.028

Zilles, K., & Amunts, K. (2010). Centenary of Brodmann's map – conception and fate. *Nature Reviews Neuroscience*, *11*(2), 139–145. http://doi.org/10.1038/nrn2776

Index

10–10 system, see International 10–10 system
10–20 system, see International 10–20 system
10–5 system, see International 10–5 system
4 × 1 ring, in tES, 489–90, 494, 508, 513

A1, 112, 317, 495, 548, *see also*
  auditory cortex, primary
abductive reasoning, 53, 521
ABR, *see* auditory brainstem response
absorption, coefficient, of light, 410, 415, 420–1,
  424, 521, 542
  of light, in fNIRI, 409–10, 414–15, 420–1, 424,
    433, 438, 440–1, 521, 542
  of neuromodulators, 7
  of photons, in PET, 384
  of radiofrequency energy, in MRI, 347
accuracy, behavioural measure, 16, 18–19, 34, 38,
  56, 58, 491–2, 494, 521
  of CMR_{O2} calculation in fMRI, 225
  of cortical thickness measures, 334
  of dynamic causal modelling, 301
  of EEG source localization, 128
  of fNIRI, 421, 424, 452, 529, 539–40
  of manual morphometry, 318
  of MEG source localization, 135, 147, 154–6,
    158, 164, 167–8
  of MRI image registration, 348
  of multivariate fMRI analysis, 284
  of PET imaging, 374–5, 382, 398, 402
  of spatial normalization in MRI, 246, 248, 252,
    314, 323
  of streamlining in tractography, 354, 556
  of tES, 506–11, 516–7
acetylcholine, 7, 466, 500
acetylcholinesterase, 386
acoustic noise, 402, 481, 513, 538
action potential, 5–7, 9, 33, 62, 65, 93, 219–20,
  223, 228, 340, 342–3, 368, 411, 466, 484, 499,
  517, 521, 535, 540, 543–4
activation, brain, 38–9, 41–5, 47–50, 52–4, 56, 178,
  309, 315, 334, 362, 524–5, 527, 530–1, 535,
  538, 541, 543, 550–1
  brain, in EEG, 67, 69, 73, 131
  brain, in fMRI, 15, 31–2, 216–17, 219–21,
    223–6, 230–1, 237–8, 240–2, 246, 248, 250,
    252–4, 257, 259, 261–2, 269–81, 283–8,
    299, 301–4
  brain, in fNIRI, 408, 418, 436, 438–9, 441
  brain, in MEG, 137, 154, 160, 162–3, 165–8, 173
  brain, in PET, 41–5, 372, 382, 385, 391–2, 400
  brain, in tES, 501–4, 519
  brain, in TMS, 461, 466
active electrode, 81, 84–5, 94, 521, 526, 550
active electromagnetic shielding, 521
active motor threshold (aMT), 455, 463, 521–2
activity, brain, 2–4, 6–7, 9–11, 15–17, 20–2,
  26–34, 45, 47–50, 52, 57–8, 308, 310, 339,
  366, 368, 521–6, 530–40, 543–4, 549, 552,
  554, 556–7
  brain, in EEG, 20, 26–30, 62–5, 67–9, 72–4,
    76–7, 79, 84–5, 90, 92–3, 102, 104, 111,
    113–14, 118, 124, 126, 128–30
  brain, in fMRI, 30, 178, 180, 216, 219–24,
    226–30, 251, 253, 256–8, 261, 273–4, 279,
    283–4, 286–7, 289–92, 294–9, 301–4
  brain, in fNIRI, 405, 411, 417, 422–3, 429, 432,
    435, 437–9
  brain, in MEG, 134–5, 137, 143–4, 148, 150–1,
    153–6, 158, 160–2, 165–6, 168–73, 175
  brain, in PET, 30, 372, 382, 385–7, 390–6,
    398–400, 402
  brain, manipulating, 31–3, 444–6, 453, 455,
    460–1, 463–5, 468–70, 472, 476, 478–81,
    484, 491–2, 494, 498–506, 517–9
  physical, of research participants, 320
activity–dependent model, 501–3, 519, 521, 543
adaptation, fMRI design, 276–9
  neural, 263–4, 277
  256, 302, 304, 390, 522, 533, 543
adaptive mean amplitude, 121, 522
ADC, *see* apparent diffusion coefficient
additive factors design, 36, 38–40, 48, 57,
  269, 522
additivity, of haemodynamic response function,
  240, 262–5

adenosine triphosphate (ATP), 219–21, 226, 522–3
Adrian, E.D., 62, 64
AECI, *see* anodal excitation–cathodal inhibition model
aerobic metabolism, 219–21, 224, 522, *see also* oxygen metabolism
affine linear registration, 244–6, 248, 250, 252, 254, 314, 323, 357, 522
age, 45, 387, 405, 421
    as factor in fMRI, 225–6, 228, 291
    as factor in fNIRI, 421
    as factor in structural MRI, 320, 326, 328, 332, 335
    as variable in analysis, 49
    effects on cortical thickness, 332
    in brain stimulation, 510, 512, 517, 519
    incidental findings, 209
    of research participants, 321
agonist, 6, 460, 466, 499–501, 522–3
air conduction, for audio stimulus presentation, 151
air travel, 389
alcohol, as fixative for brain tissue, 338
    effects on tES responsivity, 512
    for cleaning skin (EEG), 92
Aldini, Giovanni, 445
Alekseichuck, Ivan, 494–6
algorithm, clustering, 294
    fMRI analysis, 242
    for EEG artifact removal, 113–4
    for ERP quantification, 120
    for fNIRI analysis
    image reconstruction, 233, 396, 527
    in computational neuroanatomy, 300, 309, 312, 315, 319–20, 322, 326, 330–4, 526
    in DTI, 348, 356, 358, 366
    in eye tracking, 113
    in surface–based cortical thickness analysis, 333–4
    machine learning, 15, 285,
    motion correction (fNIRI), 428–9, 528–9
    motion correction (MEG), 148
    motion correction (MRI), 238–9, 348
    source localization, 127–8, 134, 153–6, 158–9, 165–7, 173, 175
    spatial registration and normalization, 244–5, 248, 250, 252, 322, 432, 522, 544, 554
    TMS–EEG artifact removal, 475
aliasing, 110–11, 150, 430, 522, 544
alpha, frequency band in EEG, 77–80, 90, 92, 94, 106, 108, 114, 126, 146, 517, 534
    particles, 388
alpha (EEG rhythm), in tES, 492–3, 492–3, 498
Alzheimer's disease, 38, 179, 226, 291, 372–3, 385–7, 398, 401
Amassian, Vahe, 456–7
America, 87, 339

American Sign Language (ASL), 259
Ampère's circuital law, 29, 31, 86–7, 134, 136, 172, 522, 551
amplifier, differential, 82, 84
    EEG, 62–4, 80–2, 84–6, 90, 93–4, 100, 148, 474–5, 522, 525, 529, 536, 552
    EEG, in TMS, 473
    fNIRI, 420
anaerobic metabolism, 219, 221, 522–3
anaesthetic, topical, in tES, 512–3
    489, 515, 519–0
analgesic, 478, 480, *see also* Ibuprofen
analysis, fNIRI data, 426–36
    independent components, *see* independent components analysis (ICA)
    issues in fMRI reproducibility, 282
    mass univariate, 123–4
    multi–voxel pattern, 284–8
    multivariate, in fMRI, 284–8
    of cortical thickness, 330–4
    of deformation–based morphometry, 327
    of DTI data, 338, 346–9, 351–2, 357–63, 365–9
    of EEG, in frequency domain, 77, 79–80, 124–6
    of ERP data, 81, 94, 98–9, 102–5, 108, 114, 120–6, 129–0
    of fMRI data, 179, 197–8, 217, 228–9, 237–8, 240, 242–3, 248, 250, 252, 256, 258, 264, 266, 271, 273–6, 278, 280–7, 289–90, 292–9, 301–5
    of fNIRI data, 422, 424, 426, 428–9, 431, 433–6, 439
    of MEG data, 134, 148, 152–3, 162, 167–71, 173–4
    of PET data, 393–5, 399
    of structural MRI data, 308, 322, 326–7, 329–31, 335–6
    of tensor–based morphometry, 329
    of tES data, 488, 491–2, 506, 511–13, 517, 519
    of TMS data, 472, 474, 476
    of variance, multivariate, 327
    of voxel–based morphometry data, 324
    representational similarity, *see* representational similarity analysis (RSA)
    tract–based, 359–60
    univariate, 123, 169, 280, 282, 284, 303–4, 359, 541–2
analysis, of variance, *see* analysis of variance (ANOVA)
    statistical
analysis of variance (ANOVA), for DTI data, 359
    of fNIRI data, 434, 436
    of PET data, 395
    repeated measures, 395
    43, 103, 169, 171, 280, 302–3, 324, 327, 359, 395, 434, 436, 535

anatomical, connections, 16, 304, 338–40, 348, 355–6, 358, 361–2, 367, 369, 470
  constraints in source localization, 127, 155, 157, 160, 164
  labels, 286, 292
  landmarks, 244, 252, 283, 314, 318
  localization, 28, 396, 402
  MRI scan, 155, 157, 160, 164, 191, 194–5, 237, 314–15, 394–8, 432, 451–2, 481, 506, *see also* T1 weighting
  organization of brain, 2, 11, 15, 26, 64–5, 246, 250
  structure, 34, 40, 194–5, 241–2, 308–10, 312, 318–19, 398
  targeting, of tES, 490, 506, 508
  tracer, 339
anatomy, of brain, 15, 26, 148, 154, 235, 239, 242–3, 246, 250, 252, 283, 312, 314, 320, 338, 356–7, 363, 367, 396, 432–3, 441, 479, 510, 512, 516–17, 519, 548
aneurysm clips, 208, 477
angiography, MRI, 398
angular momentum, 180, 183, 522, 536, 542
animacy, 47–8, 285–8
animal, 13, 221, 278, 309, 339, 363, 365, 388, 404, 445, 465, 485, 493, 507, 514, 550
anisotropic, 342, 349–50, 352, 367, 523
anisotropy, 338, 342, 349, 351–2, 354, 357, 367–8, 532, 534
annihilation, 373–6, 383, 400–1, 523, 526, 531, 547
anodal excitation, 489, 499, 501, 519, 522–3
anodal excitation–cathodal inhibition (AECI) model, 499, 501, 519, 521–3
anode, 486–91, 493, 497, 499–500, 507–10, 513, 516–19, 523, 537, 545
ANOVA, *see* analysis of variance
antagonist, 6, 460, 466, 499–500, 523
Antal, Andrea, 492–4, 497, 502–3, 506, 510
antenna, artifact in MEG, 151
anxiety, imaging with PET, 387
  treatment with electrical stimulation, 485
  treatment with TMS, 479
APD, *see* avalanche photodiode
aphasia, 23, 333
apparent diffusion coefficient (ADC), 349, 522–3
apraxia, 458
arcuate fasciculus, 338
arms race, neural, 56
artery, 23, 223–4, 398
artifact, aliasing, 522
  correction, 114, 130, 152, 347–8, 429, 431, 523, 538, 542
  decay, 475, 529
  defined, 523
  head movement (in EEG), 90
  in diffusion–weighted MRI, 346–8, 367
  in DWI, 347–8, 531

  in EEG, 20, 28–9, 70, 86, 89–92, 98, 101–2, 105, 108–14, 120, 129–30, 544, 553
  in fMRI, 233–40, 251–3, 292, 294, 525, 538, 541, 542, 546, 554
  in fNIRI, 412–13, 428–31, 440–1, 539
  in MEG, 146, 150–2, 156, 172, 174
  in MRI, 207
  in PET, 383, 533
  in structural MRI, 336
  in TMS, 471–2, 474–6, 480, 530, 552, 557
  methods for correcting or removing, in EEG, 111–4
  methods for reducing, in EEG, 87–92
  muscle, 151, 475–6
  ocular, 89, 112–14, 544
  physiological, in fMRI, 237, 294
  susceptibility, 233–40, 251–3, 541, 552
ASL, *see* American Sign Language
aspirin, 514
association cortex, 523
association fibres, 339
associationist school, 338
astrocyte, 221–3, 251, 253, 523
astrocyte–neuron lactate shuttle hypothesis, 221, 523
atlas, 55, 243, 250, 283, 310, 312–13, 357, 359, 448, 452, 548, *see also* MNI152
ATP, *see* adenosine triphosphate
attention, of participant in study, 19, 24, 39, 58, 68, 71, 75, 79, 99, 225, 260, 492, 494
  studies of, 18–19, 26, 33, 80, 99
  visual–spatial, 99, 321, 467, 469
attenuation correction, 396–8, 402, 523
attrition, in structural MRI studies, 321
  321
auditory, comprehension, 24
  cortex, 40, 47–8, 69, 166, 173, 285, 391, 548, *see also* A1
  speech
  stimulus, 37, 39–41, 46, 68–70, 75, 80, 89, 91, 100, 114, 145–6, 153, 163–4, 166–8, 270, 275, 444, 468, 538
auditory brainstem response (ABR), 68, 168, 227
autopsy, 11
avalanche photodiode (APD), 379–80, 379, 416, 425, 523, 553
axial gradiometer, 141–6, 152, 159, 172, 174, 524
axial plane, 195, 524, 528
axon, 4–6, 8, 26, 28, 64–5, 127, 135–6, 158, 191, 308, 339–43, 363, 365, 367–9, 465–6, 521, 524, 530, 536, 543, 547, 558

b (parameter in DWI), 345–51, 523–4
B_0, 182–3, 185, 189, 193, 210, 212, 344, *see also* magnetic field
baby, imaging with fNIRI, 406

back–projection, 382–4, 400–1, 524, 533
BaF$_2$, *see* barium fluoride
banana, shape of optical path in fNIRI, 71, 104, 408, 417–18, 438
band–pass filter, 105, 108, 524, 544
Bandettini, Peter, 178, 217–18, 228, 278
barium fluoride (BaF$_2$), 380
barrier, to water diffusion, 310, 342, 385, 388
basal ganglia, 386, 392, 470, 559
base rate, of brain activation, 53
baseline, activity, 49, 220–1, 225–8, 256–60, 497, 503
   condition, 40, 47–8, 225, 256, 260, 262, 269–73, 302, 304, 392, 394, 524, 551
   current, in tES, 497
   estimation in fNIRI, 428, 430, 436
   in ERP, 72, 116, 118
   in MEG, 167–8, 173
   in TMS, 462–3, 470, 476, 524, 542,
   of HRF, 227–8, 237, 251, 259, 262, 265–6, 302–3, 406, 453
   period, 72, 118, 168, 173, 175, 258–9, 273, 279, 285, 289, 413, 536
   scan, in DWI, 345, 347,, *see also* b (parameter in DWI)
basis function, 246, 248
Basser, Peter, 339
Bates, Elizabeth, 23–4
battery, analogy with EEG dipole, 84
   in tES, 486, 488–9
   64, 81, 516
Bavelier, Daphne, 259, 272
beamformer, 156, 162, 164–6, 168–70, 524
becquerel (Bq), 388
beer, 29
Beer–Lambert law, 420–1, 439, 521, 524, 529, 541–2
behaviour, complements to measures of, 22, 24, 26, 52, 544, 558
   ethical issues in studying, 54–6
   habituation, 390
   in disease states, 291, 339
   in neurostimulation studies, 444–4, 462, 467, 469, 480, 485, 491–5, 502, 504, 513, 517, 537, 540
   influences on, 49
   methods to study, 11, 16–22, 26, 33–4, 269, 521, 549–1, 558
   relationship to neuroimaging data, 321
   response collection in neuroimaging, 102, 151,
   study of, 2, 4, 16, 47, 274–5, 470–1,
Behrens, Timothy, 296, 361–2, 365, 369
BEM, *see* boundary element model
benzodiazepine, 386
Berger, Hans, 62
Bestmann, Sven, 510

beta, frequency band in EEG, 77–8, 94, 126, 534
   weight, 280
beta amyloid (β–amyloid), 385–7, 398, 400–1
beta weight, 280
between–subjects design, 36, 45, 49, 57–8, 524
BGO, *see* bismuth germinate
bias current, 139–0
Binder, Jeffrey, 270
biochemistry, 554
biology, 369, 503
biomarker, 291
biophysical model, 225
biphasic pulse, 453, 524
bismuth germinate (BGO; Bi$_4$Ge$_3$O$_{12}$), 380
black and white stripes, *see* sine wave grating
bladder, in radiation safety, 389
blank screen, 21, 39, 269, 271, 269, 279
blinding, 468, 498, 513–14, 517
blink, 28, 68, 70, 89, 91–4, 112–4, 129–30, 151, 172, 174, 475, 523, 544
block detector, 379–81, 524
blocked design, 257–62, 266, 284, 298, 302–3, 525
blocking, 474–5, 500, 525, 552
blood, cell, 225
   cerebral flow rate (rCBF), 221, 385
   effects in DWI, 345–6
   flow, 2, 31, 221–2, 224–5, 345, 372, 385, 393, 398, 400, 410, 430, 523, 535, 558
   oxygenation, 27–8, 31, 33–4, 52, 180, 218, 251, 253, 281, 405–6, 436, 525, 548
   volume (tHb), 406–7, 434
blood oxygenation level dependent (BOLD),
   calibration, 225–6, 229, 251, 253, 525
   contrast, 216, 218, 237
   effect, 217–18, 222, 226, 546
   EPI, 241
   fMRI, 218–19, 221, 224–8, 230, 235, 237, 244, 269, 279, 293, 304, 393, 406–7, 438, 525, 536, 555
   linearity, 258, 262–4
   measurement with fNIRI, 407–11
   negative, 270
   paradox, 218–9
   physiological basis, 218–6
   quantification with fNIRI, 407
   relationship to neural activity, 227–30, 296
   response, 46, 225–6, 228, 230, 251, 257, 261, 264–8, 271, 281, 284, 296, 299, 301–2, 400, 406, 438–9, 471, 523, 553
   signal, 216, 218–19, 221, 224–9, 235, 237–8, 242, 251, 253, 256–8, 260, 263, 265–73, 279, 284–5, 289, 291–2, 297, 299, 302–4, 366, 402, 406–7, 413, 432, 434, 436, 468, 472, 480, 526, 530, 537
   timing, 227–30

variability, 228–9
see also haemodynamic response function
blood supply, 222
blood vessel, 10, 23, 27, 191, 208, 217–18, 221–4, 226, 346, 352, 398, 407, 410, 421, 440, 513, 558
blood volume, 221, 223, 226, 406–7, 434, 438
blood–brain barrier, 385, 388
Bode, Stefan, 45–6
body piercing, 208
BOLD, *see* blood oxygenation level dependent
Boltzmann radiative transfer function, 433
Bonferroni correction, 170, 281, *see also* multiple comparison correction
bootstrapping, 171, 525, 544, 546, 549
bore, of PET scanner, 381
194–6, 207, 238, 345, 381, 471
boredom, during resting state, 270
Bortoletto, Marta, 502
boundary, between grey and white matter, 321–2
cytoarchitectural, 312–5
3, 11–12, 156–7, 191, 233, 277, 311–12, 318–19, 322, 330, 333, 432, 507, 525, 533, 555
boundary element model (BEM), 156–7, 432, 507, 525, 533
boxcar design, 257, 525
Boynton, Geoffrey, 21–2, 261
Bq, *see* becquerel
brain, –behaviour relationships, 2, 544
–scalp distance, 437
activation, 31, 38–9, 42, 44–5, 49–50, 52, 56, 69, 160, 166, 168, 216, 219, 221, 230, 240, 259, 261, 270, 280, 301–2, 385, 400, 408, 439, 524–5
activity, 2–3, 9–10, 16–17, 20–2, 26, 29–34, 45, 47–8, 50, 52, 57–8, 62–3, 68, 72, 74, 76, 79, 84–5, 90, 102, 104, 111, 113–14, 118, 126, 129, 134, 144, 150, 154, 158, 162, 170, 172–3, 175, 178, 216, 219–20, 261, 274, 289, 291, 294, 308, 390–3, 405, 422, 429, 439, 444–5, 453, 463, 465, 468–9, 478, 480–1, 484, 491–2, 494, 498, 518–19, 521, 523, 532, 534–5, 537, 539–40, 543, 552, 556
adult, 9, 27, 244, 342
anatomy, 26, 148, 154, 367, 432, 441
area, 8, 11, 15–16, 21–3, 26, 28–9, 32, 39, 41–2, 44–8, 52–4, 57–8, 63–4, 72, 76, 79, 94, 160, 165–6, 169–70, 219, 223, 226–30, 251, 256–7, 260, 264–5, 268–70, 272–3, 275–8, 281, 283, 285–7, 289, 291–2, 294, 296–7, 299–304, 308–9, 318, 334–5, 338, 340, 353, 363, 366, 369, 393–4, 411, 432, 445–6, 448, 452, 460, 464–5, 467–9, 472, 479–81, 489–94, 499, 501–3, 506, 508, 517, 519, 521, 523, 526–7, 536, 539, 542–3, 551

damage, 2, 11, 22–3, 32, 472, 477, 514, 544, 558, *see also* lesion
development, 9
electrical activity, 2, 9, 33, *see also* electroencephalography
extraction, 320, 335, 525
function, 3–4, 6, 9, 15–16, 32–3, 55, 338, 520, 535
human, 3–4, 9, 15–16, 22, 28, 64, 221, 310, 312–13, 352, 369, 372, 385, 445, 509, 537, *see also* Human Brain Project
imaging, 2, 16, 22, 24, 26, 29, 44, 47, 55–6, 192, 195, 220, 240, 308, 310, 330, 332, 335, 385, 405, 438, 440, 445, 546, 548, 553, 555
injury, 22–3, 32
organization, 10, 13, 22, 240, 310, 314, 426, 527, 535, *see also* cytoarchitecture, myeloarchitecture
pathology, 23
region, 7, 9, 13, 22, 33–4, 44, 53–4, 58, 63, 70, 72, 79, 93, 128, 148, 153–4, 165–6, 170, 173, 179, 227–8, 251, 253, 262, 264, 270, 275, 278–9, 285–6, 289–90, 293–4, 296–304, 309–10, 315, 335–6, 339–40, 342, 353, 366, 385, 393, 400, 418, 433, 439, 445, 454, 460–1, 465, 467–8, 472, 476, 479–81, 491, 493–4, 503, 510, 512, 516, 518–19, 526–7, 530–1, 533, 535–7, 541–2, 544–5, 548, 551, 557, 559
response, 21, 37, 44, 55, 262, 390, 537
stimulation, 444–5, 467, 480–1, 485, 516, 520, 544
structures, 4, 309, 319, 328, 529, 556, 559
tissue, 11, 189, 191, 240, 335–6, 363, 409, 411, 418, 430, 465, 525
tumour, 209, 360
versus vein debate, 224, 407
volume, 162, 166, 173, 175, 231, 248, 251, 325, 328, 336, 347, 349, 473, 524, 529
Brain Products LLC, 64, 81, 475
brainstem, 10, 68, 168, 175, 227
brassiere, 151
brightness, 21, 37, 44, 58, 70, 72, 98, 128, 191, 199, 260, 421, 504, 527, 548–9, *see also* luminance
Broca, Paul, 11, 13, 15, 41, 52, 309, 313–14, 445–6
Broca's area, 15, 41, 52, 313–14, 446
Brodmann area, 310–1, 313–4
Brodmann, Korbinian, 11–14, 309–11, 314, 412
Brownian motion, 342–3, 345–6, 363, 366–8, 525
Brunoni, Andre R., 445, 492, 520
brute force approach, 356, 525
Burdach, Karl, 338
burn, 208, 219, 414, 473, 477, 515–16, 519
butterfly plot, 116–7, 146
by eye, 22, 70, 172, 312, 353

C1 (ERP component), 83, 412
Ca, see calcium
cadaver, 361, 363–5, see also corpse
caffeine, 225, 228, 251
Cajal, Ramon y, 7–8
calcium (Ca), 5–6, 219–20, 223, 466, 499–500, 517, 519
calcium ion channels, 466, 517
calibrated BOLD, 216, 225–6, 251, 253, 525
calibrated bold fMRI, 225–6, 525
cannabinoid, 386
cannabis, 512
capillary, 218, 222–4, 228, 253, 346, 407, 523
car, 71, 278, 280
carbamazepine, 466
carbon dioxide (CO_2), 219, 526, 537
cardiac gating, 347, 525
categorical variable, 37–8, 57, 525, 532
cathode, 486–91, 493–4, 497, 499–500, 507–10, 513, 516–19, 526, 537, 545
caudate nucleus, 470–1
CBF, see cerebral blood flow
cellular structure, 11, 191, see also cytoarchitecture
central sulcus, 10, 15, 248, 250, 314, 456, 506, 526
cerebral blood flow (CBF), 221, 224–6, 385, 398, 400, 410 see also regional cerebral blood flow
cerebral cortex, 4–5, 7–8, 10–11, 13, 15, 28, 33, 135–6, 155, 157, 160, 168, 173, 318–19, 322, 362, 408–9, 411, 418, 446, 510, 523, 526, 528, 536, 543, 548–9, 554–5, 558
cerebral metabolic rate, of glucose (CMR_{glu}), 221, 385
of oxygen (CMR_{O2}), 221, 385
cerebrospinal fluid (CSF), 250, 526
contrast, 28, 127, 191–3, 203, 210, 237–8, 241, 244, 321, 340, 342, 394, 396,
electrical conduction, 484, 507–8, 510, 515,
flow, 346
segmentation, 320, 322, 324–5, 330–3, 335, 352, 432, 546, 555–6
cerebrovascular disease, 226, 387
cerebrovascular reserve (CVR), 226, 526, 528
CES, see cranial electrotherapy stimulation
Chance, Britton, 404–5
channel, in EEG, 81, 92, 106, 108, 112, 115–16, see also electrode
in fNIRI, 416–8, 419–20, 426–34, 436, 438–0, see also optode
in MEG, 146, see also magnetometer, gradiometer
in MRI head coil, 194, 234–5,
in PET scanner, 379–80, see also scintillation detector
ion, 5–6, 65, 219–0, 411, 439, 466, 480–1, 499–501, 517, 519
chemistry, 404

children, head movement in fMRI, 240
MRI safety, 209
11, 17, 30, 172, 439, 508, 515
chromophore, 409–10, 414, 427, 429, 440, 526, 528
cigar, shape of DTI ellipsoid, 349–0
cingulate gyrus, 44, 448
cingulum, 338
Claudius (Roman emperor), 445
closed field, 65–6, 154, 526
cluster, 11, 242, 282, 360, 528, 535
CMR_{glu}, see cerebral metabolic rate of glucose
CMR_{O2}, see cerebral metabolic rate of oxygen
CNR, see contrast–to–noise ratio
co–registration, in MEG, 147–8
of fNIRI and MRI data, 432–3
PET–MRI, 398
CO_2, see carbon dioxide
Coca–Cola, see Coke
cochlear implant, 152, 400, 402, 406, 478
code multiplexing, 420, 526, 542
coefficient, absorption, 410, 415, 420–1, 424, 433, 521, 542
apparent diffusion, see apparent diffusion coefficient (ADC)
in statistical analysis, 280
cognitive, activity, 220, 290, 308, 492, 524, 526
behavioural, 19
conjunction, 273, 275, 526–7
deficit, 23, 544
enhancement, 58, 518
function, 4, 22, 26, 33, 77, 277, 308, 372, 445, 491–2, 549
impairment, 387
neuroscientist, 15, 27–9, 31, 48, 385, 405
operation, 29, 34, 41, 53, 57–8, 93, 130, 269, 273, 304, 334, 527, 551
performance, 32, 56
process, 2–3, 22, 29, 34, 39, 52, 56–8, 72, 93–4, 129, 269, 275, 302, 551
psychologist, 372
psychology, 3, 38, 59
science, 18, 21, 24–5, 34, 36, 47, 280, 547
state, 476
structure, 269
task, 314, 492
training, 492
Cognitive Neuroscience Society, 3
Cohen, David, 134
coherence, 169, 186, 188–9, 192, 230, 504–5, 526, 555
coil, gradient, in MRI, 345, 348
in MEG, 140–2, 146–8, 150, 172, 524,
receiver, in MRI, 184–6, 188, 192–4, 197, 210, 212–13, 233–5, 240, 322, 546
transcranial magnetic stimulation (TMS), 32, 446–54, 459, 461–2, 465, 467–8, 471, 474–6, 479–81, 533

coincidence detector, 373, 375–6, 381–3, 401, 526, 529
Coke, 56
colour, 52–3, 146, 163, 241, 277, 279, 317, 351–2, 362, 418, 421, 450–1, 472–3, 536, 559
comfort, 92, 480, 489
commissural fibres, 339
commissure, 243, 250
component, C1, 83, 412
   ERP, 62, 65, 67, 69–78, 93–5, 98, 100–1, 103–4, 108–10, 113–17, 120–30, 148, 526, 531–2, 546
   ERP, evoked by TMS, *see* TMS–evoked potential (TEP)
   error–related negativity (ERN), 71
   in MEG, 168–9, 173
   independent, *see* independent components analysis (ICA)
   latent, 128
   lateralized readiness potential (LRP), 76, 539
   left anterior negativity (LAN), 71, 104
   memory, 20
   mismatch negativity (MMN), 261
   N1, 69–71, 74, 120, 128, 456
   N170, 69–71, 100, 116–8
   N2, 71, 74
   N250, 116–7
   N400, 71–2, 75, 103, 109, 122, 125–6
   of magnetic field, 141–3, 146, 172, 174, 424, 545–7, 557
   P1, 69–71, 74, 83, 112, 116–17, 120, 128, 441, 456, 546
   P1–N1–P2 complex, 69, 71, 128
   P2, 69–71, 74, 83, 109, 112, 128
   P3 (or P300), 71–2, 75, 83, 107, 260–1, 390, 495
   P600, 71, 104, 109, 125
   principal, *see* principal components analysis (PCA)
   transverse, 192, 557
Compton scattering, 374, 376, 526
computational model, 285–6, 288, 433, 506
computational neuroanatomy, 309, 319–22, 329, 335–6, 357, 526, 529, 556, 558
   contrast weighting, 321–2
   data acquisition, 321–2
   experimental design, 320–2
   processing steps, 320–2
   spatial normalization, 320, 322–9, 332–4
   spatial smoothing, 323
   tissue segmentation, 320–2
computed tomography (CT), 22, 377, 388, 395–7, 402, 526–8, 557
concentration, calcium, 219, 499
   chemical, 30
   fat, 340
   grey matter, 322–6, 328–9, 335–6, 536, 558

haemoglobin, 217–19, 221–5, 253, 406–7, 409, 414, 421, 424, 426–7, 434
hydrogen, 209
measurement, using spectrophotometry, 404, 406, 410, 420–1, 426–7, 434, 438–9, 521, 524, 535, 542, 554
neuromodulator, 400, 402, 470
oxygen, 27, 30
radioactive material (in PET), 372, 388, 400, 402, 524, 547
sodium, 219, 499
water, 28
conceptual processing, 270
condition–rich design, 278–9, 527
conditioning stimulus (CS), 458–9, 527–8
conduction, delay, neural, 340
   electrical, 65, 89, 93, 151, 168, 340, 343, 465, 506–7, 515, 543
   saltatory, 65
conductive loop, 208
conjunction analysis, 273–6, 302, 304, 526–7, 530
connecting the dots, 353, 555
connection, between scalp and electrode in EEG, 80, 85, 90, 92, 94, 114,
   filtered, 87
   grounded, 92
   long range, 340
   neuroanatomical, 4–5, 7–9, 16, 26, 28, 87, 91–2, 289, 304, 338–41, 366, 411, 461–2, 465, 470, 499, 517, 526–7, 537, 543, 549
   short range, 340
connectivity, effective, *see* effective connectivity
   functional, *see* functional connectivity
connectome, 16, 309, 314, 338–41, 369, 527, 537, 549
connectomics, 309, 337–9, 341, 343, 345, 347, 349–51, 353, 355, 357, 359, 361, 363, 365–7, 369, 527, 537
continuous theta burst stimulation (cTBS), 463–6, 477, 527–
continuous variable, 36–7, 57, 525, 527
continuous wave (CW) imaging, 414–15, 420–2, 424–7, 429, 437–41, 527–9
continuum, 37, 46, 329, 340, 393, 525, 527
contrast, –to–noise ratio (CNR), 426, 438
   blood oxygenation level dependent (BOLD), *see* blood oxygenation level dependent (BOLD) contrast
   experimental, 36, 39–44, 48, 48–9, 52, 56–8, 168, 170, 260, 270–6, 2, 283, 302, 304, 314, 335, 391, 410, 437, 527, 530
   of CT scan, 22, 396
   of MR images, 28, 31, 189–93, 199, 203, 207, 210–13, 241–2, 244–5, 310, 320–2, 340, 394–5, 397, 527
   stimulus, 22, 44, 72, 98, 225–6, 260, 456
   T1, *see* T1 contrast

T2, *see* T2 contrast
T2*, *see* T2* contrast
weighting, 191, 245, 322, 527
control, condition, 18, 39, 41–2, 48, 257, 259–60, 264, 269–75, 289, 291, 297, 304, 320, 391, 460, 467, 470–2, 481, 525
experimental
group, 38, 49, 291, 320, 527
convolution, 124, 263–4, 301, 527
coordinates, 243, 250–1, 360, 426
corona radiata, 363
coronal plane, 196, 510, 528
corpse, 445
corpus callosum, 339, 455
correction, artifact, *see* artifact correction
attenuation, in PET, 396–8, 402, 523
motion, *see* motion correction
correction, for multiple comparisons, *see* multiple comparison correction
correlation, 24, 45–6, 148, 165, 169, 281, 284–99, 301, 303–4, 321, 366, 393–4, 429, 436–7, 494, 528, 531, 536, 542–3, 549, 552
between fMRI runs, 284–5
in functional connectivity, 289–94
correlation–based signal improvement, 429, 528
cortex, auditory, 40, 47–8, 69, 166, 173, 285, 391, 548
cerebral, 4–5, 7–8, 10–11, 13, 15, 28, 33, 135–6, 155, 157, 160, 168, 173, 318–19, 322, 362, 408–9, 411, 418, 446, 510, 523, 526, 528, 536, 543, 548–9, 554–5, 558
motor, 17, 39, 41, 67, 76–7, 218, 227–9, 242, 312, 432, 438, 448, 455, 458, 460, 476, 486, 491, 493, 497, 501–2, 506, 508, 510–12, 539, 548, 552
parietal, 290, 292, 300, 494, 502
prefrontal, 262, 296, 299–300, 365, 460, 463, 470, 488, 492
somatosensory, 137, 313–14, 331
visual, 11–12, 15, 17, 41, 52, 137, 145, 154, 221–2, 227–8, 246, 257, 261, 276–7, 286, 412, 435, 450, 456, 461, 498, 502, 547–8
cortical, columns, 11, 15, 34, 276–7, 340, 528
thickness, 28, 308, 319, 321, 325, 330–6, *see also* surface–based cortical thickness *and* voxel–based cortical thickness
cortical organization, scales, 310–15
cortisol, 7
counter–balancing, 48, 528
covert methods, 24, 26, 52
[^{11}C]RAC, *see* raclopride
cranial electrotherapy stimulation (CES), 485
criteria, stopping, in tractography, 353–4, 365–6
95, 113, 118, 131, 311, 315
cross–frequency coupling, 494, 496, 528
in tACS, 494

cross–sectional design, 320, 324, 528
crossed design, 41–2, 535, *see also* fully–crossed design
crystal, 375, 378–82, 400, 524, 529, 531, 540, 552, 554
CS, 249, 458–60, 527–8
CSF, *see* cerebrospinal fluid
CT, *see* computed tomography
cTBS, *see* continuous theta burst stimulation
Cu, *see* Curie
Cui, Xu, 437–8
curie (Cu), 388
current, Eddy, 348, 367–8, 531
electrical, 29, 31–2, 84, 86–7, 134–6, 139, 156, 172–3, 184, 186, 348, 444, 446, 450–1, 454, 465, 474, 477, 479, 481, 484–6, 518, 522, 531, 536, 541, 547, 557
cutoff frequency, 105–6
CVR, *see* cerebrovascular reserve
CW, *see* continuous wave
cyclotron, 375, 377, 401, 528
cytoarchitecture, 11, 13–14, 283, 308, 310, 312, 315, 335, 528, 536, 541, 548

D–wave, *see* direct wave
D_1 receptor, PET imaging, 386
D_2 receptor, in TMS–PET, 470–1
PET imaging, 386, 391–2
database, of neuroimaging results, *see* Neurosynth database
53, 58, 208
Datta, Abhishek, 508
Davis, Hallowell, 62
Davis, Pauline, 62
dB, *see* deciBel
DBM, *see* deformation–based morphometry
DBS, *see* deep brain stimulator
DC–DOT, *see* depth–compensated DOT
DCM, *see* dynamic causal modelling
deactivation, in fMRI, 270
decay, T2, *see* T2 decay
T2*, *see* T2* decay
decay artifact, 475, 529
decay time, 188, 379–80, 529, 542
deciBel, 20, 37, 106–7, 444, 478
decision making, 45
deep brain stimulator (DBS), 152, 444, 477–8, 515
deep neural network, 285
default mode network, 270, 290, 292, 468
deflection, 112, 526
of proton in PET, 374
deformation field, 326, 328, 521, 556
deformation–based morphometry (DBM), 319, 326–9, 335–6, 521, 528–9
deGausser, 152
delta, frequency band in EEG, 77–8, 94, 534

demand characteristics, 467, 481, 498, 513, 529
dementia, 321, 333, 398, 510, 515
dendrite, 4–6, 9, 135, 308, 340, 411, 529, 544, 557
dental work, 152, 233
deoxygenated blood, 535, *see also* deoxyhaemoglobin
deoxyhaemoglobin (deoxy–Hb), 217–19, 221–2, 224–6, 251, 253, 406–7, 409–10, 413–14, 421, 424, 427, 429–30, 434, 437–40, 528, 542
dependent variable, 36, 38, 56–7, 122, 529, 535, 538, 542, 545–6, 557
dephasing gradient, 343–4, 529, 550
depolarization, 5, 411, 499, 529
depression, 9, 32, 82, 461, 465, 499, 515, 540
   imaging with PET, 387
   psychiatric condition, in TMS, 479
   studied with tES, 515
   treatment with electrical stimulation, 485
   treatment with tDCS, 491–2
   depth–compensated DOT (DC–DOT), 433
desynchronization, 79, 98, 130, 532
detection, of coincidence events in PET, 373–5
detector ring, 375, 378, 382, 384, 400–1, 529
determinant, Jacobian, 329, 539
deviation, 100, 352, 428
diagnosis, 55, 209, 321, 373, 387–8, 391, 479
DICS, *see* dynamic imaging of coherent sources
diffeomorphic mapping, 319, 529
difference waveform, 74–6, 119, 529
differential amplifier, 62, 84–5, 93–4, 529
differential path length (DPL), 421–2, 424, 529–0
diffuse optical imaging (DOI), 406, *see also* functional near–infrared imaging (fNIRI)
diffuse optical tomography (DOT), 406, 432, *see also* functional near–infrared imaging (fNIRI)
diffusion, direction, calculation of, 349–53
   number of directions in DWI, 345–6
   tensor, 179, 237, 309, 337–40, 345, 347, 349, 351–2, 357, 367–9, 523, 529–31, 534, 539
   tensor, calculations, 349–53
   weighting, 343, 345, 348–9
diffusion tensor imaging (DTI), 179, 237, 309, 337–41, 343, 345–7, 349–53, 355–7, 359–69, 398, 523, 530–1, 534, 539
   acquisition, 343–7
   applications, 360–2
   computation, 349–53
   limitations, 342, 363–6
   preprocessing, 347–9
   relationship to functional and effective connectivity, 366
   spatial normalization, 356–8
   spatial registration, 356–8
   statistics, 356–8
   validation, 363–6
diffusion weighted imaging (DWI), 524, 530

diffusivity, mean (MD), 352, 358
dipole, 64–5, 67, 73, 89, 115, 127–8, 134–7, 142–4, 149, 155–64, 168, 173, 175, 180, 210, 530, 532, 540–1, 544
   modelling, 156, 158–60, 162, 168
direct wave (D–wave), 466, 528, 530, 538
directionality, 296, 299–301, 303, 355, 366, 531, 535
disconnection syndrome, 339
Discover magazine, 3, 373
discrete scale, 530
discrete wavelet filtering, 429, 530
disease, 22–3, 28, 38, 49, 55–7, 179, 209, 225–6, 228, 251, 253, 291, 308, 318, 320, 335, 339, 358–60, 363, 369, 372–3, 385–7, 391, 398–401, 445, 459, 519, 527–8, 544
disjunction analysis, 256, 276, 302, 304, 530
distance, between brain and scalp, 417–18, 433, 437–8
distortion, 245, 248, 250–1, 253, 315, 356, 540
   correction in EPI imaging, 233–5
   geometric, in DWI, 348
   geometric, in fMRI, 232–5
   of EPI images, 232–4
distribution of time–of–flight (DTOF), 423, 530
DLPC, *see* dorsolateral prefrontal cortex
DOI, *see* diffuse optical imaging
Donchin, Emmanuel, 75, 95, 114, 131
Donders, F.C., 38
dopamine, imaging with PET, 386, 391–
   in tES, 500
   in TMS, 466, 470–1
dorsolateral prefrontal cortex (DLPC), 262, 460–1, 470, 488, 492, 494, 498, 506
DOT, *see* diffuse optical tomography
downstream, 224, 387, 460, 469, 499, 503
DPL, *see* differential path length
drawing, 7–8, 20, 83, 100, 149, 192, 199–201, 258, 309, 311, 330, 353
drift, EEG, 90, 92, 105–6, 108, 110, 118, *see also* skin potential
   of fMRI scanner, 294
   of fNIRI signal, 430–1, 434
drug, 6, 24, 31, 49, 55, 225, 251, 373, 386–7, 461, 465–6, 485, 499–501, 512, 514, 517, 519
dSPM, *see* dynamic statistical parametric mapping
DTI, *see* diffusion tensor imaging
DTOF, *see* distribution of time–of–flight
dual regression ICA, 294
Düsseldorf (Germany), 312
dynamic artifacts, 471, 530
dynamic causal modelling (DCM), 299–302, 528, 530
dynamic imaging of coherent sources (DICS), 164
dynamic range, 225, 474, 480
dynamic statistical parametric mapping (dSPM), 162–3, 530

ear canal, 233, 541
ECG, see electrocardiogram
echo planar imaging (EPI), 216, 230–6, 239, 241–2, 245, 251–3, 346, 348, 368, 398, 472, 525, 530, 532, 540–1, 554
echo time (TE), 32, 188, 193, 198, 211–12, 232–3, 236, 344, 437, 444, 483–91, 493–5, 497–501, 503–19, 521, 530, 532, 537, 544–5, 554–5, 557
ECT, see electroconvulsive therapy
Eddy current, 348, 367–8, 531
education, 49, 320
EEG, see electroencephalography
effective connectivity, 256, 289, 294–6, 299–301, 303–4, 362, 366, 530–1, 535–6, 549
effective dose, 388–9, 531
efficiency, 42, 266, 269, 303, 531
eigenvalue, 349, 352, 531
eigenvector, 349–51, 353, 355–6, 367, 531, 534, 549, 555
EKG, see electrocardiogram
electrical, current, 29, 31–2, 84, 86–7, 134–6, 139, 156, 172–3, 184, 186, 348, 444, 446, 450–1, 454, 465, 474, 477, 479, 481, 484–6, 518, 522, 531, 536, 541, 547, 557
  energy, 453
  ground, 87, 531
  potential, 5, 29, 33, 65, 67, 69, 72, 77, 82–5, 93–4, 115, 120, 126–7, 129, 131, 134–7, 140, 149, 158, 173–4, 219–20, 343, 412, 446, 470, 474, 486, 499, 507–8, 510, 512, 521–2, 526, 529, 531, 536, 541, 546, 550, 552–3
Electrical Geodesics Inc (EGI), 81
electrocardiogram (EKG or ECG), 89, 90, 146, 151, 347
electroconvulsive therapy (ECT), 485, see also electroshock therapy
electrode, active (EEG), 81, 84–5, 94, 521, 526, 550
  cap, 64, 80–2, 84, 92, 146, 148, 473, 475
  ground (EEG), 84, 86, 92–3, 490, 529, 536
  impedance, 81, 85, 90, 92, 94, 115, 173, 474, 486, 488, 515–16, 518–19, 537–8, 553
  number used in EEG, 63
  positioning systems (EEG), 82
  reference (EEG), 84–6, 93, 114, 529, 536, 550
  reference location (EEG), 85–6
electroencephalography (EEG), 34, 68, 77–8, 86–9, 93, 101–2, 129–30, 135, 146, 151, 162, 174–5, 348, 373, 406, 437, 441, 444–5, 470, 472, 481, 521, 523, 533, 546, 554, 557–8
  artifacts, 111–4
  combined with TMS, 472–8
  components, 67–76
  data acquisition, 80–6

electrode materials, 473
epoching, 118–20
experimental design, 98–104
extracting measures, 120–3
filtering, 104–1
frequency–domain analysis, 124–6
impedance, in TMS, 473
mass univariate analysis, 123–4
movement (of participant), 102
oscillatory measures, 76–80
physiological basis, 63–7
practical considerations, 91–2
preprocessing, 104–20
re-referencing, 114–8
recording with MEG, 148–9
response collection, 101–2
setup of experiment environment, 87, 91–2
signal and noise, 86–90
simplicity of experimental design, 103–4
source localization, 126–8
stimulus features, 98
stimulus presentation, 101–2
timing, 99–101
electromagnetic, induction, see Ampère's circuital law
electromyography (EMG), 89, 102, 105, 151, 448, 455–6, 469, 531, 542, 552
electron, 82, 180, 217, 219, 373–4, 376, 379, 382, 399–400, 416, 516, 523, 526, 545, 547
electron transport chain, 219
electrooculogram (EOG), 102, 113–14, 151, 531
electroshock therapy, see electroconvulsive therapy
electrosleep, 485
ellipsoid, 349–51, 355–6
embryo, 342
EMG, see electromyography
emitter, 408, 413–20, 422–5, 427, 430–1, 433, 438–40, 526, 530–1, 534, 539–40, 545–6, 556
emitter–detector separation (in fNIRI), 408, 416–9, 424–5, 429–31, 433, 436, 439–1
encoding, frequency, see frequency encoding
  gradient, 204–7, 211, 213, 231–2, 236, 251, 253, 530, 534, 547, 554
  phase, see phase encoding
  spatial, 194–209
  step, 198, 205–7, 211–12, 231–3, 251
end feet, 223
endogenous component, 71, 531
endophenotype, 291, 531
energy, heat, 342–3, 368, 525
  metabolism, in brain, 219–1, 223, 385, 522
  of positron or photon, 373, 375, 382, see also specific energy
  resolution, 379–80, 382, 531, 540
RF, see radio frequency
specific, 373, 375, 377–9, 547

energy transfer, 190
English language, 259
enhancement, 58, 462, 518
entrainment, 492, 501, 507, 532
EOG, *see* electrooculogram
EP, *see* evoked potential
EPI, *see* echo planar imaging
epilepsy, 22, 339, 373, 387, 399, 444–5, 477, 480, 507, 515
epileptogenic, 477
epoch, 72, 104, 118, 120, 123–4, 167, 532
EPSP, *see* excitatory postsynaptic potential
equation, Beer–Lambert law, 420
   Larmor, 183, 194, 539
   330–1, 356, 433, 539
equilibrium, 186
equipotentiality, 13
   of cerebral cortex, 13
equivalent current dipole (ECD), 64, 532
equivalent dose, 389, 531–2
ERN, *see* error–related negativity
EROS, *see* event–related optical signal
ERP, *see* event–related potential
error, false positive, *see* Type 1 error
   in behavioural performance, 44
   in fNIRI measurement, 421, 424, 433, 529
   in source localization, 165, 319,
   in spatial normalization, 158
   propagation, in tractography, 354–6
error–related negativity (ERN), 71
erythema, 513, 517, 519, 532
estrogen, *see* oestrogen
ether, 485
ethics, 36, 54, 57, 516, 538, 543
event–related desynchronization (ERD), 79, 130, 532
event–related fMRI, advantages, 261, 264
   fast design, 262–4
   slow design, 262–4
   256, 258, 266, 273, 302
event–related optical signal (EROS), 30, 406, 411–13, 532–3, *see also* functional near–infrared imaging (fNIRI)
event–related potential (ERP), analysis, 99, 108, 124, 126, 436
   component, 62, 67, 69–71, 77, 93–4, 98, 101, 103, 116, 122, 130, 148, 390, 531–2
   condition, 72
   data, 98, 103–4, 108, 118, 120, 127–8, 130–1, 148, 152, 169
   effect, 68, 76, 101, 115–16, 118
   epoch, 72
   evoked by TMS, *see* transcranial magnetic stimulation evoked potential (TEP)
   experiment, 94, 98, 104, 110, 119, 130
   experimenter, 68

literature, 71, 75, 122
research, 69, 98–9, 120, 522, 534, 539, 541, 546
researcher, 48
source localization, 128
study, 108, 113, 116, 123, 260
waveform, 70–4, 121–2, 126–7, 529, 539, 546
event–related synchronization (ERS), 77, 79, 98, 130, 532
evoked potential (EP), 29, 62, 75, 80, 374, 455–7, 476, 532, 541–2, 556–7, *see also* transcranial magnetic stimulation evoked potentials
excitability, 453–4, 466, 469, 491, 493–4, 497, 500, 502, 512–13, 515, 517–9
excitation, –inhibition balance, 512
   in MRI acquisition, 178, 184–6, 188–9, 193–4, 196–7, 210–12, 230–2, 235–6, 238, 251, 253, 343, 368, 453, 479, 530, 532–3, 550, 553–5
excitation
excitatory postsynaptic potential (EPSP), 65, 223
exercise, 219, 225, 291
exogenous component, 71, 532
experience, day–to–day life, 55
   effects on brain structure, 9, 308–9
   human, 308
   learning, 44
   mental, 71
   of researcher, 27, 68, 209, 236, 334, 468
   ongoing, 270
   pain, 478
   perceptual, 21
   sensory, 467
   subjective, 21
experimental control, 467, 498, 511
experimental design, additive factors, 38–41
   between–subjects, 36, 45, 49, 57–8, 524
   blocked, 257–62, 266, 284, 298, 302–3, 525
   cross–sectional, 320, 324, 528
   ERP, 90–1, 98, 102–3, 114, 118, 123, 129
   factorial, 41–3, 57, 273, 275, 391, 532
   fMRI, 216–17, 237, 256–7, 259–61, 266–7, 269, 273, 275–6, 278, 280, 283, 298, 302–3
   fMRI–adaptation, 276–9
   fully–crossed, 41–2, 273, 532, 535
   general, 3, 18, 35–9, 528
   Hillyard principle, 48, 57–8, 98–9, 537
   longitudinal, 320–1, 324, 327–8, 528, 540, 549
   MEG, 134, 167–9
   parametric, 36, 44–6, 57, 276, 546
   PET, 372, 385, 390–2
   structural MRI, 320–1
   subtractive, 38–40
   tES, 488, 491, 511, 519
   TMS, 467–9
   TMS, 467, 469, 471–2
   within–subjects, 48–9, 58, 72, 559

experimental design
eye, blink, 28, 68, 70, 89, 91–4, 112–4, 129–30,
    151, 172, 174, 475, 523, 544
  blink, as EEG artifact, see artifacts, ocular
  blink, removal from EEG and MEG data, see
    artifacts, ocular
  channel, 112, see also electrooculogram
  in radiation safety, 389
  movement, 25–6, 89, 91, 112–13, 129, 151, 172,
    544, see also eye tracking
  naked, 76, 239, 248, 347, 409
  tracking, 24–6, 113, 532
  use in inspection of data, 22, 70, 172, 312, 353

F, see fluorine
FA, see fractional anisotropy
face, area, fusiform (FFA), 278, 283–4, 286, 288,
    see fusiform face area
  considerations in TMS, 463, 467–8, 478
  fusiform gyrus, see fusiform face area
  image, 99
  inverted
  mask, 147
  muscle, 28, 102
  non–, 260, 279, 286
  perception, 39, 259
  processing, 115–16, 119, 260
  stimulus, 116, 278, 286, 527
  upright, 69–70, 99, 115–9
factorial design, 41–3, 57, 273, 275, 391, 532
factory, analogy for brain imaging, 10
false alarm, 19, 380, 382
false detection, in PET, 374–5
false discovery rate (FDR), 170–1, 282, 436, 532–3
Faraday cage, 87–8, 533, 546
Faraday's laws of induction, 348, 446, see also
    Ampère's circuital law
Farwell, Lawrence, 75
fast optical signal (FOS), 406, 411–12, 418, 422,
    427, 430, 436, 438–1, 532–3, 535
fat, 28, 180, 188–93, 203, 210, 212, 233, 310,
    340–1, 396, 398, 410, 526, 543, see also myelin
fatigue, 92, 512, 517, 519
fcMRI, see functional connectivity MRI
FD, see frequency domain imaging
FDG, see fluorodeoxyglucose
FDR, see false discovery rate
Fechner, Gustav, 20–1
FEF, see frontal eye fields
    341, 472–3
FEM, see finite element model
    432, 507–12, 514, 519, 533
FFA, see fusiform face area
fibre, association, 339
  bundle, 339, 342, 350, 353
  commissural, 339

  crossing, 355–6
  laser, 425
  optic, 151, 440
  orientation, 349, 351–3
  pathway, 355
  projection, 338
  tracking, see tractography
  tract, 350–1, 353, 361, 364–5, 367–8, 530, 555
field, closed, see closed field
  magnetic, see magnetic field
  map, magnetic, 143, 235, 245, 348, 540
  of cognitive neuroscience, 2–3, 32–3, 36, 51, 56,
    62, 69, 71,
  open, see open field
  static, see B_0
  strength, 138, 141, 143, 147, 152, 173, 181, 191,
    194–5, 211–12, 224, 233, 343, 366, 446,
    471, 536, 539–40, 546, 555
figure–8 coil, 448–50, 467, 475, 533
filter, artifact, 108–9
  band–pass, 105, 108, 524, 544
  cutoff, 46, 98, 105–10, 130, 237, 430–1, 524
  EEG, 89
  Gaussian, 242
  high–pass, 105, 107–10, 130, 150, 199, 237, 430,
    524, 537
  high–pass, of image, 285
  in fMRI, 237–8
  Kalman, 428–30, 539
  low–pass, 88, 105, 107–8, 110–11, 120, 129–30,
    150, 156, 199, 285–6, 430, 540
  low–pass, of image, 285
  matched, see matched filter theorem
  notch, 105, 108, 130, 524, 544
  of fNIRI data, 430
  response, 104–6, 533, 557
  rolloff, 105–6, 108, 130, 196, 551, 557
  spatial, in beamforming, 162–6
  spatial, in fMRI, 240–
  spatial, in source localization, see beamformer
  theorem, see matched filter theorem
  to prevent aliasing, 110–1
  wavelet–based, 429–31
filtered back–projection, 384, 400, 533
finite element model (FEM), 432, 507–11, 525, 533
Fischl, Bruce, 248
fish, 4, 47, 445
Fitzgerald, Paul B., 460, 492
fixation cross, 269–71, 302, 304
flip angle, 184–5, 188, 193, 533
flower, 222
fluorine (F), in PET, 373, 385, see also
    fluorodeoxyglucose
fluorodeoxyglucose (FDG), 385, 393–4, 401
flux transformer, 140–1, 533
fly–through, 297, 300

fMRI, *see* functional magnetic resonance imaging
fMRI adaptation (fMRI–a), 276–9, 533, 543
fMRI–a, *see* fMRI adaptation
fNIRI, *see* functional near–infrared imaging (fNIRI)
fNIRS, *see* functional near–infrared imaging (fNIRI)
fontanelle, 508
formaldehyde, 243, 250
Formisano, Elia, 285
formula, 330, 433, 436, 524
    Beer–Lambert law, 420
    Larmor equation, 183, 194, 539
    forward inference, 52, 58
forward solution, 98, 127–8, 131, 155, 158–60, 162, 433, 441, 534
Fourier, decomposition, 178, 248
    Joseph, 199–200
    series, 76–8, 105, 534
    transform, 77–8, 94, 105, 124, 197, 199, 201–2, 211, 213, 246, 420, 427, 534, 539
Fox, Peter T., 2, 221–2, 292, 516
fractional anisotropy (FA), 288, 338, 351–3, 355–61, 363, 365, 367–8, 532, 534, 553, 556
fractional area latency, 121–2, 534
frame, 25, 240, 243, 272, 309
Freeman, Walter, 339
frequency, analysis of, in EEG, 124–6
    bands in human EEG, 76–9, 89, 94, 129, 168–9, 492, 517, 534
    domain, 76–8, 94, 105–6, 108, 124, 129, 167, 169, 415, 422, 440, 497, 533–4
    Larmor, 183–6, 190, 194–7, 206, 210–12, 233, 539, 553
    lexical, 103
    line, 87–8
    modulation, in tES, 486
    multiplexing, 419–20, 534, 542
    Nyquist, 110, 522, 544
    of RF pulse, *see* Larmor frequency
    of rTMS, 461
    plot, 80, 108, 125
    spatial, 178, 198–207, 211, 213, 242, 553
    word, 42–3, 103
frequency, domain (FD) imaging (fNIRI), 414, 416, 421–2, 424–7, 429, 438–41, 529, 533–4
    encoding, 178, 198, 204–7, 211–13, 231–3, 236, 251, 253, 343, 534, 547
    encoding gradient, 204–6, 213, 232, 236, 251, 253, 534, 547
    resonant, 184–5, 194–5, 343, 503, *see also* Larmor frequency
Freud, Sigmund, 338
Friston, Karl, 16, 246, 258, 266, 273, 296, 299–300, 305, 325, 327–8, 336
frog, 445

frontal eye fields, 471–2
frontal lobe, 10–11, 73, 233, 300, 339, 360–1, 417, 438, 463, 478, 508
frontal lobotomy, 339
FSLview, 192
full–width at half–maximum (FWHM), 240, 534–5
fully crossed (experimental design), 41–2, 273, 532, 535
functional connectivity, affected by TMS, 468
    in fMRI (fc–MRI), 229, 270, 289–92, 294–6, 298–9, 301, 303–4, 314, 316, 363, 366, 369, 398, 533, 535, 543, 552
    in MEG, 165, 169
    in PET, 393–4
    relationship to DTI, 366
functional integration, 16, 535
functional magnetic resonance imaging (fMRI), adaptation design, 276–9
    baseline, 269–73
    baseline condition, 269–73
    blocked design, 257–60
    BOLD effect, *see* blood oxygenation level dependent
    combined with fNIRI, 436–8
    combined with TMS, 471–2
    condition–rich design, 278–80, 285–8
    conjunction, 273–6
    discovery, 179, 216–8
    disjunction, 275–6
    duration of scan, 231, 236–7
    dynamic causal modelling (DCM), 299–302
    effective connectivity, 294–302
    event–related, *see* event–related fMRI
    event–related design, 260–9
    experimental design, 257–80
    filtering, 237
    functional connectivity, 289–94
    Granger causality analysis (GCA), 295–6
    graph theory analysis, 292–3
    independent components analysis (ICA), 292–4
    motion correction, 238–40
    multiple comparison correction, 281–
    multivariate analysis, 284–8
    normalization (spatial), 243–51
    physiological basis, 218–6
    preprocessing, 237–51
    psychophysiological interactions, 296–9
    pulse sequence, 203–6
    region of interest (ROI) analysis, 282–4
    spatial smoothing, 240–
    statistical analysis, 280–8
    temporal resolution, 227–9
    time–continuous design, 279–80, 285–8
    univariate analysis, 280–1
functional near–infrared imaging (fNIRI), 3, 30, 403–41, 508, 524–35, 537–40, 542, 545–6, 553, 555–7

channel count, 431, 436
combined with other imaging modalities, 436–8
continuous wave (CW), 420–1, *see also* continuous wave imaging
data analysis, 426–36
data conversion, 427
development, 404–5
fast signal, 411–13, 427, 430, 436, 438–1, 535
filtering, 430
frequency domain (FD), 421–2
instrumentation, 414–7, 4
intensity of light, 408
measurement, 405, 413–20
motion correction, 428–9
quality assurance, 427–8
relationship to ERP, 411–13
short–distance correction, 429–30
slow signal, 406–13, 419, 427, 430, 535
source localization, 426, 431–3, 437–8
spatial resolution, 405–6, 408, 417–19, 424–5
statistical analysis, 433–6
temporal resolution, 406–7, 411–16, 419–20, 422–6
time domain (TD), 422–6
types, 406, 414
validation, 411–12, 437
wavelengths used, 409–10, 413–14
functional near–infrared spectroscopy (fNIRS), *see* functional near–infrared imaging (fNIRI)
functional specificity, 278
fusiform face area (FFA), 278, 283–4, 286, 288
FWHM, *see* full–width half–maximum

GABA, 6–7, 461, 466, 480–1, 500–1, 512, 517, 519, 535
$GABA_A$, 459, 465–6
$GABA_B$, 459, 461, 465–6
Gabor patch, 286
Galen, 445
Galvani, Luigi, 445
gamma, frequency band in EEG, 6, 77–8, 94, 263, 267, 492, 494, 496, 498, 517, 528, 534–5
gamma ray, 388, 552
garden, 222
gating, 347, 474, 525
Gaussian, distribution, 240, 242
 filter, 242
 kernel, 240–2, 554
 random field theory (GRFT), 281–2, 395, 436, 535–6, 554
Gazzaniga, Michael, 2–3, 34, 339
GCA, *see* Granger causality analysis
general linear model (GLM), 103, 169, 434, 535
German language, 259
gesture, 136, 271–2
Glasser, Matthew, 14–15, 314, 316–7

GLI, *see* grey level index
glia, 4, 7, 33, 535
GLM, *see* general linear model
global normalization, 395
glucose, 180, 219, 221, 385, 387, 393, 400–1, 522, 548
 metabolic rate, 221, 385
glutamate, 6–7, 221, 223, 459, 466, 480–1, 500, 512, 517, 519, 523, 525, 535
glycolysis, 221, 223
gold standard, 22, 56, 131, 363, 365, 367, 369, 437, 445
Golgi, 7–8
gradient, coil, 345
 dephasing, 343
 direction, 196, 344–5, 529, 534, 547
 echo, 217, 346
 hardware, 235–6, 251, 554
 magnetic field, in TMS, 475
 map, 315–6
 refocusing, 344, 368, 550
 rephasing, 344, 368, 550
 reversed, 206
 slice selection, 196–7, 232, 553
 spatial, 194–7, 203, 238, 316, 348, 553
 strength, 205, 231, 235
 switching, 231, 252
gradiometer, 134, 141–6, 152–3, 159, 170, 172, 174, 524, 536, 539, 547
grammar, 15, 259, *see also* syntax
grand average, 68, 115–16, 120, 130, 536
grand mean scaling, 395
Granger causality analysis (GCA), 295–7, 299, 535–6
graph theory, 292–3, 301, 536–7, 542, 553, 558
gray (Gy; unit of measure), 231, 233, 235, 388–9, 536
Gray, Henry, 8
grey level index (GLI), 312–13, 535–6
grey matter, concentration, 322–6, 328–9, 335–6, 536, 558
 contrast, *see* contrast of MR images
GRFT, *see* Gaussian random field theory
Grill–Spector, Kalanit, 277–9
Grinvald, Amiram, 221–
ground, electrical, 84, 87
ground electrode, 84, 86, 92–3, 490, 529, 536
ground truth, 128, 153–4, 167
guidelines, MRI safety, 207–9, 347
 radiation safety, 389–90
 safety, for TMS, 473, 477–8
 safety, in fNIRI, 414
guitar, 184
Gy, *see* gray (unit of measure)
gyromagnetic ratio, 183, 536

H, *see* hydrogen
H coil (TMS), 448–9, 451
H$_2$0, *see* water
habituation
habituation, 390–1, *see also* adaptation, neural
haemodynamic response function (HRF), defined, 227, 251, 536
  filtering, 237
  in event–related fMRI, 261–9
  in fNIRI, 407–11, 434, 436, 480,
  properties, 227–9, 253, 273
  summation, 258, 262–6
  under–additivity, 262–3
  variability, 228–9, 296, 301
haemoglobin (Hb), defined, 217, 536–7
  deoxygenated (deoxy–Hb), 217–19, 221–2, 224–6, 251, 253, 406–7, 409–10, 413–14, 421, 424, 427, 429–30, 434, 437–40, 528, 542
  oxygenated (oxy–Hb), 217–19, 221–2, 224–6, 251, 253, 406–7, 409–10, 413–14, 421, 424, 427, 429–30, 434–5, 437–40, 528, 542
  tHb (total blood volume), 406–7, 434
hair, 80, 85, 94, 152, 409, 411, 413, 428, 440
half–life, 372, 375, 385, 388–9, 391–2, 401, 470, 548
Handwerker, Daniel, 228–9, 301
Haxby, James, 280, 284–5
Hb, *see* haemoglobin
HCP, *see* Human Connectome Project
HD–tES, *see* high definition transcranial electrical stimulation
He, *see* Helium
head coil, 234, 240, 322
head model, 155–7, 164, *see also* boundary element model *and* finite element model
head movement, correction, *see* motion correction
  in diffusion MRI, 346, 348, 368
  in EEG, 90, 93, 102, 106, 129
  in fMRI, 238–40, 240, 252–3, 294
  in fNIRI, 406, 410, 413, 422, 439–41, 528
  in MEG, 146, 148, 152, 174, 537
head position, 146–8, 158, 172, 174, 238, 537
headache, 445, 478, 480–1
headphones, 89, 100–1, 151
hearing loss, side effect of TMS, 478
heart rate, 24, 82, 404, 547
heartbeat, 28, 89–90, 93, 172, 174, 346–7, 413, 525
heat, 211, 342–3, 347, 368, 373, 380, 473–4, 477, 480, 525
heat energy, 342–3, 368, 525
heating, in fNIRI, 414
  in MRI, 207–9, 207–9, 213, 347
  of EEG electrodes during TMS, 473, 477–8
  of implants during TMS, 477–8
  of photodiodes, 378–9
  of TMS coil, 449, 453

Hebb, Donald O., 9
Hebbian mechanism, 462
helium (He), 135, 138–9, 144, 172, 174–5, 348
helper cell, *see* glia
hemoglobin (Hb), *see* haemoglobin
hertz (Hz; unit of measurement), 76, 82, 94, 524, 534, 552
high–definition tES (HD–tES), 489–90, 506, 508–10, 515–16, 518–19, 537
high–frequency noise, 88, 105–6, 108, 122, 156
high–frequency rTMS, 461, 479, 537, 545
high–pass filter, 105, 107–10, 130, 150, 199, 237, 430, 524, 537
Hillyard principle, 48, 57–8, 98–9, 537
Hillyard, Steve, 48, 57–8, 75, 95, 98–9, 131, 537
hippocampus, 4–5, 9–11, 15, 168, 297–8, 300, 318–19, 493–4, 551
histology, 308
hOc3d (brain region), 313
hodology, 338–9, 537
Hoge, R.D., 192, 222, 225–6
Horner, Aidan J., 262–3
Hotelling's T^2, 327
house, 285, 287, 471
HRF, *see* haemodynamic response function
Huang, Yu, 55, 465, 507
hub, 292–3, 537
Huettel, Scott, 254, 262
Human Brain Project (HBP), 312, 537
Human Connectome Project (HCP), 314, 317, 340, 537
human experience, 308
hydrogen (H), 178, 180–1, 183–4, 209–10, 212, 341, 344
hydrophobic, 342
hypercapnia, 225–6, 537
hyperoxia, 537
hyperpolarization, 499
hypothesis, 13, 43, 47, 58, 79, 103–4, 122–4, 128–9, 169, 219, 221, 278, 280, 283, 299, 521, 523, 537, 543
Hz, *see* hertz

I, *see* iodine
I–wave, *see* indirect wave
Ibn–Sidah, 445
Ibuprofen, 228
ICA, *see* independent components analysis
ICBM, *see* International Consortium for Brain Mapping
ICF, *see* intracortical facilitation
IFG, *see* inferior frontal gyrus
ill–posed problem, 126–6, 167, 405, 550
imageability, 72, 103
impedance, 81, 85, 90, 92, 94, 115, 173, 474, 486, 488, 515–16, 518–19, 537–8, 553

implant, 152, 400, 402, 406, 477–8
impulse response function (IRF), 423, 427, 436
incidental finding, 57, 209, 538
independent components analysis (ICA), 114, 129, 292–5, 413, 429, 431, 441, 474, 476, 538
independent variable, 37–8, 56–8, 524, 529, 535, 538, 541–2, 546, 557
indirect wave (I–wave), 466, 537–8
individual differences, 57, 154–5, 225, 247, 254, 308, 313–4, 318, 358, 364, 393, 432, 506, 508, 511–12, 517, 519, *see also* endophenotypes
induction, 90, 110, 348, 445–6, 465–6, 475, 514, 529, 557, *see also* Ampère's circuital law
infant, 30, 406, 408, 422, 439, 508
inference, forward, 52, 58
  in interpreting neuroimaging data, 26, 30, 32, 52–4
inference, reverse, 36, 52–4, 58, 521, 551
inferior frontal gyrus
inferior frontal gyrus (IFG), 11, 13, 15, 41, 52, 283, 297, 314, 445–6
informed consent, 54, 209, 515, 538
infrared light, 24, 30, 438, 535, *see also* functional near–infrared imaging (fNIRI)
inhibition, 69, 270, 454–5, 459–61, 464–6, 480, 489, 499, 501–2, 512, 519, 522–3
inhomogeneity, 191, 212, 217, 233, 235, 322, 348, 555
inion, 82–3, 538, 558
input–output curve, 466, 541, *see also* motor evoked potential
insomnia, 485
institutional review board (IRB), 54, 516
insulin, 7, 152
insurance, 55, 209
integrity, of white matter, 28, 343, 352–3, 359, 367, 368, 530, 534
intelligence, 56, 308
inter–stimulus interval (ISI), 101, 273, 302–3, 413, 538, 554
inter–trial coherence (ITC), 169
interaction, between brain areas, *see* functional connectivity *and* effective connectivity
  between variables, 43, 103, 259, 538
  cortico–cortical, 492, 494
  magnetic fields, 190, 197, 203, 210,
  of subatomic particles, 373
  psychophysiological, 296–300, 548–9
interleaved, 15–16, 438, 472–3, 538
intermittent theta burst stimulation (iTBS), 464–5, 538–9, 545
International 10–10 system, 82–3, 432, 448, 479, 495, 498, 506, 538, 546, 558
International 10–20 system, 82
International 10–5 system, 82
International Consortium for Brain Mapping (ICBM), 250

intracellular structures, 342
intracortical facilitation (ICF), 458–60, 499
intraparietal sulcus (IPS), 249, 283, 471–3
inverse problem, 98, 126, 129, 131, 159–61, 431, 433, 534, 538–9, 541, 550
inverse solution, 126, 155, 539
inverted face, 99–100, 117
iodine (I), 373
ion channel, 5–6, 65, 219–0, 411, 439, 466, 480–1, 499–501, 517, 519
ion pump, 219
IPS, *see* intraparietal sulcus
IR, *see* infrared light
IRB, *see* institutional review board
IRF, *see* impulse response function
ISI, *see* inter–stimulus interval
isotope, 144, 365, 385
isotropic, diffusion, 342, 349–51, 367, 539
  voxel, 346, 354, 539
iTBS, *see* intermittent theta burst stimulation
ITC, *see* inter–trial coherence

J, *see* joule
Jacobian determinant, 328–9, 539
Jacobian matrix, 328–9, 539, 556
Jasper, Herbert, 445
jewellery, 151, 208, 478
jitter, in event–related fMRI, 266–9
Jöbsis, Frans, 404
Josephson junction, 139–40, 539, 555
Josephson, Brian, 139
joule (J), 388, 536
JuBrain atlas, 312–3
Jülich (Germany), 312

K, *see* potassium *and* kelvin
k space, 178, 199–202, 204–7, 211, 213, 230–3, 235–6, 251, 253, 530, 534, 539, 547, 554
Kalman filter, 428, 539
kelvin (K; unit of measure), 138
kernel, smoothing, 240–2, 252, 323–4, 348–9, 395, 535, 539, 541, 554
ketamine, 466
ketoprofen, 514
Koepp, M.J., 391–2
Kriegeskorte, Nikolaus, 278, 280, 285–8
Kwong, Kenneth, 178, 217–8

lactic acid, 219
lamotrigine, 466
LAN, *see* left anterior negativity
language, 11, 15, 22–4, 33, 45, 53, 72, 75, 100, 122, 259, 283, 338–9, 391, 444, 463
Laplace equation, 330–1
Laplacian, *see* Laplace equation
Largus, Scribonius, 445

Larmor equation, 183, 194, 539
Larmor frequency, 183–6, 190, 194–7, 206,
    210–12, 233, 539, 553
laser, 144, 147, 422, 425, 439, 503, 545
laser diode (LD), 414, 539
Lashley, Karl, 13
late commitment, 280
latency, 69, 71, 73, 120–2, 129–30, 457, 476, 534,
    539, 546
latent component, 72–4, 128, 148, 526, 539
lateral occipital cortex (LOC), 272, 277–9
lateralized readiness potential (LRP), 76, 539
Latin, 338, 521, 526, 548
LD, *see* laser diode
lead field, 142, 159, 539
learning, effects of tACS, 494–6
    effects of tDCS, 491–2
    effects of tRNS, 497–8
    experience, 44
    in structural MRI studies, 321
    motor, in tES, 500
    process, 44
    see also long–term potentiation
    308–9
least squares estimation, 159, 539–0
Leborgne, M, 13, *see also* Broca, Paul
LED, *see* light–emitting diode
left anterior negativity (LAN; ERP component),
    71, 104
lesion, –deficit method, 22–3, 308–9, 446, 539
    –symptom mapping, *see* voxel–based
        lesion–symptom mapping (VLSM)
    location, 22, 24
    virtual, 446, 461, 463, 466, 472
    voxel–based, *see* voxel–based lesion symptom
        mapping (VLSM)
    see also brain injury
letter, 39, 69, 71, 75, 82–3, 103, 143, 260–1,
    457, 510
LFP, *see* local field potential
LICI, *see* long–interval intracortical inhibition
light, absorption, in fNIRI, 409–10, 414–15, 420–1,
    424, 433, 438, 440–1, 521, 542
    as form of radiation, 373
    as stimulus, 17–18, 21, 144
    energy, 373, 409–10, 440
    in neuroimaging, *see* functional near–infrared
        imaging (fNIRI)
    infrared (IR), 24, 30, 404, 407–11, 438, 535,
        see also functional near–infrared
        imaging (fNIRI)
    output, 379–80, 540
    particle, 373, 375, *see also* photon
    scattering, 405, 408
    sensor, 375, 278–80
    source, in fNIRI, *see* emitter
    spectrum, 410

speed, 381, 400
    wavelengths used in fNIRI, 409–10, 413–14
light–emitting diode (LED), 9, 11, 16, 22, 47, 55,
    58, 75, 81, 179, 216, 218–19, 225, 250, 262,
    315, 319, 339, 404–5, 414, 439, 445, 485, 489,
    492, 494, 497, 502, 518, 540
Likert scale, 19
Limb, Charles J., 20
line of response, 381, 383, 400–1, 540
linear mixed effects, 280, 302–3, 359, *see also*
    general linear model
linear regression, 280, 303, 430–1, *see also* general
    linear model
lobe, frontal, 10–11, 73, 233, 300, 339, 360–1, 417,
    438, 463, 478, 508
    occipital, 10–11, 41, 52, 79, 128, 145, 166,
        218–19, 277, 435, 469, 472, 493, 548
    parietal, 10, 15, 45, 47, 262, 283, 300, 438, 460,
        472, 526, 555
    temporal, 10, 23, 69, 73, 163, 166, 168, 233, 277,
        284–5, 360–1, 391, 541, 555
lobotomy, 339
LOC, *see* lateral occipital cortex
local field potential (LFP), 228
local minimum, 159, 540
localization, of EEG, ERP, or MEG sources, *see*
    source localization
Localization in the Cerebral Cortex (book), 11
localizer, 251, 253, 283, 550
Logothetis, Nikos, 227–8
long–interval intracortical inhibition (LICI), 458–1
long–range connections, 340, 526, 543
long–term depression (LTD), 9, 491, 499–500,
    523 540
long–term potentiation (LTP), 9, 465, 491,
    499–500, 517, 523, 540
longitudinal design, 320–1, 324, 327–8, 528,
    540, 549
longitudinal fasciculus, 363
longitudinal plane, 184–6, 188–9, 193, 210, 212,
    532–3, 540, 550, 555, 557
López–Alonso, Virginia, 511–2
loudness, 21, 37–8, 47–8, 58, 70, 72, 128, 527, 549
low–frequency noise, 105, 431
low–frequency rTMS, 461, 463, 479, 540
low–pass filter, 88, 105, 107–8, 110–11, 120,
    129–30, 150, 156, 199, 285–6, 430, 540
LRP (ERP component), *see* lateralized
    readiness potential
LSO, *see* lutetium oxyorthosilicate
LTD, *see* long–term depression
LTP, *see* long–term potentiation
Luck, Steven, 48, 52, 95, 98, 108, 131, 537
luminance, 44, 72, 288
luminescence, 378–9, 540
lungs, 216, 389, 536
lutetium oxyorthosilicate (LSO; $LuSiO_5$:Ce), 380

M1, *see* motor cortex, primary
machine learning, 15, 285–8, 315
macro–scale (organization of cerebral cortex), 10, 15, 33, 340
Magistretti, P.J., 221, 223
magnetic field, gradient, 142, 178, 194–5, 197, 201–2, 205, 207–8, 211–12, 232–3, 238, 240, 252, 343, 367–8, 529, 531, 540, 547, 550
  in MEG, 138–49
  induction, 29, *see also* Ampère's circuital law
  map, 143, 235, 245, 540
  of Earth, 181
  of fridge magnet, 181
  strength of MRI scanner, 181
magnetic flux, 138, 140, 174, 446, 533, 540, 547
magnetic moment, 180–1, 183, 190, 210, 212, 217, 536, 540, 542
magnetic resonance imaging (MRI), 177–9, 181, 183, 185, 187, 189, 191, 193, 195, 197, 199, 201, 203, 205, 207, 209, 211, 213, 254, 540
  2D reconstruction, 197–201
  combined with PET, 393–4, 397–9
  contrast, 191–3
  diffusion tensor (DTI), *see* diffusion tensor imaging (DTI)
  diffusion–weighted, *see also* diffusion tensor imaging (DTI)
  functional, *see* functional magnetic resonance imaging (fMRI)
  gradient, 194–7, 202–7
  k space, 199–207
  measurement, 186–207
  physical basis, 180–6
  precession, 182–3
  pulse sequence, 188, 196–8, 204–7
  resonance, 183–6
  safety, 207–9
  spatial encoding, 194–7
  structural, *see* structural magnetic resonance imaging
magnetic susceptibility, 233–4, 251, 253, 540–1, 552
magnetically permeable, 150, 541
magnetoencephalography (MEG),
  beamforming, 162–6
  combined with EEG, 148–9
  data acquisition, 138–49
  data analysis, 169–72
  dipole modelling, 158–60
  distributed source modelling, 160–2
  experimental design, 167–9
  gradiometer, 140–4
  head position, 146–8
  instrumentation, 398
  physiological basis, 135–8
  physiological noise, 151–2
  recording with EEG, 148–9
  sensors, 138–6
  shielding, 149–51
  signal and noise, 149–53
  signal processing, 152–3
  source localization, 153–67
  wearable, 144–7
magnetometer, 134–5, 140–2, 144, 147, 152, 172, 174, 539, 541, 545, 555
Magstim Inc., 449, 451
main effect, 42–3, 116, 541, 548
make–up, 152
Malonek, Dov, 221
MANCOVA, *see* multivariate analysis of covariance
manganese (Mn), 365
MANOVA, *see* multivariate analysis of variance
Mansfield, Sir Peter, 230–1
MAO, *see* monoamine oxidase
map, magnetic field, *see* magnetic field map
mask, for wearable MEG, 144, 147
  in DTI analysis, 356, 358
  in fMRI data analysis, 271–2, 541
  to reduce head motion in MRI, 240
  visual, TMS study of, 456–7
mass action, 13
mass univariate analysis, 123, 169, 282, 284, 303–4, 359, 541–2
mastoid, 69–70, 83, 85, 112, 115–9
matched filter theorem, 240, 242, 252, 323, 348, 541, 554
matching, brain shape, 23, 246, 248, 250, 314, 357, 554
  stimuli, 42, 98
matrix, cortical connectivity, 340–1
  dissimilarity, 286–8
  Jacobian, 328–9
  similarity, 286
maze, 296–7, 300
MBLL, *see* modified Beer–Lambert law
McCarthy, Gregory, 254, 261–2, 266
Mcintyre, Michael, 3
MD, *see* mean diffusivity
mean amplitude, 104, 121–4, 129–30, 152, 169, 279, 522, 534, 541
mean diffusivity (MD), 352, 358
medication, 253, 291, 477, 512, 519, *see also* drug
MEG, *see* magnetoencephalography
memory, 168–9
  effects of tACS, 494–6
  effects of tDCS, 491–2
  effects of tRNS, 497–8
  encoding, 262, 493, 551
  episodic, 270
  loss, after electroshock therapy, 485
  short–term, 269

menstrual cycle, 512–13, 517, 519
mental chronometry, 17, 75, 541, 550
mental experience, 71
mental illness, *see* psychiatric illness
MEP, *see* motor evoked potential
meso–maps, 310, 541
meso–scale (organization of cerebral cortex), 11, 13–15, 33, 310, 312, 314, 334–5, 340
meta–analysis, 360–1, 491–2, 506, 511, 517, 519
meta–data, 347
metal, artifact in MEG, 151–2
  grinding, 208
  in tattoo, 208
Meynert, Theodor, 338–9
micro–scale (organization of cerebral cortex), 11, 15, 340, 362
microscopic, structure of brain, 308–14
middle frontal gyrus, 460, 492
mild cognitive impairment, 387
Millikan, Glen, 404
mini–blocks, 264
minimum norm estimation
minimum norm estimation (MNE), 161, 541
mislocalization, of BOLD signal, 224
  of EEG/ERP signal
  of MEG signal
  of PET signal, 374–6, 380–2
mismatch negativity (MMN), 261
missing data, 321
mixed designs, 49, 58, 542
MMN (ERP component), *see* mismatch negativity
MNE, *see* minimum norm estimation
MNE–Python (software), 146, 163–4
MNI, *see* Montreal Neurological Institute
MNI152 atlas, 245, 250–2, 312, 452, 323, 357–8, 394, 452,
mock scanner, 240
model–based tract segmentation, 357, 542
modified Beer–Lambert law (MBLL), 421, 424, 426–7, 433, 524, 529, 541–2
modularity, 292, 542
molecular lattice, 188, 542
Moliadze, Vera, 493, 497, 510
monitor, video (in stimulus presentation), 25, 64, 86–9, 91, 100–1, 550
monitoring, of data during collection, 88, 92, 100, 113, 129–30, 148, 151
  of disease state or treatment, 291, 444, 507
  of participants in TMS studies, 479–80
  semantic, 40
monkey, 71, 228, 262, 339, 365
monoamine oxidase (MAO), 386
monophasic pulse
Montreal Neurological Institute (MNI), 250, 281–

morphometry, defined, 179, 309, 215–6, 542
  deformation–based, *see* deformation–based morphometry (DBM)
  manual approach, 315, 318
  semi–automated, 318–9
  tensor–based, *see* tensor–based morphometry (TBM)
  voxel–based, *see* voxel–based morphometry (VBM)
motion, –sensitive cortex, *see* V5 (brain region)
  visual, 52, 273, 450, 461, 505
motion artifact, 239–40, 367, 428–9, 539, *see also* head motion
motion capture, 20
motion correction, defined, 542
  in DWI data processing, 348
  in fMRI, 216, 238, 245, 252–3, 522
  in structural MRI, 325
  of fNIRI data, 428–9, 431, 528, 530,
  of MEG data, 144, 148
  of PET data, 398
motion–sensitive cortex, *see* V5
motor cortex, effects of tACS, 493
  in tES, 501–2
  in tRNS, 497–8
  mapping with MEG, 137
  primary (M1), 218, 229, 242, 460, 476, 493, 497, 501–2, 506, 508, 548
  stimulation with TMS, 455–6, 460
motor evoked potential (MEP), 455–6, 458–61, 466, 485–6, 491, 497–8, 511–12, 521, 541–2, 551–2
motor mapping, 455–6, 479
motor threshold, 455, 458, 469, 479, 521–2, 551
  active, *see* active motor threshold (aMT)
  resting, *see* resting motor threshold (rMT)
movement, *see* motion
movement planning, ERP component related to, *see* lateralized readiness potential
MR–active nucleus, 180, 183, 536, 539, 542
MRI, *see* magnetic resonance imaging
MS, *see* multiple sclerosis
MT, 317, 341, 450, 466
MT (brain region), *see* V5
mu, frequency band in EEG, 77, 94, 150, 534, 542
  metal, 542
MUA, *see* multi–unit activity
multi–centre research, 312, 314, 340
multi–start approach, in dipole modelling, 160
multi–unit activity (MUA), 228
multi–voxel pattern analysis (MVPA), 284–8, 303
multidimensional scaling, 288
multimodal imaging, 27, 314, 316–17, 362, 542
  EEG and MEG, 148–9
  fNIRI with other methods, 437
  involving fNIRI, 436–8
  involving PET, 372, 393–9, 400

multiple comparison correction, defined, 542
   in DTI, 359
   in ERP, 103–4, 123, 129
   in fMRI, 256, 281–2, 303–4
   in fNIRI, 434–6
   in MEG, 170–2
   methods, 532, 535
multiple comparison problem, 169–70, 282–3, 303
multiple sclerosis (MS), 209, 340, 363
multiplexing, 419–20, 440, 526, 534, 542, 556
multivariate analysis, 153, 283–5, 303, 327, 527, 541–2, 551, *see also* multi-voxel pattern analysis
multivariate analysis of covariance (MANCOVA), 327
multivariate analysis of variance (MANOVA), 327
muscle, artifact in EEG, 68, 89, 91–4, 102, 106, 114, 129–0
   artifact in EEG–TMS, 475–6
   artifact in MEG, 151
   contraction, 55, 106, 130, 445, 463, 469, 471, 478, 480–1, 523, 542, 552
   in DTI, 363
muscle artifact, 151, 475–6
music, 20, 92
MVPA, *see* multi-voxel pattern analysis
myelin, 5–6, 26, 28, 65, 191, 310, 314–16, 325, 340, 342, 367–8, 543
myeloarchitecture, 13–14, 308, 310, 312, 335, 541, 543

N-methyl-D-aspartate (NMDA), 6, 459, 466, 500–1
N1 (ERP component), 69–71, 74, 120, 128, 456
N170 (ERP component), 69–71, 100, 116–8
N2 (ERP component), 71, 74
N250 (ERP component), 116–7
N400 (ERP component), 71–2, 75, 103, 109, 122, 125–6
Na, 6, 220, 288
Na, *see* sodium
Na–K pump, *see* ion pump
naked eye, 76, 239, 248, 347, 409
nasion, 82–3, 115–17, 119, 147, 543, 558
National Research Council of Canada (NRC), 3
naturalistic, 280
naturalistic stimuli, 280
navigation, 296–7, 299–300, 452–3, 469, 479, 481, 506, 543
near-infrared neuroimaging (NIN), 406, *see also* functional near-infrared imaging (fNIRI)
near-infrared tomography (NIT), 406, *see also* functional near-infrared imaging (fNIRI)
Neisser, Ulrich, 10
neo-phrenology, 15, 256, 289,
   see also phrenology

net magnetization vector (NMV), 178, 182, 184–6, 188–93, 197, 210, 212, 343, 346, 5323, 543–4, 550, 555, 557
network, –based correlation, 292–3, 543, 552
   activity–dependent model, 503, 543
   connectivity, 16
   default mode, *see* default mode network
   discovery, 300–1, 543
   in functional connectivity, 289–94
   view of brain, 256, 289
neural, adaptation, 263, 390, 522, 533, 543
   connection, *see* synapse
   network, 285, 293, 299–300, 393, 503, 512
neuro–navigation, 452–3, 469, 479, 481, 506, 543
neuroanatomist, 8, 11, 309–12, 314–5
neurocognitive, 76, 93, 104, 153, 270, 290, 339, 437, 486, 504
neurodegeneration, 318
neuroethics, 55, 57–9, 543
neurofibrillary tangles, 386
neurohormone, 7, 543
neuromodulator, 7, 31, 33, 372, 385–7, 391, 393, 399–402, 480–1, 500, 517, 519, 543, 555
neuron, 4–7, 9, 16, 31, 33–4, 62–7, 65, 79, 135–7, 154, 158, 172–3, 218–3, 226, 228, 230, 264, 276–7, 286, 302, 304, 339–40, 368, 386, 390, 407, 411, 465–6, 484, 486, 489, 491, 499–506, 517, 519, 521, 523–9, 535, 540, 547, 549, 552–5, 557
   firing, *see* action potential
   number in brain, 4, 9
   pyramidal, 4, 158, 411, 549
neuroplasticity, 463, 486, 491
neuroprivacy, 55–6, 58, 543
neuropsychology, 11, 22, 540, 544
neurostimulation, 17, 28, 31–4, 49, 56, 58, 436, 441, 485, 542, 544, 557, *see also* transcranial magnetic stimulation (TMS) *and* transcranial electrical stimulation (tES)
neurosurgery, 2, 22, 63, 243, 252, 339, 347, 444–5
Neurosynth database, 53
neurotransmitter, 6–7, 11, 14, 31, 33, 65, 219–21, 223, 228, 460–1, 465–6, 470, 472, 499–501, 512, 521, 535, 543–4, 548, 550, 555
   excitatory, *see* glutamate
   inhibitory, *see* GABA
   recycling, 220
neutron, 180, 373–5, 385, 400, 547
Neville, Helen, 3, 48, 71
Newman, Aaron, 21, 71–2, 74, 116, 259, 272, 275
NIBS, *see* noninvasive brain stimulation
nicotine, 251, 512
NIRS, *see* functional near-infrared imaging (fNIRI)
NIRx Medical Technologies LLC, 417
NIT, *see* near-infrared tomography
nitrous oxide, 485

Nitsche, Michael, 485, 491, 494, 499, 502, 506, 520
NMDA, *see* n–methyl d–aspartate
NMV, *see* net magnetization vector
Nobel prize, 7, 139, 230
node, 65, 292–4, 300–1, 537, 544, 553, 558
noise, effects on tractography, 353–4, 365–6
  high–frequency, 88, 105–6, 108, 122, 156
  in DTI, 348, 354–6, 359
  in EEG, 86–90
  in EEG, 67–8, 73, 76–8, 80–1, 84–94, 98, 101–2, 104–6, 108, 114, 120, 122, 126, 128–0
  in fMRI, 237, 240–2, 252, 277–8, 281–2, 294
  in fNIRI, 404, 410–11, 413, 426, 428, 430–1, 434, 436, 438, 440–1
  in MEG, 134–5, 141–2, 147, 149–52, 154–6, 162–3, 168, 172–5
  in MRI, 186
  normalization, 162–3, 530, 544, 554
  in PET, 379–80, 400, 402
  in structural MRI, 323
  in tES, 486, 497, 502–4, 506, 513, 517, 519
  in TMS, 455, 471, 478, 481
  low–frequency, 105, 431
  random, stimulation in tES, *see* transcranial random noise stimulation (tRNS)
  ratio, *see* signal–to–noise ratio *and* contrast–to–noise ratio
non–invasive brain stimulation (NIBS), 444, 479, 520, 543–5, 552, 558, *see also* transcranial magnetic stimulation (TMS) *and* transcranial electrical stimulation (tES)
nonlinear registration, 246–7, 254, 323, 357, 544
nonparametric statistics, 171, 525, 544, 546, 549
noradrenaline, 466, 480, *see also* norepinephrine
norepinephrine, 7, *see also* noradrenaline
normalization, global (in PET), 395
  linear affine, 323
  noise, 162–3, 530, 544, 554
  nonlinear, 323
  nonlinear, in DTI, 357
  of PET data, 395
  spatial, in DTI, 356–8
  spatial, in human connectome project, 314–5
  spatial, in structural MRI, 320, 322–9, 332–4
  spherical, 248–50, 332–4
  surface–based, 248–50, 332–4
notch filter, 105, 108, 130, 524, 544
noun, 37, 41–3, 72
NRC, *see* National Research Council of Canada
nucleus, 180, 183, 373–5, 385, 470, 536, 539, 542
null event, 266, 273
Nyquist frequency, 110, 522, 544

O, *see* oxygen
o–tDCS, *see* oscillatory tDCS

obsessive–compulsive disorder (OCD), 479
occipital cortex, lateral, 12, 39, 69, 77, 90, 154, 227, 272, 279, 313, 470
see lateral occipital cortex
occipital lobe, 10–11, 41, 52, 79, 128, 145, 166, 218–19, 277, 435, 469, 472, 493, 548
OCD, *see* obsessive–compulsive disorder
ocular artifacts, 102, 113–14, 544, *see also* blink
oddball, 260–2, 266, 390–1, *see also* P3, mismatch negativity
oestrogen, 7
offline, defined in neuroimaging, 545
  effects of TMS, 465
  filtering, 110
  inhibitory protocol, 463, 544
  processing of DTI data, 345
  removal of artifacts, 174
  tES protocols, 491–2, 500–1, 503, 519
  TMS protocols, 463–4, 470–2, 481
offline, facilitatory protocol, 464, 545
Ogawa, Seji, 178, 217–19, 257
Ohm's law, 486–7
ongoing experience, 270
online, 53, 207, 313, 463, 470–3, 481, 491, 500, 516, 519, 545
  defined in neuroimaging, 545
  MRI safety video, 207
  purchase of tES system, 516
  tES protocols, 491, 500, 519
  TMS protocols, 463, 470–3, 481, 545
online, inhibitory protocol, 463, 545
open field, 65–7, 94, 135–7, 172, 174, 230, 545
operational definition, 56, 545
opioid, 386
Opitz, Alexander, 507
OPM, *see* optically pumped magnetometer
optic chiasm, 363
optical imaging, *see* functional near–infrared imaging (fNIRI)
optical path, 408, 415, 418, 438
optical signal, 30, 404–6, 410–12, 422, 424, 426, 432–3, 436, 438–9, 532–3, 553, *see also* functional near–infrared imaging
optical tomography, 406, 431–2, 439, 545
optically pumped magnetometer (OPM), 144, 147, 545
optode, separation in fNIRI, *see* emitter–detector separation
  30, 408, 410–11, 413–14, 416–19, 422, 425, 427–30, 432–3, 436, 438–41, 528, 545
orbitofrontal cortex, 233, 448
ordinal scale, 522, 530, 545
orientation, of current relative to MEG sensor, 142–4, 149
  of dipoles, 67, 69, 89, 127–8, 131, 158–9, 163–4, 173–5, 534, 538

of magnetic field in TMS, 450–1, 465, 476
of proton, 181–2, 184, 212, 540, 543, 548
tuning, in representational similarity analysis, 286
tuning, of neurons, 276–7
orientation, of white matter tracts, 340–1, 343, 350–8, 367, 523, 530
orthogonality, in DTI, 349–2
oscillation, 79, 126, 186, 492–3, 501, 516, 526, 528, 532, 547, 551, 557
oscillatory tDCS (o–tDCS), 486–7, 497, 545
outcome measure, 23, 512, 529, 545
outdoor scene, 168, 280
ovaries, 389
oxidative phosphorylation, 219
oxygen (O), concentration, 218, 224–5
  extraction fraction, 225, 545
  in blood vessels, 27, 30, 216–9, 223–4, see also blood oxygen level dependent (BOLD)
  in PET, 31, 39, 372–4, 385, 394, 401
  measurement with spectrophotometry, 404
  metabolism, 221–2, 224, 385, 401, 522, 525
  saturation, 218, 406, 424, 434
  tank, danger in MRI, 207
  transporter, see haemoglobin
oxygenated blood, 30–1, 222, 226, 228, 269
oxygenated haemoglobin (oxy–Hb), 217–19, 221–2, 224–6, 251, 253, 406–7, 409–10, 413–14, 421, 424, 427, 429–30, 434–5, 437–40, 528, 542
oxyhaemoglobin, 217–19, 221–2, 224–6, 251, 253, 406–7, 409–10, 413–14, 421, 424, 427, 429–30, 434–5, 437–40, 528, 542
oxytocin, 7

p value, 50–1, 169–71, 281–2, 532–3
P1 (ERP component), 69–71, 74, 83, 112, 116–17, 120, 128, 441, 456, 546
P1–N1–P2 complex, 69, 71, 128
P2 (ERP component), 69–71, 74, 83, 109, 112, 128
P3 (ERP component), 71–2, 75, 83, 107, 260–1, 390, 495
P300 (ERP component), see P3
P600 (ERP component), 71, 104, 109, 125
pacemaker, 152, 478, 515
pain, side effect of TMS, 478, 481
  studied with tES, 515
pair production, 374, 545
paired–pulse transcranial magnetic stimulation (ppTMS), 454, 458–62, 545, 548
pancake, shape of DTI ellipsoid, 350, 355
parallel component, 141–2, 545, 547
parallel imaging, 234, 546
paramagnetic, 217, 365, 540, 546
parametric design, 36, 44–6, 57, 276, 546
parcellation, 14, 315, 317, 335, 362, 369

parietal cortex, 290, 292, 300, 494, 502
parietal lobe, 10, 15, 45, 47, 262, 283, 300, 438, 460, 472, 526, 555
Parkinson's disease, 22, 209, 386, 459
Parkkonen, Lauri, 168
partial volume effects, 330, 334, 349, 352, 357–8, 546
passive electromagnetic shielding, 546
Passow, Susanne, 393–4
path length, differential, see differential path length
Paulus, Walter, 485, 493–4, 497, 502, 510
PCA, see principal components analysis
peak, –to–peak amplitude, 120–1, 546
  60 Hz, 106, 108
  activation, 261, 279
  amplitude, 120–2, 130, 152, 169, 522, 546
  difference (ERP), 75
  latency, 71, 121–2, 130, 539, 546
  of activation, in source localization, 166
  of ERP, 67, 69, 71–2, 74, 100, 116–8, 120—3, 126, 127, 129
  of HRF, see haemodynamic response function
Pellerin, Luc, 221, 223
Penfield, Wilder, 445
Pepsi, 56
PER, see positron–emitting radioligand
perceptual experience, 21
peri–auricular points, 82, 546, 558
peri–Sylvian, see Sylvian fissure
permeability, 342, 507, 535
permutation distribution, 171, 546
perpendicular component, 142–3, 146, 524, 546
personality trait, 308, 393
PET, see positron emission tomography
Petersen, Steven, 2, 39, 41, 48, 257, 260
pharmaceutical, 399
pharmaco–TMS–EEG, 461
phase, angle, 203
  delay, 412, 415, 422, 427, 546
  difference, 201, 495
  encoding, 178, 198, 204–6, 211, 213, 231–3, 235–6, 238, 251, 253, 343, 348, 530, 534, 547, 554
  encoding gradient, 204–6, 211, 213, 231–2, 236, 253, 530, 534, 547, 554
  locking, 187, 207, 210, 492, 547
  of menstruation, 512
  of proton, 186–9, 192, 196, 202
  of sine wave grating, 201
  of waveform, 126–7, 167
  roll, 202–6, 211–12, 343–4, 347, 529, 547, 550
  shift, 126, 187, 346, 427
  synchronization, 186, 494, 526, 547
phenotype, 531, see also endophenotype
phoneme, 101, 260, 285, see also endophenotype

phosphenes, 450, 469, 479, 547, *see also* endophenotype
photocathode, 378–9, 547, *see also* endophenotype
photodetector, 378–80, 413, 437, 524–5, 530, 547, 553, *see also* endophenotype
photodiode, 100, 378–9, 416, 425, 439–40, 523, 547, 553, *see also* endophenotype
photoelectron, 378–9, 547, *see also* endophenotype
photomultiplier tube (PMT), 378–80, 416, 425, 547, 553, *see also* endophenotype
photon, counting, in fNIRI, *see* time–correlated single photon counting
  defined, 547
  in fNIRI, 408, 415–19, 422–7, 429, 431, 433, 441
  measurement, in PET, 373–82, 530, 553, 576
  production, in PET, 373–5, 545
  scattering, in PET, 374, 376, 526
phrenology, 13, 15, 256, 289, *see also* neo–phrenology
physics, of EEG, 63
  of fNIRI, 441
  of MEG, 135, 153–4, 173
  of MRI, 180, 240
  of PET, 375, 388, 399
  of tES, 503
  subatomic, 180, 372–3, 523, 547
physiological measures, 26, 547, 549
piano, 20, 184
PIB, *see* Pittsburgh compound B
piercing, 151, 208
Pittsburgh Compound B (PIB), 386–7, 398, 401
placebo effect, 467, 498, 547
planar gradiometer, 141–6, 152–3, 159, 170, 172, 174, 547
Pliny the Elder, 445
PMT, *see* photomultiplier tube
point–to–point tracking, 353, 356, 359
pointillistic noise, 240
Polanía, Rafael, 494–5, 520
polarization, 66, 173, 474–5, 484, 493, 501, 529, 535, 547
Poldrack, Russel, 52–3, 282, 305
polyphasic pulse, 453, 547
positron, 2, 31, 371–5, 377–85, 387, 389, 391, 393, 395, 397, 399–402, 523, 526, 528, 531, 546–8
  annihilation, 373–6, 383, 400–1, 523, 526, 531, 547
  defined, 547
positron emission tomography (PET), 2–3, 31, 371–402, 416, 431, 470, 523–6, 528–9, 531, 533, 540, 545, 547, 552, 554, 556
  acquisition, 380–4
  chemicals, *see* positron–emitting radioligands (PERs)
  combined with MRI, 393–4, 397–9
  combined with TMS, 470–1
  data analysis, 394–5
  experimental design, 390–93
  instrumentation, 375–80, 395–9
  physical basis, 373–4
  reading study, 39–41
  safety, 388–90
  scanner, 397
  temporal resolution, 393–4
  temporal resolution, 390–4
positron–emitting radioligand (PER), 372–3, 375, 377, 380, 382, 385–92, 395–402, 528, 546–8
Posner, Michael, 2, 39, 257
post hoc, confirmation of hypothesis, 283
  test, 43, 103, 548
postmortem, 14, 309–10, 312–14, 334–5, 339, 361, 363–6, 369
postsynaptic potential, 65, 79, 93–4, 127, 135, 223, 228, 230, 253, 340
potassium (K), 5, 219–20, 342
potential, electrical, 5, 29, 33, 65, 67, 69, 72, 77, 82–5, 93–4, 115, 120, 126–7, 129, 131, 134–7, 140, 149, 158, 173–4, 219–20, 343, 412, 446, 470, 474, 486, 499, 507–8, 510, 512, 521–2, 526, 529, 531, 536, 541, 546, 550, 552–3
power, electrical, 102
  nuclear, 389
  of light source in fNIRI, 409, 425,
  spectral (2D), 199
  spectral (frequency domain), 77–80, 94, 105–8, 110, 124–6, 129–30, 167–9, 492–3, 517, 532, 534, 548, 556
  statistical, 36, 49, 51–2, 57–8, 231, 236, 282, 298, 321, 548, 554
  stopping, 379, 554
power spectrum, 78, 106, 108
  EEG, 107
PPI, *see* psychophysiological interaction
ppTMS, *see* paired–pulse transcranial magnetic stimulation
pre–existing condition, 55, 479
precession, 178, 182–8, 195–6, 202, 204, 206, 210, 212, 343–4, 539, 547–8
prefrontal cortex, 262, 296, 299–300, 365, 460, 463, 470, 488, 492
preparation, of EEG participants, 91–2, 94
preprocessing, defined, 548
  Diffusion MRI data, 338, 347, 359–60, 366–7
  EEG data, 5, 98, 104, 120, 129–0
  fMRI data, 216, 237–8, 252–3, 256, 281, 525, 541–2, 554,
  fNIRI data, 404, 426–31, 441
  MEG data, 134, 152, 156, 172, 174
  PET data, 395
  structural MRI data, 314, 320, 556
Price, Cathy, 46, 179, 273, 391, 516

Prichard, James, 221
primary motor cortex, 218, 229, 242, 476, 493, 497, 501–2, 506, 508, 548
primate brain, 220
principal components analysis (PCA), 114, 429, 548
probabilistic atlas, 312, 548
probabilistic tractography, 356, 361, 549
production effect, 274–5
projectile, 208
projection, axonal, 340
  fibres, 338
  in PET coincidence detection, 383–4, see also back–projection
projectome, 340, 366, 527, 549
projector, 151, 558
proton, effects of magnetic field, 180–2
  in diffusion MRI, 344–5, 400
  in PET, 373–4, 547
  source of MRI signal, 180–91, 194–7, 202, 204, 206–7, 210–12, 217, 252–3, 522, 548
  see also hydrogen
psychiatric conditions, 32, 56, 338, 479, 485, 492, 512, 518
psychological conditions, 36, 48, 98–9, 129, 537
psychology, 3–4, 21, 34, 36, 38, 47, 50, 59, 276
psychophysics, 20–2, 44, 505, 549, 554
psychophysiological interaction (PPI), 296–300, 548–9
psychophysiological measures, 549
psychosis, 339, 479, 485, see also psychiatric conditions
publication bias, 51, 549–0
pulse, transcranial magnetic stimulation (TMS), 453–
pulse sequence, defined, 549
  for diffusion MRI, 338, 341, 343–8, 363, 365, 368, 529–30
  for fMRI, 216–17, 230–3, 235–8, 251, 253, 530, 554
  for MRI, general, 178, 188, 191, 194–6, 198, 204–5, 213, 527, 540, 553
  for structural MRI, 321
  in TMS–fMRI, 471, 473
  spiral, 230, 235–6, 238, 251–2, 554
pump, insulin, 152
  ion, 219–20, 226
pupillometry, 26, 549
pure insertion, 39, 259–60, 549, 555
pyramidal cell, 4, 158, 411, 549
Python (programming language), 100, 146, 163–4

quadripulse stimulation, 454, 549

RA, see relative anisotropy
raclopride ([11C]RAC), 391–2, 470

radiation, dose, quantifying, 389
  ionizing, 373
  safety, 388–90
  types, 373
391, 396, 399, 401, 414, 532, 552
radio frequency (RF), coil, 194
  defined, 549
  energy, 184–6, 188, 190, 207–8, 210, 212, 347, 400, 533
  excitation, 196, 230–1, 343, 368
  pulse, 184–6, 188–9, 191–4, 196–8, 210–13, 232, 236, 238, 240, 251, 346–7, 549–0
  receiver, 234
  transmission, 184, 188
  transmitter, 186
  wave, 30, 184, 207–8, 211, 216, 401
radon, 288, 389
random, coincidence detection in PET, 382
  diffusion of water, 342–3, 345, 366–7, 525
  events, in PET, 380, 382
  field, see Gaussian random field theory
  noise stimulation, see transcranial random noise stimulation (tRNS)
  noise, in DTI, 348, 355
  noise, in EEG, 68, 73,
  noise, in fMRI, 242, 281,
  orientation of protons, 181–2, 210, 212
  variance, 46, 557
rat, 13, 217, 463, 514
rating scale, 19, 522, 545, 550
ratio, CBF to CMR_{O2}, 224
  contrast–to–noise, see contrast–to–noise ratio
  grey to white matter, 318
  gyro–magnetic, 183, 536
  in light absorbance, 420
  oxy– to deoxy–Hb, 30, 217–8, 225, 406, 438, 535
  risk–benefit, 478
  signal–to–noise, see signal–to–noise ratio
  T1 to T2 weighting in MRI, 314
  volume, in DTI (VR), 352
Rb, see rubidium
rCBF, see blood, cerebral flow rate
re–referencing, 114–18, 129–30, 174
re–wiring, of brain, 23, see also neuroplasticity
reaction time (RT), 17–18, 32, 34, 38, 45–7, 56 126, 269, 321, 485, 491–2, 495, 497–8, 541, 550
reading, eyetracking studies of, 25
  mind, 55
  neuroimaging studies of, 39–42, 79, 274–5, 297
  out, MRI signal, see readout signal
  sentence, 68, 125,
readout signal, 187–8, 193, 204, 206, 211, 344,
REB, see research ethics board
receiver coil, 184–6, 188, 192–3, 197, 210, 234
receptor, acetylcholine, 500

benzodiazepine, 386
cannabinoid, 386
defined, 6, 550
dopamine, 386, 391–2, 470, 500
GABA, 6–7, 466, 500
glutamate, 6, 223, 500
mapping, 310, 312, 372, 385–7, 391,
neurotransmitter (general), 14
nicotine, 386
NMDA, 6, 500–1
opioid, 386
serotonin, 386, 500
recovery, from brain injury, 32
  from neural refractoriness, 101
  from stroke, 226, 456
  of HRF, 264
  system for helium, 138
  T1, *see* T1 recovery
red blood cell, 225
reference, brain, 155, 158, 243–4, 250, 252, 311, 336, 544, 554, *see also* spatial normalization *and* template
  condition, *see* baseline condition
  for fMRI motion correction, 238
  in EEG, 83–6, 92–4, 114–9, 128, 529, 536, 550
  phase, in fNIRI, 422, 427, 546
  point, in TMS neuronavigation, 452
  time series, in functional connectivity, 289, 296
  voxel, 296
reference voxel, *see* voxel, seed
refocusing gradient, 346
refocusing pulse, 345–6
refresh rate, 100, 550
region of interest (ROI), 162, 170, 282, 284, 297–8, 303, 439, 521–2, 524, 533, 535, 550
registration, based on myelin density, 314–5
  in computational neuroanatomy, 323, 325–6,
  linear, 245–6, 250, 252, 254, 522
  MEG sensors, 164
  nonlinear, 246–52, 254, 522
  of fNIRI and MRI data, 432–3
  spatial, in DTI, 348–9, 356–8, 368
  spatial, in fMRI, 244–52, 254, 320,
  spatial, in PET, 394–6, 402
  spherical surface–based, 248–52, 254
regularization, 161–2, 165, 355, 433, 541, 544, 550
Reil, Johann, 338
relative anisotropy (RA), 352
relaxation, 188–90, 193, 210–12, 230, 340, 532, 550, 555
repetition time
repetition time (TR), 191–3, 198, 211–12, 230–2, 236–8, 251, 471–3, 550, 557
repetitive TMS (rTMS), 454, 459, 461–3, 466, 470, 473, 477, 479–81, 491, 537, 540, 544–5, 550–1, 556

rephasing gradient, 344, 368, 550
replicability crisis, 50, 549–0
replicable, 37, 123, 175, 283, 298, 304, 451, 453, 551
representational similarity analysis (RSA), 285–8, 551
reproducibility crisis, 282
research ethics board (REB), 54, 516
resolution, energy, in PET
  spatial, defined, 27, 553
  spatial, diffusion–weighted MRI, 346, 375
  spatial, EEG, 63
  spatial, fMRI, 9, 15, 30, 224, 231, 240, 244, 277, 290
  spatial, fNIRI, 30, 405–6, 408, 417–19, 424–5, 432, 439–0
  spatial, MEG, 29–30, 135, 156, 160, 162, 165–6, 173, 175
  spatial, MRI, 194
  spatial, PET, 379, 382, 384, 391, 395–6, 398, 400, 525
  spatial, structural MRI, 310, 323–4, 334, 336
  spatial, tES, 489–90, 506–11, 537
  spatial, TMS, 447
  temporal, defined, 27, 555
  temporal, EEG, 28–30, 99, 122, 130, 167
  temporal, fMRI, 30, 216, 257,, *see also* haemodynamic response function (HRF)
  temporal, fNIRI, 30, 406–7, 411–16, 419–20, 422–6, 438, 440, 556
  temporal, MEG, 167, 173, 175
  temporal, PET, 31, 216, 379, 382, 385, 390, 393, 398–401, 529, 552
  temporal, TMS–EEG, 472
resonance, 177–9, 181–7, 189, 191, 193, 195, 197, 199, 201, 203, 205, 207, 209–13, 254, 503–5, 519, 540, 551, 554
resonant frequency, 184–5, 194–5, 343, 503, *see also* Larmor frequency
response, auditory brainstem (ABR), 68, 168, 227
  behavioural, 16–20, 34, 38–9, 45–6, 50, 102, 118, 444–5, 492, 504, 521–2, 537, 539, 545, 550
  BOLD, *see* blood oxygenation level dependent
  contingency, 19, 551
  device, 91, 151, 175
  filter, 104–6, 533, 557
  haemodynamic, *see* haemodynamic response function (HRF)
  line of, 381–4, 390, 400–1, 431, 524, 540
  physiological, 24–5
  sigmoid, 504–5, 552
  time, 16–17, 20, 39, 45–6, 50, 296, 517, 550, *see also* reaction time
resting motor threshold (rMT), 455, 458, 479, 551
resting state, 34, 79, 167, 270, 289–90, 295–6, 391, 393–4, 398, 524, 535, 545, 551

resting state functional connectivity magnetic resonance imaging (rs–fcMRI), 290–1, 294, 551
resting state functional magnetic resonance imaging (rs–fMRI), 290, 292, 294–6, 301, 314–15, 317, 391, 393–4, 551
retinotopic, 137, 154, 166, 548, 551
reverse inference, 36, 52–4, 58, 521, 551
reversed gradient, 206
reward system, 392–3
RF, *see* radio frequency
Riggs, Lily, 168
right–hand rule, 29, 31, 87, 134, 136, 139, 141–2, 148, 172–4, 184, 186, 208, 348, 444, 446–7, 479, 481, 522, 551, *see also* Ampère's circuital law
ripple frequency, 493, 551
rMT, 455, 458–9, 469, 472, 551, *see* resting motor threshold
Rogue Research Inc, 449, 452, 456
ROI, *see* region of interest
rolloff, of filter, 105–6, 108, 130, 196, 551, 557
Romei, Vincenzo, 461–3
root mean square, 152
rotation, 181, 238–9, 245, 252, 326, 328–9, 556
rs–fcMRI, *see* resting state functional connectivity magnetic resonance imaging
rs–fMRI, *see* resting state functional magnetic resonance imaging
RSA, *see* representational similarity analysis
RT, *see* reaction time
rTMS, *see* repetitive transcranial magnetic stimulation
rubidium (Rb), 144, 147
Ruff, Christian C., 469, 472–3, 520
run, fNIRI, 435
run, fMRI, 235–6, 238, 265, 273, 280, 283, 297, 302
running, analogy for phase roll, 204

S1, *see* somatosensory cortex
saccade, 25
safety, EEG, 84
  guidelines, 55
  MRI, 207–9, 211, 213, 247, 399
  tES, 489, 514–16, 518–19
  TMS, 455, 473, 477–8, 480–1
  20, 55, 84, 178, 181, 207–8, 211, 213, 347, 375, 388–90, 399–401, 408–9, 414, 444, 455, 473, 477–8, 480–2, 484, 489, 514–16, 518–20, 552, 556
safety, fNIRI, 408–9, 414–5
  PET, 375, 388–90, 400–1, 552, 556
sagittal plane, 192
saltatory conduction, 65
sampling rate, defined, 82, 552

EEG, 82, 110–11, 123
EEG with TMS, 474
fMRI, 27, 237
fNIRI, 413, 417, 419–20, 423, 430, 440
MEG, 167
of fNIRI, 413, 416–20, 423, 425, 430, 440
  relationship to aliasing
  relationship to aliasing, 110–11, 522, 544
SAR, *see* specific absorption rate
saturation, of EEG amplifier, 474–5, 525, 552
  oxygen, 218, 406, 424, 434
  sigmoid, 504
SBCT, *see* surface–based cortical thickness
scaling, in MRI normalization, 245
  158, 244–5, 252, 288, 326, 395, 429, 530
scalp–brain distance, 437
scattering, Compton, 374, 376, 384, 526
  light, 405, 408, 411, 415, 419, 421, 433, 529, 542
Schaefer, Evelyn, 10
schizophrenia, DTI study of, 360–1
  imaging with PET, 387
  in TMS study, 461
  studied with tES, 515
  treatment with tDCS, 492
scintillation detector, 375, 378–82, 399–401, 524, 529, 531, 540, 552, 554
scout scan, 235, 237
seed region, 290–3, 296, 368
seed voxel, 290, 356, 525
seed–based correlation, 291–2, 543, 552
segmentation, of EEG data, *see* epoch
  of fibre tracts, 357–61, 542
  of tissue types in MRI, 314, 320, 322, 324–5, 332–3, 335
segregation, 16, 535, 552
seizure, 55, 477, 481, 485, 507, 514–5
semantic, 39–41, 75, 109, 125–6, 270, 285, 333
semiconductor, 378, 416, 503, 547
sensitivity, of behavioural methods, 18–9
  of diffusion–weighted imaging, 346–7, 356, 524
  of EEG system, 84, 102
  of ERPs, 69, 104, 109, 124, 130
  of fMRI, 229–31, 252, 266, 270, 276, 282–3, 304
  of fNIRI, 408, 414, 416, 418, 422, 424–6, 430, 434, 438–0
  of MEG, 138–44, 148, 150, 154, 162, 168, 174, 533, 539
  of PET, 382, 384, 532, 552
  of PET scanner, 380–4
  of VBM, 324
  to experimental effects, *see* statistical power
  to noise, 122
  to radiation, *see* equivalent dose
  to visual motion, 461–2
sensory artifacts, 471, 552
sensory experience, 467

serotonin, 7, 386, 400, 466, 480, 500
sex, 49, 421
sham, stimulation, in non–invasive brain
  stimulation, 552, 558
sham, stimulation in tES, 488–9, 492, 494–5, 498,
  513–14, 517, 519
  stimulation, in TMS, 462, 467–9, 480–1
shape, of brain, *see* morphometry
shear, 244–5, 252
shielding, electrical, 87–8, 90
  from TMS, 437, 468, 471
  in fNIRI, 437
  in PET, 377
  MEG, 135, 149–51, 172, 174–5, 521, 541–2, 546
shimming, 233, 552
short–distance correction, 429–30, 441
short–interval intracortical facilitation (SICF),
  458–60, 499–500
short–range connections, 7, 340
shrapnel, 208, 211
SICF, *see* short–interval intracortical facilitation
SICI, *see* short–interval intracortical inhibition
Siemens AG, 179, 377, 380, 397
sievert (Sv), 389, 552, 555
sigmoid, 504–5, 552
sign language, 259
signal processing, of EEG/ERP data, 63, 102, 104,
  114, 124, 129
  of fMRI data, 237–51, 292
  104, 527, 530, 541, 548, *see also* preprocessing
signal processing, of MEG data, 152–3, 162
signal–to–noise ratio (SNR), 68, 93–4, 104, 114,
  130, 156, 158, 165–7, 169, 173, 175, 235,
  251–2, 256, 276, 303, 321, 346, 378, 380,
  384, 400, 405–6, 409, 411–13, 416, 418, 422,
  424–6, 431, 433, 437, 502, 523, 525, 529,
  531–2, 541, 552, 554
silent period (SP), 455, 466, 480, 552–3
silicon photomultiplier, 416, 553
sine wave, grating, 198–203, 206, 211, 213, 246,
  263–4, 544, 553
  76–8, 105, 198–9, 492–7
single–photon counting, *see* time–correlated single
  photon counting
single–pulse TMS, 453–6, 458, 461, 476–7,
  479–80, 553
sinus, in fMRI susceptibility artifact, 233–4
skeletonization, 358–9, 553
skin potential, 90–1, 105, 110, 129–30, 553
skull, base, *see* inion
  bumps, in phrenology, 13
  effects on EEG signal, 13, 27, 29, 63–4, 115,
    128, 137
  effects on fNIRI signal, 30, 404–5, 408–9, 432, 441
  in MEG, 136–7, 140, 155–7
  in MRI, 239, 320, 525

in tES, 484, 506–8, 512, 515
  modelling, *see* boundary element model *and*
    finite element model
  thickness, 115, 128, 432, 441, 508, 512
slice selection, 178, 196–8, 211–12, 231–3, 236,
  238, 343, 553
slice selection gradient, 196–7, 232, 553
sLORETA, *see* standardized low–resolution brain
  electromagnetic tomography
slow optical signal, 404, 406–13, 419, 426–7, 430,
  433, 438–9, 535, 553
small–world properties, 292, 553
smart watch, 404
smoking, 225
smoothing, kernel, 240–2, 252, 324, 348–9, 395,
  see also Gaussian kernel
  spatial, in diffusion MRI, 348–9, 355, 360
  spatial, in fMRI, 240–2, 246, 252–3, 281–2,
    323–4, 534–5, 539, 541, 554
  spatial, in PET, 395
  temporal, *see* filter
Snowball, Albert, 498
SNR, *see* signal–to–noise ratio
SOA, *see* stimulus onset asynchrony
sodium (Na), 5–6, 219–20, 342, 380, 466, 480–1,
  499–501, 517, 519
sodium iodide (NaI(Tl)), 380
sodium ion channels, 480–1
sodium–potassium pump, *see* ion pump
software, computational neuroanatomy,
  322, 326, 334
  DTI analysis, 347–8, 352, 357
  EEG data analysis, 105, 110, 114
  fMRI analysis, 179, 238, 250, 266, 281–2, 318
  for analyzing behavioural data, 20
  for DTI analysis, 347
  for fNIRI, 413, 426–7
  for fNIRI analysis, 426
  for MRI scanner, 217–8, 230–1, 238, 321
  for tES, 489–90, 516, 519
  FSLview, 192
  MEG analysis, 152, 161, 163–4
  MNE–Python, 146, 163–4
  morphometry, 318
  neuro–navigation, 452–3
  PET analysis, 399
  SPM, 322
  stimulus presentation, 100, 130
  Surf Ice, 161
soma, 4–5, 158, 521, 553
somatosensory cortex, primary (S1), 137,
  313–14, 331
Soterix Medical Inc, 488, 490
source localization, averaging across people, 158
  beamformer, 162–7, 524, 558
  comparison of algorithms, 166–7

comparison of EEG and MEG signals, 148–9
dipole model, 158–0
distributed models, 160–2
EEG/ERP, 98, 126–9, 131
in fNIRI, 426, 431–4, 439, 441, 545, 557
in MEG, 134–5, 148, 153–8, 163–70, 172–5, 524–5, 530, 541, 544, 554
in tES, 506–8
limitations, 153–5
of fNIRI data, 426, 431–3, 437–8
validation, 153–5
SP, see silent period
spatial, derivative, 315, 553
distortion, 234–5, 238, 245, 248, 250, 315, 348
encoding, 194, 207, 238, 253, 471, 536
frequency, 178, 198–207, 211, 213, 242, 553
gradient, 203, 238, 316, 348, 553
normalization, 158, 216, 243–5, 248, 252–4, 283, 319–20, 322–4, 326–8, 335–6, 357–8, 395, 522, 536, 544, 553–4
resolution, see resolution, spatial
smoothing, see smoothing, spatial
spatially variant regularization (SVR), 433
speaker, 87, 89, 91, 100–1, 151, 285
speaking, aloud, 41
fMRI study of, 274
in EEG studies, 89, 102
in fNIRI studies, 410
specific absorption rate (SAR), 327
specific energy, 377–8, 547
spectrophotometry, 404–5, 438–9, 554
speech, 13, 15, 17, 20, 23–4, 46–7, 52, 72, 100, 102, 270, 275, 391, 446, 461, 463
Sperry, Roger, 339
spherical surface–based normalization, 248–50, 252, 254, 332–4, 554
spike, 60 Hz, 106
artifact in fMRI, 238–9
electrocardiogram artifact, MEG, 145–6
in model of fMRI stimuli, 264
motion artifact, in fNIRI, 428–9
spiking, of neuron, 228, 340, see also action potential
spinal cord, 363, 523
spiral imaging, 230, 235–6, 238, 251–2, 554
SPM (software), 322
square wave, 112, 264, 436
SQUID, see superconducting quantum interference device
stair climbing, 219
staircase method, 21, 554
standard, atlas, 283
brain, 160, 245, 432
brain template, 28, 155, 247, 252, 254, 323, 347, 357–8, 368, 394, 553
deviation
for electrical line frequency, 87

for electrode locations, see International 10–10 System
gold, 22
safety, see guidelines, safety
stimulus, 99, 261–2, 266, 390–1
unit
unit, 407
standardized low–resolution brain electromagnetic tomography (sLORETA), 162, 554
static artifacts, 471, 554
statistic, hypothesis testing, 537
interaction, 43, 103, 259, 538
multivariate, in structural MRI, 327, 329
nonparametric, 171, 525, 544, 546, 549
nonparametric, for DTI data, 359
T^2, see Hotelling's T^2
univariate, 123, 169, 280, 282, 284, 303–4, 359, 541–2
z, see z test
statistical, analysis of DTI data, 351–2, 360
analysis of EEG/ERP data, 98, 104, 120–1, 129–0
analysis of fMRI data, 237, 252, 256, 258, 280–1, 283, 302–3
analysis of fNIRI data, 431, 433
analysis of MEG data, 169–72
analysis of PET data, 395
analysis of structural MRI data, 326, 331, 335
comparison, 152, 170, 275, 320, 324, 335–6, 352
contrast, 275
independence, see independent components analysis
map, 242, 280, 285
method, 171, 303, 313, 324, 329, 359
model, 427, 535, see also general linear model
power, 36, 49, 51–2, 57–8, 231, 236, 282, 298, 321, 548, 554
sensitivity, 109, 231, 276, 282
significance, 18, 50–1, 104, 109, 124, 169, 262, 268, 271, 275, 281, 324, 333, 511, 546, 549, 554
test, 23, 129, 170–1, 281, 302–4, 324, 434, 521, 542, 550
threshold, 163, 304, 535
statistical parametric mapping, dynamic (dSPM), 162, 530
statistical parametric mapping (SPM), 322
statistics, class, 49, 170, 281
STG, see superior temporal gyrus
stimulation, deep brain, 152, 444, 477–8, 515
electrical, see transcranial electrical stimulation (tES)
electrical, in neurosurgery, 444–5
magnetic, see transcranial magnetic stimulation (TMS)
perceptual
sham, see sham stimulation

stimulus, auditory, 100–1
  auditory, in MEG, 151
  category, in multivariate fMRI analysis, 284–8
  control, 283
  duration, 261
  features, 98–9, 303–4, 533
  intensity, 21, 45, 505, 554
  presentation, 68, 100–1, 113, 123, 130, 151, 257, 261, 264, 289
  presentation, in event–related fMRI, 261–6
  timing, 99–101, 130
  visual, 37, 44, 68–9, 80, 100, 153, 225, 229, 456, 472–3, 550
stimulus onset asynchrony (SOA), 101, 168, 261, 263–9, 279, 538, 554
stingray, 445
stochastic resonance, 503–5, 519, 554
stopping power, 379, 554
stopping rule, in tractography, 353–4
Strafella, Antonio, 470–1
streamlining, 353–7, 359, 365–8, 549, 555–6
stroke, 11, 22–4, 226, 396, 456, 458, 515
structural magnetic resonance imaging (sMRI), computational neuroanatomy, 319–4
  contrast weighting, 321–
  cortical thickness measurement, 330–4
  deformation–based morphometry (DBM), 326–7
  experimental design, 320–2
  grey matter concentration, 324–5
  morphometry, 315–19
  scales of cortical organization, 310–15
  surface–based cortical thickness (SBCT), 332–4
  tensor–based morphometry (TBM), 328–9
  voxel–based cortical thickness (VBCT), 330–1
  voxel–based morphometry (VBM), 322–5
  see also computational neuroanatomy
STS, see superior temporal sulcus
subatomic particle, 180, 373, 547
subjective experience, 21
subjectivity, 294, 312, 318–9
substance abuse, 492
subtraction method, 18, 38–9, 56, 72, 74, 257, 259, 522, 555
suicide, 485
sulcus, central, 10, 15, 248, 250, 314, 456, 506, 526
  intraparietal, 283, 472
  Sylvian fissure, 10, 15, 248, 283, 314, 555
  137, 246–7, 272, 312, 330–1, 334, 465, 472, 536
Supalla, Ted, 259, 272
superconducting quantum interference device (SQUID), 138–40, 144, 172, 174, 533, 545, 555
superficial signal, 427
superior temporal gyrus (STG), 47, 283, 548
superior temporal sulcus (STS), 249, 272
Surf Ice, 161

surface–based, normalization, 248–9, 252, 254, 314, 332, 554
  representation of cortex, 334, 336
surface–based cortical representation, limitations, 334
surface–based cortical thickness (SBCT), 319, 331–4, 552, 555, 558
surgeon, 243, 360
Sv, see Sievert
SVR, see spatially variant regularization
swing, 184
Sylvian fissure, 10, 15, 248, 283, 314, 555
synapse, 4–7, 9, 223, 308, 466, 521, 529, 555
synchronization, across neurons, 65
  event–related, 77, 79, 98, 130, 532
  of BOLD activity, see functional connectivity
  of neural oscillations, 492, 494–5, see also entrainment
  phase, 186, 526, 547
syntactic processing

t–test, 123, 169, 171, 258, 275, 280, 302–3, 324, 434, 436
T1, contrast, 190–1, 193, 210, 212
  recovery, 178, 188–93, 210, 212, 542, 555
  relaxation, 189–90, 230, 555
T2, contrast, 178, 188–93, 210–12, 217, 219, 225, 230–1, 251, 253, 314, 322, 327, 363, 397, 541–2, 555
  decay, 178, 188–92, 210, 212, 230, 542, 555
  Hotelling's (statistic), 327
  relaxation, 190, 210, 555
T2*, contrast, 230, 541
  decay, 191, 212, 217, 219, 225, 230, 251, 253, 540, 555
tACS, see transcranial alternating current stimulation (tACS)
Takano, Takahiro, 222–3
Talairach atlas, 243–4, 246, 249–50, 252, 310
Talairach, Jean, 243
Tan (patient of Broca), 11, 13, 41
tattoo, 152, 208
tau protein, 386
taxonomy, of white matter tracts, 338–9
TBM, see tensor–based morphometry
TBS, see theta burst stimulation
TCA cycle, see tricarboxylic acid cycle
TD, see time domain fNIRI
TE, see echo time
template, 28, 192, 244–8, 250, 252, 254, 312, 314, 318–20, 323, 326, 347, 357–8, 368, 394–5, 432, 544, 553–4
temporal lobe, 10, 23, 69, 73, 163, 166, 168, 233, 277, 284–5, 360–1, 391, 541, 555, see also superior temporal sulcus (STS) and superior temporal gyrus (STG)
temporal resolution, see resolution, temporal

temporal–parietal junction, 391
tensor–based morphometry (TBM), 308, 319, 327–8, 335–6, 521, 539, 555–6
  diffusion, *see* diffusion tensor
  line approach, 355–6, 556
TEP, *see* transcranial magnetic stimulation–evoked potential
Terney, Daniella, 497–8
tES, *see* transcranial electrical stimulation
TES (transcranial electrical stimulation), 484–5
Tesla (T; unit of measure), 138, 181
tessellation, 319, 332, 556, 558
test stimulus (TS), 458–60, 556–7
testes, 389
testosterone, 7
thalamus, 339, 361–2, 548, 559
tHb, *see* total blood volume
theory, Gaussian random field, *see* Gaussian random field theory
  graph, *see* graph theory
  hodological, 338
therapy, electroshock, 485
theta, frequency band in EEG, 77–8, 94, 126–7, 169, 454, 463–4, 480–1, 494, 496, 498, 517, 527–8, 534, 555–6
theta burst stimulation (TBS), 454, 463–4, 480–1, 496, 527–8, 555–6
  continuous (cTBS), 463–6, 477, 527–
  intermittent (iTBS), 464–5, 538–9, 545
thickness, cortical, *see* cortical thickness
  of MRI slice, 194, 196, 231, 233
  of scalp, 432
  skull, *see* skull thickness
threshold, statistical, *see* statistical threshold *and* p value
threshold limit value (TLV), 389, 556–7
Thulborn, Keith, 217
tickle, 488, 515
Tikhonov regularization, 433
time–continuous design, 278–80, 285, 551, 556
  –correlated single photon counting (TCSPC), 425, 556
  –frequency analysis, 77, 126, 129, 556, 558
  –frequency plot, 125
  domain, fNIRI (TD), 414, 416, 421–7, 438–9, 529, 555–6
  domain, representation of data, 76–8, 94, 105–8, 124, 126, 169
  for DWI scan, 346
  locking, 29, 62, 68, 77, 79, 82, 93–4, 118, 124, 129–30, 146, 166–7, 262, 267, 460, 463, 528, 532
  multiplexing, 419, 542, 556
  period, 25, 94, 113, 118, 289, 400, 423, 456, 476, 522–3, 541
  points, 110, 116–17, 122, 130, 167, 170, 231, 239, 258, 266, 280, 297, 320–1, 324, 327, 329, 359, 401, 413, 468, 497, 512
  scale, 7, 9, 27, 31, 230, 308, 393, 411, 430, 439
  window, in ERP analysis, 104, 110, 120–4, 129–30, 522, 534, 546, 556
  window, in fNIRI analysis, 423–5, 427, 436
  window, in MEG analysis, 152, 169–0
  window, in PET analysis, 373, 381
  window, in TMS, 471, 475
time of flight, distribution, in fNIRI, *see* distribution of time–of–flight (DTOF)
  imaging, in PET, 382, 556
time–resolved, fNIRI, *see* time–domain fNIRI *and* frequency–domain fNIRI
timing, in MRI pulse sequence, 188, 206, 210, 213, 549
  in paired–pulse TMS, 457–9
  in rTMS, 461–3, 470
  of ERP effects, 29, 69–72, 75, 93–4, 98–101, 116, 118, 120, 122–4, 126–8, 130, 526
  of haemodynamic response, *see* haemodynamic response function (HRF)
  of light in fNIRI, 414, 422, 438, 440, 534
  of MEG effects, 148, 153
  of neural activity, 226, 228, 230, 481
  of visual evoked potential, 457
  properties of crystals used in PET, 381–2
  stimulus, 99–101, 168, 531
tinnitus, 515
tissue segmentation, 320, 325, 333, 556
TLV, *see* threshold limit value
TMS, *see* transcranial magnetic stimulation
TMS–evoked potential (TEP), 476, 556–7
tomographic imaging, 426, 545, 557
tomography, computed, *see* computed tomography
  low resolution, *see* standardized low–resolution brain electromagnetic tomography (sLORETA)
  optical, *see* optical tomography
  positron emission, *see* positron emission tomography
tongue, 270, 489
tool, as stimulus in fMRI, 285
toolbox, 31
total blood volume, 221, 406, 438
total blood volume (tHb), 221, 223, 226, 406–7, 434, 438
Tournoux, Pierre, 243–4, 246, 250, 252, 310
toxicity, of anatomical tracer, 339, 365
TR, *see* repetition time
tracer, 31, 339, 361, 363, 365, 372, 385–6, 395, 401, 548
tract, 28, 179, 338–9, 343, 349–69, 523, 530, 542, 555, 557

association, 339
commissural, 339
tractography, 337–41, 343, 345–7, 349, 351, 353, 355–61, 363, 365–9, 525, 542, 549, 553, 555–7
training study, 32, 179, 321
trajectory, 232–3, 235–6, 365, 428–9, 539
transcranial alternating current stimulation (tACS), 32, 486–7, 491–9, 501, 503, 507, 511, 517–18, 532, 545, 557
transcranial direct current stimulation (tDCS), 32, 483, 486–7, 489–92, 494, 497–503, 508, 510–15, 517–18, 520–1, 523, 543, 545, 557
transcranial electrical stimulation (tES), activity dependence, 501–6
  blinding, 488, 513–14
  conduction through brain, 506–11
  consumer grade, 516
  current intensity, 487–9, 495, 497, 504, 507–8, 511–16, 518
  dangers, 484,
  defined, 484
  discomfort during, 488–9, 498
  effects of age, 508–10, 515
  effects on brain, 499–506
  electrodes, 489–90, 494, 506, 508
  experimental design, 511–14
  guidelines, 511
  high definition (HD–tES), 489–90, 494
  history, 484–6
  impedance, 488
  individual differences, 511–12
  participant selection, 511
  pharmacology, 499–501
  ramping current, 489, 513–4
  safety, 484, 514–6
  self–administration, 516
  sham stimulation, 488, 513–14
  sponges, 488–9, 506, 508, 515
  stochastic resonance, 503–6
  tACS, *see* transcranial alternating current stimulation
  tDCS, *see* transcranial direct current stimulation
  tRCS, *see* transcranial random noise stimulation
  tRNS, *see* transcranial random noise stimulation
transcranial magnetic stimulation (TMS), –evoked potential (TEP), 460, 476, 556–7
  acoustic noise during, 467
  coil, 446–53, 459, 474
  combined with EEG, 460–1, 472–8
  combined with fMRI, 471–2
  combined with PET, 470–1
  confounds, 467
  distribution of magnetic field, 446–8, 451
  effects on brain, 465–6
  experimental design, 467–9
  history, 445
  instrumentation, 446–53
  muscle contractions during, 448, 478
  navigation, 448–52
  neurotransmitters mediating effects, 459
  online vs. offline protocols, 463–5
  paired–pulse, 454, 458–61
  pulse shape, 453–
  quadripulse (QPS), 454,
  repetitive (rTMS), 454, 459, 461–3, 466, 470, 473, 477, 479–81, 491, 537, 540, 544–5, 550–1, 556
  safety, 477–9
  sensory stimulation, 444–5
  sham stimulation, 467–9
  side effects, 477–9
  single–pulse, 453, 455–9
  spatial resolution, 447
  stimulation intensity, 455, 469
  strength of magnetic field, 446
  theta burst (TBS), 454, 463–4, 480–1, 527–8, 555–6
transcranial random current stimulation (tRCS), 486, *see* transcranial random noise stimulation
transcranial random noise stimulation (tRNS), 32, 483, 486–7, 497–9, 501, 511, 517–18, 557
transition band, 105–6, 108, 551, 557
translation, 11, 238–9, 245, 252, 329
transmission scan, 396
transverse component, 192, 557
transverse plane, 184–6, 188–93, 197, 210, 212, 343, 532, 555, 557
Tri–Council Policy Statement: Ethical Conduct for Research Involving Humans, 54
trial–to–trial variance, 46
triangulation, 159, 318
tricarboxylic acid (TCA) cycle, 219
trigger port, 82
TS, *see* test stimulus
Tseng, Philip, 502
tube formula, 436
tuft, 4–5, 557
tumour, 22, 209, 360, 396–7
Type I error, 103, 303–4, 542

U–fibres, 353, 355
under–additivity, of haemodynamic response function, 262–4
undiagnosed condition, *see* incidental finding
unexpected finding, *see* incidental finding
unfolding, cortical, 248–50
univariate analysis, 123, 169, 280, 282, 284, 303–4, 327, 359, 541–2
upright face, 69–70, 99, 115–9
urine, 389

V1 (brain region), 12, 286, 288, 317, 341, 349, 351, 456, 461–2, 472, 548, *see also* visual cortex
V2 (brain region), 313, 341, 349, 351, 472
V3 (brain region), 341, 349, 472
V4 (brain region), 341, 450, 472
V5 (brain region), 272–3, 450, 461–2, 472, 502, 505
vacuum, 378, 422–3, 546
variability, between individuals, *see* individual differences
   in brain structure and organization, *see* individual differences
   in er–fMRI stimulus timing, *see* jitter
   in ERP stimulus timing, 100, 130
   in fNIRI results, 507, 511–2
   in haemodynamic response function, 228–9, *see* haemodynamic response function (HRF)
   in measurements, 104
   in reaction time (RT), 18, 45
   in results of structural MRI studies, 322
   spatial, 241
variable, categorical, 37–8, 57, 525, 532
   continuous, 36–7, 57, 525, 527
   dependent, 36, 38, 56–7, 122, 529, 535, 538, 542, 545–6, 557
   independent, 37–8, 56–8, 524, 529, 535, 538, 541–2, 546, 557
   levels, 36
variance, analysis of, *see* analysis of variance (ANOVA)
   as indicator of artifact, 429
   defined, 50
   in BOLD response, *see* blood oxygenation level dependent (BOLD)
   in statistics, 50–1, 57–8, 171, 275, 280, 544, 554, 557–8
   in timing of ERP components, 101
   of fMRI time series, *see* efficiency
   trial–to–trial, 46
vasoconstriction, 225, 558
vasodilation, 222–5, 228, 251, 253, 523, 525, 558
vasopressin, 7
VBCT, *see* voxel–based cortical thickness
VBM, *see* voxel–based morphometry
vector field, 326
vein, 218–19, 222, 224, 228, 398, 407
vein versus brain debate, 224
verb, 37, 40–3, 259
verbal response, 20, 91, 558
vertex (graph theory), *see* node
vertex (of head), 73, 82, 115–19, 558
   as EEG reference, 115–9
   stimulation in TMS, 467–8, 473
   tES electrode location, 494
   vertex (tessellation), 433, 558
verum, 467–8, 513, 558

video game, 391–2
virtual electrode, 162, 558
virtual lesion, 446, 461, 463, 472
visual, cortex, primary (V1), 12, 286, 288, 317, 341, 349, 351, 456, 461–2, 472, 548
   field, 11, 137, 154, 160, 277, 286, 435, 450, 472–3, 548
   perception, 17, 39, 44, 456–7, 547
   processing, 127
   stimulus, 37, 40, 44, 68–9, 91, 100, 114, 128, 145, 153, 225, 227, 229, 259, 273, 277, 456, 472–3, 550
visual, cortex, 11–12, 15, 17, 41, 52, 137, 145, 154, 221–2, 227–8, 246, 257, 261, 276–7, 286, 412, 435, 450, 456, 461, 498, 502, 547–8, *see also* occipital lobe
   inspection, 112, 123, 258, 352–3, 363, 427–8
   motion, 52, 273, 450, 461, 505
VLSM, *see* voxel–based lesion–symptom mapping
Vogt, C., 13, 315
Vogt, O., 13, 315
volume, blood, 221, 223, 226, 406–7, 434, 438
   conduction, 65, 93, 134, 148, 168, 173–4
   of brain structure, 318–19, *see also* tensor–based morphometry (TBM)
   of brain structures, 308, 319, 328–9
   partial, *see* partial volume effect
   pixel, *see* voxel
   ratio (VR), 352
   whole brain
voluntariness, 54
von Economo, 13, 315
voxel–based cortical thickness (VBCT), 319–20, 330–2, 334, 555, 558
   –based lesion–symptom mapping (VLSM), 24, 540, 558
   defined, 162
   in diffusion MRI, 338, 340–2, 344–6, 348–62, 367–8, 525
   in fMRI, 218, 224, 229, 231, 238, 240–1, 243, 246, 248, 251–2, 264, 266, 271, 276–8, 280–5, 290–4, 296–7, 302–4
   in fNIRI, 433–6, 438
   in MEG source localization, 165–6, 170–1
   in MRI, 194, 205–6
   in PET, 398, 400
   in structural MRI, 308, 314–15, 319, 322–32, 334–6
   in TMS
   isotropic, 346, 354, 539
   seed, in functional connectivity analysis, 290–
   seed, in psychophysiological interactions, 296–9
voxel–based morphometry (VBM), limitations, 324–5
   normalization, 323

registration, 323
software package, 322
statistical analysis, 324
technical errors, 325
319, 322, 335–6, 536, 558
VR, *see* volume ratio

Wagner, Anthony, 262
warping, 28, 235, 246, 248, 250, 252, 323, 357–8, 395
wash–out period, 385
Washington University, 2, 257, 372–
water, analogy for electricity, 84
 Brownian motion, *see* Brownian motion
 concentration, 28
 in diffusion MRI, 338, 340–5, 349, 356, 363, 365, 367–9, 523, 529–31, 539, 550
 in MRI
  light absorbance, 409–10, 420–1, 440
  molecule, 28, 180, 190, 217, 342–5, 363, 367–8, 529, 550
 source of contrast in CT imaging, 396
 source of contrast in MR imaging, 28, 180, 188–93, 203, 210, 212, 310
watering the garden, 222
Watts, James, 339
wave, continuous, *see* continuous wave (CW) fNIRI
 direct, *see* direct wave
 indirect, *see* indirect wave
 radio, 30, 184, 207–8, 216, 401, *see also* radio frequency (RF)
 sine, 76–8, 105, 198–9, 492–7
 square, 112, 264, 436
waveguide, 151, 437, 471, 558
wavelength, 144, 404, 409–10, 413–14, 421, 425, 434, 439–40, 524, 527, 534, 539, 556
wavelet, 124–5, 429, 431, 530, 558
Weber, E.H., 21
Weber's law, 21
weighting, diffusion factor, 388–9, 552
factor (radiation safety)
matrix, 162, 165
MRI contrast, 191–3, 199, 245, 397
sine wave gratings, in MRI, 199, 201–3
welding, 208
Wernicke, Carl, 309, 338–9
Wernicke's area, 47, 391
white matter, bundles, 243, 289
 defined, 8, 558–9
 in cortical thickness measures, 325, 330–3, 335–6, 555
 in PET
 in VBM, 324
 MRI contrast, 191–3, 203, 210, 237, 320–2, 394–6, 527, 546
 segmentation, *see* tissue segmentation
 tract, 338–43, 349–53, 357–8, 360, 363–5, 367–9, 523, 530, 534, 542, 553
 see also myelin
whole brain, volume, 173, 248
winding, dephasing gradient, 344
 MEG gradiometer, 141–2, 172, 174, 524
 phase roll, 206
 TMS coil, 32, 448
within–subjects design, 48–9, 58, 72, 559
wobble, 182, 210, 548, *see also* precession
word, frequency, 42–3, 103
word, reading, *see* reading
 spoken, *see* speaking
working memory, 52, 75, 257, 461, 492, 494–6, 502, 528
World War II, 404–5
Worsley, Keith, 281

X–ray, 22, 388–9, 395–6, 402, 526–7, 552, *see also* computed tomography (CT) scan

z statistic, 162, 544
zero emitter–detector separation, 424–5

CPSIA information can be obtained
at www.ICGtesting.com
Printed in the USA
JSHW071649070723
44153JS00002B/4

9 781446 296509